RESOURCES, NEEDS AND OUTCOMES IN COMMUNITY-BASED CARE

Resources, Needs and Outcomes in Community-Based Care

A comparative study of the production of welfare for elderly
people in ten local authorities in England and Wales

BLEDDYN DAVIES
ANDREW BEBBINGTON
HELEN CHARNLEY

in collaboration with

BARRY BAINES
EWAN FERLIE
MICHAEL HUGHES
JULIA TWIGG

PSSRU
UNIVERSITY OF KENT
AT CANTERBURY ■■■■

Avebury

Aldershot · Brookfield USA · Hong Kong · Singapore · Sydney

First published in Great Britain in 1990

Avebury Gower Publishing Company Limited Gower House Croft Road Aldershot Hants GU11 3HR England	HV 1481 .G52 B35 1990

Gower Publishing Company
Old Post Road
Brookfield
Vermont 05036
U.S.A.

ISBN 1-85628-130-2

Typeset at the PSSRU, University of Kent at Canterbury
Printed in Great Britain by Billing & Sons Ltd, Worcester

Contents

Part II

List of tables

List of diagrams

Preface

This is the first of two books from the comparative study of community social services for elderly people undertaken by the Personal Social Services Research Unit at the University of Kent at Canterbury.

The work is a production of welfare study; that is, it looks at the needs-related circumstances of consumers, resources allocated, and outcomes of evaluative importance in their own right. In particular, it analyses (i) how the allocation of resources and their effects on outcomes vary between consumers in various circumstances, and (ii) how the allocations differed between the twelve small areas compared. Like other larger production of welfare studies, the work combines statistical description and modelling with the analysis of the policy process based on interviews and documentary evidence. The study describes the important statistical relations of the production of welfare, how the production processes work, and why they take that form.

The book itself is an essay, not a general descriptive study; an exploration of the implications of one issue of current policy and management. The basic report to the DHSS ranges more widely (Bebbington and colleagues, 1986). Allusions to the work in DHSS publications are to that report, which was based on interim findings.

Policy issues, research questions and the policy dilemma

The *issue* is the extent to which greater spending on the neediest persons living at home will reduce the need for residential modes of care of various forms. Some believe that the need for publicly-financed residential modes of care will be much reduced simply by *targeting* home care resources better. Chapters 3, 6, and 7 confirm that targeting is too variable to be a consistent response to need, and that it is in some ways biased: some needs-related circumstances have greater or less effect on the probability of receiving services and the amounts of resources received than one might expect. However, Chapters 4 and 5 find that services have low *marginal productivities*; that consumers who receive larger amounts of service given their need-related circumstances seem after six months not to be in greatly improved circumstances in some important respects, or less likely to have entered institutions for long-term care, than consumers who receive less. Chapter 11 suggests that the innovations studied were not likely to affect the overall impact of services greatly. So in Chapters 12, 13, and 14, we argue that it will be necessary to change the content and nature of service to improve marginal productivities. That is a more formidable task than just to secure better targeting. We discuss how targeting and productivities might be improved.

These findings will surprise few who have followed the critiques of the last decade. Our community social services grew in a largely unanalysed way to serve a population which has been only broadly specified. Policy documents have claimed throughout the last thirty years that the services reduced the need to enter institutions for long-term care. However, the claim that they have done so for a high proportion of recipients has become increasingly incredible. At the same time, there has been increasing disquiet about the stress and other diswelfares born by spouses, other members of the family, and 'informal carers' generally, though we have lacked statistical information for representative samples about the numbers suffering diswelfares of some important kinds. The White Paper on community care quite clearly states the relief of carers to be an aim in its own right (Cm 849). Likewise there has been disquiet about the insensitivity to the desires and expectations of consumers. This too is reflected in developments in the best authorities. Our results fully support these generalisations, though we also find that actual recipients in the general frail population value the services they now receive, and that others think that they should be provided and subsidised from public funds.

What is new is that, for the first time, the effects have been researched. Large amounts of evidence from interviews were used to construct a large number of indicators of outcome. Only some are reported here. It is unlikely that our analyses have failed to find important and general effects, and still less likely that the effects we have failed to discover would greatly alter our general conclusions. Indeed, in some respects our strategies for the statistical analysis of the data are likely to result in the overstatement of the effects of resources on outcomes.

Our findings create a dilemma. Great effort and resources will certainly be needed to improve productivities and targeting in home care, but the scale of improvement achievable is uncertain. More and better service has a Pandora effect; high priority demand increases as what is made available becomes more consumer-responsive, and resources are better matched to the varied and complex needs. The Pandora effects of better home care may be less easy to control than high priority demand for residential care. However, meeting high priority demands by publicly financing residential care will certainly be expensive, while investing well in the improvement of the targeting and productivities of home care could substantially reduce total expenditure, and that investment would extend choice and improve the quality of life of many clients.

Acknowledgements

This has been a large and complex study. It could not have been conducted without the commitment of managers, researchers, social workers, home help organisers, community nurses and clerical staff in local health and social services authorities. Many must remain anonymous. Among those who deserve special mention are: Doreen Allen, Adrien Antoine, Ken Aspinall, Maurice Bates, Steve Clarke, Martin Cooper, Ken Cox, Linda Hammond, Norman Hodgson, Kay Jackson, Andrew Jenney, Keith Leatham, Gerda Loosemore-Reppen, David Martin, Rhydfen Morgan, Anne Parkes, Patrick Pope, Robert Pope, Pam Satterthwaite, Tom Thompson, and William Warburton. Jane Ritchie, Jenny Hyatt, and Jude England of SCPR were helpful in every way.

Of the authors, Andrew Bebbington contributed most to the detailed design of the project: to the sample design, to the general design of the questionnaires and the detailed development and adaptation of the instruments within them, and to the liaison with SCPR. He has been a senior collaborator throughout the project. Additionally he liaised with some authorities, collected data and interviewed in areas and wrote Chapter 4. Helen Charnley was the one author to have worked full-time on this project for several years, again collecting and analysing evidence, liaising with authorities, producing the first drafts of Chapters 6 and 7, and contributing to the team effort in innumerable ways. Mike Hughes initially processed the data and wrote the first draft of Chapter 5. Barry Baines has latterly had charge of the project's complex statistical databases, and with Bleddyn Davies produced models. Bleddyn Davies drafted chapters not otherwise attributed and helped to shape and revise the analyses and drafts. Ewan Ferlie liaised with authorities, collected data, and drafted all of Chapters 9, 10, and 11, save for a few paragraphs about statistical analyses. Julia Twigg likewise collected data, liaised with authorities, and drafted Chapter 8. Ken Buckingham and Sheila Kesby visited authorities to collect the information required for some of the costing. Robert Walker and Mia Yee worked on and influenced the project during its design stage and for a short while thereafter.

Man-Sum Tong and Andrew Fenyo provided a great deal of assistance with computing. Diagram 14.2 and page 362 use some statistics of costs to informal carers which Ann Netten estimated in her work for *Community Services and the Social Production of Welfare* (PSSRU, forthcoming 1991). Angela Fitzpatrick assisted with the collation of some of the information, and with indexes, the glossary, and proof-reading.

Special thanks are due to Anita Whitley, who has been secretary and research assistant, general archivist and custodian of avalanches of typescript and manuscript, the patient detective tracking clients and references with equal dedication. Certainly not least, Jane Dennett, with help from Anita and Nick Brawn, has supervised the technical preparation and typesetting of the book and its presentation to our publishers.

Officials at the DHSS have helped in many ways. We are grateful to Hazel Canter, Su Moylan and Jenny Griffin; and to Jack Barnes, who agreed that we should undertake a major study of the relations between resources, needs and outcomes in the community social services long before others recognised it would become a key issue.

On reading the book

We have laboured long and hard to make the messages of this book clear to everyone who has the time to think about it carefully. The messages are at too many levels to reduce it to a short statement. We know that parts of the book are demanding, and few can make the time to read it thoroughly. So advice on reading it may be appropriate. Read the first two and the last two chapters first. Make full use of the detailed contents pages and the index. Look at the 12-page booklet about the main results and their messages – *Resources Needs and Outcomes in Community Services: an Overview*, copies of which are available (free of charge) from the Executive Officer at the PSSRU.

Bleddyn Davies

1 The study and its context

This is the first of two books. Each shows how resources used in community social services affect the wellbeing of elderly consumers and their informal carers. In the language of our 'production of welfare approach', the books do two things:

- They estimate the relations between inputs and outputs. They show how the relations vary between persons and households with different need-related circumstances and between the systems operating in twelve small areas scattered across England and Wales.
- They explain the variations by exploring the relations between structures, policies, practice and processes, the allocation of resources, and the outputs which flow from them.

To our knowledge, this is the first study in the international literature on social policy for the elderly both to estimate and to explain the relationship between means and ends in a dozen forms of standard provision. Certainly it is the most ambitious yet published in its range of measures of inputs, need-related circumstances and outcomes, and in its use of analyses of structure, policy and process as an integral part of the investigation. These characteristics make this book and its sequel quintessential production of welfare studies. In this, they have been designed to be like the first two books about the PSSRU's community care projects, *Matching Resources to Needs in Community Care* (Davies and Challis, 1986) and *Case Management in Community Care* (Challis and Davies, 1986). They too explore the relations between needs, resources and outcomes and explain them by the analysis of structures, policy and process. As we shall see in the concluding chapter, the arguments developed in the four books are complementary.

This chapter introduces the study in two ways. Section 1 lists some of the questions which the analysis sets out to answer, provides some contextual notes to the questions, and sketches the design of the study. Section 2 outlines what we see to be the critical policy issues which the answers to our questions should illuminate. Our capacity to tackle them is what can make or mar the immediate practical usefulness of the book. So Section 2 defines the issues to which we must return in the concluding section.

1 Project questions and design

1.1 Questions

In particular, the study either describes or provides the information to deduce:

- Who gets what: how the quantities of services consumed vary with need-related circumstances and need-affecting events. The quantities are measured both in the number of physical units and by the opportunity cost to the principal agencies and to consumers and their principal carers.
- What the non-resource outcomes are for consumers (dependents and their informal carers). The outcomes studied include probabilities of admission to institutions for long-term care, client morale, carer stress, and what consumers perceive to be the benefits of receiving services.
- What improvements in outcomes are associated with additional units of inputs of various types: the 'marginal productivities' of inputs.
- What are the effects on marginal productivities of need-related circumstances.
- What different mixes of inputs produce similar levels and mixes of outcomes: the observed 'substitutability' of inputs in the production of outputs.
- What are the costs associated with various levels and mixes of outcomes, and the increased costs associated with improvements in outcomes: 'average' and 'marginal' costs. Again the effects of need-related circumstances on average and marginal costs are studied.
- How targeting, outcomes, marginal productivities, average costs and marginal costs vary between the areas.
- How the nature and effects of innovatory schemes in the areas vary.

These are fundamental features of community-based care. To attempt to describe them requires no justification. However, there are some special reasons why the description is particularly important at this time.

1.1.1 The outcomes of variations in inputs

The achievements of high-cost residential care have been disappointing. Also we shall show that a big gap exists between the average costs of residential care and community-based packages. It is critical to know whether the community services produce (or with sufficient resources *could* produce) a wide enough range of outcomes to a sufficient degree to make feasible the effective substitution of community-based for residential-based care. It is just as important to know how to extend the range of effects and magnify their scale as it is to describe what is achieved. For this it is useful to compare systems. However, the variations are also likely to depend on the need-related circumstances, so that needs, resources and outcomes cannot be separated in the analysis.

1.1.2 The substitutability and appropriate substitution of inputs

An argument about substitutability and substitution reads like a brain-teasing parody of academise. However, it is too important to omit and difficult to simplify. Substitution is about what actually occurs. Substitutability about what might potentially occur.

Davies and Challis (1986, Chap. 1) argue that there is potentially a vast range of sources for the services which dominate social care, and that there is therefore great potential substitutability between inputs from different sources. The importance of the argument is that inputs which one might expect to be usable in ways which make them highly substitutable can vary greatly over time and space in their cost to the agency and to society. If resources can be used to produce inputs which are potentially substitutable, the variations in the relative prices of the inputs can be exploited to yield more welfare from social expenditures.

However, one must not take for granted the actual substitution, and still less the appropriate substitution of service inputs. Resources may be used in ways which make the service inputs they produce less substitutable than they could usefully be. Also the actual substitution of service inputs which are in fact substitutable might not be achieved. And the substitutions made can be inefficient by failing to take into account the relative costs of substitutes. So it is important first to understand the degree of substitutability which exists and the reason why substitution potential is not realised. For instance, is a gap between potential and actual substitutability due to structures and assumptions which are easy to change? Or is it due to almost irremovable features of care contexts? Second, if service inputs are substitutable, do the agencies in fact achieve input mixes which maximise the outputs from the available finance? As we shall see in the final chapter, comparing what this study shows to happen generally with what happens in community care experiments demonstrates that the distinction between substitution and substitutability is critical to the economics of developing community-based care and helping it to achieve its full potential for those who would otherwise have to receive residential-based care. We hope that this book and its sequel will clarify the distinction and show how important it is for thinking through the development of home care.

1.1.3 Responsiveness to variety and changes in needs

Again, Davies and Challis (1986, Chap. 1) argue great variety in need-related circumstances of persons at risk of admission to long-term care and, given the fragmentation and complexity of services, the difficulty of matching resources to the needs of the individual. So how finely are interventions tailored to individual needs, and how are the interventions altered in response to need-affecting life events? Does the evidence support the Davies-Challis developmental bias thesis: the argument that a bias towards unnecessary admission to institutions for long-term care has been reinforced because the post-war growth in resources has been used to increase the level, range and quality of services but not greatly to improve the effectiveness of the performance of the core tasks of case management, though this has been made more important by the greater range of community-based services and their greater potential contribution to the quality of recipients' lives? Is there support for the argument that resources would be more productively used if concentrated on those in greatest need or at highest risk of avoidable admission to institutions for long-term care?

The argument of Davies and Challis (1986, Table 1.1) laid great stress on variety. Indeed, it associated variety with the complexity of need-related circumstances and the likelihood of sudden changes. It argued that these were not rococo features seen in only a few cases. They were so frequently encountered and so important in determining responses that assumptions and arrangements should be built around them. We should investigate the argument, because service structures and procedures are not those which would take best account of variety, complexity and instability of needs, and we suspect that many managers make quite different assumptions about needs. The success of the White Paper's reforms could be greatly diminished if action is based on the wrong assumptions. So, for instance, we must ask whether responses reflect consumers' individual desires and perceptions about what would most contribute to adding to the quality of life at home – that is, do the responses attempt to meet higher as well as lower Maslow (1970) needs? Or are the responses narrowly focused on providing services to compensate for the more obvious functional incapacities? Do the responses build around the structures and expectations of life of the dependent and those closest to them and help them all to function better by their own criteria? Do the responses focus sufficiently on the nature and quality of service, and do they result in the matching of inputs mobilised from many sources? Or do the assumptive worlds lead to a narrow concern with the allocation of standard services? Of course it is simplistic to postulate stark opposites. However, it is important to use the study to compare the varieties of standard practice with the assumptions and arguments worked through in our community care experiments.

1.1.4 *The effects of system differences*
Differences between local authorities have widened during the last decade. So also have differences in the circumstances of their populations. One would expect variations in priorities and assumptions to be reflected by such differences as the rise of centre parties, the apparently greater volatility of political control, the emergence of hung councils, and the style and content of the new urban politics. The provision of community care is

essentially redistributive in nature in the sense in which the concept is used in political science (Lowi, 1972). Indeed, some academic writers seem to see it almost entirely as a redistributive matter, and in important respects, redistribution in one dimension only: they describe it simply as a women's issue. But the differences might also be expected to affect the technical relations between resources and outcomes: the resources required to achieve outcomes might differ partly because need-related circumstances of populations might vary in ways which are difficult to capture in models, and partly because authorities seem to attach different priorities to the trade-offs between the aspects of efficiency we distinguish and other things they think to be important; for instance, the involvement of and control by elected representatives, and factors affecting the style of provision which do not greatly measure the outcomes treated as important in the narrower social welfare paradigm. And of course large variations in technical efficiency have long been seen as a problem requiring solution. The reforms of the 1970s were expected to eliminate much of the variation by, among other means, eliminating small authorities, Crossman famously arguing the trade-off between scale, efficiency, and democracy when justifying the Royal Commission on Local Government. However, the reforms of the 1970s did not solve the problem. There is still evidence that big variations in technical efficiency remain (Audit Commission, 1985).

Such matters beg broad questions – questions which are too broad to deal with fully in this essay, though the evidence we have collected can illuminate some of them. We start with some ground-clearing matters. Do the area 'systems' for which we have collected evidence appear to vary greatly in efficiency? Does the differential variation between aspects of efficiency and the outcomes achieved reflect policy priorities and local values, organisational differences (for instance, patch or specialist social work organisation), the relative emphasis placed on organisational control and the mix of devices used to achieve it, or the effort made to secure inter-agency working at middle management level and in the field?

1.1.5 The effects of innovations on equity and efficiency
Our work is like that of others in suggesting that the nature of efficiency-improving innovations have changed during the last decade (Davies, 1981; Davies and Ferlie, 1982; Davies and Ferlie, 1984; Ferlie, 1982; Ferlie, Challis and Davies, 1983; Ferlie, Challis and Davies, 1984; Ferlie, Challis and Davies, 1985; Ferlie, Challis and Davies, 1989). It is clearly worth while to describe changes in their logics and natures, and show how environments influence the rate and type of innovations. However, our earlier work left us dissatisfied in at least one important respect. We had little direct evidence about process and outcomes, but were forced to make inferences from circumstantial evidence. The evidence collected in this study is for few innovations and beneficiaries. But it at

least allows us to ask whether there is evidence that the most common forms of innovation have affected efficiency for clients of the schemes and had a substantial beneficial impact on the system as a whole?

These are examples of the questions addressed by the project. Their analysis requires both the modelling of statistical data and other forms of enquiry yielding generalisations of different levels. It is on the illumination of one by the other that the most interesting ideas for creating implementable policies depend.

1.2 Study design

The main features of the design are summarised in Table 1.1.

The statistical analysis of needs, resources and outcomes required a substantial collection of evidence whose content was obtained in several ways.

- Persons in a sample of 589 recipients of community-based services were interviewed by Social and Community Planning Research (SCPR) applying a PSSRU-designed questionnaire, survivors in the community being re-interviewed approximately six months later. The sample was

---

Table 1.1
Study features

Focus on needs, resources and outcomes
- Statistical description and modelling analysis.
- Explanation and illumination by studying structures, policies, assumptive worlds, practice and processes.

Databases
- Interviews with 589 consumers at referral or at major change in support package.
- Interviews with 443 of the consumers approximately six months later.
- Interviews with 210 'principal carers' of the consumers contemporaneously with the second consumer interviews.
- Resources for consumers tracked until death, admission to an institution for long-term care, or second consumer interview.
- Data about consumers collected over six months from SSD workers most likely to perform core tasks of case management using the case review instrument.
- Data about relocation, mortality, and utilisation after three years.
- Analysis of SSD and community health service documentation.
- Interviews about structures, policy process, practice, and assumptive worlds with agency personnel; e.g. social work team leaders, area officers, SSD headquarters policy-makers, participants in innovatory social service schemes.
- Analysis of secondary data bases: e.g. 1985 *General Household Survey*, CIPFA and DHSS statistics.

drawn to represent levels of services received, household structures, and physical ability. Precisely which elderly member of the household was the consumer was left an open question at that stage. All were interviewed. The estimation of the degree of shared benefit was deferred to the subsequent analysis. The interview schedules were designed to provide evidence for some of the crucial indicators of the main types of production of welfare factors: resource inputs, 'quasi-inputs' (primarily exogenous circumstances and characteristics of recipients and systems likely to affect the allocation of resources and the relationships between resources and outcomes); the building blocks for indicators of 'intermediate outputs' (consequences of resource inputs significant because of their expected contribution to outcomes important in their own right) and 'final outputs' (consequences of value in their own right). A sample of 210 non-recipients comparable in household structure and physical disability was also interviewed twice.

- An attempt was made to define a principal non-spouse informal carer for each household on the basis of replies to questions about who provided regular unpaid help. The interview schedules covered the pattern of support, the involvement of others and the effects of care-giving; again contributing data for the construction of indicators for quasi-inputs, resource inputs and outputs. The analysis was to estimate the degree to which the persons interviewed provided care inputs and were primarily sources of help or beneficiaries of social service intervention. Moreover, brief interviews were undertaken to provide information about death and institutionalisation.

- Quantities of care inputs from the formal agencies consumed by households were tracked over the evaluation period. Other data were collected from the agencies to help us estimate the unit and marginal costs of inputs.

Ad hoc collections from NHS acute and community service providers were also made, principally to support the thematic analysis of cause and effect.

- For each recipient, interviews were conducted with the social services personnel most likely to perform the core tasks of case management: social workers, home help organisers, and in some cases, day care managers. The data were collected using a modified case review instrument at the time of the client interviews, and covered aspects of case management (including aims and the allocations of resources) and outcomes. The case review data also provided information for statistical analysis of needs, resources and outcomes.

- Interviews were conducted with representative personnel from the ten authorities: home help organisers, social workers, team leaders, area officers, planners at social services department (SSD) headquarters, and participants in innovative schemes. Also interviewed were National

Health Service (NHS) personnel: representatives of community nursing management and district planners. The interviews were supplemented with documentary collections about policy and practice. Data were also collected about levels of referral bombardment and patterns of service allocation.

Volume 1 of the Interim Report of the project gives more detailed accounts of the collections and data on response (Bebbington, Charnley, Davies, Ferlie, Hughes and Twigg, 1986). Also it analyses need-related circumstances and area variations in them. Volume 2 consists of the instruments used.

2 A climacteric in community care of elderly people?

The late 1980s may well prove to have been a climacteric in the history of the long-term care of elderly people. First, important enquiries into long-term care have been published: the report of the Firth Committee (DHSS, 1987a) published hard on the heels of earlier committees on the financing of residential care; the reports of the inspection of home care by the Social Services Inspectorate (SSI) (DHSS, 1987b, 1988a); various studies by the Audit Commission (1985, 1986a, 1987); the report of the Wagner Committee (1988), reports from the House of Commons Social Services Committee (1985) and other parliamentary committees; and above all, the Griffiths Report (1988). But these are only milestones on a journey which started with the assumptive changes in the politics of the late 1970s. Earlier milestones show how the broader ideas worked their way into the care of elderly people: the inauguration and tenacious advancement of at least some features of the Financial Management Initiative, the establishment of the Audit Commission, the transformation of the DHSS Social Work Service into the Social Services Inspectorate, the articulation of a new conception of the primary role of the social services departments in the then Secretary of State's speech to the Joint Social Services annual conference in Buxton (Fowler, 1984). Policy changes in housing, education and other areas of local government have shaken the confidence of those who would wish to resist the new arguments. Financial pressure and the development of for-profit provision financed from public funds have undermined their ability to do so.

It is the intellectual and assumptive aspects of the climacteric that are of most interest here. Four aspects particularly affect our analysis of community-based care of elderly people.
• Local authorities and the Department of Health (formerly Department of Health and Social Security) expect community-based services to become an alternative to residential-based care for many clients.

- Well-publicised analyses have catalogued important respects in which there are shortfalls in the efficiency of the services.
- Some of the analyses have produced coherent and general diagnoses of the causes of the shortfalls in efficiency, and use the diagnoses to lead to strategic proposals for improving performance.
- Radical argument is being developed about what will and should be the characteristics of the economy of social care and the roles of the SSD in it, not just on the analytic fringe of policy-making but also in the social services departments and other policy agencies themselves.

These have large implications for community-based care of elderly people. We must consider each of them if we are to use our data most effectively for policy argument.

3 The substitution of community-based for residential modes of care

The Social Services Inspectorate report *From Home Help to Home Care* (DHSS, 1987b) begins the substance of its summary thus:

All eight authorities were pursuing policy change towards the provision of more flexible and intensive personal care service for people who will otherwise require institutional care (DHSS, 1987b, Summary, para. 2).

The SSI Report defined three key issues: effectiveness, efficiency and 'community care'. It asked:

Is the home help service to be the backbone of a support service offering practical and personal care for people who under previous policies would have been cared for in institutions, or are different kinds of domiciliary care and support services required for such policies to be fulfilled? (DHSS, 1987b, para. 1.2.4)

The SSI did not question whether the policies had changed. It asserted that they had. The report's focus was the implications of the change. In this, the SSI was working through a logic of earlier policy analyses of great impact. The major premise of the Audit Commission's *Managing Services for the Elderly More Effectively* (1985) was that long-term residential care is an expensive indivisible resource, so that authorities should aim to use it more efficiently by better deploying resources in community-based modes of care. Again, the opening words of the Wagner Report were:

People who move into a residential establishment should do so by positive choice ... An important implication of this is that there need to be real and valid alternatives on offer ... there is no valid choice if old people are driven into a residential establishment because domiciliary services are skimpy (Wagner, 1988, pp.7-8).

The community social services were not designed from their inception to substitute for long-term care in institutions. Histories (Parker, 1965; Sumner and Smith, 1969; Means and Smith, 1985) show them to have been rather reluctantly and absent-mindedly produced by the growth of the welfare state. They were the Cinderellas of the social services: left to cook and scrub, imprisoned by structures which ensured a biased and slow development, despised by siblings with more fortunate professional histories which followed the narrowing of the foci for professional development on social work after the defeat of Eileen Younghusband's (1959) apparently broader conception, and ignored by the punch-drunk managers from whom they needed avuncular if not paternal support, yet valued almost unquestioningly by local politicians and so not easily reformed or redirected.

Having to find their market for themselves, and in the case of the home help service, located in an unglamorous section of a local health department receiving little attention from the most senior officers, they came to be seen almost more as a general support for elderly persons than as a service to prevent admission to residential care. In many areas, the allocation of a small amount of service was seen as one of the comforts of old age for the frail elderly in general. So a substantial minority of recipients did not claim it to be difficult to perform for themselves the tasks undertaken by domestic helps (B. Davies, 1981) – higher proportions during the 1950s than fifteen years later (Bebbington, 1979).

The two objectives – making unnecessary the admission to institutions of persons whose quality of life and care could be better outside but who in the absence of appropriate home care would be at high risk, and the provision of modest support for a more general population of frail elderly persons – required different targeting and service content. However, the dilemmas created by the conflicts between the objectives were not recognised for two decades or more. During the early 1960s, chief officers of welfare and health departments did not see the need for residential care and community social services to be interdependent: they were not perceived to be close substitutes (Davies, 1968; Sumner and Smith, 1969). Indeed, recognition of that was slow to emerge. Such powerful advocates as Townsend and Wedderburn (1965) promoted the case for their expansion more as collectively-financed and state-provided consumer goods, whose benefits were mainly immediate and which should be enjoyed as a right by a wide range of citizens, than as cost-effective investments to reduce the demand for residential-based care targeted on the smaller number at most risk of admission. Townsend was a quarter of a century ahead of his time in the form of shelter-with-care he advocated, but the emphasis of the argument was not on substitution for residential care. Neither did Bevan place the emphasis on the substitution for residential care at the time of the debate on the National Assistance Bill. However, some contemporaries clearly saw the importance of the potential substitutablity of community for residential care. Alderman Messer, chairman of the National Old People's Welfare Council, questioned Bevan's policy in the debate on the Second Reading of the National Assistance Bill, arguing that people should not enter residential care as long as they could manage in their own homes and that the need was for more highly developed domiciliary services. Alice Bacon had commented in the same debate that suitable housing provision for old people would be needed. Bevan's view seemed to be that residential homes should be left to find their own place in the market without so much as subsidisation, although it was necessary to sponsor supply:

The whole idea is that the welfare authorities should provide them *and charge an economic rent for them,* so that any old persons who wish to go there may go there, in exactly the same way as many well-to-do people have been accustomed to go into residential hotels (House of Commons, 1947, col. 5, our italics).

These nuances were ignored in the euphoria which followed the demise of the Poor Law.

So the prerequisites for making admission to institutions unnecessary for those at high risk were neglected. The ideas and structures built up over the last forty years are making it more difficult to create the capacity to meet that objective. The constraints include the expectations of citizens, consumers and politicians; and the political gains which might be made by playing on the expectations; and the assumptions and skills of service personnel and the structures and procedures in which they operate. For this study, the most important constraints are those on what the supply of additional resources can achieve. The first paragraph of this section quoted a question posed by the Social Services Inspectorate. The question suggests doubts about whether simply increasing resource levels will sufficiently reduce demands for residential care. During the 1980s, attention has been focused on the concentration of resources on the neediest as a prerequisite for achieving the substitution of community-based for residential care. That SSI question suggests the importance of another issue: improving the nature of the services in a way which increases the beneficial impact of resources – or which improves their 'marginal productivities,' if we use the convenient jargon of the economist.

The SSI issue can be put in a different way. It is of great importance to policy to analyse which of the following four scenarios best describes the characteristics of the services.

- The existing targeting propensities of the services and the relations between ends and means are such that merely by increasing expenditure on them, the services would be able to cope with a substantial shift to a more community-based system. This implies that the community services would use the additional resources to provide services of a kind, at a time, in a way and for the persons which would make them an effective substitute for residential care at no greater cost.

- Changes are required in targeting propensities – that is, the persons receiving services and the quantities of the resources allocated to consumers in different circumstances – but given these, the services would be able to substitute for residential care at no greater cost.
- The 'marginal productivities' of inputs will have to be increased although targeting is satisfactory. By marginal productivities we mean what is produced from resources given input mixes and levels and the need-related circumstances of consumers.
- Changes are required both in targeting propensities and in the 'marginal productivities' of inputs into the services.

The four situations are judgements in descending order of optimism. The first would merely require more of the same; lineal development but not the acceleration of the new managerialist revolution and the determined reconstruction of the community services around a new balance of ends and means. Both the second and third require investment; the allocation of resources without immediate return on activities not contributing directly to the production of welfare. The third would demand a much higher ratio of investment to consumption expenditure than the second. Unlike the second, it would require that the investment effort reach parts unaffected by the tight implementation of targeting criteria and allocation guidelines. In particular, it would affect what, when and how tasks were performed, in a way which produces consequences analogous to the 'Heineken effects' in the community care experiments (Davies and Challis, 1986; Davies and Missiakoulis, 1988). So the balance of policy effort should be quite different in each of the four situations. And to the extent that the third exists, success would require antidotes to the fatal mixture of management optimism, overload, vagueness about the logics connecting arrangements and desired outcomes and an insufficiently broad repertoire of devices which are described clearly enough to be replicated.

To which of the four scenarios reality conforms is one subject of the book. We review the evidence in Chapter 12. The other subject is how policy and practice should be developed given the scenario which proves to be most realistic. That is the focus of Chapters 13 and 14.

4 Overview

The chapter has argued that:

- The next five years may well prove to be a climacteric in the long-term care of elderly people, and particularly for community-based care since it is likely that an attempt will be made to meet the substantial growth in needs and demands more by the development of community-based than residentially-based modes of service.

- It is critically important to know whether increasing expenditures on the community-based services will be sufficient to cope with the increased demands, whether increasing expenditures with improved targeting will be sufficient, or whether it will also be necessary to achieve a great improvement in the marginal productivities of services. The second has proved difficult. The third will require great effort, but the need for it has not been seriously discussed.

2 Inequity and inefficiency: diagnoses and prescriptions

Chapter 1 postulated four scenarios to which reality might correspond. What would distinguish between them are targeting propensities and the marginal productivities of service inputs for outcomes important to persons who are most dependent on community services. Both targeting and productivities influence inequities and inefficiencies. This chapter first reviews evidence and argument about the nature of the inequities and inefficiencies. Then it discusses diagnoses and prescriptions.

1 Allegations and evidence about inequities and inefficiencies

Determining which analysis most accurately describes the reality depends on knowing the nature of inefficiencies and inequities. Since the late 1970s, the growing body of policy-analytic argument and research has spread an understanding about the nature and causes of inefficiencies and inequities. Produced partly by DHSS-financed research units and local authorities themselves, some of the argument has had direct influence on policy-making.

Most directly influential have been analyses by the Audit Commission, the new Social Services Inspectorate of the DHSS and the House of Commons Social Services Committee. (The remit of the National Audit Office covers central government expenditure, and so the National Health Service. However, it works through implications for other policy agencies, and it uses much the same style of policy analysis as the Audit Commission.) All four reflect a new priority to improve efficiency through better management: a 'new managerialism' (Davies, 1987). The work of the Audit Commission, an independent body, has complemented the new efficiency focus of the Social Services Inspectorate of the DHSS. The Audit Commission has developed and disseminated broad policy argument illustrated with particular cases and the narrow generalisations which are the stuff of agency management. The SSI worked within similar frameworks but developed the fine-grained argument about policies, resources, structures and processes on which the development and implementation of policy most directly depend. The same new managerialist doctrines are being applied throughout public administration by means of such instruments as the Financial Management Initiative. The language and ideas promoted by the Audit Commission and the SSI are heard in local authorities to an extent which would not have been predicted five years ago.

It is unnecessary to undertake another literature review of inequity and inefficiency in the long-term care of the aged (see Goldberg and Connelly, 1982, and more recently, Davies and Challis, 1986, Chap. 2.). However, it is useful to list and classify allegations by the nature of the inequity or inefficiency to which they relate, and to state some of the arguments about the more general and pervasive processes which cause them. The aspects of inefficiency distinguished in the classification have been used in earlier production of welfare studies. This project was so designed as to measure the relative efficiency of systems in four of the five aspects.

The allegations are made in a large literature. What is particularly interesting is to see which have been made in those policy documents most widely seen in local government. We now turn to allegations made in these documents.

1.1 Horizontal target inefficiency

Ensuring that resources are productively used has come to dominate managers' thinking. The degree of horizontal target inefficiency is a measure of unmet need; and much need remains invisible and not fully comprehensible without *ad hoc* investigations to identify and estimate it. Most new managerialist writing is strongest in its treatment of the more visible forms of inefficiency. However, there are exceptions. One example is the Audit Commission's argument (1985, paras 54, 90) that too few resources are allocated for the relief of carers and that earlier identification and help is necessary. A later chapter in this study considers the mixture of providers' motives; the relative priority of (i) relieving strain on carers likely to 'burn out', or to cease giving care for other reasons, and so to preventing the admission of dependants into institutions, or (ii) of relieving carers who are bearing a grossly inequitable burden but who are likely to continue to do so without additional support. A second example is the Audit Commission's allegation that psychiatric, medical, geriatric and social services have failed to establish the clear joint policies which would prevent physically disabled persons with behaviour disorders or severe dementia from being seen by each agency as primarily the responsibility of others.

Estimates suggest horizontal target efficiency in the home help service to be lower than vertical target efficiency by any of a variety of targeting criteria. Partly this is because the service is allocated in response to referrals and little outreach is undertaken. Partly it is because allocations are not based on carefully constructed, precisely formulated and transparent policies subject to open review and requiring widespread justification. Horizontal target inefficiency is particularly serious among complex cases, including many of those needing larger quantities of several services and most at

risk of admission to institutions for long-term care. Many among such
cases will not be attracted by the services available unless the service is
thought by consumers to contribute directly to improving the quality of
their lives as they see it, and unless the response is created in stages,
each step building on the goodwill created by the services' helpfulness
at the last stage. (See for instance, Davies and Challis, 1986, chapters 6
and 7). Applying a targeting criterion intended to reflect actual allocation
practice as closely as possible, Bebbington and Davies (1983) estimated a
degree of horizontal target efficiency for the home help service in 1980
of little more than one-third. The Social Services Inspectorate (DHSS,
1987b) criticised the criterion for being excessively generous given the
present balance of needs and resources in social care. However, adopting
the apparently more restrictive criterion developed by the Audit Commission (1985) paradoxically yields a lower estimate of the degree of
horizontal target efficiency: 14 per cent. The estimate by the Audit Commission's 'High Public Sector Dependency' criterion is lower either because
in practice the home help service operates criteria which are in some
(though arguably inappropriate) ways more restrictive than those of High
Public Sector Dependency membership, or because the Audit Commission
data are unreliable. The replication of our reanalysis of the 1980 General
Household Survey (GHS) with the 1985 GHS data shows for three definitions
of the target group that (i) vertical target efficiency remained greater than
horizontal target efficiency for all target groups and local authority types
save one (the exception being a definition based on personal disability
for London boroughs); and that (ii) horizontal target efficiency did not
diminish between 1980 and 1985 (Bebbington with Moennadin, 1989).

1.2 Vertical target inefficiency

Allegations abound. Possibly the most common is that the level of input
to those at greatest risk is insufficient to diminish greatly their probabilities
of admission to institutions for long-term care. This is in spite of most
local authorities seeing the prevention of admission to institutions for
long-term care, particularly residential homes, as an important, and possibly
the most important, objective of community services (DHSS, 1987b).
Nationally in 1980, perhaps only one-fifth of home help resources were
consumed by persons in 'severe need' by the criteria used in calculating
the Rate Support Grant (Davies and Challis, 1986, p.4). Also some groups
in particularly great need receive inadequate attention; for instance persons
suffering from dementia and related diseases. Conversely many recipients
are not too disabled to perform the tasks undertaken by the services
without great effort. For instance, Howell, Boldy and Smith (1979) found
that home helps in Devon and Cornwall spent only 2 per cent of their
time on personal care. The evidence is for a wide range of locales and
refers to periods between the late 1970s and mid-1980s. (See for home

help, Marks, 1975; Gwynedd County Council, 1977; Hurley and Wolstenholme, 1980; Bebbington and Davies, 1982; Audit Inspectorate, 1983; Carpenter, 1983; Audit Commission, 1985; and for other community services, Brotherton, 1975; Bedfordshire Social Services Department, 1978; Hounslow Social Services Department, 1981; Johnson, di Gregorio and Harrison, 1981; Means, 1981; Camden Social Services Department, 1983.) The Audit Commission (1985) argues that it is difficult to select the 10 per cent of the Low Public Sector Dependency recipients at high risk, and so to justify provision to members of the group on the grounds that it will prevent admission to residential care. Arguments about input mix efficiency are associated with allegations of vertical target inefficiency.

However, not all agree about the implications for policy. The Social Service Inspectorate (DHSS, 1987b) have argued (and quantified) the case for concentrating resources and adapting the services to what is required by those at greatest risk. Without concentration and adaptation, they argue, the needs of the larger numbers at greatest risk are unlikely to be met from the resources expected. But Dexter and Harbert (1983, p.27) lucidly describe the dilemma: whereas the cost of a greater concentration of domestic help on those at greatest risk is clear – a reduction in the quality of life due to the removal of services from others – its preventive impact is an unproven assumption. Similar disagreements exist about whether to concentrate the targeting of meals services, day care, and the provision of sheltered housing. (Compare L. Davies, 1981; Booth, 1978; Audit Commission, 1985, para. 113; and Johnson, di Gregorio and Harrison, 1981, for meals services.) Rereading descriptions of the services in the 1960s and their policy histories (Davies, 1968; Sumner and Smith, 1969; Clarke, 1984; Means and Smith, 1985), one can see how slow central government was to argue that the promotion of community services for large numbers of people in low need would inevitably make less likely the development of effective intensive services for those at high risk of admission to institutions. By the time of the DHSS community care study, the contradictions were clear and so were central government priorities (DHSS, 1981c). However, the pattern of development of the previous two decades had made it politically and managerially difficult for authorities to accept or implement them.

Bebbington and Davies (1983) estimated degrees of vertical target efficiency of the home help service for 1980 using various targeting criteria. It was 77 per cent for England and Wales as a whole using the criterion which most closely reflected the pattern of utilisation. The replicatory analysis of the data from the 1985 GHS suggested little change – if anything a small fall – in vertical target efficiency (Bebbington with Moennadin, 1989). Taking High Public Sector Dependency as the criterion, using the Audit Commission's data, and net (not gross) expenditure as the index of resources, suggests that the degree of vertical target efficiency varied between the seven authorities studied from about 50 to 75 per cent. High vertical target efficiencies were associated with low expenditures on community services. But the correlation is inexact. For instance, low expenditure was compatible with a degree of vertical target efficiency only one-fifth higher than for an authority spending more than three times as much; and the Audit Commission (1985, p.2) reported that in four of the seven authorities studied, one-half or more of the expenditure on community services was made on those not obviously needing them, but that in two out of the four the spending on the most dependent on public sector support was lower than average.

1.3 Input mix inefficiency

Among the allegations most commonly made and often supported with evidence are:

- Health, housing and social services are inadequately coordinated. The role of the social services department in the decision to develop sheltered housing is argued to be insufficient. They are not universally involved to a sufficient degree in the training of wardens and the selection of residents. For instance, the social services are not universally represented on allocation panels. Very sheltered housing accompanied by community services should be more purposefully and frequently used as an alternative to residential care (Audit Commission, 1985, para. 77). The provision of social, community nursing and medical services for clients is inadequately coordinated.
- Insufficiently intensive inputs are made to persons with one carer carrying a heavy burden: intensive inputs could prevent 'burn-out' or an overwhelming incentive to take an opportunity to obtain residential care. More use should be made of carer self-help groups. Authorities with high expenditures on community services should consider focusing their spending so as to encourage the mobilisation of informal care, not to imply to relatives, friends and the voluntary sector that their efforts are no longer necessary (Audit Commission, 1985, paras 61, 65).
- Incontinence services are inadequate (Audit Commission, 1985, para. 90).
- Packages are not adjusted to the needs of groups at particularly high risk; for instance the moderately disabled with no local support from friends or relatives (Audit Commission, 1985, para. 54). The response to the changing needs of individuals is 'too little, too late' and inappropriate in nature.
- More expensive services are used for tasks which could be performed as well more cheaply. For instance, home helps are used to collect the pension or do the shopping (Audit Commission, 1985, para. 69).

- The circumstances in which phased care can most effectively make admission to institutions for long-term care unnecessary have not been worked out and embodied in effective policies and procedures.
- The allocation of resources between the geographical areas of authorities does not achieve the prerequisites for making the best use of resources over the authority as a whole.
- Meals provided by voluntary organisations are provided less intensively and seem to be less integral to the package of support services for the client than meals provided by the social services department itself (Audit Commission, 1985, para. 112).
- The services are unavailable at the times required; for instance out of office hours, at weekends, and during holidays.
- The tasks performed for those at high risk are not those which would most make it unnecessary to provide residential care.
- Increases in provision during the 1970s were not geared directly to providing a genuine alternative for those at the margin of need for residential care (DHSS, 1981a, para. 1.10). Trends in the allocation of services have not reflected changes in need distributions among the populations in private households (Wenger, 1984).

1.4 Technical efficiency

Allegations include:
- Services are provided in a manner which allows the skills of dependants to deteriorate rather than to be reinforced and complemented. Services are sometimes provided 'merely because they are available' or as a token response made because no more appropriate response seems feasible (Audit Commission, 1985, para. 66).
- Policy and procedures for home help deployment are inadequate, for instance, about the circumstances in which an area home help should be used so as to minimise travelling costs and those in which a specialist home help could be used to undertake personal care. Again, the routing of transport for meals and day care services fails to minimise travel time and costs.
- Little attention has been given to alternative methods of meal preparation such as 'cook-chill' methods, although assessments in some authorities suggest that great improvements are possible in technical efficiency through reducing delivery costs and improving quality (Audit Commission, 1985, para. 114).
- Insufficient ingenuity has been used in reducing the costs of transport to day centres and making the most effective use of day centre capital (Audit Commission, 1985, para. 110).
- Too few departments had established contracts offering guaranteed hours for sufficiently high proportions of home helps, it being argued that the dependence on home helps working short and irregular hours

increased the need for management inputs and so the costs of producing outputs (DHSS, 1987b, para. 2.5.5). (However, Davies and Coles, 1981, found that the proportion of home helps working for less than 1,000 hours a year had no impact on cost variations within the authority investigated.)

1.5 Output mix inefficiency

The concern with carer stress is only partly instrumental: social workers and others seek to improve the welfare of carers to a degree greater than is necessary to prevent admission of clients to institutions or to improve client welfare, and do so in circumstances in which client benefits will be small. The Audit Commission (1985, para. 66) comments that insufficient information about benefits is provided to carers and that authorities should clarify their policies about the support of carers compared with providing services for elderly people, and advocates more carer support groups.

The most general and coherent arguments about output mix efficiency have not emerged from the new managerialist analyses but from feminist critiques. For instance, Finch (1984, 1986, 1987a,b) describes feminists' major line of critical questioning to be 'the incorporation of women's unpaid labour as front-line carers for elderly people (almost always their relatives) who might otherwise have been cared for in a residential institution'. In practice, community care is family care, and family care is women's care. Comparing findings for Bethnal Green in the early 1950s and the early 1980s, Finch (1987a) suggests that kin relations remain mainly, if not exclusively a matter for women. Women are imprisoned by informal care. Among the reasons are that 'caring defines women's identity in our society ... it is through caring in an informal capacity ... and through formal caring as nurses, secretaries, cleaners, teachers and social workers that women enter and occupy their place in society' (Graham, 1983). Men see morality in terms of the respective rights of individuals whereas women see morality in terms of networks of relationships within which there are responsibilities, the principal responsibility being to ensure that no one gets hurt (Finch, 1987a, p.28; Gilligan, 1982); and women in our society are defined as people for whom altruism is the natural mode of operating, and so is enforced in the sense that much in social life is built on the assumption that women will behave thus and should be encouraged to do so by policy (Land and Rose, 1985). However it would be wrong to argue that social care of elderly people is almost entirely a women's issue. As the OPCS (1988) illustrates, men contribute large inputs, particularly for spouses. Moreover to some degree the dependence on women in later generations is an accident of demographic history. Population projections suggest that higher proportions of very elderly persons will in the future be male, implying more care from elderly husbands, whose tending input can be too easily forgotten (OPCS, 1988a,b). But of course the feminist case is basically unanswerable.

Therefore provision should take the form of residential care, or to express Finch's argument more accurately, a form of accommodation providing shelter with domestic and nursing services for those needing them (Finch, 1986). However, most people, particularly women, would prefer care *in* the community to care *by* the community for their elderly dependants: packages of care which take the dependent individual out of the home for a large part of the time (West, Illsley and Kelman, 1984) – though not residential care itself, for reasons which the analyses of the comparison groups of the community care projects make clear (Challis, Chessum, Chesterman, Luckett and Woods, 1988).

1.6 The allegations and the focus of the new managerialist critique

Our attempt to classify the arguments contained in the new managerialist literature yielded the interesting result that few relate directly to output mix efficiency. Beyond assertions about the importance of avoiding unnecessary admission to institutions for long-term care, the argument of even the most sophisticated analyses of the new managerialists is imprecise and unsystematic about what do and should comprise the 'final outputs' of the community services, the outcomes of intervention which should be valued in their own right. It is still less precise and systematic about the importance which should be attached to each. It is also imprecise about what outcomes, final or intermediate, must be achieved for the final outputs to be produced. That is hardly surprising within a decade of the commencement of the attack on the pervasive vagueness of the assumptions about ends, means and their relationships in social care.

2 New managerialist diagnoses and prescriptions

Some of the more general new managerialist argument has produced impressively coherent analyses of causes and how performance might be improved. The reports of the Social Services Inspectorate on the home care services (DHSS, 1987b, 1988a) contain the best-grounded analysis of structure and process in the community social services. The most general new managerialist argument is the visionary Griffiths Report (1988), which anticipated the implications of increasingly mixed supply and financing economy of social care.

2.1 The reports of the Social Services Inspectorate

The SSI reports on the home care services argued that:

- A policy of community care requires more intensive and personal care to more dependent people who would otherwise be likely to require institutional care (para. 2.1.1.) The growth in the group most at risk is too great to be accommodated without large increases in resources unless home care services abandon their traditional high acceptance practices (para. 2.2). The 1988 report added that charging practices could also affect the resources available and that the inspection had revealed 'a great variety of charging policies' (DHSS, 1988a, paras 4.2-4.4).
- The authorities studied provide to an unequal degree all the prerequisites for the successful development of a home care service which reduces the probability of admission to residential care of large numbers of the more dependent: the statement of underlying principles. The prerequisites were argued to be the formulation of strategic objectives; the specification of organisational arrangements for services and work structures for staff in line with these objectives; statements of eligibility criteria and priorities to guide resource allocation practice; and management processes which are conducive to 'collective ownership' by all staff of principles and objectives, and which facilitate innovation and change from the ground up (para. 2.31-2.35). In most authorities, policy development is 'characteristically incremental' (para. 2.3.5).
- The service is highly responsive to referrals so that available resources are spread across as many recipients as possible, the quantity of resources allocated to each recipient being low, so restricting the capacity to move from domestic work to the performance of the physical and social care tasks required to provide an alternative to institutional care: 'intensity' (provision per recipient) is sacrificed for 'cover' (number of recipients per population at risk) at any given level of resources (para. 2.4, summary para. 3), the intensity of service varying little once referrals have got through the eligibility gate (para. 2.4.12).
- Discretion in the performance of core tasks of case management is routinised as a way of coping with everyday pressures, since those who exercise it operate at the bottom of long hierarchies down which clearly formulated messages about policies and procedures do not travel well, if at all, and they face a constant bombardment of demand. Rules and procedures become a means to ensure the flow of clients through service processes rather than a framework for determining efficient resource use or effective outcomes for clients (para 2.5.1). Outreach to areas of unmet need is unusual (para. 2.5.2). Assessment practice is rarely linked to detailed policy guidance, organisers learning 'rules of the game' rather than assimilating formal guidelines, making fairly standard allocation responses on the basis of sparse documentation, and rarely refusing to allocate services (para. 2.5.3). Collaboration in care planning is rudimentary and haphazard. Monitoring and review rarely

result in the reduction or withdrawal of service (para. 2.5.4). The size of caseloads limits the performance of the core tasks of case management.

- Caseloads of home helps and organisers and the range of tasks are excessive; infrastructural support inadequate, and few organisers are trained, at a time when the increased disability of clients makes case management more complex and the moves towards personal care create a need for increased supervision and support of home helps and organisers (p.6).
- There is neither the specificity and control entailed in top-down approaches nor the participative service planning required for bottom-up approaches (para. 2.7). The supply of resources is insufficient (para. 2.8). The core tasks of case management are insufficiently well performed for high efficiency (para. 2.9).

In brief, therefore, the argument is that authorities face a strategic choice between cover and intensity; that the structures, policies, procedures and assumptive worlds combine to give excessive emphasis to cover and inadequate attention to intensity; and that the low level of intensity is a sign of the inadequate matching of resources to needs which prevents home care services from being real alternatives to residential care.

The danger is no longer that authorities are unaware that the home care services are in need of modernisation and reform. Indeed, the social services agencies seem almost too ready to accept the allegations, and the outside world is in danger of underestimating what the home care services have contributed. The reaction of the social services press to the SSI report on the home care services in 1989 was interesting. *Community Care* headline read: 'SSI Slates Home Care Services'. The magazine's account merely summarised some of the report's argument. *Community Care*, one of whose functions is surely to articulate a social services perspective, did not attempt a reasoned assessment of the SSI evidence and argument.

2.2 Are the SSI arguments generally valid?

The first SSI inspection covered only eight authorities and the second studied another six. However, many would agree that the argument continues to apply to most authorities. Indeed, the argument may be more valid now than during the period for which some of its more quantitatively testable propositions were first stated, because the balance of needs and resources is less favourable now than during the 1950s and early 1960s (Davies, 1968, 1971a,b; Davies, Barton, McMillan and Williamson, 1971). Bebbington showed that during the 1970s, the intensity of provision fell despite the growth in proportions of disabled elderly persons in private households and the big expansion in residential provision (Bebbington, 1979). Diagram 2.1 extends the analysis. It shows trends in cover, intensity and unit costs over fifteen years. Intensity declined steadily until the break in the series in 1982. However, cover was extended only negligibly. (The

Diagram 2.1
Cover, Intensity and Unit Cost
England and Wales, 1971-84

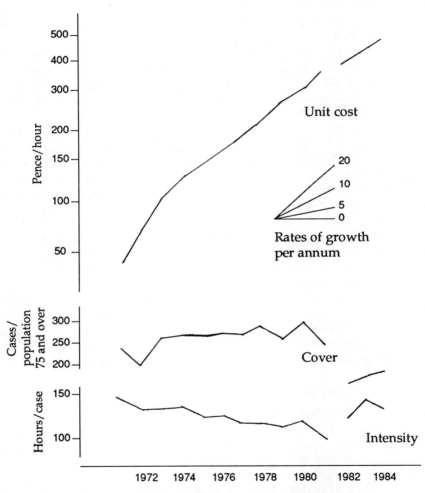

Note: Statistical discontinuity between 1981 and 1982
Sources: *Health and Personal Social Services Statistics*
Health Statistics for Wales
CIPFA: *Social Services Statistics: Actuals*
Population Trends

absence of an appropriate price deflator makes the growth in unit costs difficult to interpret. Dexter and Harbert (1983) describe the large changes in the terms and conditions of staff and suggest that a large part of the apparent growth in resources was consumed thereby.) What is clear from the diagram is that the reduction in intensity has not purchased the extension of cover; merely its maintenance.

The earlier studies showed that the patterns of inter-authority variation in the 1950s and 1960s were neither the outcomes of chance variations nor of random authority or departmental influences. They quite clearly reflected pervasive and powerful influences on the authority; influences affecting values and priorities, and what would be rational political and policy responses to historically-determined and externally-determined environments. Political scientists may still disagree about the placing of such influences in causal sequences (Sharpe and Newton, 1984). However, what is incontrovertible is that these and other comparative statistical studies exploring influences on policy outcomes showed that the patterns could not be understood apart from the broader environment of the authority and its area. It was a new message, an antidote to the case study of policy and politics in a single authority or to the comparison of a small number of authorities which led scholars to stress authorities' uniqueness; for instance, 'above all, the decisive factors shaping the political process were the elected members and officials. Each town is unique ... Most of all, each town throws up its own unique individuals' (Jones, 1969, p.347) and 'Any county borough with over 75 years of history behind it can make out a good claim to be regarded as *sui generis*' (Peschek and Brand, 1966, p.8). Authorities responded more similarly to their environments than had been thought. If true today, this is significant for national policy-making. Where we can identify the incentives to which authorities' behaviour responds, the local implementation of national policy demands that the national policy includes the appropriate structuring of those incentives which the central government can manipulate. This is particularly so if the incentive is created by a policy variable whose effect is narrow. Where the common response reflects more partisan ideological assumptions, successful local implementation demands conversion by example. But successful attempts to change perceptions and behaviour also demand that the central government acknowledges the inevitability of variety in the interpretation of ends and of what constitutes desirable means.

We have therefore explored what influences affect the basic parameters of local variation in home care: Cover (recipients per population at risk); Intensity (service units received per recipient); and Unit Costs (gross expenditure per recipient); and their product, Gross Expenditure (gross expenditure per population at risk). (Unlike the SSI, we distinguish Unit Costs because they are likely to reflect the way in which the technical operating characteristics of the service reflect area and population char-

Table 2.1
Influences on local variations in home care:
Gross Expenditure, Cover, Intensity and Unit Costs

Gross Expenditure: Appendix Tables A2.1 and A2.2

- *Variations in Gross Expenditure were overwhelmingly used to provide variations in Cover*, as they have been for 40 years. Variations do not much affect Intensity and Unit Costs as the simple correlations show. However, authorities may meet demand in full as suggested by the SSI's investigation of the services at work, but the relative variations (coefficients of variation) in Cover and Gross Expenditure imply that authorities do not do so without some compensating variation in Intensity and Unit Costs. So variations in Gross Expenditure are insufficient to compensate fully for variations in demand.
- *The general fiscal position of authorities did not seem to influence Gross Expenditure greatly.* Indeed, Gross Expenditure seems to be slightly higher (not lower) in authorities whose rates have increased most since 1979 because of grant redistributions or untypical expenditure increases.
- *Other things being equal, Labour-controlled authorities tended to spend 6 per cent more.* Also *the greater the volatility of party representation (and so, by hypothesis, electoral competition), the lower Gross Expenditure tended to be.*
- *Authorities with higher proportions of their populations aged 75 and over tended to spend less*, a 10 per cent variation in the proportion being associated with a 1.2-1.5 per cent variation in expenditure.
- *Authorities recovering high proportions of their spending through user charges did not tend to have higher Gross Expenditures.*
- *Higher spending on home helps was not associated with lower spending on residential homes or day care.*
- *The influence of variations in the DoE index of local authority labour costs was greater than required to compensate for purely cost variations*, assuming that variations in home help wage rates were correlated with and no greater than variations in local government wage rates in general. A model predicted logged Gross Expenditure to be as much as 14.5 per cent greater with an index score higher by 1 per cent; an estimate of over-compensation which exceeds those in PSSRU investigations of influences on more aggregated expenditures on the elderly.

Cover: Appendix Tables A2.3 and A2.4

- *Cover was inversely correlated with the proportion of the population aged 75 and over and the provision of residential homes*, despite the apparent goal of providers to Cover all eligible cases. Cover more than other variables would be expected to be influenced by indicators of need-related characteristics and the provision of alternative modes of care.
- *Conservative-controlled authorities may tend to provide lower Cover, Labour-controlled authorities higher.*
- *Cover greatly influences other features of local provision*: there were negative correlations with the ratio of younger to older elderly consumers, perhaps reflecting lower need thresholds where Cover is greatest; and with the ratio of organisers to cases, perhaps reflecting a lower priority to tight control of resources in authorities providing greatest Cover.

Table 2.1 (continued)

Intensity: Appendix Table A2.5

- Although there is a simple correlation only with the ratio of the number of hours paid for to hours received, the partial correlation between Intensity and the ratios of organisers to home helps and cases are negative. However average ratios are high and the relative variation is not great.
- *Intensity tends to be lower where high proportions of home helps work part-time*: an excessive reliance on part-time helps might not only be inefficient (SSI, 1987), but also reflect low Intensity.
- *Intensity is partially correlated with population sparsity*: perhaps organisers react to higher ratios of travel to service time by raising Intensity. However, travel accounts for substantial proportions of paid time, even in the south-eastern county studied by Davies and Coles (1981) but is argued to be reducible (Gwynne and Fean, 1978).
- *Intensity seems to be uninfluenced by political, fiscal, and employment-related variables, the provision of substitutes and the proportion of the population aged 75 and over.*

Unit costs: Appendix Table A2.6

- *A 1 per cent variation in the DoE index of local government wage rates is associated with as much as 3 per cent variation in Unit Costs.* Most of the variation in the index is beween London boroughs and other authorities.
- *Unit Costs tended to be higher in authorities held by the Conservatives in 1974, 1979, and 1986, having a consistent swing to the Conservatives, and the greatest volatility in party composition.*
- *Unit Costs are sensitive to service operating characteristics.* Allowing for Intensity, a high ratio of organisers to cases raises Unit Costs, the fixed costs of the organisers being spread less thinly; an effect also found by Davies and Coles (1981). Unit Costs are also lower in authorities with higher Intensity and authorities with high ratios of hours paid to hours received. A 1 per cent difference in the ratio is associated with a difference in Unit Costs of 28 per cent.
- *Partial correlations with fiscal variables are apparent when allowance is made for service operating characteristics.* Higher Unit Costs were associated with large increases in the proportion of expenditure financed from rates and the excess of expenditure over Block Grant target.
- *The level of provision of substitutes appears not to affect Unit Costs.*

acteristics outside the control of the authority as well as local policy.) The appendix to this chapter (pp.403-12) describes the modelling and its results. Table 2.1 summarises the results.

The results of the modelling suggest:

- The SSI generalisations are broadly valid. Our results elaborate and qualify some of the SSI generalisations. For instance, they show that variations in Gross Expenditure are insufficient to cover demand without reducing Intensity and Unit Costs; that the recovery of higher proportions of gross expenditure by consumer charging may in principle allow the higher levels of gross expenditure required to increase demand, but that in practice authorities have not used the recovered expenditure to finance high spending; that although managers use their budget allocations to maximise Cover, Cover does not vary with the provision of substitutes or demographic pressure – indeed, Cover may more reflect the demand consequences of current expectations generated by past levels of provision; and that as the maximand of the front-line allocation process, Cover, need thresholds, and the effort to target resources more intensively seem to be associated.

- Service operating characteristics which SSDs can substantially control have a considerable influence on the patterns focused on by the SSI. But several of the more general factors which are outside the control of the SSDs and of policy-making in social care have less effect than might be expected.

Examples of the effects of operating characteristics are the associations between Cover, the ratio of younger to older elderly cases, and the ratio of organisers to cases; the relationship between Intensity and the proportions of home helps working part-time; the effect of the ratio of organisers to cases and Unit Costs given Intensity; and the relationships between Unit Costs and the ratio of hours paid for and the hours received.

One might expect a trade-off between the increased Unit Cost required to finance higher ratios of organisers to cases, and the increased intensity of (and in other ways improved) targeting and care made possible by the more careful management permitted by the increase in organisers. Such beneficial consequences are used to justify increased staffing in other areas of long-term care and in secondary prevention in general. For instance, Vetter (1987) has elegantly demonstrated a high negative correlation between the provision of geriatricians and the average length of stay of elderly patients in hospital beds for Welsh counties. He argues a causal connection: 'some bed-use statistics in geriatric care appear to be critically dependent on staffing levels. This does not appear to be the case in better-staffed specialties.' The reduction in costs due to the bed-days saved can be offset against the greater overhead costs incurred by employing more geriatricians. However, although our models suggest a partial correlation of the right sign between Intensity and the ratio of organisers to cases, the average ratio is too low and the variation in the ratio is insufficiently large for one to believe that Intensity can be greatly affected by the inter-authority differences.

- The relative unimportance of purely demographic pressure is well illustrated in Table 2.1. So also is the rarity of the influence of more pervasive fiscal indicators on Gross Expenditure and Intensity.
- Party representational variables strongly influence Gross Expenditure and Cover. This must in part reflect ideational influences. Though showing great continuity over long periods, how policy issues are

interpreted can be influenced by policy argument from the outside, as the experience of the Audit Commission illustrates. Also, our indicator of political competition, the index of representational instability, does not have a pervasive effect, and actually has a negative partial correlation with Gross Expenditure, although one might expect the home care services to be of sufficient symbolic importance and to be closely enough identified with the interests of an important voting bloc for changes in home help spending and charging to be sensitive issues in electoral politics.

So authorities' service policies seem not to have been tightly constrained by either of two types of factor: (i) influences which are in the short run outside the control of the authorities; or (ii) influences which either cannot be influenced by the national community of policy-makers in social care or have their impact almost irrespective of the assumptive worlds of that policy community.

3 Social services departments and the economy of social care

3.1 The Griffiths argument

The themes of the Griffiths Report of most relevance to this study are (i) the emphasis on the performance of core tasks of case management and concentration of the responsibility, authority and accountability for performing them; and (ii) features of the wider context most likely to influence the effects of equity and efficiency of the way the tasks are performed: the reconstructed financing system intended to achieve neutral incentives between alternatives of equivalent cost-effectiveness, continuity of incentives, and the removal of arbitrary limitations on choices; a budgetary approach to management at all levels based on close accounting for resources with machinery for identifying the results of local activity; centrally-approved local plans with grant incentives to develop and implement them with clearer statements of objectives and priorities; and operating assumptions in which the 'first task of publicly provided services is to support and where possible strengthen these networks of carers' (para. 3.2), the second is to fill gaps in caring networks, and the third is that 'the primary function of the public services is to design and arrange the provision of care' (para. 3.4).

Griffiths called the concentration of the responsibility for performing and managing the performance of the core tasks of case management 'a keystone' of his proposals. British recognition of the importance of the performance of the case management tasks is recent. In the early 1980s, the concept 'core task of case management' and how core tasks related to aspects of efficiency meant nothing to academics, managers or field social care professionals. However, the Griffiths Report was not the first official report to adopt the analysis. The Audit Commission had described case management and the development of individual care plans to be 'at the very centre of effective and efficient care' by 1987 (Audit Commission, 1987, paras 48, 49). The 1987 report of the Social Services Inspectorate described their performance to be 'of central interest', and identified the creation of 'case management frameworks' to be one of five preconditions for policy change to have real impact (DHSS, 1987b, paras 48, 49), an emphasis reflected in their report in 1988 (DHSS, 1988a). The Wagner Report recommended that anyone for whom residential care might be an option should have available to them a nominated social worker whose primary task would be to act as their agent, and that authorities should develop systems of delegated budgeting whereby the nominated social workers would exercise direct control over financial resources (Wagner, 1988, paras 3.6, 3.16).

The Griffiths Report made the performance of case management a primary aim:

The role of the social services authorities should be reorientated towards ensuring that the needs of individuals ... are identified, packages of care are devised and services coordinated; and where appropriate a specific care manager is assigned (Griffiths, 1988, Introductory letter to Secretary of State, para. 24).

The report argued that the performance of each of the core tasks was necessary for broad community care objectives to be translated into action for individual people (para. 3.8), and recommended that a care manager should be assigned wherever 'a significant level of resources' was expected (para. 6.6).

This concentration of responsibility was to be in the context of the intention to 'align responsibility for achieving objectives with control over the resources needed to achieve them so that there is a built-in incentive and the facility to make the best use of the resources available' (para. 5.6). For example, the PSSRU community care models give case managers authority to dispose of a budget against which a wide range of services are notionally or actually charged, applying the same array of unit costs as the case managers themselves use in care planning (Davies and Challis, 1986, Chap. 1). That and other features of the structural and procedural framework in the PSSRU models are intended to provide incentives progressively to improve the equity and efficiency of care outcomes.

Although consumers were to pay the full cost of services, the report recommended that case management itself should be free of charge to users. It would be paid for from the community care grant (Griffiths, 1988, para. 6.33). The importance of this has been emphasised in BRITSMO argument (Davies, 1986a; Davies and Challis, 1986; Davies and Goddard, 1987): the greater the influence of the case management agency on the flows of demand and so the flows of resources tied to the demand, illustrated in the chart of the white paper, the less likely is market failure and the greater is the influence of the lead agency over supply and financial interests.

Griffiths recognised but did not grasp one of more vicious nettles. Inevitably there are unresolved dilemmas in proposals which retain a boundary between health and social care agencies and so problems of making the best use of both sets of resources. Griffiths argued that his recommendations were a more satisfactory solution than the mandatory imposition of new common structures: the definition of responsibilities, the insistence on performance and accountability, and emphasis on results and the collation of evidence about them within agreed resources and time-scales (1988, Introductory letter, para. 20). The report recommended that:

Special attention should be given to services at the point of delivery, with the aim of putting into practice at that crucial point the proposals on the identification and assessment of need, consultations with carers and those being cared for, design of care packages, setting of priorities, and monitoring (para. 6.15).

Others had proposed arrangements which would have made it easier to achieve the concentration of case management responsibility for both long-term health and social care (for example, Ferlie, Challis and Davies, 1985; Audit Commission, 1986a; Hunter, 1988). In effect, they had proposed a health/social care agency for long-term care. However, Griffiths recommended financial incentives to agencies to develop the types of joint working reflected in projects reported by the Audit Commission (1986a), and some PSSRU community care projects (Davies and Challis, 1986) and care in the community schemes (Renshaw, Hampson, Thomason, Darton, Judge and Knapp, 1988).

3.2 Implications for the study

Three features of the economy of social care implicit in Griffiths' (1988) scenario are of importance to the arguments of this study: supply is to be sectorally 'mixed'; the financing of services is to be sectorally mixed and the subsidy of services is to be selectivist; and the evolution of the local care economy is to be guided by the politically accountable local social services authority within a framework set by national policy.

- Services are to be supplied 'by the public or private sector according to where they can be provided most economically and efficiently. The onus in all cases should be on the social services to show that the private sector is being fully stimulated and encouraged and that competitive tenders or other means of testing the market are being taken' (Griffiths, 1988, Introductory letter, para. 24). The proposals 'are aimed at stimulating the further development of the mixed economy of care' (para. 3.4). 'Social services authorities should not be allowed to become monopolistic suppliers of residential and non-acute nursing home care' (para. 6.49). 'They should look rigorously at the comparative costs of domiciliary services ... and seek out the most efficient services there too whether from the private, voluntary or statutory sectors' (para. 6.50).

- 'It seems right that those able to pay the full economic cost of community care services should be expected to do so' (para. 6.33). 'Public finance [for residential care] should only be provided following separate assessments of the financial means of the applicant ... and of the need for care' (para. 6.39). 'Planning needs to take account of the possibilities of individuals beginning to plan to meet their own care needs at an earlier stage in life' (para. 6.60). 'Many of the elderly have higher incomes and levels of savings in real terms than in the past. ... This growth in individually held resources could provide a contribution to meeting community care needs. Wider availability of information would assist individuals in planning ... There are already a number of interesting schemes for encouraging owner occupiers to use their equity to provide income which can be used to pay for services in retirement and I believe that similar innovative schemes should be encouraged' (para. 6.61). 'Encouraging those who can afford to plan ahead to do so should help to ensure that public resources are concentrated on those in greatest need' (para. 6.62). 'I therefore recommend that central government should look in detail at a range of options for encouraging individuals to take responsibility for planning their future needs. This examination should include evaluating the potential of innovative service models, such as social maintenance organisations ... and the incentives available through taxation and insurance systems for encouraging individual and corporate planning in this area' (para. 6.63).

The economy of social care postulated by Griffiths extends what Norman Fowler, as Secretary of State, called in his Buxton speech an 'enabling role' (Fowler, 1984). The label never did justice to the potential, indeed the demands, of the role. Griffiths and others make it clear that the local social service authorities will have to be more proactive, able to use a wider repertoire of means in the pursuit of a broader range of ends, and in doing so be more able to apply local political values to their task of managing the evolution of the local care system than is implied in the 'enabling' metaphor. More recently, one hears a variant of the 'enabling' metaphor, 'the managing authority'. The context is the provision of services by contracting with independent suppliers. It reflects the influence on senior managers and policy-makers of the assumptions and techniques of the new managerialists. However, the metaphor understates (i) the con-stitutional right and practice of authorities to make political choices about priorities, and (ii) their duty to work for the improvement of equity and efficiency in the system as a whole, not just for those for whose provision they are paying or acting as brokers. All these duties have in common the prevention or correction of 'market failure', broadly interpreted. The branch of public policy whose focus is the prevention or correction of market failure is 'trade and industry' policy. Therefore what we propose is the metaphor 'lead agency responsible to the central government and local citizens for developing and implementing local trade and industry policies for long-term social care' (Davies and Challis, 1986; Davies, 1986a).

Appropriate charging levels and relativities are critically important to the efficiency of a mixed economy. Prices give the signals to which the wide range of independent producers and the consumers of widely differing wants and needs respond. This is particularly so if much if not most of the public funding of consumption is channelled from the bottom up, either directly through consumers by means of such social security entitlements as attendance allowances, or through case managers with their own budgets acting as brokers for the consumers, as proposed in the white paper on community care (Cm 849, 1989, Chart 7). Prices could acquire an altogether more profound importance in the new bottom-up financing system. Griffiths strongly argued that mixing the supply economy of welfare would encourage competition. The most important form of competition should be in the variety of provision, since if the quality control exercised by authorities is adequate, actual quality variation in essential features of the basic services should not be great, at any rate among consumers of publicly-financed services. But there may also be real price competition. Indeed, there is a danger that the social services authorities may stimulate excessive price competition. They may channel demand to those willing to meet it at the lowest price in the short run in markets where excess demand will have been followed by surplus capacity among suppliers just at the time when the contracts are first issued under the new arrangements, and when, therefore, suppliers may be tempted to shave prices and profits more than is compatible with improving, even maintaining, quality in the long-run. And faced with tight budgets and having little experience of specifying and controlling quality at arm's length, managers might both be vague about quality and unable to ensure its adequate delivery.

Two difficulties of developing good charging policies for publicly-provided services are already clear: charge-setting in public services has to be based on information from inappropriate accounts; and the simple nostrums of elementary economics do not necessarily apply when the prices of some important alternatives are clearly unrelated to the costs of supplying additional units of service, or producers and consumers do not bear the costs and benefits of the two activities.

The first problem has recently received attention in discussions about internal markets and the pursuit of greater efficiency in the National Health Service. Griffiths' comment was that:

... the present lack of refined information systems and management accounting within any of the authorities to whom one might look centrally or locally to be responsible for community care would plunge most organisations in the private sector into a quick and merciful liquidation (1988, Introductory letter, para. 28).

The last chapter of *Matching Resources to Needs* (Davies and Challis, 1986) illustrated the extent of the costs of community social services for elderly people hidden from view by the structure of accounts of local authorities and other agencies. The appendix to Chapter 5 (pp.422-9) illustrates how difficult it is to compute cost figures for authorities with variations in accounting conventions and different organisations of functions.

One of the authors has discussed the second problem in the context of another area of social policy whose assumptive world changed (Davies, 1978). Readers will recognise the intellectual origins of the PSSRU community care models in the arguments of that study. The change in perception was similar to that in long-term social care. The old assumptions were (i) public provision, (ii) at a price unrelated to greatly varying resource costs, (iii) to users without alternatives, and (iv) with similar needs and wants. The new assumptions are that (i) the service provided by public agencies are some alternatives among many and (ii) that it is offered to potential consumers with complex preferences and greatly differing needs and wants. The argument showed the relevance both of a deeper understanding of the costs of provision and of the economic theory of optimal pricing, as well as the complexity of the influences on the uptake of means-tested services (Davies, 1978).The theory of optimal pricing derives arguments about what would be the prices of publicly provided goods and services when the prices of their close substitutes and complements diverge from those resulting from long-run competitive equilibrium. It shows that the optimal prices might be difficult to deduce. The problem is exacerbated because other prices in the market may to varying degrees be regulated or in other ways affected by the action of the authorities, quite apart from their channelling of demand. For instance, authorities may regulate the level of some prices. (It was at one time common for American states to limit the rate of return on capital allowable in the fixing of prices for nursing home beds paid for by Medicaid.) Also authorities might limit the supply of some types of service by compulsorily licensing providers and their facilities. Since for many services, the supply will be limited by decisions about licensing based on bad guesses in the past, the authorities themselves might have contributed to higher prices for some types of service. All this illustrates that pricing policies should not be seen apart from other features of the trade and industry policy for the area. However they should be a central feature of that trade and industry policy.

3.3 *Local influences on charge income*

So there are formidable technical problems in developing pricing devices and mechanisms and the wider trade and industry policy to which they should belong. An examination of the variation in the Expenditure Recovery Ratio, the ratio of income from charges to gross expenditure, begs the question whether local authorities should continue to set not just charges but even the most general criteria for developing charging policies. Unlike the 1977 report, the report of the SSI's 1988 inspection described variations in the ratio. It also questioned whether the charging policy of authorities was a coherent response to the needs for equity and efficiency in the service:

> It is important for managers not only to consider the implications for income generation of different charging policies, but also to review the consequences for technical efficiency (will a particular charging policy render the service management and delivery process unduly complex?), and for allocative efficiency (what will be the likely effects of price signals on user behaviour?) (DHSS, 1988a, para. 4.4).

Authorities are in fact increasing the proportions of their gross expenditures covered by user charges. Hampshire recouped 21 per cent in 1987/8. Seven others of the 117 recovered more than 15 per cent and sixteen more recovered between 10 and 15 per cent. The percentage increases in some authorities were striking, even in authorities whose recovery was substantial in 1987/8. Some increased their recovery by several hundred per cent even among those whose charges yielded substantial amounts at the beginning of the decade. Of those recouping more than 1 per cent in 1977, eight more than trebled their recovery ratios, and another eight increased it by between 200 and 300 per cent. Examples are Durham (increasing the ratio by 400 per cent from a ratio in 1977 of 3 per cent); Hereford and Worcester (by 416 per cent from 4 per cent); and Suffolk (by 429 per cent from 2.3 per cent). Of course, the recovery ratios are systematically overstated because local authority accounting conventions do not include in gross expenditure on a service a substantial part of the overhead costs of the provision. The appendix to Chapter 5 suggests that the understatement of gross expenditure might be 15 per cent or more in some of our authorities. The ratios of income from charges to service out-turn have been rising in other countries also; including those like Sweden and the Netherlands which attach a high priority to expenditure on welfare. For example, in the Netherlands the ratio of charge income to the sum of that and the central government subsidy rose from 7.9 per cent in 1980 to 9.8 per cent in 1986 (van den Heuvel, 1989).

However, the recovery ratios for 1987 in some authorities are high compared with those for several other countries. The ratio of fees paid by recipients to gross expenditure on home help in Stockholm fluctuated between 4.8 and 5.7 per cent in Stockholm between 1984 and 1988 (personal communication from the Municipality of Stockholm, 1988). In a country whose balance between selectivism and universalism is intermediate by international standards, the ratio for 'home-making' in British Columbia was 3 per cent. However, the ratio may be as high as 50 per cent in many areas of Manitoba (Kane and Kane, 1985, p.128). Indeed, British recovery ratios are high by American standards. According to the 1982 US Long-term Care Survey, only 12 per cent of disabled elderly people living in the community and receiving formal services paid some of it directly from their own pockets, and among that 12 per cent the median expense was $40 (less than £20) a month. (However, some 10 per cent of those with out-of-pocket expenses made payments of over £400 per month; Technical Working Group, 1986). It is now an aim of the State of Massachusetts to recoup a higher proportion of expenditure, but they are starting from levels which are not high by British standards.

It is not only in the home help service that the recovery ratio is high and increasing. The ratio exceeded 75 per cent for meals-on-wheels in seven authorities, and was more than 50 per cent in 26. It had more than trebled in three, and more than doubled in eight. The ratio for day care in 1987 was more than 50 per cent in three, and had more than doubled in 21. The ratio for residential care in local authorities' own homes, the product of applying what is in principle a uniform national assessment (though one which anecdotal evidence in some of our research has in the past suggested to be subject to local variation in application), was more than 40 per cent in 27 authorities in 1987, and had increased by more than 50 per cent in ten authorities.

These changes are large. They reflect changing political values and so a different balance between universalist and selectivist devices for controlling allocations and the response to complex incentives interpreted at the local level through varying ideological spectacles. But local authorities' discussions about charging policies have not been informed by systematic analysis of the impact of policy features on potential clients and informal supporters of varying circumstances. The issues described by Judge and Matthews (1980) and Parker (1976, pp.359-74) may still describe SSD perceptions. An interesting feature of that mapping of the assumptive world was that in SSDs as in local education departments (Davies, 1978), unlike public enterprises, no attention had been paid to the development of rules for pricing so as to avoid allocative inefficiency. Perhaps therefore it is more interesting to look also for other influences on the Expenditure

Recovery Ratio. Tables 2.2 and 2.3 summarise the results of models exploring influences on the Recovery Ratio. The modelling is described in more detail in tables in the appendix to this chapter. Table 2.2 describes the results of models exploring the influence of representational, fiscal, need-related population characteristics and features of local charging policies on the Recovery Ratio for home help. The simple correlations were higher with the representational variables than with any others save the charging policies themselves. The crude indicator of the incidence of poverty in the population, the unemployment rate, was uncorrelated with the Ratio, and showed no sign of influence in the modelling. The influence of the representational and fiscal variables suggest that authorities' charging policies were not mainly a response to the prevalence of poverty in their populations nor greatly constrained by that.

This impression was tested in later modelling reported in Table 2.4. The modelling compared the Recovery Ratios for the more important community social services in 1977/8 and 1987/8. It focused on the influence of representational characteristics of authorities and the prevalence of poverty in their populations. The greater the influence of the former in relation to the latter, the more the charging policy is determined by the application of partisan ideology and the less it reflects the circumstances of priority users. A failure to find partial correlations sufficient to estimate a convincing model would suggest arbitrariness in charging policy. It is clear that the predicted values of the ratios for *home help* are sensitive to political representation and to the prevalence of low income both in 1977

Table 2.2
Analysis of expenditure recovery ratio for home help in 1986: the influence of need-related, fiscal, party representational and service characteristics (Appendix Table A2.7)

Authorities recovering a high proportion of their gross expenditure from charges tend to have low gross expenditures.
The effects of political and fiscal factors worked through the features of charging policy; indicators of charging policy being substantially correlated with some of the political variables. Minimum charges per week and the existence and level of a flat rate charge are particularly highly correlated with the recovery ratio. Authorities with swings to the Conservatives tended to have lower recovery ratios, possibly because of time lags in policy change.
Since the indicator of the prevalence of poverty in the area appears not to have a large influence on the recovery ratio or indicators of charging policy, the ratio may not have been tightly constrained by the poverty of the target populations.
There is a weak negative partial correlation between the recovery ratio and the relative increase in total local expenditure financed from the rates. This may reflect the priorities of councils which chose high spending levels in relation to their grant-related expenditures at the cost of losing grant.

Table 2.3
Analyses of expenditure recovery ratios in 1977 and 1987: the effects of political characteristics and high proportions of target populations in poverty

Home help ratio, 1977
The model has considerable statistical power
- Areas with high proportions of their general population receiving supplementary benefit tended to have lower recovery ratios, but the difference was less among authorities with higher populations.
- The greater was Labour representation, the lower the recovery ratios.

Predicted recovery ratios for home help, 1977:

LABPC	Supplementary benefit (per cent of mean)		
	60	100	140
20	5.8	5.3	5.1
37.0 (mean)	4.0	2.8	2.5
60	2.6	1.4	1.5
80	2.0	1.2	0.5

Home help ratio, 1987
Two models of similar and substantial statistical power tell the same story:
- *Authorities controlled by the Conservatives (CONCON) tend to have higher ratios.*
- *The greater is Labour representation, the lower tends to be the ratio.* The effect declines at higher levels of UR1. The combined effect of LABPC and UR1 is to reduce the ratio, but to a diminishing degree as LABPCxUR1 increases.
- *The more prevalent is target group poverty, the lower tends to be the ratio.*

Predicted recovery ratios for home help, 1977:

LABPC	UR1		
	10	21.6 (mean)	30
20*	13.7	12.5	11.7
47.7	8.8	6.8	6.0
60	8.2	6.2	5.8
80	7.5	5.9	5.6

* Assuming Conservative control for authorities with LABPC=20.

Proportionate increase in home help ratio, 1977-1987
The model is as statistically powerful as the models for 1977 and 1987.
- *The percentage increase in the ratio was lower in Conservative controlled authorities and highest in councils where Labour regained control between 1977 and 1987.* The political complexion of the council did not affect the response of its charging policy to the prevalence of low incomes in the target group.
- Authorities with high proportions of the target group with low incomes tended to have low increases in their recovery ratios. So also did authorities having a relatively great increase in the proportion of the target group with low incomes.

Meals-on-wheels ratio, 1977
The model is weak
- Authorities controlled by Labour tended to have low recovery ratios.
- Recovery ratios tended to be higher the greater the proportion of the general population with low incomes.

Table 2.3 (continued)

Meals-on-wheels ratio, 1987

The model is less weak than for 1977 but not as strong as the equivalent models for the home help ratios.

- *The prevalence of low incomes (UR2) was negatively correlated with the ratio. However, the male unemployment rate was positively correlated with it.*
- *Extensive exploration failed to find an association with any of the indicators of the political composition of the Council or its volatility, either alone or in combination with low income variables.*

Proportionate increase in meals-on-wheels ratio, 1977-87

The model is as powerful as that for 1987.

- *Representational volatility combined with a change to Conservative control is associated with greater increases in the recovery ratio.*
- *Relatively great increases in the prevalence of poverty were associated with greater rises in the recovery ratio.*

Day care ratio, 1977

It proved impossible to discover relationships between the ratio and the political and low income variables.

Day care ratio, 1987

The power of the model is between those for the equivalent meals and home help ratios.

- *Low income and political variables did not have a general effect, but high prevalence of low income (UR1) was positively correlated with the ratio in solidly Labour councils (SOLIDLAB).*

Proportionate increase in the day care ratio, 1977-87

Thorough exploration failed to find any associations between the increases in the ratio and the political and/or low income variables.

Authorities' own residential homes, 1977

The model is of intermediate power.

- *Authorities controlled by Labour at all dates tended to have lower recovery ratios.*
- Among authorities controlled by Labour at all dates, recovery ratios tended to be lower for authorities with higher proportions of their general populations of low income, the effects being less for authorities with the highest and lowest proportions.

Authorities' own residential homes, 1988

The model has much the same power as for home helps.

- *The stronger Labour representation (LABPC), the lower was the ratio.*
- *The more prevalent was low income (UR2), the lower was the ratio.*
- *The lowering effect of the prevalence of poverty was less in solidly Labour councils (SOLIDLABxUR2).*

Proportionate increases in the ratio for own residential homes, 1977-87

The model was statistically of intermediate strength.

- *The proportion of the seats held by the Labour party and the loss of control by the Conservative party between 1977 and 1987 were associated with lower ratios though Labour-held councils in all three years 1974, 1979 and 1984 (SOLIDLAB) had greater increases.*
- *Exploration failed to find evidence of a response to the prevalence of low incomes.*

and 1987. The sensitivity of councils in 1987 to the prevalence of low incomes is itself affected by their political composition. (The model for the ratio of the 1987 to the 1977 ratios suggests the same conclusion. However, although it fits well, the coefficients are unstable.) The models for *meals-on-wheels* suggest a low degree of responsiveness to the prevalence of low incomes. The partial correlation for 1977 is positive, the wrong sign to suggest a responsiveness of local policy to population circumstances. Representational variables had some influence in 1977 and affected the percentage increase in the ratio. Again authorities with high proportions of their populations in poverty did not tend to have low *day care* ratios; indeed, the ratios varied arbitrarily. Again the models for *authorities' own residential homes* suggested that representational variables had a greater and more consistent effect than the prevalence of low incomes.

So one overall conclusion is the great and almost omnipresent influence of partisan ideology on the policies which affect the ratios; an influence which in several cases affected the response to the prevalence of low incomes itself. Recovery Ratios are not primarily the outcome of responses to local situations which make the charging policies adopted the most likely to improve the equity and efficiency of resource allocation. The analysis continues.

3.4 *The responsiveness of home help hours consumed to the price of the marginal hour*

Charging policies should not conflict with the aims of the service. Among the aims of the service is that consumption should not be deterred among those who would gain most from it. For most commodities, it is assumed that the consumers are the best judges of what the benefits of additional expenditure would be. Indeed, it would be an invasion of their rights to make arrangements which deprived them of their right to choose what to consume as long as the rights of others were not affected by their decisions, and if the relative prices of commodities are proportional to their costs to society of producing them – or if the relative prices are optimal by the criteria of the 'theory of the second best' (Lipsey and Lancaster, 1956). Many, possibly most, consumers of home help are able to evaluate the benefits of more, less, or indeed no home help; at any rate they are no worse at doing so than at judging whether to spend more or less on food, clothes, presents for the grandchildren, and other things.

However, there are important objections to the general argument. First, it might be argued by some that the level of state income support for elderly people has emerged historically partly because it is assumed that local authorities provide income in kind. If so, there has always been much territorial injustice because local policies have always differed in the extent of provision and subsidisation of commodities. This is not an argument we can engage here. Secondly, it is argued that the powers of some clients to choose (and to articulate their choice) is impaired. These would be likely to be in the higher dependency groups. Thirdly, society would be affected if as a consequence of under-consumption, the persons were later to require services which were more costly to public funds. These too would be likely to be the more dependent of the potential users. So the degree of responsiveness of consumption to the price to the consumer is of importance for the determination of local charging policies. And the responsiveness of the number of hours consumed to the price of additional hours among the most dependent is of particular importance when it is a policy aim to ensure higher consumption by recipients at high risk.

The evidence is scant, crude, and mostly old. Judge and Matthews (1980) reviewed the state of the argument. They quote the Hunt survey (1970) that found that more than one-half of home help organisers thought that some potential clients were deterred from consuming the service at all because of the charges and that other consumers gave up because of the charge; and that three-quarters of organisers thought that it deterred some from seeking the service. They quoted a survey in Devon which showed that the shortfall in hours consumed compared with those judged ideal by the organiser was greatest among payers, implying that price affected the amount consumed among recipients. There seems to be a shock effect of increasing charges (Judge and Matthews, 1980; Hyman 1980). Data obtained by asking consumers about their utilisation given the price of meals-on-wheels at different levels suggested to Judge and Matthews (1980, p.116) that the price elasticity might vary with the price level. More recently Evandrou and Winter (1988) have used the General Household Survey with great ingenuity. They estimate that the price per hour (but not whether or not a charge is made) affects whether and how much home help is consumed. The model estimated a general effect over all recipients. It did not particularly seek effects varying with the need-related circumstances of recipients. However, inferences are difficult from general cross-section data which provide only crude indicators of factors influencing consumers' marginal valuations and managers' allocation judgements.

Results of an analysis of this study's data are summarised in Table 2.4. (More information is provided in the appendix to this chapter, pp.403-12.) The main policy question tackled in this study is whether attempts to increase allocations would successfully reduce the need for residential care. Therefore our analysis particularly focused on (i) whether the amount consumed during the period of the study would reflect the price of the marginal unit rather than whether the price would affect the probability of consuming any service at all; and (ii) whether the effects varied with the dependency and amount of social support received.

Extensive modelling investigation yielded no sign that among recipients, variations between the ten authorities in the price of an additional hour of service affected the number of hours consumed. There were no signs of statistically significant effects for any of the need types. This seemed to be compatible with the information collected about individual cases in discussion with first-line managers. Therefore our data does not suggest that higher charges for the marginal unit of service would make unlikely higher consumption either of those whose particularly at risk of admission to institutions for long-term care (at higher cost to public funds) or of those whose capacity for independent judgement is likely to be impaired. We would have expected powerful effects to have been evident from this data base, since it is the richest available and allows analysis through time. However, we have seen that the evidence of the few studies available conflicts.

However, such analysis is too crude to be a substitute for investigations collecting major *ad hoc* collections of data like that on which the study by Davies (1978) was based. If we are to make a care economy based on Griffiths principles work well, we should be undertaking such investigations.

Table 2.4
Summary of the results of the modelling to investigate the responsiveness of quantities consumed by users to variations in the price to them

The dependent variable was hours of home help consumed. Some 57 need-related predictor variables were used, including the main predictors of being at risk of admission to an institution for long-term care at the time of the first interview and changes by the end of the study period. They included client and informal carer circumstances and characteristics, the utilisation of services which might be partial or total substitutes, and clients' perceptions of the tasks done and the adequacy of their performance. Appendix Table A2.11 shows the list of variables. The population analysed was a group of 119 recipients who consumed home help for 12 weeks or more and who were not recipients of supplementary pensions or housing benefits.

The primary foci were the hypothesised effect of the price of the marginal weekly hour of help consumed and its variation with the need-related circumstances of the consumer. This was separately estimated for each recipient, taking into account their financial status and first-line managers discretion to waive charges where that was thought desirable. The ten authorities provided substantial variations in these marginal prices. The effect of income was also explored.

The principal results were the rejection of the hypotheses that consumption would be reduced by higher marginal prices, that the effect of the prices would be more greatly to reduce the demand of those of low need, and with the easiest access to substitutes, and that consumption would increase with income. The only effect significantly greater than zero at the 5 per cent level was a negative partial correlation with income.

4 Overview

The argument of this chapter has been that:

- There have increasingly been allegations that the resources could be used in ways which would produce more equitable outcomes with greater efficiency.
- Increasingly coherent and convincing argument supports the allegations, and explains the causal processes which cause inequity and inefficiency. Paradoxically, the changing balance of needs and resources may have caused the processes described by the Social Services Inspectorate (DHSS, 1987b) to have had the most deleterious effects during precisely the period when one might have expected new managerialist argument and intervention to have been of beneficial influence. Statistical analysis presented in the chapter supports the general arguments about processes. However, it also shows the crucial importance of local discretion and traditions. Good national policy must recognise that behind the local variations lie irresistible forces and immovable objects and that its success must depend on how far it helps local policy-makers to accommodate or exploit them.
- The Griffiths Report postulates a sectorally mixed supply and financing economy of welfare characterised mostly by full-cost user charging mitigated by subsidies for those able and willing to establish their eligibility by satisfying a means test. Charging policies will be of great importance to equity and efficiency, and policy for them must be part of a wider local trade and industry policy, since prices will be affected by the lead agency in so many ways. However, statistical analyses show variations in the ratio of charges to gross expenditure (the Expenditure Recovery Ratio) to be little constrained or influenced by local circumstances which are outside the control of the authority or by factors which would affect the relative efficiencies of charging policies. Moreover, the data of this study, in some ways the best ever collected for estimating the responsiveness of demand among existing consumers to variations in price, has found no sign that the quantity consumed tends to be lower the higher the price to the user of the marginal unit. This too suggests that a policy of increasing the concentration of resource inputs on the neediest would not be vitiated by pricing policies which imposed a charge for additional units consumed by users. But further analysis is required to establish appropriate charging policy. Similarly, it will be necessary to develop systems which minimise the depressing effects of means-testing on the uptake of services by those in need.

Part I

3 Who gets what?
Need-responsiveness in service targeting

This chapter tackles two targeting issues. One is whether there are clear relationships between the quantities of services consumed and general indicators of need-related circumstances. The circumstances of most interest are those which predict (i) the probability of admission to residential care; (ii) the degree of diswelfare of users and their carers; (iii) disability; and (iv) the adequacy of informal support. Second, we investigate whether allowing for specific need-related circumstances by statistical modelling greatly elaborates and qualifies the generalisations based on the broad indicators.

Statistical modelling describes the associations between service types and levels, and the need-related circumstances of recipients. It shows the relationship between quantities of services consumed and a crude categorisation of need. Also it presents partial and multiple correlations of service quantities with a wide range of indicators of need-related circumstances. It does so for the main community social services: home help (including home care and the peripatetic warden service provided in one of the areas); meals-on-wheels provided or substantially funded by the SSD; day care services (including day care in residential homes); social work; and short-term residential care received by 29 persons and designed to help them remain in their own homes in the longer term. Similar analyses are presented for the total cost of community social services. The modelling strategies are designed to find whatever relationships exist between needs and consumption.

These analyses throw into relief the results of research on what allocators themselves claim to be the criteria used to allocate services. For instance, it is said that as well as performing tasks for persons who are too frail to do so for themselves, home helps are used for the monitoring of clients in the hope that breakdown of arrangements will be avoided and admission to residential care will be averted or delayed; to encourage and motivate clients and work with them and others to restore lost skills; to relieve loneliness and act as confidantes; and to perform personal care tasks (Goldberg and Connelly, 1982; Hedley and Norman, 1982; Dexter and Harbert, 1983). In addition to nutritional sustenance, meals-on-wheels are said to be allocated to provide social contact for and 'surveillance' of elderly persons living alone. Day care, it is claimed, is allocated partly to stimulate and reduce the loneliness and social isolation of the dependent but also to relieve the strain on carers and provide a general resource base from which such services as bathing, chiropody and meals can be provided (Carter, 1981). As well as assessing needs and performing other brokerage tasks, social workers counsel the bereaved and provide advice to carers (Rowlings, 1981; Davies and Challis, 1986). The most cost-effective allocation of services would be different for each function. The analyses reveal whether those already likely to be at high risk receive a higher priority in practice than others.

So the analysis is of the simple associations shown in Appendix Table A3.2 (pp.417-21), and of partial and multiple correlations of quantities of services with need-related circumstances. Section 1 describes the indicators of need-related circumstances. Section 2 reports the associations with indicators of need-related circumstances of individuals, and Section 3 assesses whether authority and area characteristics have effects additional to the individual circumstances. Some conclusions are presented in Section 4.

1 Need-related circumstances

Indicators of these circumstances are summarised in Appendix Table A3.1 (pp.413-16) and described in this section. The simple associations between these variables and service allocations are shown in Appendix Table A3.2 (pp.417-21).

1.1 A need typology: disabilities and functional deficits

Simple analyses show the levels of services allocated to those in different categories of a need typology (MYTYPO). The categories are defined and illustrated in Table 3.1. The typology is based upon measures of functional ability to perform the activities of daily living and the availability of informal support to compensate for disability (Bebbington et al., 1986).

While physical ability determined the functional ability of most clients, mental incapacity affecting the performance of daily tasks was also taken into account in determining the classification of need types. These dependency indicators were established at the beginning of the study period at the time of assessment by social services personnel. Other dependency-related characteristics are included separately in the multivariate analyses of service allocations. They include functional abilities to perform housework and personal care tasks, continence both of urine and faeces, confusion and behaviour problems. These characteristics were established both at the beginning of the study period and approximately six months later.

1.2 Life events

Evidence of the potential effects of major life events on states of wellbeing, and on other outcomes has become widely developed and documented in recent years (Brown and Harris, 1978; Henderson, Byrne and Duncan Jones 1981). Contact with SSDs often follows adverse life events such as hospitalisation or the loss of supporting relatives, and social services practitioners respond to the consequences of those events in their initial judgements of need. During the first and second set of interviews, elderly respondents or their proxies were asked about recent major events including accidents and injuries to themselves or others close to them, movement of all household members, financial circumstances, accommodation and other personal events. The data allowed an examination of initial responses by practitioners, and of later assessments and adjustments to service provision.

1.3 Social interaction and social integration

Social interaction and integration relate to wellbeing in a number of ways, reflected in the development of different approaches towards the 'measurement' of social interaction. Social contacts may be viewed as resources ensuring physical safety and security, and emphasis placed simply on the number and frequency of social contacts (Miller and Ingham, 1976). They may also be viewed as contributing to more complex aspects of quality of life. Weiss (1969, 1974) stresses both the availability of opportunities for social interaction and the perceived adequacy of those interactions for the individual concerned, allowing for differences in need between people with varying preferences for gregariousness or solitude. The availability of a close attachment figure, a confidante, is recognised to be crucial to wellbeing for some individuals. The availability of such figures is often threatened in later life by illness or death of a spouse, siblings or close friends. Henderson, Byrne and Duncan Jones (1981) have built on the work of Weiss in studies of social interaction among psychiatric patients and elderly people living in the community. They have confirmed the importance of both factors: opportunities for social interaction and the availability of a close attachment figure.

Many services are intended to relieve loneliness and social isolation. One example is day care. Another is the role of social workers in counselling the bereaved. Home helps are seen as providing companionship as well as fulfilling other duties, and those delivering meals-on-wheels are said to provide social contact (Goldberg and Connelly 1982). Respondents were asked about the availability of, opportunity for, and adequacy of social interaction, and about confiding relationships at the beginning and end of the study period.

Table 3.1
The need typology

Need type	Definition	Case illustration
0	**Independent.** 15 per cent of cases. People independent with respect of the main domestic tasks necessary to maintain an acceptable degree of sustenance, warmth, cleanliness, security.	
1	**Long interval needs.** With potential/actual support. 16 per cent of cases. People who are unable to perform one or more domestic tasks which require to be undertaken occasionally (less often than daily), but who have potential help.	Mr L. is 70 and lives alone. He had a 'minor' stroke last year and although he says could do most domestic tasks if he had to, he finds going out and managing steps difficult. He is well supported by friends and is visited regularly by his daughter in whom he can confide.
2	**Long interval needs.** Lacks potential support. 10 per cent of cases. People who are unable to perform one or more domestic tasks which need to be undertaken occasionally (less often than daily), and who lack adequate potential help.	Mr M., aged 84, lives alone and has partial hearing. He is quite mobile and goes out walking every day. Although he can manage to get himself drinks and snacks, he has difficulty managing cleaning and cooking himself a main meal since he is not used to doing these tasks. He has been well-supported in the past by his daughter, but she has recently become ill and has had to go into hospital.
3	**Short interval needs.** With potential/actual support. 16 per cent of cases. People who are unable to perform one or more domestic tasks which require to be undertaken frequently (more often than daily), but who have potential help.	Mr N. is 71 and lives alone. He has failing eyesight and is diabetic. He finds bathing, dressing and getting in and out of bed difficult. He cannot easily get out to do shopping but he can do light cleaning tasks. He cannot cook a main meal or snacks but he can make himself a cup of tea. He is well supported by his sister who cooks for him, and he also has friends whom he sees regularly.

Table 3.1 (continued)

Need type	Definition	Case illustration
4	**Short interval needs.** Lacks potential/actual support. 21 per cent of cases. People who are unable to perform one or more domestic tasks which need to be undertaken frequently (more often than daily), and who lack adequate potential help.	Mrs O. is aged 85 and lives alone in her own house of which she is very proud and does not want to leave. She is blind in one eye and suffers from leg ulcers which have to be dressed by a district nurse three times a week. She used to share her home with her son but he died suddenly last year. He used to do the shopping and lots of jobs around the house. Mrs O. no longer goes out now that her son cannot take her. She finds a number of domestic and self-care tasks very difficult, and some she cannot manage at all. Her niece visits her once a week and she sometimes asks the paper boy to run errands for her. She worries that she will not be able to continue coping living alone.
5	**Critical interval needs.** With potential/actual support. 11 per cent of cases. People who are unable to perform crucial self-care tasks which need to be undertaken frequently and at short notice, but who have potential help.	Mr P. is aged 77 and lives with his wife aged 67. She is quite fit and able to take care of the domestic tasks in the house and to care for herself. Mr P. had a stroke recently and was in hospital for some time. He is housebound and can do almost nothing for himself. A district nurse calls twice weekly to bath him, and he also receives physiotherapy. Mr and Mrs P. are closely involved with a local church community and friends/volunteers call daily. These friends are available to sit with Mr P. while Mrs P. goes out, and to take them both out.
6	**Critical interval needs.** Lacks potential/actual support. 19 per cent of cases. People who are unable to perform crucial self-care tasks which need to be undertaken frequently and at short notice, and who lack adequate potential help	Mr Q. is 78 and lives with his wife who is 80. He suffered a stroke some years ago and is confined to a wheelchair, having lost the use of his legs. Although Mrs Q. helps him in and out of bed, she has considerable difficulty herself in looking after the house. A district nurse calls to bath Mr Q. about once a month. Mr and Mrs Q. are rather isolated, having no contact with friends or relatives. Mr Q. worries about becoming too dependent to be cared for at home and is conscious of overburdening his wife.

1.4 Other client characteristics and circumstances

The perceived needs of elderly people and possible responses to those needs were influenced by a range of characteristics. These included household structure, housing conditions, neighbourhood factors, gender and attitudes towards the receipt of services. The last has not usually been taken into account in analyses of utilisation but its importance has been demonstrated in the work of Steinberg and Carter (1983) and Davies and Challis (1986).

1.5 Informal care

The role of informal carers, relatives, neighbours and friends as substitutes for the provision of services also features in our examination of 'Who Gets What', although conceptually informal carers may feature in the production of welfare model as part of a set of substitute services, or as part of a set of non-resource inputs. The difficulty arises from the range and intensity of functions they perform. Some activities have clear resource consequences but others do not. Personnel in SSDs see carers differently: as resources, as co-carers or even as co-clients (Twigg 1989). As potential substitutes for social services inputs we examined the role of carers in helping elderly people with housework, meal preparation, getting up and going to bed. Social support of a less task oriented nature forms part of the set of social interaction variables.

1.6 Substitute services and other sources of support

The rationale behind the allocation of a social service may depend on the inputs of other elements in a care 'package'. Services can complement (be used in a manner in which the input of one combines with the input of another to produce the outcomes required), or substitute (be partial alternatives) for one another. Other public, private and voluntary agencies provide substitute or complementary services, and the levels of input of these services are taken into account in our multivariate analyses of service allocations.

2 The patterns of association

The samples for modelling service inputs consist of the households receiving the relevant service in the case of individual service models and all households for the model of service packages. For home help and social work services which are allocated to households, rather than individuals, separate analyses have been performed for elderly people living alone. Two sets of cases have been excluded from the analyses: those for which there is insufficient information to calculate a reliable measure of service receipt, and two cases receiving disproportionately high levels of home care services over a short period following hospital treatment for acute conditions but with long-term implications for self care ability.

Social work support has been classified into high, medium and low levels judged on the basis of case records, time allocation sheets completed by practitioners and discussions with case managers providing information about the nature and extent of activities undertaken. Definitions of the level of input are given in Appendix Table A3.3 (p.421).

2.1 Home help and home care

Table 3.2 shows the mean, median and modal allocations of home help services to households with differing levels of need taking first the need

Table 3.2
Weekly number of hours of home help and home care received[a]
by need type of most and least dependent
client member of household[b]

Need category	Mean	SD	Med.	Mode	Min.	Max.	Recipients %[c]	N
Low need								
of most dependent client	2.1	1.6	2.0	2.0	0.34	7.0	92	12
of least dependent client	2.2	1.5	2.0	2.0	0.06	7.4		
Long interval, supported								
of most dependent client	2.6	1.6	2.0	2.0	0.71	8.0	85	73
of least dependent client	2.9	2.0	2.0	2.0	0.12	11.0		
Long interval, unsupported								
of most dependent client	4.0	8.1	2.0	2.0	0.68	44.2	93	52
of least dependent client	3.8	7.1	2.0	2.0	0.07	44.2		
Short interval, supported								
of most dependent client	3.4	2.7	2.6	1.5	0.14	14.0	84	70
of least dependent client	3.5	2.8	2.4	2.0	0.14	14.0		
Short interval, unsupported								
of most dependent client	3.9	3.2	3.0	2.0	0.11	21.0	89	90
of least dependent client	4.2	3.4	3.5	6.0	0.15	21.0		
Critical interval, supported								
of most dependent client	3.3	2.4	2.2	2.0	0.64	10.1	73	43
of least dependent client	3.9	2.6	2.8	4.0	0.86	10.1		
Critical interval, unsupported								
of most dependent client	4.9	3.8	4.0	6.0	0.20	17.3	86	56
of least dependent client	5.0	4.0	3.9	7.0	0.20	17.3		

a Average over the duration of consumption.
b Single elderly people are included as both the most dependent and least dependent client.
c Percentage of the 'client sample'.

category of the most dependent client in a household and then the least dependent client. Home help is the foundation on which most care packages are built, and most clients, whatever their need category, receive it. But the effects of variation in need category of the most dependent household member on mean consumption are anomalous. There is little variation in the modal, or most commonly occurring allocation, apart from the group with critical interval needs who are unsupported. This group consists disproportionately of recipients of special intensive home care schemes. This is a depressing indicator of the degree to which patterns of consumption of home care services were contributing to the prevention of unnecessary admission to residential care. Two hours a week of home help are unlikely to reduce the probability of admission of unsupported clients with short interval needs to institutions for long-term care, and two hours a week is unlikely to defer the burn out of supporters of clients with critical interval needs. There is clearly vast variation in the service levels within each group. The median and modal allocations suggest a stronger relationship with functional incapacity. While consumption does rise consistently with increasing levels of disability for unsupported clients, the increase is not steep. If SSDs wish to use the home care service to prevent or delay admission to residential care, there should surely be a steeper rise in consumption with increasing disability.

Table 3.2 contains other anomalies. For instance, the median (and maximum) allocation to supported clients with critical interval needs is less than the median and maximum consumption for supported clients with short interval needs. The patterns look more convincing if classification is made by the least rather than the most dependent client in the household. However, the table confirms that variety of need is not matched by variety in consumption, and that there is substantial input variation which cannot be explained using this typology of need despite its origins as an aid to service provision by geriatricians (Isaacs and Neville 1972).

The models presented in Tables 3.3 and 3.4 provide additional insight. First, the adjusted R^2 in Table 3.4 is much higher showing a firmer pattern of consumption for those living alone. The independent variables also give us further clues about patterns of allocation and consumption. SSDs vary in the priority they give to the interests of carers, but the presence of supported groups in the models implies that informal carers are treated as substitutes for home help. This picture is confirmed by the simple associations in Appendix Table A3.2 (pp.417-21), showing significantly more home help allocated to unsupported clients with short and critical interval needs, and significantly lower levels of service to clients with informal carers performing housework tasks.

The models also provide further clues about allocation criteria. Some variables are what might be hoped and expected: for instance, lower levels of self-care ability, inability to do housework, and inadequate informal

Table 3.3
Regression analysis of the levels of home help and home care services allocated to all households

Dependent variable: hours per week of home help, home care and warden services

Explanatory variable	Coefficients before inclusion of area variables	Coefficients after inclusion of area variables
Negative attitude to service receipt	0.78 **	0.61 *
Dependency characteristics		
Self care ability at beginning of study period	−0.11 ***	−0.12 ***
Short interval needs, inadequately supported at beginning of study period[a]	0.81 ***	0.81 ***
Critical interval needs, inadequately supported at beginning of study period[a]	0.81 **	0.73 *
Life events		
Death of spouse shortly preceding study	1.90 ***	1.75 ***
Financial problems at beginning of study period	−0.94 **	−0.83 **
Hospitalisation during study period	−0.80 **	−0.81 **
Social interaction		
Square of change in number of people for elderly person to turn to in times of difficulty during study period	0.18 *	0.18 *
Substitute services		
Receipt of meals-on-wheels during study period	0.33 ***	0.33 ***
Receipt of social work during study period	0.38 ***	0.40 ***
Nursing input at end of study period	0.21 ***	0.21 ***
Day hospital attendance during study period	0.79 *	0.61 NS
Area variables		
Area 2 Inner London		0.05)
Area 3 Outer London		1.71)
Area 4 Metropolitan District		0.82)
Area 5 Metropolitan District		−0.05)
Area 6 Metropolitan District		1.09) NS[b]
Area 7 English Shire		0.43)
Area 8 English Shire		0.41)
Area 9 English Shire		1.01)
Area 10 Welsh County		0.28)
Constant		2.47 ***

R^2=0.48 (0.43) Adjusted R^2=0.43 (0.40) Residual mean square=3.38 (3.54)
F=9.91 *** (14.88***) Figures in brackets indicate values before the inclusion of area variables.

Number of persons: 246

Significance levels: *** $p < 0.01$, ** $0.01 < p < 0.05$, * $0.05 < p < 0.10$
  a Applies to most dependent member in household.
  b The result of a test of the significance of combined area effects (F=0.88 NS)

support among those with short and critical interval needs are correlated with higher levels of service receipt. The death of a spouse is also associated with higher than average allocations of service suggesting a response to emotional needs. An examination of the case notes of seventeen people experiencing such a loss shortly prior to the study showed organisers responding to expressions of depression and loneliness as well as to the disability of the remaining partner. Four cases were widowers unused to doing housework or cooking. Of those losing a spouse during the study period, all but two were perceived to be the more dependent partner and continued to receive higher allocations of home help. There are also signs of attempts to compensate for the loss of important potential supporters (a circumstance which the findings in Tables 4.12 and 4.13C of the following chapter suggest may achieve greater marginal productivities, i.e. greater benefits from increased inputs). Service receipt tended to be lower among those with larger numbers of persons to turn to in times of difficulty, and higher among those who received fewer visitors to their homes, indicating either or both declining capacity and lessening social support.

In other ways, the models do not remove some of the anomalies observed in Table 3.2, neither do they indicate that resources are being concentrated where their marginal productivities are highest (for instance, compare the higher marginal productivity for MYTYPO3, those with short interval needs who have informal support, in Tables 4.12 and 4.13B of the following chapter).

The positive correlations with other service inputs suggest that consumption of several of the services is a common response to basically similar circumstances. In particular, recipients of community health services consumed more home help, a picture presented even more sharply by the simple associations between home help receipt and (i) community nursing and (ii) day hospital attendance. Of 80 clients receiving both home help and community nursing services only two received less than the average amount of home help. Both were well supported by informal carers, and one was offered home help but refused it. Again, of those receiving both home help and day care, only two received less than the average allocation of home help. One objected to paying the charge and limited her consumption accordingly, and the other had strong informal support from members of the family living in the same building. Similarly, higher consumption of home help is associated with higher levels of social work support and greater allocations of meals-on-wheels.

The models also show the significance of attitudes among service recipients about service consumption. The expression of reservations about social services intervention is associated with higher levels of home help. Clients expressing negative attitudes were often either confused, lonely or depressed or were heavily dependent on informal carers. A clear positive attitude towards social services is also associated with higher consumption

Table 3.4
Regression analysis of levels of home help and home care services allocated to elderly people living alone

Dependent variable: hours per week of home help, home care and warden services

Explanatory variable	Coefficients before inclusion of area variables	Coefficients after inclusion of area variables
Gender	0.58 *	0.52 NS
Negative attitude to service receipt	1.72 ***	1.85 ***
Positive attitute to service receipt	0.62 *	0.75 **
Poor housing conditions (interviewer assessment)	0.68 *	0.76 **
Dependency characteristics		
Short interval needs, inadequately supported at beginning of study period	0.61 *	0.65 *
Critical interval needs, inadequately supported at beginning of study period	1.05 **	0.89 **
Confusion at beginning of study period	−1.26 **	−1.68 ***
Ability to do light housework at beginning of study period	−0.68 ***	−0.67 ***
Square of ability to do light housework at beginning of study period	0.24 ***	0.27 ***
Life events		
Death of spouse shortly preceding study	2.09 ***	1.86 ***
Hospitalisation during study period	−0.75**	−0.66 *
House repair problems during study period	−1.24 **	−0.93 NS
Social interaction		
Change in regularity of visitors to elderly persons' home during study period	−0.25**	−0.20 **
Substitute services		
Receipt of meals-on-wheels during study period	0.18 **	0.16 *
Receipt of social work during study period	0.34 ***	0.35 ***
Nursing input at end of study period	0.16 ***	0.18 ***
Area variables		
Area 2 Inner London		−1.61)
Area 3 Outer London		0.79)
Area 4 Metropolitan District		0.24)
Area 5 Metropolitan District		−0.68)
Area 6 Metropolitan District		−0.04) NS[a]
Area 7 English Shire		−0.52)
Area 8 English Shire		−0.51)
Area 9 English Shire		0.76)
Area 10 Welsh County		−0.31)
Constant		3.69 ***

R^2=0.70 (0.65) Adjusted R^2=0.63 (0.61)   Residual mean square=2.27 (2.43)
F=11.13*** (15.18***) Figures in brackets indicate values before the inclusion of area variables. Number of persons: 148
Significance levels: *** $p < 0.01$, ** $0.01 > p < 0.05$, * $0.05 > p < 0.10$
a The result of a test of the significance of combined area effects (F=1.18 NS)

of home help for elderly people living alone. However, it is only in conjunction with other need-related characteristics that strongly held feelings about receiving social services demonstrate their significance. Alone, they show no direct association with levels of service receipt.

2.2 *Meals-on-wheels*

Table 3.5 shows no clear pattern of increased allocations of meals-on-wheels to clients with increasing levels of disability, and the modal allocations reflect the widespread availability of meals-on-wheels on a twice weekly basis.

Table 3.5
Weekly number of meals-on-wheels received[a] by need type of most and least dependent client in household[b]

Need category	Mean	SD	Med.	Mode	Min.	Max.	Recipients %[c]	N
Low need								
of most dependent client	3.0	1.8	3.5	0.03	0.03	5.0	31	4
of least dependent client	2.9	1.8	3.9	0.03	0.03	5.0		
Long interval, supported								
of most dependent client	3.0	2.2	2.0	2.0	0.29	7.0	21	18
of least dependent client	3.3	2.5	2.0	2.0	0.29	10.1		
Long interval, unsupported								
of most dependent client	2.5	1.7	2.0	2.0	0.40	7.0	38	21
of least dependent client	3.5	3.2	2.0	2.0	0.40	14.0		
Short interval, supported								
of most dependent client	3.1	1.5	3.3	2.0	0.07	6.0	28	23
of least dependent client	2.9	1.6	3.0	2.0	0.07	6.0		
Short interval, unsupported								
of most dependent client	4.1	3.0	2.9	2.0	0.37	7.0	30	30
of least dependent client	3.2	2.2	3.9	0.13	0.13	7.0		
Critical interval, supported								
of most dependent client	2.7	2.1	2.0	0.13	0.13	7.0	14	8
of least dependent client	3.2	2.2	3.9	0.13	0.13	7.0		
Critical interval, unsupported								
of most dependent client	4.0	2.8	3.1	2.0	0.98	7.1	46	30
of least dependent client	3.4	1.9	2.3	2.0	0.98	7.0		

a Average over the duration of consumption.
b Single elderly people are included as both the most dependent and least dependent client.
c Percentage of the 'client sample'.

The model presented in Table 3.6 shows allocations to be substantially influenced by higher-level dependency characteristics, although breakdowns of the significant variables show a complex picture. Those in the middle range of ability to do light housework tasks receive higher allocations of meals than those with lower-level abilities. An examination of individual cases confirms the mismatch between self-care abilities and allocation of meals revealing (i) the most highly dependent clients receiving alternative,

Table 3.6
Regression analysis of allocations of meals-on-wheels
Dependent variable: numbers of meals-on-wheels per week

Explanatory variable	Coefficients before inclusion of area variables	Coefficients after inclusion of area variables
Dependency characteristics		
Ability to do light housework at beginning of study period	–0.37 ***	–0.27 ***
Change in ability to perform self-care tasks during study period	–0.11 **	–0.06 NS
Square of change in urinary incontinence during study period	0.99 **	0.63 *
Square of change in faecal incontinence during study period	0.86 *	0.68 *
Life events		
Financial problems at beginning of study period	1.78 ***	0.98 *
Substitute services		
Receipt of social work during study period	–0.36 ***	–0.10 NS
Day hospital attendance during study period	1.84 ***	0.83 NS
Area variables		
Area 2 Inner London		–3.41)
Area 3 Outer London		0.25)
Area 4 Metropolitan District		–1.81)
Area 5 Metropolitan District		–2.26)
Area 6 Metropolitan District		–1.81) ***a
Area 7 English Shire		–1.57)
Area 8 English Shire		–2.69)
Area 9 English Shire		–2.67)
Area 10 Welsh County		–0.86)
Constant		5.56 ***

R^2=0.61 (0.32) Adjusted R^2=0.53 (0.27) Residual mean square=1.56 (2.44)
F=7.81*** (6.04***), Figures in brackets indicate values before the inclusion of area variables.
Number of persons: 96
Significance levels: *** $p < 0.01$, ** $0.01 > p < 0.05$, * $0.05 > p < 0.10$
  a The result of a test of the significance of combined area effects (F=5.90)

more intensive forms of service or high levels of informal support where meals are provided to reduce carer strain, and (ii) among the less physically dependent, allocations associated with factors including loneliness, specific health conditions such as diabetes, and a lack of experience of cooking.

2.3 Day care

Day care may be provided in day centres or in residential homes for elderly people, and patterns of provision vary between authorities. Claims associated with the provision of day care and outlined at the beginning of this chapter indicate that the service is intended to cater for clients with a range of characteristics such as loneliness, confusion or those with informal carers requiring relief. Not all day care establishments offer care for all such client types, tending instead to cater for particular groups. These analyses of day care services are, however, general and seek to discover the degrees of association between actual consumption of day care and the purposes for which it said to be provided.

Table 3.7

Days per week of social services day care received,[a] by need type of most and least dependent client in household[b]

Need category	Mean	SD	Med.	Mode	Min.	Max.	Recipients %[c]	N
Low need	–	–	–	–	–	–	0	0
Long interval, supported								
of most dependent client	0.8	0.6	0.9	0.3	0.3	3.6	15	13
of least dependent client	0.9	0.7	0.9	0.4	0.04	2.0		
Long interval, unsupported								
of most dependent client	1.0	1.0	0.9	0.3	0.3	3.6	16	9
of least dependent client	1.2	1.1	1.0	1.0	0.03	4.4		
Short interval, supported								
of most dependent client	0.9	0.7	1.0	1.0	0.03	3.0	22	18
of least dependent client	1.0	1.0	1.0	1.0	0.03	4.4		
Short interval, unsupported								
of most dependent client	1.4	1.8	1.0	1.0	0.03	7.0	27	27
of least dependent client	1.4	1.8	1.0	1.0	0.03	7.1		
Critical interval, supported								
of most dependent client	1.2	1.1	1.0	0.03	0.03	4.4	17	10
of least dependent client	1.0	0.7	0.9	0.03	0.03	2.0		
Critical interval, unsupported								
of most dependent client	1.0	0.7	1.0	1.03	0.03	2.1	29	19
of least dependent client	0.6	0.6	0.9	1.0	0.03	2.0		

a Average over the duration of consumption.
b Single elderly people are included as both the most dependent and least dependent client.
c Percentage of the 'client sample'.

Table 3.7 shows some variations in the mean allocation of day care to those in different need categories, but virtually no variation in the median allocations. Maximum allocations do not increase consistently with increasing levels of need, indeed those with critical interval needs receive less day care than nearly all others.

The model in Table 3.8 shows the significance of dependency factors and adverse life events associated with allocations of day care.

Lower allocations are made to those suffering urinary incontinence with even lower levels for those who are regularly incontinent. Day centres, often run by volunteer staff and geared up to providing a service for those who are socially isolated are usually unable to cope with more dependent clients, notably those who are incontinent or more than mildly confused. Two of the need type categories, 4 and 6 contribute to the model, both indicating higher than average allocations of day care. Bivariate analysis of need type by day care allocation confirms high allocations to those with short interval needs and inadequate informal support but demonstrates that critical interval needs and inadequate informal support as a single characteristic is associated with the lowest allocations of day care save for clients with long interval needs. This may of course be related to difficulties in preparing for and getting to day care establishments, problems which will be more severe for the most highly dependent. Changing ability to care for oneself is also a significant factor but shows a non-linear relationship with levels of day care. The greatest changes in ability, whether improvements or deteriorations, are associated with higher levels of day care. The only exception involved the onset of regular incontinence unmanageable without assistance, a factor already discussed as being associated with lower consumption of day care. At first sight, these relationships appear ambiguous, if not perverse, but examination of the individual cases revealed the explicit use of day care to relieve carers. Further evidence of this use of day care is offered by the direct association between allocations of day care and the presence of confusion (shown in Appendix Table A3.2 on pp.417-21) with more day care being provided for those showing symptoms of confusion.

Of the two life events in the model, accidents or injuries preceding the study period are associated with higher levels of day care. An examination of this phenomenon again reveals the presence of confusion and the aim to relieve overburdened carers. In contrast, hospitalisation during the previous three months is associated with slightly lower than average levels of day care. The significance of the allocation of aids, also associated with lower levels of day care, raises the issue of access to day care and the difficulties encountered by physically dependent people in taking advantage of services outside their own homes.

Table 3.8
Regression analysis of allocations of day care services either in day centres or in elderly persons' homes

Dependent variable: allocated days of day care service per week

Explanatory variable	Coefficients before inclusion of area variables	Coefficients after inclusion of area variables
Dependency characteristics		
Short interval needs, inadequately supported at beginning of study period[a]	0.82 ***	0.78 ***
Critical interval needs, inadequately supported at beginning of study period[a]	0.52 *	0.46 NS
Urinary incontinence at beginning of study period	–0.40 **	–0.40 **
Square of change in self-care ability during study period	0.01**	0.01 **
Life events		
Accident/injury shortly preceding study period	1.31 ***	1.37 ***
Hospitalisation during three months preceding study period	–0.67 ***	–0.59 **
Substitute services		
In receipt of aids during study period	–0.25 **	–0.27 **
Area variables		
Area 2 Inner London		–0.54)
Area 3 Outer London		0.15)
Area 4 Metropolitan District		0.40)
Area 5 Metropolitan District		0.16)
Area 6 Metropolitan District		0.43) NS [b]
Area 7 English Shire		–0.06)
Area 8 English Shire		0.33)
Area 9 English Shire		–0.29)
Area 10 Welsh County		0.39)
Constant		0.93 ***

0.49 (0.42) Adjusted R^2=0.35 (0.36) Residual mean square=0.74 (0.73)

F=3.61*** (7.22***) Figures in brackets indicate values before the inclusion of area variables.

Number of persons: 77

Significance levels: *** $p < 0.01$, ** $0.01 > p < 0.05$, * $0.05 > p < 0.10$

a Applies to most dependent member in household.

b The result of a test of the significance of combined area effects. F=0.89

2.4 Social work support

Table 3.9 shows the greater frequency of social work inputs to households with inadequate social support, indeed over 60 per cent of clients with critical interval needs who were supported informally received no social work support at all. Levels of support were highest for those with critical interval needs who lacked adequate informal support.

Table 3.9
Client households with social work receipt, by household need[a] (%)

Need category	Social work input				Total	
	None	Low	Med.	High	%	N
Long interval, supported	74	23	0	2	100	86
Long interval, unsupported	66	25	9	0	100	56
Short interval, supported	59	22	16	4	100	83
Short interval, unsupported	55	27	15	5	100	101
Critical interval, supported	61	20	10	8	100	59
Critical interval, unsupported	43	29	23	5	100	65
N	277	110	55	21		463
%	59.9	23.7	11.9	4.5	100	

a The need category of the household is defined by that of its most dependent member.

Regression analyses of social work allocations are shown in Tables 3.10 and 3.11 and explain more than half of the variation in allocations with reference to the need-related variables contained in them. The models illustrate how physical incapacity is only one aspect among those taken into account in targeting social work time. Clients judged to be living in poor housing conditions received more social work than average, and men living alone received higher allocations than women. Again, taking other factors into account, it is not those without support networks who receive larger inputs. This picture is strongly confirmed by the simple correlations between levels of social work support and variables reflecting levels of social contact and adequate informal support. An examination of the evidence from individual cases suggests that those who are depressed and confused consume more social work effort, and that substantial time is taken by the post-hospital assessment of clients thought to be 'at risk', a nebulous allocation criterion discussed in Chapter 7.

Table 3.10
Regression analysis of levels of social work support to all households
Dependent variable: social work input[a]

Explanatory variable	Coefficients before inclusion of area variables	Coefficients after inclusion of area variables
Positive attitude to service receipt	-0.28 *	-0.33 **
Household composition: living alone	1.02 ***	0.91 ***
Household composition: elderly couple	0.76 **	0.70 *
Dependency characteristics		
Short interval needs, adequately supported at beginning of study period[b]	0.49***	0.60 **
Change in ability to do light housework during study period	-0.07 NS	-0.09 *
Life events		
Moved house shortly before study period	0.70 **	0.78 **
House repair problems shortly before study period	0.45 NS	0.61 **
Illness shortly before study period	0.48 **	0.47 **
Social interaction		
Regularity of visits by elderly person at beginning of study period	-0.27 ***	-0.24 **
Square of change in number of people to turn to in times of difficulty during study period	0.14 **	0.14 **
Area variables		
Area 2 Inner London		0.18)
Area 3 Outer London		-0.07)
Area 4 Metropolitan District		0.75)
Area 5 Metropolitan District		0.76)
Area 6 Metropolitan District		-0.01) ** c
Area 7 English Shire		0.24)
Area 8 English Shire		0.20)
Area 9 English Shire		0.15)
Area 10 Welsh County		0.04)
Constant		1.69 ***

R^2=0.51 (0.41) Adjusted R^2=0.37 (0.33) Residual mean square=0.36 (0.38)

F=3.68*** (5.21***) Figures in brackets indicate values before the inclusion of area variables.

Number of persons: 86

Significance levels: *** $p < 0.01$, ** $0.01 > p < 0.05$, * $0.05 > p < 0.10$

 a Social work input is a three level indicator (low medium high) and is defined in Appendix Table 3.3.

 b Applies to most dependent member in household.

 c The result of a test of the significance of combined area effects. F=1.95.

Table 3.11
Regression analysis of levels of social work support to elderly people living alone

Dependent variable: social work input

Explanatory variable	Coefficients before inclusion of area variables	Coefficients after inclusion of area variables
Gender	−0.74 ***	−0.54 **
Dependency characteristics		
Critical interval needs, inadequately supported	−0.46 **	−0.29 NS
Ability to do heavy housework at beginning of study period	−0.21***	−0.28 ***
Square of change in self-care ability during study period	0.02 *	0.02 *
Change in state of urinary continence during study period	−0.46 ***	−0.38 **
Social interaction		
Square of change in number of people to turn to in times of difficulty during study period	0.29 ***	0.21 **
Area variables		
Area 2 Inner London		−0.13)
Area 3 Outer London		−0.16)
Area 4 Metropolitan District		0.46)
Area 5 Metropolitan District		0.77)
Area 6 Metropolitan District		0.08) *a
Area 7 English Shire		−0.06)
Area 8 English Shire		0.23)
Area 9 English Shire		−0.11)
Area 10 Welsh County		0.66)
Constant		4.09 ***

R^2=0.57 (0.45) Adjusted R^2=0.40 (0.38) Residual mean square=0.34 (0.36)
F=3.44*** (6.49***) Figures in brackets indicate values before the inclusion of area variables.
Number of persons: 55
Significance levels: *** $p > 0.01$, ** $0.01 > p < 0.05$, * $0.05 > p < 0.10$
  a The result of a test of the significance of combined area effects. F=1.71

2.5 Short-term residential care

Table 3.12 presents a picture of the allocation of short-stay residential care
to 24 elderly individuals from nine of the ten authorities, categorised by
need. It shows allocations of short-stay care increasing with dependency
and clients with informal supporters receiving more than those without
supporters. Reasons for allocating short-stay care varied, arranged
specifically as respite care for either client or carer, as a one off short-stay
in an emergency or as an intermittent or phased sequence in a programme
using different modes of care. The small numbers of recipients make

Table 3.12
Number of client households where short stay in residential care is provided, by household need

Need category	Cases receiving short-stay care	Total N
Low need	0	13
Long interval, supported	2	86
Long interval, unsupported	1	56
Short interval, supported	8	83
Short interval, unsupported	3	101
Critical interval, supported	6	59
Critical interval, unsupported	4	65
N	24	463
%	5.2	100

multivariate analysis impossible, so that our examination of need-related
characteristics involved bivariate analyses of allocations with variables
thought *a priori* likely to influence allocation of short-stay care. These
included mobility, dependency-related characteristics, social isolation,
adverse life events, the involvement of carers, and since the use of
short-stay care is inevitably associated with social worker involvement,
the variables which were significantly linked to the allocation of social
work support. Table 3.13 presents the few variables which are significantly
and directly associated with the allocation of short-stay care. A client
living in a poor neighbourhood was admitted to a rotational bed to offer
his wife relief, and received a much higher than average level of short-stay
care. A client whose wife was in the last stages of a terminal illness had
also been admitted to offer his wife relief and again received a higher
than average level of care. Neither of these is among the twelve losing
confidantes during the study period who received on average lower levels
of short-stay care. So too did those who exhibited confusion at the
beginning of the study period. The other variable significantly associated
with levels of short-stay care is a change in the number of people visited

by the elderly person during the study period. This applied to three cases, two involving elderly couples with one partner highly dependent on the other who showed signs of being overburdened. In one case a wife who had received short-stay residential care was admitted to hospital and as a result, her social contacts were restricted to those able to visit her there. In the other, the dependent husband who had received short-stay care died, leaving his wife free to resume a social life outside the house. Here, the relationship between the use of residential care and social contacts outside the house applied to different partners. The third case involved an elderly woman cared for by her daughter who took her mother to her own home daily. Short-stay care was provided to offer the daughter some relief, but, during the course of the study, social work intervention resulted in a successful housing transfer enabling the elderly woman to live next door to her daughter.

Nearly all the cases receiving short-stay care involve the relief of informal carers, ranging from overburdened spouses to relatives and other carers living outside the household but providing high levels of basic care.

Table 3.13
Allocation of short-term care: multivariate analysis of variance

Variable	Significance (probability)	N[a]
Dependency characteristics		
Confusion at beginning of study period	0.08	15
Life events		
Loss of confidante during study period	0.09	12
Social interaction		
Change in regularity of visits by elderly person during study period	0.06	4

a Total number of people receiving short term care during the study period was 29

2.6 Overall costs of community social services

Tables 3.14, 3.15 and 3.16 summarise the results of analyses of the overall costs of community social services.

The pattern in Table 3.14 shows that the mean consumption of community social services rises less steeply with increasing dependency for old people who are informally supported than for those without adequate informal support. Expenditure on households whose neediest client was supported but of critical interval need was on average little more than expenditure on households whose neediest client was supported but of short interval need. Indeed, the median expenditure was lower for those with critical interval needs implying that a minority of these clients received relatively very high levels of resources.

Table 3.14 also compares expenditure on community social services with total expenditure on community health and social services. Including the community health services results in a pattern of consistently rising expenditure, both mean and median, with increasing dependency, although the rise is steeper for those without informal supporters. The inclusion of

Table 3.14
Average weekly cost of (1) all community-based social services and (2) community health and social services by need category of most dependent client in household[a]

Need category	Mean	SD	Med.	Mode	Max.	Min.	N
Low need							
Community social services	11.64	6.40	10.99	4.77	27.63	4.77	11
Community health and social services	12.94	7.06	11.97	4.77	27.63	4.77	10
Long interval, supported							
Community social services	9.88	6.72	8.01	6.89	28.37	0.39	62
Community health and social services	12.69	11.64	9.05	0.42	76.52	0.42	59
Long interval, unsupported							
Community social services	10.35	7.49	6.96	0.25	31.82	0.25	41
Community health and social services	13.86	14.62	8.65	0.25	69.70	0.25	39
Short interval, supported							
Community social services	17.73	15.46	13.43	0.49	88.43	0.49	67
Community health and social services	22.26	21.22	16.14	1.21	109.71	1.21	64
Short interval, unsupported							
Community social services	18.57	14.80	13.62	0.43	72.46	0.43	70
Community health and social services	26.20	25.98	17.94	0.43	155.34	0.43	69
Critical interval, supported							
Community social services	18.32	23.35	8.85	0.20	106.80	0.20	47
Community health and social services	31.28	37.16	17.44	0.20	198.57	0.20	45
Critical interval, unsupported							
Community social services	25.35	22.75	19.34	2.29	119.88	2.29	55
Community health and social services	46.29	54.73	32.79	2.29	295.34	2.29	51

a Recipients for twelve weeks or more. Differences between numbers of cases reflect the number of cases for which NHS data are unavailable.

community health services also makes the picture of overall allocation look less anomalous. For instance, the median expenditures for both services imply that informally supported clients with critical interval needs receive equivalent health and social services resources to those informally supported clients with short interval needs, unlike the expenditure on community services alone.

Tables 3.15 and 3.16 illustrate three major features.

(i) Around 40 per cent of the variation in expenditure on community social services can be explained with reference to the need-related characteristics in the models. The models were developed by testing sets of hypothesised relationships derived from our knowledge of the theory and practice of allocation procedures mentioned at the beginning of this chapter. It is clear that the variations are far from random.

(ii) The complexity of the relationships between overall service allocations and disability. For clients with informal support, service consumption is negatively correlated with disability. This is an even more perverse result than was found for the comparison group of the Thanet Community Care Project (Davies and Challis 1986), where lower allocations of community based services were made to those with critical and long interval, than with short interval needs. Like the Thanet results however, particular disabilities such as incontinence, and consumption of nursing and day hospital services, as well as the more general indicators of need are significantly associated with levels of services received.

(iii) Greater quantities of resources consumed by those living alone and smaller quantities by those with informal supporters.

3 Area variations in service provision

The consequences of living in a particular area are associated differently for each service. For the home help service, area differences add little to the explanation of variations in allocations, although they do add to explanations of variations in allocations of the other services. Values of R^2 were raised by 29 per cent for meals-on-wheels, 7 per cent for day care, 10 and 12 per cent for social work support to all households and single person households respectively, and 8 and 9 per cent in respect of the volume of all services to all households and single person households.

Table 3.15
Regression analysis of the total volume of domiciliary services allocated to all households

Dependent variable: log of adjusted weekly cost of services adjusted for inter-area price differences

Explanatory variable	Coefficients before inclusion of area variables	Coefficients after inclusion of area variables
Household composition – living alone	0.17 **	0.16 **
Dependency characteristics		
Long interval needs, adequately supported at beginning of study period[a]	−0.24 **	−0.20 **
Short interval needs, adequately supported at beginning of study period[a]	−0.30 ***	−0.25 ***
Critical interval needs adequately supported at beginning of study period[a]	−0.37 ***	−0.35 ***
Ability to do light housework at beginning of study period	−0.14 ***	−0.12 ***
Change in ability to do light housework during study period	−0.06 **	−0.05 **
Square of change in ability to do light housework during study period	−0.03 **	−0.02 **
Ability to do heavy housework at beginning of study period	−0.08 ***	−0.09 ***
Change in ability to do heavy housework during study period	−0.08 ***	−0.10 ***
Square of change in state of faecal incontinence during study period	−0.22 **	0.23 **
Life events		
Health problems at beginning of study period	−0.12 *	−0.11 NS
Accident/injury to close person shortly preceding study period	0.26 *	−0.28 **
Accident/injury during the study period	0.29 **	0.28 **
Substitute services		
Nursing input at end of study period	0.03 ***	0.03 ***
Day hospital attendance during study period	0.33 ***	0.27 **
Area variables		
Area 2 Inner London		−0.04)
Area 3 Outer London		0.37)
Area 4 Metropolitan District		−0.12)
Area 5 Metropolitan District		−0.38)
Area 6 Metropolitan District		−0.09) ***[b]
Area 7 English Shire		−0.12)
Area 8 English Shire		−0.15)
Area 9 English Shire		0.12)
Area 10 Welsh County		−0.12)
Constant		3.29***

R^2=0.47 (0.39) Adjusted R^2=0.42 (0.35) Residual mean square=0.24 (0.27)
F=9.15*** (10.83***) Figures in brackets indicate values before the inclusion of area variables. Number of persons: 273. Significance levels: *** $p < 0.01$, ** $0.01 > p < 0.05$, * $0.05 > p < 0.10$
a Applies to most dependent member in household
b The result of a test of the significance of combined area effects. F=4.30

Table 3.16
Regression analysis of the total volume of domiciliary services allocated to elderly people living alone

Dependent variable: log of adjusted weekly cost of services.

Explanatory variable	Coefficients before inclusion of area variables	Coefficients after inclusion of area variables
Owner occupation	0.14 *	0.14 *
Dependency characteristics		
Ability to do light housework at beginning of study period	–0.15 ***	–0.15 ***
Self-care ability at beginning of study period	–0.05 ***	–0.05 ***
Change in self-care ability during study period	–0.06 ***	–0.04 ***
Change in state of urinary continence in study period	0.16 *	0.13 *
Social interaction		
Number of people to do errands/favours at beginning of study period	–0.11 **	–0.10 **
Substitute services		
Attendance at day hospital during study period	0.24 *	0.25 *
Area variables		
Area 2 Inner London		–0.50)
Area 3 Outer London		0.07)
Area 4 Metropolitan District		–0.20)
Area 5 Metropolitan District		–0.54)
Area 6 Metropolitan District		–0.34) **a
Area 7 English Shire		–0.48)
Area 8 English Shire		–0.44)
Area 9 English Shire		0.02)
Area 10 Welsh County		–0.24)
Constant		3.79) ***

R^2=0.51 (0.40) Adjusted R^2=0.46 (0.38) Residual mean square=0.21 (0.24)
F=9.77*** (15.42***) Figures in brackets indicate values before the inclusion of area variables.

Number of persons: 168

Significance levels: *** $p < 0.01$, ** $0.01 > p < 0.05$, * $0.05 > p < 0.10$
a The result of a test of the significance of combined area effects. F=2.19

3.1 Differences between areas

3.1.1 The home help service

Differences between areas in the mean consumption of home help and home care services are not significant, although there are differences in allocation policies, for example in relation to informal carers. In some areas the service is committed to the support of carers. In contrast there are others in which the service is not allocated to households from which younger relatives go out to work during the day. At one extreme we found an example of a home help provided to clean only rooms occupied exclusively by the elderly person in a household. There are also differences between areas in the intensiveness and extensiveness of provision. Authority 8 has a policy of targeting its services to those most in need and it provides the highest average allocation of home help services. Authority 4 provides the second highest allocation of home help, not the effect of targeting, but of high levels of expenditure. At the lower end of home help provision, Authority 1 has high levels of expenditure but explicitly aims to provide its services extensively, while Authority 7 has the second lowest average allocations despite its targeting policies.

3.1.2 Meals-on-wheels
The significant differences in the allocation and consumption of meals reflect local arrangements. At one extreme Authority 8 operates its services under the auspices of the WRVS who offer a minimal twice weekly service, the choice simply being between one or two meals a week. At the other, Authority 4 organises its own meals service and can offer meals five days a week with provision for seven day delivery where judged essential. Between these two extremes is a host of arrangements involving five day schemes and the advanced delivery of frozen meals. Alternatives to mainstream local authority provision also varied between areas and included the voluntary provision of Sunday 'meals on heels' by a local probation service, private provision of 'dial a meal' services, luncheon clubs for those able to reach them and the formalisation of 'good neighbours' to prepare meals in more isolated areas.

3.1.3 Day care
Area differences in the allocation of day care services are not significant. Despite the wide variation in arrangements with different emphases placed on provision in day centres and elderly persons' residential homes, allocations rarely exceeded twice a week. Many of the services were used spasmodically, more physically dependent clients needing to feel sufficiently fit and motivated to attend.

3.1.4 Social work services
Area differences in levels of social work support are significant, reflecting the variety of forms of organisation studied: patch teams in Areas 1 and 2, specialist teams in Areas 3, 6, 9 and 10 and the sub-office of Area 4, generic teams in the main office of Area 4 and Areas 5 and 6, and intake/long-term teams in Areas 7 and 8. Despite policies in most areas of employing only qualified social workers, much work with elderly people was still carried out by unqualified social workers or social work assistants.

The qualified workers, specialist or otherwise, were largely responsible for the assessment of cases judged at referral stage to be more complicated. Activity in many social work cases was geared to the arrangement of specific social services for the support of clients or carers, followed by withdrawal of social work support and the monitoring of cases by other personnel such as home helps or day care staff. Little counselling was visible despite the enthusiasm of some practitioners to provide this kind of professional service, and in one area referrals were made to a local branch of CRUSE, a voluntary agency specialising in bereavement counselling. Social workers expressed regret at the policies of rapid case closure evident in many of the study areas.

3.1.5 *The overall cost of community care services*
The total volume of services provided to individuals and households differs significantly between areas. Areas 3 and 9 both had clear targeting policies to provide the highest levels of input to all households in which elderly people lived alone, despite their very different profiles. Area 3 is an outer London borough with a high level of expenditure on community services for old people, and Area 9 a northern shire county with low levels of spending in this respect. The next highest service levels were provided by Area 4, a metropolitan district in the north east. This area aims to spread services widely, but its high level of expenditure allows it to allocate a comparatively 'intense' service to its clients. Area 8, another shire county follows a policy resistant to the use of long-term residential care and aims to target its services tightly, screening incoming cases through an intake team, and offering a specialist team of workers for elderly people. This area provides the fourth highest level of support. Areas 1, 2 and 6 provide the middle range of service packages to their clients although Area 1 performs better in relation to elderly people living alone. These areas are very different from one another in character. The first is a high-spending inner London borough aiming to spread its services widely through patch modes of working. Area 2, a low-spending inner London borough concentrates its expenditure on elderly people in residential services and encourages the use of the private sector. Area 6 is a low-spending metropolitan district with a policy to target services on those most in need. Among the lower providers of social services support are Areas 7 and 10, both high-spending shire counties. Area 10's specialist commitment to elderly people through the development of a specialist resource group integrating home help and social work services is diluted by policies of providing services to a high proportion of its elderly community, while Area 7 which aims to target its services closely, making use of special intensive care schemes in close cooperation with health service personnel, fails to achieve its policy goals. Its poor showing in this study suggests that these special services meet the needs of very few

people indeed, leaving the majority of recipients with low levels of input. The lowest level of service packages occurs in Area 5, a medium-spending metropolitan district. This authority has a mainstream home care service geared to providing services for heavily dependent people in their own homes, but it had not succeeded in its attempts to end or minimise the practice of 'fortnightly cleaning', the allocation of three hours home help time once a fortnight for domestic cleaning.

4 Conclusions

Two general conclusions arise from the analyses. Several more relate to specific services.

4.1 General conclusions

- Our first general conclusion is that service targeting is indeed poor. This has implications for vertical target efficiency and input mix efficiency. While there are substantial variations in the amounts of community social services consumed by individual clients, there are only small differences in average consumption between those in different need categories. Within most need groups the majority of recipients receive low levels of service and higher allocations to others in the same need group are largely unrelated to their broader need related circumstances. The differences between need groups provide little evidence of sophistication in targeting services on those who are most at risk of admission to residential care, or on those imposing the greatest burdens on informal carers. The multivariate analyses provide a more powerful searchlight to seek evidence of attempts to make best use of resources. We have been able to offer explanations, particularly for elderly people living alone, for substantial proportions of variation in the allocations of services. Many of the independent need-related variables in the regression equations have coefficients which would make good sense in a system attempting to make the best use of resources. However, some seem to be anomalous, and others beg questions. In reading the tables which summarise the results it must be remembered that demonstrating the best use of resources does not rest simply on explaining a high proportion of variation with reference to the independent need-related circumstances. It also requires that the resources are allocated to activities associated with outcomes that are highly valued in relation to their costs. So it is important to seek evidence of relationships between allocations and specific need-related characteristics. The analysis of the relationships between service inputs and outcomes are presented in the following chapter.

- Average consumption of services differs considerably between areas. This variation has been attributed to inefficiency (Audit Commission, 1985), however, these analyses have shown that much of the variation is associated with differences in the need-related circumstances of clients. Again, the degree to which the correlations with need-related circumstances reflect commitment to and success in achieving equity and efficiency in the allocation of resources will become clearer only when the evidence of the later chapters is absorbed.

4.2 Other conclusions

- There are larger differences between areas in the average consumption of home help/care by those sharing households than by those living alone, for whom the allocation criteria are more consistent. Although this may reflect the history of a service whose central role has been to provide a relatively standard package for persons living alone, it confirms the concerns expressed by the Audit Commission (1985) about the failures to identify carers in need of relief, and to provide insufficiently intensive inputs to elderly people with one carer carrying a heavy burden. It also suggests that attention could usefully be applied to developing clearer criteria for allocating home care to elderly people sharing their homes with others, allowing outcomes for carers to become a valid and explicit part of the care delivery system.
- It has been less easy to explain for the variations in allocations of the other services. Although there are substantial differences between areas in their arrangements for delivering meals-on-wheels and day care services, little explanation can be offered by differences in need characteristics. For day care, indicators of social interaction do not feature significantly in our multivariate analysis, even though it is widely claimed that day care is allocated to prevent social isolation and to provide company. Perhaps the facilities used to counter social isolation are lunch clubs, social clubs and drop in centres where places are not specifically allocated. In the case of day care we must also remember not to confuse allocation with consumption, indeed, many of those allocated a place attend only once or twice. Indicators of reliance on informal care are also absent from the model of day care allocation, although the relief of carers is said to be an important allocation criterion. It is possible that the relief was for spouses whose caring inputs are inadequately reflected in our data collection. Another reason may be the practical and psychological difficulties which prevent those who are allocated places from using them. These problems confirm our earlier argument about inefficiencies in the mix of inputs to form packages of care, in particular, the practice of offering available standard services as a token when no appropriate alternative seems immediately available.

- Social work consists mainly of indirect work (Barclay 1982). The arrangement of services following crises or more general adverse life events is followed by quick withdrawal of the social worker. We see here confirmation of the allegation that packages of care are not adjusted to needs, and that responses to changes in circumstances came 'too little, too late' (Audit Commission, 1985, para 54). In only very few cases is there evidence of counselling for clients or carers. Despite different styles of social work teams with different emphases on prevention or targeting, there is no significant difference in the levels of social work support offered between areas.

- Finally, levels of expenditure, and policies which favour either the thin-spreading or targeting of services also influence patterns of service allocation. Although authority and departmental decisions about the overall scale of budgets are based on broad impressions of need, these are only crudely measured and often have little effect on the allocation of resources. There are wide differences in the balance of resources and needs between areas even within quite small authorities. The significance of the need-related circumstances of populations is mediated by values, beliefs and assumptions about such matters as the roles appropriate for the public, private and voluntary sectors, and informal carers. Departmental policies set varying criteria for targeting services, but in a service like home help, what is interesting is that these differences have little effect on the weighting attached to need circumstances by field allocators.

4 Client-related outcomes

This chapter tackles one of the principal questions of the study: how variations in inputs of community-based social services affect welfare outcomes for elderly clients. Section 1 is a technical introduction. In it the main indicators are defined: potential outputs, that is potential consequences of direct evaluative importance; resource inputs, interpreted in the analysis as service inputs; and 'quasi-inputs', need-related circumstances of clients not greatly affected by variations in resource inputs, but possibly influencing the effects of resources on outputs. Section 1 also outlines the mode of analysis. Section 2 examines the relationship between the needs of the client, the services that were provided, and their outcomes. Section 2 also investigates whether some authorities are more effective than others in creating these benefits. Section 3 draws some general conclusions.

1 Variables and mode of analysis

Section 1.1 defines the outputs. Section 1.2 lists the services whose performances are investigated. Section 1.3 details the relevant characteristics of clients which affect the outcome consequences of services. The analytic approach is described in Section 1.4. Section 1.5 reminds us of salient features of the research design.

1.1 Potential outputs

The focus is on final outputs: outcomes of evaluative significance in their own right. This chapter focuses specifically on the benefits of social services to the immediate recipient and not to carers or others. We have investigated four ways in which community-based social services for elderly people are expected to manifest their effectiveness:
- survival in the community: reducing the need for admission to permanent institutional care and, if possible, delaying death;
- maintenance or improvement in the overall quality of life;
- improvements in aspects of life in which social services specifically intervene: lowering vulnerability and providing help with practical problems; and
- consumer satisfaction with services.

The range of potential outcomes studied in this project covers nearly all of those proposed as criteria for the effectiveness of community-based social care in the evaluation research literature, particularly in production of welfare studies. (See for example Wright, 1974; Goldberg and Warburton, 1979; Davies and Knapp, 1981; Goldberg and Connelly, 1982; Kane and Kane, 1982; Davies and Challis, 1986). These criteria in turn reflect policy statements and interpretations of the purpose of social care; for example, DHSS, (1981b); Audit Commission (1985).

Some of the outcomes can only be assessed by using evidence from interviews in which people gave subjective evaluations. The principle adopted throughout is to obtain the view of the client wherever possible. One of the strengths of this project is that the client's view can be set alongside that of the service provider, the informal carer and sometimes our own interviewer, and in some cases this allows us to qualify the account which the client gives. The variables used to measure the four domains of outcome are listed in Table 4.1.

The measurement of most outcomes implies a comparison of states at the beginning of the study when services are first provided, and approximately six months later. For the purposes of this comparison, the outcome for scaled variables is measured by the final score regression adjusted by the initial score.[1]

1.2 Indicators of resource (service) inputs

Variables measuring the volume of services and other resource inputs are shown in Table 4.2. These cover social services inputs, health care, voluntary services, private paid help and informal care used during the period of the study.

1.3 'Quasi-inputs': characteristics of recipients

These are of two kinds, shown in Table 4.3.
- Circumstances of the person at the outset: including level and type of disability, incontinence, mental state, level of social support and household structure.
- Life events which occurred during the study, and which are unlikely to be the consequence of social services interventions. In principle, events such as ill-health might be affected by the initial intervention, but our preliminary (unreported) analysis showed that in reality the amount of service provided is far more likely to be the consequence of life events than vice versa.

The list of variables included in the present analysis to characterise clients is quite short. Its brevity reflects a laborious process of simplification and elimination of variables during the preliminary analysis.

Table 4.1
Outcome variables (summary)

DSTNT A variable indication of destinational outcome after six months
  1 = Entered institutional care (49 cases in the analysis)
  2 = Died (40 cases)
  3 = Client believes social services care enabled survival in the community (91 cases)
  4 = Other survivors (332 cases)

LSX Change in client's life satisfaction score. The scale is derived from client's PGC Morale Scale score after six months regression-adjusted by the score at initial assessment: or equivalently using a proxy version. The resulting scale is Windsorised to lie in the range +− 5. Mean = 0.18, standard deviation = 2.32 (361 cases in the analysis). A positive score denotes a decline in life satisfaction.

RISK An index of felt vulnerablilty to seven adverse life events: (i) falling; (ii) becoming too dependent to be looked after at home; (iii) putting too much burden on others; (iv) being forgetful, causing accidents; (v) not eating well enough; (vi) not being able to keep sufficiently warm; and (vii) becoming unable to cope with living alone (where relevant). The index is a count of the number of these that the respondent 'often thinks about'. A high score denotes high felt vulnerability. This index is calculated for 424 individuals at initial assessment and after six months: the mean scores were 1.25 at initial assessment and 1.13 after six months, with a standard deviation of 1.4. The outcome is measured by the score after six months regression-adjusted by the score at initial assessment.

DESHELP An index of client's felt need for additional help with three activities: going to bed, meals, housework. Each of these items is scored 0 if no help is needed, 1 if occasional, 2 frequently, 3 all the time. The total index is the sum of these three items. A high score denotes high felt need. The mean at initial assessment was 1.19 and after six months was 0.95 among survivors, with a standard deviation of 1.4.

CMCURE Case manager's view of the success of intervention. This is measured as a count of the number of problems reported as resolved or the risks averted in the interview after six months with the case manager; more than five counted as five.

SDFAV A summarisation of the client's experience of the social services at the end of six months:
  1 = favourable
  2 = mixed
  3 = unfavourable
  Treated as a scale.

HHEFFECT A summarisation of the impact of the home-help service on the client after six months (client's opinion).
  1 = Enabled client to continue living at home
  2 = Possibly enabled client to continue living at home
  3 = Neither 1 nor 2, but made a great difference to client's ability to manage at home
  4 = Made little difference, but hoping to continue
  5 = Intending to give up or already given up service

Table 4.2
Resource inputs (summary)

Community social services

HHCINP — Home help and home care inputs, hours per week provided, averaged over the period. Range 0-21 hours per week, mean 2.9.[a]

HHCINPSQ — Square of the above, measured about mean

WARDINP — Street warden, proportion of the study period for which provided. Range 0.0-1.0, mean 0.02.

WARDINPSQ — Square of the above, measured about mean

SWINP — Social work input, measured on a 4 point scale
0 = None
1 = Low, of the order of 5 hours per case over the period
2 = Medium, of the order of 13 hours per case over the period
3 = High, of the order of 23 hours per case over the period
Mean is 0.59.

SWINPSQ — Square of the above, measured about mean.

MOWINP — Meals-on-wheels, meals per week provided, averaged over the period. Range 0-7, mean 0.98.

MOWINPSQ — Square of the above, measured about mean

DCINP — Day centre and day care, days per week provided, averaged over the period. Range 0-7, mean 0.24.

DCINPSQ — Square of the above, measured about mean.

STCINP — Short term residential care, number of days used to a maximum of 14. Mean 0.71.

Health services

AIDS — Number of aids/adaptations provided (including those provided by SSD and other agencies). Mean 0.76.

HOSP — Entered hospital at any time during the study. 1 = yes, 0 = no. 14 per cent did.

DAYHOSP — Day hospital care, days per fortnight being used at the end of the study period. Range 0-6., Mean 0.08.

NURSE — District nurse visits per fortnight being used at the end of the study period. Range 0-18. Mean 1.0.

Private, voluntary and informal services

PRIVHLP — Whether the client used a private nurse or home-help during the study period. 1 = yes, 0 = no. 4 per cent did.

VOLHELP — Whether a voluntary helper visited the client for any purpose during the study period. 1 = yes, 0 = no. 9 per cent did.

INFCARE — Informal domestic help was received, the average number of days per week. Mean 1.1.

Means and other statistics for variables may differ slightly from those shown elsewhere due to the restricted definition of 'client' used in this chapter.
All means of service receipt include non-recipients, counted as zero.

Table 4.3
Characteristics of clients (quasi-inputs)

Characteristics and circumstances at first interview

MYTYPO   A categorisation of clients according to the level of dependency and availability of informal support, as follows:

0 = Low need (5 per cent)[a]

1 = Long interval need (e.g. housebound) with available support (e.g visited several times weekly) (18 per cent)

2 = Long interval need without available support (11 per cent)

3 = Short interval need (e.g. unable to make a snack) with available support (e.g. visited daily) (18 per cent)

4 = Short interval need without available support (25 per cent)

5 = Critical interval need (e.g. chairbound) with available support (e.g. living with an independent person) (12 per cent)

6 = Critical interval need without available support (13 per cent)

These six categories are treated as dummy variables in the analyses.

SEX   1 = Male, 2 = Female. 70 per cent were women.

HHOLD   Household composition

1 = Living alone (58 per cent)

2 = Living with husband or wife only

3 = Other combinations

AREA   Local authority (codes 1-10)

These ten categories are treated as dummy variables in the analyses.

ADEQ   Adequacy of social contact

0 = Would like to see friends more often *or* would like someone to confide in

1 = Neither of the above

65 per cent have adequate contact.

AVAIL   Availability of support network. A scale of 0-6 indicating numbers of people outside the household (i) who would do small favours (ii) who would help in times of difficulty. A high score indicates strong support. Mean is 1.7.

CF   Mental confusion. Individuals who score 4+ on the test of mental status or who are assumed to have a similar level of confusion by the proxy. By this definition 18 per cent are confused.

Life events during the study

HEALTH   Score 1 for the onset of a health problem causing increasing disability during the period of the study (20 per cent of sample). Score 0 otherwise.

ACUTE   Score 1 for an accident or acute illness during the period of the study (10 per cent of sample). Score 0 otherwise.

DEATHSP   Score 1 if spouse died during the period of the study (4 per cent of sample). Score 0 otherwise.

Table 4.3 (continued)

FINANCE
Score 1 if there were money or tenure problems during the period of the study (7 per cent of sample). Score 0 otherwise.

ADLSELFX
Change in ADL (self care index) during the period of the study. For each of the following activities:
* get around the house
* walk outdoors
* wash face and hands
* get in and out of bed
* get to the toilet
* take a bath or shower
* dress and undress

Score:
2 = done easily
1 = done only with difficulty
0 = not done at all
A positive change score denotes an improvement.
The mean change score among survivors was 0.33 (slight improvement).

ADLHOMX
Change in ADL (managing domestic activities) during the period of the study. For each of the following activities:
* dust and tidy
* wash paintwork
* sweep floors
* do hand washing
* make a cup to tea
* cook a main meal
* do shopping
* clean windows
* do jobs involving climbing
* open screw top bottles
* use a frying pan

Score:
1 = can be done
0 = cannot be done
A positive change score denotes an improvement in ability.
The mean change score among survivors was –1.3 (decline).

INCONTX
Score 1 if client became incontinent during the period of the study (11 per cent of sample). Score 0 if remained the same or improved.

LOSSADEQ
Score 1 if client lost support during the study period as defined by ADEQ in Table 5.3 (21 per cent of sample). Otherwise score 0.

AVAILX
Change in the availability of support network, AVAIL, as defined in Table 5.3. A positive score indicates an improvement. Mean is –0.07.

CFX
Change in mental status. Score 1 if client became mentally confused during the period of the study as defined in CF in Table 5.3 (1 per cent of sample). Score 0 if unchanged.

a Means and other statistics for variables may differ slightly from those shown elsewhere due to the restricted definition of 'client' used in this chapter.

1.4 Model forms

The production of welfare approach draws on the theoretical arguments derived from the conventional economic theory of production, and is used to choose the most appropriate statistical methods to describe the relationships between inputs and outputs. In particular we describe these relationships by statistical models which are analogous to empirical *production functions* of contemporary economics. This mode of analysis allows us to estimate the marginal productivity of each of the main services in achieving outcomes. Also we can examine the behaviour of resource inputs as substitutes to or as complements of one another, and variations in the rate of return to different levels of input. There are, however, some significant differences from conventional production functions. Most important is in the emphasis on the interrelationship between services and client characteristics in the production of welfare. For example, recipients may differ in the way they are affected by services. We would expect an equitable and efficient system to yield patterns in which levels of resource inputs and quasi-inputs would affect one another's influence on outcomes in particular ways (Davies and Challis, 1986, Chaps 4, 11 and 12). Our analysis has been designed to let those complex patterns reveal themselves. Second, the models used here do not take into account variations in input prices. Modelling with complex data sets usually requires simplification. The reasons why this simplification was chosen were that the focus is not the distinction between the degree of input mix from other types of efficiency, and that we thought bias was unlikely to be great since we did not expect the actual mixes to be very sensitive to geographical variations of input price ratios. Third, we estimated an average not a 'frontier' function. We did so (i) because we are more interested in making predictions of the results of small changes in the world of SSDs as they typically are than in a world consisting of hyperefficient SSDs; and (ii) because at this stage it is not a main purpose to measure degrees of efficiency by our various criteria, but to keep relations typical of social care.

Our main models are quadratic in form (Lau, 1974); for example

$$Q = \alpha + \sum_i \beta_i X_i + \sum_{i \geq j} \sum \beta_{ij} X_i X_j$$

where Q denotes the quantity of output, X_i the quantity of both inputs and quasi-inputs, and α, β_i and β_{ij} denote parameters. When drawing inferences from this form it is important to check that one is not extrapolating, that is, inferring the effect of service combinations beyond the range of those actually observed, since this may lead to nonsensical conclusions (Fuss, McFadden and Mundlak, 1978).

In addition to the direct (main) effect of particular services and particular client characteristics on outcomes, we are also interested in their interactions.

These are represented in the model by the β_{ij} coefficients. It is not practical to include every possible term of type $\beta_{ij}X_iX_j$ in the models because of the large number of service inputs and client characteristics. Instead, attention is focused on effects involving the four main domiciliary services inputs, that is social work, the home help service, meals-on-wheels and day care. These effects are of three types:

- Quadratic effects (that is $\beta_{ii}X_i^2$) in each of these resource inputs. A positive β_{ii} indicates an input with an enhanced marginal effect at higher levels. This can imply that unless sufficient inputs are provided the effect is negligible. A negative β_{ii} suggests the opposite, a diminishing return on the amount of input.
- Interaction effects between the input of each service and the key personal characteristics as they were at the beginning of the evaluation period. A positive β_{ij} implies that the output to be expected from a service is higher for that particular client type than for others.
- Interactions between these two domiciliary services, or between these and community health inputs. A positive β_{ij} implies that two services in combination have a greater effect than would have been expected from these individual effects, and vice versa. They therefore reflect joint supply effects.

The coefficients in models of the above form are estimated by least squares regression. Two refinements should be noted:

- The coefficients β_i are automatically estimated in all analyses, but as far as possible the coefficients β_{ij} are assumed to be 0. Stepwise linear regression analysis is used so that only where the estimated β_{ij} coefficient is significantly different from zero at the notional 5 per cent level is its value cited in tables.
- The model has been adapted slightly from the usual quadratic form given above to the following form:

$$Q = \alpha + \sum_i \beta_iX_i + \sum_{i \geq j} \sum \beta_{ij}(X_i - \bar{X_i})(X_j - \bar{X_j}),$$

that is, variables are measured about their means in the terms involving β_{ij}. This enables a direct significance test of the usefulness of including the higher order terms. It is a well-known device for statistical models, though rather unusual for economic production functions. It is not fundamentally different from the usual form.

The marginal productivity curve, the increase in output derived from a single unit increase in a resource input X_i, is given by

$$MP(X_i) = \beta_i + \beta_{ii}(X_i - \bar{X_i})$$

at average levels of all other inputs.

Some benefits are essentially qualitative in nature: for example whether or not intervention has prevented entry into residential care. In this case the equation given above is inappropriate (since Q is not continuous). Here we will be interested in the probability that a qualitative benefit can be achieved at particular levels of resource input given client characteristics. The method used is discriminant analysis, which yields a set of classification functions

$$g_k = \alpha_k + \sum_i \beta_{ik}X_j + \sum_{i \geq j} \sum \beta_{ijk}(X_i - \bar{X}_i)(X_j - \bar{X}_j)$$

where k=1, ..., k denotes the set of possible outcome states: and X_i as before denotes the amount of resource input and the personal characteristics of a client. The probability that a person with any given set of characteristics will have the kth outcome is predicted by:

$$P_k = \frac{\exp(g_k - \max(g_k))}{\sum_k \exp(g_k - \max(g_k))}$$

1.5 Population studied

There are three features of the study's design that are particularly salient for the study of outcomes.

- The sample was highly stratified. In particular it avoided certain groups; for example elderly people who from the first were being assessed for long-term residential care, and those for whom social services involvement was judged likely to be once-off, or to have low cost consequences, for example the issuing of a bus pass.
- We rely on the great variation in service allocation to people in apparently similar circumstances to provide the basis of a natural experiment for assessing outcomes. A necessary assumption for our conclusions to be valid is that there are not client need factors beyond those considered in the study which are crucial to allocation decisions. The evidence for this assumption and for the variability in resource allocations given need-related circumstances was presented in Chapter 3.
- In about 50 cases, where community-based social services were provided to a couple, it is clear that one of the partners was very much the 'real' client. In such cases their partner has been excluded. A number of clients could not be re-interviewed, at least not in a comparable form, and so changes could not be observed. So the number of clients in the sample studied for the destinational outcome was 512, and for outcomes involving repeated measurement about 390. Numbers are further depleted because individual items of information are missing for some persons.

2 Results

Section 2 describes the results of our investigation of the circumstances of clients, the services provided, and the four types of potential benefits described in Section 1.1. Section 2.1 deals with survival in the community, Section 2.2 with improvement in quality of life, Section 2.3 with achievements in the tasks for which social services specifically intervene, and Section 2.4 with client satisfaction. Section 2.5 investigates why a large number of elderly clients show no benefit by any criterion. Each section is concluded by a short summary.

2.1 Destinational outcomes

Destination has not always been regarded as a final output of community care. Two things have changed this. First, in relation to death, there has been a growing awareness of the link between social environment, health and survival (Schmale, 1958; Gunderson and Rahe, 1974; Cassel, 1976; Lynch, 1977, Chap. 2). Social origins for both mental and physical ill-health are now recognised (Brown and Harris, 1978; Clare, 1982); and there is concern about the low life expectancy of elderly people suffering from mental health conditions (Thompson and Eastwood, 1981) for whom social care is nowadays considered appropriate (Bergmann and Jacoby, 1983). Ill-health generally has become recognised as a major factor for people referred for social interventions (Clare and Corney, 1982). So a reduction in mortality has become an important criterion for examining the consequences of care. Recent examples are Booth (1985, Chap. 9), who used it as one of the main criteria for assessing the effect of regime in old people's homes; and Levin, Sinclair and Gorbach (1985) who used it to assess the effectiveness of the home help service. There has been a spectacular demonstration that appropriate social interventions in the community can prolong the life expectancy of the frail elderly, and should therefore be regarded as a legitimate objective of social services interventions (Challis and Davies, 1986).

The second reason why destinational outcome has become central to community-based interventions is because of the acceleration away from residential forms of provision, particularly long-term hospital care. There have been many reasons for this. Earlier disillusionment with residential provision (Townsend, 1962), the anti-institutionalisation views of the political left and ideological preferences for 'traditional' community care on the right, the cost advantages and the preference of many elderly people for maintaining their independence, have all contributed to the pressure for keeping elderly people out of long-term institutional care (Johnson and Challis, 1983). The move to develop alternatives to institutional care has become perhaps the single most explicit objective for social services for elderly people specified in national policy documents (DHSS, 1981a,b).

The development of this policy has been documented many times, most recently by Means and Smith (1985), and it would be superfluous to repeat it here. We mention in passing the counter-views which have been expressed over the last decade about the consequences of overemphasis on this single objective to the exclusion of other objectives, particularly client quality of life and the reduction of burden on carers (Plank, 1977).

To identify the preventive impact of domiciliary care more clearly, we distinguish two groups of survivors, those clients who during the second interview said that the services they had received (home helps, meals-on-wheels, day care, short-term care but not social work) had directly contributed to their ability to continue living at home; and the remainder. So we shall compare four destinational outcome groups: those who died; those who entered long-term institutional care including hospital, local authority and private residential care; those who were enabled to remain in their own homes; and the remaining survivors.

Table 4.4 shows that, on average, clients who died or were institutionalised during the study period were high consumers of social services for the time they were in the community. The same is also true of those clients who felt that social services had enabled them to continue living at home. In part this can be explained by the higher needs of these groups. Seventy-six per cent of individuals in these groups have short or critical interval needs compared with 60 per cent of other survivors. Those who entered institutions were often confused (35 per cent showed strong evidence of confusion compared with 14 per cent of 'other survivors'); and incontinent of either urine or faeces (30 per cent compared with 22 per cent).

A comparison of particular interest in Table 4.4 is between the circumstances of those who entered institutions and those who felt that social services help had been crucial in enabling them to live at home. The initial circumstances of the two groups are very different. The key difference is level of support: *the people who are enabled to live at home by social services help are those who are disabled but who crucially lack other forms of support*, classified into groups 4 and 6 rather than 3 and 5 (see Table 4.3). Typically they live alone and they report a shortage of people available to give support or help with difficulties. Over the six months of this evaluation, which it should be recalled covers elderly people who were not initially being assessed for residential care, *institutionalisation occurred frequently where disability was combined with an unsatisfactory informal caring arrangement*. One-quarter of those who entered institutions had been living with a daughter or other close relative, whereas nobody who had been enabled to continue living at home was living in this situation. The other key distinction between those who enter institutions and those who are successfully enabled to live at home is that many more of the former are

Table 4.4
Differences among clients according to destinational outcome in initial personal characteristics and the average level of services received

	Entered institution	Died	Social services enabled client to live at home	Other survivors	Between groups significance %
Personal characteristics					
MYTYPO1	0.13	0.15	0.14	0.20	n.s.
MYTYPO2	0.08	0.15	0.06	0.13	n.s.
MYTYPO3	0.28	0.18	0.10	0.18	n.s.
MYTYPO4	0.13	0.09	0.41	0.22	< 1
MYTYPO5	0.25	0.24	0.04	0.10	< 1
MYTYPO6	0.12	0.18	0.23	0.10	5
CF	0.35	0.29	0.14	0.14	< 1
SEX	1.75	1.55	1.71	1.71	n.s.
INCONT	0.30	0.24	0.39	0.22	1
HHOLD1	0.50	0.62	0.74	0.56	1
HHOLD2	0.28	0.29	0.23	0.33	n.s.
ADEQ	0.70	0.74	0.57	0.66	n.s.
AVAIL	1.35	1.73	1.59	1.71	n.s.
Services					
HHCINP	3.51	3.64	4.45	2.33	< 1
WARDINP	0.00	0.03	0.03	0.02	n.s.
SWINP	1.03	1.12	1.11	0.79	10
MOWINP	1.08	1.18	2.39	0.61	< 1
DCINP	0.27	0.33	0.39	0.20	n.s.
STCINP	1.40	0.82	1.00	0.51	n.s.
NURSE	0.53	0.53	0.48	0.38	10
(N)	(40)	(34)	(84)	(324)	

Figures shown indicate means of the variables within each category. For example 0.13 of the people who entered institutions were initially in group MYTYPO1 (see Table 3.3). People who entered institutions had on average 3.51 hours per week of the home-help (and related) services before entry. Significance is calculated by the F-test on 3,478 degrees of freedom.

showing signs of mental confusion whereas the latter suffer only from physical problems which may include incontinence.

Mrs Adams[2] is a typical example of someone who was successfully enabled to remain at home. She lived alone, was very depressed, had no social contact other than an occasional visit from a niece who lived 200 miles away. Severe diabetes had left her housebound and nervous of walking even indoors. A social worker visited to assess her for day care following a period of hospitalisation. She arranged for home help to be increased to daily, day care once a week, meals-on-wheels daily, a telephone and a zimmer frame. The purpose was specifically to maintain Mrs Adams at home for as long as possible. A district nurse also visited. Six months later her health was still bad, but her morale was higher. She was particularly happy with the opportunity to socialise through day care, while the home help was described as 'like a daughter to her' and was her main contact on the telephone.

The key question of this section is, given that clients who died or were institutionalised were high consumers of services, what evidence is there that providing high levels of service is effective? We answer this by checking whether the initial circumstances of these clients are sufficiently worse than average to explain the higher resource allocation. The rationale for the analysis was explained in Section 1.4: discriminant analysis is used to differentiate between the four destinational groups, and to predict the probability that a client with given characteristics will have each of the four outcomes. From this we can deduce whether differences in service usage make a significant difference once need circumstances are taken into account.

Table 4.5 shows the classification functions produced by discriminant analysis. Among the individual services, home helps, meals-on-wheels and social work all have a significant impact on final destination after allowance is made for the client's characteristics. In order to make clear what this effect is, Table 4.6 calculates the probability of each destination, for different levels of each of these services, for a hypothetical individual who in all other respects is average. (An explanation of this was given in Section 1.4).

A number of interesting conclusions may be drawn from Table 4.6. The home help service and meals-on-wheels are treated together, since our sample excluded people who were assessed for meals-on-wheels alone. It is evident that even for clients who are similar at the outset, high usage of these two services is a predictor of eventual death or institutionalisation. Often the reason for this is that as the client's problems get more acute, more and more services are drawn in.

Mr Bennett was described by his social worker as 'a difficult old man'. He had angina but was not particularly disabled. However, when his wife became ill with cancer, his daughter asked social services to take him into residential care. Instead, the social worker decided to provide five hours' home help and two days per week of day care for him. Mrs Bennett went into hospital for three weeks, during which he was given a short stay in residential care. Afterwards, his day care was increased to all day, three times a week and meals-on-wheels were introduced three times a week. Then, for reasons

Table 4.5
Discriminant analysis between four destinational outcome groups on the basis of initial circumstances and services provided

	Entered institution	Died	Social services enabled client to live at home	Other survivors
Constant	−27.74	−28.44	−28.67	−24.80
MYTYPO1	15.44	15.40	15.40	14.98
MYTYPO2	17.59	18.14	17.07	17.34
MYTYPO3	16.48	16.20	16.11	15.84
MYTYPO4	14.59	14.63	15.98	14.81
MYTYPO5	18.38	18.52	16.16	16.51
MYTYPO6	15.39	16.22	15.86	15.28
CF	3.45	3.70	1.71	2.46
SEX	9.70	8.92	9.48	9.62
INCONT	1.06	0.74	2.52	1.35
HHOLD1	10.22	11.18	11.56	10.75
HHOLD2	13.37	13.95	14.41	13.96
ADEQ	4.62	4.68	3.99	4.15
AVAIL	1.05	1.21	1.14	1.13
HHCINP	0.26	0.26	0.20	0.09
WARDINP	17.80	7.41	27.44	14.21
SWINP	1.49	0.35	0.64	0.29
MOWINP	0.07	0.01	0.58	0.01
DCINP	0.87	1.25	1.15	0.66
STCINP	0.00	0.02	0.13	0.03
HHCINPSQ	0.00	−0.01	0.01	0.00
WARDINPSQ	−16.76	−4.75	−26.29	−12.32
SWINPSQ	−0.41	0.71	0.33	0.62
MOWINPSQ	0.06	0.08	0.05	0.04
DCINPSQ	0.05	0.03	0.10	0.11
NURSE	0.48	0.51	0.12	0.29
(N)	(40)	(34)	(84)	(324)

a These functions may be used to predict the outcome for any individual, using that individual's values for each of the above variables to compute the four discriminant scores and predicting according to the highest score.

b A discriminant analysis using the variables listed below gives Wilks $\lambda = 0.64$, equivalent to 36 per cent of total variation explained.

c Pairwise, all groups are significantly different from one another except: Entered institution and Died, and Died and Other survivors.

d 69 per cent of all original observations are correctly classified by the discriminant functions obtained using priors equal to group sizes. The discriminant functions add little insight to univariate analysis and are not reproduced here. The within-group covariance matrices are significantly different so some caution must be observed in interpreting these results.

e The linear discriminant functions for the four groups are as follows:
Entered Institution (40)
Died (34)
Social services enabled client to live at home (84)
Other survivors (324).

Table 4.6
Predicted destinational outcome of a 'typical' social services client, given different levels of domiciliary services

Service	Entered institution %	Died %	Social services enabled client to live at home %	Other survivors %
No home help, no meals-on-wheels	3	4	5	88
Two hours home help, no meals-on-wheels	4	5	5	86
Four hours home help, two meals-on-wheels p.w.	5	6	17	72
Eight hours home help, five meals-on-wheels p.w.	6	7	61	26
No social work	3	6	9	82
Low social work	3	6	10	81
Moderate social work	15	7	12	67
High social work	84	2	3	11
(N)	(40)	(34)	(84)	(324)

Reading along rows, the above figures give the predicted probability of each destinational outcome, using the discriminant equations of Table 3.5. The predicted probabilities are calculated by taking every variable at its mean value, except the indicated service input.

that are unclear, Mr Bennett was admitted to hospital with hypothermia. His wife and daughter were reluctant to have him home again, and only did so when the home help was increased to daily. There was continued family tension and frequent rows, which culminated in his abrupt death following a seizure.

But sometimes the resource allocator provided an initial high level of services on the basis of a hunch about the case which seems independent of measurable characteristics.

Mrs Cooper was 87, lived alone, was cheerful but had difficulty walking and had a home help once a week. She had seriously burnt one leg on a hot-water bottle, after which a district nurse started to visit twice weekly. Then she fell, and needed stitches in her head. At the start of the study, the hospital asked for a reassessment, and the home help organiser commented after her visit that although Mrs Cooper was quite independent in her home and had good support from neighbours and a son who visited weekly, a high level of services would be appropriate to ensure that she could have good prospects of long-term survival in the community. So home help was provided daily, ostensibly to light her coal fire, and meals-on-wheels twice weekly. The organiser was sufficiently concerned to revisit regularly, and two months later she reported that the son no longer visited, the neighbours were less supportive, and she was alarmed by the deterioration in Mrs Cooper's condition. A week or two later she died.

It is necessary to be cautious about taking clients' reports about the preventive effect of services too literally.

Mr Davis's claim to be unable to manage housework after his wife left him led to four hours per week home help. But the organiser was sceptical especially when she found out that Mr Davis was learning to drive, and reduced the allocation to three hours. Mr Davis was very upset about this and insistent in our interview that the service was essential to maintain him at home.

What also stands out from Table 4.6 is the impact of high levels of home help and meals-on-wheels for a 'successful enabling to remain at home' outcome. People who got four hours or less of the home help service were unlikely to think that social services contributed significantly to their survival in the community.

The high involvement of social work shown for people institutionalised, as shown in Table 4.6, reflects the standard procedures for admission to residential care that all local authorities adopt. *What is far more significant is the lack of involvement of social work in successful preventive care.* There were only thirteen clients in total for whom moderate or high levels of social work were combined with high levels of other services (five hours or more per week of home helps, five meals-on-wheels per week, or five day centre visits per week), and where the outcome was described by the recipient as successfully preventive. Mostly these were clients of special home care schemes: five of the thirteen came from Area 3 which had a specialist team for elderly people with high commitment to intense preventive work, and was running an experimental home care scheme during the period of the study.

The final question about destinational outcome is whether there are differences between local authorities, particularly in successfully enabling the client to live at home rather than dying or becoming institutionalised. Table 4.7 shows that there were considerable differences between areas in the destinations of clients in the study – as shown in the 'actual' column. The proportion of people who died or were institutionalised varied from 5 per cent in Area 1 to 26 per cent in Area 3. But what happens when allowance is made for differences between areas in the characteristics of clients and services? Table 4.7 also shows the predicted number of people in each category using the formulae in Table 4.5. These

Table 4.7
Destinational outcome for each local authority, compared with predicted value from discriminant analysis

Area and type	Entered institution		Died		Client believed social services enabled him/her to live at home		Other services	
	Act.	Pred.	Act.	Pred.	Act.	Pred.	Act.	Pred.
1 Inner London	1	2.9	2	2.3	13	10.4	36	36.4
2 Inner London	3	4.3	2	2.4	4	7.1	33	28.3
3 Outer London	8	5.4	5	3.1	15	12.3	21	28.2
4 Met. District	4	2.9	6	3.1	6	5.6	28	32.3
5 Met. District	8	3.8	7	4.9	9	8.8	42	48.5
6 Met. District	5	5.7	5	4.3	6	5.1	31	31.9
7 English Shire	7	5.9	3	4.9	3	6.5	39	34.7
8 English Shire	5	4.0	3	4.5	10	7.7	35	36.8
9 English Shire	4	7.1	6	4.0	10	8.2	36	36.7
10 Welsh County	4	6.1	1	4.9	15	12.6	31	28.2
(N)	(49)		(40)		(91)		(332)	

$\chi^2 = 24.70$ on 18 degrees freedom (combining 'died' and 'entered institution') is not significant: This suggests that predicted values fit reasonably closely.

predicted figures closely match the actual figures, implying that *the differences of effectiveness between areas are due to the type of client being served and in the resources provided, and not to differences in technical efficiency* resulting from the management or quality of services.

2.1.1 Summary
Since those who died or were institutionalised were 'high uptake of service' cases, it is difficult to assess objectively whether the amount of service input enables people to continue living at home. But judging from clients' own opinions this is certainly true of the home help service, particularly when it is combined with meals-on-wheels, although less than four hours' home help per week has little effect. Differences between local authorities in the numbers of clients who died or were institutionalised are due to the type of client taken on and to the amount of service provided, and not to differences in the quality of care or the calibre of service providers.

2.2 Life satisfaction
Challis (1981) and Davies and Knapp (1981) identified a number of general outputs of social care which are associated with quality of life, including life satisfaction (morale); independence (control over the pattern of one's

life); social integration; compensation for and the relief of disability; and nurturance (living standards). All of these have been examined in the present study (c.f. Bebbington et al., 1986, Chap. 5). The conclusions drawn were similar and generally these outputs did not appear to be influenced by social services inputs in any consistent manner. So here we comment only on life satisfaction.

Reviews of measures of the subjective wellbeing of elderly people have been given by Challis (1981), Davies and Knapp (1981), Kane and Kane (1981), Larsen (1978), and Lohmann (1977). Three distinct approaches particularly within the American literature have predominated in recent years: Neugarten, Havighurst and Tobin's (1961) Life Satisfaction Ratings and Index; Bradburn's (1969) Affect Balance Scale; and Lawton's (1975) Philadelphia Geriatric Centre (PGC) Morale Scale. The last of these has been adopted for use in the present study. The individual items are anglicised as proposed by Challis and Knapp (1980). A factor analysis of this scale based on project data and reported by Bebbington et al. (1986, Chap. 5), produced very similar results to Lawton's original analysis. An equivalent measure was required for subjects interviewed by proxy, and this reference reports a surrogate version which proved useful in the initial analysis.

At the outset, the morale of the client group was low, significantly lower for example than the comparison sample of disabled elderly people not in contact with social services. It was quite closely linked to the client's circumstances: varying from a PGC score of 5.6 for those in low need (MYTYPO group 0) to 9.8 for the critical interval need group (MYTYPO group 5). A high PGC score indicates lower morale. Over the course of the study there was a slight improvement in morale in all groups, averaging 0.4.

Table 4.8 shows the regression model relating service inputs and client characteristics to the morale outcome. The fit is poor. A few terms are statistically significant, and it would be unwise to base firm conclusions on them. It appears that clients who have had hospital or short-term residential care have the most favourable morale outcome, whereas more day care may be associated with the opposite effect.

In fact it is difficult to identify more than a few clients who are like Mrs Adams, where a long-term improvement in morale can be unambiguously attributed to social services care. More typically, morale is raised by short-term expectations, and on occasion this can backfire.

> Mrs Everett did not get on very well with her family, and after a stroke her daughter, with whom she had been living, refused to have her back. It took four months to arrange alternative housing, during which time she stayed in hospital. When we first saw her, she was excited about the prospect of getting a home of her own, though privately the social worker thought that residential care was really

Table 4.8
Equation predicting decline in life satisfaction from needs and resources

Item	Regression coefficient	Significance level (%)
HHCINP	−0.55	—
WARDINP	1.28	—
SWINP	0.15	—
MOWINP	−0.07	—
DCINP	0.62	1
STCINP	−0.14	1
AIDS	−0.13	—
HOSP	−0.74	5
DAYHOSP	−0.20	—
NURSE	−0.04	—
PRIVNUR	−0.28	—
PRIVHWK	−0.50	—
VOLCARE	0.48	—
INFHELP	0.11	10
MYTYPO1	0.00	—
MYTYPO2	−0.32	—
MYTYPO3	−0.38	—
MYTYPO4	−0.13	—
MYTYPO5	0.81	—
MYTYPO6	0.60	—
SEX	−0.02	—
HHOLD1	0.84	—
HHOLD2	0.77	—
ADEQ	0.10	—
AVAIL	−0.08	—
CF	−1.05	5
HEALTH	0.56	10
ACUTE	−0.16	—
DEATHSP	1.31	—
FINANCE	1.32	1
ADLSELFX	−0.07	—
ADLHOMX	−0.05	—
INCONTX	0.29	—
LOSSADEQ	0.75	5
AVAILX	−0.21	10
CFX	1.44	—

R^2 = 0.19 (Adjusted: 0.08) Sample size = 339
  Significant negative coefficients indicate factors producing an improvement in life satisfaction.

more suitable. Six months later, the social worker was visiting fortnightly, home help was provided two hours a week, and day care twice weekly. Though she was being successfully maintained in the community, the daughter and the remainder of her family had withdrawn completely. Mrs Everett was desperately lonely as well as guilty and anxious about her family. 'My life is one long hell. I've got to struggle to do everything'.

These findings may be contrasted with those of Davies and Challis (1986, Chap. 9) using the same PGC Morale Scale. They found that the Community Care Project produced greater improvements with large inputs than did standard provision. There may be at least two reasons why this present study found that variations in inputs makes little significant impression on morale. First, the Thanet Community Care Project explicitly aimed at the improvement of morale (Davies and Challis, 1986, pp.14-17) and care packages were designed to achieve this. While by implication most conventional services have this objective, it is rarely made explicit or acted on. As the figures in Section 2.3 show, it was unusual for social workers or home help organisers to mention this general area as an objective of their intervention, and only 8 per cent of those interviewed afterwards said that they thought the client had made improvement in this respect. For example, the case of Mr Farley, cited in Section 2.5, illustrates how, in the eyes of many service allocators, low morale on its own is not sufficient reason for intervention.

Second, Davies and Challis (1986) attribute their success in improving morale very largely to the provision of someone who can act as a close confidante. In our present study, *conventional services were almost never successful in creating good interpersonal relationships, except between the client and members of their own staff*. Between the first and second interviews, 35 clients reported gaining a confidante (excluding home helps and other staff), compared with 70 who lost and did not replace their existing confidante. But even when a confidante is gained as a result of social services intervention, often the relationship is not on a firm enough footing to be effective, as the following example illustrates.

Mrs Gray lived with her son. After a stroke, she had difficulty with housework and getting about, although her actual reason for approaching social services was a claim that her son was withholding her pension. The social worker felt her main problem was depression and feelings of lack of support, and commented 'She needs companionship and stimulation which will improve the quality of her life'. Mrs Gray liked the day care provided twice a week, although she would have preferred a family placement. At the end of six months, the relationship with her son was improved, and he was now regarded as someone in whom she could confide. She was pleased with social services help and said she felt it had lessened the burden on her son. The son told a different story. He was contemptuous of the support that had been given, and attributed the improvement to the fact that he had lost his job and so had more time with his mother. But the evidence suggested that there were still many problems. Our interviewer commented that the home had become dirty and neglected. Mrs Gray's morale was three points lower than it had been. There had been no follow-up by the social worker.

On average, the *gain* of a confidante is not associated with a rise in morale, which remains significantly lower for this group than for those who had a confidante throughout.

2.2.1 Summary
There is little evidence that conventional services have a favourable long-term effect on morale, or indeed on any other subjective measure of quality of life. This contrasts with recent findings from the Thanet Community Care Project (Davies and Challis, 1986). It is suggested that this may be because explicit action of proven effectiveness, such as helping to establish a close supporting relationship, is rarely part of a conventional intervention.

2.3 Achievement of service objectives

2.3.1 The service objectives
Improvement in length and quality of life in the community are the most final of the benefits which community-based personal social services seek to create. But our evidence, like that of many other studies, suggests that the factors which primarily affect these are largely beyond the influence of conventional services. Health (Palmore and Luikart, 1972; Larue, Bank, Jarvik and Hetland, 1979), the quality of social relationships (Strain and Chappell, 1982; Baur and Okun, 1983) and living standards (Larsen, 1978) have been identified as the key determinants of quality of life.

The evidence of the domiciliary care study is that in practice the aims of service allocators where these are made explicit are geared to the achievement of short-term goals that are more within their control.

In *Growing Older* it was argued that 'the primary role of public services is an enabling one, helping people to care for themselves and their families by providing a framework of support' (DHSS, 1981a, p.38). We have shown that one active and successful role of domiciliary social services is to enable people to remain living in their own homes. But beyond that, we find that the rationalisations for intervention revolved around two main issues. The first was to intervene in a situation in which an elderly person was felt to be at risk. Chapter 7 describes how social services departments have become preoccupied with the preventive function, particularly where the client is felt to be threatened in a way which might have repercussions for the department itself. Forty-six per cent of all clients in our study were described as being at risk in one sense or

another, of which the commonest single group were those at risk of falling
(17 per cent). Exactly one-half of those at risk were considered as being
unsafe to leave alone without at least regular monitoring.

The second type of reason for intervention was to meet an outstanding
welfare shortfall. This is evident in answers to a direct question about
the overall purpose of the proposed course of action, to which the following
were the most frequent responses: to undertake domestic tasks, food
preparation (36 per cent); the relief of carers (23 per cent); to defer need
for residential care (18 per cent); the relief of loneliness (15 per cent); to
improve functioning, mobility, health (15 per cent); monitoring, surveillance
(11 per cent); to provide emotional or general support (6 per cent);
rehabilitation, skills training (6 per cent); to improve morale, lessen depression (4 per cent); to improve personal cleanliness (3 per cent).

The great majority of these are concerned with direct treatment for
specific needs or finding solutions to specific problems. So in this section,
the achievement of service objectives is assessed in three ways.

Reducing client's felt vulnerability to adverse life events
Clients were asked about nine individual fears which are relevant to
problems of elderly and disabled people. The interview with the proxy
covered the client's fears. These items, and the answers to them, are
summarised in Table 4.9. Factor analysis (reported by Bebbington et al.,
1986, Chap. 5) reveals they form a single, though rather weak factor. A
score was computed of the number of 'often' answers to the set of fears
items at initial assessment and after six months for each client. The output
variable for the analysis is the score after six months, regression-adjusted
by the score at initial assessment.

Reducing welfare shortfall with the main daily living activities
Clients were asked at the outset and again after six months whether they
felt they needed extra help with getting up and going to bed; with food
preparation and cooking; and with housework. These questions were also
asked in proxy form. We have identified providing help with such tasks
as the most frequently cited reason for social services involvement, and
the major justification for the home help service and meals-on-wheels.
Answers to these items are summarised in Table 4.10. We analyse this
factor in two ways. The first is to identify those people who had a
problem at the time of the first interview and to differentiate those who
were successfully helped (that is, need was reduced in at least one respect)
from those who were not. The second is to measure improvement
quantitatively by computing a scale DESHELP as defined in Table 4.1
from the summation of items. The output variable is then the score after
six months, regression-adjusted by the score at initial assessment.

Table 4.9
Clients' felt vulnerability to various risk factors

Do you ever think about....	At initial assessment			After six months		
	Often	Occas-ionally	No	Often	Occas-ionally	No
	%	%	%	%	%	%
(i) Falling down at home and not being able to get up again	23	25	52	20	26	54
(ii) Becoming too ill or dependent to be looked after at home	19	29	53	15	31	54
(iii) Putting too much burden on the people who help you	19	20	61	13	18	68
(iv) Being forgetful and perhaps causing accidents, e.g. forgetting to turn off the kettle	15	14	70	9	19	72
(v) Not eating well enough	8	8	84	4	8	88
(vi) Not being able to keep yourself sufficiently warm in winter	14	7	78	9	11	80
(vii) If living alone, being able to go on coping with living alone	11	12	77	8	15	77

Sample size is 436 at each time except item (iii) with 381 at initial assessment and 369 after six months (not asked in proxy form). For item (vii), people not living alone are classified as 'No'.

Resolving or ameliorating problems generally

The approach so far in this chapter is to judge the effectiveness of interventions by clients' own accounts. But resource allocators have special skills in identifying problems and, as Crosbie (1983) has shown, on occasion view the situation rather differently from the client. (Indeed, the interests of the client and of the department are not always the same; for example when residential care is sought but the department wishes to support care in the community, as in the case of Mr Bennett above and Mrs Jones below.) So we have taken this opportunity to look at service allocators' views about the effectiveness of the intervention in resolving the original problems for which services were provided.

In the final interview with social workers and home help organisers, questions were asked about changes in a number of domains: improvement

Table 4.10
Clients' felt need for extra help with certain activities of daily living

	At initial assessment %	After six months %
More help needed when getting up or going to bed		
No	89	89
At certain times	9	9
All the time	2	2
(N)	(514)	(396)
More help needed to help eat		
Eats adequately, no extra help needed	77	86
Eats inadequately, but no help wanted	19	11
Eats inadequately, needs help at times	3	2
Eats inadequately due to lack of help	1	1
(N)	(512)	(385)
More help needed with housework		
No	64	71
On special occasions only	15	12
At times	13	9
All the time	9	8
(N)	(515)	(397)

or decline with specific problems such as loneliness and with a number of risks such as falling. We are here taking a particularly instrumental view of social work activity, in line with the goal-centred approach advocated for example by Goldberg and Warburton (1979). This approach relies on the worker having maintained contact with the client or having reassessed the client reasonably close to the time of our second approach. This was often not true. And in such cases the easy assumption of many resource allocators was that if they had had no further contact, problems had been resolved; but as we shall see this is by no means realistic. Because there were many home help clients in particular who had not been reassessed, we accepted organisers' reports from their own home helps where these had been actively sought. Even so, *there were cases where the social worker or home help organiser did not know enough about the consequences of the intervention for us to code whether or not problems had been resolved.* For the remainder, the outcome measure is a count of the problems resolved or risks reduced. The results are summarised in Table 4.11.

Table 4.11
Service providers' views about problems reduced or solved and risks ameliorated

	No. of clients
Number of problems reduced or risks ameliorated[a]	
None	186
One	73
Two	36
Three	9
Four	3
Five or more	2
The main problems reduced or solved[b]	
Loneliness	26
Depression	25
General health	18
Mobility	18
Overburdened carer	17
Disability with daily living activities	11
Behaviour problems	9
Accommodation	9
The main risks ameliorated[b]	
Falling, accidents	18
Unable to cope	8
Undernourished	7
Depressed, suicidal	6
Loss of carer	6
Isolated	5
Self-neglect	4
Hypothermia	3

a There is no information on 14 people who were still in the community.
b Number of clients mentioned.

2.3.2 Results

Tables 4.9, 4.10 and 4.11 show that in respect of each of felt vulnerability, need for additional help, and general problems, there is an overall improvement over the period of the study for clients who remained living in the community. However, it is a minority of clients who are successfully helped. The question is, what services have the greatest effect and for what type of client? This may be answered in general terms by the three statistical models shown in Table 4.12 which link these outcomes to services and to client characteristics. The main features of these models are described in the following subsections.

Change in felt vulnerability

As was seen from Table 4.9, there is a slight but statistically significant reduction in felt vulnerability over the period of the study in most individual items. (There was no similar reduction in a comparison group of disabled elderly people who were not service recipients.) Each of the main social services is associated with change in felt vulnerability, although the average effect is quite small. We have already referred to one explanation of why this is so: the service level may be responsive to vulnerability, rather than vice versa. For example, for certain clients, a high level of input may be symptomatic of a continuing problem. For this reason, to get a more genuine outcome variable, we have also looked specifically at people with fears at initial assessment which were ameliorated. Of 283 people who reported frequent concern with any of the seven risk factors, by the second interview 178 (63 per cent) were showing a resolution in at least one of those which had formerly troubled them. Some of the following conclusions about individual services are based on this indicator.

(i) Social work is actually associated with lower than average reduction in felt vulnerability, though the effect is very slight. Sixty per cent of social work clients showed a resolution of at least one fear compared with 65 per cent of those who did not get a social worker. We must infer that social work does not serve effectively to reduce fears of vulnerability.

(ii) The home help service and meals-on-wheels have a positive effect. But the marginal effect is very small. Table 4.12 shows that each extra meal on wheels per week reduces vulnerability by 0.1 on the scale. Applying the formula described in section 1.4, the marginal effect of each hour (per week) of the home help service is

$$-0.12 + 0.02 \times \text{hours}$$

implying decreasing returns to scale, since a high score on the scale indicates low output. Table 4.13A uses the formula of Table 4.12, column A to illustrate the predicted effect on the scale of felt vulnerability of typical combinations of the two services. Even the highest levels produce an average improvement of less than one point of the scale. Meals-on-wheels are, not surprisingly, most relevant to people who feel at risk of not eating adequately – although, curiously, few recipients were actually worried about this. Fifteen out of the 88 clients who received meals-on-wheels throughout were initially very concerned: all but one no longer had this worry after six months.

Reduction in client's desire for extra help
Change in the felt need for extra help with daily living activities – 'felt welfare shortfall' – is influenced more by the availability of informal care, voluntary care and private nursing help than by social services support, except that the provision of meals-on-wheels significantly reduces problems concerning eating. The marginal effect of meals-on-wheels is again to improve the score on the scale by about 0.1 per extra meal. The only

Table 4.12
Regression equations predicting the achievement of service objectives from needs and resources

Item	Column A Felt vulnerability (RISK)		Column B Felt welfare shortfall (DESHELP)		Column C Service provider's view (CMCURE)	
	Coeff.	Sig. (%)	Coeff.	Sig. (%)	Coeff.	Sig. (%)
HHCINP	−0.06	–	0.03	–	0.10	1
HHCINPSQ	0.01	1	0.01	10	−0.01	10
WARDINP	−0.48	–	−0.29	–	0.41	–
SWINP	0.24	–	0.05	–	0.42	1
SWINPSQ	−0.05	–	−0.01	–	−0.19	5
MOWINP	−0.10	5	−0.09	5	0.03	–
DCINP	−0.01	–	−0.05	–	0.09	–
STCINP	−0.00	–	0.01	–	0.03	10
AIDS	0.01	–	0.00	–	0.03	–
HOSP	0.34	10	0.21	–	−0.05	–
DAYHOSP	0.02	–	−0.17	–	−0.05	–
NURSE	−0.02	–	−0.00	–	0.00	–
PRIVHLP	0.33	–	−0.60	5	0.10	–
VOLCARE	0.14	–	−0.53	1	−0.11	–
INFHELP	−0.02	–	0.05	–	0.03	–
MYTYPO1	0.44	–	−0.27	–	−0.02	–
MYTYPO2	−0.02	–	−0.26	–	0.00	–
MYTYPO3	0.52	–	−0.06	–	0.13	–
MYTYPO4	0.45	–	−0.55	5	−0.12	–
MYTYPO5	0.31	–	−0.54	–	0.05	–
MYTYPO6	0.25	–	−0.14	–	−0.20	–
SEX	−0.25	–	0.05	–	−0.04	–
HHOLD1	0.12	–	−0.27	–	0.16	–
HHOLD2	0.04	–	−0.25	–	−0.32	–
ADEQ	−0.00	–	−0.35	5	−0.02	–
AVAIL	−0.05	–	−0.19	1	−0.01	–
CF	0.30	–	0.62	1	−0.06	–
INCONT	−0.06	–	0.24	–	−0.05	–
HEALTH	0.35	10	0.13	–	0.10	–
ACUTE	0.14	–	0.08	–	−0.21	–
DEATHSP	0.42	–	−0.37	–	−0.26	–
FINANCE	0.47	10	0.09	–	−0.24	–
ADLSELFX	−0.08	1	0.00	–	0.00	–
ADLHOMX	0.03	–	−0.03	–	0.01	–
INCONTX	0.15	–	0.42	5	−0.26	–
LOSSADEQ	0.37	5	0.21	–	−0.10	–
AVAILX	−0.05	–	−0.16	5	0.07	–
CFX	1.13	–	0.38	–	−0.91	10
DCxHHOLD1	0.62	1	–	–	–	–
HHCxMYTYPO3	–	–	0.27	1	–	–
HHCxLOSSADEQ	–	–	–	–	0.14	1
Constant	−0.14	–	0.61	–	0.45	–
R^2	0.21		0.30		0.24	
(N)	(365)		(368)		(262)	

other domiciliary service to have an effect is the home help service, but this effect is barely significant in Table 4.12, column B, and indicates that the marginal effect of each hour of service is

$$-0.03 + 0.02 \text{ hours}$$

for clients in MYTYPO group 3 and

$$-0.23 + 0.02 \text{ hours}$$

for clients in other dependency groups, again implying decreasing returns to scale. Table 4.13B illustrates the combined effect of home helps and meals-on-wheels for different types of client, based on the formulae of Table 4.12, column B. For people with high needs, or without other sources of support, the more domiciliary services are provided, the greater the reduction in their problems. However, for low need clients with some existing support (MYTYPO group 3), extra provision of services may actually be associated with an *increase* in the need for help. The following is a case illustrating the vulnerability of clients in this group and how services may become drawn in.

> Mrs Hobson is blind and rather deaf but with no other major problem. She could look after herself quite well, although her husband had been doing most routine housework for some years. A daughter nearby also helped with the heavier tasks, but with a young family and a full-time job her support was limited. Three hours per week home help was provided when Mr Hobson went into hospital for an operation, and when cancer was diagnosed this became permanent. Six weeks before we revisited, Mr Hobson died. Mrs Hobson was very depressed and unable to answer our questions. The daughter, who was interviewed on Mrs Hobson's behalf, was doing all the cooking and taking her mother home at nights. Although the home help allocation had been doubled, the daughter felt that a great deal more would be essential to enable Mrs Hobson to survive in the community in the long term.

Not surprisingly, social work and day care have no effect on felt need for extra domiciliary help.

Service allocators' judgement about problems ameliorated
The service allocators who were asked about improvement in clients' circumstances were almost exclusively social workers and home help organisers, and so it is perhaps not surprising that in the formula of Table 4.12, column C, these two services are both associated with favourable outcomes. The marginal effect of the home help service is considerably greater for people who lost friends or a close confidante during the study. The marginal effect of each hour per week of the home help service is

$$0.04 + 0.02 \text{ hours}$$

for those who lose support (LOSSADEQ) and

0.18 + 0.02 hours

for the remainder. Again this implies decreasing returns to scale (a high score on this scale indicates high output). The negative coefficient of SWINPSQ in Table 4.12, column C also implies decreasing returns to scale for social work input, but the arbitrary nature of this measurement of social work precludes a detailed analysis. What these results imply is that

Table 4.13
The predicted effect of the home help service and meals-on-wheels on output variables, from the formulae given in Table 4.12

A. Change in felt vulnerability (RISK) (Mean = 0.00, S.D. = 1.38)

Home help	Meals-on-wheels	Average change score
None	None	0.09
Two hours per week	None	0.07
Four hours per week	Two per week	−0.25
Eight hours per week	Five per week	−0.50

B. Change in felt need for extra help (DESHELP) (Mean = 0.00, S.D. = 1.28)

Home help	Meals-on-wheels	Average change score for client type 3	for other types
None	None	−0.63	0.14
Two hours per week	None	−0.18	0.04
Four hours per week	Two per week	0.14	−0.15
Eight hours per week	Five per week	1.03[a]	−0.34

C. Service provider's view of problems resolved (CMCURE) (Mean = 0.63, S.D. = 0.94)

Home help	Meals-on-wheels	Average score Clients who lost informal support	Others
None	None	−0.38	0.03
Two hours per week	None	0.09	0.21
Four hours per week	Two per week	0.56	0.41
Eight hours per week	Five per week	1.31	0.59

Figures represent outcomes scores after six months, (taking into account score in the same variable at initial assessment and all other factors), e.g. no home help and no meals-on-wheels implies an increase in felt vulnerability of 0.29 *above* the average.
a Very high levels of domiciliary services are unusual for clients in this category.

allocators' opinions about whether problems are solved are influenced more by whether services were provided than by how much was provided. The home help service is regarded as particularly effective for those people who lost friends or a close confidante during the period of the study. There is marginal evidence of a favourable opinion about the effect of short-term care. A disturbing feature of this model is that it illustrates how weak is the link between clients' own statements of their change in circumstances and service providers' views of favourable outcomes. (The one exception, mental confusion, was in fact partly gauged by the service allocators' opinion.)

Area differences

Given the circumstances of the client being cared for, and the services provided, there remain strongly significant differences between areas in the reduction of felt need for extra help among clients, as is shown in Table 4.14.

The authority with the best record is also the one with the best-established tradition of informal care while the worst is a loose-linked inner city area with weak informal care. This reinforces the conclusion that it is inputs other than community social services resources which are most crucial in

Table 4.14
Differences between areas in achieving service objectives

Area and type	Change in felt vulnerability (RISK)		Change in felt need for help (DESHELP)	
	Mean score	(N)	Mean score	(N)
1 Inner London	−0.24	43	0.03	43
2 Inner London	−0.30	26	0.41	27
3 Outer London	0.50	33	−0.04	31
4 Metropolitan District	−0.01	30	0.09	28
5 Metropolitan District	−0.07	45	0.10	48
6 Metropolitan District	0.32	33	−0.18	32
7 English Shire	−0.02	36	0.18	35
8 English Shire	−0.35	36	−0.25	38
9 English Shire	0.14	41	0.30	39
10 Welsh County	0.07	38	−0.60	36
Average s.d.	1.19		1.03	

Figures represent the mean residual for each authority derived from the estimating equations described in Table 4.12. A *negative* score indicates a *lower* than expected outcome score; i.e. *high* efficiency.
An F-test indicates significant difference between areas at the 10 per cent level for felt vulnerability and at the 1 per cent level for felt need for help.

improving the welfare of elderly people. Also reported in Table 4.14 are differences in reduction in risk, even though these are not quite statistically significant. Area 3, which has the poorest record in risk reduction, has an active policy of taking risks to keep very disabled people living in the community, and this corresponds to their success in the high proportion of people from this area who consider that social services averted the need for institutionalisation. There were no differences between areas in resource allocators' evaluations of outcomes.

2.3.3 Summary

Reducing risk and meeting the need for help with specific tasks are seen by social workers and home help organisers as the main purposes of providing help. Clients showed a small but significant improvement in both these respects. The home help service and meals-on-wheels had the most effect. The apparently slight effect of services is attributed to the complexity of the forces at work. Service allocators were themselves asked whether they thought outcomes for cases to be successful in the sense that problems were solved. Success was associated with the provision of home helps or social work involvement. There is some indication of decreasing returns to scale in the achievement of these objectives, implying that providing greater amounts of services would not necessarily improve outcomes *pro rata*. There was a significant difference in the reduction of felt need for extra help between areas, even after allowing for differences in the clients treated and the type of service provided. But it seems likely that this may be due to the availability of informal care locally rather than to social services.

2.4 Consumer satisfaction

Consumer satisfaction is for many practitioners the touchstone of success in an intervention – and indeed implicitly it is the chief criterion for many research evaluations. Therefore it is of note that in the present study client satisfaction as defined in Table 4.1 was not correlated with the other measures of outcome that we studied. An important implication of this is that a service can be successful by the criteria which social services departments would apply, even when it is not appreciated!

Mrs Irving was in her eighties, blind and very hard of hearing, living with two sons who were out from 6.30 a.m. to late in the evening. She was unable to manage any housework and usually saw no-one and had nothing to eat or drink all day. She was described by our interviewer as very dirty and undernourished when she was first visited. It is not known who referred her, possibly a neighbour. Mrs Irving did not want to have help, but was extremely lonely, and admitted she did not eat. The social worker's assessment concentrated on her loneliness for which day care was provided once a week, but a home help organiser also visited and arranged meals-on-wheels five times weekly and a home help once a week. After six months many of her immediate problems were resolved. She was no longer ill-fed, and her morale was higher, too. But, when asked, she said she was dissatisfied with meals-on-wheels. 'I'm pleased I get some help I suppose. The helpings are too small, only fit for a baby. But it's nice to have a visitor.'

The reverse side of the coin is that many clients are satisfied when other benefits are less clear, but we shall postpone discussion of these cases to Section 2.5.

Two aspects of consumer satisfaction have been investigated.

- *Clients' overall satisfaction.* This is a summarisation of clients' feelings about their experiences with the social services departments during the first six months, whether or not services are still received. Clients' overall satisfaction is measured by a three-part assessment based on an open-ended question, at the end of the time period, about their experience with social services generally. Answers for those who were interviewed at the second stage were coded as exclusively favourable (74 per cent); mixed (12 per cent); unfavourable (10 per cent), while 5 per cent were unclassifiable answers. For analysis, this has been treated as an interval scale with the indicated scores.

- *Service impact.* Recipients of each service were asked about the impact on their lives of that service, although only for the home help service is the sample size sufficiently large to be reported here. At the end of the study period, two questions were asked of clients who had been allocated the home help service at the outset. These questions were: (a) Without the home help service would you have been able to continue living at home? (b) If yes, how much difference has it made to you? (Part of the answer to part (a) has already been examined in Section 2.1. The five-point index devised from these questions is shown in Table 4.1, and is treated as a scale for the purpose of analysis.

Both these scales are essentially ordinal, but for the purpose of summarising what factors produce consumer satisfaction it is convenient to treat them as if they were interval scales. Table 4.15 shows the statistical model linking these measures of client satisfaction to resource inputs and client characteristics. In both cases, these factors clearly help to explain client satisfaction. Some of the key results are summarised in Table 4.15.

- Client's overall satisfaction with services is greatest for those people who were less disabled at the outset (MYTYPO groups 0, 1 and 2). In particular, dissatisfaction is greatest for critically needy people *who have some informal support* (MYTYPO group 5). One-half of the responses in this category were less than favourable. Also the results imply that elderly clients living with family (HHOLD type 3) are less satisfied

Table 4.15
Regression equations predicting consumer satisfaction from needs and resources

Item	Satisfied with services (SDFAV)		Impact of home help service (HHEFFECT)	
	Coeff.	Sig. (%)	Coeff.	Sig. (%)
HHCINP	−0.09	1	−0.28	1
HHCINPSQ	0.01	5	0.02	1
WARDINP	0.04	–	0.26	–
SWINP	−0.01	–	−0.06	–
MOWINP	−0.03	–	−0.03	–
DCINP	−0.27	1	−0.28	–
STCINP	−0.00	–	0.00	10
AIDS	0.04	–	−0.10	–
HOSP	0.04	–	0.34	10
DAYHOSP	−0.06	–	0.01	–
NURSE	0.01	–	0.00	–
PRIVNUR	−0.19	–	0.69	–
PRIVHWK	0.08	–	0.91	5
VOLCARE	0.02	–	0.03	–
INFHELP	−0.02	–	−0.01	–
MYTYPO1	0.25	–	−0.63	10
MYTYPO2	0.28	–	−0.52	–
MYTYPO3	0.34	10	−0.38	–
MYTYPO4	0.36	5	−0.84	5
MYTYPO5	0.73	1	−0.51	–
MYTYPO6	0.43	5	−0.91	5
SEX	−0.14	10	0.18	–
HHOLD1	−0.29	10	−0.46	–
HHOLD2	−0.40	5	−0.34	–
ADEQ	−0.31	5	−0.05	–
AVAIL	−0.06	10	0.08	–
CF	0.09	–	0.29	–
INCONT	−0.08	–	−0.35	10
HEALTH	0.04	–	−0.16	–
ACUTE	−0.01	–	−0.21	–
DEATHSP	0.27	–	−0.15	–
FINANCE	−0.22	10	−0.17	–
ADLSELFX	−0.01	–	0.05	–
ADLMOMX	0.00	–	−0.17	5
INCONTX	−0.10	–	−0.17	–
LOSSADEQ	0.14	–	−0.05	–
AVAILX	0.00	–	0.08	–
CFX	0.82	10	0.20	–
Constant	2.12	1	4.52	1
R²	0.29		0.37	
(N)	(283)		(193)	

See Table 4.1 for a definition of the actual variables. Negative coefficients indicate greater satisfaction and greater impact.

than average. However, where there is expressive informal support, such as a close confidante (ADEQ), then satisfaction remains higher. These findings are curious. Several factors may be of influence. (i) For many of the other outcomes we have discussed, it has been the *most* disabled who had most to gain from service provision. Speculatively, this appears to offer evidence that services fail to respond in sufficient measure to variations in the extent of client need, so that the less needy are relatively overprovided and hence more likely to be satisfied. Evidence of this lack of responsiveness has been demonstrated in Chapter 3. (ii) Additionally, or alternatively, those people who are less disabled, and for whom services are not so crucial, are self-selecting clients. Among these, those who do not like services either do not get services allocated or do not remain recipients for long. Continuing to consume the service implies satisfaction. We shall discuss this further in Section 2.5. (iii) The result of less favourable outcomes for elderly people with some informal support parallels our findings for other outcomes. As Crosbie (1983) found, when social services intervene in a situation already involving informal carers where there are conflicting interests at stake, the outcome is often unsatisfactory to everyone.

- Client's overall satisfaction with services is raised by provision of the home help service and by day care. Day care had little impact on other outcomes, but again, a large proportion of those people allocated day care barely used it so actual recipients are self-selecting. So perhaps it is not surprising that over 90 per cent of recipients clearly liked it. Day care is most liked by those people of comparatively low disability who are isolated and appreciate the opportunity to meet others. Table 3.8 suggests that they do not receive larger quantities than others.
- The results for the impact of the home help service are quite different. Table 4.15 does not give a sufficiently clear picture of how this impact is related to the amount provided, so it is further illustrated by Table 4.16 which shows a statistical model predicting which category of impact the client is likely to report, given the amount of service provided. This table shows how strong the relationship is, and indicates that *a minimum of three hours per week is required to ensure 50 per cent probability of high impact* (Groups 1 and 2) while seven hours per week is required for a similar probability that the client will regard the home help service as essential to survival in the community. To some extent the circumstances of the client determine the impact – Table 4.15 indicates that the impact is greatest with the most disabled *unsupported* clients (MYTYPO4, MYTYPO6); but by and large these results suggest that the impact appears to depend more on the amount of service than on the client's circumstances. Note incidentally that the apparent effect of private home help in reducing impact occurs because in some areas clients who could

afford to do so were encouraged to switch from local authority home helps to the private sector.

- There is very little difference between areas in favourable responses to the social services as a whole, given client circumstances and the services that were provided. By contrast, Table 4.17 shows *there are considerable differences between local authorities in the impact of the home help service.* That is to say, with similar clients, and with similar amounts of the home help service, some areas achieve higher impact. In fact, Areas 2, 3, and 10, three of the four most successful areas in this respect, were running enhanced home help services and the fourth successful area, Area 8, was running only a mainstream service. Although Area 7 was also running an enhanced form of service, this particular scheme was proving less successful.

2.4.1 Summary

Consumer satisfaction is not correlated with other benefits, and there are clients who appear to derive clear benefit from services who are not satisfied, and vice versa. The less disabled on the whole express the greatest satisfaction – it is suggested that this is because the less disabled who approach social services are a self-selecting group. In contrast, the impact of the home help service (the client's view of what would happen if the service was not provided) increases dramatically the more that is

Table 4.16
Predicted level of impact of the home help service
given average weekly volume of input

Level of input	Amount of home help (hours)					
	2	4	6	8	10	12
Enable client to remain at home	0.10	0.22	0.39	0.61	0.82	0.93
Great difference	0.30	0.41	0.38	0.26	0.12	0.04
No apparent sign of impact	0.22	0.20	0.15	0.09	0.04	0.02
Little difference	0.23	0.14	0.07	0.04	0.02	0.01
Given up	0.15	0.03	0.01	0.00	0.00	0.00

The figures show the estimated probability of being in each of the five categories signifying impact, given the amount of home help provided, e.g. recipients of twelve hours per week have a 93 per cent probability of being in the top impact group.

These figures have been estimated from the following model fitted to data:

Prob (Outcome 'j' given service volume 'L')

$\alpha \exp (\beta_{1j} \times h + \beta_{2j} \times h^2)$

where h denotes the number of home help hours and β_{1j} and β_{2j} are chosen such as to minimise Wilks λ .

Table 4.17
Differences between areas in the impact of the home help service

Area	Impact of home help service	
	Mean score	(N)
1 Inner London	0.25	33
2 Inner London	–0.17	22
3 Outer London	–0.20	26
4 Metropolitan District	0.05	27
5 Metropolitan District	–0.09	42
6 Metropolitan District	–0.01	26
7 English Shire	0.32	29
8 English Shire	–0.26	33
9 English Shire	0.55	24
10 Welsh County	–0.29	36
Average standard deviation	1.05	
Significance	0.04	

Figures represent the mean residual for each authority of the production function given in Table 4.15. A *negative* score indicates a *high* impact score, i.e. *high* technical efficiency.

provided, and is greatest in those areas that were running enhanced home care schemes.

2.5 Clients who did not benefit

We have put forward a number of criteria for successful outcome: the need for institutional care was averted, life satisfaction was increased, the client felt less vulnerable, the client's welfare needs were met, or the service allocator felt that problems had been resolved. Out of 428 clients who survived throughout the study, 324 (76 per cent) had benefited in at least one of these respects. We are excluding client satisfaction alone as a benefit for this analysis. So some benefit was evident for the vast majority of clients, even by the crude criteria of success which this study has been able to apply. Nevertheless, there is a significant proportion of clients for whom we were unable to identify any benefit, and this group would undoubtedly have been larger if we were to add cases where it is doubtful whether the benefits reported, particularly improvement in life satisfaction, were really due to social services help.

In theory, it is of course possible that the client has benefited in some way other than those listed. But this study has been comprehensive in its coverage of long-term benefits, and we can point to no examples where a client has had an obvious long-term benefit which is not at least reflected in any of those above. However, sometimes there may be a short-term benefit, or sometimes it may be a carer rather than the client who is the real beneficiary.

It is worth examining these outstanding 104 cases who seem to have benefited little, because they highlight some of the problems with social care in a way that has previously received little attention. The vast majority of studies of domiciliary services, particularly for the home help service, have created an impression of a successful service. But this is very often based on evidence of consumer satisfaction which is almost universally favourable among participants (a typical example is Levin, Sinclair and Gorbach, 1985). *Our findings have indicated that consumer satisfaction is not a good guide to whether some of the broader aims of social services provision are being achieved*, and in terms of these broader aims, the truth is rather less rosy. The point is that studies of consumer satisfaction tend to draw attention away from the fact that clients of community social services, specially long-term clients who are most easily reached by 'consumer' studies, are a highly self-selected group. People who do not like services, particularly those who are less dependent, either are not offered them or quickly drop out.

First, there are two groups of clients for whom some 'legitimate' explanation of why no benefit was received might be offered:

- There are 27 cases where one member only of a couple appeared to benefit. In such cases it seems to be usually the less disabled person initially who gains. In addition there are another five cases where the client was living with others, and it is possibly for their benefit that the intervention was intended.

- Apart from the people who died or entered institutional care, a significant proportion suffered a rapid decline in their ability to cope with living in the community. About one-third of all clients reported an accident, an acute illness or a steady decline in their health over the period of the study. Adverse health events appear to constitute a case of *force majeure* but in fact the majority still had some benefit from social services by the criteria we have set. Of the 21 who did not, the circumstances are usually more complicated. The following case is a poor advertisement for social services, illustrating a number of common problems, but in particular how difficult case closure can be even when a service is not considered effective.

Mr Farley was living alone and approached social services for help with the shopping as he had recently found walking outdoors difficult. A neighbour had being doing this for him, but a small allocation of home help and meals-on-wheels was made as the home help organiser felt that this would support the neighbour and a niece who was also helping. Three months later Mr Farley collapsed and was hospitalised for a month. Afterwards he felt depressed and vulnerable, and though his health was no worse than before, seemed unable to cope with the daily routine. The home help was increased considerably for a brief period after hospitalisation but the home help organiser subsequently made efforts to reduce the amount of service, against the wishes of both Mr Farley and his niece, not just by a planned reduction in the allocation but also by surreptitiously changing his home help repeatedly and giving him short hours. 'His problem is that his motivation is much less. He has lost his spirit'. The niece said that she no longer felt obliged to ask for help from others now that social services were involved, and she visited less regularly. So it is likely that providing services was actually counter-productive as a means of retaining carers in this case. Mr Farley had become very dependent on the service. 'I'm pleased to get as much help as I can. I wish they would leave my home help alone and not keep taking her away'.

Seventy-five of the original clients who survived were no longer clients at the end of the study, despite an initial assumption that they would be long-term. In most cases where the client is no longer getting services, the problem has been resolved or help is now received elsewhere. But there are 28 cases where the social services simply failed to meet the client's needs. In 22 of these, there was virtually no involvement, the client giving up very quickly. The following is a little more complicated.

Mrs Jones was 91, living alone and with restricted mobility though not quite housebound. She was finding it difficult to manage financially. Her GP referred her for a place in residential accommodation. Contact with the DHSS to provide financial help was arranged and a walking aid, telephone and commode supplied, but Mrs Jones was persuaded to consider day care twice a week rather than residential care. However, transport was unavailable, although it was promised as soon as possible. She missed two visits, went once and then gave up. 'I don't know how they expect me to get there when I can't walk, and anyway I didn't really want to go out, specially in the winter'. Mrs Jones was only visited once by the social worker, and after the aids and financial arrangements were completed the case was closed. The social worker mistakenly believed the home help service was involved. When she was revisited, Mrs Jones had become housebound and deaf. She was very dependent on an elderly daughter-in-law and said she would still like residential care. Yet she readily expressed gratitude and satisfaction with all that had been done for her though her daughter-in-law considered that she had been let down.

While some who failed to benefit gave up, there remain 44 people who continued to get services though neither they nor anyone else appears to derive any great benefit. In the majority of cases, what happened is that a small home help allocation was made, possibly after a hospitalisation, and it was allowed to carry on. Examples occur in all areas although are more understandable in those authorities which have a universalistic attitude to service provision and a commitment to preventive care. These are cases for which the client's satisfaction is the main justification for continuing.

Mrs King suffered from anaemia, and the district nurse visited to give a daily injection. Her son began to feel she needed some domestic assistance, and asked for a home help assessment. The social worker who visited was not sure whether there was a real need for home help, but allocated her two hours per week as well as a weekly visit to a day centre '... mainly to keep an eye on her. I will revisit in a month or so to see if the home help is really helpful'. It is not clear why the district nurse's visit could not be used to monitor Mrs King, but this was not an area with close liaison with community health services. The social worker had still not revisited six months later. She commented: 'I believe Mrs King turned down our offer of day care. I haven't heard from the home help so I assume that is going all right'. In fact, Mrs King was attending the day centre quite frequently. 'I like meeting my friends. We have a sing-song and there are outings arranged for us'. The home help was felt to be not crucial to her as she could always get help from her family, but she appreciated the weekly visits for the company. However, loneliness was not a problem, and her morale was high throughout.

The case of Mrs King illustrates a point made earlier, that there are many clients who are satisfied with services, so for lack of systematic reassessment they are often retained, even when no broader outcomes are being achieved.

2.5.1 Summary

Twenty-four per cent of the clients who survived in the community throughout the study did not seem to have benefited greatly. In some cases a partner benefited and in others the service had been discontinued, but in nearly half these cases, services were still continuing. Typically, this was because the services suited the clients well even if they were not essential to meet their needs; and no reassessment had been done.

3 Conclusions

Outputs are here defined as variables of evaluative significance which might have been positively affected by variations in resource inputs. Of the potential outputs studied, few were proved unambiguously. In particular, service volumes for more dependent and problematic elderly clients may be adjusted to their worsening state, so that ultimately greater input is correlated with worse output. This is particularly true for some of those more general outcomes which best characterise what domiciliary social services are aiming to achieve: avoidance of institutional care and maintenance of life satisfaction. So we cannot necessarily conclude that community social services have little effect because the results of our formal analyses generally demonstrate weak links between the quantity of input and the amount of output. However, it can be seen from the table describing predictors that we sought to allow for changes in circumstances. Also we have not found evidence of general, large, and timely adjustment of resources in response to changes in needs during the subsequent 30 months. So it is possible that our estimates may understate marginal productivities, but we have no reason to believe that they do so sufficiently generally and to a large enough extent to affect our general conclusions. Therefore, despite these difficulties of interpretation, a number of general conclusions about the outcomes of social care can be drawn from this analysis and from the examination of case studies.

3.1 Most clients benefit

The great majority of clients who were studied had benefited in at least one of the following respects: they believed, usually with considerable justification, that domiciliary service was enabling them to continue living in the community; their morale had improved; in their own opinion they were less vulnerable; the need for extra help was less; or the service provider believed problems were reduced. We emphasise this point because it is inevitable that by its focus on the less satisfactory cases, the present chapter may otherwise appear to paint a too pessimistic picture of the genuine achievements of social care. Even so, of 427 people studied who were the primary recipients of interventions and who survived throughout the study, no fewer than 104 (24 per cent) felt that services neither had a preventive effect, nor improved life satisfaction. The people did not report any worries overcome nor problems with domestic management solved, nor could the service allocator cite any specific benefits. Yet nearly half of this group were continuing to receive services. Our detailed investigation of this group has illustrated two characteristic problems of case management: points which have been made before but which are worth reiterating through this study. Attention has been drawn to the failure to implement routine assessment (DHSS, 1987b). Service allocators often have weak criteria for judging successful outcomes and so for deciding whether it is worthwhile to continue with service provision. Because no clear criteria for terminating domiciliary services are given to the client, it becomes too traumatic to withdraw a service which the client wants to retain. As a result, 'routine' reassessment is pointless and often skipped.

Despite all the lip-service, the lack of collaboration between field agencies involved in a single case remains chronic. In the great majority of cases, social services resource allocators often had only the vaguest idea of what health services provision was being made – sometimes even of what else their own department was doing – and then only at the point of assessment. The result is duplication of effort particularly in preventive care.

3.2 Benefits are greatest for those lacking support

The greatest effect of domiciliary services is for people who lack support, who are out of contact with informal supporters. But the solutions are rarely sought by creating a framework of support. The impression given by many of our case examples is that social services serve more to reduce dependence on sources of support that are regarded as inadequate or unsatisfactory than to buttress existing care networks. Domiciliary care seems capable of coping successfully with people of very considerable physical disability including incontinence (although not so well once senile dementia becomes a factor). Social services are at their most problematic when dealing with a collapsing support system and it is this situation, rather than severity of disability, which is most likely to result in entry to institutional care.

3.3 Home care has the most beneficial effect

Of the individual services we have examined, undoubtedly home help/home care has the most beneficial effect on outcomes, although both meals-on-wheels (when provided in sufficient amounts) and day care are beneficial in certain respects. Other services such as phased care and street warden schemes were not sufficiently well-represented in the study for us to draw clear conclusions. Results for social work are ambiguous for reasons given above.

3.4 Different levels of service are needed for different outcomes

Our results are sufficiently strong to conclude that home helps and meals-on-wheels will only have real impact, at least in the view of recipients, in enabling them to continue living at home if they are provided in sufficient quantities. Reduction in vulnerability and welfare shortfall can be achieved at all service levels, and whether or not the client is satisfied with service provision seems to depend very little on how much is provided. Indeed, client satisfaction is not a good guide to whether the main objectives of social care, as we have defined them, are achieved. Part of the explanation for this is that it is easy to go on providing a low level of service when the client is happy regardless of whether they bring other benefits.

3.5 Some authorities are more successful than others

Our conclusions about the technical efficiency of departments are mixed. Given similar clients, and assuming that they provide similar services, authorities will be equally successful in maintaining very dependent elderly people in the community. (Although as we saw in Chapter 3, in reality departments do not make the same decisions for people with similar needs.) In this most important of respects, supposed differences in quality between the services offered by different local authorities do not have an effect on outcome. This conclusion is a common one for evaluative research on social services for elderly people; most recently, for example, Booth (1985) drew a similar conclusion about the lack of impact of quality of care on outcomes in old people's homes. The implication is that improvements in the efficiency of social services departments are more likely to come from better strategy in case selection and resource allocation – that is improvements to target efficiency, input mix and output efficiency – than by attempts to improve technical efficiency. This hypothesis remains open to further investigation. However, in other respects, particularly in the extent to which specific needs are met, there is evidence of differences in outcome between different local authorities. Our conclusion in this case is that for clients in similar circumstances, even if similar services are provided, some authorities are better than others in reducing the felt need for help with the activities of daily living, and with the impact on the lives of elderly clients of the home help service. We have not investigated why this is so, but it is worth noting that Areas 3, 8 and 10 are the most successful, and these were the three areas which were operating a client-specialist model of field organisation.

Notes

1 The regression adjusted outcome score is the deviation of scores on the second occasion from those predicted by regression analysis from a knowledge of scores on the first occasion. This is advocated by Nunnally (1975) among many others, as the preferable method of measuring change. The reason for preferring this approach to a simple difference in scores is that generally such change scores are correlated with the initial score: those who were worst at the beginning are more likely to improve and *vice versa*, for reasons solely connected with the way in which measurement error produces 'regression to the mean' with the causal factors at work. However, regression adjusted scores do not have the desirable feature that a positive score generally denotes an improvement, a negative score a decline. Occasionally in the text we revert to analysis of simple change scores for ease of interpretation.

2 Clients' names throughout are, of course, fictitious.

5 Needs, costs and outcomes

This chapter analyses variations in costs, the need-related circumstances of clients, and changes in circumstances which might be affected by social service inputs. The aim is to estimate the costs of final outputs for persons with varying need characteristics.

The costs are 'opportunity costs' to the social services department: the value of the resources which might have been used for other purposes. The variable is weekly costs averaged over the study period. The variable covers the five major sets of services: domiciliary services (including home helps, home care assistants and community wardens); meals-on-wheels; day care; short-term residential care; and social work. (None of the remaining services would contribute to the total costs of a client by more than about 25 pence per week.) Much early costs analysis focused on the estimation of an average revenue account cost for a recipient for each service separately, ignoring costs hidden by accounting conventions. Such work as that of Wright, Cairns and Snell (1981) advanced the state of the art by estimating opportunity costs for modes of care for persons of varying dependency, taking into account important hidden costs such as the costs of capital.

The potential final outputs and need-related circumstances explored were described by as many as 200 variables. In practice, 90 or so were explored beyond a preliminary stage. The 'quasi-input' variables describe disability and health-related circumstances, housing amenities and condition, income and socio-economic group, social networks and contacts, attitudes to service, utilisation of health and other services, and significant life events. The variables were based on data about the situation at the first client interview and before, the period between the interviews, and at the time of the second interview. The important evaluative changes in circumstances which might be affected by social service inputs, 'potential final outputs', include several which the literature suggests might have beneficial consequences achievable through community-based inputs.

The analysis was based on a group of clients who (i) lived alone throughout the study period, (ii) completed a full interview at both the beginning and the end of the period, and (iii) were in contact with the department throughout the period. The group excluded those suffering confusion to a degree which prevented them from being interviewed, persons with informal carers living outside the household, and those having only a brief encounter with the department. Of the remaining group of 184, twelve were excluded either because the interview information was incomplete or because service input could not be adequately costed.

(The latter difficulty arose because in the absence of case managers it was difficult to trace changes in utilisation for all clients.)

1 Cost estimation, prices, outputs and quasi-inputs

1.1 Cost estimation

The appendix to this chapter (pp.422-9) describes in more detail the methods used to make the costs estimates for each service.

1.2 Prices

The modelling experimented with two sets of price indices covering variations in the general price level: the Department of the Environment labour price index and the index for health and social services compiled by Begg, Moore and Rhodes (1983). The results were not sensitive to the choice of index. The results reported below are based on the use of the latter. The variation in the price level was handled by deflating costs by the index. *Community Services and the Social Production of Welfare* (PSSRU, 1991) will consider the implications of cost functions with more elaborate price indicators.

1.3 Quasi-inputs

The appendix to this chapter describes the quasi-inputs which actually contributed to the description of cost variations.

1.3.1 Physical dependency
Chapter 3 describes the classification of physical disability in three categories: 'long interval need', 'short interval need' and 'critical interval need'. In our analysis these were coded as three dummy variables. Therefore we are comparing the costs of being in one of these categories compared with those in the 'independent' category. In addition other particular aspects of dependency were included. Notably these identified specific disabilities – such as partial sight or blindness, poor hearing, loss of limb – and the level of incontinence (none, urinary or faecal).

Mental aspects were covered by a mental score test used at the beginning of the questionnaire and also on the interviewer's assessment of the elderly person's responsiveness etc. However, the sample actually used in our analysis demands a low score in the test indicating little or no confusion and thus it might be expected that those aspects would not feature in our models.

1.3.2 Life events
The life events are outlined in Chapter 3.

1.3.3 Housing
This covers the state of housing in which a person lives and the amenities that are available. Thus we are concerned with both the upkeep of the structure of the house and the cleanliness of the rooms. Also of importance is the availability of essential amenities such as an inside toilet and a bath or shower. Consideration was given to the provision of purpose-built housing for the elderly and the availability of a warden and/or an alarm system.

1.3.4 Socio-economic status
Social class was included as well as other basic demographic descriptions such as age and sex. In the questionnaire details of income from all sources were requested although this had a poor response compared with other questions. Therefore we took as economic indicators the type of consumer luxuries in a home ranging from fridge/freezers to televisions and washing machines. In addition the interviewer was asked to classify the immediate neighbourhood of the elderly person as to whether they considered it poor, average, well-to-do or rural.

1.3.5 Care provided by other agencies
As we have already suggested, the uptake of care provided by other agencies has been considered as exogenous quasi-inputs for the purpose of our analysis so as to allow for the substitution of care provision between agencies. In particular we considered the inputs of the health services, voluntary groups, private (paid) support and also that of the informal care network. For the first two agencies, we restricted our attentions to the types of service provided (for example, community nursing, day hospitals, social clubs) and recorded whether they were used at the beginning and at the end of the study period and, if so, the volume provided. This seemed to capture long-term inputs. To assess the *ad hoc* take-up of these services we also asked the client, and used information provided by professionals as to the usage between the interviews.

In contrast, the substitution of care provision by the private and informal sectors was considered to have more important consequences for social services costs for those individuals for whom these sources were available. We therefore assessed the volume of input from both forms of care by type of activity provided (housework, meal preparation and personal care). Again this was on the basis of the two interviews with the elderly person.

1.3.6 Social network
The emphasis is on the availability of a social network both in terms of contact and social interaction and also of people on whom the client can call in times of particular need. This contrasts with the measures above which concern actual physical support provided. These were measured

by asking about the regularity of meeting with both friends and relatives, the availability of a confidante and of people to call upon. Identical questions were asked at initial assessment and after six months.

1.3.7 Other quasi-inputs
Two other sets of quasi-inputs were considered. First we attempted to discover something of the elderly person's attitude to help. This was summarised to describe those who had distinctly positive attitudes, negative attitudes or apparent indifference. Secondly, for each output measured (as will be described shortly), the level at the start of the study period was included.

1.4 Potential outputs

To be classified as an output, a state (i) must be an 'outcome', that is, have been substantially influenced by resource and/or endogenous non-resource inputs; (ii) must be judged to be of significance for the evaluation of the costs and benefits and/or the equity and efficiency of provision. A framework for the analysis of outcomes for services for the elderly has been elaborated in several production of welfare studies (Challis, 1981; Davies and Knapp, 1981; Davies and Challis, 1986). This analysis focuses on five dimensions: (i) satisfaction with the level of help received; (ii) perception of being 'at risk'; (iii) subjective wellbeing; (iv) satisfaction with social contact; and (v) perception of independence. Between them, they relate to all but one of the dimensions distinguished in earlier production of welfare studies: nurturance, compensation for disability, independence, morale, social integration and family relationships.

The potential outputs were measured by the change in the elderly person's response to a set of questions asked at both the first and the second interviews. Scores for (i), (ii) and (iii) were adjusted to reflect variations in the length of time between the interviews. The adjustment was not made to outputs (iv) and (v) as these were based on questions with binary responses.

The correlation between pairs of output indicators was weak with none of them significantly different from zero. Each output indicator was constructed so that increasing values reflect an improvement in state with respect to that output.

The indicators are related but not identical to some of those described in Table 5.1. Therefore some description is necessary.

1.4.1 Satisfaction with the level of help received
Three questions were framed in the same manner but were addressed to different needs for help relating to getting up and going to bed (indicators of personal care needs), to home care activities such as cleaning, and to the preparation of meals. They followed questions about whether anyone

helped with that specific need and if so who. Thus they may be seen to reflect the client's satisfaction with the level of care provided across all sources and not with formal provision. A score of 0 to 3 was given according to their level of satisfaction with each type of help. These were then summed to give a total satisfaction score both at the beginning and the end of the study of between 0 and 9. The adjusted difference was used as the output.

This output covers a wide area of issues. In particular it addresses aspects of nurturance and compensation for disability (two of the output dimensions distinguished by Challis) since it assesses the fulfilment of the basic needs of the elderly person for daily living and the client's perception of the quality of care being received. (However, it does not cover the effects of treatment for disability, which production of welfare studies classify as an output of health service interventions.) The collection of evidence included open-ended comments about this dimension. Therefore the data available summarise the elderly person's perception of the shortfall in either the volume or quality of care provided. As such the data are the most directly related to service performance of the final outputs considered and, consequently, might be expected to be the most highly correlated with cost.

The nearest equivalent in Table 4.1 is SDFAV.

1.4.2 Perceived risk

The second aspect of nurturance is the provision of warmth and security. This we assessed by asking a series of questions to find out whether the person thought about those things which often concern elderly people and if so how often. The concerns mentioned were: (i) falling down at home and not being able to get up again; (ii) becoming too ill or dependent to be looked after at home; (iii) putting too much burden on the people who help you; (iv) being forgetful and perhaps causing accidents, like forgetting to turn off the kettle; (v) not eating well enough; (vi) not being able to keep sufficiently warm in winter; (vii) being burgled and/or attacked; (viii) people pressing you to move somewhere else; (ix) not being able to go on coping living alone.

These were then factor-analysed. We sought a scoring system that was interpretable and that was stable over time. It was found that the concerns (vii) and (viii) introduced considerable instability. These differ from the remaining concerns as they reflect the impact of others on the individual's life rather than worries of not being able to cope. When (vii) and (viii) were removed, a single factor model fitted well and was particularly stable where a score of zero represented the concerns often thought about and one for other responses. This scheme was therefore adopted with the output being measured as the adjusted change between initial assessment and the second interview.

The equivalent indicator in Table 4.1 is RISK.

1.4.3 Subjective wellbeing: PGC Morale
The indicator is similar to LSX described in Table 4.1.

The Philadelphia Geriatric Centre Morale Scale is well-established as a measure of psychological wellbeing (Lawton, 1975). It was developed to measure three aspects of the life of the elderly person: 'an acceptance of the unchangeability of the life that has passed', 'self-acceptance' and 'a positive attitude to the environment'. However, there has been some debate whether one or three underlying factors are found in practice. In our factor analysis we found that a model with one factor worked well and was stable between initial assessment and the second interview. There was also some suggestion of a model with three or four factors, although the structure of these was not stable over time. These results are similar to those of possibly the most sophisticated analyses of the dimensionality of the scale. Consequently we have adopted a single factor model in which each of the 17 questions are scored one if the response is indicative of higher morale and zero otherwise. Again an adjusted change in the score was computed.

1.4.4 Satisfaction with social contact
A need for social services interventions for socially isolated elderly people has been found (Townsend and Wedderburn, 1965; Tunstall, 1966). Social integration might therefore be included among the potential outputs of social services. We asked a number of questions to try to assess the volume and nature of a person's social contact. However, we have adopted just one question to measure this attribute. This question was about the elderly person's *satisfaction* with the level of contact with friends and relatives. As each individual's needs for contact are likely to vary in terms of volume and type this was felt to be more indicative of the person's own assessment of adequacy of contact. In addition it is likely that a social services intervention can have an impact on satisfaction without necessarily affecting either volume or type of contact (at least as far as these concern friends and relatives).

Three possible answers were allowed: a desire for contact 'more often', 'less often' or 'as it is'. In practice only three clients responded 'less often' at initial assessment and none after six months, so we combined the catagories of 'less often' and 'as it is.' Output was measured by three dummy variables which taken as a set describe the possible changes within six months of initial assessment.

1.4.5 Perception of independence
The focus was whether the elderly person felt that they had control over their own life. As in the case of 'satisfaction with social contact' above,

this was somewhat crudely assessed by a pair of questions which together gave a measure of the client's strength of feelings about how much other people ran their day-to-day life. In practice the vast majority of clients (90 per cent at both interviews) felt that they were satisfied with their control. Again, therefore, we presented this output as a set of three dummy variables representing the change in satisfaction level between initial assessment and the second interview.

It is clear from our discussion of the outputs measured that the first three are somewhat better measured than the final two. It is always a problem in such a study to obtain sufficient breadth of information about both the quasi-inputs and the outputs without having an excessively long interview which, itself, will affect the validity of the answers given. In our analysis we have therefore concentrated on the first three and, as we shall see, even more so on the first and the third: satisfaction with the help given and the change in morale as measured by the PGC Scale.

2 Modelling and its results

2.1 Form and variable selection

2.1.1 Form

This section describes the statistical estimation of the cost function. The analysis proceeds in stages developing the model as we go and looking at various hypotheses on the way. As we have already mentioned, the dependent variable examined is the average weekly opportunity cost of providing the client with a package of services with an adjustment for inter-authority price variation. We then considered the natural logarithm of this so as to remove the heterogeneity that was apparent without it (in particular increasing variability in costs with increasing cost).

As we had no *a priori* grounds for choosing any particular functional form, f, we used the simplest: a linear function of effects. The logarithm transformation then also has a useful interpretation as follows. The model estimated is

$$\ln {}^{C}p = b_1 x_1 + b^2 x_2 \dots + b_n x_n$$

where x_1 to x_n are the quasi-inputs and outputs of interest. Taking exponents of both sides gives

$$C = p \, e^{b_1 x_1} e^{b_2 x_2} \dots e^{b_n x_n}$$

Thus the cost is a product of the effects and we can easily compute the factor by which any level of a particular value of each x_i ($i = 1, 2, \dots, n$) increases costs. Notably, if any x_i is a dummy variable (taking the value 1 if a characteristic relates to the individual of interest and 0 otherwise) then the exponent of b_i represents the cost factor of this characteristic. A major advantage of this approach using a multiplicative model is its expected stability over time, despite changes in absolute costs.

2.1.2 Estimation procedure and variable choice
The approach adopted consisted of several steps: (i) enter dummy variables representing the areas; (ii) enter the outputs being considered and the corresponding scores at initial assessment; (iii) enter the needs grouping variables of interest; (iv) enter the variables describing the services received from other care agencies (including the informal network); (v) using a stepwise variable selection procedure (p-value for entry = 0.15, p-value for removal = 0.20) consider all other quasi-inputs of interest; (vi) using a backward variable removal procedure (p-value for removal = 0.20), consider removal of any variables entered in steps (iv) and (v).

The first step was necessary. It very quickly became clear that there were quite substantial differences in cost between authorities and that this was having an adverse effect on the assumptions underlying the statistical analysis. Therefore a dummy variable for each of Areas 1 to 9 was included: the estimated coefficients and the associated cost factors thus describe the cost in an authority relative to the cost in Area 10. Area 10 was taken as the reference point. The *relative* values of the area cost factors compare the level of costs between areas for a common set of outputs and quasi-inputs. Ideally these might be taken as measures of efficiency, though clearly that interpretation must be made in the light of caveats about the varying degrees of centralisation.

The set of variables forced into the model regardless of their significance was limited to the outputs and needs grouping variables of interest. For all other variables, a low degree of significance ($p > 0.20$) was demanded for removal. In principle, this could have admitted a large number of variables. In practice that did not happen: a similar set of variables tended to appear in all the models and this method of variable selection appeared to maintain stability in the estimates of effects. The approach also allowed more marginally significant effects to feature in the model. This usefully admitted those characteristics that might have an important effect on cost at least in magnitude but were less common characteristics in the sample and hence for which there was lower power to detect their impact at higher levels of significance. Step (iv), the forced entry of the variables recording the involvement of other agencies, also seemed desirable as it might be expected that they would have a substitution effect on social services costs. However, step (vi) enabled their removal if such an effect did not approach any formal level of significance.

One other constraint was placed on the modelling. If a polynomial term (for example, squares, cubes) was considered for inclusion, it was entered with all the lower-order terms included regardless of its level of significance.

This was also felt to be desirable as there are very rarely occasions when higher-order terms are theoretically appropriate in this context in their own right: including them as such would define a very special relationship that would be hard to justify.

2.2 Model one: satisfaction with help as output and quasi-inputs at initial assessment

The first model includes just the potential output describing the satisfaction of the client with the level and quality of help being given (irrespective of its source). As has been mentioned, this output is the most directly related to service provision of those presented, and so might be expected to show the greatest correlation with cost.

In addition, we impose a very strict restriction on the class of quasi-inputs admissable. With the exception of the care provided by other agencies only the levels of quasi-inputs at initial assessment were considered. Conceptually, the basis for this is extreme. We assume that after initial assessment, the social services have intervened with all the elderly people being studied here and so should be able to take charge and control each person's situation. Certainly this might be the case for such effects as improving the situation with respect to inadequate housing. However, social services might not be expected to foresee and control all the factors described by the quasi-inputs; notably 'life events'. The model describes the extent to which the state of an individual at the time of social services intervention predicts the cost-output relationship for the following seven months.

Table 5.1 shows the estimated coefficients for the effects included in this model.

2.2.1 Costs and potential 'outputs'
Diagram 5.1 shows how the cost factor varies with increasing satisfaction with the help provided. It is clear that costs increase with the level of output achieved, but only when there is a *positive* output. However, the effect is quite the reverse when there is a *negative* output: the bigger the drop the greater the cost. In principle, increased output levels require more resources (Davies and Challis, 1986, p.184). Clearly the variable only partially met the logical preconditions for being an unambiguous indicator of 'output'. A more complex specification included the interaction of this output with the needs category of the elderly person (combining the independent people with those in the long interval needs category as there were few of the former). This is modelled in the same framework as model 1. It made no change to the quasi-inputs included in the model. Diagram 5.1 shows the pattern of cost factors found for each of the needs categories. The curve for the critical needs group shows increasing costs with increasing output over a wide range. In stark contrast, the short

Table 5.1

Average weekly opportunity cost with client's satisfaction with help (interacting with dependency group) as output, with pre-study and in-study quasi-inputs

Dependent variable: logged price-adjusted weekly opportunity cost.

Variable	Coeff.	Std error (coeff.)	P-value
Output			
Needs: long/independent			
satisfaction with help	0.0287	0.0439	0.52
square of satisfaction with help	−0.0050	0.0209	0.81
Needs: short			
satisfaction with help	−0.0500	0.0625	0.43
square of satisfaction with help	0.0084	0.0216	0.70
Needs: critical			
satisfaction with help	0.1950	0.0713	0.01
square of satisfaction with help	0.0538	0.0198	0.01
Quasi-inputs			
Satisfaction with help at initial assessment score	−1.0106	0.4825	0.04
Square of satisfaction with help at initial assessment	0.0775	0.0303	0.01
Needs group:			
independent/long at initial assessment; short after six months	0.4054	0.1382	0.00
independent/long at initial assessment; critical after six months	−0.0359	0.2477	0.89
short at initial assessment; independent/long after six months	−0.1575	0.1586	0.32
short at initial assessment; short after six months	0.1533	0.1100	0.17
short at initial assessment; critical after six months	0.3928	0.1876	0.04
critical at initial assessment; independent/long after six months	−0.1604	0.2541	0.53
critical at initial assessment; short after six months	0.0984	0.1632	0.55
critical at initial assessment; critical after six months	−0.0463	0.1778	0.79
Informal support: personal care	−0.1860	0.0427	0.00
Private support: with housework	−0.3411	0.2023	0.09
NHS support: community nursing	0.4140	0.0889	0.00
Day hospital	0.6205	0.1390	0.00
Incontinent of faeces	0.4898	0.1115	0.00
Regularity client visits friends/relatives at initial assessment	−0.0335	0.0233	0.15
Availability of someone to do favours at initial assessment	−0.1138	0.0613	0.07
Availability of someone to do favours after six months	−0.1067	0.0622	0.09
Availability of confidante after six months	0.2777	0.0976	0.01

Table 5.1 (continued)

Variable	Coeff.	Std error (coeff.)	P-value
Manual social group	0.2838	0.0956	0.00
General difficulties with housing/neighbours at initial assessment	–0.5318	0.1638	0.00
Death of spouse prior to initial assessment	0.5118	0.1631	0.00
Death of household member (not spouse) prior to initial assessment	–0.6015	0.2460	0.02
Other person had serious accident/illness prior to initial assessment	–0.6839	0.2300	0.00
Away from home (not holiday or hospital) within six months of initial assessment	0.5486	0.2483	0.03
Area variables			
1 Inner London	0.2504	0.1535	0.11
2 Inner London	–0.4954	0.2141	0.02
3 Outer London	–0.0249	0.1703	0.88
4 Metropolitan District	–0.2583	0.1581	0.10
5 Metropolitan District	–0.5902	0.1505	0.00
6 Metropolitan District	–0.0712	0.1523	0.64
7 English Shire	–0.6709	0.1577	0.00
8 English Shire	–0.3186	0.1439	0.03
9 English Shire	–0.2550	0.1624	0.12
Constant	5.3147	1.9599	0.01

R^2=0.66 Adjusted R^2= 0.56 Residual mean square=0.20 F=6.35 (P=0.00)

interval needs group shows predominantly decreasing costs with increasing output. Finally the independent and long interval needs group has relatively constant costs across all levels of output. For the critical interval needs group, satisfaction with help received may be interpreted as an output in the sense used by Davies and Challis, but it can not be so interpreted for the other two needs groups.

2.2.2 Costs and quasi-inputs

Faecal incontinence
Diagram 5.1 illustrates variations in costs between need groups. However, the diagram understates the cost effects for most members of the critical interval group as it plots the cost factor derived for the output and constant effects alone. However, both Tables 5.1 and 5.2 show cost effects for those suffering incontinence of faeces; a characteristic which itself places a person in the critical interval group. What Diagram 5.1 describes is the cost factor for housebound people of critical interval need but without the one characteristic entering the equation and automatically qualifying for critical interval status: incontinence of faeces. Faecal

Diagram 5.1
Cost factors in achieving changes in the client's satisfaction
with the help provided for each needs group

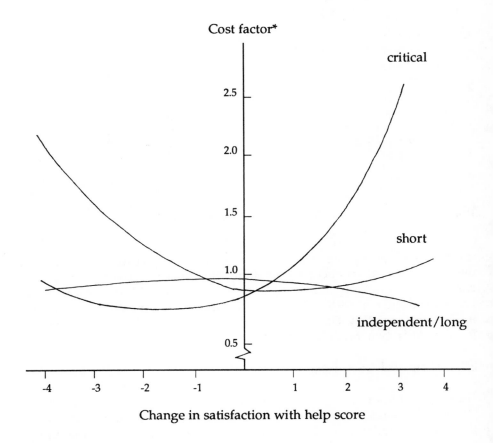

Change in satisfaction with help score

Note: * Cost factor relative to no change in satisfaction with help score for the
         independent/long interval needs group

incontinence has an additional factor raising costs by about 45 per cent. Given a larger sample, it might have been preferable to separate the critical interval cases according to whether they suffered from incontinence of faeces.

Support by other agencies or persons
Informal help with personal care and private help with housework both substitute for the social services. Informal support with meal preparation and health service interventions indicate higher costs to the social services. At first, this might appear unexpected. However, throughout our analyses it was clear that these variables did not describe substitution effects but indicated the greater disability of the elderly people receiving these forms of support. In particular their exclusion brought in variables describing health problems, although these were never so useful in the model. Similarly, the quasi-input describing regularity of visits *to* friends and relatives seemed to describe mobility, as its counterpart describing visits *from* friends and relatives was never significant in any model estimated. Consequently, these four variables together with the incontinence one must be taken as a set with the needs categories, if the purpose of the model is to predict costs rather than to compare hypothetical individuals who differ only by one or two characteristics.

Life events in the period immediately prior to the first interview
All the effects are negative. This suggests that they have cost-reducing effects, since they all describe events which do not indicate increasing disability to the elderly person. This would be expected if the role of the social services is predominantly to meet the needs caused by disability. The events included in the model are those associated with social worker involvement providing short-term counselling and an advice/information service.
We shall defer discussion of the area effects until the fourth model.

2.3 Model two: satisfaction with help as output and quasi-inputs over time

The first model with quasi-inputs predominantly reflecting the client's state at the first interview only explained 56 per cent of the variation in costs to the social services department over the study period. Maintaining interest in satisfaction with help as the only output we shall develop a second model which relates cost to this while admitting variables describing quasi-inputs both at initial assessment and over the subsequent study period. This treats life events as exogenous random shocks; life events occurring and conditions arising that are beyond the control of the social services department. In particular, we include dummy variables so as to describe cost variation by changing needs group. The fitted model is shown in Table 5.2. The inclusion of quasi-inputs over time has increased the level of variation explained to 66 per cent.

2.3.1 Costs and 'outputs'
How costs vary with 'output' remains similar to that found in the earlier model with only the effect for recipients in the critical needs interval category showing significantly non-zero positive coefficients. There is a significant and substantial negative correlation between the level of satisfaction with help at the first interview and subsequent costs. Thus people who had the highest score (nine) have a cost factor of only $e^{-9.0954}$ compared with the level of those who were very dissatisfied (score 0) whose factor would be unity. This suggests that the social services costs and hence their assessment of the level of service provision corresponds well to the perception of the elderly person themselves. The score at the second interview did not achieve significance at any formal level when included in the model in addition to the score from the first. This is, however, to be expected when the change in scores is also included as the output and when, for over 50 per cent of those studied, no change in score was recorded (that is, output was zero).

2.3.2 Costs and need-related circumstances
Table 5.2 gives costs factors with other 95 per cent confidence intervals for need groups. It is clear that increasing disability entails greater costs and conversely decreasing disability entails lower costs. There is consistent monitoring and a substantial response by the social services to the physical dependency of single elderly people. The relationship may be stronger than it might seem at first glance for several reasons.

Table 5.2
Cost factors and 95 per cent confidence intervals associated with changing needs categories

Needs category at first interview	Needs category at second interview		
	Independent/ long	Short	Critical
Independent/long	1.00[a]	1.50 (1.14, 1.97)	0.96 (0.59, 1.57)
Short	0.85 (0.63, 1.17)	1.17 (0.94, 1.45)	1.48 (1.02, 2.16)
Critical	0.85 (0.52, 1.41)	1.10 (0.80, 1.52)	0.95 (0.67, 1.35)

a by definition of the dummy variables included in the model.

- The confidence intervals reflect the uncertainty in estimating the factors for the small number of people making the big changes from the critical to the long/independent category or *vice versa*.
- The cell describing critical interval need at both interviews consists almost exclusively of persons with faecal incontinence, only a handful of clients similarly affected appearing elsewhere in the table, so that a more representative factor for this cell might include the incontinence effect giving a factor of 1.56. The large effect of faecal incontinence on the cost factor for the critical interval needs group will be recalled.

2.3.3 Costs and other quasi-inputs

The set of quasi-inputs included in the model has expanded from those in our first model. Three features of those additional ones included are important.

(i) Three measures of quasi-inputs describe the availability of an informal social network to which the elderly person can turn. The *existence (and number) of people of whom the elderly person can ask help with small favours* reduces social services costs in addition to that provided by the more intensive informal support (often by one friend or relative) with personal care. The *existence of a confidante* is associated with increased costs. Once again, as with the health service inputs, this may be describing the person's needs for such support and related help more than the existence of the confidante itself.

(ii) Two additional life events have a substantial positive correlation with cost. *Death of the elderly person's spouse* in the period prior to initial assessment had a very significant effect. (It is perhaps surprising that it did not appear in our first model.) The implication of bereavement and often of someone who gave a lot of support and shared tasks in the household is clear. *Being away from home between the interviews for reasons other than hospitalisation or holidays* was also associated with substantially increased costs. The interpretation of this is not clear. Indeed its inclusion might be debatable if it is picking up the cost consequences of short-term residential care for clients. This, however, was not the case for the majority of people responding positively for this quasi-input.

(iii) The manual or non-manual classification included here proved to be as good an indicator of socio-economic group as using all the five or six classes generally employed. This variable appeared to be acting as a measure of income. Its inclusion might therefore be of political interest. As an income measure it would then be indicative of higher *gross* costs to the social services and hence generally more service volume input to the less well-off client than someone with a higher income. This might mean that social services departments target or less consciously bias their service allocation to the less well-off. This may reflect policy, insensitive assessment, or factors affecting need too subtle to be modelled. Alternatively, it might refer to the reduction of the demand by some consumers in response to user charges paid by those of higher income.

(iv)Perception of independence. The effects are not significant but, if anything, higher costs have a negative effect with clients feeling that their ability to run their own life has been diminished.

(v)Subjective wellbeing: PGC Morale Scale. In contrast to the three measures above, the average weekly change in the subjective wellbeing score has a highly significant effect in the model. However, like the client's satisfaction with help described in the first model and the pattern for risk described above, the coefficients essentially suggest a declining cost with increased morale. There is a small upturn for higher positive changes (above a change of about 0.17) but very few clients achieved changes above about 0.4 where the cost factor is 1.06. Also of interest here is the lack of effect of the level of wellbeing at the first interview. Thus change clearly influences costs whereas absolute values apparently do not. However, such a subjective score of wellbeing is measured relative to the individual and whereas changes, particularly declines, might be considered by society to be undesirable, a static state will go largely unnoticed.

The remaining models focus on satisfaction with help and subjective wellbeing. Modelling with all five measures found that the remaining three never had significant effects, whether or not their interaction with other measures and quasi-inputs was considered.

2.4 Model three: needs group interactive effects with changes in satisfaction with help and subjective wellbeing

The purpose of this model was to explore the interaction of the needs group at initial assessment with the change in subjective wellbeing to see whether the latter behaved as an output within any category. Table 5.3 shows the fitted model and Diagram 5.2 the pattern of cost factors across the range of average weekly change in wellbeing scores. The figure demonstrates well the pattern of relationship between the cost factor and 'output' variable common to the three needs categories. All exhibit cost factors very close to unity for positive (beneficial) changes in outcome while they show increasing cost factors with both dependency level and the rate of decline in wellbeing.

2.5 Model four: area effects and area/change in subjective wellbeing interactive effects

So far we have made no mention of the area effects necessarily included and estimated in each model described. The study's interest in efficiency requires discussion about how these should be interpreted. Certainly the cost effects partly reflect the consequences of relative inefficiencies for individual clients. However, cost factors are not the result of inefficiency alone.

The degree of *centralisation of the authority in management and administration* distorts the cost variables and causes apparently lower cost factors in such centralised authorities as Area 2. The effects of *substitute services* by other agencies are not properly taken into account. They might be assessed by considering either the multivariate regression modelling of all the constituent accounts or by including area interaction teams with the volumes of service provided by other agencies. At the time of writing, the comprehensive information needed for other agencies' inputs was not available. However, it would be difficult to tease apart the full efficiency consequences of cooperation, or lack of it, between different agencies. Suffice it to say

Table 5.3
Effects of adding each of the remaining outputs[a] to model 2 together with their associated scores at initial assessment

Output set included	Coeff.	Std error (coeff.)	Sig.
Perception of risk			
Risk output	−0.7625	0.9102	0.40
Square of risk output	−1.4247	7.1264	0.84
Risk score at initial assessment	−0.2573	0.1593	0.11
Square of score at initial assessment	0.0256	0.0159	0.11
Subjective wellbeing			
PGC output	−1.2528	0.3336	0.00
Square of PGC output	3.5111	1.1846	0.00
PGC score at initial assessment	0.0030	0.0397	0.94
Square of score at initial assessment	−0.0010	0.0020	0.64
Satisfaction with contact with friends and relatives			
Dissatisfied at initial assessment and after six months	0.1508	0.1118	0.18
Changed from satisfied to dissatisfied	0.1971	0.1246	0.12
Changed from dissatisfied to satisfied	0.1254	0.1194	0.30
Perception of independence			
Dissatisfied at initial assessment and after six months	−0.1135	0.2953	0.70
Changed from satisfied to dissatisfied	0.0800	0.1714	0.64
Changed from dissatisfied to satisfied	−0.0602	0.1956	0.76

a Note that positive output is interpreted as an improvement in a client's status.

Diagram 5.2

Relative cost factors for average weekly change in subjective wellbeing by needs category at first assessment

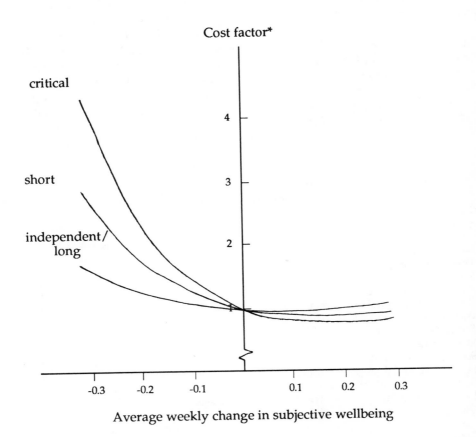

Average weekly change in subjective wellbeing

Note: * Cost factor relative, within needs category, to a zero average weekly change in subjective wellbeing

that the effects of joint service provision by the health and social services could influence the magnitudes of the cost factors for the areas. This is particularly so for Area 7. Cooperation is well-established there between health and social services and may account to some degree for the low cost factor.

Results with *outputs/area interactions* have not so far been discussed. No significant improvement in the model was obtained using interaction terms for satisfaction with help with area. However, interaction terms for subjective wellbeing with the area did have some effect.

Given the sample size and the large number of areas studied, the full set of area/needs category/subjective wellbeing outcome effects cannot be realistically pursued. We have therefore included just the interactive effects of area and wellbeing with the intention of comparing this with the development of the second model when subjective wellbeing was included without an interactive term. The model explained 72 per cent of the variation in cost. A present model with additional area/wellbeing interaction terms explained 75 per cent: an insignificant improvement in fit. The cost effects for the terms are shown in Table 5.4.

Diagram 5.3 illustrates the relationship between the cost factor and change in subjective wellbeing for each area and for the model across all areas. The curves are plotted only for the range of changes experienced by study clients in the respective areas. Although the coefficients shown in Table 5.4 have wide confidence intervals, the graph does indicate two important features: (i) for all areas, costs increase monotonically for more negative change; and (ii) there is no clear relationship between cost and positive changes in subjective wellbeing. This is similar to our experience with the cost/satisfaction with help relationship presented earlier, at least for the independent/long and short interval needs categories. Also recorded in Table 5.4 are the area cost factors themselves. Including the area/change in wellbeing interactive effects affected their relative values, though not their ordering. However, given that improved wellbeing is not associated with higher costs, the change in area cost factors between models cannot be interpreted as reflecting different cost/output relationships between the areas, although areas do differ in their costs of providing for the hypothetical identical client. We shall discuss area variation in the next section.

3 Results and the production of welfare

The last section explored propositions about the interrelationships between costs, outputs, dependency and potential for informal support put forward as signs of an equitable and efficient system; and analysed by Davies and Challis (1986, Chaps 4 and 11). The results have demonstrated that the cost influences of both dependency and the informal support received are

Table 5.4
Average weekly opportunity cost with client's satisfaction with help and client's subjective wellbeing as outputs, with pre-study and in-study quasi-inputs

Dependent variable: logged price-adjusted weekly opportunity cost.

Variable	Coeff.	S.E. (coeff.)	P-value
Outputs			
Needs: long/independent			
satisfaction with help	0.0499	0.0415	0.23
square of satisfaction with help	–0.0084	0.0193	0.66
subjective wellbeing	–0.6252	0.4505	0.17
square of subjective wellbeing	2.9697	1.4716	0.05
Needs: short			
satisfaction with help	–0.0340	0.0573	0.55
square of satisfaction with help	0.0240	0.0208	0.25
subjective wellbeing	–1.6692	0.5193	0.00
square of subjective wellbeing	5.5267	2.6108	0.04
Needs: critical			
satisfaction with help	0.1875	0.0676	0.01
square of satisfaction with help	0.0295	0.0186	0.12
subjective wellbeing	–2.5310	0.8251	0.00
square of subjective wellbeing	6.8778	3.2708	0.04
Quasi-inputs			
Satisfaction with help score at initial assessment	–1.3677	0.4476	0.00
Square of satisfaction with help at initial assessment	0.1054	0.0279	0.00
Subjective wellbeing score at initial assessment	0.0294	0.0386	0.45
Square of subjective wellbeing score at initial assessment	–0.0023	0.0020	0.26
Needs group:			
independent/long at initial assessment; short after six months	0.4551	0.1309	0.00
independent/long at initial assessment critical after six months	–0.2162	0.2271	0.34
short at initial assessment independent/long after six months	–0.1341	0.1556	0.39
short at initial assessment; short after six months	0.2863	0.1120	0.01
short at initial assessment; critical after six months	0.1444	0.1929	0.46
critical at initial assessment; independent/long after six months	–0.1633	0.2333	0.49
critical at initial assessment; short after six months	0.3839	0.1680	0.02
critical at initial assessment; critical after six months	0.1056	0.1780	0.55
Informal support: personal care	–0.1886	0.0456	0.00
Informal support: preparing meals	0.0456	0.0217	0.04
Private support: personal care	0.4894	0.3536	0.17
Private support: with housework	–0.2936	0.1916	0.13
NHS support: community nursing	0.3058	0.0849	0.00

Table 5.4 (continued)

Variable	Coeff.	S.E. (coeff.)	P-value
NHS support: day hospital	0.3826	0.1407	0.01
Incontinent of faeces	0.4607	0.1044	0.00
Availability of someone to do favours at initial assessment	-0.0962	0.0607	0.12
Availability of someone to do favours after six months	-0.1247	0.0582	0.03
Availability of confidante after six months	0.3575	0.0911	0.00
General difficulties with housing/ neighbours at initial assessment	-0.6882	0.1591	0.00
Other person had serious accident/ illness at initial assessment	-0.5197	0.2182	0.02
Death of spouse at initial assessment	0.4734	0.1509	0.00
Death of household member (not spouse) at initial assessment	-0.6735	0.2289	0.00
Death of other person at initial assessment	0.2637	0.1146	0.02
Elderly person had accident within six months of initial assessment	0.5105	0.1697	0.00
Financial problems within six months of initial assessment	0.3597	0.1644	0.03
Difficulties with neighbours within six months of initial assessment	-0.5059	0.2790	0.07
Health problem causing disability before at initial assessment	0.1505	0.0827	0.07
Manual social group	0.3594	0.0952	0.00
Elderly person has telephone	-0.3560	0.0900	0.00
Elderly person is owner-occupier	0.2055	0.0790	0.01
Area variables			
1 Inner London	0.5176	0.1541	0.00
2 Inner London	-0.4365	0.2110	0.04
3 Outer London	0.2691	0.1645	0.10
4 Metropolitan District	-0.2589	0.1498	0.09
5 Metropolitan District	-0.4253	0.1426	0.00
6 Metropolitan District	-0.1622	0.1411	0.25
7 English Shire	-0.6298	0.1552	0.00
8 English Shire	-0.3974	0.1377	0.00
9 English Shire	-0.2704	0.1512	0.08
Constant	6.0633	1.8299	0.00

$R^2=0.76$ Adjusted $R^2=0.65$ Residual mean square=0.16 F=6.72 (P=0.00)

Diagram 5.3

Relative cost factors for average weekly change in subjective wellbeing by area and over all areas

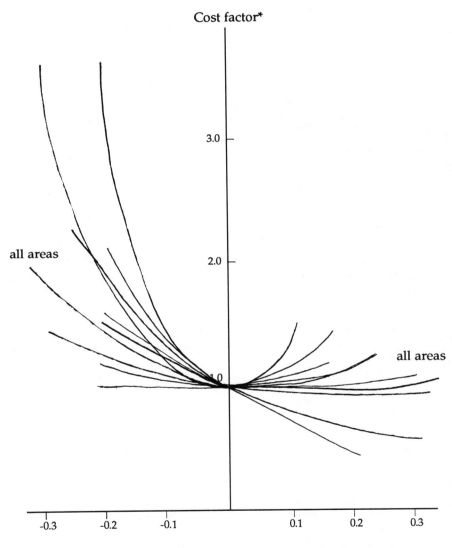

Average weekly change in subjective wellbeing

Note: * Cost factor relative to no change in subjective wellbeing

Table 5.5
Area and area/subjective wellbeing output effects from the model also including satisfaction with help output and quasi-inputs over time

Dependent variable: logged average weekly opportunity cost.

Area and type	Effect	Coeff.	S.E. (coeff.)	P-value
1 Inner London	constant	0.6164	0.2007	0.00
	wellbeing output	−1.8846	1.4451	0.20
	square of wellbeing output	0.6252	6.9916	0.93
2 Inner London	constant	−0.4005	0.2670	0.14
	wellbeing output	0.3777	2.3151	0.87
	square of wellbeing output	34.1717	24.6224	0.17
3 Outer London	constant	0.3075	0.2475	0.22
	wellbeing output	−1.3856	1.3170	0.30
	square of wellbeing output	11.1873	12.5172	0.37
4 Metropolitan District	constant	−0.1618	0.1683	0.34
	wellbeing output	0.0054	1.1356	1.00
	square of wellbeing output	0.0729	2.6947	0.98
5 Metropolitan District	constant	−0.3808	0.1621	0.02
	wellbeing output	−0.0794	1.0956	0.94
	square of wellbeing output	14.1271	5.1356	0.01
6 Metropolitan District	constant	−0.4382	0.1963	0.03
	wellbeing output	−1.1528	0.8459	0.18
	square of wellbeing output	10.0950	4.9928	0.05
7 English Shire	constant	−0.4075	0.1764	0.02
	wellbeing output	−0.5317	1.7515	0.76
	square of wellbeing output	1.5623	7.2672	0.83
8 English Shire	constant	−0.2875	0.1813	0.12
	wellbeing output	0.1669	1.1527	0.89
	square of wellbeing output	4.8996	8.9667	0.59
9 English Shire	constant	−0.0105	0.2272	0.96
	wellbeing output	−2.8491	0.9268	0.00
	square of wellbeing output	−3.2057	7.2874	0.66
10 Welsh County	constant	0.0[a]		
	wellbeing output	−0.5635	0.6886	0.41
	square of wellbeing output	2.3055	2.6869	0.39

R^2=0.75 Adjusted R^2=0.60 Mean square error=0.18 F=5.02 (P=0.00)
a Constants for each area are relative to area 10: hence constant for area 10 is zero.

as expected: increased physical needs lead to increased costs and an available informal care network tends to reduce costs. In addition, other quasi-inputs relating to life events appeared in the models with cost factors in the directions that might be expected. However, increased expenditures did not produce all of the potential outputs postulated; indeed the only effect was the increased satisfaction with help over time for people with critical needs. Clearly, studies using the production of welfare model which 'asserts that resources and non-resource inputs determine the outcomes of social care activity' (Davies, 1985) must distinguish potential from achieved outputs.

Our results contrast sharply with those of the Thanet Community Care Project, an experimental case-managed community care scheme whose comparison group received the standard provision of social services (Davies and Challis, 1986). It is interesting to consider other reasons why the patterns revealed in this study differ. First, the costs of varying levels of output for that project and standard provision were compared only for positive changes (see, for example, Davies and Challis, 1986, Table 11.2) because only a small minority of the experimental group suffered declines in psychological wellbeing and quality of care (Table 11.6). Our results also included some minimal positive correlations between costs and indicators we have treated as outputs for those for whom there was an improvement in state. But the state of most of the recipients in our study either remained unchanged or declined, and for them the correlations between costs and changes in state were negative.

Second, the community care approach is goal-centred, the workers being conscious of precisely those goals whose achievements were measured by the indicators of potential need in this study. Indeed, the workers contributed to their selection. It is hardly surprising that they used resources to impact on the output variables, and that increased resources were associated with higher outputs.

Third, for the comparison group of the community care project, admission to residential homes resulted both in higher costs and improvements in at least some aspects of their quality of life and care; so that for this group also, costs and outputs were correlated. The analyses reported in this chapter excluded those admitted to residential homes; and the accounts given in other chapters do nothing to suggest that criticisms of the lack of goal-centredness of community-based services are misplaced.

The reactions of field allocation to constraints on resources may also help to account for the absence of effects of resource variations on potential outputs. In a climate of financial constraint, the allocators and others in the organisation may give the highest priority to responding to the circumstances of those in most rapid decline. They might attach a lower priority to those for whom inputs would stabilise their state, and they might attach still lower priority to those for whom larger inputs would be associated with improved status. Also, policies and behaviour differ in important respects between areas. Area variations may well be an important part of the explanation of the small effects of differences in resource levels. The pattern of variation between areas yielded in Model 4 illustrates the argument. Area 4 claims to operate a policy of spreading services thinly over as many persons as possible. In consequence, the levels of provision for each recipient might be too low for variations in resources around the average in the authority to have much effect on potential outputs; a situation recognised by the Audit Commission (1985). The patch social work teams in Area 1 might monitor more effectively, intervene more effectively to stabilise states without the extensive use of community-based services, and so again show little sign of a positive correlation between costs and state. Such area variations in policy might well influence the relationship between costs and client state. So we must consider how output should be measured if the main aim is to give the highest priority to those in most rapid decline. Certainly, positive improvements compared with the baseline should have a lower weight.

Part II

6 Case management

1 Introduction

Official reports now recognise how ineffective is the performance of the core tasks of case management, how the ineffectiveness reduces the equity and efficiency of social care, and how improvements in their performance could be important in implementing community care policies (Audit Commission, 1987; DHSS, 1988a). This study is the first to undertake a systematic review of their performance in community-based services for the elderly.

The basic concepts and the core of the theoretical argument can be stated briefly. Several core tasks are distinguished and described in Table 6.1, the most useful classification depending on circumstances. The effectiveness of the performance of each core task contributes to one or more aspects of efficiency as is indicated in Diagram 6.1 which also lists and defines the core tasks. Of course, it is not argued that greater effectiveness in their performance will necessarily improve efficiency, indeed the community care experiment embodied devices not only to allow the more effective performance of the core tasks but also to provide incentives to perform them in ways which would improve equity and efficiency (Davies and Challis, 1986, Chap. 1).

2 Patterns of practice: sources of efficiency and inefficiency in systems

The general characteristics of service provision for elderly people have been described most recently by Hunter, McKeganey and MacPherson (1988) for Scotland; by Goldberg and Warburton (1979) and Goldberg and Connelly (1982); and most fully by the Social Services Inspectorate (DHSS, 1987b). This chapter describes aspects of service provision important to equity and efficiency and of particular interest in the context of the literature. The core tasks of case management described are well recognised under various names within social services departments. However, neither managers nor practitioners used case management or any equivalent concept, and perhaps partly as a result we could find little evidence of the systematic planning and coordination of the performance of the range of core tasks.

Appendix Tables A6.1 to A6.6 (pp.429-35) provide an overview of the performance of the tasks comparing the twelve systems.

Table 6.1
Core tasks of case management

Case finding	The recruitment of appropriate cases. The role of health and social services are contrasted in cases which subsequently receive services from both agencies with referrals from health to social services being commonplace but rarely occurring from social services to health.
Screening	Ensuring the appropriateness of referrals to the system. Little screening actively occurs in social services, and is carried out largely by GPs in the community health services.
Assessment	The identification of needs, in particular the unmet needs in social services: all too often assessment is for particular services. For community nursing assessment is carried out almost exclusively by nursing sisters.
Care planning, service packaging and gap-filling	The setting of goals, devising of plans and ensuring the availability of the resources required or substitutes. Mobilising resources to fill gaps in informal/social services provision.
Monitoring, re-assessment and adjustment	Enabling an awareness of and responsiveness to changing circumstances and needs.
Closure	In circumstances where individuals are no longer in need of the services that can be provided or arranged by the agency in question.

2.1 Case finding

The effectiveness of the performance of case finding can be substantially influenced by the field team itself. Various arrangements were made to increase the identification of individuals in need. Such arrangements included (i) the outposting of individual teams to outlying towns and villages in rural areas and neighbourhood estates in the inner city; (ii) individual practitioners operating from local facilities such as general practitioner surgeries, hospitals and day centres; (iii) the establishment of formal liaison arrangements with other agencies; and (iv) the encouragement of voluntary activity. Such arrangements were widely believed to promote

Diagram 6.1
Principal causal connections between case management tasks and aspects of efficiency

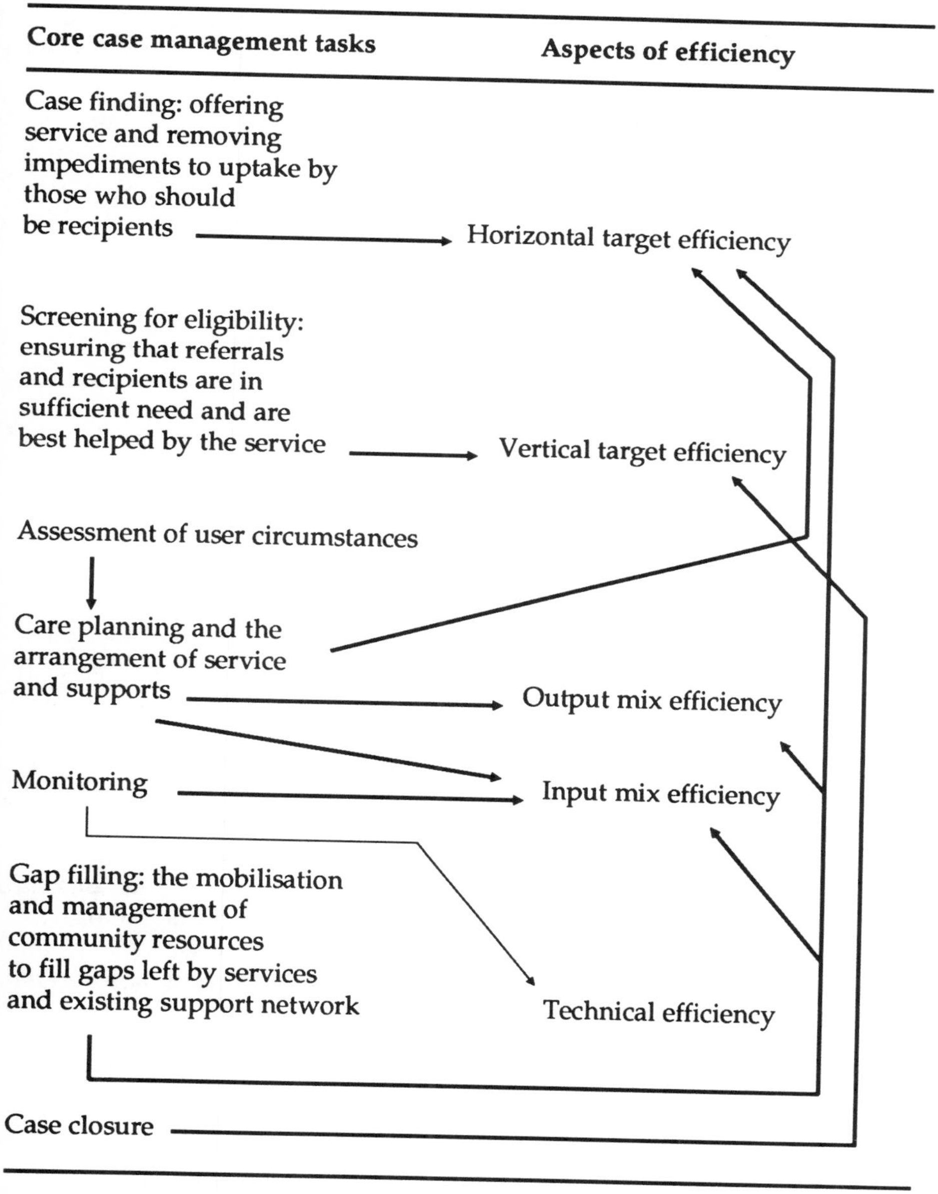

Core case management tasks	Aspects of efficiency

Note: Arrows signify direct causal relationship. Thin line signifies an indirect effect.

greater effectiveness in identifying those in need. A social work assistant spoke about the setting up of a volunteers' group:

I think the elderly find it easier to come in than they did ... we have attempted to get out into the community and establish links with them. Part of that is the establishment of a volunteers group which does an awful lot in the community ... it all helps to establish links and it breaks down the mystique between them and us. (Area 6)

Practitioners also referred widely to the value of devices to increase potential contacts such as proximity to other service providers, by sharing office space or adjacent buildings. While this improved accessibility, it did not always improve relations. Conflicts and tensions were reported despite close contact. Indeed, they were sometimes created or exacerbated by it. These tensions highlight differences in attitudes between different workers. An assistant social worker described the experience of an open plan office shared between home help staff and social work staff:

That can sometimes be a hazard, the home helps think they can just pop over ... I mean it's nice, but it takes time because you can't just brush them along, and if you're in the middle of something that needs all your attention, sometimes it's a bit off-putting. (Area 2)

2.2 Screening

Screening arrangements varied both in terms of the practitioners who carried out screening and in the discretion exercised by those practitioners. While some spoke of following through referrals as far as possible while on duty, others spoke of 'collecting only basic information' and 'passing it on as quickly as possible', leading to delays in decision-making over appropriate action. Some areas had adopted the practice of permitting only qualified workers to be responsible for dealing with referrals, while in others all practitioners took their turn 'on duty'. The development of intake teams has made the activity more specialised and could be expected to lead to greater efficiency in the screening of cases and their redirection where appropriate. This is not always the case, however. In one area an intake team was responsible for taking all referrals including those for the home help service. This led to the duplication of work, and the displeasure of the organisers who claimed: 'It's creating more hassle than it's relieving us.' (Area 8)

In contrast, in some other areas home help clerks regularly received initial referrals and while the information gathered was only minimal, the practice did conform to the assumptions and practices of the organisers, one of whom commented:

The clerk can take referrals. She knows what information we want and she makes a note of it. (Area 3)

All areas used standardised referral forms with varying degrees of effectiveness. The prescribed use of standard forms did not always ensure the thorough completion of the forms, and in only one authority with a computerised information system were referral forms returned if not completed properly. Many practitioners spoke of their inability or unwillingness to complete all the details on such forms. Some felt that they had insufficient time to gather information beyond that given by the referrer. Some were unwilling to pursue points not felt to be directly relevant. Also home help organisers tried to remember much of the information without recording it.

2.3 Assessment

2.3.1 Assessment in general

As indicated earlier, effective screening preliminary to (or as part of) an assessment process directly influences vertical target efficiency, ensuring that those people who receive services are those who need them. A system offering services in response to demand rather than need, or offering an inappropriate service in the absence of an appropriate one is inefficient in this sense. Assessment is an activity often indistinguishable from initial screening. A home help organiser described the situation in her area saying:

On the whole, home care is pretty catholic in the way it accepts its referrals. What we try to do is to visit each referral as speedily as we can because often we're given very little information. (Area 1)

This observation fitted well with reports that in nearly all areas over 95 per cent of referrals to home help organisers led to service allocation. Responsiveness in the home help service also refers to the speed of response, with organisers usually reaching new referrals within a couple of days. In emergencies, home helps were sent out immediately and only cases known to be 'non-urgent' might wait more than a week to be seen. The pace of response points to the difficulties in achieving thorough assessments of need (Carpenter, 1983). While such responsiveness may be the result of unforeseen circumstances, it also occurs as a consequence of failures of communication. A home care organiser told a familiar story about a referral:

A hospital social worker will ring you and will say something like 'I can't tell you anything about this lady, because she's in the ambulance on her way home'. (Area 5)

Among social work staff the tendency for referrals to be passed on as quickly as possible has already been noted. Another reason given for combining the screening and assessment processes was how referrers requested services. One social worker commented:

Often we find that somebody might come to us about someone they feel needs a home help simply because that's the only way they know they can make contact with us. They don't know what to say other than 'my mother needs a home help'. (Area 10)

And a home help organiser referred to general practitioners passing referrals via their receptionists:

All he's given the receptionist is that this person needs home help. And she doesn't really know what's wrong with her because the GP hasn't given her the information. (Area 10)

In only three of the study areas was explicit attention paid to carrying out need-related or problem-based assessments. These areas had different forms of team organisation and varying policies about the status of workers carrying out assessments but in all of them attention was focused on the assessment process *per se*. In contrast, a great deal of demand-led and service-led assessment was observed. A specialist team for the elderly allocated 'day care cases' to a particular social work assistant 'for assessment', as did a generic team that had developed guidelines specifically for the general assessment of elderly people. Similarly in another area, qualified intake workers, aided by special assessment forms for elderly people 'assessed for day care'.

The use of standard assessment forms or special guidelines used in some areas, and designed to improve the collection of relevant information, did not always affect practice decisions. Details of physical health and illness, while often recorded, did not lead to a clear view of their implications. Real multidisciplinary assessment was rare, and joint working on assessment between social services practitioners and health professionals was conspicuous by its absence in the mainstream services. Referral patterns demonstrated flows from health to social services. However, this did not ensure contact between personnel at stages beyond the referral. Within social services departments joint assessments between social workers and home help organisers were reported in only one area and between social workers and occupational therapists in another.

Recording of the availability of informal carers tended to relate to their potential for helping rather than a consideration of their own needs and the effect such needs may have on their capacity to continue caring. Liaison with informal carers during the assessment process was rare unless they happened to be present during assessment visits, despite anxieties expressed particularly by home help organisers about the denial or exaggeration of informal care inputs reported by elderly people.

The picture we have of assessment is that it is hurriedly and unsystematically undertaken, lacking in thoroughness, and largely uninfluenced by departmental attempts at standardisation. However, the intake team in one area was experimenting with a new assessment form for the elderly. It was described as:

Much more complicated and much more time consuming. It's about fourteen sides and about seven sides of functional rating, though that's useful and it's quick because you can tick their abilities in certain areas like washing, dressing, walking, feeding; useful practical information. But there's also about five sides on information about family, background, employment, etc. (Area 8)

The use of the form, initiated by the specialist workers in the long-term team met with expressions of ambivalence about its use, but has subsequently been adopted in modified form, and is described in the area as a major step forward.

2.3.2 Assessment for users of both health and social services

Assessment is undertaken by nursing sisters for community health and by social workers and home help organisers for social services. In practice, there is little inducement for the practitioners involved to take a problem- or need-based approach to assessment. A common source of frustration was that even if such assessment was made, the resources required were not within the control of the practitioner and inevitably the client would have to be passed to another practitioner for a further assessment, probably by different criteria. For example, as one community nurse said:

What I do find rather irritating is that with regard to meals-on-wheels and home help and things, even if a trained nurse makes a referral, they still won't take it on until they've done their own assessment.(Area 1)

The result is that the great majority of assessments are made in response to requests for specific services. Real multidisciplinary assessment was rare and joint working on assessment by health and social services only occurred with panels for residential care and in a few small-scale innovatory schemes.

2.4 Care planning, service packaging and gap-filling

Services from a number of sources may be involved in developing a total 'package' of care for an individual and there is widespread acknowledgement of the need for coordination. In practice, however, services tended to be coordinated within, rather than between agencies with social workers acting as 'bankers' rather than 'brokers' of services. The concept of 'key worker' was reported to be taken less seriously than in cases involving children. Discussing the coordinating role, a social worker said:

It's not strictly made out as it would be in a child abuse case where a register's held and somebody's actually designated as a key worker, but I think that people will look to you as being the key worker especially when things start breaking down. (Area 5)

The reality of coordination involving services outside the social services department could best be described as 'arranging' services or 'liaising' with existing service providers. Another social worker specialising in working with elderly people described his involvement in coordinating services as something happening:

Very rarely nowadays. We usually find that most elderly people have already got services from health. It's only very rarely now that we find they don't have and then we liaise with them for things like incontinence pads and things like that. (Area 9)

Difficulties in contacting community nurses were expressed in some rural areas. One home help organiser expressed her frustration:

They're very difficult to get hold of, they phone in and leave very unclear messages and it's ever so difficult to get back to them because you can never get in touch, they're not based anywhere. (Area 8)

Documentary planning tools such as weekly 'care plans' were used by community nurses in most areas but much less often by social services practitioners. There were exceptions such as the home care section which made use of a seven-day chart to ensure continuity of care. Often the community nurse 'plans' are left in patients' homes and might in theory form a medium of communication with the other visiting services, but are rarely used in this way. The use of a cover chart was not, in any case, without its problems:

It takes a lot of time does that, planning out what particular service or what particular person's going to take what day. (Area 5)

Social work practitioners were involved as advocates for clients with housing and social security problems where rules of eligibility are applicable. A largely secondary activity was the arrangement of alternative specialist services or volunteers for gardening, decorating, transport or to provide company, filling gaps in provision left by the limitations of the formal services of the department.

The allocation of departmental resources was a more usual activity among practitioners. Constraints on the power of field personnel to allocate resources varied between areas and services. The provision of telephones, of some day care places and of all residential care places was subject to specific criteria, with either local or central panels scrutinising applications. In some cases these panels were multidisciplinary and advised practitioners about alternative forms of assistance while others acted simply as gate-keepers or referees to decide between competing cases. Services with minimum, vague criteria such as day care and meals-on-wheels were often allocated as an 'easy option', even in areas with intake and specialist teams with implied skills of assessment.

Home help organisers were largely free to allocate home help and home care services in the way they thought appropriate within the limits of financial budgets. Management did not define specific criteria, allowing discretion within the framework of informal criteria. In addition to home helps, all organisers could effectively allocate meals-on-wheels and many were responsible for and free to allocate a variety of additional services including community wardens, night sitters, formalised 'good neighbours' and incontinence laundry facilities.

Home help services vary in the tasks performed and the times at which they are undertaken. All but one of the areas claimed to prescribe the tasks in individual cases, although such prescription was either so loose as to be adaptable, or it was not followed in practice. The exceptional area asked clients 'to explain their greatest needs to the home help when she comes'. All areas had rules proscribing 'forbidden' tasks. Gardening, spring cleaning and decorating were generally discouraged. They were described as 'the three deadly sins' in one area, which also 'banned' nursing tasks. The 'grey area' of personal care (see Chapter 8) was subject to debate in all areas and home helps and nurses were widely reported to be carrying out tasks beyond their job descriptions. Greater variation among areas was noted in the degree to which it was legitimate for home helps to act as companions, motivators and encouragers. An organiser from an area trying to develop problem-based assessments reported:

Recently I've dared to be a little more broad ... before I might have said that this wouldn't be your job, but you would do this that and the other ... now I'm thinking more in terms of things like encouraging clients to go out and to go with them shopping so they can still choose their own things. (Area 4)

Areas also varied in the times at which help could be offered. Two areas were able to offer 24-hour cover for limited periods by using night care aides and home care aides or a special home care scheme. Others limited help to daylight hours to avoid risks of physical assault to helpers returning home, while others provided help during the mornings, allowing additional help only for the essential tasks of fire lighting and meal preparation. The provision of more intensive personal care services requires greater flexibility in the use of time, and while some areas provided separate home care services, others offered personal care as part of the mainstream service. In one area with a traditional, morning domestic service, managers expressed hopes that the introduction at national level of the care assistant grade for home helps would allow them to move towards greater flexibility in service provision.

Despite claims made about the role of social work practitioners as direct workers and counsellors (Barclay, 1982), we found only limited evidence of such involvement with elderly clients or their carers. General statements were made about this aspect of work:

I never discount the fact that there's always a social work service to be given, it's not just seeing it in terms of day care, home help and what have you. (Area 5)

But pressure of work and active policies of case closure limited the amount of direct work undertaken. Social work staff were more likely to be involved as counsellors in situations where there were tensions between elderly people and their carers. Bereavement counselling was mentioned as an activity by a number of workers in response to general questions about direct work, but not one which figured significantly in their caseload activities and one area made specific use of CRUSE, a voluntary counselling service.

Direct work among home help organisers was limited by other aspects of their jobs, and it was therefore unsurprising that all organisers we spoke to complained of having too little contact with clients.

2.5 Monitoring and reassessment

Monitoring progress is often given as the sole reason for sustained involvement with elderly clients, particularly in the home help and meals services. While this may be a legitimate aim of intervention, monitoring achieves little unless it incorporates reassessment or alerts practitioners to the need for reassessment. This implies active intervention, and while procedures for reviewing cases often exist, in practice, current pressures and crises effectively devalue the reassessment process, resulting in the failure of resources to match changing needs. Some services have informal means of monitoring, an example being home helps who often feed back information about their clients to home help organisers.

Accounts of monitoring and reassessment activities varied widely among social workers. In one area, monitoring was described as 'an unrealistic concept', with pressure to close cases quickly and with 'emphasis on crisis management not prevention'. Two other areas followed active review systems, although one of these was largely concerned with monitoring individuals in day care or residential places. Clients receiving day care and residential care services were more commonly reviewed only once to check the suitability of the placement. The other area with an active review system had a specialist long-term team, operating a 'bank' system whereby cases were raised for review at regular intervals. This team also made use of 'task-time sheets' as a means to identify gaps in an elderly person's care network.

Reassessment in the home help service was subject to standard procedures in all study areas. Eleven areas reported procedures of six-monthly reviews although all but one failed to meet these standards. The twelfth area which operated its service with separate personnel for administration and client contact had a twelve-monthly review target which it did meet. Two areas attempted to carry out follow-up visits to clients within two weeks of putting a home help in, but they described this as part of the assessment process, the result of their 'own professional standards' rather than any departmental procedure. Active reassessments of elderly people receiving the home help service occurred either where clients made explicit demands, where specific problems arose, or in cases where the organiser was 'just passing anyway'. The area making use of seven-day cover charts subscribed to a practice of actively reviewing cases while stressing that this could take the form of contacting key people by telephone, and need not involve time-consuming visits. All areas relied on feedback from individual home helps although this was not always felt to be appropriate, and it was widely recognised that reassessments on the basis of a home help's contact, while often leading to an increase in service, would rarely lead to a reduction. An organiser in one of the areas concentrating on problem-based assessments commented: 'I feel we rely far too much on home helps' assessments'. (Area 4)

Contacts between health and social services were sparse, despite the fact that most referrals were from health to social services. Table 6.2 shows that for the 177 clients receiving both health and social services, contact (by letter, telephone, one-off visit) was made between community health workers and SSD case managers in less than half the cases during the study period. Regular liaison, or case conferences occurred in only twelve cases.

Monitoring and reassessment appear to be activities carried out for the most part by default and the widespread use of informal monitoring systems such as the use of home helps, day care, or meals service personnel is not without its problems. Active reassessments of need seem most likely

Table 6.2
Contact between social worker (or home help organiser) and community health services[a] during six months for 177 elderly clients

	Number of clients	Percentage of clients
Regular liaison or joint case conference	12	7
Any other contact	69	39
No contact	96	54
Total	177	100

a Community health includes GP and community nursing

to occur when prompted by clients or their carers, and are thus often associated with specific life events. This practice clearly caused the inefficient use of resources, individuals continuing to receive services when they were no longer in need, and the less effective use of services where the increasing needs of undemanding clients go unnoticed.

2.6 Case closure

Closure of cases among the social work teams invariably required the approval of a senior social worker or team leader, and was actively pursued in the majority of areas with a pattern of brief intervention often involving the arrangement of services followed by social worker withdrawal. An intake worker described the nature of work with elderly people: 'We're not there for very long. We're usually in there doing assessments, providing a service and then moving on, closing the case or passing it through to the long-term team.' But he went on to comment:

The long-term team and the intake team don't have an easy meeting place where they would transfer. Seniors in the long-term teams want to protect their workers from heavy caseloads and are therefore going to be reluctant to take on cases unless it's quite clear there's a long-term application. (Area 8)

A social worker in a traditional generic team saw case closure as something that should happen:

... where there is no further need for social work help or involvement in any other form like coordinating services. [However,] that may well be influenced by pressures of other workload and external pressures mainly. (Area 5)

This was among the majority of areas with policies of short-term intervention, and the use of 'caseload management' to control workloads for individuals by fast turnover of cases. A more general expression of the process of case closure was 'where services are set up and running' and early closure was specifically mentioned when additional services, particularly home helps, were involved. In such cases other parties were usually informed and the home help service used as a 'front-line warning system'.

Case closure in the home help service is much more clearly defined. Few circumstances result in withdrawal of the service, so that of clients who consumed home help and who were still living at home after six months, 82 per cent still recieved the home help service; and of those no longer getting the service, more than half said that it was because they no longer wanted the service rather than because it had been withdrawn. In one set of circumstances clients recover after acute episodes, or alternative forms of care are provided. Here, it is usually the client or carer who initiates the withdrawal of service. In another, clients behave unreasonably towards home helps. Instances most commonly described involved sexual aggression of male clients towards female home helps or continual drunkenness, illustrated by an organiser who withdrew home help from '... a grotty old man who probably I could say was sexually attacking home helps and spent three parts of his life roaring drunk, and you couldn't keep any home help in there' (Area 8).

Other forms of behaviour not tolerated by organisers were repeated accusations of stealing, often associated with problems of confusion where organisers were usually willing to replace a home help in the first instance, or more general clashes between a client and home help. There was one instance of withdrawal where a white client refused to have a black home help. Instances seen to represent the inappropriate use of a home help's time also led to closure, either where a client's living environment was thought to present a health risk to the home help, and thus to warrant the attention of environmental health services, or where home helps were consistently being left to deal with double incontinence of clients. In these cases, withdrawal was seen as a way of pressurising other more appropriate service providers to become actively involved. 'Case closure' for the other main community services – meals-on-wheels and day care – was invariably at the choice of the client.

Patterns of case closure contrasted sharply between the social work and home help services. Social workers often closed cases when their continued intervention was thought unlikely to be effective. This is consistent with findings about the effectiveness of brief and extended social work (Reid and Shyne, 1969). However, closure also occurred where alternative services had been set up. The implication for case management is the separation of responsibility for the range of core tasks, with the implicit danger that formal monitoring and reassessment may not take place unless specifically demanded. In contrast, closure of cases in the home help service is a rare phenomenon. However, this in itself does not promote reassessment activity. It may lead to the allocation of resources to those with lower levels of need, and so the failure to allocate resources at appropriate levels for those in greater need.

3 Conclusion

This analysis confirms the deleterious effects on the equity and efficiency of provision of two independent factors: (1) service provision is fragmented, and so (2) the fragmentation and vagueness in responsibility and accountability for the performance of the core case management factors causes a failure to match resources to needs.

3.1 The fragmentation of services

Attempts to meet the welfare needs of elderly people rely on good communication and effective packaging of services to avoid the inefficiencies which arise from overlap or gaps. Poor communication and tensions between health and social services personnel were evident between hospitals, the home help service and community nursing services, affecting the coordination of services for those being discharged from hospital and cooperation in providing services to the same individual.

The separate consideration of the case management role of social work practitioners and home help organisers has been forced by their separate structures. We found no real evidence, even within shared office space, of the integration of social work and home help services for elderly people, though it is widely advocated.

3.2 Fragmentation of the performance of the core tasks of case management

This examination also confirms a lack of 'case management' activity, with no single individual taking the role of 'case manager'. The only exceptions to this were special schemes in two areas offering augmented home care services for very frail elderly people (see Chapter 11). In one area, the scheme was, and remains, small-scale. The other scheme was established in two areas. It was jointly financed by health and social services, and aimed to provide care for people on the margins of need for residential care. Staffing is multidisciplinary, key workers are appointed, assessments are structured to encompass a wide range of needs, formal treatment plans are drawn up, and regular reassessments take place. However, the scheme was limited in scale and became silted up leading to the operation of a waiting list. Replication of the scheme to cover all areas in the authority had been accompanied by the degeneration of some of its key features, in particular the focus on effective case management through the appointment of key workers, giving way to a concentration on the personal care content of the service, essentially sacrificing its flexibility. In this way, the gap-filling capacity of the scheme came to conflict with its effectiveness in performing purely case management tasks.

Mainstream services in all areas showed 'weak points' in the overall management of cases not only in the transfer of responsibility from one stage to the next but also in the nature of the performance of the different case management tasks. Waiting lists for allocation to social workers and the divided management between intake and long-term teams caused silting up. The tendency to assess for services rather than needs can lead to the inappropriate provision of services and limited awareness of the inflexibility of existing services, preventing imaginative approaches towards negotiating alternative sources of help outside the department. The nature of monitoring and reassessment activity suggested a failure to be able to respond to the changing needs of individuals in any planned way, 'crisis management' being the order of the day in most social work teams, while 'prevention' was the watchword in the home help service, justifying increases in service provision, but rarely reductions.

Social services departments are aware of the diverse and changing nature of client needs. Their effectiveness in meeting needs, however, is constrained both by formal, organisational structures and by the existence of separate services with different channels of access. Particularly at field level, different structures have been used to attempt to provide care more effectively, but they have had the effect of simply relocating gaps in the system. The separation of services is likely to persist, though possibly to a diminished extent. Perhaps fixing the locus of responsibility for the effective performance of the core tasks of case management must be implemented in order to offer a better chance of ensuring continuity of appropriate care and the achievement of better outcomes.

7 Risk and decision-making

1 Introduction

Our initial examination of service allocations to clients (Bebbington and Charnley, 1985) in common with other studies revealed high drop-out rates among clients allocated day care places (Bligh, 1979) and to a lesser extent, meals-on-wheels (Means, 1981). Closer scrutiny of these cases found processes of assessment more closely resembling tests of eligibility for available services than considerations of need, and a commonly-held belief that it is better to offer an inappropriate service than to offer no service at all. This behaviour was an insurance against being criticised for having failed to respond to referrals of elderly people or their carers seen to be 'at risk' in some way. This chapter analyses the influence of allocators' perceptions of 'risk' and shows how these affect – and in some respects distort – the equity and efficiency of outcomes.

Section 1 considers the place of risk as a concept in the care of old people. Section 2 addresses the problem of uncertainty and the importance of accountability as factors influencing decision-making. Section 3 draws upon interviews from the domiciliary care study to consider clients' and workers' perceptions of risk, and organisational responses to risk. Finally, the hypotheses derived from these accounts are tested by statistical analyses which illuminate the need-related characteristics influencing judgements of risk, and the importance of such judgements in the allocation of services.

2 The place of risk in the care of old people

In the social work literature, 'at risk', 'acceptable risk' and 'risk management' are familiar terms. Specific attention was paid to 'risk' in social work during the 1970s, following the death of Maria Colwell (DHSS, 1974). The interest has spread to other than 'children at risk'. The probation service (National Association of Probation Officers, 1977), and the British Association of Social Workers, drew up guidelines and policies for dealing with 'risk'. They acknowledged that one role for social workers is 'understanding and accepting the degree of risk which the client is prepared to take, and balancing this with the sometimes over-reaction of society' (British Association of Social Workers, 1977). Discussing social work with elderly people, Crosbie (1983) summarises the central elements of the social work role as 'the negotiation of resources, acceptable to clients and supporters, for the management of risk'.

Managing risk involves notions of protection (Rowlings, 1981) and so arguments about the appropriate balance between protection and freedom, the right of individuals to choose where and how they live. Norman (1980) has examined the relationship between rights and risk in old age. Discussing the stereotyping of old age, and the consequent use of such stereotypes to patronise and infantilise elderly people, she identifies what amounts to the denial of civil liberties. Freedom to choose has been an element in the case for the development of community care. Innovation in the care of those living in the community (Ferlie, Challis and Davies, 1983) has been described as giving elderly people freedom to make the *wrong* choice and as embodying the concept of acceptable risk as the price to be paid for individual freedom of choice (Isaacs and Evers, 1981). However, others have suggested that community care can amount to inadequate care for elderly people living in their own homes 'in situations of high personal risk, distress, and miserable environment' (Plank, 1977).

The concept 'risk', applied to social work and to old age, creates complicated dilemmas for elderly people, their families, professionals and wider society, partly because 'risk' is diversely interpreted. Brearley (1982; see also Brearley, Hall, Jefferys, Jennings and Pritchard, 1982) focuses on two central elements in understanding risk; estimation and evaluation. Drawing parallels with the world of commercial insurance, *estimation* is defined as involving an awareness of the range of possible outcomes, and a consideration of the probability that each outcome will occur. To *evaluate* risk on the other hand is to attach values to each of the possible outcomes. In addressing questions of risk assessment and the determination of acceptable risk, Rowe (1977) has pointed to the difficulties arising from the imprecise nature of the values upon which decisions are based. Analysing the role of regulatory agencies in the field of public safety, he develops a classification of the value judgements of affected parties whose views must be taken into account in choosing a course of action. 'Technical' value judgements are made by experts in the appropriate field, while 'societal' value judgements made by individual members of the public are reflected in the strength of popular opinion. 'Managerial' value judgements which interpret societal judgements, are made both by those involved in the technical aspects and others such as managers who are responsible for dealing with the consequences of particular courses of action.

While addressing problems of a rather different nature, there are useful parallels to be drawn between these judgements, and those made in the assessment of risk in social work with elderly people. Here, the technical judgements are usually made by such workers as medical or paramedical practitioners, social workers and home help organisers. Societal judgements may be made by informal carers, local communities, pressure groups and more broadly through the media. Managerial judgements will often rest with the staff of health and social services departments who frequently act as a focus for the concern of others. In the case of public safety issues, individual value judgements form part of the larger societal judgement. Social work with elderly people, however, involves a recognition of the individual's judgement in its own right as part of the principle of self-determination and this may not always be congruent with the wider societal view. Decisions made about a particular course of action following the estimation and evaluation of risk will be influenced in part by the degree of perceived risk but also by actors' perceptions of their personal responsibility, legal liability or level of accountability in the event of a negative outcome, that is, something going wrong.

3 Risk and uncertainty: the problem of accountability

Despite widespread concern regarding the risks to which elderly people are subject, there is a large degree of uncertainty about appropriate responses to situations of perceived risk. This reflects uncertainty as a central element in risk (Rowe, 1977; Brearley, 1982; O'Brien, 1986), and leads to difficulty in offering clear guidelines for practice (Mortimer, 1982). Such difficulties have been discussed in relation to the role of doctors in making rational decisions about acceptable degrees of risk where the problem is seen as one of 'calculating odds' carrying with it inherent dangers of inaccurate calculations for the professional (Klein, 1973; O'Brien, 1986). Goldberg and Connelly (1982) see this view of risk taking being applicable in social work and Rowlings (1981) points out the complications that can arise from varying perceptions and interpretations of risk by such different professionals as social workers, doctors and home help organisers. These complications, in addition to those of the sometimes conflicting interests of elderly people, their carers, and professionals, highlight the problem of accountability.

Accountability is concerned with responsibility for particular actions or non-actions. The issue of accountability in social work has been widely documented by Goldberg and her colleagues in the development of the case review system (Goldberg and Fruin, 1976; Goldberg, Warburton, McGuinness and Rowlands, 1977; Goldberg, Warburton, Lyons and Willmott, 1978), and has been given special consideration by the British Association of Social Workers (1977). In a discussion of professional discretion, Adler and Asquith (1981) argue that professional decision-making is subject to particularly weak forms of public accountability and control, and they view social workers' decisions about what kind of help, if any, should be given, as being largely immune to any form of democratic accountability and control. This contrasts with the view of many social workers who express anxieties about being ultimately responsible, the feeling that 'the buck stops here' (Stevenson and Parsloe, 1978). Such anxieties have been expressed in relation to the consequences of taking positive action:

We had one old lady who went into a home (she was not keen to go), and she just gave up and died (Stevenson and Parsloe, 1978, p.232).

They are also expressed in relation to the consequences of failure to protect vulnerable people living in the community. These particular anxieties are twofold, involving not only the reluctance of wider society to accept the risks inherent in a policy of community care, but also the concern to defend elderly people from the pressures of their carers or other professionals to move from their own homes to accommodation affording greater protection (Rowlings, 1981).

It might reasonably be expected that professional supervision might offer practitioners assistance in making appropriate decisions in situations involving considerable risks. Indeed, the roles of supervision and workload management in accountability have been addressed explicitly in the social work literature (Bamford, 1982). Rather than clarifying problems, however, the supervision relationship is often characterised by a lack of clear lines of accountability. Rowlings comments:

The confusion that surrounds the meanings of responsibility and accountability make for difficulty in clarifying the extent to which senior staff can be expected to encourage or even permit their subordinates to take the risks which may be important, possibly crucial, if the client is to be allowed any control over different aspects of his life (1981, p.88).

This absence of clear lines of accountability is regularly paralleled by a lack of systematic recording procedures, particularly for elderly clients. While it is clear that there is intermittent demand for the development of procedures following particular incidents or scandals, such demand tends to die down without any apparent improvements having been made (Stevenson, 1981a). An example is the use of 'at risk' registers for elderly people, by social services departments, often initiated in response to deaths, or fear of deaths arising from hypothermia. Many of these registers have been discontinued having become outdated, and because they carry a suggestion of interference in the private lives of individuals. Goldberg and Warburton claim a positive role for a case review system in accountability, and they offer the words of a social worker operating the system in evidence:

The area is in a strong position to be held accountable for our decisions about what work is done and what work is not done. People may disagree with our reasons, but we can account for what is happening and that is important (1979, p.122).

4 The domiciliary care study

Our collection of evidence covered various aspects of the meaning and response to perceived risk. The meaning of risk was discussed in interviews with managers and practitioners. Clients and their case managers were also asked specifically about risk factors. Information on the elements of risk in individual cases has been used to examine the factors contributing to practitioners' perceptions of risk, and the consequences of such perceptions in terms of service allocation.

4.1 Clients' perceptions of risk

A most important aspect of risk is the perception held by elderly people themselves. There are wide differences for instance in the very low statistical probability (1 per cent) of elderly women being the victims of street crime, and widespread fears of vulnerability to such violence (37 per cent) (*British Crime Survey*, 1983). Our finding is that 39 per cent of the sample of elderly people felt at risk of being burgled or attacked prior to service intervention. There are many examples too where elderly people perceive themselves to be at low, or no risk – for instance of not eating adequately – when in the view of a professional worker they may be judged to be at risk. It is the perceptions of elderly people themselves that are likely to offer the key to ensuring that any services provided, as well as being judged appropriate by the professional, will also be acceptable to the client.

The examination of risk as an outcome for clients formed part of structured interviews held with elderly people both before service interventions and again six months later. Respondents were asked about their fears of being at risk of falling, becoming ill or dependent, overburdening carers, being forgetful and causing accidents, not eating well enough or keeping warm enough, being burgled or attacked, being pressed into moving and being unable to continue living alone. The fear expressed most often by the clients immediately prior to service interventions was that of being physically at risk due to frailty, a fear affecting nearly a quarter of the sample. These fears were largely unaffected by service interventions although significant reductions in fears were noted in risks related to food, warmth and accommodation, and were closely associated with the receipt of home help and meals-on-wheels.

4.2 Practitioners' perceptions of risk

4.2.1 Case reviews
Case managers views of risk were sought as part of a case review exercise, carried out for each client in the study immediately prior to service intervention and again six months later. Following Crosbie's (1983)

approach, social workers and home help organisers were asked open-ended questions about risk, first whether clients were thought to be at risk, and if so what form(s) this risk took. Unlike Crosbie, however, our case reviews were carried out by telephone interviews between researchers and case managers. This method was used to reduce the burden on individual case managers some of whom had a number of clients in the study, and also to encourage the fullest possible accounts of various aspects of each case. Many respondents experienced difficulty in answering questions about risk, and were uncertain whether some clients were at risk or not. Responses such as 'yes, in the same way that all old people are at risk', and 'no more than any other elderly person' were common and reflected the uncertainty that pervades the concept of risk.

Case review information was available for 481 cases of which 46 per cent involved individuals thought to be at risk, 11 per cent marginally at risk and 36 per cent not at risk. Answers were not given for 7 per cent of cases. The percentage of those thought to be at risk or marginally at risk (57 per cent) resembles Crosbie's findings where 58 per cent of cases were said to be in some kind of danger or at risk (1983, p.129). Responses to questions about the nature of risk covered a range from very specific to wider, more general descriptions. Table 7.1 shows the rank order of risks reported by case managers, and the distribution of risks among different household structures.

Table 7.1
Risks reported by case managers

Risks related to	Number	Per cent of those living alone	Per cent of couples	Per cent of those living with younger others
Falling/unable to get up	79	74	15	11
Forgetfulness/confusion	34	79	21	0
Specific health conditions	35	60	37	3
Loneliness/social isolation	31	74	13	13
Not eating well enough	27	85	7.7	7.5
Burden on carers	44	32	50	18
Too ill/dependent to live at home	21	57	29	14
Frailty causing accidents	19	63	26	11
Self neglect	13	85	15	0
Unable to continue living alone	14	100	0	0
Non-specific risk	13	77	23	0
Being burgled/attacked/conned	14	93	7	0
Depression/suicide	11	82	9	9
Not keeping warm enough	9	78	11	11
General risks of old age	10	80	0	20
Being pressed into moving	8	62.5	12.5	25

Number of cases = 457

These responses reflect widespread concern about the possibility of falling and being unable to get up, but also about over-burdening carers, specific health conditions, confusion, social isolation, and not eating properly. Responses in the categories of 'general risks of old age', 'general self-neglect', and 'non-specific risks' occurred in 44 cases. This confirmed a significant degree of uncertainty about the nature of risk with the inherent dangers of failure to articulate appropriate ways of managing or controlling that risk.

For the clients remaining in the community six months later, case managers were asked again about these risks. Responses were given for 289 cases of which only 29 per cent were thought to have experienced a change in respect of the risks mentioned previously. Table 7.2 illustrates the nature of those changes. Sixty-two per cent were reported not to have experienced any change and case managers for 9 per cent of cases indicated they did not know whether there had been any change in risks. Service interventions seemed to make little difference, no changes being reported in just over two-thirds of cases. In those cases where some change was experienced, the case manager felt that risks had been reduced or resolved (67) more frequently than they had worsened (16) or new risks been mentioned (22).

Table 7.2
Change in risks perceived by case managers
after six months' intervention

Risks related to	Increased	Reduced/resolved	New risk
Falling/unable to get up	5	13	0
Forgetfulness/confusion	6	4	0
Specific health conditions	0	5	5
Loneliness/social isolation	1	6	1
Not eating well enough	0	8	4
Burden on carers	0	9	3
Too ill/dependent to live at home	2	3	3
Frailty causing accidents	0	1	0
Self neglect	0	4	0
Unable to continue living alone	1	1	1
Non-specific risk	1	2	1
Being burgled/attacked/conned	0	1	0
Depression/suicide	0	7	0
Not keeping warm enough	0	3	0
General risks of old age	0	0	2
Being pressed into moving	0	0	2
Total	16	67	22

No. of cases = 289

4.2.2 *Interviews with practitioners*

The subject of risk was also pursued in focused interviews with practitioners and managers in each area. The interviews sought to identify some of the value assumptions of those responsible for making decisions about service allocations and broader issues of case management. Respondents were asked specifically about their understanding of the term 'at risk' in relation to elderly people, although in many cases it had already been used spontaneously. While responses were variable, each respondent recognised and acknowledged the use of the term and most were concerned to stress acceptance of the rights of individuals to take risks. However, such acceptance was often conditional upon the elderly person having sufficient knowledge to be able to recognise not only the risks, but also the implications of those risks. The acceptance of risk-taking was described as being important in retaining the quality of life for some elderly people, and as respecting the right of individuals to choose, including the right to refuse services.

Practitioners' perceptions of elderly people 'at risk'

Conflicts of professional opinion about risk were mentioned between social workers and home help organisers, home helps, general practitioners and wardens of housing complexes, each group attaching different meanings to the term. Conflicts with informal carers were rarely mentioned in the same vein, although comments on the role of social workers in helping carers manage risk, or accept risk, were widespread:

I find that risk is very much something that I'm trying to explain to carers ... by giving them aids and adaptations to lower that risk ... by giving them ideas about how they could minimise the risk, and taking away their anxiety while maintaining the older persons.

Other professionals, social workers say, are less willing to take risks. One social worker related his experience:

It's a phrase I get from the GPs. It is a term I use, but what I say is, there's an acceptable element of risk, and again, has anybody asked the individual concerned are they happy? And we must accept it if they want to live in whatever conditions they choose ... that is their right.

Another social worker described the unwillingness of wardens to tolerate, or attempt to manage risky situations:

I'll give you a case, a lady of 91 and they've threatened to evict her. It's an almshouse, Christian almshouse would you believe. She keeps falling. Now the old lady doesn't want to go into a home, at the moment anyway, and is prepared to take that risk.

This elderly tenant had previously caused concern by constantly leaving her gas cooker on, and the social worker had managed this hazardous situation by changing her cooking facilities, thereby reducing the risk of an explosion which was also acknowledged as presenting a risk to those living nearby.

Specific risks mentioned most frequently in interviews were related mainly to physical dangers such as falling, particularly where the elderly person lived alone and may be unable to summon help, physical abuse by 'carers' and hypothermia. One instance of hypothermia illustrated the problems and risks associated with the use of 'new technology' (Stevenson, 1981a) designed ironically to increase convenience and to reduce risks:

We were called out last winter to a little old lady living in a rather nice flat. She'd been sitting in front of a typical two bar electric fire all night trying to get warm, but she hadn't switched the bars on. She was trying to get warm from the glow and she didn't understand that she had to switch the bars on separately, and she was hypothermic by the time we got to her.

Confusion was also seen widely as a risk-raising element particularly when it led to wandering or leaving gas on with the possibility of causing an explosion. Also concern was expressed over elderly people seen to be vulnerable because of their inability to avoid being tricked or conned, due to poor sight, a lack of awareness of the current value of money, or excessive trust in strangers wishing to enter their homes. Psychological and emotional risks such as becoming isolated or depressed were mentioned spontaneously by only one social worker reflecting the greater importance attached to physical risks (Rowlings, 1981). Such concentration on physical risks is in part the result of the overwhelming concern to preserve life and in part a reflection of the fact that physical risks are seen as being easier to identify and tackle. It has been argued that a principal concern of social workers is 'hazard management' (Brearley, 1982) and the provision of a safe or 'prosthetic environment' (Wasser, 1971). In contrast, social isolation was mentioned as a specific problem for elderly people in 17 per cent of cases, and home help organisers in seven of the ten areas felt that loneliness was the biggest single problem for old people. Indeed, many of the organisers felt the prevention of social isolation to be a legitimate role of the home help service.

Risks to practitioners

As well as describing risks for their elderly clients, practitioners were also mindful of the risks to which they felt themselves exposed. A level 3 worker summed up the situation:

It's more to do with how people perceive us and how we sort of look to the outside world. If we are involved with an elderly person and that person is found on the floor either seriously ill or dead, the headline will be 'What was Social Services doing?' That's the kind of risk we're involved in.

Aggressive and violent behaviour of clients towards front-line workers also featured. Increasing attention has been paid to this area recently following the deaths of social work staff in the course of their work. Although elderly people do not feature in these incidents, a study of social workers at risk (Brown, Bate and Ford, 1986) considers circumstances that might lead to violent reactions from elderly clients. These include inappropriate patronising behaviour towards old people, states of confusion misinterpreted and, as a consequence, 'badly handled', resistance to compulsory removal to hospital, and more generally, instances of intimate personal caring carried out by an individual unacceptable to the elderly person concerned.

The domiciliary care study revealed no such incidents nor any such expressions of potential risks among social work staff. However, home help organisers described aggressive forms of behaviour among some of their clients as being a reason to withdraw the service. These cases usually involved drunken behaviour or sexual harassment by elderly men towards female home helps. Not only were the home helps seen to be at risk in these cases, but also the elderly clients whose service had been withdrawn.

These various expressions of concern underline the complex nature of risk, with meanings and interpretations differing between actors and situations. What constitutes a risk for one person may not do so for another; ensuring a safe situation for an elderly person may give rise to risks for carers; attempts at controlling risks for elderly people may result in risks for social workers. The problem lies in the challenge to respond appropriately and to minimise the risks for all concerned. Responses to risk can be divided into two broad categories in the context of providing social services for elderly people: the management of risk in practice and the development of policies and procedures for dealing with situations of risk.

4.3 Responses to risk

4.3.1 Policies and procedures

Nearly all areas in the domiciliary care study experienced specific incidents involving elderly people which had given rise to particular concern. Only one area claimed an absence of incidents and, even here, anxiety was expressed in the response 'touch wood, no, not yet'. Three areas cited incidents of accidents in old people's homes, but the overwhelming concern in responses to this subject was of the relative lack of action and continuing consequences following such incidents, when compared to the field of child care. One respondent reported:

We've had a number of elderly people die of hypothermia at home, alone, and that has caused a ripple in the local press. 'How could this possibly happen?' And then it's gone. It hasn't been like Tyra Henry or the death of a child in care.

Another respondent, in an authority with no experience of major scandals, described the prevailing attitudes towards elderly people at risk as being:

Not in the sense of having laid down priorities and procedures to deal with it ... if a child care case is referred there's a booklet that thick telling you exactly what to do and how to do it. We don't have that for any other client group.

Notions of responsibility for serious incidents were referred to in different ways by several respondents. At one end of the spectrum the organisation is seen as being devoid of responsibility as long as efforts have been made to resolve a particular situation:

We've had one or two (scares) ... usually after investigation it's proved that we've done our level best to do something for someone and they've refused the service. We had a man die last year, but frequent contact had been maintained with him and although we'd been almost forcing our services on to him, he was getting rid of the services as quickly as we'd managed to put them in.

At the other end of the spectrum are 'at risk' registers for elderly people, although they were not a common feature in the study areas. In one area, the operation of such a register was thought to 'prevent panics' since certain cases on the register were subject to routine case conferences. The register distinguished between three levels of risk, with those in the highest category being raised at each register meeting, attended by a multidisciplinary team of health and social service workers. Other areas had no formal registers although several informal procedures for monitoring elderly people thought to be at risk were evident. One team leader kept a list of elderly people who would be vulnerable to isolation in bad weather conditions, and held case conferences for elderly people consistently refusing services. Another area operated a priority scale with clients at serious risk of abuse or self-neglect at the top, elderly people being included if 'they are at a life-threatening stage'. The inclusion of elderly people among all clients seen to be 'at risk' took on a different meaning in another area operating a system of caseload management for social workers. Under the system, any case containing an element of risk would score an extra point; however, cases involving elderly people could not score more than one point by definition. Another respondent expressed the opinion that it would be good practice to keep a list of people at risk of hypothermia, and another felt a register could be useful to help in cases of 'granny bashing'.

The use of registers also evoked numerous negative comments with a number of respondents eager to point out dangers associated with keeping registers: 'people are wary of registers', 'it would lead to unrealistic expectations', and 'it's the same as any register ... people think that because someone's name is on an at risk register, that in fact protects them, and it doesn't'.

Organisational responses to risks directly affecting staff were limited to the home help service where organisers were involved in withdrawing, or refusing to commence service delivery in cases where clients' houses were thought to represent a health hazard. Although this was reported to have happened only rarely in the study, it drew attention to guidelines governing the content of the home help service. For instance, many home help sections would not sanction home helps cleaning windows or doing other jobs that involved climbing, giving medication to clients or providing some sorts of personal care, such as getting an elderly person out of bed. Such activities were seen as potential risks to the home helps, either in terms of their personal safety or, as in the case of client medication, in terms of personal responsibility and organisational accountability.

4.3.2 The management of risk

The management of risk implies a recognition of the risks to which an elderly person may be exposed, and an attempt to respond appropriately to those risks. Risk management involves the identification and assessment of risks, the development of a planned course of action designed to lessen, control, or eliminate the risks identified and a form of monitoring to allow for the reassessment of risks. Actions may range from the provision of comparatively simple aids or adaptations allowing particular activities such as getting in and out of the bath to be made less hazardous or replaced by a safer alternative, to the removal of the elderly person to a 'safe' environment. The difficulties in making a clear assessment of risk increase with the degree of uncertainty about the risks to which the client is exposed. Stevenson (1981a) contrasts ideas about risk taking for elderly people and children, and identifies the lack of a comparable set of developmental norms for ageing, since processes are more diverse and less precisely timed than for children. This absence of a set of 'normal expectations' makes for greater difficulty in estimating the likelihood of being exposed to a specific risk, and leads to a correspondingly greater degree of uncertainty. If clients are not prepared to accept workers' views of risks, the problem becomes one of ensuring that the client has been given, and understood the appropriate information, and has been offered help in managing the risk. The right of clients to refuse services offered is widely acknowledged, though not always accepted, and alternative attempts are often made to monitor what are thought to be high risk situations:

If they (people at risk) are still wanting to stop at home even though they may be at risk, then we'll provide as much domiciliary care and probably day care, so we can monitor the situation.

Problems for practitioners do not end with the estimation of risks, which may not be shared by the client, nor with the development of care plans designed to manage risks since these may not meet with the client's approval. The refusal of elderly people to accept social services can give rise to particular anxiety since it removes the easiest method of monitoring what are perceived as 'risky situations', and such refusals may lead to specially convened meetings where matters of accountability are clearly spelled out. This may be an appropriate way of averting 'scandalous crises' since it is widely acknowledged that occasional routine visits are rarely appropriate, either as a means of support, or as a way of anticipating approaching crises (Goldberg and Warburton, 1979). Where it is less clearly perceived that an elderly person is at risk, the management of that risk is subject to greater degrees of uncertainty preventing the anticipation of unforeseen circumstances and effective care planning.

4.4 *Uncertainty and risk: the case of hypothermia*

An example of uncertainty in risk can be found in the case of hypothermia, a subject mentioned frequently by social work respondents during interviews, although it was raised as a specific risk in case reviews for only ten elderly clients in the study. This concern among social work practitioners reflects the risk of exposure to allegations of negligence should an elderly person die of hypothermia (Shanas, Townsend, Wedderburn, Friis, Milhoj and Stehouwer, 1968). Little is known about the aetiology of hypothermia increasing the difficulty for social workers in making realistic estimates of the risks involved. Hypothermia, literally a fall in the temperature of the inner body, has been the subject of attention in attempts to distinguish social factors associated with it and to identify factors that might help to prevent it (Wicks, 1978). No clear answers have been established to explain why some people fail to maintain deep body homeostasis, but a number of factors have been identified as increasing the likelihood of this happening. Among these are increasing age, low body weight (associated with age), living alone (since there is no one available in the event of an accident) and receipt of supplementary benefit. However, possession of an electric blanket is associated with decreased risks of hypothermia.

A study by Bradshaw, Clifton and Kennedy (1978) which traced the histories of 203 elderly people found dead in their own homes, using the records of the coroner's court, found that only 0.7 per cent of these people had died of hypothermia. The vast majority had died of heart, cerebro-vascular, circulatory, respiratory or hypotensive diseases, generally considered to be beyond the responsibility of social services departments, with 12 per cent dying after an accident or suicide. The majority of the deaths involved elderly people living alone, or having been left alone, for example, when their spouse had been hospitalised, and the majority were last seen by neighbours or relatives rather than by statutory services. Of those who died as the result of diseases, two-thirds were known to be suffering from potentially fatal conditions, but a third were not known to be at risk in this way. Of those who committed suicide, half were linked with bereavements and subsequent depression. In their conclusions, the authors drew attention to the lack of evidence to support a case for the extensive development of services to prevent 'found deaths', and they point to the dangers of active interventionist policies which may interfere with the lives and deaths of those who prefer to remain at home. They stress, rather, that social policy should be geared towards allowing old people valid choices predicated upon relevant and accurate information, influenced by the state of knowledge of physical, mental and environmental factors. Even in the absence of complete knowledge to enable perfect estimation of risks, information is often available to act as an indicator of vulnerability. Wicks' (1978) study, for instance, suggests some specific indicators for hypothermia. It is important that practitioners seek appropriate information which may be available from a variety of sources – old people themselves, their carers and other professionals – in order to make the best possible estimate and assessment of risk.

5 Risk: the statistical evidence

Given the great uncertainty associated with perceptions of risk, we have attempted to address two issues. The first is the need-related characteristics of clients that contribute towards judgements of risk. The second is the effects of risk judgements on the allocation of services. These two questions have been pursued using multivariate statistical techniques.

5.1 Practitioners perceptions of risk: logit analyses

Taking 'at risk' (defined as case managers' perceptions of their elderly clients as being at risk or not prior to the recent social services intervention)[1] as the dichotomous dependent variable, multivariate logit regression was used to examine the simultaneous effects of various need-related client characteristics on judgements of risk. These characteristics consist of those used in the modelling of service inputs in Chapter 2. This allows us at a later stage to compare patterns of service delivery to those people considered to be at risk with those not thought to be at risk. A final stage of the process is the inclusion of dummy variables representing the areas in the study. This enables us to look at any differences associated with living in, and being served by particular social services areas. The analysis is carried out first for all households, then selects out those elderly people who live alone, and finally those who live with other household members, either spouses or younger families.

The results of the logit analyses are shown in Tables 7.3, 7.4 and 7.5. A note on the use of logit analysis, including the procedure for calculating the probability of being judged 'at risk' for an elderly person with particular characteristics, is included in the appendix to this chapter (pp.436-7). Variables with positive coefficients increase the probability of being considered at risk, and *vice versa*. For example, Table 7.3 suggests that an elderly person with critical interval needs and inadequate informal support is more likely to be considered 'at risk', other things being equal, and an elderly person who has recently moved house is less likely to be considered 'at risk'.

5.1.1 Explanatory need-related characteristics
The interpretation of coefficients is of course open to much debate. However, it is useful to consider whether significant coefficients reflect departmental policies, lower-level informal policies and/or the assumptive worlds of practitioners.[2]

5.1.2 Predictive power of the equations
Table 7.3 refers to all households. It shows the coefficients of independent variables which are significant in the case managers' perceptions of 'risk' both before and after the area variables have been included. Three of the independent variables cease to be significant once the area variables are included. Tables 7.4 and 7.5 are similar but refer to elderly people living alone and those living with others respectively. More variables are significant in the equation for all households than in the equations for different household compositions. The fewer significant variables, the easier it is to understand the factors taken into consideration by case managers in making judgements of risk.

The probability of being considered at risk for any client in the study is 55 per cent. That is, case managers reported 55 per cent of clients to be at risk prior to service intervention. The probability of those living alone being considered at risk is 54 per cent and for those living with others 56 per cent. The equations allow us to make correct predictions in 65 per cent, 71 per cent, and 64 per cent of cases for each of the groups. Need-related characteristics have greater predictive power for elderly people living alone. For them we can make an accurate prediction of the probability of being considered at risk for nearly three-quarters of the sample population.

5.1.3 Area effects
Area variables actually reduce the explanatory power of the equation for people living alone, but add to the predictive power of the equations for the whole population and for those living with others, increasing the percentage of correct predictions to 72 and 73. There seems to be little

variation between area in judgements about single elderly people, but considerable variation for people not living alone. This suggests differences in formal and/or informal policies towards elderly people living with carers, and towards their informal carers. Other analyses of the relationship

Table 7.3
Logit analysis predicting the likelihood of being considered 'at risk' prior to intervention: all households

Dependent variable perceived to be at risk: 0 = No   1 = Yes

Independent variables	Coefficient (excluding areas)	Coefficient (including areas)
Dependency characteristics		
Long interval needs, inadequate informal support	−0.707**	−1.030***
Short interval needs, adequate informal support	+0.813**	+0.791**
Critical interval needs, inadequate informal support	+1.347***	+1.174**
Evidence of confusion	+1.102**	+1.069**
Ability to perform self-care tasks	−0.086*	−0.068 NS
Ability to perform light housework	+0.212**	+0.182*
Urinary incontinence	−0.701***	−0.762***
Recent life events		
Health problems	−0.707**	−0.476*
Moving house	−0.075***	−1.099**
Period spent away from home	+2.022*	+1.512 NS
Poor relations with neighbours	+1.671**	+1.719**
Accident or injury to a close friend	+1.050*	+1.222*
Substitute services		
Community nursing input	+0.764***	+0.944***
Attendance at day hospital	+0.957*	+0.802 NS
Area variables		
Area 2 Inner London		+1.410**
Area 3 Outer London		+0.668 NS
Area 4 Metropolitan District		+1.175**
Area 5 Metropolitan District		+1.987***
Area 6 Metropolitan District		−0.227 NS
Area 7 English Shire		+0.533 NS
Area 8 English Shire		+0.215 NS
Area 9 English Shire		+1.265**
Area 10 Welsh County		+0.621 NS
Constant	−0.249	−1.058*
Percentage of correct predictions	65	72

Significance levels: * 0.1 > p > 0.05; ** 0.05 > p > 0.01; *** 0.01 > p; NS Not significant

N = 369. Proportion judged to be at risk = 55%

Table 7.4

Logit analysis predicting the likelihood of being considered 'at risk' prior to intervention: single person households

Dependent variable perceived to be at risk   0 = No   1 = Yes

Independent variables	Coefficient (excluding areas)	Coefficient (including areas)
Dependency characteristics		
Long interval needs, inadequate informal support	−1.305***	−1.750***
Critical interval needs, inadequate informal support	+1.352*	+0.677 NS
Evidence of confusion	+1.903**	+2.811**
Urinary incontinence	−0.834**	−0.916**
Recent life events		
Hospitalisation	−0.745*	−0.475 NS
Substitute services		
Community nursing input	+1.341***	+1.777***
Attendance at day hospital	+1.717**	+1.902**
Voluntary help	+1.417*	+1.205 NS
Area variables		
Area 2 Inner London	+0.602	NS
Area 3 Outer London	−1.946*	
Area 4 Metropolitan District	+0.006	NS
Area 5 Metropolitan District	+1.264	NS
Area 6 Metropolitan District	−1.143	NS
Area 7 English Shire	−0.264	NS
Area 8 English Shire	−1.232	NS
Area 9 English Shire	+0.644	NS
Area 10 Welsh County	+0.453	NS
Constant	+0.026	−0.015 NS
Percentage of correct predictions	71	70

Significance levels: * $0.1 > p > 0.05$; ** $0.05 > p > 0.01$; *** $0.01 > p$; NS Not significant

N = 178. Proportion judged to be at risk = 54%

between service allocations and client dependency suggest both significant mismatches between dependency and service allocation for cases where spouses or other informal carers were present in the household, even if they were not in a position to offer adequate help, and that some of the need-related characteristics of the carers seem to influence allocation (Bebbington et al., 1986; Netten, 1988).

Table 7.5

Logit analysis predicting the likelihood of being considered 'at risk' prior to intervention: those not living alone

Dependent variable perceived to be at risk: 0 = No   1 = Yes

Independent variable	Coefficient (excluding areas)	Coefficient (including areas)
Dependency characteristics		
Critical interval needs, adequate informal support	–1.198*	–1.223*
Ability to perform self-care tasks	–0.140***	–0.149***
Recent life events		
Specific illness	–0.821*	–1.323**
Health problems	–1.286***	–1.348***
Social interaction		
Number of people to turn to in times of difficulty	+0.610***	+0.902***
Area variables		
Area 2 Inner London	+2.274***	
Area 3 Outer London	+2.978***	
Area 4 Metropolitan District	+3.247***	
Area 5 Metropolitan District	+3.139***	
Area 6 Metropolitan District	+0.834	NS
Area 7 English Shire	+1.452*	
Area 8 English Shire	+1.279*	
Area 10 Welsh County	+0.907	NS
Constant	+1.706	–0.112 NS
Percentage of correct predictions	64	73

Significance levels: * $0.1 > p > 0.05$; ** $0.05 > p > 0.01$; *** $0.01 > p$; NS Not significant

N = 191. Proportion judged to be at risk = 56%

5.2 The effects of being judged 'at risk' on the allocation of services

These effects were investigated in two ways. First, the residuals from the regression equations of service allocation detailed in Chapter 3 were compared for those judged by allocators to be 'at risk' and 'not at risk.' T-tests were used to test the significance of the difference between the mean residuals for the two groups. This exercise was carried out initially for each separate service, home care, meals-on-wheels, day care and social work support, and then for the service packages as a whole. Secondly, being 'at risk' or not was entered as a dummy variable in the regression analyses of individual service allocations and service packages, thus testing

the significance of risk judgements, their likely contribution to the
explanation of variation in service allocations, and the effects of being
judged at risk on the significance levels of the need-related characteristics
The analyses of residuals are shown in Table 7.6. The 'at risk' group
on average received higher allocations of the home help and home care
services, lower allocations of meals, day care and social work support.
Taking the services overall, the 'at risk' group received significantly larger
packages of service. Differences in allocations between the two groups are
also significant for home care services to all households and social work
support to those living alone, although here this is only the case when
the area effects are included. The inclusion of the 'at risk' dummy variable
in the original regressions confirms this picture. Table 7.7 shows that it
contributes significantly to the equations for levels of provision of home

Table 7.6
Analysis of residuals: summary of the effects of
being judged 'at risk' on service allocations

Service	Household[a] structure	No. of cases 'At risk'	Not 'at risk'	Areas	Allocation to 'at risk' group	T Value	
Total package	All	168	132	Exclude	More	3.67***	
		168	132	Include	More	3.77***	
	Single	95	73	Exclude	More	1.67*	
		95	73	Include	More	1.73*	
Home care	All	149	120	Exclude	More	2.28**	
		149	120	Include	More	3.05***	
	Single	92	72	Exclude	More	0.60	NS
		92	72	Include	More	1.09	NS
Meals-on-wheels	All	75	28	Exclude	Less	−0.83	NS
		75	28	Include	Less	0.44	NS
Day care	All	39	30	Exclude	Less	−1.33	NS
		39	30	Include	Less	−0.84	NS
Social work	All	81	40	Exclude	Less	−0.50	NS
		81	40	Include	Less	−0.58	NS
	Single	41	21	Exclude	Less	−1.64	NS
		41	21	Include	Less	−2.38**	

Significance levels: * $0.1 > p > 0.05$; ** $0.05 > p > 0.01$; *** $0.01 > p$;
NS Not significant
a For home care, social work, (services provided to households rather than individuals) and service 'packages', separate analyses were carried out for all households, and those living alone.

care services, social work support to elderly people living alone and total service packages with the amount of variation explained in service allocations being increased by up to 5 per cent.

6 Summary and conclusion

This chapter has reminded us that the concept of 'risk' is important in the assumptive worlds of social services personnel, particularly of front-line workers. Any analysis of the performances of core case management tasks must therefore engage it. The contribution of this chapter has been: (i) to suggest how need-related circumstances are associated with risk judgements and so some of the associations on which to base theoretical arguments; (ii) to show the vagueness and elasticity of the concept of risk in the minds of field workers allocating services; and (iii) to show that risk judgements by front-line allocators do indeed affect service allocations.

Table 7.7
The effects of the inclusion of being judged 'at risk' in the regression analyses

Service	Household[a]	Areas	Coefficient of 'risk'		% variation explained excl. risk	% variation explained incl. risk
Total package	All	Exclude	-3.98***		33.6	37.1
		Include	-4.35***		42.3	46.0
	Single	Exclude	-1.82*		43.9	45.1
		Include	-2.31**		51.6	53.4
Home care	All	Exclude	-2.11**		38.8	39.9
		Include	-2.39**		42.4	43.8
	Single	Exclude	-0.51	NS	63.0	63.1
		Include	-0.47	NS	67.1	67.3
Meals-on-wheels	All	Exclude	0.76	NS	38.7	39.0
		Include	-0.88	NS	62.3	62.6
Day care	All	Exclude	1.37	NS	48.2	49.9
		Include	0.79	NS	57.8	58.4
Social work	All	Exclude	0.48	NS	40.3	40.5
		Include	0.66	NS	48.1	48.3
	Single	Exclude	1.80*		46.7	49.8
		Include	2.51**		59.0	64.3

Significance levels: * $0.1 > p > 0.05$; ** $0.05 > p > 0.01$; *** $0.01 > p$; NS Not significant

a For home care, social work (services provided to households rather than individuals) and service 'packages', separate analyses were carried out for all households, and those living alone.

This has been a first attempt at the analysis of a complex phenomenon. Perhaps more sophisticated analyses will demonstrate larger effects than an additional 5 per cent of service allocation explained.

Our evidence suggests an overwhelming desire of practitioners and managers to protect old people, their carers or themselves. Significantly higher levels of services are allocated to those judged to be at risk. The protection of each of these groups gives rise to dilemmas. Ensuring the physical safety of elderly people may at the same time serve to restrict their freedom and reduce their independence. Actions taken to reduce the physical burden on informal carers may increase feelings of guilt surrounding the failure to meet personal expectations of what is the proper role of a carer. Both these forms of protection illustrate the widespread problem of the trade-off between health and safety and quality of life. In protecting themselves from public criticism, practitioners and managers become 'risk averse', and may trade work satisfaction for personal and professional security.

Practitioners experience even more complex dilemmas in attempts to protect clients, carers and themselves simultaneously. The dilemmas lie in the tensions between the desire to protect vulnerable individuals and the desire to ensure individual freedom of choice, and concern to protect oneself from criticism in the event of a tragedy. All these considerations influence the practitioner's choice of appropriate action. The freedom of clients, carers and workers to determine their own needs and to take their own risks is reduced if the consequences present risks for another party. The complications of family dynamics often make it difficult to separate clients and carers in this sense. Some carers for instance may be less inclined to respect an elderly person's wishes for independence if this introduces risks to the carer or her family associated with the burden of caring, while other carers continue to shoulder the burden of responsibility and physical caring to the detriment of their own health. To fail to do so would lead to unacceptable levels of guilt and feelings of inadequacy. The study has yielded several examples of people who tried day care once, but then decided they would rather be at home with their partner or family.

The responses of social workers to these sets of conflicting interests vary according to their perceptions of the risks to which they themselves are exposed. An example of this phenomenon can be seen in the way social services departments respond to elderly people who have supportive informal carers. There is less likelihood of social services intervention when it is thought that carers are unlikely to collapse under the strain of caring or withdraw their support. Earlier interventions to support carers are likely if the situation is perceived as containing the risk that care may be withdrawn. The home help service operates largely on the basis that small amounts of service on a weekly or fortnightly basis will avoid the risk of a crisis demanding unpredictable intervention on a much larger scale.

Social work supervisors and managers modify or veto any plan of action which might cause the department to be seen as having failed to protect. This is more clearly done in child care. However, it is also present in social work practice with elderly people. As one social worker put it:

With social work, whether it's with the elderly or with children, the key thing is to cover yourself so that if there is an inquiry of any kind by a relative or a councillor or whoever, you can always say you did the maximum possible within various limitations.

Inquiries into the deaths of people known to social services departments almost invariably comment about problems of communication between agencies. Hopefully, the desire of social workers to demonstrate that they have done the 'maximum possible within various limitations' is a foundation on which could be based more sophisticated practice, including better communication and coordination with other agencies and individuals. Too often, workers now seem to take the 'easier option' of offering an available service to satisfy minimum bureaucratic criteria of responsibility and accountability, resulting inevitably in less equitable and efficient use of resources.

Notes

1 Although for many clients this was their first involvement with social services, others were receiving additional or different services as the result of a major reassessment.

2 This treatment is limited to perceptions of risk *prior* to service interventions. It has not been possible to examine perceived changes in risk following service interventions on the same basis. This is in part due to the smaller number of elderly people still living in the community six months after intervention. More importantly, many case managers changed during the six month period and in many cases there had been little or no contact with clients (and consequently little or no knowledge of changes in the clients' states of risk) for significant numbers of cases where the case manager remained the same.

8 The interface between the NHS and the SSD

1 Introduction

The interface between health and social services has been recurrently identified as a problem area in the care of elderly people. Literature on the subject, however, has tended to concentrate on the higher levels of interaction, choosing to look at joint planning or joint finance (Booth, 1981; Glennerster, Korman and Marslen-Wilson, 1983), at the macro level of decision-making and at organisational structures (Brunel Institute of Organisation and Social Studies, 1974). These levels are important, and issues relating to them are discussed in Chapter 10. Where the literature has taken the practitioner level as its main focus, it has tended to concentrate on higher status groups. Thus work on the interface between the two systems from a social services perspective has looked at doctor/social worker relations (Huntingdon, 1981). Where multidisciplinary work within a health-service perspective has extended to include social services, it has tended to concentrate on liaison with the 'social worker', ignoring the fact that trained social workers are in fact relatively little involved in the provision of care to elderly people. The really significant agency in their support is the home help service.

For this reason any adequate examination of the interface at practitioner level needs to take as its principal focus the relations between the home help and the community nursing services. It is at this point furthermore that the potential for input substitution is at its highest. This applies both between agencies and between types of personnel employed by agencies. As Chapter 11 confirms, this area of the interface has been the focus of much innovatory activity. Various forms of specialist and augmented home care services have developed in an attempt to resolve the recurring service discontinuities and irrationalities of provision, particularly in relation to personal care.

The problems of the interface between the two systems, however, do not simply arise in relation to organisational structures, though these are important. The area of personal care itself raises issues that derive from the character and definition of the tasks involved. Recent literature on health and social services has often been preoccupied with organisational features and with formal structures to the detriment of cognitive and ideological structures. This has at times led to a neglect of some of the important background definitions of the situation; and it is precisely the failure within departments to understand and deal with such cultural features that can lie behind failures in policy implementation. The fuller understanding of these aspects is therefore of central importance to the success of managerial initiatives.

The material presented here is drawn from the analysis of interviews undertaken with community nurse managers, home help organisers, and personnel at other levels of the social services and health authorities across the areas. Community nurse managers were interviewed partly because they are the first-tier managers, able to discuss policy initiatives while still in contact with the realities of practice on the ground, and partly because their level is broadly equivalent to home help organisers, although in practice such equivalence across the two systems do not exist. (In many ways, the home help organisers work more closely with the district nursing sisters.) The interviews, which were qualitative, were structured around a number of discrete topics, one of which was the boundary of tasks between the two services.

The structure of the chapter is as follows. Section 1 gives an account of the boundary of tasks as it lies between the district nursing and home help services in ten local authority areas. It looks at where the boundary lies, and how it is defined. As we shall see, the central issue here is that of personal care, the management of the body. Section 2 develops an argument which draws on a larger tradition of analysis deriving from an anthropological perspective that seeks to interpret the body as a social phenomenon, looking at its social construction and the meanings that are attached to it. In Section 3, insights derived from this tradition are used to comment on the issue of personal care within social services explaining features of the current situation and of institutional attempts to transcend some of these difficulties.

2 The boundary of tasks: the district nursing side

Looking first at the district nursing side, it is clear that from the perspective of the nurse-managers tasks fell into three broad categories. First there were those of an unambiguously medical character, requiring a trained nurse. No detailed questions were asked about these in the interview. Second, and in contrast, there were tasks of a clearly non-nursing type, but which were still relevant to the wider situation. Here questions were asked about making meals, doing shopping, sitting with a patient while a carer popped to the shops, and contacting DHSS about financial or benefit problems – all known informally to exist. On the first three, answers emerged across the areas relatively consistently. Nurses would pop to the shops if a patient had no food in the house, and they would similarly make a snack, certainly a cup of tea as part of making a patient comfortable; but neither were really nursing tasks and should only be done on a one-off basis. In some areas, nurses had traditionally done some shopping but only in their own time, and this was contrary to current ideas of practice. The sitting question evoked a very definite no, with strongly expressed remarks about the pressures of time. There was greater variety over the benefit/finance question. Some respondents regarded contacting DHSS as quite appropriate, something nurses were trained and encouraged to do, though a majority felt that while it was quite appropriate to recognise and act on such a need, this should be done by referring to social services or, more often, to a health visitor.

The third group related to intermediate tasks: tasks that are nursing tasks in the context of other medical problems, but that standing alone have a more ambivalent status. Helping to get the patient up and dressed and, above all, bathing are the classic examples, and were time and time again referred to by both the district nurse and the home help respondents as the *grey areas*. Such tasks are of course fully nursing tasks in the classically defining locus of the hospital. Performed within the patient's own home, however, they take on a slightly different character. This is something to which we shall return.

The auxiliary grade is of course employed largely to do such tasks as bathing and dressing, but the existence of auxiliaries does not necessarily ensue the availability of such support to frail elderly people. It is important to understand the effects of work patterns. Community nursing has increasingly developed an internal hierarchy. Though there are local differences, this broadly consists of sisters who carry the caseload, do assessments and direct the work of the team; enrolled nurses who do not have case responsibilities but perform similar nursing duties to the sisters; and auxiliaries, the untrained grade who do tasks such as baths, though in some areas also perform simple nursing duties. The emergence of such a hierarchy and the provision of an auxiliary grade is a development of the last ten years (DHSS, 1986). This hierarchy has not, however, produced a full corresponding hierarchy of tasks. Bathing and dressing and the other more diffuse care tasks are still widely undertaken by trained nurses, particularly in the context of other medical tasks. Thus although Dunnell and Dobb's analysis of the work patterns of nurses in the community found that some four-fifths of the time of auxiliaries were spent on routine nursing care, personal care and the supervision of the patient, up to a third of trained nurses' time was similarly spent (Dunnell and Dobbs, 1982). This shared pattern of activity is further reinforced by the common work patterns, whereby a full sister must substitute once a month for any regular auxiliary visit. This pattern of monitoring and reassessment clearly draws provision back towards the medical focus.

What this means essentially is that despite the existence of the auxiliary grade and the general agreement that bathing and washing are appropriate district nursing tasks, there is in fact no overall provision for these needs. A personal care or bathing service as such does not exist. Any use by social services personnel or others of the term 'bath nurse' or 'bathing auxiliary' produced distinctly shirty answers from the nurse managers, who felt the assumptions in such terminology were inappropriate.

It is in this area of personal care furthermore that pressure of resources is being felt. Under severe financial constraint, one health authority in the sample had withdrawn completely from 'social baths'. In another, bathing was limited to patients who also had medical needs. Two other authorities restricted them very closely, and questions in one of these authorities were answered – almost parried – in terms of encouraging relatives to do their bit, and fears of ending up bathing half the town. Two more respondents – both in inner London – believed that the growing pressure from acute discharges inevitably threatened their capacity to continue social baths.

2.1 The structure of policy: the district nursing side

Three points need to be made here concerning the way policy is structured from the nursing point of view. First, when talking about the definition of the boundaries, it is important not to make the district nursing response appear clearer than it is in fact. The 'rules' concerning the boundary of provision are far from codified. Rather they are *ad hoc*, implicit and fragmented. It was hard in the interviews either to elicit a policy rule or to establish guidelines of practice. Pursuing exactly what was involved in a 'social bath' or when such would be offered did not result in clear information. Particularly when dealing with categories of patients whose needs are only marginally medical, the situation is one of considerable leeway and of individual discretion, in which the current level of an individual sister's caseload, rather than any *explicit* policy, was clearly a central defining factor.

Furthermore, it was difficult to get district nurse respondents to talk about what they do or do not provide on the margins of need. They recognise unmet need, but shy away from any clear definition. For example one respondent when pressed as to what nurses would or would not do for a patient became distressed and could only respond by saying:

If a patient *needs* something then we would ... I mean I don't know, I can't really explain it. We are trained to do anything that somebody needs.

This holistic response to the patient's needs was repeated in a number of interviews, and clearly touched a chord in nursing values. In a parallel way, a direct question asked in the interviews with community nurse managers concerning priorities tended to be unproductive, with respondents answering either very narrowly in terms of insulin injections, or at the other end rejecting the concept altogether or replying with statements like: 'we like to think that all our patients have priority'.

However, decisions about priorities and about appropriate tasks clearly are made. They are, however, negotiated on a model that is characteristic within the health sector, whereby overall levels of provision are set, leaving the subsequent allocation decisions to be dispersed into a series of professionally defined judgements about individual patients. They are thus defined not so much by policy rules as by professionally bounded decisions. This structure of decision-making around professional discretion at the individual level raises problems for the management of the boundary between the two services, for as we shall see that of social services is constructed rather differently.

Lastly in this area of the definition of boundaries, the concept of 'training' is central. Personal care tasks were frequently described as not requiring a qualified district nurse: 'a doubly qualified, highly skilled person'. One nurse manager commented: 'It is difficult because you will always get staff that'll say: I have not trained to do that. Full stop.' It is clear that this concept of training is to some degree at odds with holistic nursing values. It is important here, however, to distinguish between assessment and provision. It is clear that although district nurses increasingly employ a holistic language that recognises the wider social, material and emotional context of the patient and that is enshrined in the Nursing Process and the post-1974 restructuring of the district nursing training, it is about holistic *assessment* rather than holistic *provision*. Thus at the same time as there has been increased involvement and awareness by district nurses of the social needs and contexts of their patients, there has been increased specialisation and division of labour both within the district nursing service and in relation to other social care agencies.

2.2 *The nature of decision-making: the home help side*

Turning now to the home help side, it is clear that the rules concerning the boundaries are constructed in a very different way and are contained within a different form of decision-making. In relation to home help rules, these can be seen as existing at three levels. First there is explicit policy, set down in procedures manuals and operational statements. This formal policy level largely consists of either very general accounts of the purpose of the service or very specific injunctions forbidding certain things. Such prohibitions often result from an unfortunate incident. These rules are essentially protective rather than purposive in character, designed to prevent scandals rather than achieve outcomes. The second level consists of implicit policy rules, created and sustained in this case mainly by the home help organisers. These are defined operationally in judgements about services, but are rarely codified. They exist as part of the culture of the office, absorbed and shared by individuals as part of their work practices.

Finally there are the judgements of front-line service providers, in this case the home helps. These draw on the official accounts of the job, but are also influenced by the more general social and cultural definitions that home helps bring to the understanding of their jobs. The importance of these will become apparent when we look at the content of personal care tasks.

2.3 The boundary of tasks: the home help side

Turning now to the actual rules, it was clear from the interviews that most of the explicit regulation concerning the definition of home help tasks related less to such issues as personal care than to employment considerations of the health and safety at work variety – not doing high dusting – or to activities like outdoor work on the house or garden, which are not conceived of as part of the home help role, structured as it is around female tasks.

Related to these areas of employment terms and legal responsibilities was the question of medication. Should home helps be involved in giving medication? On both the home help and district nurse sides the answers were very varied, from the emphatically not, to the positively approving. Part of the difficulty is that giving medication has such variable meanings from simply passing a glass of water to the client, to taking responsibility for the timing and accuracy of doses; and as a result a number of respondents on both the district nursing and the home help side made clear qualifications as to levels of appropriate involvement. Those district nurses that favoured home help involvement tended to cite the model of the caring relative, and regard the home help as a parallel untrained lay figure, and this perception was extended beyond the provision of medicine to include other tasks in the grey area of home nursing. From the home help side, however, this generalised concept of the lay person was less convincing and the boundary between domestic and professional tasks not obvious. As one home help organiser commented: 'what constitutes washing that you could expect anyone, a caring relative, to do, and what constitutes washing you need a professional to do is very difficult'.

The emphasis on training is an essentially *nursing* point of view, and it leaves aside factors that are much more to the fore in local authority concerns – employment terms, legal responsibilities and consequences. It provides one of the examples of how the categories deriving from the different ideologies cut up the world in different ways: for the nurses the essential contrast is between trained and untrained, with the untrained category undifferentiated; whereas for social services, it is as much between formally and informally undertaken tasks. (This incidentally is an area similarly misunderstood by carers who are often confused and resentful when home helps are forbidden to do tasks that carers have to undertake on a regular basis.) More significant than these questions of medication and gardening were the issues around the boundaries in relation to personal care. Questions were asked in the interviews about dressing, bathing, washing, emptying commodes and clearing up after incontinence: what sorts of staff did and should perform these tasks.

Although two local authorities had consciously decided to restructure the mainstream home help service as home care, with the clear acceptance of responsibility for personal care, this was at the time a minority approach. A more common response, found in four out of the ten authorities, was the development of separate elite services. These frequently based their service around a composite worker, though sometimes employing joint assessment. Though the provision of personal care was often part of the package, the origins of many schemes lay in the resolution of other service difficulties, notably those relating to hospital discharge, and this was frequently reflected in their origin in joint finance monies. These services were often on a small scale, taking only few clients, and tended to become quickly silted up. Their contribution to the *overall* situation was therefore limited, though they were often of considerable political importance internally. Some of these innovative services are discussed in Chapter 11.

Returning to the predominant model, that of the mainstream service, policy relating to personal care, despite its importance, tended to remain inchoate, and was either deliberately left vague, or defined by policy rules that were widely evaded. Thus one respondent when asked what her authority's policy in relation to personal care was, replied that the policy was: 'you don't get involved', but added that in practice people of course did. 'Turning a blind eye', was how two other respondents described it. Data from the main questionnaires, where clients were asked what home helps did for them, showed that personal care tasks were in practice undertaken in at least nine out of the ten authorities.

The situation at the employment level of home helps appeared to be very mixed, with a high degree of discretion being exercised by staff. Thus taking the case of bathing – the task most often the focus of inter-agency dispute – although none of the local authorities explicitly required home helps to do baths, and many explicitly forbade them, it was clear that many home helps did assist clients in this way. This was described as occuring in seven out of the ten authorities.

This picture was confirmed from the district nursing side, where managers reported that home helps did give baths 'out of the kindness of their hearts', although they were strictly forbidden to. Comments were also made on the nursing side, though in rather less favourable terms, in relation to willingness of home helps to empty commodes or clean up after incontinence. Once again the aspect of individual discretion was emphasised. Thus in an inner London area, according to the nurse manager, home helps 'would not see that [emptying a commode] as their job, though there might be individuals who would.' Similarly another respondent commented on cleaning up after incontinence: 'it just depends entirely on the home help.' In another area the perception was one of greater willingness, but again at the level of individual discretion:

You get occasionally individuals [who do not], but it is not because of social services, its because of individuals.

The aspect of discretion clearly related not only to the attitude of the *particular* home help, but of the particular home help in response to a *particular* client. Where personal care was mentioned, it was frequently accompanied by comments about there having been built up closer relations between the helper and the client. It was clear that the defining feature was that these were voluntaristic relationships, structured around choice, personality and friendship, rather than around professionally defined roles.

Some authorities did now recruit on the basis that personal care was an integral part of the definition of the job, but the majority, while expressing a wish to 'welcome' staff willing to undertake these tasks, did not explicitly recruit on that basis. One authority clearly anticipated union resistance to any move in that direction, and a number of organisers were aware that they had on their books home helps who had joined on a different employment basis:

In practice ... some of the home helps who've been with us a long time who are used to doing cleaning on a weekly basis have found it quite difficult to adapt to a new way of thinking. As they say to us – which I think is quite fair – 'I chose to do the home help job when it was a different one to the one it is now'.

2.4 The interface

Turning now to the negotiation of the interface between the two systems, it was clear that in many localities personal care issues had been a source of friction and sometimes ill-feeling: 'We get friction from time to time, I mean we have to be honest about this.' Even in an area where there was a 'close relationship' and where home help organisers 'got on very well' with community nurses, bathing was still an area that was: 'A bit sort of precarious ... a grey area which hasn't yet been sorted out.'

Two areas had attempted to tackle the problem directly; and it did appear in general that relations were better where there was some intermediate service, but in the majority of cases the situation remained vague. There was as a result a marked lack of knowledge as to the other side's exact rules and practices, with some contradictory statements being made as to what the other side did or did not provide. These uncertainties were compounded by the differing role and character of policy in the two systems.

It was not the case furthermore that the relationship between the two systems, either as a result of an explicit policy or through the pragmatic developments of practice, was in any sense a homoeostatic one. Thus there was in the majority of areas little evidence that either side structured its services in close response to the availability of the other. In two areas, indeed, both the home help and district nursing services had vacated the middle ground of personal care. No assumptions about any 'necessary' existence of such coverage should be made.

3 Personal care and the structuring of instinctual life

So far we have looked at personal care tasks in terms of the boundaries between agencies, but as important is the actual character of the tasks performed.

Personal care is characterised by *touching, nakedness, contact with excreta* – areas all of which bear strong elements of taboo, and that are widely employed to mark the boundaries between states of privacy, intimacy and the public realm. As such, they are part of the wider social process of the management of the body. Disability disrupts that management in ways that threaten social identity. Attempts by social services and other helping agencies to overcome such disabilities take place within the context of a wider set of cultural assumptions and meanings. It is necessary to understand these, for it is the problems of the negotiation of these that underlies many of the difficulties that social services departments, in particular, face in this area.

It is useful here to draw on a tradition of analysis familiar in anthropology that derives from the work of Marcel Mauss (1935). Mauss is concerned to display how bodily behaviour is culturally learnt behaviour. It belongs therefore within the wider expressive system. Later developments of the approach are found in the work of Douglas (1973, 1975). Polhemus and others provide a review of the tradition (Polhemus, 1978; Benthall and Polhemus, 1975) and Turner develops its role within sociology (1984). The work of Foucoult has been particularly influential in this area, as had that of the earlier and pioneering Norbert Elias (1978).

Elias is concerned to explore the social structuring of instinctual life. In condensed form, his argument centres on the imposition and gradual internalisation over the early modern and modern period of rules on modesty, on the retreat from the directly bodily, on the shift in what he terms the shame frontier, and the growth in the sphere of the private. Elias traces these developments in the West through changing rules and assumptions across a series of activities. These include eating and table manners, sleeping arrangements, access to nakedness and touching, and the treatment of bodily effluvia. Across these spheres he traces the growing imposition of social restraint on physiological expression, whereby individuals are increasingly separated and defined vis-à-vis each other. As a product of this separation, areas like touching, nakedness, shared sleeping are given a narrower more exclusively erotic definition. Barrington Moore in his cross-cultural study based on a review of anthropological literature similarly roots developments of autonomy and privacy in bodily categories around excreta and sexuality (Moore, 1984).

These changes are according to Elias internalised at a deep level, so that rules that have in the past had to be spelt out in conduct books are now so much part of the mental structures of modern society as to be effectively invisible. They are part of the assumed pattern of 'natural' behaviour, and thus exist at a level below conscious discourse. Elias, by tracing the evolution of such behaviour over time, is able to demonstrate how shifts in the definitions of behaviour occurred prior to the hygiene explanations that are frequently employed to justify them. Such explanations are, as it were, overdetermined. What we are faced with when looking at the changes concerning, for example, shared eating – the growth in separate utensils, the abandonment of eating with the hands – or the rules concerning spitting or excreta, are not medical rules based on hygiene categories, but social rules concerned with intimacy, autonomy, solidarity, and the social expression of these. This applies just as profoundly to the tasks of personal care.

Personal care tasks are intimately connected with the bodily expression of these values of privacy, autonomy and adulthood. Personal care tasks can be defined as those tasks that an adult would normally perform for him or herself without assistance. They are bodily tasks, and are in general performed privately. Loss of autonomy in these areas is frequently experienced as an erosion of adulthood. This occurs not only in the minds of individuals, but more widely in the social context, and can result in elderly people being drawn into models of interaction that deny their adulthood and effectively reconstruct them as infants. The degree to which conscious good practice within care provision has to attempt to reverse these category changes testifies to the power of the social symbolism.

Home help work of the traditional non-personal care type encompasses tasks – housework, shopping, meal preparation – that in ordinary social life are freely done for others. These can be performed either by means of the formal economy through the division of labour, purchased meals, paid-for laundry, or through the informal sector, usually through the sexual division of labour within the family. In either case, there is a prior model for their public, social production. They are tasks that can be relatively straightforwardly performed, and their transfer to a public service agency raises few problems. But the tasks of personal care are different, and models derived from ordinary social life – which is the basis for the traditional home help role – provide only uncertain means for the negotiation of these boundaries.

It is for this reason that personal care is so often conceived of as nursing activity, despite the fact that the skills required are not in any real sense medical. What the medical model offers here is the means for the negotiation of these boundaries through the restructuring of the *social body* into the *medical body*. This is achieved in ways that enable medicine to renegotiate the rules of intimacy and to achieve a form of neutrality. This renegotiation is achieved symbolically through the traditional means of technical language, of starched uniforms, and of the hygiene rules and explanations which we have already noted operating so powerfully in this field.

This background in turn explains some of the features found in the social services situation.

4 Personal care within the local authority setting

In social service departments, there is a relative lack of debate or formalisation around the subject of personal care, despite the fact that it is a key element in the development of services for frail elderly people. Indeed community care can be regarded as meaning precisely this – the development of social care models within the community for what was previously medicalised and institutionalised. Developed discussion of these themes is, however, rare either at authority level or in research or practice literatures. Dexter and Herbert, for example, in their book on the home help service (1983) note briefly the existence of uncertainty over the appropriateness of personal care tasks, but fail to discuss the character of the problem. Personal care relates to areas of experience that have been bleached out of formal managerial discourse. It fits more easily into the informal sub-worlds of joking and of childhood. It belongs to the female world that men attempt to transcend, and it fits with unease therefore into spheres of discourse dominated by such approaches (Miller, 1976). Ungerson (1981) had developed a parallel theme in relation to gender patterning of such tasks in the context of informal care.

This also explains the aspects of discretion and choice noted earlier. The rules are not codified or spelt out and certainly not insisted upon because the area is an awkward one, beyond the normal social definitions. Because there is no enabling ideological structure like that of the medical model in relation to district nursing, home helps, where they do give personal care fall back onto personal relationships, on particularistic rather than role-specific aspects. This underlies the recurrent emphasis on the personal relations built up between the home help and the client.

Lastly there is the aspect of venue. The fact that these are tasks performed in the client's own home is central to their interpretation. We have already noted how personal care tasks are fully nursing tasks when performed in the classically defining locus of the hospital. And this is not just a product of dependency, but relates to the ways in which hospitals are total environments. Total environments deny the existence of boundaries of autonomy, privacy and adulthood. Of course, good practice emphasises the importance of allowing patients or residents such areas, but it does so essentially against the grain. These are not features residing inherently within the situation, they are not part of its natural social logic; in so far as they exist, it is by conscious construction. This in part explains why personal care is much less of an issue within Part 3 homes than within the home help service. In the Part 3 context, which contains aspects of the total environment, the problems are more ones of resource levels than of social roles. By contrast, personal care within the client's own home involves difficulties that are absent within the total environment. Ironically, it is the resources and power that reside in such territorial autonomy, its capacity to underwrite independence and continued authenticity, that can prevent individuals being cared for in ways that would enable that independence to continue.

9 Inter-agency planning and services

1 Introduction

The boundary between health and social care has proved difficult both to draw and to move for all three priority groups. The perception of a continuing reliance on hospital provision and of underdevelopment of community-based alternatives has led to a continuing search for countervailing policy levers. The creation of the joint planning mandate, the introduction of joint finance and of the Care in the Community initiative are successive examples of centrally sponsored attempts to grapple with this continuing local problem. In many ways services for the large and diffuse elderly client group fall uneasily into this joint planning framework. Thus the pace of change in services for elderly people is much slower than in services for those with mental handicaps where there are now projected hospital closures, new models of community-based provision and the recruitment and socialisation of cadres of staff equipped with a distinctive normalisation ideology. Few such changes are apparent in services for the elderly, where there have been for the most part only incremental adjustments to service systems and continuing difficulty in achieving well-established objectives, such as increasing the proportion of geriatric beds on district general hospital sites or introducing personal care roles within social care agencies.

1.1 No lead agency

Part of the reason for the slow pace of development lies in the nature of interorganisational exchange which entails uncertainty about how the costs of service development will fall. Development imposes substantial costs on an organisation in terms of initial investment, planning time, role renegotiation, changes to external boundaries and uncertain returns. It could be argued that the recurrent search for 'joint' provision is a chimera, and to avoid underinvestment in development, the costs and benefits of this process need to be internalised so that the organisation which undertakes the initial costs of development should expect to accrue any benefits. The perceptions of agency responsibility and hence organisational cost/benefit expectations vary significantly between the three priority groups. For both mental health care groups, lead agency models are emerging which will substantially internalise development costs and benefits with SSDs taking on a lead agency role with mentally handicapped people (House of Commons Select Committee on Social Services, 1985; Griffiths,

1988) and the NHS retaining a similar status with those with a mental illness. Services for the elderly client group remain scattered between the two agencies and unamenable to such structural reorganisation. While the NHS may respond to rising demand by offloading long-term care responsibilities in the grey area where medical and social care meet, it will retain core interest in a client group which accounts for a major component of bed admissions throughout the acute sector as well as on geriatric wards. No single agency is thus likely to win lead agency status, with consequent responsibility for the development of a 'trade and industry policy' for the client group (Davies, 1986a).

Thus responsibility will remain divided between the two agencies and such development as does occur will be based on interorganisational exchange. Attempts to get two agencies with different interests, ideologies and organisational shapes to work together are bound to run into continuing difficulties. The employment of powerless lateral coordinating bodies or 'reticulists' (Friend, Power and Yewlett, 1974) as an alternative to joint planning is likely to run into difficulties as mainstream managerial and professional hierarchies reassert control when conflict arises.

1.2 An incentives-led control strategy

A second difficulty in establishing effective joint planning lies in the nature of the incentive-led control strategy adopted by the centre (Etzioni, 1961). Some of the American Great Society social policy programmes revealed severe weaknesses in federal supervision of grants and ability to secure compliance at local level (Cohen, McCann, Murphy and van Geer, 1973). Similar issues arise in the joint finance programme where the centre recognised that social care agencies were unlikely to agree to transfer responsibility from health care agencies in the absence of compensation, but has little power to monitor or direct the local spend. The design of appropriate incentives is thus fraught with difficulty as a control device as the incentives offered may be insufficient to alter behaviour, or so excessive as to erode the cost advantages of input substitution.

The tapering effects of joint finance schemes represent a powerful disincentive to local authorities, especially where they are faced by rate-capping. The more generous dowry arrangements introduced to support long-stay hospital patients without a time limit apply to mental health care groups more than to the elderly. Regional incentives (such as capital top slicing, revenue funding formulae and bridging funds) are also skewed towards the mentally handicapped (West Midlands Regional Health Authority, 1984).

Therefore it is difficult to ensure compliance at local level and that the joint finance spend is 'legitimate'. Criticism has come from the House of Commons Public Accounts Committee (1983) which concluded that the NHS had often played a reactive role in the joint finance process with little consideration of objectives, monitoring or evaluation. The Committee argued that 100 per cent long-term grants could badly distort service development:

> The dangers are those of undermining the incentive towards efficiency in the specially assisted schemes and of distorting local priorities in favour of those schemes as compared with others which might be more cost-effective but would mean a greater cost for local ratepayers.

The extent to which social care agencies are able to dominate the process of exchange and win such transfers of resources depends on the attitude of the health service bargainers which appears since 1983 to have become more directive.

Evidence which could shed light on the nature of joint planning and of joint finance is taken from structured interviews undertaken with senior SSD and NHS planners in ten different areas. Section 2 considers the issue of interorganisational exchange and the dynamics of joint planning. In Section 3, obstacles to joint planning for elderly people are analysed in greater detail. Different experiences of joint planning are described in Section 4.

2 Inter-organisational exchange and joint planning

2.1 Inter-organisational exchange

Joint planning represents a special case of interorganisational exchange which has long-term consequences and commitments. Such exchange relationships are often seen within a power-dependence framework, with the dependence of an organisation defined as proportional to its need for the resource controlled by the other agency and inversely proportional to the availability of the resource elsewhere. At this macro level, there appears at first glance to be a power imbalance in favour of the NHS: the SSD will find it more difficult to secure substitutes for NHS services than the NHS to find substitutes for SSD services.

Such a power imbalance has repercussions for the choice between strategies which can be adopted to manage the process of exchange:
- An *authoritative* strategy in which the dominant agency dictates the terms of the exchange relationship (Hasenfeld, 1983). For such a strategy to succeed, the leading agency must be in such a strong position that the subordinate agencies are unable to withdraw from the exchange relationship. Such a strategy seems unlikely as an aggressive NHS attitude in joint planning negotiations could well result in an SSD withdrawal which would harm NHS interests.
- A *complementary strategy* where different organisations agree responsibility for defined sets of functions and avoid the uncertainty associated with

blurring the boundaries between services. Such complementary provision helps to establish a clear division of inter-agency labour and reduce uncertainty, while providing linkage and referral channels between agencies. Contracting out of schemes to the voluntary sector (for example, Age Concern) is another example of such an approach. Agreeing such complementary provision represents a minimal but possibly widespread approach to joint planning.

- A strategy of *coalition* (Hasenfeld, 1983) where agencies pool resources to create joint ventures. Coalition-based strategies arise where the coalition is much more powerful than the sum of its parts, where the interests of agency members are compatible in the long-term, and where there is a high probability of payoff to each member of the coalition. It is unlikely that these conditions apply to many joint planning exercises where agencies are likely to resent loss of autonomy, the diversion of investment from single agency services, and the bargaining and communication costs required to establish joint services.
- A non-strategy of *passive hostility* where each agency attempts to minimise long-run involvement while preserving lip-service to the concept of joint planning and maximising short-run individual agency gains.

This typology makes it possible to map interorganisational responses at a macro level. But the nature of joint planning for elderly people is also influenced by the distinctive nature of the client group and it is to this topic that we now turn.

2.2 Joint planning and elderly people

The drive for increased collaboration in the care of elderly people reflects two special arguments. The first is based on input substitution, with social care seen as substituting for health care at cheaper cost to the public purse. This retrenchment argument is decreasingly echoed in the mental health field (House of Commons Select Committee on Social Services, 1985) where community care is increasingly seen as requiring real growth in resources. Services for elderly people have been characterised by a longstanding concern with reducing long-term hospital geriatric care, increasing throughput in geriatric wards and reducing so-called 'bed-blocking' (prolonged hospitalisation unrelated to medical needs) through securing access to alternative long-stay care facilities. Estimates of the degree of bed-blocking vary from one locality to another. Coid and Crome (1986) found that about 10 per cent of acute beds were occupied by elderly bed-blockers, often unable to secure alternative long-term care arrangements. This input substitution argument has formed the kernel of attempts to develop innovatory community-based services: Tinker (1984) thus drew attention to the considerable costs involved in unnecessary stays in hospital and the cost advantages of community-based innovations.

The knock-on effects of faster discharge policies in the hospital sector on social care as well as primary care services are substantial. Thus DHSS (1985b) indicates that the number of average beds available daily fell from 403,500 in 1973 to 343,000 in 1983, with falling average lengths of stay in such key specialties as general medicine and surgery. Despite increases in the elderly population, the number of geriatric beds fell marginally throughout this period, with a consequent reduction in the average length of stay from 101.5 days to 57.1 days between 1973 and 1983.

The second distinctive argument is based on the multifaceted needs of many elderly people which are often unspecific but take the form of dependency syndromes, involving social, psychiatric and physical components. The development of affective psychiatric disorder late in life can be linked to physical disorder (Bergmann, 1982) as well as to such social factors as bereavement or social isolation. As SSDs adopt policies aimed at maintaining more dependent elderly people at home, so it becomes even more difficult to draw the boundary between medical and social care. Davies and Challis (1986) describe an SSD-based community care project designed to maintain in the community elderly people who would otherwise have been eligible for Part 3 accommodation. Nearly all cases exhibited multiple pathology. Risk of falling was common. As Bergmann (1973) argues, falls should be seen as the culmination of increasing difficulty in coping at home, self-neglect, unsteadiness and lack of a support network. Over one-third of cases suffered from incontinence of urine and 7 per cent from incontinence of faeces, levels which required health services input. The experimental group also experienced substantial levels of both affective and organic psychiatric disorder. The management of dementia requires a mix of techniques derived from psychology (reality orientation) as well as social care-based inputs. Not only may considerable levels of 'tending' care be necessary for dementing elderly people, especially those living on their own, but Bergmann, Foster, Justice and Matthews (1976) found that families looking after dementing elderly people often required planned support through advice from social workers and the provision of relief care.

These arguments for collaboration are based on a macro 'governmental' perspective. At a lower agency level, questions of self-interest dominate attempts to engage in joint planning, and agency and 'governmental' interests frequently diverge. This interorganisational game can be defined as a positive, zero or negative sum. Negative sum games are likely to lead to withdrawal and breakdown of the process of interorganisational exchange. Within zero sum games, the joint planning process will be dominated by attempts to shunt costs between agencies or budgets. It is only when joint planning is defined as positive sum that a substantial move towards joint models of provision is likely.

3 Obstacles to joint planning

However, there are reasons for supposing that the interorganisational game will rarely be defined as positive sum.

3.1 Different problem definitions

The policy problem is defined rather differently by the two sides. This is not to say that there is a straightforward conflict of interest, but rather a mixture of conflictual, compensatory and cooperative elements which may be resolved differently according to local balances of forces. Let us consider the likely problem definitions of each side.

3.1.1 The health service

Specialist services for elderly people are seen as part of a wider priority group problem, complicated by the scattering of elderly patients throughout the acute sector (in such settings as ophthalmology and orthopaedics) as well as geriatric wards. Hospital inpatient enquiry figures (DHSS, 1985a) indicate that some two-thirds of the average beds used daily in the non-psychiatric sector are now occupied by people over 65. Within the psychiatric sector, the percentage of elderly admissions rose from 20 per cent in 1973 to 31 per cent in 1983 (DHSS, 1985b). Elderly patients with organic mental illnesses are cared for inadequately in standard community care models, instead often requiring the development of new forms of long-term residential care. So a redistribution of resources from the acute sector to priority group services may take as much as it gives for elderly patients.

Priority group policies as a whole are characterised by attempts to transfer responsibility to community-based agencies, including SSDs. The elderly care group fits with greater difficulty into this policy framework than services for mentally ill or handicapped people and are hence often 'left until last' in planning terms. By contrast, services for mentally handicapped people are smaller-scale, do not often utilise acute medical inputs, respond to relatively stable patterns of need, and have sustainable resource implications where there are moves to a higher unit cost, community-based mode of provision.

In terms of priorities between the three client groups, NHS interest is now concentrated on the projected rundown and closure of large mental handicap and illness hospitals. Over the last five years, services for elderly people have slipped in priority in comparison with services for the mental health groups in many districts. Substantial top slicing has created reserved regionally-based funds for mental handicap services (West Midlands Regional Health Authority, 1984) which have further accelerated the pace of development. The secondary status of joint care planning for elderly people could result in an NHS-led attempt to skew resources away from elderly groups to mental health care groups, flushing out the differences in priorities between the two sides. Reflecting national concerns, the NHS has an increased interest in monitoring the joint finance spend and districts seem increasingly reluctant to accept bids which could have been funded through the SSD base budget. In some inner city districts, the development of priority group services awaits the rationalisation of the acute sector which remains the primary focus of interest.

The centrepiece of policy for elderly people at district level often is securing a greater district general hospital presence for geriatric services (in the face of resistance from the acute sector) as a means of achieving increased throughput. DHSS normative guidelines have now been withdrawn and regional targets are often less elaborate for services for elderly groups than for services for people with a mental handicap; confined to increasing the proportion of geriatric beds in district general hospitals (for example to 30 per cent of all geriatric beds). Regional policy in Trent, for example, is to provide a minimum of three geriatric beds per 1000 population on district general hospital sites (Trent Regional Health Authority, 1984). Expansion of community nursing staff and of day hospital places is an important area where regional normative guidance may be given.

Such hospital-based moves towards quicker discharges and fewer long-term geriatric beds have repercussions for a range of community-based services: private and public sheltered housing, the private and voluntary residential care sectors, and the social security budget as well as social care and primary health care services. Given this interest in a wide range of possible substitute services, districts are often anxious to widen joint care planning team (JCPT) membership to include housing, education and voluntary organisations as well as SSD representatives. Issues of particular concern in the NHS/SSD interface include the allocation between the agencies of personal care tasks and the level of dependency which can be managed in Part 3 accommodation.

3.1.2 The social services department

Elderly people are seen as essentially problematic because of their role as major resource consumers, and hence are given higher priority by managers than by professionals who have historically retained a child care orientation. Elderly client groups often come higher up the SSD planning agenda than mental health care groups which are much less significant in terms of referral numbers to the agency. SSDs are particularly unsure about their role with people with a mental illness. Unlike the NHS, however, there is no nationally validated planning system, and so policy-making is less explicit. Normative targets for service provision are rarely utilised and policy aims often remain at a global level. Nevertheless there have been general moves away from further expansion of Part 3 residential accommodation typical of the pre-1976 period of expansion, when the priority was the replacement of antiquated plant. A contraction in the number of Part 3 places relative to a growing 75-plus population has a number of consequences for social care agencies: greater utilisation of the private and voluntary residential sector as substitute forms of residential care, investment in higher residential care staffing levels to cope with rising levels of long-term dependency, and the construction of more personal care roles within the home help service.

In relation to the NHS, SSDs are likely to have a number of objectives. They will be anxious to limit the transfer of responsibility following from a rundown in the long-term bed stock, or at least to negotiate appropriate compensation for additional functions undertaken. The agreeing of post-discharge procedures and the introduction of short-term post-discharge services assumes importance given the achievement of faster throughput on the NHS side. In response to lower growth rates in the base budget, SSD objectives frequently include securing external funds (such as joint finance) for quantitative and (more rarely) qualitative development of community services. Such innovatory schemes are argued to be appropriate not only for post-hospital discharge but also to prevent admission to hospital, although the health side wish to see the development of firmer targeting criteria. However, there are benefits to be maximised through joint planning with the NHS as well as costs to be minimised. At least in districts which are gaining under RAWP, the SSD will want to improve access not only to expanding district general hospital sites but also enhanced primary care services. In loser districts, on the other hand, relations can be soured by an accelerated programme of hospital closures and moves to a more directive health management style which accords less priority to consultation procedures, or by the inability of the health side to commit any new money. Thus one SSD respondent in an Inner London area where health districts were major losers commented:

The health authorities are under such tremendous pressure not only to save a lot but to save it fast. They're subject to such pressures from the region and so on, that we're constantly faced with astonishing turnabouts.

Where community services are expanding, SSDs may want to negotiate additional nursing inputs to increasingly dependent Part 3 residents or improve access to community psychiatric nurses to help maintain dementing elderly people in the community, and to improve relations between the community nursing and home help services. On the other hand, given a traditional cultural fear of 'medical domination', SSDs may also tread warily when more radical proposals for the joint management of services are raised.

3.2 Different organisational shapes

The shape of health and social care organisations demonstrate important differences which may erode the joint planning capability, irrespective of differences in intent as seen through diverging problem definitions. Most obviously the lack of coterminosity results in differences in the catchment areas of the two agencies. Local authorities seem to find it difficult to negotiate in wider forums where disagreements might be publicly exposed to other departments. Lack of coterminosity also entails substantial time costs when an agency is faced with a number of counterparts, resulting in choices in the deployment of planning time.

Differences in the hierarchical position of staff is another source of mismatch. At a professional level, the comprehensive field coverage of consultant geriatricians is not mirrored in the far more limited brief of social workers. There is also role mismatch at planning level, especially in decentralised SSDs where the joint planning function had often been delegated to area officers who were not able to commit the department. As one NHS planner said of the SSD side:

They can't commit new resources or change policy or anything or plan without reference to the centre and that has been a problem for us which I think we are working through.

SSD elected representatives are readier to intervene in detailed decisions, with the result that even senior officers find difficulties in committing their departments, especially in politically volatile or hung authorities. In particular there was political unease about officer-led joint strategies which could significantly alter the definition of local government responsibilities. Politicians may also be anxious to limit the tapering effects of joint finance on base budgets. As one NHS planner put it:

Their politicians like to see a balance of recurring and non-recurring schemes, and some of the non-recurring schemes that they want to put into the programme we don't feel are terribly relevant to joint funding.

An additional distortion flowed from the use of the old area health authorities as a shadow collaborative tier discharging the joint finance function. An unintended consequence of the failure to involve districts was SSD domination of bids and a consequent silt up of expenditure. As one NHS respondent remarked:

Before restructuring, joint planning was social services-led in the AHA [area health authority] days and there was no joint care planning team, the senior offices met to service the JCC [joint consultative committee] and decided what issues should be put to them.

3.3 Flows of resources

Actual and anticipated flows of resources are central to the process of interorganisational exchange and vary substantially from one locality to another. As flows of resources were determined not only by the state of the joint finance budget but by wider resource patterns, the position of health districts vis-à-vis the RAWP redistribution and degree of pressure on SSD base budgets through ratecapping helped shape these wider expenditure climates. There was a greater incentive for SSD collaboration in gainer districts where new facilities were coming on stream. In loser districts, on the other hand, SSDs will often be fighting more defensively to protect levels of provision and resist transfers of responsibility. As well as variation in objective flows of resources, SSD subjective attitudes varied. For example, approaches to tapering were not consistent, and tapering was much more acceptable in some areas than others. Where tapering was disliked, there was an obvious temptation to load expenditure onto capital and non-recurrent schemes.

4 Experiences of joint planning

Our interviews with planners revealed very different experiences of joint planning. In some areas it was seen as a major influence on service planning, while in others it remained marginal. These experiences can be mapped by analysis of the content of formal plans, the structure of liaison, and the use of joint finance. Each item will be considered in turn.

4.1 Joint strategies

One method of measuring formal strategic intent is through the content of planning documents. However, a minority of documents on either side focused on joint planning which thus remained marginal to mainstream planning activities. Where documents did refer to joint plans, there were two levels of response. The first was a narrow development of particular models of provision which required substantial planning time, in particular developments within Part 3 establishments towards more nursing inputs. Some areas had gone beyond that to formulate broader joint strategies or raise ideas for the joint management of services (although such joint management as was evident was confined to small-scale innovations). For example, one strategic plan referred to the crucial role of the community-orientated geriatric unit in the district general hospitals. The plan stressed liaison with the SSD and other community services, and proposed a number of new developments including a multidisciplinary crisis intervention team, community care schemes, joint assessment and relief for carers, provided in conjunction with Age Concern. Proposals for joint budgets and eventually administration were also floated.

It was sometimes difficult to know how seriously these joint strategies were taken by the mainstream hierarchies. As one NHS respondent indicated:

> The so-called strategy for the elderly is a very valuable document but it isn't a strategy. What it does is describe existing services and throw up ideas about where services might go and identifies good practices. I don't think either authority has been able to respond yet saying 'right, this is really in broad terms where we are going'. The local authority by virtue of its nature does not really go in for strategic planning anyway ...

Another NHS respondent in an area where joint strategy plans had been developed for all three priority groups focused on the implementation problem:

> The difficulty comes from here on in. You've got your group objectives. They are going to cost a bit ... we are into a lot of expense over a long period and a very difficult road to get there.

Plans could also be used for more critical comments about the behaviour of other agencies. An important area of contention was staffing levels in Part 3. One NHS district plan commented acidly of problems in Part 3 provision:

> The permanent staffing levels are considered inadequate for residents with other than low levels of dependence and there are examples of some reluctance to accept such help from community services as can be made available by way of additional support.

4.2 *The structure of liaison*

While the formation of a JCC and JCPT is mandatory, areas varied in the extent to which there were functioning client group-based subteams, with some districts exhibiting minimal compliance which could eventually lead to regional intervention. As an SSD respondent indicated:

> They were so under-resourced in the health service that they decided that they were not going to have any planning teams, but there were certain groups that they were worried about, – in their case the mentally handicapped, in our case the elderly – so they set up *ad hoc* working parties which they refused to call planning teams.

Subteams sometimes had a strategic remit, and one area in particular reported the formation of joint strategies across all priority groups, with the subteams retaining a developmental role in the implementation phase. Often these subteams displayed many of the problems encountered by marginal lateral groups such as lack of focus, excessively large and disparate membership, a consensus management style based on professional representation, and no control over resources. Often the focus of such groups oscillated between micro questions (such as laundry) and macro strategies which were not implemented by the mainstream agencies. One respondent reported of an elderly subteam in an health district dominated by teaching hospitals:

There's a lot of frustration in the team, not in terms of being paper-bound, but in terms of decisions or resources coming through or having a great deal of influence on other specialties.

Another SSD respondent remarked on the confused focus of the subteam for elderly clients:

They have been a talking shop about things like patients' laundry and registers of people receiving services and shortages of district nurses. On occasions that has been interspersed with quite important policy issues ... and the result is that important things don't get adequate attention and the unimportant things drive everyone insane.

There was a perception that such subteams were unable to put a 'big bid' together, and strategically significant change would be handled by senior personnel in both mainstream agencies. When issues blow up (such as contested hospital closures) then the subteam would also be marginalised as senior personnel again became involved.

In a number of areas there were attempts by health planners to take a lead in tightening the management of the joint planning process through smaller core membership, reporting systems and the delegation of explicit tasks. An NHS respondent argued:

The big change we will be wanting to make to joint planning teams is that they have a very distinct relationship with operational management and a clear brief of what they are doing, there's got to be product, they've got to have tasks ...

4.3 Use of joint finance

The previous section drew attention to the role of resource flows in determining processes of interorganisational exchange. It was the deployment of joint finance which frequently energised the wider joint planning process, by providing a potential incentive for the SSD to collaborate and a separate budget as a focus for activity. The attitude of SSDs towards joint finance varied, with some anxious to make full use of, while others resisted, tapering. Thus an NHS respondent pointed out the advantages of joint finance for SSDs at least in the short term:

It's provided a great lever within the district to start shifting resources, it gives you an offer you can't refuse because it's free in the short term.

The response to joint finance was not always so positive. One SSD respondent in a radical right-wing authority reported political objections to joint finance:

Joint finance is a rude word here. Not only our Chairman but probably a majority of our members would not touch it. It is immoral we are told. It is *immoral*. It is a bribe, it is a temptation, it is an inducement on the local authority to incur expenditure that it would not otherwise do.

Local government manpower controls could also prove an obstacle, as an NHS respondent indicated:

When they got manpower controls, they were not prepared to take any joint finance scheme that had a revenue commitment to them, so we went through a period when social services were not interested in taking up joint finance at all. And we had money available.

Where relations were less good, the SSD would characteristically load its bids onto the capital rather than the revenue side. Tapering was managed better in those SSDs which had produced clearer rules structuring the use of joint finance:

This Council takes the decision if it agrees to joint financing, it will agree to the revenue consequences, so they consider lots of projects on their merits, not so much the question of their being virtually free in the first few years. And similarly with capital projects, the central policy and resource plan takes account of the revenue effects of capital projects.

When the joint financing function was held at area level before 1982, a vacuum sometimes emerged which was filled by SSD bids, focussing on building up mainstream services as a supposed buffer against hospital admission. One NHS respondent outlined differences in interpretation between the two sides:

There is this slight tension between us and the County on the basis of care in the community, that we tend to think about joint finance advancing care in the community, when they see it in the broader context of keeping people out of hospital.

Pre-1982 SSD domination of joint finance expenditure also resulted in a silting up of joint finance which was only now being unpicked. For example, in one area the AHA joint finance programme had been dominated by a five year home help development programme which was based on quantitative expansion rather than qualitative change. The NHS side was now attempting to build up other areas of spending.

The nature of the joint planning and joint finance relationship thus diverged substantially from one area to another. Clearly the process of interorganisational exchange was not crudely determined, but remained sensitive to local variation and hence could result in either strategic or marginal change.

5 Conclusion

Clearly there are defining upper limits to the degree of jointness which has been created through joint planning. Jointly managed services are not apparent, except for some small-scale innovations which are responsible to joint management committees. A coalition-based approach to interorganisational exchange was thus not apparent. Despite this, the experience of joint planning remained locally variable. In some areas there is a tradition of passive hostility and hence little interest in joint planning outside the use of joint finance for incremental projects. In other areas, more cooperative strategies were apparent, although implementation remained problematic. New models of joint provision in personal care and high dependency residential care were emerging.

The indeterminacy of this process of interorganisational exchange reflects ambiguity in the power relationship between the agencies. In some areas the SSD had historically dominated the planning process, while in others the NHS was now taking more of a lead. An authoritative strategy was not a realistic option as the other agency could withdraw into a hostile passivity. Joint finance remained at the heart of the joint planning process, and the design of more appropriate incentives is likely to remain the focus of centrally-based attempts to sponsor more collaboration at local level.

10 Organisational variation

Within a climate of delegated local discretion and historical professional neglect of services for elderly people, SSDs may be expected to vary substantially both in the way in which they deliver such services and ultimately in the efficiency with which they deploy given resources so as to create client welfare. Unlike child care services, there is not the legislative mandate, the tradition of central control nor the developed professional norms to standardise forms of provision. Although the measurement of organisational shape is more complex than analysing endowments of resources, it is interesting to note continuing evidence of large variations in the amount and balance of local expenditure on social services for elderly people (Audit Commission, 1985).

In seeking to explain variation in performance between local systems, we first face the descriptive problem of identifying the key dimensions which differentiate between systems. This specification is a tricky task, as one can ascribe importance to very different questions of structure, strategies of organisational control, formally expressed goals (that is policy) and work culture as sources of system variation. The distinction between analyses based on formal or alternatively informal aspects of organisational life reflects a basic choice between structurally or culturally-based explanations of organisational behaviour.

There has been little British analysis of the organisational design of human services organisations, with most organisational theoretic work concentrated in the private sector (Pugh and Hickson, 1968; Pettigrew, 1985). Some human services organisation analysis has been undertaken but usually at plant rather than system level, designed to establish associations between formal measures of organisational structure and measures of good practice (Raynes, Pratt and Roses, 1979). Thus a high degree of centralisation at home level is often thought to be associated with poorer forms of practice. The dominant focus of analysis within this plant level tradition is on the quality of care given by direct care staff, rather than the more diffuse effects of the higher tiers of an organisation. The measurement of organisational characteristics also remains at a primitive level with only a subset of the dimensions identified by the Aston School being operationalised (Davies and Knapp, 1981). System-level analysis is located within a much wider organisational network, looking both laterally at links between operational units and vertically in terms of the relationship between different tiers, such as the degree of concordance between higher-tier policy and lower-tier action.

The central question which will be explored in this chapter is therefore the nature of organisational control apparent in the delivery of services for elderly people. Formal structure provides only one mechanism which can be used to influence organisational personnel, often representing merely a definition of upward lines of accountability. A much wider range of control mechanisms may be employed by the higher tiers of an organisation (Ouchi, 1971) aimed at securing control either over output or – even more difficult – over behaviour. Behaviour control is most appropriate for workers with predictable workflows which can be subjected to decision rules; output control where there is an unavoidable element of discretion. The development of control strategies requires considerable investment by higher organisational tiers in securing compliance. Lower tiers may retain sufficient power resources to sabotage top-down control mechanisms, given that they may impose time costs or threaten practice autonomy. The result is that certain sectors of the organisation may be prioritised by higher tiers for the development of effective control mechanisms, reflecting differential political, professional or resource importance. Such fragmented control systems fit with the concept formulated by Weick (1976) of the SSD as a 'loosely coupled system' (Challis and Ferlie, 1986) where different teams operate with wildly divergent workflows, models of practice and task environments. It is not immediately obvious which client groups are most likely to attract the greatest top-down investment in control mechanisms. While child care cases exhibit the greatest political and professional salience, the resource implications of services for elderly people (especially decision-making at the point of entry into long-term residential care) might be expected to attract managerial interest in altering the pattern of front-line resource allocation.

Section 1 considers the nature of human services organisations, and the obstacles to devising effective strategies of organisational control. The chapter then moves on to consider empirical material relating to control mechanisms in the systems in the study. Section 2 outlines the different models of organisational structure found, while Section 3 goes on to examine alternative control strategies. Section 4 analyses the processes of formal goal setting in policy statements for elderly people. In conclusion, the difficulties of securing formal organisational control are restated with greater consideration of the role of informal organisation.

1 Human service agencies as organisations

Classic Weberian bureaucracies designed to process a mass workload display a rational and hierarchically-based authority system, task specialisation, and discipline governing conduct in office (Weber, 1947). Issues of organisational structure and of control thus arise. Yet the ideal-typical Weberian model is most appropriate where tasks are routine (Perrow, 1972) rather than non-uniform, and where there are no professional groups employed on the basis of accredited expertise (Hasenfeld, 1983). Human service organisations share some of the features of the Weberian bureaucracy but also important divergences. They remain hierarchical organisations, with lines of management ascending to the Director and the Committee of elected representatives which sets policy guidelines. Social work staff are case accountable through supervision. Attempts to design more 'participative' models of organisation (Whittington and Bellaby, 1979) have as a consequence foundered given a dominant interest in devising formal line-management arrangements in newly formed departments. Structural reorganisation is a continuing theme in many departments (Challis and Ferlie, 1986).

Human service organisations display other work features incompatible with classic bureaucratic models of organisation. First, the work technology is indeterminate both because of client variability and because of competing practice ideologies and patterns of professional socialisation and deployment. No doubt there are measures which can be taken to reduce technological indeterminacy and foster standard practice through improved training, setting up incentive structures, providing professional peer review or changing the mode of team organisation. Social work has been slow to follow medicine in developing empirically established practice rules. Davies and Challis (1986) thus describe a project which developed grounded practice norms for intervention with particular subgroups (such as demented elderly people or elderly alcoholics). They argue that there has been understatement of the potential for increasing the degree of technological determinacy of the relations between resources, need-related characteristics of recipients and outcomes. Such an increase in technological determinacy would, however, require substantial professional investment, both in a training and employment context. At present, the pattern of work undertaken with elderly people varies substantially from one area to another in grade mix and practice style.

Second, important segments of the organisation are dominated by personnel with professional qualifications: Challis and Ferlie (1986) found that 86 per cent of area social workers in their sample of teams were qualified. The proportion of social workers who are qualified has risen substantially over the last decade. Because of the division of professional prestige, social work with elderly people is often the last work setting to be colonised by qualified social workers, remaining the province of unqualified social work assistants who operate according to a prescribed output model.

Producer groups vary in the degree of self-regulation and occupational closure they are able to achieve, ranging from ideal-typical professions such as physicians, through semi-professionals (such as social workers) to para-professionals (such as hospital attendants) (Etzioni, 1969). Semi-professionals are confusingly subject both to managerial and developmental work cultures. Thus SSDs are led by managers, but employ semi-professionals. Social workers are line-managerially case-accountable and have to work within prescribed procedures and organisational guidelines, although there is also an expectation of development through professionally-based supervision or peer review. For these reasons supervisory procedures are unusually muddled, reflecting confusion about the role of the senior social worker as a first-tier manager or as a professional adviser. The processes of bureaucratisation and professionalisation represent alternative and perhaps contradictory control mechanisms, given the widespread evidence of alienation of professionals and semi-professionals within bureaucratic organisations (Kakabadse, 1982). The first control mechanism relies on task specification, routinisation and the formalisation of procedures, the second on internalised norms and self-regulation (Hasenfeld, 1983).

A third feature of human service organisations where services are delivered 'free' at the point of consumption is that of persistent overload at front-line level resolved through the adoption of standard operating procedures (both legitimate and illegitimate) designed to bring demand back into line with supply. The combination of high caseloads, the organisational costs of securing full information, and limitations on staff time results in the passing of substantial discretion down into the hands of 'street-level' bureaucrats (Lipsky, 1980). Internal organisational conflict will arise where such street-level personnel seek to preserve their autonomy, while managers attempt to implement formal work targets. The greater the overload which is managed by front-line workers, the more difficult it will be to devise effective control strategies. Thus work settings with high bombardment rates (such as intake teams or area teams) may pose greater difficulties for the implementation of control mechanisms than second-tier specialist teams with a more managed referral process.

A final difficulty in establishing control mechanisms in human service organisations lies in task dissimilarity across work units. Thus the SSD can be broken down into a number of subsystems, each with different control strategies. These subsystems are 'loosely coupled', as components

...are somehow attached, but that each retains some identity and separateness, and that this attachment may be circumscribed, infrequent, weak in its mutual effects, unimportant and/or slow to respond (Weick, 1976).

SSDs often display unclear systems of line-managerial control, shown in dual lines of management and ambiguous 'consultative' arrangements. However, the poor lateral communication and coordination between teams reflects real differences in patterns of work and models of practice. Thus it may be easier to devise control strategies over pandepartmental operational questions (such as personnel policy) rather than over professionally related issues, where the degree of control sought or achieved may also vary from one setting to another.

2 Formal structure

SSD organisational design has often been seen as a choice between a limited number of formal models of organisation. Thus SSD directorates have been conventionally organised along either functional or geographic lines, although a client group mode of organisation represents an emerging third alternative (Challis and Ferlie, 1986). A major problem with functional splits has been poor communication between residential and fieldwork sections, and a tendency for minor issues to ascend to high cross-over points, but a geographical mode of organisation can entrench quantitative and qualitative inequality. As yet we know little about the performance of the growing number of Elderly Divisions.

There has been a recent awareness that such crude structural choices represent extremely weak levers of control, and an increasing interest in questions of organisational process (Challis and Ferlie, 1988). A number of authorities now report 'value for money' reorganisations, slimming down middle management, but at the same time introducing clearer accountability and reporting systems. Other authorities have undergone decentralisation exercises, increasing the range of resources held at area level.

At team level, too, a variety of formal structures are on offer. The dominance of the generic team characteristic of the post-Seebohm period has been eroded, but there are three alternative lines of development. The first is towards the adoption of intake teams as a screening device, although there are often difficulties in negotiating transfer to silted up and child care-dominated long-term teams or 'revolving door' patterns of case closure and reopening. The second model consists of patch-based working (Hadley and McGrath, 1984) which in its most developed form involves substantial change to both roles and style of working. Such features as small area working, interweaving with local statutory and informal resources and role blurring are thought to be particularly appropriate for constructing a support network for elderly people. Note also the stress on the depro-fessionalisation of care and the emphasis on basic tending tasks. The third model consists of client group specialisation either at team level (Davies and Challis, 1986) or at individual practitioner level within generic teams. The need to win the confidence of external agents who act as key referral points and to improve practice with problematic subgroups (such as those with dementia) represent powerful arguments for client group specialisation.

Home help organisers can also be managed in a variety of ways: responsible to a senior central officer, to an area officer or subject to dual management. Dexter and Harbert (1983) suggest that central control leads to a greater range of services, although this may be bought at the cost of poorer relations with area teams and hence difficulties in establishing effective case management.

Table 10.1 contains information on the formal structures of the systems of the study. Most directorates were organised either along client group or functional lines, and only one authority had a divisional tier during the period of fieldwork. Team structures were scattered across generic, patch and client group modes of deployment, with one team maintaining an intake/long-term system. Home help organisers were organised in a range of ways: centrally accountable, locally accountable or subject to dual management. Information was also sought on the structure of NHS unit management teams which were organised in a variety of ways, but rarely did services for elderly people form a package allocated by one person.

Such cross-sectional information needs to be studied in conjunction with knowledge of the evolution of the systems. A substantial degree of change in fieldwork structures is now apparent at both headquarter and team levels (Challis and Ferlie, 1986, 1987). Table 10.2 indicates that the most significant shifts in this group of authorities have been towards the delegation of responsibility for an increasing range of resources to local level and the adoption of a client group-based mode of fieldwork deployment. The shift towards specialist working has been gathering momentum since the mid-1970s, but the devolution of resources is a more recent development. However, such reorganisations are complex and partial: Authority 5 has devolved responsibility for day and rotating care, but centralised control over home care. The switch from structural to these more process-based forms of reorganisation which focus on issues of decentralisation and service integration reflects the realisation that departments or teams with identical formal structures behave in different ways. Thus patch teams vary in their brief from modest enhancements in the degree of small area case allocation to more radical attempts to renegotiate basic roles (Challis and Ferlie, 1986). The pattern of work behaviour is more likely to be shaped by subtler patterns of organisational control than crude changes to formal structure.

3 Strategies of organisational control

3.1 Conceptualising strategies of organisational control

All organisations are likely to employ control mechanisms designed to push the behaviour or output of staff in a 'legitimate' direction, but the extent and nature of these mechanisms will vary from one setting to another (Greenwood and Hinings, 1976). Nor is it clear whether control strategies are positively or negatively associated. Preliminary evidence

Table 10.1
The formal structure of systems (1984)

Area and type	Directorate structure	Team structure	Home help org. management	NHS UMTs
1. Inner London	Functional	Generic/ patch	Dual management	Community health, dental, hospital
2. Inner London	Client group/ functional	Generic/ patch	Centrally managed	Mental health, community, acute units
3. Outer London	Client group	Client group	Centrally managed	Community/ mental handicap, mental illness, acute
4. Metro-politan District	Functional	Moving from generic to client group	Area officer accountable, Principal officer has advisory function	Hospital, mental health, community
5. Metro-politan District	Functional	Generic	Centrally managed	X Six units on mixed care groups and hospital lines (inc. geriatrics) Y DGH, mental illness, geographic
6. Metro-politan District	Functional	Generic	Dual management	Hospital, community
7. English Shire	Functional	(i) Geo-graphic (ii) Intake	Area officer accountable	Mental illness, community, city hospitals
8. English Shire	Operational	Client group	Locally accountable	X Acute, mental handicap, elderly, community Y Mixed functional/ geographic
9. English Shire	Operational/ geographic; divisional tier	(i) Client group (ii) Generic	Dual management	X DGH, community Y Acute, elderly, mental illness, mental handicap, community
10. Welsh County	Client group	Client group	District officer accountable	Geographic, mental health

Table 10.2
Evolution of formal SSD structures

Area and type	Directorate structure	Team structure	HHO management
1. Inner London	Stable.	Elderly specialist appointed.	Stable.
2. Inner London	1985: move to a purely functional split.	1985: department-wide reorganisation; devolution of responsibility for home help/day care. Formation of elderly team.	1985: reorganisation; transferred line management responsibility from the centre to the area.
3. Outer London	Stable.	1981: department-wide move to specialist teams.	Home help service has recently moved to a 'patch' system.
4. Metro-politan District	Stable.	Move from generic to specialist teams.	Stable.
5. Metro-politan District	Stable.	Responsibility for day and rotating care has been devolved. Greater focus on the elderly.	1981: reorganisation; transferred line management responsibility from the area to the centre.
6. Metro-politan District	Complex 'value for money' reorganisations.	1985: delegation of control over residential and day care to the districts.	Attempts to centralise management failed.
7. English Shire	Projected divi-sionalisation.	Stable.	Stable.
8. English Shire	Stable.	1981: shift from patch to client group mode.	Stable.
9. English Shire	Strengthening of divisional tier.	(i) 1983: move from intake to elderly team (ii) Stable.	1984: team attachment.
10. Welsh County	1980: move from geo-graphic to client group.	Stable after 1975 when specialist team was formed.	Stable.

suggests the latter, as Greenwood (1978) found that SSDs are subjected to formalisation as a control strategy, but not other forms of control. The following potential control mechanisms can be examined:

- The extent of *centralisation,* or the retention of decision-making powers at the higher tiers of an organisation. The centralisation of decision-making over resource allocation is the crudest form of control mechanism. Thus the Audit Commission (1986a) suggests that decentralisation of authority for the allocation of community services should be accompanied by the centralisation of residential care allocation mechanisms so as to alter the 'lines of least resistance' facing front-line resource allocators. But widespread centralisation is unlikely to be utilised as a control strategy because of overload at higher tiers which become swamped with case-level issues. Given the rapid growth of SSDs since 1971, both in terms of employees and in terms of the range of services delivered, a lesser rather than a greater degree of centralisation seems likely given a desire to push responsibility downwards towards lower crossover points. A high degree of centralisation can also have negative effects on other aspects of organisational performance, especially given professional personnel. Thus Aiken and Hage's (1966) study of American health and welfare agencies found an association between a high degree of centralisation and worker alienation. This was confirmed within the British context by Kakabadse and Worrall's (1978) study of nine SSDs which found a negative relationship between the level of centralisation and job satisfaction.
- The extent of *standardisation* or the use of formal rules and procedures. Pugh and Hickson (1968) define a procedure as an event which has a regularity of occurrence and is legitimised by the organisation. Although the scope for front-line decision-making can be reduced through the specification of such decision rules, the extent of standardisation varies between agencies. For example, recruitment procedures may be standardised or may be delegated for local decision. There may be standard operating procedures covering initial assessment, reassessment and case closure, or the social worker may be able to use discretion. Prescribed arrangements for case visiting may be seen as a guarantee of due process in risky cases, even if the outcome of the case is unpredictable. Yet the cost of standardisation may be worker alienation. Thus Kakabadse and Worrall (1978) found significant negative relationships between fulfilment of primary work role and job codification, rule observation, the presence of a rules manual and the presence of job descriptions. Under conditions of chronic overload, the enforcement of procedures will be difficult as front-line staff develop their own routines for cutting down workload.
- The extent of *formalisation* or documentation of actions undertaken. The proliferation of forms designed to structure and record the nature of

worker/client contacts is a noticeable feature of control strategies in human service organisations (Hasenfeld, 1983). Line managers may also expect to have access to written accounts of visits undertaken. The extent of information recorded will vary between agencies, as will the degree to which such information is structured or remains open ended. The status of such documentation is unclear as workers control much of the information flow and may reduce the flow of information further under conditions of excess demand. Nevertheless, Greenwood (1978) found that SSDs tended to be controlled through a process of formalisation, rather than standardisation or centralisation and suggested that this control strategy was appropriate for retrospective defence in risky cases (such as child abuse) rather than for the control of future events.

- The extent of *professionalisation* or self-regulation on the basis of accredited knowledge and internalised norms. The management of semi-professionals (such as social workers) poses particular difficulties, because of the blurring of professional and managerial power structures. A strategy of professionalisation requires at the very least a qualified workforce and a capacity for practice development through peer review, based on shared concerns.

- The extent and nature of *political control*. This is of a different conceptual order, being not a type but a source of control which may result in higher levels of centralisation, standardisation and formalisation. Upward accountability to a committee of elected representatives is a primary control characteristic of local authority departments (Greenwood and Hinings, 1976) and politically derived goals will be much more prominent than in private sector firms. The degree of political organisation will vary between systems, with councillors playing a passive, case-level role in some departments, but undertaking a more goal oriented approach to programme formulation and implementation in others.

3.2 *Measuring strategies of organisational control*

The analysis is based on material gathered through the course of structured interviews (lasting between an hour and an hour and a half) undertaken with a sample of respondents from a number of tiers ranging from assistant director to social work assistant in each of the study authorities. About ten respondents were interviewed in each system. A central feature of these interviews was to gather material which would illuminate strategies of organisational structure and control. However, there are major theoretical and methodological difficulties. There have been a few previous attempts to measure organisational dimensions within SSDs, but such work as has been undertaken has shown bias towards the measurement of those aspects of the organisation which have private sector analogues (such as personnel procedures) rather than the core resource allocation mechanisms of human service organisations. A second weakness is the retreat from the examination of organisational procedures needed for the mapping of the structure of an organisation to the reporting of subjective sentiment. The approach adopted in this study was as follows.

First, we have to define which aspects of the department's work are to be measured. The SSD system can be broken down into a number of very different client group-based subsystems, retaining some pandepartmental standard procedures, such as personnel or recording functions. We need therefore to consider not only work features associated specifically with the elderly subsystem but also those pandepartmental areas of work which impinge across all client groups through we should not consider items of work specific to other client groups, such as children. While this distinction is relatively easy to maintain at practitioner level, it becomes harder to sustain higher up the hierarchy where there are cross-cutting policy responsibilities.

Second, measures should focus on the central work features of the human services organisation. Of key interest are residential, day care and home help resource allocation procedures together with arrangements for the recruitment of personnel. Measures should not be based on aspects of work which are peripheral to the functioning of the organisation, nor on aspects of practice rather than of formal control.

Third, while each of the control strategies was operationalised into a number of items, no scaling exercise was undertaken as we were unable to assign equivalence to each of the items. It may be that some items (such as the allocation procedure for residential care) should be weighted more heavily than others.

Summary information is contained in Tables 10.3 to 10.7 with fuller information available in Bebbington et al. (1986). Table 10.3 considers the extent of *centralisation*. Thus systems varied in their interpretation of the role of area officers, the composition of interview panels, Part 3 and day care allocation procedures and the extent to which home help organisers and social workers referred decisions on individual elderly cases upwards. Despite the importance of the resources involved, Part 3 mechanisms were not always centralised but involved a number of complex mechanisms, including a local multidisciplinary panel or a centrally-based panel to which areas had 'quota' nomination rights. While home help organisers rarely referred individual cases upwards, social workers would often have to secure the agreement of their senior to case closure, while social work assistants would often refer up extensively.

Table 10.4 indicates a generally low degree of *standardisation*. Departments were more likely to have developed procedures manuals for child care cases than for the elderly. There were rarely written procedures for home help organisers. Even when review procedures had been formally agreed,

Table 10.3 – Centralisation

Item	Area 1	Area 2	Area 3	Area 4	Area 5	Area 6	Area 7	Area 8	Area 9	Area 10
(i) Role of area officers	Restricted – not on directorate.	Mixed – recent delegation of home care to areas.	Restricted – not on directorate.	Areas are 'fairly autonomous'.	Little policy input or resource control.	Latest reorganisation expanded the role of district managers. (Missing information)	Reorganisation will put divisional officers on the directorate.	Areas officers are 'mini-directors'.	Powerful divisional tier.	Centralised, resisted at district level.
(ii) Interview panels	Most panels include central representatives. Job descriptions have been centralised.	Panels include central representatives.	(Missing information)	Local except for the most senior appointments.	Senior appointments include central representatives.	(Missing information)	Central representatives for the senior appointments.	Locally based.	Area/divisional panels.	Committee Chair is involved in senior appointments.
(iii) Part 3 allocation	Centralised	Locally-based panel.	Mixed – central panel, but areas have 'quotas'.	Centralised.	Centre has permanent beds – areas rotating care.	Centrally based except for rotating care.	Locally agreed procedures.	Locally based.	Area based.	Centralised.
(iv) Day care allocation	Centralised.	Officer-in-charge has discretion.	Centralised.	Allocation has recently been decentralised.	Locally controlled.	(Missing information).	Local procedures – but central transport section important.	Locally based.	Area based.	Day centre – local. Part 3 day care – central.
(v) Home help organiser upwards referrals	Case closure.	'Dodgy cases'.	To abate charges.	No supervision available.	Case closure or referral.	Very rarely.	Rarely – residential care assistance.	Very rarely.	When budget is overspent.	'Difficult cases'.
(vi) Social worker upwards referrals.	Extensive referrals to seniors in difficult cases.	Case closure and 'out of the norm' cases.	Active supervision. Case closure goes to area office.	'High risk' cases.	Case closures go to senior.	SWA should; specialist worker most unlikely to.	Extensively – reviews, case closures.	Senior has to countersign.	9a frequent discussion; 9b inter-agency dispute.	Detailed central control over resources.

Table 10.4 – Standardisation

Item	Area 1	Area 2	Area 3	Area 4	Area 5	Area 6	Area 7	Area 8	Area 9	Area 10
(i) Is there a procedure manual?	Yes – little for elderly.	Yes – more for elderly.	Yes – for every social worker.	Yes – each manager has a copy.	Yes – less for elderly.	No – procedures only in child abuse.	Yes – but needs updating.	(Missing information).	Yes – less for elderly.	Home care manual projected.
(ii) How are social workers notified of changes in procedure?	Procedures manual: training.	Procedures manual; via team leader; training.	EPH manual has not been updated.	(Missing information).	Procedures manual; service circulars.	Poor communications.	Communication is improving.	(Missing information).	Procedures manual.	Memos via district officer.
(iii) What is the complaints procedure?	Serious complaints go to Personnel.	Serious complaints go to Director.	Eventual recourse to a Councillor Appeals Panel.	Serious complaints go to Director.	Can go to Director – most at area level.	Senior management likely to get complaints from councillors.	Most at area level – except from MPs.	'Nothing has to go to County Hall'.	Serious complaints could go to Director.	Most dealt with locally.
(iv) Department guidelines on time period between allocation and assessment?	No – but informal norms on the home help side.	No official guidelines but social workers operate informal norms.	Home help organiser expected to respond 'within 24 hours'.	No.	Local home help guidelines.	Not on social work side.	Home help – within three days. Social work – at risk' cases have priority.	Social work: 'unrealistic' department guidelines. Home help: local guidelines.	9a 'Informal expectation'. 9b More formal team guidelines.	No.
(v) Is there a caseload weighting system?	No.	No.	No.	No.	No.	No.	Yes.	In intake teams.	9a No 9b Yes	No.
(vi) What is the procedure for supervision?	Once a fortnight – this slips.	Once a week for level 1/2; level 3 can choose. Goal setting.	SWAs are actively supervised – some daily.	Fortnightly for SWAs; monthly for other staff.	Levels 1/2 are weekly/fortnightly. Level 3 on a consultative basis.	Unqualified are seen fortnightly; qualified are seen monthly.	Weekly or fortnightly.	Weekly or fortnightly.	9a Once a week for level 2. 9b Once a month for level 3; more for level 2.	Every two weeks – but slips.

(vii) Written procedures for home help organisers?	No.	No.	Local and central guidelines.	(Missing information).	No.	(Missing information).	Only for assessment and reassessment.	(Missing information).	For child minders and play groups – not home help.	Home care manual in preparation.
(viii) Is there a review system?	Social work review has fallen into disuse. Home help review slips.	Home help reviews slip.	Six-monthly home help reviews slip.	Six-monthly home help reviews slip. Social work 'building in reviews'.	Six-monthly home help reviews slip. Local day care reviews.	Six-monthly home help reviews slip. Social work moving towards review.	Six-monthly home help reviews slip. Social work review system.	Home help – follow up and review visits (these slip). Social work – basic system.	Six-monthly home help reviews slip. Social work – post part 3 admission.	Home help – annual review. Social work – no.

they would often be eroded in practice, as would supervision arrangements in some authorities.

The extent of *formalisation* is considered in Table 10.5. A distinction has to be drawn between the provision of structured documentation for resource allocation and more open-ended casenote recording. Part 3 documentation was the most extensive, although in some authorities even this documentation either remained rudimentary or was not completed in practice. Other resources were allocated on the basis of much simpler documentation. The lack of documentation at central level meant that a variety of local-level documentation had been designed. Areas varied in their emphasis on casenotes as an instrument of formalisation, and in some it emerged as a major area of control.

Professionalisation as a control strategy is considered in Table 10.6. In all but two of the areas all social workers were qualified, although one Inner London Borough had brought in a new equal opportunities policy which was moving away from that position. In nearly all these areas, however, social work assistants continued to perform much of the work with the elderly. In some areas nearly all the work with the elderly, except for Part 3 allocation decisions, was undertaken by assistants at this level resulting in a pattern of close supervision and a high level of upwards reporting. In about half the areas, there was a specialist team for elderly people or special interest group which had the potential for acting as a focus for peer review and professional development, although specialist teams could also be dominated by para professionals (as in Authority 10).

Summary information on the nature of the political regime in the study areas is considered in Table 10.7. The two Inner London authorities were both active in the pursuit of policy issues, and one in children's case-level issues. This authority had centralised recruitment procedures as part of an equal opportunities policy. Although this was the most politicised authority, there was a more general development of policy for the elderly at political level, if only because of resource implications.

The level of active control sought over services for elderly people was thus generally low. Part 3 allocation tended to be more centralised and require fuller documentation, although even here the picture was mixed. Services for the elderly displayed few guidelines and often procedures emerged informally at local level. Imposed procedures (such as review visiting) were eroded by excess local workload. The use of structured documentation designed to force changes in assessment behaviour was less common than the gathering of open-ended casenote material as a retrospective defence strategy. In some systems retrospective case recording assumed major importance: moves to more proactive systems were less common (Davies and Challis, 1986, chapter 3). Professionalisation as a

Table 10.5 – Formalisation

Item	Area 1	Area 2	Area 3	Area 4	Area 5	Area 6	Area 7	Area 8	Area 9	Area 10
(i) Extensiveness of Part 3 documentation	23 items - countersigned by team leader.	(Missing information).	Simply designed - team leader countersigns.	Detailed 4-page form. Countersigned by senior.	Detailed, structured, 9-page document.	(Missing information).	Simple 2-page form - more complex form is rarely used.	Comprehensive 14-page document.	Unstructured 10-page document.	(Missing information).
(ii) Extensiveness of day care documentation	7 items.	(Missing information).	6 items.	Detailed 3-page form. Countersigned by senior.	2-page structured form.	(Missing information).	Simple 1-page form - local supplements.	Simple 2-page form.	Part 3 forms are used.	(Missing information).
(iii) Extensiveness of home help application	Simple 'own cards'.	No assessment instrumentation.	Well-developed assessment instrumentation.	Form is financially based.	4-page structured planning document.	2-page structured form.	Simple form. Special project documentation is more extensive.	Comprehensive 2-page structured form.	2-page divisionally based assessment form.	(Missing information).
(iv) Elderly at risk register?	No.	No.	No.	No.	No.	No.	No.	No.	(Missing information).	Yes.
(v) Recording system	Standard open-ended forms.	No formal assessment/review instrumentation.	Casenotes - no standard review procedures.	Senior keen to improve recording.	Casenotes - no automatic review by senior.	Local procedures manual.	7a Caseload weighting system 7b Special project.	(Missing information).	Home help assessment documentation.	At risk register.
(vi) Written reports submitted to the senior?	Might read records 'at intervals'.	Caseloads usually written up in summary form.	No - 'if he wants to see, then he reads my files'.	Resource allocation decisions go up.	No, but case closures go to senior.	More so on the second team.	Through the review system.	Through counter-signing.	Every report goes to the Area Officer.	Casenotes; counter-signing.

Table 10.6
Extent of professionalisation

Area and type	Are all social workers qualified?	SWAs?	Elderly special interest group?
1 Inner London	Yes – but there is a new equal opportunities policy	Yes – do much of the elderly work	Yes
2 Inner London	Yes	Yes – do much of the elderly work	1985 – specialist team
3 Outer London	Yes	Yes – important role	Specialist teams
4 Metropolitan District	Yes	Yes – do a lot of elderly work	Moving to specialist teams
5 Metropolitan District	Yes	Yes – seen as Aides	No
6 Metropolitan District	No	Yes	No
7a English Shire	Yes	Yes – do much of the elderly work	No
7b English Shire	Yes	Yes	No
8 English Shire	Yes	Very few	Specialist team
9a English Shire	Yes	Only one	Specialist team
9b English Shire	Yes	Only one	No
10 Welsh County	No	Large number	Specialist team

control strategy lacked viability because of the continuing role of social work assistants, working under the close control of seniors.

4 The department as a goal-directed organisation

We have so far only considered organisational structure and control strategies as influences on work behaviour, but the setting of formal goals or policy represents an alternative vehicle of control. Thus Child (1972) has focused on the 'strategic choice' open to higher-level decision-makers as a source of organisational control. Although some have argued that

Table 10.7
Nature of political regime

Area and type	Regime	Style
1 Inner London	Left Labour	Interventionist in both policy and case level issues (esp. children).
2 Inner London	Radical Conservative	Strong interest in expenditure implications.
3 Outer London	'Managerial' Conservative	Interventionist in child care, but less in the elderly.
4 Metropolitan District	High-spending Labour	Interventionist – refers issues to Policy Subcommittee.
5 Metropolitan District	Marginal – liberal Conservative tradition	Policy interest in elderly services.
6 Metropolitan District	Marginal – low-spending tradition	Focus on 'value for money' considerations.
7 English Shire	Conservatives lost control in 1985 – now 'hung'	Conservatives traditionally resisted formal policy statements.
8 English Shire	Conservatives lost control in 1985 – now 'hung'	Decision-making has become less predictable.
9 English Shire	'Traditional' Conservative	Increasing interest in elderly policy and also managerial issues.
10 Welsh County	'Traditional' Labour	Greater interest in case level than policy issues.

the concept of an organisational 'goal' is meaningless, as it is not organisations but individuals and to a lesser extent subgroups which have goals, there is usually a dominant coalition which sets formally accredited goals. Departments are here not seen as confederations, but as likely to require an overall statement of mission and establishment of domains. Of course there is a struggle for interpretation going on between different interest groups, only one of which at any one time can be seen as the dominant coalition (Cyert and March, 1963). Thus Chandler's (1962) work on American industrial history argues that strategy can determine structure, defining strategy as the specification of basic long-term goals and objectives, and the adoption of courses of action and the allocation of resources necessary for the carrying out of these goals. Gerard (1987) argues similarly for British voluntary organisations. Operationalised goals should therefore provide targets against which performance can be monitored. Such goal setting is even more important as a control mechanism in inter-agency bodies such as joint care planning teams which do not have vertical line-management hierarchies to act as an alternative source of control. In some of the study authorities, the development of SSD strategy for the elderly was led by the JCPT.

SSDs have traditionally placed little emphasis on policy development, exhibiting a greater degree of interest in the handling of 'tricky cases' than the formulation of strategy. Unlike health districts, there is no requirement to produce strategic or operational plans and as a consequence much less elaborate planning capacity. The emphasis on 'statutory' work within SSDs reflects a culture in which service programmes are seen as unchanging and determined by statute, and in which room for local system development is limited. Such procedural changes as do occur are often based on badly handled cases. Child abuse cases in particular have had major department-wide repercussions.

Local planning capacity has been geared to reflect national interest in capital loan sanction and periodic long-term, input-led, planning exercises such as ten-year plans. There has been only a gradual move away from reliance on crude national norms and towards appreciations of the local system. Glennerster, Korman, Marslen-Wilson and Meredith (1982) found that attempts to plan for a client group in a comprehensive sense were rare, and were often based on the assumption of growth. The result has often been a policy vacuum, filled by local implicit policies and resulting in a slow rate of change. The need for the formulation and periodic review of strategies for the elderly has been picked up by other studies (Audit Commission, 1985; DHSS, 1987b).

However, there are countervailing forces. Departments which experienced the demands of local corporate management in the early 1970s were often the first to change from a policy-free culture, but the diffusion of a widespread normative commitment to community care, the downturn in the historic rate of growth and the increased role of external finance have sharpened the policy focus. Policy development for the elderly often springs from an awareness of their major importance as resource consumers, and the desire to promote new forms of community care as an alternative to residential care. The central problem is thus the management of strategic change. However, this strategic aim requires detailed operationalisation and may be pursued through a number of alternative lines of development. Choices have to be made about which sectors to invest in and whether new roles and patterns of working have to be created.

Table 10.8 summarises information on formal policy for elderly people in the ten study authorities. First of all it shows authorities now have a strategic conception of community service development as it has become progressively clearer that traditional residential care-led strategies are not viable in a colder expenditure climate. In the late 1970s, therefore, there was a shift in policy paradigm in many localities. The implications are now being worked out in fuller detail. Such shifts do not only impact on those services where new growth is concentrated but have systemic consequences, as the local health and welfare system as a whole has to be turned round. In some areas, the formal expression of this policy shift is still rudimentary. Nevertheless, plans often include both quantitative expansion (the traditional input-led approach to planning) and qualitative change, most notably diversification within domiciliary care, improving the skill level of the social work service offered to elderly people, and experimenting with high dependency forms of residential care, sometimes in conjunction with NHS inputs. Qualitative and process-based changes have of course proved more difficult to implement than quantitative or structural shifts.

The extent and nature of the shift from residential to community care policies varied. Some SSDs are reducing the number of Part 3 places, or have taken a policy decision not to build any more, while others talk more guardedly of a 'balanced' policy with major roles for both the residential and community sectors. In other areas interest is growing in private sector residential care (often funded through the social security budget) or new forms of sheltered housing provided jointly with the housing department as an alternative to traditional residential care. Development is concentrated in the domiciliary care sector where there is an important shift to personal care roles, with the process of change in fieldwork services being both slower and more indirect. Nevertheless the improvement of assessment for service (notably residential care) and the achievement of a case management function across service boundaries was an important line of development, as our earlier work would lead us to expect (Ferlie, Challis and Davies, 1984). Services for elderly mentally infirm people also emerged as a major policy issue, where a requirement was sometimes seen for more residential care as well as community-based provision, such as day care. Although there were frequently generalised commitments to improving joint working (especially with the NHS), specific action was rarer and more narrowly defined. Joint assessment was a common focus for development, particularly for residential care resources. The joint administration or management of services was conspicuously absent, although experiments in joint provision were beginning to emerge, particularly through nursing inputs into high-dependency Part 3 homes.

Policy implementation has increasingly been seen as inseparable from policy creation. Longstanding conflicts between professions, agencies or politicians result in policies which may appear to be formally agreed nevertheless being contested. The likelihood of dissensus is greater in zero

Table 10.8
SSD policy for the elderly

Area and type	Policy
1 Inner London	An SSD strategic review of 1982 indicated a reduction in the number of Part 3 places and a switch of these resources to sheltered housing, domiciliary care and improved Part 3 staffing ratios. Plans for the extension of sheltered housing have been hit by ratecapping.
2 Inner London	No integrated policy document, but a clear line of development from residential care. A Part 3 closure has been used to finance rate reductions rather than (as planned) to improve community services. Pandepartmental adoption of specialist fieldwork for the elderly. Number of small centrally controlled domiciliary care innovations.
3 Outer London	During the 1970s, priority was given to building up the low level of residential care. Policy now stresses improved social worker skill, diversification within domiciliary care and centrally sponsored innovation. A Multidisciplinary Care Assessment Panel has also been started.
4 Metropolitan District	A joint strategic review of 1984 indicated the main SSD lines of development as: (i) to improve staff training and the introduction of problem-based assessment; (ii) to increase in the number and range of carer support schemes; (iii) to pilot a GP attachment scheme; (iv) to support an elderly fostering service; (v) to provide more residential care places for the elderly mentally infirm and more short-term and rehabilitative work; and (vi) to provide role diversification in domiciliary care.
5 Metropolitan District	While there is no integrated policy statement, two major policy changes have taken place. The domiciliary care review of 1980 included commitments (i) to provide sufficient support to facilitate post-hospital discharge; (ii) to improve interservice coordination; (iii) to prioritise personal care tasks; and (iv) to consider more specialist roles. Qualitative change has proved difficult to manage in some areas. Fieldwork policy changed in 1983, indicating a shift to client group specialisation at area level.
6 Metropolitan District	The SSD produced a strategic plan in 1985 which set the following objectives: (i) to expand and differentiate the home care services; (ii) to improve the quality of day care; (iii) to explore alternatives such as very sheltered housing; (iv) to provide a further mobile meals round; and (v) to strengthen inter-agency liaison.

sum games where resources are being taken away from some services to finance growth in other services. Policy implementation sometimes displayed gross failures, with systems which attempted to move resources instead discovering that they lost them as factors unpredictably intervened.

Table 10.8
continued

Area and type	Policy
7 English Shire	Despite SSD reluctance to produce formal policy, a JCPT statement has been agreed which reflects current lines of development: (i) a shift from residential to domiciliary services; (ii) improved multidisciplinary assessment for service; (iii) experimental higher dependency forms of residential care, in conjunction with the NHS; and (iv) the introduction of personal care roles within the home help service. SSD services for the elderly mentally infirm are developing in the light of projected hospital closure, current thought favouring special residential care and local day care groups.
8 English Shire	The major line of development sprang from a research study which found poor assessment for residential care resources. Central policy now states (i) all areas should operate a problem-oriented assessment for elderly cases; (ii) intensive community services should be made available as an alternative to Part 3 admission, as long as the total cost does not exceed that of Part 3; (iii) a home help organiser report should be mandatory for all Part 3 applicants; and (iv) the Part 3 waiting list should be rigorously controlled. There was no evidence of need for a general expansion of the home help service, but rather of more targeted services.
9 English Shire	Traditionally residential care-led, policy has swung to domiciliary care as new building became increasingly unlikely. A joint financed home help development programme included: (i) an expansion of the basic home help service; (ii) redistribution to redress historic inequality between areas; (iii) increase in the number of organisers to allow team attachment; and (iv) moves to a more flexible and varied service. There was also an expansion of the meals-on-wheels service. Qualitative change has proved difficult to implement, although experiments in community care are now being considered.
10 Welsh County	There is little tradition of formal policy-making. Community care is preferred because it reflects consumer choice rather than because it is seen as cheaper. Residential care should only be used when there are no feasible community options. Increased resources have been allocated to home care and day care within Part 3, but overall the ethos is traditionalist.

As central government, other agencies or local politicians could thus change the rules in the middle of the game, the incentive is to produce limited, low profile, sole agency strategies which internalise the decision-making process and hence reduce uncertainty. Sometimes difficulty arose because policy was ambiguous or excluded key topics. As rationing decisions were often delegated to professionals rather than specified at a policy level, professionals retained substantial ability to re-interpret policy guidelines in the light of their own agenda.

5 Conclusion

Questions of structure, strategies of organisational control and of policy formulation all focus on the formal aspects of organisations. Yet all organisations – especially human services organisations – retain an informally-based definition of organisational life where routines and coping mechanisms are developed by front-line staff as a response to excess demand both on resources and on time (Lipsky, 1980). Informal patterns of communication, cooperation and conflict arise which prevent the standard application of top-down guidelines. Changes in structure may not result in changes in practice, as old work cultures may continue to dominate. Systems develop distinctive histories which result in pre-eminence being accorded to particular client groups or methods of working. The enforcement of organisational control strategies remains problematic. While higher tiers may be anxious to reduce overload, the alternative strategies of control in a decentralised department are imperfect. New assessment documentation may be devised, but not be fully completed. Standard procedures (such as review visiting) may slip. Case recording may be done schematically or at intervals. Changes in formal policy (especially commitment to qualitative change) may have only weak effects on practice, except in small-scale specially financed innovation insulated from mainstream work norms.

Despite the widespread importance of the informal 'shadow' organisation, the higher tiers possess power resources, so that the implementation of formally legitimated programmes can display greater as well as lesser success. Webb and Wistow (1980) focus on policy *explication* and the securing of *compliance* as key aspects of the implementation process. Although their work was on the pattern of central/local relations, the concepts can also be utilised at local level to explore the relations between SSD headquarters and front-line units. By 'explication' is meant the formation of operationalised policy goals and the transmission of policy sub-goals to appropriate front-line units. However, explicit medium targets are very rarely set out in SSD plans. Aims are global, ambiguous and rarely tied to finance, timetables or evaluation. Policy transmission is also often poor, with front-line staff and first-tier managers often claiming ignorance of even the main lines of formal policy.

Reliance on central command is at best a risky control strategy in increasingly overloaded agencies anxious to delegate micro decisions to lower tiers, particularly in loosely-coupled organisations (Weick, 1976). Webb and Wistow's (1980) discussion of compliance strategies drew on the distinction formulated by Etzioni (1961) between the application of sanctions for non-compliance, the offering of incentives, and the moulding of normative structures. While it is difficult to see how sanctions could be applied in this context, financial incentives can be offered by tying growth money to specific programmes, although the funding may not be on a large enough scale or a long enough timescale to produce the desired response. There are, however, other forms of incentives which can be used to secure compliance. Professionalisation rests on a strategy of normative control, but this is poorly developed in services for the elderly. Semi-professionals might be particularly expected to resent the widespread bureaucratic constraints on behaviour and their inability to prescribe resources. Davies and Challis (1986) describe a compliance strategy in an experimental project which rested on the decentralisation of control over resources to social workers within a centrally controlled budget limit which provided the shadow prices of resources. While the organisation grants greater autonomy over day-to-day work, it also provides them with incentives to cost-effective resource allocation.

We have therefore found little evidence of organisational control in the provision of services for elderly people. There is recourse to structural reorganisation, but at the same time a recognition that alterations to formal structure leave many of the key organisational processes untouched. The policy-making function remains undeveloped and the professions have traditionally shown least interest in services for the elderly. Within large-scale human service organisations, traditional mechanisms of organisational control remain difficult to devise and enforce. This is not to say that more indirect control strategies cannot be devised which depend on: first, clearer policy formulation and explication at central level; second, normative control based on professionally-led developments in practice; and third, the provision of incentives at both area and individual level for more cost-effective behaviour. In order to reflect the special nature of human service organisations, the centre may thus become decreasingly interested in direct command and more concerned with the engineering of local contexts.

11 Innovation

Such human service organisations as social services departments encounter two contradictory pressures. The first is the push to restructure patterns of service provision in response to perceived loss of organisational performance following demographic or environmental change, increased or decreased flow of resources, new legislative mandate, or the revision of received professional practice. But there is also a countervailing and constraining pull generated by the conservative nature of these agencies as organisations (Booth, 1978). They often are dominated by issues of procedural equity rather than policy formation and implementation, screen out environmental signals, are risk-averse and have relied on a consensus management style. Such conservative forces have been strengthened by a tradition of entrenched and continuing services rather than experimental and time-limited programmes. The perception of a failure to manage change has gained currency: a report on the management of the National Health Service argued that a decreasingly favourable balance of supply and demand entailed 'the ability to move much more quickly' (Griffiths, 1983, para. 8).

Of course, such statements need decoding. There is a need to understand the dominant streams of innovatory activity, each of which has its own history and defines the change agenda in a characteristic manner. Above all, there remains the question of whether the new service system can be said to be 'better' than the old. Section 1 of this chapter examines the concepts of change, innovation and efficiency-improvement as means of approaching this question. Sections 2 and 3 consider in more detail the schemes encountered in our study, and the extent to which they can be said to contribute to efficiency improvement. We conclude by considering the centrality – or otherwise – of the process of 'innovation' within human services organisations.

1 Change, innovation and efficiency improvement

Some of the literature on innovation sees the type of innovation as of less interest than the motors of change. Thus predictors of the rate of innovation such as organisational structure or patterns of funding or the nature of the implementation process frequently assume central importance (Davies and Ferlie, 1982, 1984). This chapter, however, follows another tack (Ferlie, Challis and Davies, 1984): the type rather than the predictors of innovation will be considered as central. 'Innovation' is defined here as the adoption of a product, service or technology perceived to be new by the adopting organisation (Hage, 1980). Hence the problem is seen not in terms of original social invention, but of local adoption. In contrast, organisational 'change' involves a wider set of less visible alterations to the pattern of service, such as redistribution of resources between existing heads or structural reorganisation (Hasenfeld, 1983). A further distinction can be made between radical and incremental product innovation, depending on whether a major redesign or minor modification of service is effected. Radical innovation promises larger benefits to the adopting agency, but also greater costs in terms of resource investment, time and effort.

We consider the extent to which innovation leads to 'better services' by examining its contribution to the improvement of each of the different dimensions of efficiency. Innovation may contribute to none, some or all of these dimensions. Although greater input mix efficiency has been the major objective of national policy, there is an important link with greater output mix efficiency if community services are to respond credibly to higher dependency levels. The implications of each of these dimensions for the design of services will be considered in turn.

1.1 Input mix efficiency

This is currently the dominant policy objective, reflecting interest in input substitution and cost compression. There is thus evidence of a distinct cost hierarchy between hospital, residential and community-based modes of care (Audit Commission, 1985; Tinker, 1984). Further cost information will be presented later in the paper. Historically seeing the problem of requisite service design as a crude choice between these three alternative modes of care, this balance of care argument has moved on to consider wider role change within the community-based sector. Such input mix objectives form a major thrust behind moves to post-hospital discharge schemes, personal care services and more rehabilitative work within residential care. A new input mix question is the expansion of publicly-financed but privately-provided residential care without adequate screening or assessment on entry. There are also attempts to substitute informal or voluntary resources for public provision, with increased interest – at least at formal policy level – in supporting informal carers. Little is known about the interaction between formal and informal systems, and in particular whether formal care sustains or drives out informal inputs. Nor is it easy to substitute voluntary for formal care, both because of limits to the tasks undertaken by volunteers and because pressure group-orientated agencies within the voluntary sector often build up provision for client groups accorded low priority by the public sector, effectively acting as advocates and pump primers for public provision. So the input mix question is considerably more complex than a crude choice between defined modes of care might suggest.

1.2 *Output mix efficiency*

Shifts away from residential care have long been advocated on effectiveness as well as efficiency grounds (Townsend, 1962). In studying the effectiveness of innovations, a full experimental/control before/after design provides the best information. Where this is not available, for example because of small numbers, proxy process-based measures thought to be associated with valued outcomes can be used. Such process criteria should aim at high specification and detailed operationalisation (Donabedian, 1982) including cost control as well as quality of care measures. Thus justification of admission, or continued stay, and the use of cost benchmarks form important elements of an *efficiency* dimension, while an *effectiveness* dimension can be explored through such indicators as verification of the diagnosis, the performance of diagnostic and therapeutic procedures required by this diagnosis, and the avoidance of service under-utilisation.

Such process measures should be related to a theory of client need and of requisite service response. Following Isaacs and Neville (1976), Chapter 3 thus distinguishes between three need categories into which elderly clients can be categorised, based on the interval between necessary episodes of help. Thus 'long interval' (often domestic care needs) have to be performed daily or less frequently. The exact time when these tasks have to be performed is unimportant, and no special skill is required. 'Short interval' personal care tasks must be performed every few hours by day, although help is not required at an exact time, and no special skill is required of the helper. 'Critical interval' needs (such as incontinence of urine or faeces, dementia, or a tendency to fall) arise at short and unpredictable intervals requiring continuously present, skilful and accept-able help. The need of elderly people can be further measured by the degree of solitude or the period of the day during which the elderly person is left alone (Isaacs and Neville, 1976).

In order to manage higher dependency levels, community-based services can move along two dimensions related to output mix efficiency. The first is based on enhanced *service content*, especially the performance of personal care tasks at specific times or outside normal working hours (such as getting up or putting to bed, feeding, toileting or the administration of medication). The precise definition of such personal care tasks depends on local circumstances, particularly the pattern of relations between the home help and district nursing service. The other dimension relates to the extent of *case management* tasks such as assessment, the negotiation, planning and arrangement of individual care plans, and monitoring and re-assessment (Davies and Challis, 1986). Important signs include prob-lem-based assessments, key workers, case conferences, and liaison with other providers (especially in health agencies). The establishment of multi-disciplinary teams is an interesting but problematic development, requiring appropriate authority structures and legitimating ideologies (Webb and Hobdell, 1980). The construction of daily care plans to meet the critical interval needs of elderly people with dementia is another key area.

1.3 Technical efficiency

Moves to increase technical efficiency rarely involve service innovation but depend on the rationalisation of existing services. New technology may provide an opportunity for service innovation designed to increase technical efficiency, such as alternative methods of delivering prepared meals (Audit Commission, 1985). The cost improvement programmes being undertaken by the National Health Service are a good example of attempts to improve technical efficiency.

1.4 Vertical target efficiency

A common criticism of services from a selectivist viewpoint has been not only the neglect of vertical targeting, but the failure to develop assessment instrumentation which would make such targeting possible. The home help service is relatively insensitive to differences in need, while social work activity with the elderly client group has historically consisted of the routine visiting of large caseloads, rather than task-centred casework (Bebbington et al., 1986). Better vertical targeting at programme level can take the non-innovatory form of devising policy guidelines for existing services, or the innovatory design of new services targeted on particular subgroups. At individual level, better targeting can proceed through structured assessment documentation which attempts to introduce consistency into the needs judgement. Re-assessment enables case managers to respond to changes in need but is presently crowded out by the pressure of work, despite sharp fluctuations in the level of need shown by some clients.

1.5 Horizontal target efficiency

Although innovatory activity is dominated by input mix objectives, an alternative line of development – currently subordinate – consists of securing mechanisms designed to increase uptake. This universalistic, expansionist objective dominated the Seebohm Report (Cmnd 3703, 1968) which set up social services departments, basing them on generic rather than specialist fieldwork teams. More successful case-finding activity has been a longstanding preoccupation of agencies through the needs surveys of the early 1970s to the renewed interest in interweaving with community resources and the informal sector apparent in the Barclay Report (1982). Some innovations are specifically designed to improve casefinding: thus

Hadley and McGrath (1984) associate shifts to patch-based working with changes in the role and style of fieldwork teams involving the development of neighbourhood networks and outreach activity so as to blur the boundary with the local community. Other outreach measures include remote alarm facilities or neighbourhood resource models of residential care. Such direct outreach may be less common than limited and 'non-innovatory' changes such as attachment to NHS settings as a means of generating referrals.

2 Types of innovation

Each of the twelve areas was asked to nominate services which they classed as 'innovatory' for inclusion in the study. Forty client households coming on to these schemes during the period of fieldwork were followed through for an initial period of six months. Table 11.1 contains basic details of the twelve schemes included in the study.

Three clear groupings of schemes emerged which can be considered in turn.

2.1 Augmented home care

Six innovations came into this category, creating new roles which crossed the boundary between the domestic care tasks traditionally undertaken by the home help service and the basic nursing tasks provided by nursing auxiliaries. This overall shift, however, hides local variations in role definition. First, job descriptions in the six schemes differ. Sometimes such descriptions are loose, referring only to the personal care 'expected of a relative' or to the 'laying on of hands'. In such cases the primary qualities expected are personal ones of flexibility, reliability and initiative rather than formally accredited skills. In other cases there are more formal parallel incorporations of basic social work and nursing roles. Another important feature is the move to an out-of-hours service: one scheme operated from 8 a.m. to 8 p.m. seven days a week, while another visited clients three times a day to ensure cover. Although such increased flexibility is often formally agreed within the project remit, it also arises informally and not without difficulty in response to the raised expectations of other service providers. There is a potential clash between the interests of producers and consumers in such schemes where home carers take on an extended range of duties and of times worked, not surprisingly leading to protracted negotiations with public sector unions uneasy with a countercultural emphasis on flexibility and a quasi-familial mode of care. There is also (Chapter 8, Section 3) a potential clash between the perception of nurses (seeing the personal care question as a distinction between trained and untrained personnel) and home help organisers, who think much more about the greater legal liability of formal employees, as opposed to informal carers.

Home care innovations may be located in a central specialist team, in local specialist teams controlled by home help organisers or integrated

Table 11.1
Basic description of project innovations

Project	Description
1. Early discharge team	Among other tasks, it provides intensive, short-term, post-hospital discharge care. Basic personal, domestic and rehabilitative care is provided.
2. Community care assistants	Carers are expected to provide domestic, personal care and basic nursing tasks. They provide cover from 9 a.m. to 9 p.m. (including weekends) and may visit several times in a day.
3. Home care scheme	This is a joint home help, community nursing and social work project. The local hospital will admit scheme clients where necessary, given geriatriciana approval.
4. Elderly family placement scheme	To provide a further short term care resource, within a family setting. Carer personality rather than skills was seen as crucial to the matching process.
5. Elderly family placement scheme	To provide short-term family placements. Extremely physically or mentally frail old people are not considered suitable. The carers receive social work support.
6. Nightsitting/ tuck-in service	Night sitters provide care for the terminally ill, and also carer support. A 'tuck in' service has recently been added, which is home help based and does not serve clients needing nursing care.
7. Home care project	The project leader is supported by three key workers (a social worker, a district nursing sister and a psychiatric nursing sister). There are also home care assistants to provide domestic and personal care.
8. Home care project	Fifteen per cent of home help hours can be spent on an intensive personal care and out-of-hours service, provided by mainstream home helps.
9. Rotating residential care	This is a short-term and rotating residential care service, which has informally evolved from holiday relief. Clients should not be highly dependent.
10. Residential rehabilitation unit	To provide alternatives to long stay residential care where family care has broken down or for post-hospital care (often following a stroke). Not a separate budgetary head.
11. Residential rotating care	To provide short term support to isolated elderly persons, or stressed carers, or to act as an introduction to long-term residential care. No special resources.
12. Residential rehabiliation unit	To provide an alternative to long stay residential care, or to provide carer respite. No special resources. There is also an (underreferred) carers' resource group.

with the mainstream service. Central location may facilitate the development
of a distinctive philosophy and methods of working at the cost of poor
relations with other services, while integration with the mainstream service
preserves lines of communication and shared management but may also
lead to the degeneration of the innovation and the erosion of new service
roles. Straddling the boundary between domestic and nursing care, tasks
are defined differently according to local patterns of working. Meal preparation, washing and dressing are usually seen as the province of home
care aides, while injections remain the responsibility of district nurses. In
the middle come tasks such as bathing and the administration of medication
which can be handled by either side, but frequently the nursing service
attempts to 'offload' such tasks on input mix grounds. Successful home
care innovation, often small-scale in itself, may have important spin-off
effects through improving the relations between mainstream home help
and district nursing services: the quality of cross-service referrals improves
and joint assessment visits can be arranged for borderline cases.

2.2 New forms of residential care

Four schemes came into this grouping, reflecting increased interest in
blurring the traditional boundary between community-based and residential
care. Short-term residential care has been expanded in recent years (Allen,
1982) as a means of offering carer relief or 'topping up' for isolated clients,
but other forms of residential care have also emerged. Two of these
schemes grew out of short-term and holiday relief programmes into phased
care. Bottom-up in terms of sponsorship, small-scale and requiring no
special finance, these schemes represented an incremental extension of
existing practice. In one scheme, assessment for service was by an
unqualified social work assistant, in the other by a qualified social worker
who used the scheme as preparation for permanent admission. The other
two schemes in the group (also small-scale and bottom-up) were based
on rehabilitation units which prepared residents for discharge. Demanding
higher levels of risk than traditional residential care, such projects depend
on changing staff attitudes as well as securing physical plant. Staff in one
scheme were reported to be strongly committed to the new style of
working, while in the other there was confusion about aims and objectives.
It is also instructive to consider possible initiatives in residential care
which were not captured by the study. There were no reports of high
dependency schemes involving nursing as well as social care inputs, nor
of a resource centre model of provision involving outreach to the neigh-
bouring community.

2.3 Boarding out

The remaining two schemes were both boarding-out innovations, where an elderly person lodges with a family which provides care. The growth of boarding-out schemes for elderly people indicates technology transfer from a more advanced child care field to a lagging elderly sector, involving substantial fieldworker support to a client group where such skills have not been widely employed. As late as 1980, Thornton and Moore (1980) concluded that boarding-out provision for elderly people was extremely limited in scope. The resurgence of interest springs from the desire to develop alternatives to short-stay residential care, a service which has sometimes experienced uptake problems. Both schemes offered short rather than long-term care, although rotating care (a series of short-term care episodes) could emerge informally if a relationship formed between carer and client.

How did these two schemes define the tasks appropriate to the paid carer and in particular the degree of manageable dependency? In one scheme the service offered by the carer was defined as 'substitute family care', and personality rather than caring skills was seen as important. The clients placed were expected to be of low dependency. The other scheme also referred to the 'care expected of a relative'. Reluctant to define a specific target group, the scheme protocol noted that as carers became more experienced so they could be expected to take on more dependent clients.

These three groupings accounted for all the innovations included in the study. This narrow spectrum of innovatory activity was public sector-based, and excluded developments with the private and voluntary sectors. The only report of activity with the informal sector consisted of an under-referred carer support group blighted by constraints on transport. Given strong input mix objectives, it is surprising that only a couple of schemes reported a well-developed case management orientation where there were stronger links with nursing than hospital services. Even within the public sector, the scope and rate of change was limited. No developments were reported in day care, the boarding-out schemes displayed a short-term care remit, there were only incremental changes reported in residential care, and although the pace of change seemed fastest in domiciliary care, the development of services for those with critical interval needs (especially for the demented) was weak.

3 The twelve innovations and signs and symptoms of efficiency improvement

Each efficiency dimension is considered in turn, except for technical efficiency where there was no report of activity.

3.1 Input mix efficiency

Nine of the schemes reported input mix objectives, varying from a highly focused post-hospital discharge scheme to the creation of a more general community-based buffer zone. The objectives are summarised in Table 11.2. As might be expected, greatest interest was shown in substitution for residential care (financed locally), although substitution for hospital care was also apparent, especially where there was joint finance input. One home care team had indeed been set up explicitly to reduce 'bed blocking' in local hospitals. No explicit attempt to substitute for psychiatric inpatient care was reported.

Table 11.2
Input mix efficiency objectives

| Project | Substitute for: | | | |
	Hospital care	Part 3	Nursing home	Not specific or 'institutional' care
1. Early discharge team	Yes			
2. Community care assistants		Yes		
3. Home care scheme		Yes	Yes	
4. Elderly family placement scheme		Yes		
5. Elderly family placement scheme				
6. Nightsitting/tuck-in service				Yes
7. Home care project	Yes	Yes		
8. Home care project				Yes
9. Rotating residential care				
10. Residential rehabilitation unit	Yes	Yes		
11. Residential rotating care				
12. Residential rehabiliation unit		Yes		
Total	3	6	1	2

Table 11.3 presents evidence about SSD cost structures, although work identifying additional costs incurred by the NHS in supporting these clients at home is still proceeding. The method is the tracking and costing of all SSD inputs (not just the innovatory services identified) received by

the clients so as to establish an SSD weekly cost. Gross costs are used throughout.

Overall, clients were maintained at home at considerably less cost to the SSD than residential care, as is shown in Table 11.3. The exception to this (although numbers are very small) was the elderly fostering scheme, where the SSD was increasingly having recourse to the social security budget as a means of lowering the substantial costs incurred. Such high unit costs could well be common in small-scale schemes with low caseloads and high start-up costs. Marginal costs are decreased through expansion, but such a process of acceptance and growth is by no means automatic. Sitting-based schemes may prove a particularly costly form of innovation, best provided for particular subgroups for whom they represent an effective form of care (such as those who are terminally ill). Many of these schemes were explicitly targeted on elderly people at the margin of admission for residential care, and therefore managed clients with high degrees of dependency.

Table 11.3
Estimated gross costs to SSD of supporting elderly clients receiving 'innovatory' services

Type of innovation	Number of client households	Weekly gross cost to SSD per client
Home care	18	21.89
Elderly fostering	2	173.93[a]
Rotating care[b]	12	33.18
Total	32	35.62

a DHSS is now asked to help meet charges through board and lodging allowance.
b includes allowance for capital (7 per cent discount rate).
The 1984-85 average gross cost per Part 3 resident week was £107.12 (excluding allowance for capital).
Missing information = 8
Source: CIPFA 1984-85, *Personal Social Service Statistics (Actuals)*

3.2 Output mix efficiency

Table 11.4 describes features likely to influence output mix efficiency. Most schemes reported an enhancement of service content through moving away from long interval, domestic care-based services to more out-of-hours working, personal or nursing care. Basic nursing was undertaken by home carers in some projects, while in others the nursing service arranged to go in alongside the home help service. Enhancements in case management were usually based on the attachment of social workers (usually in domiciliary care settings), the introduction of problem-oriented assessments or an active review policy. Strong key worker roles with the authority to

Table 11.4
Output mix efficiency

Area	Service content						Case management				
	Rehabilitation	Out-of-hours	Personal care	Sitting	Nursing care	Family care	Social work attached	Problem-based assessments	Review	Case conferences	Liaison with other services
1 Inner London	Yes	Yes	Yes		Yes			Yes	Yes	Yes	Yes
2 Inner London		Yes	Yes		Yes		Yes				Yes
3 Outer London		Yes	Yes		Yes		Yes	Yes		Yes	Yes
4 Metropolitan District		Yes				Yes	Yes	Yes	Yes		
5 Metropolitan District		Yes		Yes		Yes	Yes	Yes			
6 Metropolitan District		Yes	Yes	Yes							
7(i) English Shire		Yes	Yes		Yes		Yes	Yes	Yes		
7(ii) English Shire		Yes	Yes						Yes		Yes
7(iii) English Shire											
8 English Shire	Yes						Yes	Yes	Yes		
9 English Shire							Yes				
10 Welsh County	Yes						Yes				
Total	3	8	6	2	4	2	8	6	5	2	4

allocate a range of services did not emerge, however, and only two schemes reported the use of case conferences as a means of improving liaison. So there are clear limits on the achievement of better case management roles. Both rotating care schemes, for example, functioned as discrete responses to a particular bottleneck.

For each of the 33 clients receiving an innovatory service, information was collected on the number of services with which there had been contact over a six-month period. In only five cases had no other services been involved. In thirteen cases, one or two other services had been involved. In ten cases, three or four other services had been involved, and in five cases, five or more other services. In nearly half the cases (fifteen), there had been contact with NHS services across agency boundaries. Such contacts tended to take place informally, with little structuring from higher tiers.

3.3 Vertical target efficiency

Table 11.5 describes features likely to affect vertical target efficiency. At programme level, explicit targeting was present in ten schemes, while in the other two goals were informally stated. The most frequently mentioned target groups consisted of those on the margins of admission to institutional care (seven schemes) and carers (eight schemes), although these groups were extremely broadly defined. At individual level, enhanced assessment and re-assessment provision was evident in about half the schemes, although others had tried to improve provision and had failed.

3.4 Horizontal target efficiency

The relevant features are described in Table 11.6. Although no scheme was primarily based on casefinding objectives, casefinding emerged as an important theme in a number of schemes which took steps to boost referrals. Four schemes reported problems with underreferral, usually from other practitioners. New schemes could quickly acquire a reputation for underreferral which could be difficult to shake off, although one scheme reported the opposite problem of overreferral which led to a cooling of relations with other service providers who were not able to refer on appropriate cases. The concern for casefinding did not lead to a radical renegotiation of roles.

4 The twelve innovations in their organisational context

Schemes could address similar issues, yet display very different histories. One boarding-out scheme failed during the period of fieldwork, the other developed further into a night sitting service. One home care scheme has

Table 11.5
Vertical target efficiency

Project	Margins of admission	Carer relief	EMI	Isolated elderly	Terminal care	Post hospital discharge	Enhanced assessment	Reassessment
1. Early discharge team	Yes				Yes	Yes	Yes	Yes
2. Community care assistants	Yes		Yes					Yes
3. Home care scheme							Yes	
4. Elderly family placement scheme	Yes	Yes		Yes			Yes	Yes
5. Elderly family placement scheme				Yes	Yes		Yes	
6. Nightsitting/tuck-in service	Yes	Yes						
7. Home care project	Yes	Yes	Yes				Yes	Yes
8. Home care project	Yes	Yes						Yes
9. Rotating residential care		Yes						
10. Residential rehabilitation unit		Yes		Yes		Yes	Yes	
11. Residential rotating care		Yes						
12. Residential rehabilitation unit	Yes	Yes					Yes	Yes
Total	7	8	2	3	2	2	6	5

Table 11.6
Horizontal target efficiency

Project	Case finding		
	Other practitioners	Direct with potential clients	Under-referral
1. Early discharge team			
2. Community care assistants			
3. Home care scheme	Yes		Yes
4. Elderly family placement scheme		Yes	Yes
5. Elderly family placement scheme	Yes	Yes	
6. Nightsitting/tuck-in service			
7. Home care project	Yes		
8. Home care project			Yes
9. Rotating residential care			
10. Residential rehabilitation unit			
11. Residential rotating care			
12. Residential rehabilitation unit	Yes		Yes
Total	4	2	4

remained a small-scale local resource (despite a major contribution to easing pressure on hospital beds), a second has developed into a large-scale central team, while a third has been generalised throughout the social services department concerned. Replication may go hand in hand with degeneration where roles with initial distinctive characteristics of flexibility become routinised. Scheme 3 (a bottom-up scheme) was perhaps the boldest in improving joint working at operational level, yet had not been replicated. Indeed, the replication of schemes which seek to alter work norms may be much more difficult than those which spring from structural change, yet such changes to work culture are central to the achievement of case management objectives.

Table 11.7 presents information on some organisational characteristics of these schemes. While most schemes have been set up in the last six or seven years, others have evolved gradually from traditional services. Scheme 6 is a good example of a flagging scheme which has been given

Table 11.7: Some characteristics of innovations

Project	Date	Scale	Location	Finance	Initiation	Process of expansion
1. Early discharge team	1978	105 elderly clients	Central specialist team	Joint finance	Top down	Yes
2. Community care assistants	1980	30 clients (80-90 per cent elderly)	Central specialist team	Base budget joint finance	Top down	Yes
3. Home care scheme	1979	Maximum 15	Local multi-disciplinary group	Base budget	Bottom up	Yes
4. Elderly family placement scheme	1982-1984	6 carers	Area teams	Base budget	Bottom up	No
5. Elderly family placement scheme	1982	30 carers	Central specialist team	Base budget	Top down	Yes
6. Nightsitting/ tuck-in service	Circa 1970	20+ clients	Dual central/local	Base budget joint finance	Top down	Yes
7. Home care project	1979	80 clients	Local multi-disciplinary team	Base budget joint finance	Top down	Yes
8. Home care project	1984	15 per cent home help hours	Area home help service	Joint finance	Top down	
9. Rotating residential care	Traditional holiday service	5 beds	Area team	Base budget	Bottom up	
10. Residential rehabilitation unit	1980	7 places	Mainstream Part 3 home	Base budget	Bottom up	No
11. Residential rotating care	Traditional holiday service	5 beds	Area team	Base budget	Bottom up	No
12. Residential rehabilitation unit	Traditional rehabilitation resource	3 bedsits	Mainstream Part 3 home	Base budget	Bottom up	No

a new lease of life by a newly-adopted local policy commitment to community care. The scale of these innovations varied wildly, with bottom-up schemes in particular remaining small-scale projects and unlikely to report a process of expansion. There was joint finance involvement in five of the schemes.

Six of the schemes were centrally sponsored, and six locally. The main problems with top-down innovation relate to implementation difficulties, especially the negotiation of new roles and styles of working among resistant staff, while bottom-up innovations find difficulty in securing resources or referrals because of the lack of organisational legitimacy. An alternative third mode of innovation consists of nationally-based change, such as the recent national regrading of home helps into care assistants. The interpretation of this regrading may well vary from authority to authority, reflecting the extent to which personal care roles have already emerged.

A major organisational question concerns the linkage between health and social care agencies. At case level, there was evidence of active contact (not always satisfactorily resolved) in about half the cases. Yet managerial and professional hierarchies nearly always defeated attempts to construct more lateral forms of organisation. Thus nursing officers might encourage the formation of home care roles within SSDs, but at the same time assert that such workers should come under nursing control. SSDs, with the aid of joint finance, were sometimes willing to sponsor post-hospital discharge schemes, as long as they remained accountable to SSD line managers. Nevertheless, the lack of joint management did not preclude a high level of inter-agency contact at case level.

There have been pleas for organic moves to joint management of services, most notably for mental health care groups (House of Commons Social Services Committee, 1985, para. 96) but also more generally (Audit Commission, 1986c). A joint management solution, it is argued, would dispense with the need for complex joint finance and planning arrangements. Only two schemes showed signs of moving towards a joint management model. Scheme 3 is run on a day-to-day basis by a joint management group which accepts clients on to the scheme but does not have direct line-management responsibility for special resources. A social worker coordinator (responsible to the area officer) is available as a key worker. Nevertheless, there are continuing barriers to joint working even at operational level: the district nursing sisters do their assessments independently and there was often little liaison between them and the other agencies involved.

Scheme 7 was initially funded through joint finance under the responsibility to a joint management group which met every four months. The project leader is accountable to an SSD manager, now that the project is base budget funded. Both schemes in effect demonstrate the difficulty, under present circumstances, of establishing joint management arrangements with responsibility for resources as opposed to coordinating or advisory bodies.

5 Outcomes and technical efficiency

The innovations studied differed, even the innovations of the same type. The number of cases for which we have full data is small. However, we have sought two forms of evidence of success of such a high degree that it can be revealed even with the small numbers: (i) higher scores than would be expected given service levels and quasi-inputs; and (ii) evidence about location after six months and again two years later.

5.1 The test for superior technical efficiency

Here we examined the recipients of innovative intensive home help/care schemes who remained in the community for at least six months: nine cases in all. The residuals for these cases from equations for final outputs reported in Chapter 4 were compared with residuals for a one-in-six sample of consumers of standard services. In effect, therefore, we sought an 'innovation effect' to explain that part of the variation in the final outputs which was not explained by variations in the resource and non-resource inputs found to be influential in the analysis of Chapter 4. So the innovation effect sought is additional to any benefits which work through the resource input effects revealed by the models, and is therefore an improvement in 'technical efficiency' requiring an increase in one or more forms of productivity. The differences in the residuals for the two groups of consumers were tested using analysis of variance.

The difference in the mean residuals between the groups was in the direction compatible with the beneficial innovation effect only for one output: users' felt vulnerability to risks. (The equation showing the effects of service levels and quasi-inputs on it are described in Table 4.12). There was no sign of the hypothesised effect for life satisfaction (the LSX of Table 4.1), consumers' desire for extra help (DESHELP), the user's degree of satisfaction with the experience of social services (SDFAV), the client's assessment of the impact of home help and home care (HHEFFECT), and the field worker's view of the success of the intervention (CMCURE). The failure to show superior technical efficiency for these other outputs was unlikely to be due to the small number of cases studied. The difference in means was in the opposite direction to that required to suggest the superior technical efficiency of the innovatory schemes for all the variables other than RISK, the one variable for which there is a significant difference in the direction implying higher technical efficiency.

Caveats abound: small numbers; a narrow range of output indicators; the implicit assumption that the production relations are anatomically similar in the innovatory schemes and standard provision so that the same estimated production function can be applied to both; the comparison of groups whose multivariate distributions on some of the predictor variables, particularly home help/care inputs, are quite different; the ambiguity of the final outputs: is an expressed desire for more help in some cases a positive indicator of final output and in others a negative indicator? However, these results, though in no sense conclusive, must not be dismissed. They are too compatible with the conclusions of the research to be ignored, and they are the first direct estimates of differences in the technical efficiency of innovative social care schemes derived from a production function.

5.2 *Location and input levels after six months and two and a half years*

The comparison of locational outcomes after one and three years does not contradict the impression created by the analysis of relative technical efficiency. The proportions who had died or had been admitted to institutions were more than three times as great among consumers of the innovatory home care schemes (schemes 2, 3, 7 and 8) after six months. The proportions were still much higher after three years. However, their circumstances would have predicted higher mortality or institutional admission. Since the number of cases was small and the number of likely predictors is legion, no attempt was made to exaggerate the importance of this inadequate evidence by matching the cases receiving innovatory service with others on predictors of mortality.

More interesting is what the recipients of the innovatory services were consuming after six months and two and a half years. Contrary to expectation, and what must surely be required for an adequate level of support, only a low proportion were consuming more than a modest amount of community service inputs. All those consuming more than the equivalent of six hours of home help a week after six months, and all but one after two and a half years were recipients of only one of the four schemes. Again one is reminded of the strictures of the short-term intensive home care schemes alluded to in the final section.

6 Conclusions

A hidden assumption in this chapter is that the management of innovation is indeed a major issue for health and welfare agencies. It is not enough for change to happen, but this change process should be aligned with strategic objectives, and demonstrate signs of efficiency improvement.

However, the centrality or otherwise of the process of innovation depends on the degree of change perceived as necessary in order to respond to the prior or anticipated shift in the relevant environment. Where the task environment is relatively stable, innovation is unlikely to be seen as a central managerial task. However, a combination of demographic, financial, professional and external agency factors indicate an environment which is far from static, even if not displaying the accelerated rate of change evident in mental health care groups.

The global concept of change can in turn be broken down into two quite separate notions of the rate and scope of change, the first being a quantitative and the second a qualitative concept. Agencies could be experiencing change along neither, one or both of these dimensions. The most common shift at local level has been from a situation of rapid quantitative growth and minimal qualitative change characteristic of the early 1970s to one of pockets of qualitative change which now face replication problems. Innovatory activity is of greatest salience to agencies when there is a perception that both the rate and scope of the change process are accelerating or alternatively need to be accelerated further. Such change processes may vary not only between localities but between client groups. In the British context, services for mentally handicapped people show a high degree of change, with new community-based services, models of care and newly trained staff coming onstream across a broad front within an accelerated time-scale. In contrast, the change process for the much larger and more diffuse elderly client group lags, with new models of provision fitfully emerging.

As we have seen, the change process is dominated by well-established streams of argument and activity. Alternative modal shift and outreach objectives compete for dominance, with the former currently pre-eminent given concern for cost compression. Input substitution has emerged as a major theme, with some evidence available that costs to the SSD in programmes designed for elderly people at the margins of admission are substantially lower than those of residential care. Yet such schemes remain small-scale alternatives to institutional care. Services for elderly people are still dominated by residential facilities, unlike services for people with a mental handicap where an extensive programme of hospital closures is now planned. There was little evidence of joint working with voluntary or informal sectors, despite their contribution to non-institutional care for elderly people. Nor are there reports of developing new forms of regulatory technique vis-à-vis an expanding private sector (Davies, 1986a). Indeed a major source of cost escalation has been the considerable recent growth of private care funded through the social security budget without screening on entry. Input substitution-based innovation has proceeded at a slow rate, has involved a narrow spectrum of activity, and has depended on cost-shunting between agencies as well as cost reduction.

Community care, it is sometimes said, can be cheap but also extremely nasty. Process-based measures of output mix efficiency represent one means of assessing the effectiveness of care where sample numbers are too small for quasi-experimental evaluative design. The provision of 'tending' care is central to many of the innovations, either in the form of home care roles or substitute family care. Activity was often concentrated on the enhancement of service content rather than case management. Small-scale projects were most unlikely to maintain dependent elderly people at home in isolation from other community services, either based in the SSD or in the NHS. Yet few explicit case management roles emerged, although improved informal coordination could represent a scheme objective. Improved joint working is likely to be central to the achievement of modal shift objectives, in order to avoid unplanned discharge, revolving door readmissions and failure to meet multiple needs. Not only were there few developments in case management roles at operational level, but joint management arrangements with control over resources were also absent, reflecting the power of vertical hierarchies.

Some schemes reported a gradual process of expansion and differentiation, but only Scheme 8 had been replicated on a county-wide basis, although the extent to which the special hours were taken up varied from one area to another. The dilemma which faces change groups in adopting either an exclusive or inclusive stance (Pettigrew, 1985) is apparent here. An exclusive innovating group coheres around specific values and goals which reject mainstream work norms. Such ideological coherence may be gained at the expense of poor relations with more traditional agencies. Innovators with an inclusive orientation are less likely to challenge established work cultures, but face the possibility that they may be broken by the mould rather than vice versa.

Traditionally capital and residentially care led, SSD policies for the elderly shifted to the adoption of revenue and community care-based global aims in the late 1970s. Unlike earlier dashes for growth, such policies assumed a considerable degree of role change. Many of the innovations included in the study in effect represented a preliminary working out – usually on a small-scale – of the type of service changes implied by such general community care policies. One challenge now is to maintain the momentum: to expand the coverage of the schemes, to effect a transition to stable (often base budget) finance and to ensure that replication is not accompanied by degeneration as a more inclusive change strategy is adopted. The other is to ensure that they do actually improve the equity and efficiency of outcomes. The results in Section 5 suggest that such improvement cannot be taken for granted.

Part III

12 The four scenarios reconsidered

Chapter 1 suggested that 1988 might be a climacteric in the history of the balance of care, postulating four alternative scenarios with quite different implications for policy priorities. The first section re-examines the results to assess which scenario most closely conforms to our results. The second section considers alternative strategies in the light of the analysis.

1 The scenarios

The scenarios postulated were:

- The existing targeting propensities and relations between resources and outcomes are such that the system would become substantially more community-based simply by increasing expenditure levels by an achievable amount.
- Given changes in targeting propensities only – that is, who gets what service in what quantities – the system would become substantially more community-based given a politically achievable increase in public expenditure.
- The 'marginal productivities' of inputs will have to be increased, though targeting is satisfactory.
- To become substantially more community-based given the achievable increase in spending would require greatly improved 'marginal productivities' of inputs, more and larger increments of beneficial outcomes from the additional unit of resources, as well as improved targeting propensities, unless the welfare of consumers is to fall and care burdens become more inequitably distributed.

These scenarios beg for quantitative definition. Also they imply the judgement that substitution for institutional long-term care should be the highest priority for community social services. However, they help to focus the discussion because they have policy implications which are different in kind. If reality is little different from the first, not much more than additional spending and the evolution of the services on their present path would be necessary. Managers can sup with the new managerialism with as long a spoon as circumstances permit. If the second is nearer to reality, managers must engage some issues defined by the new managerialists, and develop and implement some of their technical ideas. In particular, they must invest in the development of devices better to match resources to needs. In current Audit Commission (1987) and SSI

(DHSS, 1987b) argument, this above all means improving the effectiveness of the performance of the core tasks of case management. Since it is not just a matter of ensuring that all and only the appropriate persons obtain services, but also that the mixes and levels of inputs are adjusted to their needs and are varied in response to changing circumstances, this will require substantial investment in training and the development of policies, frameworks, procedures and technical devices to assure the quality of case management. However, it will require sensitive and skilled technicians, certainly not magicians; and not the fundamental retraining of some staff and the redeployment of large numbers. If the third scenario is most realistic, more pervasive change will be needed, and the investment of resources and effort will have to be correspondingly greater. The fourth scenario will, if anything, require more effort to handle than the third.

2 Which scenario fits?

We review the evidence around the two foci of the study which differentiate the scenarios: (i) targeting propensities and the dynamics which determine them, the interplay of structures, procedures, field-level assumptive worlds and agency policies which determine them; and (ii) 'productivities' and their causes. Table 12.1 summarises some of the more important results of the study about each.

2.1 Equity, efficiency and targeting propensities: who gets what and why?

It is a useful simplification to focus on Cover and average Intensity. Others have described the interplay of structures, policies and assumptive worlds by which Cover and Intensity are determined, particularly the Social Services Inspectorate (DHSS, 1987b, 1988a). So this study has focused on some key features of the dynamics which determine them. Some of the findings are of great practical importance.

2.1.1 The balance of needs and resources
Chapter 2 showed how the new managerialist critique focuses on one form of target efficiency only: vertical target efficiency, the proportion of resources consumed by those in the target group. Compared with the feminist critique, there are few mentions of horizontal target inefficiency (persons in the target group who do not actually consume services), and then the allusions are not to a general problem but to particular case types.

Chapter 2 also shows that in 1985 levels of community social services were inadequate both to cover populations in need by the reasonable targeting criteria currently discussed in the literature and to secure higher average Intensity. We have argued this before from the re-analysis of data for 1980 (Bebbington and Davies, 1983). However, calculations based on apparently more stringent criteria proposed by the Audit Commission confirm the finding; and the SSI reached a similar conclusion by another route (again see Chapter 2).

2.1.2 *The equity and efficiency of targeting*

The causal dynamics which determine Cover and Intensity may be deeply rooted. Indeed, they have been working in much the same way for perhaps a quarter of a century (Chapter 2). One basic relationship in the dynamic is the balance between demand and resources: the budget allocation to the service in relation to demand. Modelling in Chapter 2 shows that Gross Expenditure is the main influence on Cover. Diagram 2.1 showed that the balance did not become increasingly favourable to a degree which allowed Cover to be increased steadily. So average Intensity fell towards what in the UK is seen as the conventional minimum of two hours a week. (The Swedish conventional minimum is lower, one visit a fortnight.)

At the time of the collection of our data about needs and resources (1985), the new managerialist attempts to change targeting propensities seemed from our analysis to have hardly begun to have measurably large and general effects on targeting for the majority of recipients who lived alone. This was so despite great variations between the authorities studied in their apparent interest in, and type of, targeting policies; and the systematic attempt of several years' duration by some departments to change them (Chapters 3, 6 and 7). Indeed, the account of the performance of the core tasks of case management given in Chapter 6 suggests that levels of management above the first tier were almost irrelevant to the choices made by allocators when resolving the targeting dilemma of stretching resources to cover demand. That average Intensity varies little between areas now (and twenty years ago) reflects this (Davies, 1968, Appendix 2, Table 2). It is mainly on what therefore appears to be a marginal clientele, those sharing households with others, that policy and resource differences had an impact on targeting. (Later paragraphs comment on the parallel result that variations between authorities in their commitment to applying new managerialist effort to home care were similarly unmatched by large differences in average and marginal productivities.)

The more refined is the targeting analysis, the more sensitive targeting appears. However, the pattern is clearly improvable for many reasons. The patterns in Chapter 3 and Table 12.1 show both sins of omission and commission. Table 12.1 contains inferences the evaluative significance of which need not be spelt out in the text. Particularly important is the contrast between anomalous patterns of correlation with disability and need types, and the sum of these agency inputs and the inputs of informal

Table 12.1
Targeting results: an overview

Home help/care consumes most expenditure on community social services. Estimates for a range of targeting criteria show horizontal target efficiency to be lower than vertical target efficiency: that is, the proportion of persons in need actually receiving service is lower than the proportion receiving service who are not in need. So the reallocation of resources from those not in need would be insufficient to provide what would be required to achieve complete coverage of those in need (Chapter 2).

The analysis of average consumption of home help/care by need type suggests that the patterns are more rational than has been suggested by some on the basis of cruder analyses. However, variations in needs are not precisely matched by variations in consumption. (i) There is little variation between need types. And (ii) high need groups consuming low quantities beg questions about equity and efficiency (Table 3.2).

Much of the variation between authorities in average quantities of services consumed reflects variations in the need-related characteristics of the recipients: allocation criteria and the factors influencing the quantity demanded vary less between areas than would be supposed from an examination of mean intensities of provision. However, the partial correlations between utilisation and need-related circumstances also suggest anomalies and confirm that targeting is not highly sophisticated (Chapter 2). An examination of the single correlations also confirms this.

Statistical modelling to explain the utilisation of home help/care shows: (i) by how much the supply of informal care affects the quantities of service consumed; (ii) the greater predictability of the utilisation of persons living alone than of persons sharing households and the smaller area variations in consumption norms for persons living alone; (iii) the specific nature of some of the need-related

carers; a contrast due mainly to the similarity between this British pattern and that in Cleveland, Ohio, referred to below.

2.1.3 Association between group characteristics and marginal productivities: an efficiency criterion

The study has produced evidence of many kinds about the finesse with which equity and efficiency in targeting are systematically sought and successfully achieved. Results in Part I are particularly interesting because they estimate the associations between the circumstances of consumers and both marginal productivities themselves and the utilisation of services.

Table 12.1 (continued)

circumstances which affect utilisation, and so the likelihood that cruder analyses will overstate inequity and inefficiency (Tables 3.3 and 3.4). However, the modelling again reveals apparent anomalies and a utilisation pattern which is incompatible with the best use of resources given the marginal productivities estimated in Chapter 3.

Some of the same generalisations apply to the consumption of meals-on-wheels. In particular, there is a mismatch between self-care abilities and the pattern of consumption. Only a minority of clients in any need group receives them, and there are apparently anomalous variations between groups in the proportions (Tables 3.5 and 3.6). The same generalisations are valid *a fortiori* for the patterns of day care, whose utilisation is also characterised by a high proportion of those recommended for service not actually taking it up or soon ceasing to consume it (Tables 3.7 and 3.8). Again, only a minority of clients of any need group received regular social work, the median social work time being less than half an hour a week for all groups. However, there were clear and illuminating patterns of associations between the quantity of social work received and need-related circumstances (Tables 3.9, 3.10 and 3.11). Too few clients received short-term residential care for the study to reveal interesting patterns.

The analysis of the total cost of the resources consumed showed that (i) differences between need types are greater for those with little informal support, and (ii) differences between need types are much greater and more systematically related to the degree of need for the total of the costs of community health and community social services than for the costs of community social services alone (Table 3.14). Like the analyses of home help utilisation, the modelling of the total costs confirms the importance of a group of heavy users of health and social services, reinforcing the importance for equity and efficiency of good field coordination of the two sets of services. Although the modelling suggests how utilisation reflects particular needs, it also reveals apparent anomalies.

We can therefore apply an important criterion of efficiency not previously used in studies of home care. Efficiency requires that more resources are allocated to those whose circumstances increase the value of the beneficial outcomes produced by the inputs. In general, therefore, one must assume that efficient allocations would show positive associations between utilisation by people with a particular characteristic and marginal productivities which are higher than average for people with that characteristic. Negative associations would be found between utilisation and circumstances accompanying low productivities. There would be no association with other circumstances. We have argued elsewhere that we would expect the costs of improving outcomes to be strongly associated with user circumstances in a system making the best use of resources and that the absence of such associations indicates variable performance, an aspect of inefficiency (Davies and Challis, 1986, pp.183-9).

There is an important caveat to this argument. Beneficial outcomes are not necessarily of equal value. Our criterion is valid only if the outcomes compared are equally important. We have not directly estimated the utilities attached to outcomes and their combinations. It is true that some of the indicators of potential outcomes used are based on a composite judgement about the effects of resources and the value of these effects. Examples for which the modelling was successful are DESHELP (consumers' perceptions of their need for more help) and SDFAV (the degree of satisfaction with the community social services received). But others are indicators of consequences themselves, and take no account of the marginal valuations of consumers or others whose perceptions are a legitimate source of valuation judgements. For these, a judgement about efficiency demands that we consider whether the value of additional benefits of the kind in question is different as well as whether the allocation is associated with the marginal productivity.

2.1.4 The criterion applied to client outcomes
Table 12.2 summarises the marginal productivity effects shown in Chapter 4 and their interaction effects on quasi-inputs. The table distinguishes *general* from *target group* effects. The latter are estimates of the difference made to marginal productivities by consumer circumstances, and so are the effects to which we seek a targeting response in the utilisation evidence. There are three effects: (i) the lower marginal productivity of home care inputs for DESHELP among consumers with short interval needs and higher levels of informal support (Need Type 3); (ii) the higher marginal productivity of home care for CMCURE (the number of problems judged by the field supervisor to be resolved by the services) among those who felt that their informal social support was less adequate at the second than at the first interview (LOSSADEQ); and (iii) the negative correlation of the marginal productivity of day care in the reduction of clients' perceived risks (RISK) among persons living alone. The evidence is complex and so the judgement about efficiency is difficult. However, a judgement seems to be possible in two of the three cases.
(i) The evidence is too ambiguous to make a clear judgement about the efficiency implications in the first. Clients of Need Type 3 do have a lower *probability of receiving* home help/care than members of other groups (Table 3.2). But it is not obvious that the *quantitites consumed by users* of home help/care are lower. The mean consumption is higher for Type 3 than for any group other than those with critical interval needs and relatively little

Table 12.2
Marginal productivities[a] of services for user outcomes

Marginal productivities	LSX	RISK	DESHELP	Outputs CMCURE	SDFAV	HHEFFECT
General effects						
Home help/care (HHCINP)	—	—	—	$0.16 - .02X^a$ Maximum: 8	$0.02X^{*a} - 0.15$ Maximum: 7.5	$0.04X^a - 0.40$ Minimum: 9.8
Street wardens (WARDINP)	—	—	—	—	—	—
Meals-on-wheels (MOWINP)	—	-0.10	-0.09	—	—	—
Day care (DCPINP)	—	—	—	—	-0.27	-0.28
Short term residential care (STCINP)	-0.14	—	—	—	—	—
Social Work (SWINP)	—	—	—	0.03	—	—
Voluntary helper (VOLHELP)	—	—	-0.53	$6.48 + 2.38X^a$	—	—
Private nurse or home help (PRIVHELP)	—	—	0.60	—	—	0.91
Number of aids and adaptations (AIDS)	—	—	—	—	—	—
Nurse (NURSE)[b]	—	—	—	—	—	—
Day hospital (DAYHOSP)[b]	—	—	—	—	—	—
Hospital (HOSP)[b]	-0.74	0.34	—	—	—	0.34
Targeting effects						
Home help/care for MYTYPO3	—	—	0.27	—	—	—
Home help/care for LOSSADEQ	—	—	—	—	—	—
Day care for HHOLD1	—	0.62	—	0.14	—	—

X   Denotes the output variable in question.
a   Estimates significantly different from zero at the 10 per cent level in direction appropriate for variable with a 1–tail test, save for HOSP, DHOSP, and NURSE to which a 2–tail test applied.
b   Treated as exogenous, a quasi-input output predictor.

informal support, a high need group by the two most important general criteria. Although the modal consumption is relatively low for Type 3 users (Table 3.2), the modelling suggested higher quantities consumed by Type 3 users, allowance being made for their other circumstances. Perhaps service allocators assume less informal help to be provided than is the case. Or perhaps the judgements of allocators about the impact of the services might have been distorted by the unappreciated effects of circumstances associated with outcomes for reasons unconnected with service inputs; that is, by improvements not due to inputs but wrongly attributed to them. (Attributing recovery actually due to spontaneous remission to medical treatment is an example of this type of perceptual distortion.) Or again, that the quantities consumed appear to be no lower for this supported group might be due to strain on carers, and so be a response either to equity judgements or to the probability that informal carers will give up and so to a longer-run view of efficiency. However, the relationship between carer Malaise and service quantities is tenuous, making such judgements unreliable.

(ii) The evidence is clearer in the second case. There does seem to be an efficient targeting response to the higher marginal productivity for CMCURE of home help/care among those who perceived their social support to be less adequate at the second interview. Table 3.3 shows a partial correlation with a decline between the interviews in the number of persons whom the client judged they could turn to when in difficulty: a response to a precisely relevant change during the relevant period. However, there is a much clearer response to the situation at the time of the first interview and to events prior to it, as one would expect from a system with weak monitoring of client circumstances. Again the generally negative effect of the loss of social support (LOSSADEQ) itself for life satisfaction and RISK might have disguised the benefits of home help/care from some of the allocators.

(iii) The evidence also seems to point to a clear conclusion in the third case. In this instance, it is that there is *prima facie* evidence of inefficiency. It will be remembered that day care appeared to have lower marginal productivity in the reduction of felt vulnerability (RISK) among clients living alone. However, the unsupported need types had higher probabilities of being allocated day care (Table 3.7). Again, among those who actually consumed it, the quantities tended on average to be no less and for some levels of disability seemed to be greater (Tables 3.7 and 3.8). Perhaps the lower marginal productivity is disguised by some of the beneficial effects of higher levels of informal support; for instance, the effects of AVAILX on change in life satisfaction (Table 4.8), the effects of Type 4 membership, ADEQ, AVAIL, and AVAILX on DESHELP (Table 4.12), the partial correlation of living alone, ADEQ, and AVAIL with SDFAV (Table 4.15), and the association of Types 4 and 6 membership with HHEFFECT (Table 4.15).

Table 12.3
Distribution of principal carers by Malaise score

| Score | Carers of clients[a] Non-spouse Twelve areas[b] % | Carers of non-clients | | |
		Non-spouse Twelve areas[b] %	Non-spouse Salisbury %	Spouse Salisbury %
0	15	25	17	16
1	15	12	20	16
2	16	10	17	9
3	12	12	17	11
4	7	13	7	13
5	6	3	7	16
6	5	7	7	4
7	5	10	7	4
8	5	4	3	5
9	3	0	0	0
10	6	2	0	2
11	2	2	0	2
12	2	0	0	0
13	0.5	2	0	0
14	0.5	0	0	0
15 and over	0	0	1	4
All scores				
%	100.0	100.0	100.0	100.0
(N)	(245)	(99)	(30)	(56)

a Clients: Mean = 4.1; s.d. = 3.7. Non-client sample: mean = 3.3, s.d. = 3.2. Quine and Charnley (1987) compare means for various carer groups: parents of children with severe mental handicap (Quine and Pahl, 1985); parents of ESM(S) children from the 1970 Cohort study, mean = 5.7, s.d. = 5.1, number = 78; parents of severely disabled infants, mean = 6.1, s.d. = 5.1, number = 6.1; parents of children with severe mental handicap, mean = 5.8, s.d. = 4.1; number = 200 (Bebbington and Quine, 1986; Quine and Charnley, 1987); mothers of children with physical disorders other than brain disorder, mean = 3.67; s.d. = 3.5, number = 106 (estimated from Rutter, Tizard and Whitmore, 1970, Table 21.8); mothers of children with psychiatric disorders, mean = 6.1; s.d. = 4.5, number = 107 (Rutter, Tizard and Whitmore, 1970). Salisbury non-spouse sample, mean = 3.0, s.d. = 3.1.; Salisbury spouse sample: mean = 3.8, s.d. = 3.7 (Challis, Tong and Traske, 1988).

b The data base for this study. Neither the client nor non-client sample has been re-weighted to achieve a distribution of a simple random sample.

2.1.5 The criterion applied to carer outcomes
New evidence must be presented here to assess whether targeting takes into account variations in marginal productivities for carer outcomes. The most general measure of outcomes for carers we have is the score on the Malaise Inventory (Rutter, Tizard and Whitmore, 1970). In effect, the authors claimed that the inventory performed both the functions distinguished in the literature: an indicator of likely degree of disturbance and/or distress; and an indicator of the probability of what is sometimes called 'caseness'. Relevant to the latter function, Rutter et al. claimed that the Inventory 'differentiated moderately well between parents with and without psychiatric disorders' (Rutter, Tizard and Whitmore, 1970, p.340). In an unpublished letter to Lyn Quine, Professor Rutter suggested that scores of 5 or 6 are outside the normal range and indicate stress (Quine and Pahl, 1985, p.503).

Table 12.3 and Diagram 12.1 show that despite the services received by their dependants, a substantial minority of the non-spouse principal carers of clients of the community social services have high levels of stress, and so do substantial minorities of carers not receiving community social services. However, our data may exaggerate the proportions with high stress levels because our sampling was designed to estimate relationships between needs, resources and outcomes rather than to yield unbiased estimates of means and distributions and so was weighted with clients of high dependency; and, similarly, the non-client sample was selected to be comparable to the client population. The effect of our sampling design may not be great, a comparison of the distribution for

Table 12.4
Targeting effects for carer outcomes
**Marginal cost to the social services of reducing Malaise and effect
threshold[a] levels of the Malaise score**

Client circumstances	Equation	Effect
One person household, not MYTYPO3	1.44 − 0.27 M	5.3
Multi-person household, MYTYPO3	1.23 − 0.27 M	4.5
One-person household, MYTYPO3	2.88 − 0.27 M	10.6
Multi-person household, not MYTYPO3	−0.13 − 0.27 M	< 0

a The effect threshold is the value of M above which additional resources are partially correlated with reductions in Malaise.
b Average weekly opportunity costs to the social services department for the 208 households with clients receiving home care for more than twelve months. The coefficients reflect a modelling strategy designed to find effects of increased resources on Malaise reduction. The cost function from which the above equations were derived is described in Table 2 of Appendix 12.
'Type 3' denotes that the most dependent client in the household has short interval need with potential/actual support.

Diagram 12.1
Distribution of principal carer's Malaise score

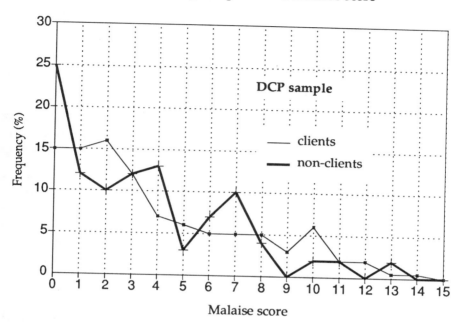

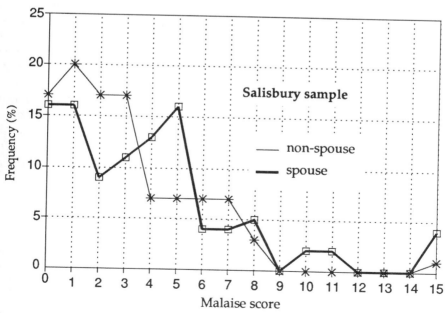

Note: In the Domiciliary Care (DCP) sample, all principal carers were non-spouse.

our non-client sample and the Salisbury sample suggests (Challis, Tong and Traske, 1988). (The Salisbury data also suggest that it is essential to develop argument about the targeting of spouse carers suffering from high stress.)

Our modelling focused on the costs to the social services department of relying on the standard community services to reduce Malaise scores to below the level suggested by Rutter to indicate abnormal stress. We therefore have estimates of marginal costs, not of marginal productivity. There are two effects analogous to the 'targeting effects' distinguished in Table 12.2: effects for multiple person households and for MYTYPO3 clients (those with short interval needs and lesser informal support). Table 12.4 shows the equations for marginal costs for combinations of MYTYPO membership and household composition. The slope term does not differ between the equations. Differences in marginal costs between groups are entirely due to variations in the constant for the marginal cost equation. It can be seen that the marginal costs of stress reduction are least for multiple households with other than MYTYPO3 dependants, but are also low for other multiple households. Chapter 3 yielded little evidence that more was allocated to such households. So there is little indication of the responsiveness which would be needed to make the best use of resources for the relief of non-spouse principal carers.

So this analysis confirms the conclusion suggested by the other evidence in the study. There are indeed signs that targeting on clients reflects a calculus which takes into account equity and efficiency more than is suggested by cruder statistical analysis. It is all too easy for senior managers and policy analysts to underestimate the quality of judgements of untrained personnel in a world which is not directly visible to those at some distance from it. The services' field managers are archetypal 'street-level bureaucrats', as the Aberdeen and SSI studies remind us (Hunter, McKeganey and MacPherson, 1988; DHSS, 1987b, 1988a,b). But also the statistical evidence suggests a degree of sophistication which could be improved, and some of the targeting priorities which might be an improvement. This seems even clearer for outcomes for non-spouse carers than for clients. We consider this again after we consider the marginal productivities in their own right.

2.2 Targeting and the field coordination of community health and social services

Those needing high intensity health and social care are a critical target group. Effective care for them should be one of the litmus tests for the national and local development of systems. The difficult issues raised by the group are among the most convenient to ignore. For this group, health and social care needs are interdependent. Changes in targeting are likely

Table 12.5
Clients' perceptions of reasons for referral to the community social services and front-line managers' perceptions of problems by occupation of front-line manager

Reason or problem	Reason for referral Front-line manager:		Perception of problem Front-line manager:	
	Home help organiser %	Social worker %	Home help organiser %	Social worker %
Specific health condition[a]	83	75	70	42
General self-care problems	84	56	96	73
Mental health problems	6	18	26	51
Bereavement and/or loneliness	20	32	11	41
Various personal and financial problems	22	22	7	23
Burden on informal carers	16	19	13	29
Not sure why referred	3	7	_b	_b
Number of cases	(294)	(175)	(271)	(136)

a Including discharge from hospital

to increase the interdependence by increasing the proportion of all recipients who are functionally incapacitated. However,

- The study shows that it is the community health services more than the community social services whose provisions are most responsive to variations in functional capacity. Chapter 3 showed that the gradient of community service spending with disability group was not steep; less steep than the expenditure on community health services (Table 3.14). That may be the result of the community health more than the community social services occupying the grey territory of ambiguous responsibility, the provision of service to undertake personal care tasks. The territory may be grey, but its strategic importance to the equity and efficiency of long-term care is indisputable. Also, there are clear signs that fiscal pressure is forcing health authorities to vacate the grey area. Social care must fill the gap.
- Others have shown that inadequate and delayed access to medical treatment are exacerbating the needs for long-term social care.
- Our evidence shows that the utilisation of acute inpatient beds is higher than might have been expected for what was selected to be a group of long-term care recipients.

So the coordination of acute and long-term care must be an important factor in evaluating plans for the future.

We must therefore (i) ask whether equity and efficiency is best served by a pattern of targeting in which the community social services are not highly responsive to the functional incapacity of clients, leaving more of the response to the community nursing service; and (ii) discuss the implications for the performance of core case management tasks. Answers to these questions have important practical implications.

What makes this of great and probably growing importance is the interdependence of need and the overlap between health and social services among those for whom institution-based care is inappropriate.

The evidence is of various kinds.

Untreated medical conditions and the impact of improved access. An example of the evidence is that 17 per cent of persons on the waiting list for old people's homes suffered untreated medical conditions. The effects of treating them can greatly affect the probability of admission (Brocklehurst, Carty, Leeming and Robinson, 1978). Likewise, well-timed and effective health visiting can influence subsequent care needs and outcomes (Vetter, Jones and Victor, 1984). Neill, Sinclair, Gorbach and Williams (1988) list other studies showing the same kinds of effect. In common with the screening and assessment literature, they suggest that good health and social care (the Thanet Community Care Project is an example of the latter) increases the demand for acute short-term treatment but reduces the need for long-term care in institutions. That there are these gains to be made suggests that we may have paid in more than one way for establishing a system of long-term care not dominated by the cultures of health-related professions: untreated illness among users whose timely access to health care is insufficiently aided by community social services staff; and in consequence a greater need for personal care than would otherwise be necessary.

The prevalence of disabilities among consumers. Table 12.5 shows the proportions of our client sample for whom health and disability were reasons for referral. Those coming nearest to performing the core tasks of case management claimed that ill health and disability were problems for more than one-half of cases. The proportions of clients claiming this are higher; perhaps because users emphasise what they perceive as the more socially acceptable reasons; for example, disability and physical disease rather than depression. Of home help cases, 48 per cent were referred by a health agency. So too were 44 per cent of day care and social work cases. Of the 177 cases receiving both health and social services, 60 per cent had been referred by health care personnel. An analysis of all client recipients showed that those consuming both community health and social services tended to have critical interval needs, particularly those with low informal support (12 and 18 per cent of the critical interval groups compared with 6-7 per cent of the others), and short interval cases with low support.

The proportions of consumers receiving both community social services and community health services. The General Household Survey for 1980 suggested that of the recipients of either the community nursing or community social services, a fifth received both. Of our home help consumers, 7 per cent were also receiving personal care from the community nursing service. Nevertheless, of the persons aged 75 and over in contact with community nurses nationally, approximately one-half were also recipients of social services. Of community nursing visits to study clients, 30 per cent involved only personal care, and an OPCS survey found that 38 per cent of community nursing time was spent on 'basic nursing' (Dunnell and Dobbs, 1982).

A logit analysis of (254) survivors in the community among our client sample illustrates the importance of recent hospitalisation and functional incapacity (Baines and Davies, 1989a). Hospitalisation in acute wards during the initial study period of six months, an indicator of incapacity to undertake personal care tasks, and the membership of the short interval need group with low social support (MYTYPO4) correctly predict whether clients would consume community health as well as social services for some 71 per cent of cases, all the coefficients being significantly greater than zero at the 1 per cent level. Such hospitalisation itself correctly predicts whether clients would receive both community health and social services for 75 per cent of cases without additional information in the case of the 45 cases who were low users of social services. The replacement of the hospitalisation predictor by a predictor defined as hospitalisation only among those with a principal informal carer improved the prediction, but merely negligibly. Also this effect of hospitalisation among persons with a principle carer is in same direction as the hospitalisation variable. So the presence of a non-spouse principal informal carer does not diminish the effect of hospitalisation on the probability of receiving both community health and social services, at least during the study period. This is an intriguing result, because the degree of informal support available certainly did not itself seem to contribute to the explanation – though it might have affected the probability of hospitalisation, or worked with the hospitalisation to further increase the predictability of joint consumption. If the provision of informal support does not affect the probability, one must wonder both about the criteria for case selection of the community health services and whether the social services transmit what must be crucial information to the health services. The logit prediction of whether users of larger quantities of community social services were joint consumers confirmed that the effects of incapacity to undertake personal care tasks were a more powerful predictor among those with critical interval need than was functional incapacity taken with the extent of informal care. It was only among those with short interval needs that the extent of informal care made a powerful difference.

Primary health care knowledge about social service needs. Hooper (1988) argues that already, for 95 per cent of cases, the primary health care team can readily obtain the information necessary to provide precise referrals to case managers of long-term community care. What they lack is the incentive to mobilise and act upon it. Other evidence suggests that in some practices elderly patients may now have few undiagnosed and untreated conditions (for example, Taylor and Ford, 1983; Ebrahim, Hedley and Sheldon, 1984; Hendriksen, Lund and Stromgard, 1984a).

What may be more valid is the argument that with the right incentives and technical devices and assistance, general practices could yield the needed information. Partly this could be accomplished by changing the perspective of physicians and their practice colleagues. The provision of the incentives, obligations, technical devices and suggested routines could help in this. No doubt, it is helpful that the new contracts for general practitioners require annual visits for persons aged 75 and over. But other approaches could help. Carpenter and Demopoulos (1988) have illustrated how volunteers drawn from among the younger retired can be trained to use a straightforward screening schedule to produce reliable lists inexpensively.

Acute care utilisation by community social services/community health services users. Perhaps the most striking evidence is the relationship between the utilisation of community social services and stays as hospital inpatients. During the quarter preceding the most recent referral, 48 and 44 per cent of home help and day care/social work clients respectively had been inpatients; and of the clients who had been in hospital during that quarter, one-third were re-admitted at least once during the six months between our first and second interview. So their community care was an episode alternating with institutional care. Unfortunately we lack the data which would allow us to infer the proportion which Gavett, Drucker, McCrum and Dickinson (1985) would describe as 'ambiplex', but it would be surprising if there are not some who would satisfy these criteria. (See the discussion of their great impact on the economics of care and its implications in Davies and Challis, 1986, p.535.)

These are precisely the changes one would expect from bed reductions, the focus of modern geriatrics on active treatment with short inpatient stays, the low rates of growth of utilisation of community social services by populations aged 75 and over revealed in successive General Household Surveys, and the growing pressure on acute beds in other wards. We have seen it before, and in other countries. An example is the impact of shortening stays in the USA after the introduction of diagnostic related groups. Many recipients of community social services have disabilities which make them unacceptable in residential care.

Though this study does not provide evidence about changes through time, needs are interdependent for increasing proportions of cases. Moreover, it is the health services which determine the demand for social services more than the reverse. 60 per cent of the recipients of social services are referred by health service personnel, but only 8 per cent of clients in our study were referred on to community health services.

Here the point is that the pattern of targeting we have discovered is not what one would expect to achieve the best matching of resources to needs given this interdependence of health and social care. It is the community health services for which the quantities of inputs increase most with increasing disability, but arguably the quantities of community social services should do so to at least the same degree. This is what relative costs would dictate assuming perfect substitutability. We estimated that unit costs were greater for auxiliary nursing than home help, as they were in the Thanet Community Care Project (Davies and Challis, 1986, pp.420, 428). The most interesting comparison is for the Darlington Community Care/Care in the Community Project (Challis, Darton, Johnson, Stone, Traske and Wall, 1989). The cost estimates were for home helps (£4.22/hour), SRNs (£11.04/hour), nursing auxiliaries (£5.34/hour) and home care assistants (varying from £4.22/hour during weekdays through £5.28 during weeknights, £5.81 during weekend days to £7.40 during the night at weekends). So community health service nursing auxiliaries appeared in 1986 to be more costly by 25 per cent than home care workers during normal working hours. The recent pay settlement for nurses has widened the gap, just as the improvements in the terms and conditions of home helps in 1985 might have done the opposite. However, the *prima facie* case for encouraging social care agencies to undertake non-technical personal care is surely strengthened by the cost differential as much by their potential for developing its management.

However, we return to the discussion of implications for case management and service development below.

2.3 Efficiency and the 'marginal productivity issue'

Our content analysis of the new managerialist critique of the community social services suggested that the outcome effects of additional resources are not seen as a problem of the same pervasiveness and generality as the improvement of vertical target efficiency. There is not a word in the lexicon of the new managerialist critique of community care which connotes 'marginal productivity'. Any perceived marginal productivity problems are particularised; for instance, the failure to achieve a good balance between household and personal care. Some may remember the age of innocence when the generality of targeting issues were first being recognised, and when the policy world found the general concept of target efficiency alien, incomprehensible, unimportant and unmemorable. This study suggests that the 'marginal productivity problem' is as important as targeting.

2.3.1 Consumer effects

Again Table 12.2 summarises our evidence about effects on clients. The individual effects need not be discussed in detail as they were in Chapter 4. The general point is that the marginal productivities are so few and so low that it would be surprising if they were not improvable: nineteen small fish, some of use only to some types of consumer, are a poor catch from such a deep and extensive trawl. (The positive marginal cost effects in Chapter 5 are not included. However, Chapter 5 also is a monument to a heroically thorough search for very small needles in a big haystack.)

The general features of the marginal productivity effects are as follows:

- Variations in inputs affect perceptions rather than the actual probability of admission to institutions, at least over the period so far studied.
- Few potential outcomes seem to be affected. The analysis discussed in Chapter 4 investigated many potential outcomes. The ones reported are the only effects found.
- We sought in vain for some effects of central importance to the success of a policy which combines improved achievements for the quality of life and care of consumers with shifting the balance of resource allocation to community-based modes of care. Our quest for morale effects would have done credit to Sir Galahad. There are no Heineken effects (Davies and Challis, 1986; Davies and Missiakoulis, 1988). Without such effects, it seems difficult to envisage interrupting the process described by Tobin and Lieberman (1976), by which elderly people gradually become demoralised and those in contact with them come to believe that admission to an institution is the only (though undesirable) alternative, despite the guilt carers often then feel (Challis and Davies, 1986; Challis et al., 1988). Again, there are no effects on functional capacities to perform the personal and 'instrumental' tasks of daily living.
- Several of the marginal productivity effects are greater at higher than at minimal inputs. Examples are the effects for home help and social work shown in Table 12.2. For instance, the additional cost of improving HHEFFECT by one point is four times greater with an input of two than eight hours. (The departure from linearity would have been in the opposite direction had it been a distortion due to the constrained minimum value of HHEFFECT.) The high values of the maxima and minima are of great practical importance. Marginal productivities rise though at a diminishing rate over almost the whole of the observed range of variation in inputs. The marginal productivity for social work is judged (by social workers) to rise increasingly with levels of input.
- The marginal productivity estimates are low. The biggest measurement errors are in the dependent not the resource (independent) variables. We tried to allow for changing circumstances during the study period. Unless the distribution of errors is particularly perverse, the values are unlikely to have been biased downwards very substantially.

2.3.2 *Effects on principal non-spouse carers*

Again we look at the implications of the cost function derived to estimate the costs of reducing the Malaise score to the level above which strain is thought to be abnormal.

The modelling showed that:

- The effects of resource variations were large enough to swamp specification measurement errors and reveal a positive effect only at a higher level of stress for most users. This is shown in the last column of Table 12.4 (see section 1.2.1.) The thresholds shown there are the levels of Malaise beyond which the resource effects become visible.
- The effects of resources on Malaise were weak. Resources seemed to have a virtually negligible effect on the stress of carers of persons with short interval needs living alone; an important target group for the community social services.
- Any effects of variations in inputs from the community health services are invisible. (Jones, Victor and Vetter, 1983, likewise found that community nursing reduced carer stress less than community social services.)

We are left uncertain about whether there are substantial effects which are dwarfed by other causes of variations in stress, or there are only small effects at low stress levels. The stress has often accumulated for many reasons and over a long period of time. Some of the causes of stress are quite unrelated to social care itself. Social work and care are unlikely either to affect some of the causes and unlikely to have much impact on the processes by which the objective reality works through to perceptions, as has long been argued. So it is unsurprising that others too have failed to find that standard services produce positive effects (Gilleard, Belford, Gilleard, Whittick and Gledhill, 1984 and Newbigging, quoted in Gilleard). However, some have discovered positive effects (for example, Gilhooly, 1984). Yet others have found effects of receiving a service rather than not doing so, or receiving one mode of service rather than another; for example, the comparison groups in Challis and Davies (1986), Challis et al. (1988); and Levin, Sinclair and Gorbach, (1985). So have we (Bebbington et al., 1986). This is unsurprising: differences in modes of care are above all differences in the balances of outputs, while input differences within a mode of care with inflexible responses to individual needs may mean nothing but more or less of the same. If the objective was particularly to relieve carer stress, resources would anyhow be differently used in an efficient system (Ratna and Davis, 1984). Some authorities are showing how to tackle carer stress directly.

However, this is grossly to oversimplify what should be the aims of care. It is a gross oversimplification to investigate only the stress effects of caring, and the costs of alleviating it. *Community Social Services and the*

Table 12.6
The effects of intensity variation on outcomes
Predicted scores with existing marginal productivities and costs

Client circumstances[a]			High intensity[b]				Costs[c] to		Lesser intensity[b]				Costs[c] to	
Need Interval	Informal Support	Whether Confused	SD-FAV	HH-EFFECT	DES-HELP	CM-CURE	SSD (£)	CHS (£)	SD-FAV	HH-EFFECT	DES-HELP	CM-CURE	SSD (£)	CHS (£)
1. Critical	Lesser	Yes	1.4	2.0	1.1	0.4	41.11	28.00	1.4	2.5	1.1	0.6	28.23	4.80
2. Critical	Greater	Yes	1.1	2.8	Sat[d]	0.7	39.71	28.00	1.1	3.2	Sat[d]	0.9	28.23	4.80
3. Short	Lesser	Yes	1.4	2.0	0.3	0.7	32.44	28.00	1.6	2.7	0.3	0.8	22.11	4.80
4. Short	Greater	Yes	Fav[d]	2.9	0.8	0.9	30.07	28.00	Fav[d]	3.6	Sat[d]	1.0	22.11	4.80
5. Critical	Lesser	No	1.3	1.9	0.5	0.8	36.06	28.00	1.4	2.3	0.5	0.9	23.18	4.80
6. Critical	Greater	No	Fav[d]	2.6	Sat[d]	1.0	33.66	28.00	1.1	3.1	Sat[d]	1.2	23.18	4.80
7. Short	Lesser	No	1.3	1.9	Sat[d]	1.0	27.42	16.00	1.5	2.6	Sat[d]	1.0	26.86	4.80
8. Short	Greater	No	Fav[d]	2.7	0.2	1.2	25.02	16.00	Fav[d]	3.4	Sat[d]	1.2	26.86	4.80

a   The following table shows the assumed client circumstances for each client type in the main table.
b   Values of service intensity predictors in Tables 4.12 and 4.15 (Chapter 4) fixed as follows.

Table 12.6 (continued)

Client circumstances (see Table 3.3)	Client type							
	1	2	3	4	5	6	7	8
ADEQ	0	1	0	1	0	1	0	1
AVAIL	0	4	0	4	0	4	0	4
INCONT	1	1	0	0	1	1	0	0
ADLSELFX	-3	-3	0	0	-3	-3	0	0
ADLHOMX	-5	-5	0	0	-5	-5	0	0
INFHELP	2	7	1	3	2	7	1	3

Also assume female clients, living alone, without financial problems or accident or acute illness or onset of health problem, death of spouse or diminution of social contact or availability of support, or change in degree of confusion during the first evaluation period.

Service intensity

Inputs Clients per week	High for client type								Medium for client type							
	1	2	3	4	5	6	7	8	1	2	3	4	5	6	7	8
HHCINP	8	8	6	6	8	8	6	6	5	5	3	3	5	5	3	3
SWINP	3	3	3	3	1	1	1	1	3	3	3	3	1	1	1	1
MOWINP	7	5	5	3	7	5	5	3	5	3	5	3	5	3	5	3
NURSE	7	7	7	7	7	7	4	4	4	4	4	4	4	4	0	0

c   Opportunity costs to the social services departments in median cost authority. Opportunity costs of community nursing to the NHS.
d   Fav denotes most favourable response on SDFAV. Sat denotes that the client desires no more help in any of the three areas of care.

Table 12.7
The effects of Audit Commission packages on client outcomes
Predicted scores with existing marginal productivities

Client Circumstances[b] Need Interval and Informal Support	Home care only						Audit Commission packages[a] Home and day care					
	Outcomes[c]				Costs to		Outcomes[c]				Costs to	
	1 (1)	2 (2)	3 (3)	4 (4)	SSD (£)	CHS (£)	1 (5)	2 (6)	3 (7)	4 (8)	SSD (£)	CHS (£)
Confused												
Critical needs												
1. Less support	1.6	3.1	1.1	0.6	20.04	8.00	Fav[d]	1.8	1.2	1.0	94.93	8.00
2. More support	1.2	3.8	Sat[d]	1.0	20.04	8.00	Fav[d]	2.5	Sat[d]	1.3	93.73	8.00
Short interval needs												
3. Less support	1.6	2.8	0.3	0.8	20.04	8.00	Fav[d]	1.6	0.4	1.1	93.73	8.00
4. More support	Fav[d]	3.6	Sat[d]	1.0	20.04	8.00	Fav[d]	2.4	Sat[d]	1.4	93.73	8.00
Not confused												
Critical needs												
5. Less support	1.5	2.9	0.4	0.9	15.01	8.00	Fav[d]	1.6	0.5	1.3	89.90	8.00
6. More support	1.2	3.7	Sat[d]	1.2	15.01	8.00	Fav[d]	2.4	Sat[d]	1.6	88.70	8.00
Short interval needs												
7. Less support	1.5	2.7	Sat[d]	1.0	15.01	8.00	Fav[d]	1.4	Sat[d]	1.4	88.70	8.00
8. More support	Fav[d]	3.5	Sat[d]	1.3	15.01	8.00	Fav[d]	2.3	Sat[d]	1.1	86.11	8.00

a The Audit Commission (1986c, Table 20 and pp.104-6) specifies packages of community nursing, home care, day care and sheltered housing. Other inputs are specified by the authors.

b Definitions of client types as in note 1 of Table 12.6.

c Outcomes are 1. SDFAV; 2. HHEFFECT; 3. DESHELP; 4. CMCURE

d Fav denotes most favourable response on SDFAV. Sat denotes that response indicates that client satiated, desiring no more help in any of the three areas of care.

Table 12.7 (continued)

The following columns show the service inputs assumed for each group.

Columns and rows	Inputs					
	HHINP	WARDINP	SWINP	MOWINP	DCINP	NURSE
Home care only						
Rows 1, 2, 3, and 4	2.5	0	3	5	0	2
Rows 5, 6, 7 and 8	2.5	0	1	5	0	2
Home and day care						
Row 1	2.5	0	3	2	5	2
Rows 2, 3, and 4	2.5	0	3	1	5	2
Row 5	2.5	0	1	2	5	2
Rows 6 and 7	2.5	0	1	1	5	2
Row 8	2.5	0	0	0	5	2

Social Production of Welfare (PSSRU, 1991) will investigate the marginal productivities of services for a variety of outcomes.

So marginal productivities seem to be disappointingly low both for consumers and carers. We know of no direct estimates of the marginal productivities of comparable services in other countries, and no one to our knowledge has diagnosed a general marginal productivity issue. However, the literature abounds with criticisms of services which suggest marginal productivities to be less than those attainable. Denmark, for instance, which offers the needy a more intensive service and which appears, to judge by non-recipients' opinions, to have achieved almost total horizontal target efficiency, nonetheless presents a whole catalogue of problems (Holstein, Due, Almind and Holst, 1989). Some of these problems would certainly lower marginal productivities seriously. Examples are interventions too late to have an impact, the absence of rehabilitation activity, inadequate coordination between hospital and home care agencies, excessive rigidity by the professionals, and lack of knowledge by the professionals about persons with poor psychic resources. Swedish and French commentators comment on the rigidity of their service provision (Nyckektal Och Matt, 1988; Ankri, Isnard and Henrard, 1989). The low marginal productivities of some of the intensive American provision is visible to the naked eye of anyone who has visited cases with their case managers and discussed provision issues with agency managers and independent observers.

2.4 The effects of varying inputs on outcomes

It is useful standard practice to show what alternative combinations of service inputs would cost. *Matching Resources to Needs in Community Care* and *Case Management in Community Care* (Davies and Challis, 1986; Challis and Davies, 1986) advanced the art by showing the cost to various parties of combinations of 'final outputs', outcomes of evaluative importance in their own right. This study's contribution is to show (i) what service inputs would be necessary to achieve desired levels of important final outputs; and (ii) what would be the implications for final outcomes of levels of service inputs, assuming marginal productivities to remain the same. This is the focus of the section.

2.4.1 Effects for clients

Tables 12.6 and 12.7 predict effects on four of the outcomes: SSDFAV, HHEFFECT, DESHELP and CMCURE. They are described in Chapter 4 and Table 12.2 above. We take these because the equations of Chapter 4 suggest positive marginal productivities at some levels of input. It would, of course, have been more interesting had we been able to find marginal productivities for other important outcomes, particularly those with the clearest interpretability and lowest measurement errors.

Client types
Our focus is the discussion of the viability of relying on more intensive community services as a substitute for residential care during a period when the supply of the former is increased compared with the latter. So we discuss the implications of the production relations of care for hypothetical clients who are either at higher risk of admission to institutions for long-term care or who are in other ways in the most severe need.

The predictions are discussed for eight client types. The types represent short and critical interval needs, higher and lower level of informal support, and whether or not the client is confused. The characteristics of each type are defined in the first column of the tables and a note to Table 12.6. Because they are less vulnerable and have lower probabilities of institutional admission, we do not postulate types with long interval needs. That they are less vulnerable is confirmed by the data of this study. Indeed, membership of MYTYPO1, the group having long interval needs and greater informal social support, is one of the most powerful predictors of a low probability of admission to an institutional mode during the subsequent two and a half years. In a logit model predicting the probability of survivors over two and a half years being admitted to an institution for long-term care, membership of MYTYPO1 was one of the four most powerful predictors, with an effect significant at the 1 per cent level for a single-tail test (Baines and Davies, 1989b, Table 1). Again, we have seen that few with long interval needs receive large inputs.

The most important of the types postulated for our argument are those which have the highest probability of entering institutions or subsequently consuming large quantities of health and social services. Among survivors over three years, a four-variable logit model predicting admission to institutions suggests the great importance of confusion and incontinence. The latter has an effect significant at the .001 level, the former at the .01 level. The first four types are postulated to be confused. Types 1, 2, 5, and 6 are postulated to be incontinent. Also the probability of MYTYPO6 clients entering institutions was twice as great as for clients in general. Types 1 and 5 are MYTYPO6. So of the eight groups in Tables 12.6 and 12.7, six are postulated to be confused and/or incontinent, and so highly vulnerable. The importance of the critical and less supported short interval clients was also confirmed by logit modelling predicting who among the heavy consumers use both community health and social services. Membership of MYTYPO4 increased the probability; and additionally the inability to perform personal care tasks – a variable discriminating most between persons with short and critical interval needs – also shows that capacity to perform personal care tasks was a powerful predictor.

Audit Commission packages

Table 12.7 shows outcome scores predicted for each of the hypothetical client types. The packages were those suggested in the Audit Commission's *Making a Reality of Community Care* (1986c). An interesting feature of the proposed packages is the low input of home care, 2.5 hours a week. The predicted outcomes show interesting patterns.

• SDFAV is an inverse indicator of outcomes: the lower the score, the better the outcome. It is unsurprising that consumers who have substantial informal support tend to be more satisfied with the impact of the services. That is because the packages are imperfectly varied to compensate for the variations in informal support. For the recipient with less informal support, the package consisting only of home care leaves the consumer with mixed feelings about the service. However, the combination of home with day care for five days per week would tend on average to make the perception of the service highly favourable.

Table 12.8

Number of hours of home care predicted to achieve target outcomes, assuming fixed packages of other services and client characterisation

Group and Need Interval	Client circumstances[a]		Outcomes		
	Informal Support	Whether Confused	SDFAV Target=1	HHEFFECT Target=2	CMCURE Target=1
Without day care					
1. Critical	Lesser	Yes	b	9.0	b
2. Critical	Greater	Yes	b	b	b
3. Short	Lesser	Yes	b	6.7	b
4. Short	Greater	Yes	3.2	b	b
5. Critical	Lesser	No	b	7.0	b
6. Critical	Greater	No	b	b	c
7. Short	Lesser	No	b	5.3	1.0
8. Short	Greater	No	2.1	b	c
With day care					
1. Critical	Lesser	Yes	c	1.6	c
2. Critical	Greater	Yes	c	4.3	c
3. Short	Lesser	Yes	c	0.8	c
4. Short	Greater	Yes	c	3.6	c
5. Critical	Lesser	No	c	1.1	c
6. Critical	Greater	No	c	3.7	c
7. Short	Lesser	No	c	0.3	c
8. Short	Greater	No	c	2.9	c

a Groups defined in the notes to Table 12.6 (medium inputs) except for home and day care.

b The equation predicted that the target would be unattainable at any level of Home Care Input.

c Equation predicts target to be achieved with zero home care input.

- HHEFFECT is also an inverse indicator: the lower the score, the better the outcome. The best possible score is 1. At that level, home help inputs would on average be thought by clients to make a great difference to clients and possibly to have enabled them to continue living at home for most groups. Unsurprisingly, those clients who are the most disabled, particularly the confused, are predicted to think that home help inputs have least impact. Those with greater informal support would think its impact to be smaller. However, the effects of packages consisting only of home care would clearly be seen to fall far short of obviating the need for admission to residential care among all the short and critical interval groups. On the other hand, the richer package which includes day care is predicted to have a greater effect, indeed the predicted value suggests a satisfactory outcome for those with less informal support.
- A score of 0 on DESHELP would indicate that the user thought that no more help was needed. This is, of course, an ambiguous indicator: consumers may feel that they receive enough because the service is not designed to tackle their pressing unmet needs and greater consumption would for that reason contribute little to their welfare. The maximum score possible would be 9. Even with the low input of home help, clients with greater informal support respond by thinking that they would not require more help. However, critical interval clients with less informal support thought that a shortfall existed in some of the three care areas. The addition of a richer day care package could and did seem to have little additional effect.
- CMCURE is a direct indicator: the higher the score the better the outcome. It is a count of the views about the number of problems resolved or risks averted. The views are of those most frequently performing case management tasks. The largest effect would be indicated by CMCURE with a score of 5. The models predict that on average the home care package would not resolve even one problem among confused clients with fewer informal care inputs and lucid clients with critical interval needs, and less informal support. The field managers claimed no more for this thin package for any of the groups. Indeed they made only modest claims for the home care with day care package. Again this was thought to be more successful among those with greater support.
- The opportunity cost estimates for the personal social services are for the median cost authority for each of the resource elements in the footnote on Table 12.7. The contrast in costs between intensive day care and other packages is large. We discuss the costs to public funds of residential care in the next chapter.

Table 12.7 is characterised by low gradients. Package differences have small effects. So also do need-related circumstances. Perhaps consumers and field managers have narrow and limited expectations about the impact of the services, and the former may be easily satisfied.

The comparison of the results for the two most interesting outcome indicators reveals a paradox of great potential importance in a consumer-responsive system. Clients with more informal support think that the home help service contributes less to their welfare. However, case managers think that the services accomplish more for those with greater informal support. The pattern is clear also in Tables 12.7 and 12.8.

Higher intensity need-related packages

Again the packages, like the client characteristics, are consistent but arbitrarily chosen. The Audit Commission packages in Table 12.7 postulate low levels of home care. Table 12.6 postulates higher levels, and varies the levels with the circumstances of users. The high intensity inputs are near the upper end of the inputs of standard services. The opportunity costs to the social services department are correspondingly higher. The high opportunity costs to the community health services reflect the high assumed allocations of community nursing. Arguably this would be a level of input needed by only a low proportion of cases of this kind.

Again the results illustrate the low marginal productivities but also the general goodwill with which the services are perceived.

- Predicted SDFAV scores are little different for the greater and lesser intensity packages, in other words, the varying service quantities seem to make little difference. Those whose perception is most favourable tend to have greater informal support.
- However, the greater intensity and the tailoring to needs does have an effect on HHEFFECT. Even the high intensity packages achieved scores of no more than 2, except for lucid persons with less informal support and confused clients with less support and critical interval needs. A score of 2 indicates that the client thought that the home help received *may* have enabled them to continue living at home. This should surely be the minimum target among these high need groups, particularly those with less informal support. But it is encouraging that the more intensive tailored packages would on average produce a response that the service had made a great difference to the client's ability to function at home.
- The more intensive package did not reduce the predicted level of DESHELP to one or less for confused persons with less informal support and critical interval needs. Again, unmet need is perceived to be greater among confused clients with short interval needs and greater informal support. Table 12.6 suggests that the desire for more help is enhanced by higher levels. Perhaps this reflects the better balance of tasks undertaken in systems providing larger inputs; a reflection of the basic ambiguity of the indicator described in the discussion of Table 12.6.

- The implicit goals of the services are better measured by CMCURE, the indicator based on the first-line managers' opinions about the number of problems resolved and risks averted, though the lack of standardisation of judgements must reduce its reliability. The high intensity package is predicted to have least effect on the problems of persons with critical interval needs with less informal support.
- Again we defer a consideration of the relative costs of the community services and residential-based care.

Packages tailored to achieve target outcome levels
The most interesting question is what levels of inputs would just achieve reasonable target outcomes. Table 12.8 contains such estimates. The computations are based on the argument that the crucial variable resources are home care and day care. The first part of the table shows what inputs of home care the equations of Chapter 4 suggest would achieve reasonable target outcomes in the absence of day care. The targets postulated are modest. The second part shows the required hours of home care assuming the five-day input of day care specified in the Audit Commission's packages. The hypothetical clients are the eight for whom predictions were made in Tables 12.6 and 12.7.

- Without the day care, the shape of the relationship between home care inputs and the clients' perceptions of its impact on them (HHEFFECT) suggests that there are groups for which merely adding hours will not cause clients to judge that the effect of services is so great as to have possibly enabled them to continue living at home. These groups are all those with greater informal support. Other clients might attribute their ability to live in the community to the services they receive, but usually to a set of substantially different inputs rather than to vast inputs of a traditional service. However, the target score of 2 is not highly demanding. A target score of 1 might be more compatible with achieved substitution, given the tendency of elderly people to be excessively grateful for small mercies.
- Intensive day care transforms the predicted quantities of home care required, as might be expected. However, a target of 1 would still be unattainable save for types 5 and 6.
- Again, the results of setting a target of 1 for SDFAV (a favourable perception of the services by clients) suggest that the target is unattainable for most groups. The exceptions are persons with short interval needs and greater informal support. However, these results, like those for home care, illustrate the implications of the low and, in the case of CMCURE, SDEFFECT and HHEFFECT, diminishing marginal productivities summarised in Table 12.2.
- The field managers are not sanguine. Setting a target of 2 for CMCURE (a count of the number of problems resolved or risks averted) yields

Table 12.9

Estimated weekly costs to the community social services of reducing Malaise Inventory score of non-spouse principal carers of sample clients to 5[a] (£ in 1985 prices)

Client circumstances	Client behavioural disturbance						Number of clients in sample[h] (n)
	Median Per person with M greater than 5[b] (£)	Median Absolute increase[c] (£)	Median Relative increase[d] (%)	Median Group costs[e] (%)	Median Total costs[f] (%)	High Per person with M greater than 5[g] (%)	
Type 3 client sharing household	28.12	1.34	5.0	4.6	0.2	37.38	6
Type 4 client living alone	25.74	1.96	8.2	2.7	0.6	35.00	36
Type 4 client sharing household	25.78	4.68	22.2	9.4	0.7	35.04	11
Type 6 client living alone	26.89	4.44	19.8	6.5	1.1	36.15	19
Type 6 client sharing household	31.47	5.41	20.8	16.1	0.8	40.73	5
Carers of other than Type 3, 4, or 6 clients	14.35	1.44	11.1	3.1	4.8	23.61	120

a   Predicted from Table 2 of Appendix 12.1 with non-Malaise predictors set at means or median values.

b   Predicted average cost of a score of 5 for carers whose actual score exceeds 5.

c   Difference in cost predicted with a score of 5 and with actual cost for carers with a score exceeding 5.

d   Difference in predicted cost with a score of 5 as a percentage of predicted cost with actual score for carers with a score exceeding 5.

e   Predicted cost of reducing to 5 the scores of carers with scores in excess of 5 as a proportion of costs of the entire group. This estimate may be sensitive to the difference between the study's sample and a simple random sample of clients.

f   Predicted cost of reducing to 5 the scores of carers with scores in excess of 5 as a proportion of the costs of the entire client sample. This estimate may be sensitive to the differences between this sample and a simple random sample.

g   Predicted average cost of a score of 5 for carers whose actual score exceeds 5 and a high client Behavioural Disturbance score of 6.

h   The number of persons in the client sample indicates how well-founded is likely to be the effect shown in the equation on which these estimates are based.

estimates of the home care inputs required by the confused above the levels provided unless intensive day care is provided. With intensive day care, input of home care is predicted to be unnecessary to achieve the target for any group. However, the results suggest that intensive day care makes little difference to the amounts of home care needed for those who have more informal support: that is groups 4 and 8. Setting the modest target of 1 suggests that small quantities are required.

We must not overstate the predictive value of the results in Tables 12.6, 12.7, and 12.8. That is not to suggest that the results are unimportant. Some of the results are interesting only because they are analogous to a *reductio ad absurdum* in a mathematical proof, that is, they show that only at unprovided levels of input. Also, the paradox that clients think that the home care service accomplishes most when they are less well-supported while case managers think the opposite could have important implications. However, the results speak with forked tongues about the impact of day care: many who are prescribed day care soon drop out and those who continue to consume it are those who most appreciate it or whose carers benefit: a self-selecting group. So we cannot infer that wholesale referral to intensive day care would improve the matching of resources to needs.

More generally, it will be remembered that we could not find clear evidence of resource effects for Morale, ADL or IADL, the duration of survival in the community, and the other effects crucial to shifting the balance of care. Some of these are the outcomes for which the marginal

Table 12.10
Predicted weekly costs in 1985 prices of reducing Malaise Inventory scores of non-spouse carers with scores in excess of 5 and whose dependents have high and low Behavioural Disturbance Index scores and live alone[a]

| Behavioural Index score | Per carer[b] (£) | Predicted costs | | |
		Increase compared with previous row[c] (£)	Relative increase compared Actual M[d] (%)	Relative increase compared with previous row[e] (%)
0	18.90		17.0	
1	20.75	1.95	15.2	9.8
6	30.01	9.26	10.0	44.6

a Assuming type 4 dependent living alone.
b Predicted average cost of a score of 5 for carers whose actual score exceeds 5.
c The entry in the cell for row k is row k of col. 2 *less* row (k-1) of col. 2.
d Increase in cost of reducing M from actual score to 5 as percentage of cost with M at actual level.
e Increase in cost of reducing M from actual score to 5 as percentage of cost of so doing for group described by previous row.

productivities are of critical policy importance. The marginal productivities which we have found are weak. Some of the outcome indicators to which they refer are ambiguous. We have been looking for needles in the haystack armed only with the statistical equivalent of a metal detector. Also, for that reason, true values of the marginal productivities are likely to be imprecisely estimated by our analyses and, for the same reason, the predictions made from the equations must not be used to support any but the most general arguments.

2.4.2 Costs of reducing carer stress

Table 12.9 shows how much extra it would cost to reduce the Malaise score to the level of 5 suggested by Rutter to be a threshold above which exists abnormal stress. The table distinguishes client groups whose definition reflect the interaction terms between Malaise and other factors in the equation shown in Appendix Table A12.2 (p.440). The table implies that the absolute cost of stress reduction seems to be small for most groups partly because high proportions of the carers with scores above 5 have scores not much greater than this value. However, the percentage increase required is estimated to be substantial for some groups: up to one-fifth. Indeed, the relative increase is substantial in relation to the entire spending on clients sharing households, perhaps because it is only when carer stress levels are high that multiple person households tend to get services. The merely 'moderate' validity and imperfect reliability of the indicator might well cause the true values of the estimates shown in column 2 to be twice as large as the values shown there, judging from the estimates by Bebbington and Quine (1986), Rutter, Graham and Yule (1970) and Rutter, Tizard and Whitmore (1970).

The Malaise score confounds the consequences of the stress-inducing dependency characteristics of the clients, other stress-inducing circumstances, and the characteristics of the carer. Like some other studies, our data suggest that the latter two sets of factors are important in relation to the first. So perhaps the costs of reduction of Malaise to 5 is best captured by adding the estimated cost of Malaise reduction (shown in column 2 of Table 12.9) to the difference in estimated cost of Malaise reduction for those with high and the median scores on the Behavioural Disturbance index assumed in computing column 1. The latter is £9.26. The result is shown in the penultimate column of Table 12.9. Taking this basis suggests that the costs are much higher. The figures seem more credible. Again the true value should reflect the attenuation of slope terms due to errors in the Malaise and Behavioural Disturbance indicators. Since the reliability and validity of the latter are likely to be greater than for the Malaise Indicator scores, the understatement of costs in the last column is likely to be less than the factor of two suggested by the first.

Again, we should apply the rule of thumb that more resources should be allocated to groups for whom the costs of welfare improvements are least in the absence of clear equity and valuation arguments implying otherwise. Column 2 of Table 12.9 suggests that the costs of Malaise reduction would be smallest (i) when the client has short interval needs, lives with others and has a high level of informal support; (ii) when the client has short interval needs, lives alone, but has little informal support; and (iii) when the client has long interval needs. There would seem to be good equity grounds for allocating more to the first group, but not the second. Only if there are clear grounds for believing that early intervention will prevent serious deterioration can a case be made for the third. The results discussed in Chapter 2 suggests that Type 3 clients living with others are not allocated much less than others whose own needs are much greater. Perhaps one reason why the differences between need types is shallow is that particularly in some of the authorities, account is taken of the contribution that provision makes to carer stress for the group. However, the evidence of Chapter 2 is ambiguous, and our evidence about the process of handling cases yields many examples where such responsiveness is unlikely.

Table 12.10 compares the costs of reducing the Malaise Inventory score to 5 at different levels of the Behavioural Disturbance index. We have seen that the costs of doing so for the 37 per cent of carers of clients with a Behavioural Disturbance score of zero are predicted to be £11.12 less than the costs for the 5 per cent of clients with a disturbance score of 6. The percentage increases in spending required are substantial. They are lower at higher levels of Behavioural Disturbance because the modelling did not yield an interaction effect between Behavioural Disturbance and Malaise, and the actual spending on clients with high Behavioural Disturbance scores are greater.

These estimates of the costs of Malaise reduction again suggest low rather than high marginal productivities. But they must be treated cautiously. They are a first attempt to ask an important question about a complex issue which can only be tackled by the analysis of new data designed to make estimates of the marginal cost of stress reduction for carers. We must bear in mind (i) the caveats mentioned above and in the appendix (pp.438-41), (ii) that stress is also caused by circumstances and characteristics other than informal caring, and (iii) that stress reduction is only one of the desirable outcomes for carers.

These results confirm the doubts raised by the estimates of marginal productivities. It is not obvious that simply increasing resource inputs is likely to achieve the outcomes needed to enhance consumer welfare in a system increasingly reliant on community-based modes of care unless many and big marginal productivity lances are put into the haystack.

3 Conclusion

We must repeat: it would be easy for the careless reader to infer from this discussion that the receipt of community social services does not have beneficial effects. This is not so. Our interim report is only one analysis to reveal positive effects. Our point is that it is the effects of increasing resource levels (given consumer circumstances) which are most important for achieving effective service with a changed balance between institution-based and community-based modes of care. These effects are estimated from the coefficients of Table 12.2 reviewed here. They are few and weak. Because they are weak they are probably an unreliable basis for predicting the initial short-run effects of changing input levels. They can be more appropriately used to construct an argument reinforcing the need to invest in the management of change. That is the use we shall make of them when we consider ways forward.

The evidence suggests that the fourth scenario is the most realistic. Community services seem to be underfunded, their targeting requires improvement and, in important respects, their marginal (and average) productivities are low. We have been arguing that targeting should be more clearly focused since the mid-1970s. The new message is that we must also improve marginal productivities.

13 Some ways forward: (1) raising productivities and matching resources to needs

In this chapter, we discuss two types of activity necessary to secure improvements: (i) raising service productivities and (ii) matching resources to needs. Raising service productivities and better matching resources to needs by more effectively performing the core tasks of case management are complementary strategies. At first sight they seem to be heuristically separable and separable also in the policy action which can achieve them. The focus of the former is changing individual units of service input: the building blocks of the care plan. The latter is the architecture of the care plan: what building blocks are used and how they are fitted together. But this separability is only partial. Section 1 explains the interdependence of the two strategies. Section 2 discusses raising service productivities. Section 3 argues the case for focusing more on matching resources to needs by ensuring the better performance of core case management tasks in two ways: first, by summarising what this study tells us about the way the core tasks were performed in the late 1980s (Section 3.1), and then by basing propositions based on the results of the PSSRU community care projects and American experiments. Sections 4 and 5 of the chapter develop and illustrate the application of a logic for designing arrangements for improving the performance of the core case management tasks.

1 The interdependence of the strategies

The separability between the two strategies of raising service productivities and better matching resources to needs exists for two reasons. The contribution to outputs of each building block depends on how and when it is used. (i) Better performing the core case management tasks (to achieve better matching) includes mixing inputs to exploit the marginal productivities of inputs and their relative prices, so obtaining the desired outcomes at less cost. That is, they improve marginal productivities. (ii) Better performance of the core tasks leads to the greater exploitation of the targeting effects of the kind sought in Table 12.3. That is, it improves technical efficiency. For instance, good case-finding allows service at the time when the targeting effects are most favourable: when their marginal productivities are highest, before avoidable deterioration occurs. (iii) In our models, case managers are encouraged to have a broader view of goals. So they choose the goals which are most important to clients and public policy, among them being to reduce probabilities of inappropriate admission to institutions for long-term care. Therefore the inputs they assemble are those with average and marginal productivities which deliver what is needed for the system to accommodate to the community-based care of persons who would formerly have entered institutions. That is, better performance of the core case management tasks improves output mix efficiency. A system in which the case managers influence a high proportion of the demand creates incentives to managers in providing agencies to raise marginal productivities in the ways needed, since they are aware that decision-makers are well informed about what other competitors are providing.

Better performance of the case management tasks can improve the intrinsic qualities of the building blocks themselves. That is, they introduce competition in one or both of the main forms distinguished by economists. In the short run, they provide a mechanism by which a selection can be made between alternative sources of the same or substitute inputs, and so stimulate price or quality competition, the process explored by the neoclassical writers following Marshall and J.M. Clark. And in the long run, they create the conditions in which there is a market into which other suppliers can enter with new and more efficient ways to match ends and means for at least some of the beneficiaries – the argument stressed by Schumpeter and the Austrian school. Modern theory has it that it is enough for entry to be probable for there often to be an anticipatory adjustment of behaviour which will cause suppliers to attempt to improve their efficiency. Contestability is the name of the competitive game (Baumol, 1982). Indeed, the local market for the particular good need not be occupiable by more than one supplier at a time, as Kendall (1989) reminds us. To borrow a quotation from Beales (1981) in Coursey, Isaac and Smith (1984):

... competition *for* the market disciplines behaviour almost as effectively as would actual competition within the market. Thus, even if operated by a single firm, a market that can be readily contested performs in a competitive fashion'.

The essence of a strategy based on securing the better performance of case management tasks is that it uses the strengths of each form of provision in relation to the particular case. Therefore no one service has to have high productivities with respect to all the important outcomes, simply with respect to some. For instance, the community care experiments did not immediately and directly transform the marginal productivities of the home help or day care services which existed before the projects were started. They made use of the strengths of the existing services, mixing them more effectively. The standard services had useful levels of average productivity for some important outcomes but low marginal productivities for some of those and for other important outcomes. Moreover it was inconvenient to mobilise higher levels of input of some of these services and expensive to do so at the times when they were most needed. So the case managers used their budgets to create new gap-filling services with complementary average and marginal productivities. Since the new inputs were flexible and various, the case managers virtually specified what their average and marginal productivities for each important output would be.

So the main immediate effect of the introduction of case management was neither the anticipatory nor the reactive adaptation by the existing suppliers, though there was evidence that managers and union representatives were clearly nervous about the potential for competition. No doubt the reasons included that needs were unmet and were rising fast. So instead of substitution, the first effect was the invention of a complementary device for raising and deploying inputs. Later, price and quality competition did result in substitution. The budgets of the home help service grew more slowly to help to finance the community care budgets spent on helpers. Also the case managers acquired the main role in selecting admissions to Part 3 homes, generic social workers and others losing influence. Still later, the authority encouraged the development of for-profit and voluntary providers, and case managers were instructed to refer demand to them. It was an advantage that responsibility for case management policy and the supplying sections were separated below the level of a general manager with a responsibility for an area with a population of more than 200,000. Therefore there was less incentive to restrict the freedom of case managers so as to protect the budgets and turfs of providing sections.

The central fact is that a strategy which did nothing to improve the performance of core case management tasks would have to raise marginal productivities for a wider range of outcomes in each service, an unnecessarily formidable task.

2 Raising productivities

We must distinguish the task of raising *average* from *marginal* productivities. Useful improvements may affect the former at the existing level of inputs without increasing the latter. Some authorities have indeed made changes which might greatly improve productivities at some levels of input but which could leave marginal productivities for some outcomes unsatisfactory outside a narrow range. The changes include attempts to produce some of the benefits of better case management without investing greatly in actual case management arrangements. Examples from the contemporary developments in our sample authorities are (i) confining the provision of services to those satisfying a set of prospectively-determined and concrete criteria of eligibility for service like a minimal degree of physical disability and some types of domestic structure; (ii) giving personal care priority over household care; (iii) computerising administrative tasks to give first-line managers time to perform more of their limited variant of case management; (iv) allocating services for only a number of weeks; and (v) limiting the tasks which can be undertaken to those thought to contribute most to the desired outcomes, and limiting the number of hours on the basis of average lengths of time taken to perform each of the approved tasks, including restricting the number of rooms cleaned and forbidding the use of paid time to shop or collect pensions. Other changes we observe in our authorities may simply affect technical efficiency for some outcomes only and they, too, are unlikely to affect marginal productivities for other important outcomes. Examples are devices to reduce the ratio of travelling to direct service costs, or the introduction of cook-freeze technology. Some authorities are investing more in their capacity to perform case management tasks. A common example which falls short of actually investing the authority responsibility and accountability over a wide span is to encourage case conferences among workers and their first-line managers. It is not necessarily inadequate to tackle average productivity alone, leaving marginal productivities almost unaffected. To repeat: with the capacity to perform case management tasks well, it can make sense to treat many of the existing services as foundations of standard depth on which to build superstructures adapted to consumer needs. However, that gap-filling was substantial. The gap-filling superstructure in Thanet accounted for one-third or more of the total costs to the SSD, despite the subsidisation of much of it.

Some authorities are clearly tackling *marginal* productivities directly. The national renegotiation of terms and conditions of 1985 at least removed major structural obstacles to the local development of services in ways which would increase marginal productivities. Possibly the most common feature of attempts to affect them amount to the creation of new services. The most common form of innovation in the mid-1980s, this study confirms, was the intensive home care service. However, this was not necessarily accompanied by a change in the tasks performed and the manner of performance of the tasks (for example, with rehabilitative and independence-fostering intent). Perhaps with some Celtic hyperbole, Victor and Vetter (1988) entitled their paper on one intensive home care scheme 'Rearranging the deckchairs on the Titanic'. The results in Chapter 11 suggest that, typically, schemes did not achieve high marginal productivities at the levels of inputs at which they were operating. Again some of the devices amount to improving the performance of case management tasks but within the narrow span of a single service. An example is the introduction of senior home help organisers to match tasks and time better to needs and/or alert organisers to the need for re-assessment. But of course investment in training and development is the main theme.

So focusing on case management might be the most effective way of raising the marginal productivity of all inputs taken together. But can one achieve the greater part of the benefit which flows from strong and flexible entrepreneurial case management by other and less contra-cultural means? That is not obviously so. Track records have been doubtful for one type of device: the limitation of targeting by concrete *a priori* eligibility criteria, the limitation of the tasks undertaken, and allowing sufficient time only for the concentrated performance of the tasks. A second device is organisational consolidation. Europeans sometimes misapply the lessons of the success of On Lok (Zawadski and Ansak, 1981; Zawadski, 1984; Zawadski, Shen, Yordi, and Hansen, 1984; Shen, Takeda and Hennessy, 1985; On Lok, 1987; Zawadski and Eng, 1988). Though the success was mainly due to organisational consolidation, its achievement by that means reflected problems of a kind rarely found here; and insufficient account is taken of other features of the particular milieu for which it was designed. It is more useful to see it as a managed care model combining finance and supply for a deprived but geographically concentrated and socially close-knitted ethnic minority developed in an extremely fragmented system. The US has had to rely excessively on means other than organisational consolidation. In contrast, the only powerful tool used in the UK has been organisational consolidation for twenty years and longer. The new focus on case management is intended to provide additional incentive-related devices for achieving the goal: a device which permits a plurality of suppliers with safeguards against cost escalation.

One reason for the failure of the first two types of device is the inconvenient complexity of the need circumstances which create the risk of serious welfare shortfall and/or raise the probability of admission to institutional care. Depression and apathy among those at risk is so common as almost to be pervasive. Depression, apathy, 'giving up' and the admission to institutions are clearly associated. There is often the need to put into operation a 'Heineken process' (Davies and Challis, 1986; Davies and Missiakoulis, 1988) to improve morale if admission is to be avoided. Both that and the tactics for helping people to receive the service which will achieve most may require the use of paid time on tasks which fall outside the high priority personal and household tasks. In the commune in Denmark studied by Hendriksen, Lund and Stromgard (1984b), some 13 per cent of the time was spent in conversation.[1] However, it is true that it might often be possible to find a cheaper way of instigating the Heineken process.

It is also the case that for many it is unnecessary to achieve Heineken effects. But one of the main reasons for the success of the PSSRU community care experiments is that they have reduced the bias in the system against basing plans on the variety and complexity of need-related circumstances of clients. They redefine assessment, replacing the confusion of (i) screening for service eligibility with (ii) diagnosis and (iii) the consideration of how to intervene and what resources to use, with the separation of the three elements as heuristically distinct core tasks of a broader case management approach. In doing so, they shift the nature of assessment in several related ways: from perfunctory to thorough; from a narrow focus on some functional disabilities to a broader consideration of problems of living in the way the clients and carers desire, and so from establishing eligibility for some or a narrow range of service to a general identification of needs, wishes and values; from a concern mainly with presenting problems to an attempt to understand and intervene in causal processes, and so to the formulation and testing of hypotheses over time; from the once-off event to a continuous process or, at any rate, a discontinuous process backed by the periodic reappraisal of continuously accumulated evidence. These are changes which can be recognised in literatures about assessment in all caring professions.

The national intake and documentary (LIER) system in the Netherlands and the similar system in the State of New York apply a standardised scoring system to a standard assessment schedule to allow persons who do not themselves see the clients to make level of care decisions. This provides no incentive to assessors to make the best use of limited institutional places. It provides no counterweight to the tendency to err on the side of trying to ensure that one's own clients have no more resources, though this may be at the expense of others; and so, in effect, encourages those making the assessment to attempt to fit the scores to their overall need judgements. Therefore it can be an inefficient means of reducing the probability of admission to institutions for long-term care (Becker, 1982; van Sonderen, Suumeijer and van den Heuvel, 1985; Davies and Challis, 1986, p.113).

3 The case for better matching resources to needs: empirical evidence

The case for investing in the better performance of core case management tasks is partly empirical, partly logical. In this section, we (i) review the performance of case management tasks described in earlier chapters, and (ii) use evidence from PSSRU and American community care experiments to derive propositions about arrangements focused more on case management.

3.1 Study evidence about the performance of case management tasks

The analysis in Chapter 6 confirms what others have argued. There is little sign that the performance of the core tasks of case management is adequately planned, coordinated and managed, despite the importance of their effective performance for the equity and efficiency of outcomes. We suggest there is inertia in the practice of field-level allocators in the face of large changes requiring new assumptions and major adaptations of policy, procedures and practice.

3.1.1 Structural issues: 'span', 'scope', and 'organisational locus'

The span of core tasks has been adequate in British arrangements for community services: in principle, the same worker has been able to undertake case-finding, assessment and re-assessment, care planning and the associated counselling and service arrangement, monitoring, and termination planning. However, the professional training of the workers who allocate the largest resources has been negligible or rudimentary, and has been heavily focused on practical home-making skills (Davies and Challis, 1986, Chap. 2). Moreover the average number of cases is so large, the caseload is so heterogeneous, and the range of tasks other than case management performed is so wide, that it is impossible to perform the core tasks with the thoroughness needed by the most important cases. We know of some systems with narrower spans of control, though we have not collected evidence about their equity and efficiency systematically; for instance, in Sweden, home help managers have between 70 and 80 clients (Wallberg, 1988). Chapter 6 describes how workers in one area described monitoring to be 'an unrealistic concept', how the failure to re-assess was general although the average length of time over which cases had received service was long: five years in the case records examined by the SSI (DHSS, 1987b, Table 6.4). Unlike some of the American case management systems we have observed in operation and described in Davies and Challis (1986), there are no checks and balances to help to improve field performance: no peer review and no arrangements to achieve accountability for developing and operating a coherent targeting policy by means of conforming to formalised norms of good practice (Davies and Challis, 1986, Chap. 3).

The scope of the authority over service allocations by any one worker who might coordinate resources is too narrow. It is restricted even within the social care agency. Social services personnel rarely coordinate activities with those responsible for the allocation of other community services. This appears to be so even for that group of recipients of both health and social services who are large consumers of resources and are at higher risk of mortality or admission to institutions for long-term care: a group of special significance for improving community care. Within that narrow scope, the field coordinators are unaided by budget norms or limits for case types reflecting practice norms.

These weaknesses have been exacerbated because of the absence of a systematic attempt to use the organisational locus of persons charged to perform core case management tasks as a device to help achieve better horizontal and vertical target efficiencies and an improved balance between them. In short, the managers have not in the past applied a theoretical apparatus about what affects case management performance to design systems which fit the opportunities and constraints of their contexts.

Neither have managements appeared until recently to have begun to grapple with one of the key issues for improving the performance of case management tasks: working out for different contexts how to find structural ways of encouraging an emphasis on performing case management tasks well in a culture previously dominated by the direct provision of service; and the circumstances where this benefit of separating the case management function and its management from the direct provision of service is more than outweighed by the risk of duplication in a system with this separation of functions. Initially, articles in the professional magazines about the organisation and training implications of the Griffiths Report hardly ever seemed to discuss this as an issue despite the clarity with which Griffiths defined the core case management tasks, and related case management to the primary roles of the SSD so as to ensure provision for needs using public money to the best effect.

3.1.2 Analytic vagueness, 'risk', practice norms and allocations
It is certainly not new to allege that first-line managers and other field personnel are analytically vague (Goldberg and Connelly, 1982; Davies and Challis, 1986, pp.33-45). Two points are important: the logical and practical distinctions between consistency, equity, and efficiency; and the vagueness of some of the concepts which influence allocations.

Consistency, equity and efficiency
Consistency is not the equivalent of equity and efficiency. For instance, the equations predicting resource allocations in Chapter 3 might have fitted well, but they might show little response to some need-related circumstances which many would judge to be of great importance, and there might be few of the 'targeting effects' suggested in Chapter 12 to be prerequisites for efficiency. In that case, the allocations would be consistent but neither equitable nor efficient.

The distinction is obvious. However, agency managers have not always made it. We have mentioned the discussion in some SSDs of firm allocation norms based on crude need-related criteria, and how the implementation of such criteria might actually yield lower degrees of equity and efficiency than systems providing indicative guidelines but leaving subtle need judgements about allocations to case managers working with carefully chosen budget caps and budget averages. Indeed, one impressive American programme succeeded admirably in improving consistency. However, only by its own contestable definitions could it be said to have raised equity and efficiency. The programme was the Equity Project conducted in several counties in San Francisco Bay (Pruger, 1987, p.159). The study provided workers with predictions of the average amounts of community care services allocated to persons in apparently similar circumstances according to the agency's standard disability-focused data collection. This and the project's other activities raised the proportion of allocations explained by the circumstances from levels not unlike those reported in Chapter 3. Increases over three years in the proportions of allocated resources explained varied between 19 and 67 per cent across the three counties. So by some criteria consistency certainly increased.

However, one can argue that it also increased equity and efficiency if one assumes that the aims of service fall far short of making admission to institutions unnecessary. Effectiveness in making admissions to institutions unnecessary requires that efficiency take into account not just resource inputs but outcomes. The number of days spent in institutions is one outcome, and is affected by improved morale, better quality of care, and effects on carers and others. The more complex the 'people change' required, the more creative the deployment of resources must be, the more resource decisions must be left to those for whom user circumstances are least vicarious, but the more difficult it is to achieve either the appearance or the reality of consistency and standardisation.

Pruger defines the goals in a way which excludes 'people change'. Miller and Pruger (1977) adopt the classification of the functions of social welfare agencies into two kinds: 'maintenance' and 'people change' (Hasenfeld, 1974). If the goal is merely people maintenance, the equity criterion can be defined entirely in terms of inputs. But even with this assumption, it is logical to identify consistency by Pruger's criteria with equity, only if one assumes that the allocation criteria of the agency are above question, and that the data measure the circumstances they define without error. The former makes with a vengeance the assumption for which sociologists criticise the designers of formal evaluations: that the simple latent and manifest goals reflected in crude measures are the only criteria which are (and should be) taken into account in the argument. That is not the world of this study and other PSSRU work, with its description and explanation of outcomes for sets of interest groups, and its separation of evaluative argument and prescription from descriptions of phenomena with a range and detail which go far beyond any allocation guidelines produced in agencies. And equity likewise cannot be treated as simple consistency in the application of the agency's guideline estimates.

Conceptual vagueness in allocation decisions
Analytic vagueness and prescriptive idiosyncracy are often associated. This is confirmed in Chapter 6. But to reduce the prescriptive idiosyncracy without analysing the rationales important in workers' operating ideology is to risk achieving a uniformity which rides roughshod over equity and efficiency.

Chapter 7 empirically analyses a concept in the lexicon of field workers which is both vague and a seemingly important determinant of allocation judgements, and so of targeting: the concept 'risk'. Chapter 7 shows 'risk' to be vaguely conceived by workers. The concept is a dangerously elastic justification for allocating resources. The way in which risk was discussed in general and in relation to the study cases suggests that workers insufficiently think through what is the nature of the risk, and how it might be avoided or managed. There is no obvious way in which the service interventions would affect some of the risks identified by workers. Again there were examples where the workers but not the client perceived a risk, a result which echoes some American findings (Sager, 1979). It is important to understand the various meanings of the concept, and to assess its importance in the determination of allocations. However, the statistical analysis in Chapter 7 demonstrates that workers' perception that a case is 'at risk' significantly affects service allocations. Clearly, good targeting demands that managers must ensure the development and implementation of good practice norms about the identification of risks and their management. Chapter 7 contributes to this by showing the relative importance of individual risk types and some of the correlates of risk. However, it also requires the precise tailoring of interventive strategies to the details of the situation using such tools as that developed by Barrowclough and Fleming (1986), and with it a larger 'clinical' component in the training of case managers.

3.1.3 The interdependence of health and social care needs
Chapter 12 has already discussed how user circumstances should make targeting decisions in the community health and social services interdependent – indeed, almost certainly, increasingly interdependent. For clients receiving both services, the social services seemed almost to be an extension of primary and community health care. Chapter 6 touched on the complaints of health personnel about the inadequacy of the community support services. The study found that the processes did not work in such a way as to suggest that the core tasks of case management were being most effectively performed for the system as a whole.

For instance, communications between social care workers, the primary health care team and the community nursing personnel and the informal carers were not usually close, perspectives were not shared between the carers, agency personnel did not generally coordinate the criteria they applied in making assessments; they did not systematically coordinate resources to achieve cover efficiently and to produce a strategy to achieve care goals; and communications were often not good with hospitals, particularly hospital social workers. Indeed the chapters describe almost incompatible perspectives, and imply ambivalences and anxieties about turf. Indeed, perhaps it is for such cases that the system is performing worst. Yet this is a group which contains a disproportionate number of persons at high risk of unnecessary admission to institutional care and admission to hospitals. It is precisely the group for which case management must best be performed.

The patterns of innovation over the period show that this was appreciated by service providers. Chapter 11 confirmed that the most common form of innovation of the early 1980s was the intensive home care service, others demonstrating it being Cloke (1983), Davies and Ferlie (1982, 1984), Ferlie (1982), Ferlie, Challis and Davies (1984, 1985, 1989), Goldberg and Connelly (1982), Salvage (1985) and Tinker (1984). Another type of innovation focused on the same or similar target group was the geriatrician-sponsored case-managed social care of persons at high risk (Ferlie, Challis and Davies, 1985).

The evidence from this study of the high proportion of the joint consumers of community health and social services who return for other episodes in acute wards again suggests the need for larger rather than smaller case management inputs; for policies and procedures which give particular priority to smoothing the transitions between acute medical care and community services; and for more training in the identification of signs of treatable disease for case managers from social service backgrounds.

Currently no one seems to be putting in sufficient time to perform the core tasks. The study suggests that the actual levels of social work input were smaller than was found in Seatown by Goldberg and Warburton (1979). We found less evidence of counselling for the bereaved and others who had suffered a serious and traumatic life event, and little evidence of work on relationships, despite evidence that such problems were common. In fact, the intensity of inputs by social workers tended to be low, and as Chapter 2 suggests high proportions of elderly people had no contact with them. In this, our results resemble those of Vickery (1981).

3.2 Evidence from community care and other experiments

The argument for strengthening the capacity of the system to match resources to individual needs does not rely only on *a priori* argument and the evidence from standard community services. The latter provides only circumstantial evidence that the ineffectiveness of the performance of the core tasks causes shortfalls in equity and efficiency in general, and unnecessary admission to institutions for long-term care in particular. For the direct evidence, we must compare the performance of community care projects and their comparison groups drawn from the recipients of standard community services.

However, the PSSRU modes provide only indirect evidence about models whose case managers carry larger caseloads and whose style is therefore likely to be more like the 'administrative' case management models described in Chapters 3 and 13 of Davies and Challis (1986). For these we must infer what we can from American experience. The evidence of the PSSRU community care projects and American research suggests the following propositions, among others:

(i) The implementation of PSSRU-type models can greatly improve outcomes for clients and carers. Table 13.1 compares results from three

Table 13.1
Results over one year of the Thanet, Gateshead and Darlington[a]
Community Care Projects

Outcome	Thanet	Gateshead	Darlington
Location			
Difference in per cent in own home (E-C)	+35	+27	+54
Difference in per cent in institutions (C-E)	+16	+35	+85
Client morale: probability of difference in group means arising by chance			
Overall morale	.001	<.08	.04
Satisfaction with life development	.002	<.05	NS
Depressed mood	.007	<.01	.006
Quality of client care			
Need for extra care	.025[b]	<.001	<.001
Burden on carers			
Expressed burden	.03	<.05	c
Strain	.09	<.001	c
Mental health problems	.09	<.001	c
Costs to SSD and NHS over period			
Cost saving (per cent)	+3[d]	−68[de] +3[df]	+6[d]

Sources: Davies and Challis (1986); Challis et al. (1988, 1989).
a Over 6 months not 1 year
b Lowest significance level for any aspect
c Indicator differences complicate comparisons
d Opportunity costs with 5 per cent discount rate in Thanet, revenue costs with capital allowance for hospitals in Gateshead, and revenue costs in Darlington.
e Inner City
f Other areas

community care experiments. The Gateshead experiment was a replication of the Thanet experiment, though it was applied in an environment which constrained some forms of entrepreneurial mobilisation of community resources, and partly for this reason had a higher ratio of home care costs to residential care costs than Thanet. The Darlington project was targeted at those for whom the alternative was more likely to be long-term hospital-based nursing care and a high proportion of the clients were recruited from hospital wards. Budget-holding case management itself was only one ingredient in its innovatory mix, which also included multifunctional community care workers and close coordination in a multidisciplinary team. Indeed, the case management arrangements were only adopted at the suggestion of the central government fundors, and were dropped as soon as the evaluated phase was over. So its relevance was to show how case management could contribute to multidisciplinary working by adding clarity of responsibility without imposing impossible demands.

The comparisons in the table are not comprehensive. Readers can refer to published material to investigate the similarities more closely. What the table shows is that dramatic gains in client and carer welfare are attainable with skilled and entrepreneurial case management and appropriate arrangements for it. Moreover, community service can be substituted for residential-based modes for cases of high degrees of disability without increasing costs to the health and social services.

(ii) The implementation of PSSRU-type models can achieve the improved outcomes at no greater costs. Davies and Challis (1986) clearly showed that the main benefits of the Thanet project over the first year were in the improved care and wellbeing of clients and informal carers. Indeed the difference in the average costs of the matched experimental and comparison clients was not large enough to be statistically significant at the 5 per cent level. Data for the subsequent three years confirmed that cost savings were not the main benefit since the discounted present value of the cost savings over four years (at a 5 per cent rate of time preference) was only £301 at 1967 prices. However, the cost saving substantially exceeded the discounted present value of the additional case management costs over the period. The discounted present value of the additional case management costs would have been £243, assuming that the ratio of case management to total social services costs during the first year remained the same over the entire period. Assuming that the ratio halved after the first year, when the initial assessment and care arrangement took place, the value would have been £160.

The replications in Gateshead and Darlington showed much the same for clients and carers and the social services department: clear and large benefits for dependents and their carers were achieved at much the same cost to the social services. However, the costs to the National Health Service were proportionately much greater. And as Table 13.1 and Challis et al. (1989) show, the mix of benefits were not quite the same as in Thanet, where there were stronger effects on client morale, and large mortality effects, partly because of exchange effects which to some degree depend on circumstances and attitudes not directly determined by the experimental inputs into the community care project itself (Challis, Chessum, Chesterman, Luckett and Woods, 1988; Challis, Darton, Johnson, Stone, Traske and Wall, 1989; Challis, Chessum, Chesterman, Luckett, and Traske, 1990). (The effects on carers are not easily compared between Thanet and other sites, since the number of principal carers studied in Thanet was small.) The difference in costs in Gateshead was much affected by clients from the inner city. Compared with standard provision, community care there cost more to the SSD, and considerably more to the National Health Service. However, community care appeared at first sight to increase the probability of remaining at home over one year by at least the same extent, since whether the place of residence was in the inner city has not so far been used as a criterion for matching in the Gateshead analysis and the costs to the social services of length of survival, morale and quality of care appeared not to be different for clients from the inner city.

One should not consider the cost savings of PSSRU community care models independently of the benefits. The PSSRU logic is constructed around the assumption that they are interdependent. The logic reflects the assumption of the production of welfare approach: the assumption that generally, the greater the resources allocated, the better the outcomes. So the community care logic postulates a trade-off between cost savings and the degree and nature of outcomes for clients and carers.

The logic is more formally stated in Chapter 14. The logic includes that costs of home care are directly determined by parameters specified at the design stage and thereafter directly modified by managers with the balance between costs and benefits in mind: average weekly home care budget per case; weekly budget limit for a case; and caseload per case manager. We assume (i) that the higher the budget and budget caps, the greater are likely to be the home care expenditures, and (ii) the greater the expenditures, the better are likely to be the outcomes given needs. The outcomes affected include those which primarily determine the cost savings.

Evidence suggests that assumption (i) is valid: higher budgets and budget caps cause higher spending, even in the short run. Experience from the PSSRU community care experiments illustrate the influence on the spending decisions of case managers of caps and average budgets. So does American evidence. For instance, Carcagno, Applebaum, Christianson, Phillips, Thornton and Will (1986, pp.241-2) wrote about the influence of the average budget per case in the channelling projects based on the financial control model:

the very fact that a special review occurred on all cases over [the average budget per case] resulted in the case managers using the figure as an *individual* cap. Indeed, they were strongly advised by their supervisors to do this. In some cases, they reported, they even modified the plan of care for an individual to keep it under the ... figure. Another factor dictating caution was their feeling (1) that each client should be far enough under the cap to allow for emergencies, (2) that keeping most clients under the cap allowed the occasional one to go well over, and (3) that the extent of future cost inflation was very uncertain.

The validity of assumption (ii) that higher home care spending causes lower spending on institutional modes depends more on the details of policy and other factors. There is evidence of this from individual projects. We await the results of our comparative study of community care projects to see whether variations in average costs in home care have affected the determinants of costs savings in the way the logic postulates.

It is particularly misleading to separate cost savings from other outcomes in the PSSRU experiments because we have used the power to influence costs in a particular way. An attempt was made to fix the parameters of the model at levels which make the improvement in the equity and efficiency of long-term care partly self-financing (Davies, 1990b).[2]

(iii) In the PSSRU approach, case management costs are substantial in relation both to other costs of community-based care and the total costs to the care agencies. This we can see from the ratios of case management to other community support costs. In Thanet, case management comprised 29 per cent of the total opportunity costs of community support costs paid for by the social services department, whereas for the comparison group it was little more than 21 per cent (Davies and Challis, 1986, Table 10.2). The higher proportion reflects the setting of the parameters of the models. The focus of the PSSRU community care model was perceived to be the entrepreneurial and client-responsive performance of the core tasks of case management with a caseload which includes many complex and unstable cases. It was by investing more in the performance of the core case management tasks in the resourceful and client-focused way that the beneficial outcomes were to be achieved.

The proportion of the total costs to the agencies accounted for by the time of case managers is also substantial. It, too, has been similar in several experiments: a feature which might be interesting to the designers of schemes. Davies and Challis (1986) showed that the case management activities cost approximately 19 per cent of the total opportunity costs to the social services department of the community care clients during the first year (Davies and Challis, 1986, Table 10.2). The cost was the equivalent of 5 per cent of all costs to public funds and 4 per cent of our estimate of the social opportunity cost. Challis, Chesterman, Traske and von Abendorff (1990) show that in the Gateshead social care model, the proportion of revenue account costs to the social services department was 18 per cent. Of course, case management costs could have been expected to be much the same given the similarity of case managers' caseloads. The similarity of other spending on care for the persons living at home is more interesting. Case managers' expectations about home care inputs seemed to resemble the patterns established in Thanet, which was the training ground for the next round of projects.

Davies and Challis (1986) distinguished health/social care models from social care models. The same case managers worked in the Gateshead health/social care extension of the main project as in the main project itself, and the team leader covered both projects. Again, therefore, the case management practice was based on the Thanet project. So it is interesting to compare proportions for the Gateshead health/social care extension with other health/social care models. In the Gateshead extension, case management cost 11 per cent of the total of health and social services costs and 11 per cent of the total of health and social services costs in the Darlington project (Challis, Chesterman, Traske, and von Abendorff, 1990).

So there is clear continuity in case managers prescriptions in the community care projects. But the nature of the case management activity in community care projects was different from the standard provision received by the comparison groups. Whereas in the Thanet family, the case management activity was mainly to achieve better care and quality of life for persons living at home and those supporting them, the activity for comparison clients was focused on admitting persons to institutions.

(iv) More 'administrative' case management models can yield benefits and probably be less expensive, though one must suspect that one gets what one pays for. The PSSRU results are for case management schemes whose caseloads are low, and in which complexity and instability are assumed for the caseload. Chapter 3 of Davies and Challis (1986) described administrative case management models. These can appear attractive to British authorities facing the dilemmas of narrowing their targets, and tempted to make case management universally available to those in substantial need. Fortunately, the Department of Health does not require assessment and case management to be made universally available in 1991, the year in which the new financing arrangements for residential care are to be introduced (Social Services Inspectorate, 1990, para. 3).

We lack British evidence about case management costs in administrative models with higher caseloads. What the costs might be is important for several reasons. However, there is American evidence for schemes which recruited clients who appeared typically to be more functionally disabled than the clients of most community-focused PSSRU experiments. (Compare, for instance, Carcagno et al., 1986, tables 7.4-7 and pp.189-99; Kemper, Applebaum and Harrigan, 1987, with Davies and Challis, 1986, Appendix 5.4 and Challis et al., 1990, Tables 4.1 and 5.1). This does not establish a neat association between the intensity of the case management and the extent of the gains (Brown and Phillips, 1986). Nevertheless what it suggests is important for current British argument.

One of the authors visited several such case management sites, and interviewed some case managers in each. It was clear that the best case managers were highly trained and competent. But case management practice was not as intensive as in the PSSRU projects. For instance, the caseload sizes in the channelling projects were greater than in the PSSRU projects, varying between 36 and 54. Moreover the pressure on managers and the tightly designed and (excessively) elaborate instrumentation required for the evaluation might have made the process more routinised and less client-responsive. It is suspicious that one-quarter of assessments were based on interviews with other than the clients (Carcagno and colleagues, 1986, I, 223). So the channelling projects might usefully suggest what an intermediate level of case management might cost.

On average over all the basic projects, the ratio of case management costs to the costs of provision of health and social services was 6 per cent. It was 5 per cent for the financial control models (Kemper and others, 1986, p.128).[3] However, the variations around the averages were large. Thornton, Will and Davies (1986, p.60) distinguished between the average costs of initial case management functions and of ongoing case management, and analysed the results for each project. For both types of model, the average cost per client of the initial case management tasks was twice as great in the highest cost project than in the lowest cost project. Ongoing case management unit costs varied less, the most being one-third more expensive than the least expensive for each of the two sets of models.

The managers weighing the advantages of setting parameters at the PSSRU levels or at levels more like channelling will ask about the benefits as well as the costs of the channelling projects. There proved to be design difficulties in the experiment which have made it difficult to be certain about what were the real effects of the projects (Kane, 1988). The evaluation suggested that the results were more ambiguous than the PSSRU community care experiments. The channelling evaluation showed little effects on longevity. But there was a reduction in needs considered by clients to be unmet, particularly over 12 months; increased satisfaction with service arrangements for meeting needs for help with four instrumental activities of daily living, particularly among those whose dissatisfaction had been greatest; a reduction in six environmental problems indicating physical hazards in the home, though in the 'basic' projects only; greater satisfaction with life generally, and in the basic model, reduced loneliness and a more positive attitude towards ageing, though no improvements in such other aspects of quality of life and psychological wellbeing as reported happiness and contentment; no effect on the number of hours of caring undertaken by the principal carer, though a reallocation of their time to tasks not readily undertaken by formal providers, and a small reduction in services provided by friends and neighbours; improvements in the wellbeing of principal carers by a range of criteria including fewer limitations on privacy and social life; greater satisfaction with care arrangements, but no general effects on care-giver perceptions of emotional, physical or financial strain, or their perceptions of the prevalence of serious objectionable behaviour by clients (Applebaum and Harrigan, 1986; Thornton and Miller-Dunstan, 1986; Wooldridge and Schore, 1986). Both medical and long-term care and shelter food and daily living costs were higher for experimental than control cases (Thornton and Miller-Dunstan, 1986). So a comparison of the channelling and PSSRU experiments at first sight suggests that the more intensive PSSRU approach did yield larger gains.

The British managers should also ask about case management costs and benefits in the projects antecedent to channelling (see Davies and Challis (1986, Chap.3). Some of the antecedent projects were more clearly and self-avowedly administrative case management models.[4] As with the channelling sites, the five antecedent projects compared had greatly differing case management costs per client per month. The most expensive was three times as costly as the least expensive (Haskins and colleagues, 1985). Estimates for case management costs and combined monthly Medicaid and Medicare reimbursements yielded ratios of case management to total costs of 9 per cent for the New York Home Care Project, 14 per cent for the San Diego project, 5 per cent for the South Carolina LTCP, and 15 per cent for Project Open. (Omitting the costs otherwise financed deflates the ratios compared with the PSSRU estimates.) As Chapter 3 of Davies and Challis (1986) describes, the projects had very different aims. The two projects with the smallest proportions of the costs accounted for by case management were those with the lowest proportion of case managers with specialised education or training at or beyond the bachelor's degree level and directly related to case management activity: one of the features which is most important for the differentiation of case management models, Capitman (1986) argued. The South Carolina project combines very low case management costs with outcomes which are favourable by one important criteria. It was one of the most successful of the projects judged by the criterion of preventing admission to institutions for long-term care. The project aimed to reduce nursing home admissions, targeted on those at high risk of admission, and procured more limited home care services than was typical of the projects. Its successful prevention of admission illustrates the importance of the capacity to target at those at high risk and to use case managers to contain the costs of home care packages. However, we do not know some outcomes of great importance to judging the relevance of its success to the British context. Its evaluation focused on functional capacities, mortality, informal carer involvement, and service utilisation, but not quality and life and care (Brown and Learner, 1983, p.81).

However, the British policy-maker will ask about the outcomes in general for the complete set of case management projects for the elderly: costs, effectiveness at reducing admissions to institutions for long-term care, quality of care of clients, quality of life and the burden borne by informal carers. Evidence from the antecedent projects varied too much to permit easy comparisons. For this reason, and because they compare different though overlapping sets of studies, the comparative reviews vary in nuance about what was generally achieved (Zawadski, Shen, Yordi, and Hansen, 1984; Haskins, Capitman, Collignon, DeGraaf and Yordi, 1985; Hughes, 1985; Kotler, Wright, Jaskulski and Kreisberg, 1985; Kemper, Applebaum and Harrigan, 1987; Weissert, Matthews Cready and Pawelak, 1988). However, the following propositions seem to be common to most.

- Most schemes did not reduce costs to public funds, though more saved nursing home costs. Saving nursing home costs was an explicit aim for many of the schemes. But it proved difficult to target only those at high risk of nursing home placement, difficult to effect large relative reductions in placement rates, and costly to provide the high level of community care thought appropriate. Several decreased the use of long-term care institutions. Indeed, the evaluators in some sought and found the kind of relations between variations in spending within the programme and the probability of avoiding institutional admission analysed in PSSRU evaluations; for instance, a trebling in the costs in the Minnesota PAS/ACG programme was associated with a reduced probability of entering a nursing home within a year by 5 percentage points among a group of recipients of whom one-third of survivors entered homes – a result interesting in the context of the slope of the TOTHCCOST curve of Diagram 14.4c – one might postulate for a case management system with higher caseloads than in the PSSRU experiment (Davidson, Moscovice and McCaffrey, 1989). However, few of the programmes reduced stays in institutions for long enough to reduce costs. Most reduced the number of days spent in hospitals. It is easiest to save costs by substituting home care when what is needed is a brief intervention at a relatively low level of input by American standards; but this is not the target group on which most British discussion focuses (see Section 4 of Chapter 13). The prevention of both nursing home and hospital use seemed most successful for those of only moderate needs, with good prognosis, and good informal support.

- Of the projects which evaluated changes in performing personal care tasks, as many found no improvement as improvements, though some of the projects asked about the receipt of help rather than the capacity to perform activities. Gains were often too small to be statistically significant. There were generally no effects on capacities to perform instrumental daily living tasks. There was only the weakest evidence of improved mental functioning. Those whose functioning were most likely to be improved were those whose use of nursing homes was least likely to be reduced, though they were also those whose hospital utilisation was likely to be shortened: the younger, healthier, less dependent, cognitively least impaired, with good informal support.
- Most appeared to improve quality of life in the sense of expressed life satisfaction of clients, though in few were the effects big enough to be statistically significant, despite the much larger number of clients studied than in the PSSRU experiments, where these effects were statistically significant. Likewise there appeared to be increased social activity and social interaction, though again few of the improvements were statistically significant. Quality of care as reflected in reduced unmet needs were reduced, the difference being statistically significant in most studies.
- Few of the studies reported statistically significant improvements in longevity.
- Most schemes appeared to achieve small gains in the morale or reduction in the stress of informal carers, but few of these gains were large enough to be significant. In many, the amounts of informal support were reduced. As has been argued elsewhere, the degree to which the time commitment is reduced as well as the nature of the support activities undertaken is changed very much reflects practice policy and, one would expect, on the intensity and skill of case management.
- Targeting effects were surprisingly mixed.

However, the evidence about what is attainable from case management with higher caseloads is circumstantial. It would be naive simply to accept these results at their face value, because the aims and nature of the schemes varied so much, and the evaluations frequently had limited and flawed designs which make inferences about outcomes difficult. Nevertheless, the results do suggest that more administrative models can confer benefits, but that the benefits seem generally to have been smaller and less pervasive than those of the PSSRU's more intensive models. Though not generally less costly than the standard alternatives, the cost disadvantages of the American schemes reviewed were not large. So if carefully designed to do so, administrative models might be made to confer costs savings. But caseloads per manager and the level of professional training of managers are less direct influences on costs than budget limits and averages, although they are the two characteristics which allow the practice of the more holistic and entrepreneurial as distinct from administrative case management. What it is not clear is the Heineken benefits one will generally forgo with larger caseloads. Our assumption is that the gains in welfare from the more intensive forms of case management are considerably greater. But given the nature of the evidence, our beliefs must be based as much on *a priori* argument as on hard evidence.

The great variety of the projects which limits the meaning of comparisons of their results suggests that we should innovate cautiously in the UK. Unless the policy-makers and managers have been able to work through the arguments and develop models selectively, we are in danger of having almost as many models here as among the HCFA projects; and with the variety of models, the great variety of outcomes. It is not that they were all different, but arguably equally good by their own criteria. Many unambiguously failed.

4 Matching resources to needs: some *a priori* argument

The logic of field schemes has been stated in earlier work, and is being restated in context after context in reports and papers about the PSSRU community care projects. The logic we explore in this section and illustrate in Section 5 is that of designing arrangements which fit the needs of local circumstances and clienteles. It is a logic addressing how to develop a local strategy for improving the performance of the core case-management tasks over the whole long-term care system. Space does not allow an analysis which is systematic, far less comprehensive.

Elements of this logic for management action seem to be emerging in those authorities most committed to correcting the developmental bias against performing core tasks well. However, the authorities themselves may be in danger of building biases into their approach. Much of the new British literature does nothing to safeguard them against the biases. The danger exists because managers have not yet had much time to learn a dialectic which helps them to seek out the best match between the enormous variety of possible arrangements compatible with the rigorous application of first principles, and the greatly different circumstances of client group subgroups and area contexts. Little wonder that case management has become 'something of a portmanteau term', as David Hunter (1988, p.18) remarks.[5]

Diagram 13.1 might help to focus thought on the issue. It postulates (i) a lead agency with responsibility for the equity and efficiency of the local long-term care of the elderly a Griffiths-type 'enabling' agency; and (ii) managers of a case management section of the agency working with field professionals to scan for ways of improving the performance of the core tasks.

Diagram 13.1

Logical principles for the field organisation of local case management systems

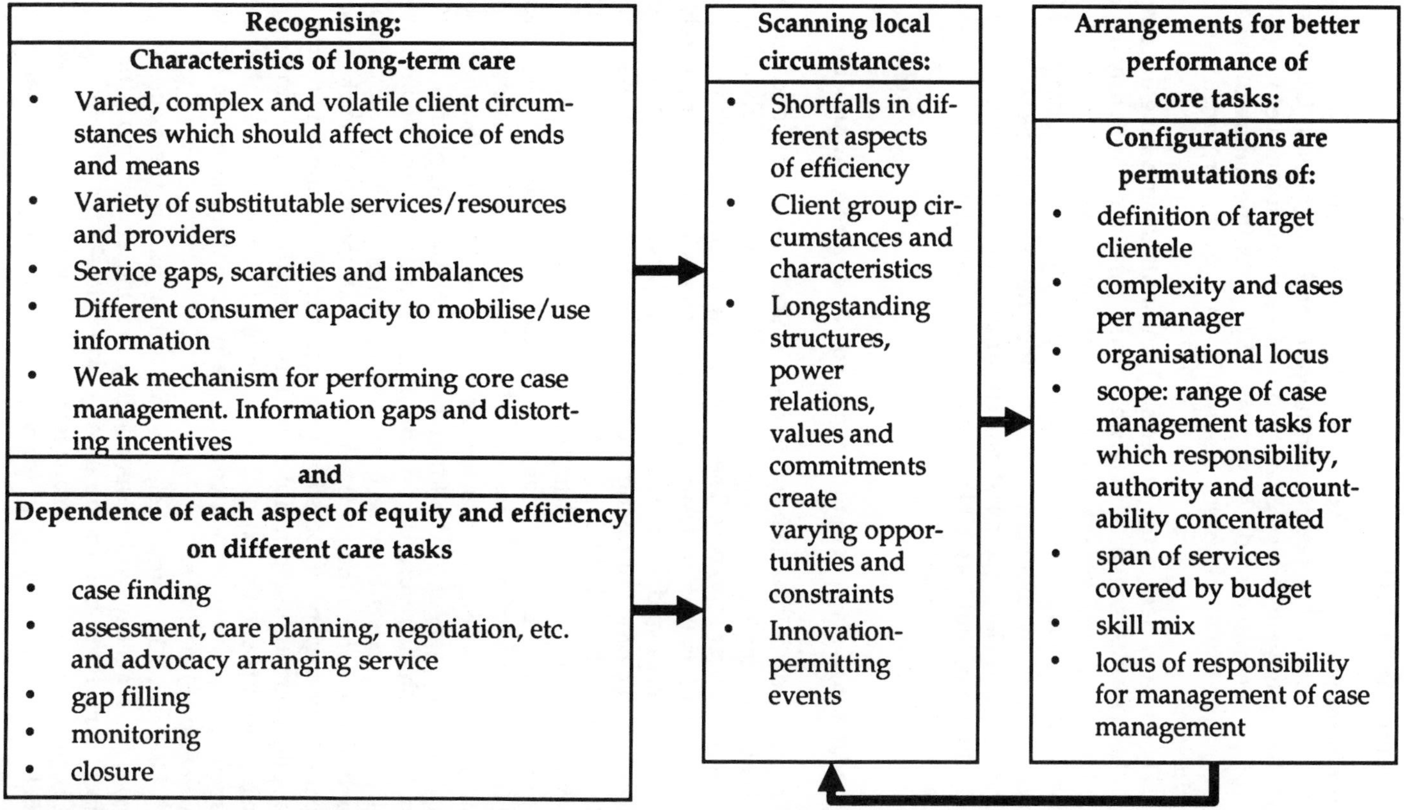

Recognising:	Scanning local circumstances:	Arrangements for better performance of core tasks:
Characteristics of long-term care	• Shortfalls in different aspects of efficiency	**Configurations are permutations of:**
• Varied, complex and volatile client circumstances which should affect choice of ends and means	• Client group circumstances and characteristics	• definition of target clientele
• Variety of substitutable services/resources and providers	• Longstanding structures, power relations, values and commitments create varying opportunities and constraints	• complexity and cases per manager
• Service gaps, scarcities and imbalances		• organisational locus
• Different consumer capacity to mobilise/use information	• Innovation-permitting events	• scope: range of case management tasks for which responsibility, authority and accountability concentrated
• Weak mechanism for performing core case management. Information gaps and distorting incentives		• span of services covered by budget
and		• skill mix
Dependence of each aspect of equity and efficiency on different care tasks		• locus of responsibility for management of case management
• case finding		
• assessment, care planning, negotiation, etc. and advocacy arranging service		
• gap filling		
• monitoring		
• closure		

Assumptions and beliefs (Boxes 1 and 2)

The degree to which managers accept as their starting point our list of fundamental assumptions should influence the entire process. The assumptions are the propositions that aspects of equity and efficiency differentially depend on the effectiveness of the performance of the core tasks of case management; the argument alluded to in the central box of Diagram 13.1, embodied in Diagram 6.1, and taken from Davies and Challis (1986). Making these axioms the starting point, they see alternative arrangements producing different mixes of benefits.

Also important to what should logically be chosen is the strength of their belief in the validity of the propositions about long-term target clienteles and service systems. The higher the proportion of target clients for whom they perceive these propositions to be valid, and the more they ascribe failures in outcomes to them, the greater should logically be their commitment to put into place strong arrangements for performing core case management tasks. For instance, if they perceive the circumstances of a high proportion of cases of high priority to be complex and volatile, they will opt for lower caseloads and highly trained case managers. If they perceive it likely that there are potentially alternative types and sources of service producing overlapping outcomes but at very different cost and they are concerned with efficiency and progressively shifting influence from providers to consumers and the case managers which represent them, they will make sure that the range of alternative inputs will be charged by the case managers to a fixed budget, that the menu of prices will reflect true resource costs, and that the average budget is realistically fixed to balance cover and benefit: in other words, they will ensure that the arrangements will embody the incentives and information contained in PSSRU models.

Conversely, if the priority were more to maintain current sources of supply rather than to extend consumer choice and improve efficiency perhaps to ensure that the range of traditional services is safeguarded, the designers would restrict case managers to a choice of basic services, not have them charge their costs to their budget, restrict their use of budgets, not make the demands made by case managers in response to consumers' wishes and needs channel resources through the service system, and not provide the case managers with information about service costs which takes full account of the hidden costs of standard services. Such a model would depend merely on focusing and consolidating responsibility for performing case management tasks without providing incentives to produce outcomes more efficiently. The model could improve effectiveness but would provide no incentive to case managers to improve efficiency. The message it would give to providers was that competition would be discouraged, so that the rerouting of finance through the case manager shown in Chart 7 of the White Paper need not threaten established practice;

certainly not achieve a major change in culture among providers and the more creative, less stereotyped responses to consumer needs and wishes.

Much of the discussion about alternative models of case management reflects unarticulated assumptions about the validity of the propositions in the second box. As in the USA, others reflect other goals of projects; for example the development of new services for neglected clienteles.

Local circumstances (Box 3)

The *a priori* beliefs and assumptions in the first two boxes affect their analysis of local circumstances. Good analysis would be explicit about the respects in which the efficiency of the system most falls short of what is required, and would be informed about the circumstances of clients and carers relevant to targeting and the potential for substituting inputs and outputs.

The managerial focus should vary with the geographical scale of the territory managed. At the most local levels, the focus should be as much subgroups within target groups as the broader groups themselves.

However, scanning must recognise that arrangements for better performing case management tasks which look good on paper must also be politically viable. So the third box also lists the assessment of opportunities and constraints and the recognition of events which affect them. Why this is essential is illustrated most clearly when we look at American experiments to divert people to home care who would otherwise have entered nursing homes. The experiments remind us that there is no such thing as a pure unadulterated model in real world programmes. It is fundamentally important that the model implemented recognises the political realities. Otherwise the programme may founder, or it may be corrupted to such an extent that it will not achieve its objectives.

But if there are constraints, there are also opportunities. One is the Malvolio effect: 'there are tides in the affairs of Man which, taken at the flood, lead on to ...' Poor Malvolio! It led to the dungeon, humiliation, and worse. What appeared to be a unique opportunity was an illusion. His virtues were of the same stamp as his vices: optimism, energy, and the willingness to act vigorously, to seize a fleeting opportunity, and to stick his head over the parapet. In less frivolous and prejudiced company, the same person as a bright-eyed and bushy-tailed young manager growing in an environment which would cultivate the virtues not the vices of their professional personality, might have been just the sort to initiate local change; the type whom the Audit Commission argued had been so important in achieving significant innovations in community care (Audit Commission, 1986c). Misleading cues and a capricious environment might transform our potential leaders into Malvolios. (We return to this theme in the next section.)

Instead the response to trends must be made to create genuine opportunities: for instance, the escalation of US Medicaid costs due to rising expenditures on nursing homes, the rise of new pressure groups, or the consciousness of the public expenditure consequences of demographic trends with unchanged care patterns. Lasting opportunities and stable incentives to take them up are also offered by events. Among the events which we have found to be particularly important are the arrival of a new local geriatrician, the announcement of a new pot of central government gold for likely schemes, the appointment of a new managerialist director of social services, and the change in the control of a council after an election.

What if there is a clear need but the circumstances are unfavourable and cannot be changed? It may sometimes be better to wait; to put the resources and effort into some more promising project. This is part of the significance of Ministers making it explicit that the modernisation of long-term care will take time; that there will be no back-sliding or arbitrary changes in direction; and that resources will be committed over the long run to achieve it. With these commitments, the managers can be sure that the local constraining circumstances will change; pressure can be brought in various ways, and professional and mass media can be used to help people to realise that they are not keeping up with changes, and to change public expectations and attitudes. In time, immovable objects can decay, be eroded, or manoeuvred around. It is not essential to act immediately, to take the tide on the flood, and so to risk becoming a Malvolio. The policy will be stable, and the manager can wait until the incentives and sanctions created by the policy are fully appreciated and come to seem irresistible. In the interim, it might well make better sense to give priority to less useful but more attainable objectives, and to arrangements which are less promising in principle but more likely to succeed in practice. But of course, the action focus of the new managerialism is to give the manager sufficient power to shift or blow up the previously immovable.

Case management arrangements (Box 3)

Arrangements themselves are permutations of such features as those described in the last box of Diagram 13.1 and others. Chapter 14 describes some as 'parameters of the case management model': quantities or quantitative specifications of relationships whose effects are statistically predictable. The features illustrated in the diagram have loomed large in the logics of PSSRU experiments.

The box describes important ways in which detailed configurations can vary between schemes and systems. It starts close to programme goals. In the PSSRU experiments, the aim has been to finance improvements in quality of life by diverting demand from residential homes in some schemes, from long-stay hospitals in others. It has not been their purpose to extend and develop home care services in general. Neither as yet have we focused on providing more effective service to particular ethnic groups.

The *diversion or extension* sought specifies the definition of the *target groups*. The goals of broad programmes include a variety of substitutions. We have often (but not always) found it useful to organise the performance of case management tasks at the lowest level with only one or two of the goals for each team. We distinguish generic from specialist case management teams according to the breadth of the target group and the related substitutions. Kent and Gateshead projects were examples of generic projects. The Darlington project was an example of a specialist project. The choice of goal and target group partly reflects clinical insight about its achievability, and translates broader target group features into more precise ideas about the characteristics of its constituent subgroups and what each needs for the goal to be attained.

The specification of the target subgroup for each team and judgements about what each requires for the goal to be met involve judgements about the complexity, variety and volatility of needs. These lead on, as the diagram suggests, to such choices as the *total size of the budget*, the *budget cap* at which cases are reviewed, and the *average number of cases per case manager*.

ACCESS and the New York LTHHCP were among American projects antecedent to the channelling projects which operated different budget caps for persons for whom the most realistic alternative institutional mode of provision differed (Davies and Challis, 1986, pp.113,129). The implementations of the arrangement in British models was discussed in Davies (1981); and the design of the health/social care extension of the social care model implemented in Gateshead acknowledged that for some clients, the realistic alternative to care at home was hospital not residential care, and this was reflected in the budget limit for them (Davies and Grimley Evans, 1982). The Gateshead extension was a small subproject opportunistically added to a larger scheme. In the context of large programmes, the practical difficulty of operating multiple budget caps is to find the rules for allocating cases to the appropriate budget limit in a way which reconciles direct judgements about complex circumstances, allocations of budgets to teams which take into account differences in case mix, and the prevention of cost escalation. The scoring systems adopted in some American states and elsewhere are too crude; see for instance, the discussion of the evidence about their distortions in the State of New York in Davies and Challis (1986). So again, it is vital to build into the design incentives for case managers not to mis-state the most likely alternative level of care, and to have guidelines which could be applied as part of regular peer review of team performance. To have the first-line manager of the case manager select the budget cap might be to balance directness of knowledge with a stake in making the best use of resources, but only if the team as a whole had an incentive not to escalate costs.

The average number of cases per case manager also depends on the tasks the team will itself perform, called in the diagram and in American case management literature, *scope* (Austin, 1983). There are two counter-vailing principles.

- Case management theory heuristically separates core tasks mainly to develop argument about each. The practice theory heavily emphasises interdependence between tasks; particularly between assessment and the others, because assessment is a process not an event, and can be informed while undertaking other tasks. So one must not separate the responsibility for assessment from responsibility for other tasks without taking steps to offset the problems thus created.
- Scope decisions can also reflect judgements about which aspects of efficiency most need improvement, and the political viability of various arrangements; what turf others are willing to surrender to the case manager. Also judgements about scope might reflect (a) the economics of operating in rural areas, some tasks being delegated to local workers outside the team; and (b) the political weakness of those who set up the arrangements. The application of the PSSRU community care arguments in a randomised experiment in up-state New York showed the more direct and intensive PSSRU methods to work better. The division or delegation of case management tasks seem generally to work worse. Some schemes described as 'case management' seem to perform only one of the core tasks of case management; for instance, the York Monitoring System, established in 1986 for dementia sufferers, and performing only a monitoring function. However, the most important issues arise in interfacing acute and the long-term case management models and in linking case management with other functions in multidisciplinary teams, as in the PSSRU health/social care models (Challis et al., 1989, 1990).

Other judgements follow, including *organisational locus*. The importance of where the team is located in the pathways into institutions has been shown to be critical in many American studies. One reason is that in practice, it has proved impossible to identify those at high risk of admission to institutions for long-term care in a way which allows recruitment to be done by rules.

Organisational locus reflects the assessment of where the shortfalls lie and affect the probability of successful targeting. The locus of the Lewisham project reflects the assumptions that access is good and assessment well performed; but that care planning, care arrangement, and monitoring required improvement. It has now become conventional for Americans to argue (as did Davies and Challis, 1986) that locating the case-managed intervention on the direct path to nursing home entry by linking it with pre-admission screening was almost a prerequisite for controlling the Pandora effect and preventing the appearance of project failure by providing intensive services for those at low risk of institutional admission. Where stigma and worse are feared by potential users, self-help and independent organisations might best perform case management tasks. The Association of Directors of Social Services' response to the Griffiths Report recognised the possibility of commissioning others to undertake case management tasks (Association of Directors of Social Services, 1988, p.5). This role is attractive to some in voluntary organisations like Age Concern. The practice of case management can be mainly a technical matter given a clear policy framework defined by a politically accountable agency. As such it can well be performed by separate agencies as long as the lead agency ensures effective quality assurance. Most British discussion about 'case management' by non-statutory agencies have been about models in which the 'case managers' focus on brokerage in the sense of informed and committed advocacy (not the sense in which, for instance, ACCESS is described as a brokerage model); and they have no authority to sanction the allocation of resources. American experience shows that independent case management agencies with the power to authorise resource use can be successful (Davies and Challis, 1986, Chapter 3). Davies and Goddard (1987) discuss alternative scenarios with competing and area monopolist brokerage agencies.

The more detailed insights into the characteristics and needs of the target subgroups should in principle determine the *span* of services over which the case manager has authority and which are covered by the budget, the *skill mix* of the team, and the *locus of responsibility for the management of case management*. However, in our experience, this too must reflect a careful political judgement. It has long been British policy to encourage authorities to have components of assessments performed by professional experts, often from health-related professions; particularly for those at risk of admission to institutions for long-term care. It would seem natural to make most teams multidisciplinary. Having the main disciplines within the team makes it depend less on goodwill and the exchange of favours, more on duty and authority. Also, some of the most valuable diversions would be from long-stay hospitals to other forms of care. For this, we have found the type of mix used in the Darlington community care project fruitful; having in or closely associated with the team a community nurse, an occupational therapist, a physiotherapist and a psychologist as well as social workers. (An extension of the Gateshead project also included a registrar geriatrician who worked to the team leader, a social worker.)

However, there are important disadvantages. There are the wellknown practical difficulties; for instance, the team can have personnel whose terms and conditions of service are determined by awards from different organisations. Case managers and care workers may have multiple accountabilities: in some models, accountability for professional matters and particular procedures to superordinate professionals; for administrative matters to the team leader and the managing agency; for case management policy to whatever mechanism exists for its development and management. Such complexity makes the field coordination and team representation of the client interest and perspective all the more difficult: it is sometimes argued about mental health teams that the voice of the clients may be lost in the clamour of the professionals claiming to speak with client insight. Again, the multidisciplinary team is a more complex organisation. It requires inputs to make it work cooperatively and well. Otherwise its gains may no more than those which come from co-locating the workers in the same offices. Clear responsibility, authority and accountability for core case management tasks may be all the more important. But direct professional supervision of case managers may be more distant if the teams consist of some who are not case managers and are best kept small. The Darlington experiment showed how case management could usefully contribute in the context of a multidisciplinary assessment team and the employment of multipurpose community care workers, but it was carefully targeted at persons at high risk of long-term hospitalisation. Whether facing the difficulties is worthwhile will depend on the welfare and efficiency gains. They cannot just be assumed without the careful appraisal of alternatives.

In the long run, we have found that the organisational environments for such projects are more turbulent and unstable. Agency managers have played games in the sense of attempting takeovers or making changes which show little respect for the integrity of the principles on which the logic depends. Schemes can be wrecked as a result. It may be a prerequisite for long-run success for case managers to be accountable to managers who are themselves responsible mainly for securing the effective performance of case management in an agency with clear lines of accountability. So it can be sensible to avoid multidisciplinary teams even if one thereby reduces effectiveness at securing important types of welfare outcome.

The power of the SSD in the case management of elderly persons will be increased by the implementation of the White Paper, the Act, and other guidance. They confirm the lead role of the SSD. They confirm the financial responsibility of the SSD. Chart 7 of *Caring for People* shows the routing of finance through the SSD to the case managers and from them to providers. It is at the core of the logic which is to accomplish the progressive shift in influence from the provider of services to those seeking care and those most directly securing it. So it will be important to ensure that agreements made by middle management at some distance from the small area covered by the case manager, and so not necessarily closely reflecting local opportunities and circumstances, do not excessively limit case managers' freedom in care planning: conservatism, even protectionism, can too easily masquerade as sensible caution, and so inhibit the cultural changes needed.

The enhanced power of the SSD is accompanied by enhanced influence of the manager compared with the care professional. Together, the effect may be an incentive to minimise the creation of multi-agency organisations employing persons from a variety of disciplines. Indeed they may reinforce the understandable tendency in some areas for the social services to create systems which commission assistance from other agencies only sparingly and for prescribed purposes.

The most common arrangement is likely to be some form of 'Go-It-Alone' (GIA) social services department model associated with specific contributions to case management tasks or elements of the care plan obtained from other professionals. So the relations between the case managers in the SSD team and other professionals might reflect a 'Don't-call-me, I'll-call-you' policy. That would reduce the influence of health-related professions and so their ability to expand into new territories. Also it would consolidate the substitution of workers employed by the SSD for health-related personnel in the grey areas of responsibilities; for instance, 'social' baths would replace 'medical' baths among those case-managed except where there was a clear medical reason. And the requests to other professionals would be for specific functions to which their skills would be most relevant; for instance, the general practitioners for the outcomes of their annual assessments, the nurses for specialised assessments which less costly workers could not be trained to undertake. The argument used by the Griffiths Report is heard the world over: the health-related professionals are scarce and expensive, and so must be used only for the tasks which they alone can perform (Griffiths, 1988). The Thanet and Gateshead projects worked well depending only on such reciprocity they could muster through exchange processes (see Diagram 1.1 of Davies and Challis, 1986). However, in the absence of specific training, there is a danger that links with health-related personnel may be too weak for the case managers to recognise when the other professionals could make important contributions. The need for them has often remained unrecognised among those admitted to residential care; though this will in the future be diminished since the circulars will require inputs from health professionals into assessments of persons for residential and nursing homes. We discuss specialist schemes for heavy and frequent users of acute services below.

Omitted from the last box of Diagram 13.1 are arrangements which the case management team itself and its immediate management have made; for instance, the primary forms which gap-filling with the budgets take. However, some of them can be central to the logic and can therefore merit an important place in the list of permutated arrangements. An example is the development in Darlington of a corps of personal care assistants undertaking tasks associated with nursing as well as more traditional social care (Challis et al., 1989). In the community care experiments, the workers have been managers of gap-filling personnel as well as performers of the core tasks more typically defined in American studies. Again the arrangements for the management of the case management can be various, as the care in the community projects well illustrate (Knapp et al., 1989). Capitman, Haskins and Bernstein (1986) list quite other arrangements as the principal scheme features of American case management projects for the elderly. Our list will certainly lengthen as our experience broadens.

5 Matching resources to needs: the logic illustrated

The scanning argument helps to evaluate some important choices.

5.1 Separation of arrangements for clienteles

The services have been expected to achieve policy goals for quite different clienteles, four of which must be clearly distinguished. The arrangements for achieving the goals need overlap little. That allows greater clarity in the prioritisation of the goals. The three goals and clienteles are: (i) the general population of frail elderly persons whose lives are enriched in some but not all cases, greatly so – by one or a few standard practical home and personal care services, but of whom few are at imminent risk of admission to institutions for long-term care; (ii) persons who are at high risk of admission to institutions for long-term care, and who could be supported in the community with a good quality of life and care without unfair diswelfares to informal carers, but for whom the design and maintenance of the most cost-effective package of care for doing this is likely to require the exercise of complex case management skills; (iii) persons who have recently suffered a health accident or other life event from which they can recover to independence given short-term rehabilitative aid and service support; and (iv) informal carers suffering unfair burdens, or burdens which they are likely to drop, causing higher long-run costs to the public health and social services agencies. The third is not a long-term care group although without the rehabilitative and support services they can be at risk of entering that group. The distinction between these and the long-term care groups are clearly made in the literature for some countries; for instance, the United States (Hughes, 1988), and Australia. The Australian Commonwealth Department of Community Services and Health have structured their subsidy system so as to encourage a higher rate of growth of services for the other groups. They are among the areas designated 'no-growth' services which may not be expanded using Commonwealth subsidies provided under the Home and Community Care

(HACC) Act: 'rehabilitative services' (directed primarily at increasing the level of functioning), 'post-acute care' services, 'palliative care services' for the terminally ill and their supporters, and services specific to disabilities other than brain failure (HACC, 1988, pp.9-11). The distinguishing characteristic is recognised to be the nature of the needs of clients (Auditor General, 1988b; Saunders, 1989). Services for the support of the carers of eligible clients are themselves eligible for subsidy (HACC, 1985).

However, the Australians are only now discovering how critical is the distinction between the first and second groups. The HACC Act of 1985 was to create a financing system which would allow a more coordinated set of services in response to needs than previous legislation, and to help to reduce the excessive reliance on residential forms of long-term care. The *Annual Report* of the Department of Community Services for 1984-5 stated the aim to be

... to provide a comprehensive integrated range of home and community care services to persons who are considered to be at risk of premature or inappropriate residential care. These may be frail aged or younger persons with moderate or severe disabilities (Department of Community Services, 1985, p.25).

By the end of the first three years, it had become clear that most HACC resources were being allocated in small quantities to those who were not in imminent danger of admission to institutions for long-term care. There was no sign that the Commonwealth and the States were withdrawing from subsidising the provision for frail elderly persons on low incomes not at high risk of admission to institutions, despite Australia's increasingly gloomy economic prospects, the influence there too of new managerialist ideas, and the realisation that case-managed care at higher levels would be beneficial for the large number at risk of institutional entry (Staples, 1989). In 1989, the Commonwealth government invited more tightly-targeted schemes, promising to meet the whole costs of demonstration projects designed specifically to assist persons 'at risk of premature or inappropriate institutionalisation' to remain in the community (HACC, 1989, p.3).

In Great Britain, too, we have only recently appreciated the differences between means and ends for (i) the general frail aged and (ii) elders at high risk of institutional admission. Our recognition of the need to support informal carers irrespective of the effects on the welfare of their dependents is still more recent and uneven, as we show in the sequel to this study, *Community Services and the Social Production of Welfare* (PSSRU, 1991). There is little reason to create whole systems of services for target subgroups. That would add to complexity without adding much to variety. Also it would reduce flexibility. But we should at least consider how best to arrange for the performance of core case management tasks for each of the three broad groups and, indeed, for some subgroups within them. There can be little doubt that it is feasible to create separate case management arrangements for (i) the general population requiring a few simple services and (ii) complex high-risk cases, including those likely to be unnecessarily or prematurely admitted to institutions for long-term care. What is more important is whether such separation of responsibility for case management is likely to be more efficient.

5.1.1 Complex high-cost cases at high risk of institutional admission
Complex cases at high risk of institutional admission do not necessarily incur high service costs when the case management tasks are skillfully performed. High-cost cases are not necessarily at high risk of institutional admission. Each of the three characteristics have many aspects and each can vary in degree. However, the three characteristics are correlated; and it is heuristically convenient to discuss arrangements for persons with varying combinations of the three characteristics together.

The advantages of separating case management from supplying service
For complex cases at high risk of institutional admission, the separation of the case management from the service supply function is likely to be worthwhile because for them there are great welfare, equity and efficiency gains possible from expert and intensive case management at arm's length from any one of the suppliers of services. There are several reasons, among them:

(i) To mix this highly skilled and intensive work with too much routine activity would be to risk creating a work environment which would make it difficult to nurture skills. Separation at the field and several layers of management above it allow the acquisition of expertise and its application to the management of case management. We elsewhere discuss the permeability of Chinese walls. Providing a career structure for case managers and their managers within the case management branch is more likely to provide the incentives to use the potential for competition between suppliers to best effect. Since generic case managers teams can cover areas of 80,000 people, and specialist teams cover larger catchments, there would be advantages in maintaining the independence of the case management section from the supplying organisations at all levels of the organisation in all but big authorities.

(ii) If the expected costs of the home care services are likely to be high, the absolute savings and improvements in outcomes which might be gained by better performance of case management tasks are more likely to make the additional costs incurred because of the separation of functions worthwhile. The gains come partly from a focus on consumer responsiveness, mainly through improved output mix efficiency and aspects of input mix efficiency which reflects greater capacity for handling potential informal carers and most resourcefully improvising care arrangements from the local economy, formal and informal.

(iii) More complex cases are likely to require services from more sources and so more intensive more coordinative activity. Also, less stable cases require more coordinative activity.

Again, the separation for some complex subgroups may be worthwhile because it helps to foster the exchange relationships with other professionals who likewise focus on client subgroups. A good example is work with confused and demented elderly people. The networks in the health services and voluntary organisations are different in the care of the demented than in the care of the more complex cases of physical disability. There are striking differences between the models for multiprofessional work and inter-agency division of labour between teams at the leading edge in the care of the confused and the support of their carers. These seem to create large differences in how, by whom, and for whom core case management tasks are performed. But they all have in common that they require a specialist case management team. Likewise the model differentiation in our programme of community care projects shows the advantages of having specialist case management teams for some of the client groups in which client circumstances tend to be complex.

Brokerage by supplying organisations
Brokerage by the same organisation which provides much of the finance and service fits in well with British assumptions. It would be the natural compromise between principled reorganisation and institutional inertia. The British welfare state was established at a time when there was a strong belief in the efficiency of consolidated publicly accountable organisations whose planning, financial control, and provision dominated 'the commanding heights' of economies; the ideals of the Morrisonian public corporation. By the late 1960s, this belief had become an unarticulated assumption in the reform of the structures providing social care. It was challenged by right and left mainly in the decade which followed, though the first intimations were already heard in the late 1960s (see, for instance, Lapping and Radice, 1968). In fact, the state-financed rise of privately-provided residential care has broken the monopoly of that mode of provision. But informal care apart, there remains a monopoly in home care. So in practice, one can envisage few authorities choosing to encourage competition among case managers in an area, and many who will be sceptical about the benefits of competition created by placing the case managers at arm's length from providers. They will instead see what used to be called the 'wastes' of competition in some of the literature which influenced our post-war trade and industry policies and structures (Meade, 1936, pp.165-8,174,178, 1948): the overlap between the assessments by case

manager and necessary appraisals by the first-line managers in provider organisations, the potential for delays, the communication requirements, the costs and difficulties of contract specification and enforcement, the costs of additional quality assurance activity made necessary to guard against exploitation by suppliers more interested in short-term gain than the fruits of long-run reputation.

However, the arrangement does not fit well into evidence about alternative regulatory models. Those who study the outcomes of regulative reform debate – for context after context – whether rules enforcing the structuring of the markets to avoid conflicts of interest are superior to regulating conduct in the market. Much recent regulative reform has replaced structural by conduct regulation. Examples are the shift from the structural separation of brokers from market-makers in financial services to the regulation of conduct through detailed new rules for investor protection. Kay and Vickers (1988) argue that conduct regulation requires information which is more difficult to acquire. It is necessary to have high-quality information about behaviour and the equity and efficiency of outcomes, and transparent processes in which conduct can easily be monitored. It is much easier and more effective to set up structures in which there are not conflicts of interest between agencies and consumers, and between the pursuit of greater equity and efficiency and accommodating pressures from colleagues providing services from the same agency. The difficulties are exacerbated at a time when old value systems based more on professional integrity are being threatened by competitive threats from new providers with varying degrees of scruple. Again, the parallel with financial services is interesting. *The Economist* was scathing about the effects of the new regulative arrangements in the City of London financial institutions. It alleged that for many the guiding principle was ceasing to be 'my word is my bond' and becoming 'catch me if you can'. Chinese walls are ineffective when cold winds blow fiercely. Closer to home, some argue that only a clear division between purchasers and providers in the National Health Service will avoid unsustainable conflicts of interest (Scrivens and Henneh, 1989). So at first sight, a quite distinct organisational separation of case management from service supply is appealing. The CMP argument is for a separation as complete as that which had existed between market making and brokerage in the City, between the roles of accountants as auditors and consultants to the same firm, or between the generation and transmission of electricity in the privatisation plans. However, Griffiths implied less separation for his major consumers for whom at least some case management input would be obligatory. The Audit Commission (1987) advocated a 'loose-tight' arrangement. Although the issue is not discussed, readers might infer that at most the building of 'Chinese walls' between the SSD's service managers and case managers would be needed. Unsurprisingly, some authorities are not attempting the separation. The arguments for separation are clear. The primary argument against it is that separation necessarily involves some duplication. We must set the costs of duplication against the long-run benefits gained by separating the case management function in an increasingly competitive supply economy of social care. The balance between the costs and forms of separation will precisely reflect the circumstances of clients and systems described in Table 13.1. For instance, the gains will be greater, (i) the more varied, complex and volatile are client circumstances, (ii) the greater the potential for substitution, (iii) the more important are service gaps and imbalances, (iv) the worse the current arrangements are seen to have performed, (v) the less expensive it is to the SSD to sponsor a large supply from independent sources, and (vi) the more the managers feel themselves to have the power to create independent case management arrangements with the design features appropriate to the client group and local system.

What arrangements are appropriate will differ between client groups. The degree of organisational separation of case management from service supply is one of the main ways in which arrangements for case management might vary. We return to the topic below. Here it is sufficient to recall that Davies and Challis (1986) describe 'lead agency' models in the USA where one agency provides case management whose policies are formulated in inter-agency agreements. However, our impression was that these arrangements reflected the weakness of the reformers and did not establish the prerequisites for a system of managed competition to work.

Meanwhile one thing is clear from some of the care in the community demonstration projects (Renshaw et al., 1988; Knapp et al., 1989) and schemes which are substantially funded by and managerially accountable to one agency and of the kind described by the Audit Commission (1986c). It was attractive to combine the performance of case management tasks with service supply. However, that was often because at the core of the alternative provision was the provision of shelter in a group facility, and in most schemes what was performed was a looser form of case coordination than full entrepreneurial case management. One reason was that many of these were focused on particular group of clients rather than attempts to set up entire new systems; systems focused more on new cases from the community face more variety in needs and alternative ways of meeting them, including arrangements other than long-term provision of shelter-with-care, so requiring more continuity in the consolidation of the responsibility for case management tasks. What the schemes illustrate is that it is vital to start with the analysis of the performance of core case management tasks, trading off effectiveness in their performance with effectiveness and efficiency in other respects. The arrangements in many of the care in the community projects did seem to allow responsiveness to the consumer. Scheme philosophy and commitment were vital influences. Knapp et al.

(1989, p.6/22) found that user influence was enhanced when case managers had control over resources. The Maidstone Community Care Project for persons with learning difficulties discharged from long-stay hospitals illustrated the combined influence of philosophy, practice policy, and case managers holding budgets. Its statement of operational philosophy offered consumers choice, as did the statement of principles in the scheme's manual. The statement of operational policy included a consumer's 'charter of care'. The evaluators observed many ways in which this sensitivity to the consumers permeated procedures and practice.

Some fear that case managers with the responsibility, authority and accountability for packaging resources would be unresponsive to client needs and wishes because their agencies would give them inadequate resources. Our experience of an authority-wide implementation of the original community care model suggests that this need not be so. A key to the realism of the budgets during that period was the influence of a standing group consisting of case managers, other senior managers from headquarters and PSSRU personnel. The group monitored performance, and proposed and discussed policy (including budget allocations). The standing group operated during the whole period from the time when other areas were invited to develop schemes based on the experimental project as one component of their standard provision, to the time when complete coverage of the authority was achieved.

There were several reasons why the authority financed expenditures per case sufficient for case managers to procure adequate service in a way which was responsive to client values, needs and wishes. The point of departure was a project producing more welfare for the same costs for a target group which was carefully defined and of high priority. The organisational locus and procedures which achieved the highly efficient targeting were easily transferred when the schemes were launched in the other areas of the county over the period of a few years. The input norms established by the original project were readily assimilated, and new case managers observed practice by experienced workers as part of their induction. Divergence from those norms through time or by individual teams was automatically revealed by the routine analyses made by the PSSRU (as technical consultants), using the data system developed for the PSSRU community care approach; and were automatically discussed in the periodic meetings between senior managers, care managers and case managers. Case managers had a clear *esprit de corps*. There were mechanisms to promote this and to discuss practice developments and problems. Though the full 'hands-on' peer review system proposed by Davies and Challis (1986) was never developed, a group of esteemed case managers (nicknamed 'the great and the good') advised management and contributed to the development of (and adherence to) norms of good practice.

These illustrate (i) that a stockade strategy of development has important advantages; (ii) that the concentration of responsibility, authority and accountability for performance core case management tasks is not enough the PSSRU community care approach is not just the introduction of 'case management' but the development of a case management system (Davies and Challis, 1986): a set of necessary and mutually reinforcing arrangements affecting many aspects of organisation, management and practice; and (iii) that in the introduction of case management systems, there are advantages in first establishing credibility with a focus on target groups of high priority with arrangements that ensure that Pandora effects are insufficiently large to allow the arrangements to threaten the escalation of overall programme budgets.

5.1.2 *Cases of intermediate cost and complexity at risk of admission to institutions*

A main feature of the logic of Diagram 13.1 is that it requires the manager to think through variations in such characteristics of cases as cost, complexity and stability of circumstances, and risk of admission. The Thanet and Gateshead models were aimed at a wide range of complex cases in the community. Unlike the Darlington and Lewisham models, they are generic rather than specialist models. Being a generic model, they are the natural starting point for models whose focus is not the high-cost, complex, unstable, and high-risk group at which they were originally targeted, but clients of intermediate cost, complexity, and risk.

Indeed, it is arguable that the reform of the SSD policy and provision for the intermediate cases is what is crucial to the modernisation of British long-term social care. (i) They are numerous. (ii) Like the high-cost complex group, what they have received another case has been provided here has been inappropriate in amount, content and style. (iii) Handling clients demands less case management skill and caseloads nearer to those which first-line managers now have. And (iv), the responsibility of the SSD for contributing to brokerage and financing has not been questioned.

One example is the evolution of policy in Kent. For a decade, Kent on the one hand maintained home help services for a general clientele. As in other authorities, the service gradually and unevenly developed from a restricted home help to a more flexible home care service. On the other, it extended the Thanet community care model throughout the county. This was targeted at high cost and complex cases at high risk of admission to institutions. However, from 1987, it produced the outline of an extended model of community care which absorbed the home care services. The new arrangements were to amalgamate its home help, social work for the elderly, and community care branches into a consolidated service. It was intended to maintain the case management flexibility and expertise of community care with case managers holding budgets. However, it was to apply these features of the Thanet model to a much broader clientele. In doing so, it would remove low need cases from its target group, referring those in lesser need to voluntary and for-profit providers. Kent sponsored the development of independent provision (County Councils Association, 1990) and it was the intention to provide quality assurance. The extension of the Kent arrangements therefore acknowledges the importance of the performance of core case management tasks, and attempts to apply a variant of the approach to the whole of the target group which it judges should be the responsibility of the local authority. Kent has separated (i) purchasing by budget-holding case managers, (ii) supply by independent agencies or 'quasi Direct Labour Organisations', supplying sections of the SSD, (iii) the planning and development of service supply and bulk supply contracting, and (iv) quality assurance and contract enforcement. The White Paper *Implementation Documents* likewise advocate separation.

The Kent model clearly focuses on the middle group with respect to complexity. This is reflected in various ways.

(i) The intended caseload size is 35, 10 more than in PSSRU community care experiments in Kent and elsewhere; and, in practice, the target caseloads have been exceeded well after the introduction of the new arrangements to areas. The Kent extension has caseloads more typical of many American case management systems. The perception of the complexity of the case management task has been described by the Director:

> We should not bamboozle ourselves that there is much more to this function than there really is. You don't need a high level of professional skill in all cases (Warner, 1990, p.4).

Defining the nature and levels of professional skill requires clear judgements firmly applied:

> introducing a care management scheme [among other things] requires a willingness to confront professional preciousness ... the issues are to do with identifying what is really professional, putting users in the driving seat, and enforcing budgetary responsibility' (Warner, 1990).

Case managers have been recruited from a variety of care and other backgrounds. Training is seen to be a vital element of the strategy.

(ii) Although the more complex cases are not excluded from the target group, special care management arrangements are not made for them. The entire target group has the same arrangements for case management: the Kent system has not developed the special case management arrangements for the complex, high-cost and high-risk cases by developing special teams for whom the

arrangements were a response to the logic of Diagram 13.1, as in the Darlington and Lewisham projects. Conversely, the targeting criteria exclude persons requiring only straightforward assistance with domestic tasks in small quantities. The criteria have been ambiguous about (and so caseload measures and budgets do not appropriately allow for) complex cases requiring only small inputs of care but larger inputs of case management activity of a more counselling kind, for instance for the support of informal carers; or cases requiring only short-term counselling and perhaps intensive resources for a short while. The evidence so far suggests that the separation made in practice is based not on risk of admission and complexity, but more on the basis of functional capacity.

5.1.3 Straightforward low-cost cases at low risk of admission to institutions

Separation of case management or division of case management labour?
There are certainly additional advantages in separating case management if what is being operated is a truly mixed competitive economy of welfare in the absence of adequate quality assurance of the nonstatutory agencies. Inadequate quality in voluntary agencies can be due to lethargy. In for-profit agencies they can also be due to the unscrupulous pursuit of profit; and so can amount to deliberate policy ruthlessly implemented. It is commonly argued that one can have greater trust in non-profit organisations because they have no incentive ruthlessly to pursue the maximisation of profits (Weisbrod and Scheslinger, 1986). But non-profit organisations can build up political goodwill and influence which allows inefficiency-inducing lethargy. The third volume of the Moreland Report (1975) described this for nursing homes in New York. So a preference for non-profit providers must be conditional; and unless the conditions are identified and met, it would be dangerous to argue that restricting the options to nonprofit providers in itself tips the balance against the separation of supply and case management.

For less complex cases at low risk of admission to institutions, there can only be smaller potential gains from the separation of case management from service supply, particularly if that is provided by the same agencies. A large part of the argument for separating the performance of case management tasks from the supply of service is that efficiency can be improved by substituting inputs if the separation is accompanied by appropriate devolution of budgets, information, and the opportunity to be resourceful. The substitutions will be inhibited if the case manager's agency has an interest in providing some kinds – or quality – of inputs only. The conflict of interest may encourage those performing the case management tasks to tolerate the knowingly inefficient, ineffective, inequitable, or customer-insensitive. But the total value of the input is much smaller. Therefore an efficiency gain of much the same proportion as for a complex case would save less. So the case for separation depends mainly on improvements in the welfare of clients and carers, not on that and improved equity and efficiency; a more difficult case to argue convincingly with the narrow evidence which SSDs now routinely collect.

Because the gains of separation may be modest, the most cost-effective arrangements may not be to fix the main responsibility for most of the tasks on a separate case management team. For publicly supported customers, the payer (the SSD) would want to ensure the greatest welfare for the budget by having a case management team at arm's length from suppliers for assessment and care planning. But that team might do no more than provide an initial assessment and care plan, and then monitor quality periodically. It might instead rely on the providing agencies to report need for small changes in provision. Many customers who pay a high proportion of the total bill and for increases in units consumed might actually not require even that level of case management. The reason is that many consumers, particularly those with articulate supporters, are well able to countervail the biases in the performance of case management by suppliers, as long as they feel that they can have some choice between suppliers whose quality is adequately assured by a reputable independent agency. However, many consumers would not be, or feel, able to assert their right to change suppliers. Therefore access to quality-assured case management provided by agencies at arm's length from the suppliers should always be available to clients. It is in the public interest that a substantial proportion of demand in the market should be brokered in this way, because the views of consumer-responsive case managers whose decisions affect a substantial part of the total market help to provide incentives to provide what is needed, and a sense of potential competition. Also direct provision of quality-assured case management will develop faster in the SSDs than elsewhere. So there is a strong case for adopting Griffiths' recommendation that the entire range of case management services should be available free of charge. (The White Paper proposes that assessment should be free, but it is ambiguous about whether that is so for the performance of the other core case management tasks; Griffiths, 1988, para. 6.33.)

However, as we have already argued, there may well be some circumstances in which the separation of what tasks of case management are necessary from supply promises small gains but certain costs of duplicated activity. For them, the still more consolidated models traditional in the UK, with for instance resource centres at the hub of a home care support wheel, may well seem best. Arguably, there is American evidence which supports this view. On Lok, a consolidated direct service model, has one of the lowest case management costs in the set compared by Capitman and others (1986).

What subsidisation and arrangements for straightforward, low-cost and risk cases?
Discussion about how much priority to attach to securing the more effective performance of case management tasks assumes that the case for state subsidisation and intervention in the market is unquestionable. Authorities are no longer behaving as if that were self-evidently true. Some appear to question whether more than modest promotion, sponsorship and regulation is needed for the provision of service to this group.

To what degree the low-risk group can hold their own as consumers is one question. The other is the degree to which their consumption should be subsidised. Relevant evidence includes two types: evidence about the benefits to dependents and carers of minimal provision, and citizen attitudes towards subsidisation.

Benefits from minimal services
The study collected data for a group of non-clients in the twelve areas. The non-clients were selected to be broadly comparable with respect to household structure and dependency (Bebbington and colleagues, 1985, pp.2/3-5). Early analysis compared outcomes for clients and the non-clients. So although the focus of our analysis has been the assessment of the impact of more rather than less inputs, the study produced some evidence about the impact of minimal services.
- Early analyses failed to reveal a significantly greater improvement in average Morale score among social service clients than among non-clients. However, the study yielded some evidence that outcomes differed more among clients than non-clients. So a larger minority of clients improved more than non-clients, judging from the answers to the question: 'Do you feel better or worse since we last saw you?' Those who claimed an improvement were particularly those who had received smaller rather than larger amounts of service (Bebbington and colleagues, 1985, p.5/13 and Tables 5/10-15).
- Clients felt a greater reduction in 'nurturance fears' – of having inadequate food and of being cold. One would expect standard home care services to engage these directly. However, clients are no less fearful of increasing frailty and loss of support. Again fears were reduced more for recipients of small amounts of service and for persons with low needs or 'long interval' needs (Bebbington and colleagues, 1985, p.5/15 and Tables 5/17-20).
- There were few clear signs that minimal levels of social services greatly influenced the feeling of social isolation (Bebbington and colleagues, 1985, p.5/18).

- The decline in ability to perform the personal tasks of daily living was significantly greater among the non-clients, but the reverse was the case for the instrumental tasks (Bebbington and colleagues, 1985, p.5/20). In both cases, minimal inputs made little difference.
- Of those describing their degree of satisfaction with the social service input, 25 per cent of the recipients of low levels of domiciliary care were dissatisfied or had mixed feelings (Bebbington and colleagues, 1985, Table 5/52).

So the overall impression is that the effects of receiving minimal rather than no services have been patchy and small. The analyses yielded few of the effects which might have been postulated, and the magnitudes of what effects were apparent seemed tiny when averaged over groups which are sufficiently large to be useful in defining targeting strategy. The results of providing minimal services are much the same as our other results, reinforcing the importance of the marginal productivity issue.

The same caveats apply as to our other results. Our study paints with a broad brush over the whole range of home care consumers and ten diverse authorities, so that our results are quite compatible with studies showing some clear gains of substantial magnitude for small groups of clients in some areas. And our results are based mainly on crude analyses of variance, like many of the studies which have inferred evidence of positive effects. (Most studies rely on the broad equivalence of clients and non-clients in ways not formally taken into account in their selection.) However, our results may in one respect be more reliable than some others: they are based on a study through time, most other studies having based inferences about the effects on life satisfaction of health status and social contacts on cross-section studies, not analysis over time (Larue, Bank, Jarvik, and Hetland, 1979; Seelbach and Hanson, 1979; Strain and Chappell, 1982; Baur and Okun, 1983; Scheidt and Windley, 1983). But we do not deny that the results reported in these paragraphs must be treated cautiously. However, there are few indications that minimal services contribute greatly to reducing the probability of admission to residential homes.

Citizen attitudes and subsidisation
The clearest rationale provided by economists for intervention in markets is some form of 'externality': a divergence between private and social costs and/or benefits. Such externalities distort the incentives facing decision-makers. There are two forms of externality which might potentially justify subsidisation. For the cases at high risk of inappropriate admission to institutions, there is the potential preventive cost-saving effect of coaxing reluctant consumers into case-managed provision. However, that is not relevant to the low-cost, low-risk consumers.

An important class of externalities could exist for persons of low risk also. It would apply when persons other than those who directly influence consumption value the benefits for others of that consumption; situations in which the utility functions of some reflect benefits to others whose consumption they do not directly influence (Hochman and Rodgers, 1959). For example, altruism can be a cause of market failure (Collard, 1978; Culyer, 1980). Culyer particularly argues the likelihood of 'specific caring' by citizens in general about the subsidisation of services for small dependent minorities. Bramley (1989, Table 9) shows that large minorities of non-users of the social care services for the elderly stated that 'more money should be spent [on them] assuming the money comes from local ratepayers' – perhaps between one-quarter and one-third. The results of a national survey were confirmed by local surveys, some in authorities whose parliamentary constituencies were Conservative strongholds. One would expect the proportions to be higher if the question had asked whether the services should be subsidised, not whether their subsidy should be increased.

Altruism is not the only possible explanation for these results, as Culyer (1980, pp.57-8) suggests in a parallel discussion of the reason for high public spending on services which are excludable and rival. Many of the non-using supporters may be informal carers or potential carers, and so perceive themselves to be likely beneficiaries. Others may wish to see increased subsidisation of these services because they might themselves be direct beneficiaries some time in the future, and see the subsidisation as an insurance premium, the exercise of an 'option demand'. More refined evidence and analysis is needed to distinguish between option demand, unmeasured current benefit, and the belief in the subsidisation of services in kind received by some dependent minorities seen as 'deserving' but poor. However, such views expressed either by those wishing to be able to exercise an option demand or by those who are selectively altruistic constitute evidence of an externality.

Bramley's results are important. However, without more refined analysis, they do no more than tell us what every councillor or reader of local newspapers knows: the (subsidised) provision of social care services for the elderly is politically popular. These attitudes are a powerful political force. They are probably more powerful at the local than at the national level, since at the local level social care is a more important item in the portfolio of areas of accountability. The values which the subsidisation reflect are unquestionably powerful in many local political cultures: 'the health of the people is the highest law' could be the motto on the emblem of more urban authorities than pre-Herbert Southwark. So there are many areas in which one suspects that public attitudes must change if subsidisation is to be reduced to a degree which will make a large contribution to financing the provisions required by those at risk of admission to institutions. Without the change in attitudes, the reduction would be bought at a high political price. It makes little political sense in the long run to fudge priorities in community care policy partly by placing the onus of awkward decisions about these priorities on local authorities, if a heavy price will subsequently be paid at that local level.

But are public attitudes based on sufficient understanding that policy-makers should be tightly reigned by them? And are they solid enough to reduce the political price of ignoring them by the active promotion of public debate? What proportion of those interviewed by the pollsters have persons of low dependency and risk in mind?

The priorities we attach to alternative uses of social resources must be for each society to decide. However, it is interesting to chart changes elsewhere. The policy argument of American liberals has been changing recently. Having found that home care programmes rarely have large effects on the use of institutions, functional capacities, the costs of care and carer wellbeing, a new justification is emerging for subsidising home care: people like them, use them, and report that they are satisfied with what they receive (Lawton, Brody and Saperstein, 1989). An editorial in *The Gerontologist* by one of the most distinguished analysts of long-term care suggests that the argument is less than persuasive. In it, Callahan (1989, pp.5-6) points (i) to all the other goods or derives that government could support that people would use, like and view with satisfaction; (ii) the trade-offs against the needs of other clienteles; and (iii) an hypothesised class bias in the source of support for expanded long-home care in the US:

long-term care services that are used, liked and produce satisfaction may be a priority for one segment of the citizenry, but massive expenditures on urban education and low income housing may be a necessity for others.

American values and circumstances are different. But we would be foolish to ignore the increasing American recognition of how difficult it is to justify the indiscriminate provision and subsidisation of home care services without measures to ensure that they have powerful effects.

Authorities face the same dilemma as American states developing channelling-type schemes faced in the 1980s. The risk of admission to institutions and case complexity involve too many factors for hard criteria to be defined by politicians and enforced by management. Yet

... simply to leave care managers to make large numbers of individual judgements without any political guidance on service eligibility seems to me an opting out of the legitimate political role it will be for local politicians to draw up these eligibility criteria (Warner, 1990, p.4).

Most American schemes of the channelling type took a similar view. However, there is a practical problem: how to define targeting criteria in such a way as not to cause wasteful Type I or Type II errors. (A Type I error occurs when someone *allocated* service does not receive benefits of the value judged to make the public costs worthwhile. A Type II error occurs when someone *not allocated* service would have received benefits which would be above the target judged to make the benefits worth the public costs.) The problem can be variously described: the complexity and instability of needs-related circumstances requiring skilled case management by workers with caseloads which allow them to give the time to it when necessary and deepen their skills; and the wide range and opacity of influences on the risks of admission to institutions for long-term care given flexible services and skilled case management of requisite intensity.

The reaction to this problem in some of the more recent American programmes (including the Wisconsin programme described below) and their evaluators have been (i) to limit (or propose to limit) the role of these preset eligibility criteria to providing a generous screening device, and leave the actual targeting and care planning decisions to trained case managers with smaller caseloads, relying on financial guidelines and carefully enforced retrospective accountability for targeting equitably, effectively and efficiently; and (ii) to have the case managers who confirm eligibility and negotiate the care package at arm's length from providers. However, the focus of the programmes has been the more complex and those at highest risk of institutional admission. We return to (i) below.

Dependent focused versus client focused cases
Again, it is feasible to separate either group from (iii) the cases where the principal objective is carer relief, though the dependents usually require straightforward support in addition. The topic will be discussed in *Community Services and the Social Production of Welfare* (PSSRU, 1991).

5.2 Degree of priority to strengthening case management

The choice is how far to give priority to improving the arrangements for the performance of the core tasks of case management compared with other policy goals. We have enough evidence about the costs of different models and their implications for performing core case management tasks to consider what the trade-offs might be between them.

Assume that the focus is a group of persons for whom residential care is the form of institutional long-term care from which diversion is sought, but for whom resources are inadequately matched to needs. Assume that most of those in the target group require a variety of services, that the situations of many of the clients are complex and might change suddenly, and that each of the service providers supply to a much wider range of clientele, feel subject to heavy pressure and provide standard and inflexible services.

The alternatives include: (i) the sponsorship of detached workers to be consumer advocates; (ii) the designation of an employee of one of the supplying agencies as the key worker; and (iii) the appointment of budget-holding case managers.

5.2.1 *Sponsorship of detached workers to be consumer advocate and broker*

Bradshaw and Glendinning found that the effectiveness of such workers tended to be undermined because of their lack of credentials with agencies. However, they felt more able to be more partisan and committed on behalf of their clients, and to take action of a kind which put agencies under pressure by means which would be unacceptable to agency employees. (The evidence was discussed in Davies and Challis (1986, pp.208-9.)

More recently, there have been so-called Case Management Projects (CMPs) for various client groups. One was for the physically handicapped. It was based on the argument that for case managers to be responsive enough to clients, they must be organisationally independent. 'commitment to the client ... the right to the same choices and say in running their lives as everybody else ... made the independence of the project essential' (Banks, 1988). The argument is important, and should be explored. The begged question is independence of whom and about what is necessary for client responsiveness.

One answer seems to be independence of suppliers. This is so partly because there are potentially conflicts of interest between suppliers, and between suppliers and consumers. For instance, the supplier who also provides would often see an interest in obtaining the additional services from their own agency when more finance was made available to cope with increased need, matching needs to services more than resources to needs. A supplier with a dominant position in the market might be able to secure consumer acquiescence and stifle the growth of competitors. There is an Australian state in which 85 per cent of the home care market is held by a not-for-profit nursing agency with long-standing community presence. It is clear that the rate of adoption of new practice and organisational devices is low. The new small competitors appear to be more flexible. It is difficult to imagine that any device short of trust-busting would allow fast modernisation. But the effort of political will required makes such a policy seem beyond the bounds of the practical (Davies, 1990a). This study has illustrated how service is now sometimes allocated as a token response though it is realised by the allocator that it is not what is really needed. Perhaps one reason why the range of tasks undertaken by British services looks narrower than in some other countries is that the concentration of the responsibilities for financing allocation and provision has not created information and incentives to managers to adjust what is done to what is needed.

Those writing about the CMP seemed to see the main reason to be that service scarcities raised difficult problems of prioritisation, and the case managers from the Case Management Project were then useful because they were independent advocates. (The context of the argument is that the CMP was for the younger physically disabled who forcefully voice their belief that providers have given their needs a low priority in resource allocation.) Other service providers saw the project as primarily providing an advocacy service. This was the main reason why they referred clients to it. 'Clients' perceptions and case records confirmed the importance of the advocacy role.

Advocacy seemed to be the most important function because of the difficulty in obtaining services (Pilling, 1988a, pp.3,4). Although the performance of core case management tasks for the clientele of the CMP case managers neither had authority to prescribe services nor the budget to purchase them. So 'having the authority to obtain services' came well down (tenth) in clients' lists of why the CMP had helped them, and 'getting things done' came fifth among the reasons why clients like the service – lower than sympathy, promptness and being easily contactable (Pilling, 1988b). The lack of authority and a budget made the CMP appreciated less for actually achieving goals than for its style, it seems. Twenty-seven per cent of its clients suggested that having power and resources would have made the service more satisfactory (Pilling, 1988b). Indeed, the absence of a budget hampered case managers in the performance of one of the most important tasks of case management: gap-filling. Pilling's results suggested difficulties in mobilising such inputs as visitors to sit and talk regularly, escorts for shopping, suitable day centres; and such gaps as getting work done though the occupational therapist. A comparison with the budget-holding case managers in PSSRU community care projects showed that these were important among the gaps filled by spending from the budget.

So in terms of Diagram 6.1, the detached advocate model might possibly improve output mix efficiency and horizontal target efficiency. But it was not designed to improve input mix, technical or vertical target efficiency.

Another case management project is targeted at moving a small number of persons from long-stay institutions (Richardson, 1990). The focus is to provide advocacy services which will guide the main service providers in their service development. The project aims to show what is needed to develop an effective service, not to improve efficiency in the use of resources. The sponsors have proved willing to allow the team to feel its way forward, insisting that all conditions are met to an almost ideal degree, and, in particular, that clients are not moulded into existing services and resources, hence the much lower rate of discharge than originally planned. However, another reason is that the suppliers of services have not responded as flexibly as hoped. Perhaps one reason is that there are not strong incentives for them to do so.

But are there circumstances in which one should question proposals that case managers should control resources? The British literature is imprecise about such circumstances. However, the doubters seem to have in mind one or a mix of circumstances in which (i) influences other than the costs to the agency and society and the benefits to consumers are likely to cause the agency to give some types of consumer a raw deal; (ii) the agencies financing provision suffer excessive fiscal stress. Let us consider each, and whether separating the performance of core case management tasks from control over resources would provide a safeguard.

Influences distorting the balance between consumer sovereignty, professional interpretation of need, and the pressure to prevent the escalation of costs

The arrangements for the finance and supply of care services reflect a balance between partially competing principles. The political costs and benefits of adopting alternative arrangements depend on the characteristics of clienteles. The political price of different balances differ between client groups. So do the efficiency effects.

One principle is *consumer sovereignty*. The financing mechanism associated with it is the cash grant or the voucher on demonstration of eligibility. A likely arrangement for commissioning supply is the independent broker when consumer circumstances are variable, not clearly analysed by the consumer without assistance, and the supply arrangements possible diverse and difficult to select and assemble. The major disadvantage of the mechanisms is that the cash grant or voucher must be made available without intensive and continuous assessments in which there is a large subjective element. The only way of reducing this is to undertake assessment activity at almost the level of intensity as would be necessary with full case management; creating either an expensive duplication of effort or client-responsive case management by another name. Therefore the eligibility criteria must err on the side of generosity. This tends to lower the degree of vertical target efficiency, many not in need obtaining the benefit. The trade-off between horizontal and vertical target efficiencies is likely to be clear if need-affecting situations are complex and volatile, and a high degree of uptake among the needy is sought. Several American states have considered voucher or grant models for the financing of community care programmes. Most have rejected them because the budgets they were willing to commit would have to be too thinly spread to provide adequate care. Only where there are indeed persons able, willing, and intensely motivated to undertake case management tasks, and circumstances are stable, is there a gain to be made by establishing a system of cash grants or needs-adjusted vouchers separate from, and additional to, a system providing case management; and there will be many cases in every client group who will need more than merely assessment and a cash grant.

However, independent advocates always press for more resources, and are unconstrained by any loyalty to the financing organisation. The principle of consumer sovereignty is therefore associated with mechanisms which escalate costs. These effects are less costly to the financing agency if the numbers at risk are small and the political gains are great, if those at risk are energetic and vocal campaigners, or if they have powerful advocates. It is no coincidence that the York Resource Worker Project (Bradshaw and Glendinning, 1984) and the CMP were both for the younger physically disabled.

A second principle is *professional, though client-responsive, interpretation of need and care provision judgements*. The characteristic mode of financing is the top-down budget to the professional agency. This too is cost-escalating though to a lower degree, depending on who it is that employs the professionals, and the prestige and influence of those professionals. So professionals acquire the power to affect resources only when problems seem to the lay politician complex, and the penalties of failure are great. The Seebohm changes themselves gave professional social workers their Seebohm charter at the end of a process which started with child care officers claiming that social work could be a more effective antidote to juvenile crime at a time when other expensive solutions were becoming discredited, and increasing rates of crime was seen as a growing embarrassment. Health professionals have likewise gained more power in the community care of the mentally ill because lay people are afraid of the consequences of mental illness but seek a treatment rather than overtly custodial solution. Again, the principle is given more weight if the number of clients is sufficiently small for cost escalation to be financed. It is less true for most persons with learning difficulties because the danger to members of society are less for most cases, and because the long-run consequences of care planning decisions can be vast.

A third principle is *cost-effectiveness in care*. This principle dominates where the consequences of failure are less socially disastrous, the problems are perceived by higher managers to be straightforward, and the number of potential clients is much greater; for instance, the elderly. It is tempting for authorities to adopt as the financing arrangement the allocation of a low fixed budget to a generalist case manager with a large caseload which precludes professional work of a high standard and high spending per case.

If this argument has some validity, solutions will reflect more than the costs to the agencies and benefits to clients and carers. There will tend to be inequities whose extent and nature will differ between client groups. It is partly for this reason that the policy systems which have most successfully minimised such inequities have ensured that the politics of community care applies arguments consistently over a wide range of client groups. Spann (1987) describes how the ideas of the independent living movement influenced the philosophy of the entire Wisconsin Community Options Programme.

But does it follow that having case managers without budgets would contribute much to minimising the inter-group inequities? The CMP argument is that the

> case manager's loyalties [should] lie entirely with the client, allowing the case manager to seek services for the client from whatever source which provides them, [and for this, the project] has to be independent; that is not a service provider itself, holding no budget, and not funded solely by either the health or local authority'.

First, the argument does not make some vital distinctions. Most fundamentally, there is a crucial difference between (i) holding a budget which can be used with great discretion and subject to management by those protected from supply agencies, and (ii) being integrated into one of the service providers and being subject to indirect pressure from, even the direct and immediate control of, the managers of service supply. The first confers the same advantages as being a consumer able to use purchasing power to select what 'commodities' and suppliers of them s/he wishes. This extends potential for choice, not narrows it. Making quasi-markets work is among other things about structuring things so that some elements are at least at arm's length from others.

Second, the evidence is that the independent 'case managers' are primarily useful as advocates. There is every reason to encourage the development of advocacy as part of the system of checks and balances needed for the equity and efficiency of the outcome of the internal quasi-markets to which the White Paper arrangements approximate. However, what is interesting to a British reader of papers for the New York Long-Term Care Planning Council is the sheer diversity of the checks and balances. Advocacy is only one check among many, though one most often heard about in current British discussion.

Third, the White Paper arrangements make it clear that responsibility is to rest with the SSD. Within the SSD, responsibility for allocations and the outcomes of care planning must meet at some level. It is much better that they should meet at the level where judgements about complex and uncertain outcomes are based on evidence which is most directly perceived; by professionals at the field level. Indeed, American 'case management' systems in which the budget is held at a much higher level tend to be those in which overwhelmingly the highest priority is to keep down costs by trying to minimise vertical target inefficiency: the receipt of service by those not in priority need. In such arrangements, the budget holder primarily accepts amends or rejects the proposed care plan compiled by others; he is like a loss adjuster authorising a claim. And if needs are complex and unstable, superficial one-off assessments based on crude criteria result in a trade-off between horizontal and vertical target efficiencies in circumstances in which horizontal target inefficiency can be quantitatively more important than vertical target efficiency (see Chapter 12 above). Authorisation arrangements by the budget holders have little to contribute to consumer-sensitive brokerage. With it, additional care must be taken not to impede the flexibility of the case manager in achieving improvements in all the other aspects of efficiency.[6]

What this discussion suggests is that depriving case managers of budgets is likely to weaken, not empower, consumers and those who see their circumstances most closely. William Laing (1990, p.16) describes the PSSRU community care model as 'the limits of Perestroika in social services departments', and his answer to the question 'can Perestroika be pushed past its limits?' is direct payments to consumers by brokerage agencies, not the provision of advocacy services without resources. The assumptions of the CMP argument would be valid only if empathy with the consumers were weaker among the front-line case managers and the middle managers holding the budgets. We lack firm evidence about this. However, casual observation suggests that this is unlikely.

Indeed, the priority to consumer empowerment is greatest not in the British CMP but, perhaps, in the budget-holding case management-based Wisconsin Community Options Program (McDowell, Barniskis, and Wright, 1990; Spann, 1987). First the programme's *ends*. What American programmes are called often speak volumes about their manifest goals though less about their true nature and achievements. Its intention has been to provide consumers – the word used in its documentation – with choices between care in nursing homes and at home, between arrangements within the home care mode, as well as between nursing homes:

the most important consumer choice ... is the choice to receive long term support outside of an institution. ... A full range of choices is available to the consumer only when there are a number of options for the provision of long term care services in the community, and when there is an expectation that consumer preferences will drive the development of services. Variety, flexibility, and even competition in the array of human services enables the consumer and the family to choose the option which best meets the needs of the elderly in her unique environment. ... The preferred concept in Wisconsin today is 'aging in place', where services and supports are organized around the individual in the place they have chosen to live throughout their old age. Long term support is intended to be as unintrusive in the life of an older person as possible, with the least disruption to relationships, habits and self-designed habitats.

Wisconsin operates on the premise that any individual, regardless of the type or extent of his or her disability, *can* be served in the community. If the assessment process determines that community care is not feasible for an individual, it is not because the person is 'too disabled' for our program, it is because the *community* has failed to provide the kinds of supports that the person would need to stay at home (McDowell, Barniskis and Wright, 1990).

In short, the programme is intended to allow people to choose 'to hold on to the normal rhythms of life throughout old age' by remaining at home irrespective of the cost, if that is what they desire.

Most of the *means* are wholly consistent with the main goal of extending client choice. (i) As in the PSSRU experiments, the central device is the concentration of responsibility, authority and accountability for the performance of core case management tasks. (ii) The style and values applied in the performance of the tasks also resembles PSSRU experiments and the oft-expressed ideals expressed for assessment in much professionally-led modern long-term care. Consumer rights and influence are safeguarded by such devices as: written notification of rights, including grievance and appeal mechanisms both at the county and state levels, representation on the principal planning and policy-making body, the state's Long-Term Care Ombudsman, in each county annual consumer satisfaction survey results are made public through the principal planning committee. The belief in the separation of powers taken with the recognition of conflicting interest has quite commonly caused American arrangements to hold decision-making in complex networks of checks and balances on individual cases. Though this sometimes kills resourcefulness, it does not seem to do so in the Wisconsin programme. Similarly the American belief in consociational as much as representative democracy has led to the mobilisation of consumer power in attempts to engineer the structure of the polity (see Chapter 14 below). Wherever possible the supervision of the 'attendants'– unlicensed supportive home care workers providing a variety of assistance like community care 'helpers' – is provided by the consumer and the spouse or other household member. (iii) As in the argument in Davies and Challis (1986), case management is separated from supply.

However, there are other goals. One is to prevent unnecessary cost escalation. The means are compatible with this end too. To achieve the substitution of home care for nursing home beds, the number of beds was capped at the inception of the Community Options Program, and the number of beds reduced by a multiple related to the ratio of the average budget per recipient to the *per diem* costs of nursing homes, so adding to the specified number of Community Options 'slots' available for counties to fill. The ratio is 0.51 compared with ratios in the Thanet community care project of 0.68, or 0.35 (if the institutional equivalent is seen as the costs of long-term hospital care, the nearest British equivalent to the American 'skilled nursing facility'). Community Options funds cannot be spent on nursing homes or on residential facilities with more than fifteen beds unless they are judged to satisfy requirements for autonomy and privacy. The combination of reducing the supply of nursing home beds in proportion to the expansion of Community Options slots has successfully changed the balance of care compared with other states. However, the ratio of spending on nursing homes to community long-term care support (including Community Options) expenditure on elderly users remained 8.5:1 in 1986.

However, there are some incentives to inefficiency.

- Not all funds for financing long-term social care are pooled. The Community Options funds are essentially for gap-filling, there being an obligation to draw on other entitlements and funds first. One of us has seen how this distorts care plans for cases in other American projects with this arrangement.
- The device to ensure targeting by counties on those in greatest need is a condition that 20 per cent of the Community Options money must be spent on plans costing at least twice the average budget per recipient. That provides an incentive to target at persons for whom care plans just above that level are appropriate. Twice the average budget per recipient approximates to the costs of institutional care. So at first sight it seems to be an incentive to encourage counties to spend at or above what would be the optimum if the distribution of recipients between modes were appropriate (see Chapter 14).
- Permitting expenditure on residential facilities would seem at first sight to allow the creation of mini-institutions. However, case managers encouraged plans which provide services from outside the facility and in other settings.
- Case management tasks other than assessment and care planning are treated as a service and so is subject to user co-payments. These provide an incentive to reduce consumption by substituting the performance of case management tasks by others (including the family) for case management by the county case managers. Since many counties have waiting lists for Community Option slots, the market share would not be increased by providing additional incentives to consumers to enroll, so that the influence of case managers' decisions would not be weakened.

So it is not to the schemes which evade issues of cost-effectiveness which we must necessarily turn for good examples of consumer-responsive systems, though some authorities here are also pioneering development in this respect (Jowell and Wistow, 1989).

Excessive fiscal pressure

Also present in arguments for having detached workers perform some of the core case management tasks is the implication that the agencies financing and setting the policy framework for case management by budget holders would suffer a degree of fiscal pressure incompatible with adequate budget caps and caseloads, or would be under pressure to shift too quickly to an entirely case-managed system. Either would compromise the quality of care and would compromise long-run development. Undoubtedly the danger is real. But again, the solution lies in the checks and balances which empower the consumer and their interest groups.

5.2.2 Designate a key worker in the main supplying agency
Concentrating the responsibility for the performance of the core tasks would be less necessary if there were a rich supply of high-quality and client-responsive services which produced all the outcomes required, if they were on offer at costs which could not be bettered, and there was a balance between supply and demand. By some definitions, key working might accomplish almost as much, at any rate in the short run, if it were unimportant continually to improve the efficiency with which outcomes are produced, and if there were an adequate balance between supply and demand. Dant, Gearing, Carley and Johnson (1989) argue that the functions of key workers can be described as precisely the performance of the core tasks of case management discovered in task analyses of American case management systems, and confirmed in the tasks of the case managers in the Thanet Community Care Project.

However, there are three significant differences. First, the diagram in Dant et al. omits the core task called gap-filling. Without a large discretionary budget, the key worker cannot undertake this task effectively. The need for gap-filling is not just a symptom of past defects in management. It exists also because of continuous change in the mix of consumers by circumstances, and change also in perceptions about ends and means. Gap-filling is the device for coping with the unpredictable consequences of change before time-consuming adaptations to the range and nature of services can be made. So gap-filling is an important and permanent task.

Second, the key worker has no incentives to mix inputs in the most cost-effective way. These incentives are given by the combination of a capped budget against which are charged the important substitutes and complements and the other arrangements of the PSSRU community care approach. Without these, the best use of resources depends ultimately on inspired guesses about relative costs and in the absence of authority, responsibility and accountability enforced through quality assurance and review, on the altruism of service personnel. Key workers typically have little of the real authority and bargaining power required to exert pressure on suppliers. Webb and Wistow (1986) have been scathing about the influence of altruism in the health and welfare agencies at a higher management level. We see no reason to suppose that it can safely be relied on at the field either. As Murphy (1988) observes, no one who depends on the voluntary cooperation of agencies rather than competition between them for resources can be held accountable for the quality of services. Or, as Hodgson and Quinn wrote: 'assessment, ... coordination, ... and monitoring ... that has no control over financial resources [are] essentially impotent' (1980, p.370). A budget-holding case manager can be held accountable for the quality of care received by a consumer in a service-rich environment. A key worker cannot.

Third, one suspects that key workers rarely perceive their role to be mainly to hold the responsibility, authority and accountability for the performance of the case management tasks, and to do so with the clarity suggested by the diagram in Dant et al. Indeed, they do not have the authority over the range of resources required, or the means to procure them. They can merely be advocates. They do not have authority even over the resources of the remainder of the team; and were these to be sufficient for most cases, they would face the conflicts of interest which arise as member of the supplying and procuring organisation; not the best arrangement for consumer responsiveness. In fact, the role is often perceived primarily to be the provision of a particular form of help (say counselling) and only secondarily as the performance of the core tasks. Compared with a case management team set in an adequate case management system, the core tasks tend not to be performed as systematically, and their performance is not rigorously managed.

Fourth, that part of new managerialist argument which has had most influence in the aftermath of the Financial Management Initiative has stressed individual responsibility, authority and accountability; not team responsibility authority and accountability. The divisions of responsibility authority and accountability within teams are often informal, ambiguous, indeed vague; and the new managerialists tend to believe that it is of the nature of things that this vagueness and ambiguity is inevitable; and that any advantages of collective responsibility cannot in general be made to compensate for the tendencies. These are sweeping assumptions. This is particularly so for clienteles for which the nature of needs make the effectiveness of professional approaches interdependent; for example, persons with mental illnesses due to long-standing chemical imbalances, and disorders which have come to be reflected in behaviours originally due to the imbalances but which have become well-established and would continue despite the removal of their original causes. In such cases, the success of medical and behavioural approaches are interdependent, and success in them requires continuous interaction, observation and communication of a kind best accomplished within one team. We are unaware of rigorous reviews of evidence about how efficient teams can be in systems which have created cultures focused on the collective; for instance Japanese industry. However, it is the assumptive worlds of the new managerialists which in the short run will influence events, and this is unquestionably individualistic.

5.2.3 *Budget-holding case managers in case management organisations*

A third level of commitment is to place responsibility authority and accountability on budget-holding case managers in a case management organisation at arm's length from suppliers and quality assurers. In principle, all the aspects of efficiency could be affected. However, the scale and nature of the effect would depend on the configuration of the arrangements listed in the last box of Diagram 13.1; particularly (i) the number of cases per case manager in relation to the complexity of case circumstances and the scope of case management tasks, as in 'administrative' compared with what Davies and Challis (1986) called 'entrepreneurial' case management; (ii) the degree to which case management tasks are delegated or shared with providers, as in what Chapter 3 of Davies and Challis (1986), following Eggert (1983), called the 'indirect' rather than 'direct' case management models.

It is sometimes argued that it would be satisfactory for case managers to have a small gap-filling budget, a list of services with perhaps some information about their costs, and some freedom to supplement a package of the standard services with resources procured using the budget. The justification quoted is that this arrangement would reduce uncertainties in the planning of standard services.

The logic is valid. But it implies priorities diametrically opposed to those in the White Paper and the Implementation Documents. The reason has been given in the last section. The main mechanism which case management provides for making the packaging of resources responsive to consumer needs and wishes and improving cost-effectiveness is the existence of a fixed budget which the case manager must use to best effect. For this to work, the budget and the budget cap must be realistic and consistent (see Chapter 14), the case manager must have realistic information about the costs and outcomes of services, the case manager must be able to use the entire budget flexibly, the whole range of complementary and alternative services must be charged against the budget, and there must be mechanisms for the retrospective review of efficiency and consumer responsiveness as well as other aspects of performance. Without these, we must rely either on management control or altruism. But the front-line managers likewise lack incentives to optimise without decentralised budgets. Simply consolidating responsibility, authority and accountability for performing case management tasks in the absence of the other elements is to remove the main mechanisms designed to deliver improved cost-effectiveness and consumer responsiveness.

Empirical evidence supports the logic. For instance, many American schemes and, regrettably, in some new Australian case management Community Options projects the case managers merely have small gap-filling budgets. They respond, and are encouraged to respond, by first drawing on resources funded from other programmes irrespective of the match between those resources and needs. Sometimes they exhaust several sources of funding with only partially appropriate resources before they are forced back on their own funds. In such circumstances, finance and the availability of services lead the system, not consumer needs and wishes. They are certainly less efficient.

The danger of such distortion will grow as the British financing economy of care becomes more complex. To build in appropriate incentives is the least expensive element in the development of good case management systems. So there is nothing to be said for simply ignoring the incentive structures and simply relying on organisational consolidation. And it happens to be completely incompatible with clearly-stated national policy. If there is really a danger of making the supply of services too uncertain to manage a highly questionable proposition where the services are performing efficiently and well, removing the incentives to consumer responsiveness and cost-effectiveness is not the way to do it.

6 Conclusions

This chapter has argued that the framework of logic we need to help us develop local strategies for modernising long-term care must take into account the diversity of clienteles and the circumstances of local systems. Examples of discussions of some of the issues which local policy-makers and planners will face have illustrated how (i) the framework of logic can be directly applied, and how (ii) the pursuit of a more equitable and efficient system involves balancing the value of benefits of establishing structures which will improve the performance of core case management tasks and structures which will yield other improvements, including increased service productivities. The discussion illustrates how the balance of advantage differs between clienteles and circumstances. In doing so, it clarifies some of the strategic choices facing SSDs and others. The selection of broad strategies and the more obvious concomitants of change will be discussed in the final chapter.

Notes

1   Their home help service also seemed to underprovide personal care, since only 6 per cent of the time was spent on it.

2   By 'partly self-financing' we have meant that the running and (discounted) development costs of the new community care approach should preferably be less, and at any rate should be no greater than, the running costs of standard provision. In effect, model parameters affecting costs, targeting and case management style were fixed, and the case managers asked to help produce the best improvements in welfare compatible with them given these parameters.

Therefore the cost savings achieved reflect no more than a guesstimate about what budget levels and totals would achieve the goal of a substantially self-financing project with improved client and carer welfare.

3   The differences between the models were described in Chapter 3 of Davies and Challis (1986). In summary, the basic model provided only case management and some discretionary expenditure for gap-filling. Like the PSSRU projects, the financial control model also built in incentives through budget capping, fixing the scale of the case managers budget and charging services to it.

4   See, Davies and Challis (1986, Chap. 3, pp.99-100 and note 6, pp.147-8) for the analysis of administrative and brokerage models compared with entrepreneurial, direct assessment, and, in mental health, 'clinical case management'. See Zawadski and Eng (1988) for an alternative and cross-cutting classification of recent case management models for the elderly.

5   That is so in the USA also, despite excellent studies and texts. See, for instance, the bibliography in Davies and Challis, 1986, particularly the work by the first major collator of knowledge on case management for the elderly, Ray Steinberg, in Steinberg and Carter (1982); and recent texts like Harris and Bachrach (eds) (1988) on case management for target groups where counselling and therapy have always had particular emphasis; and more generally, Moxley (1989).

6   One sometimes hears in British discussions an analogy between the relationship between the budget-holding 'care manager' who manages case managers and a banker. This arrangement does not fully apply Griffiths' 'fundamental' principle that the system should 'align responsibility for achieving objectives with control over the resources needed to achieve them, so that there is a built-in incentive and the facility to make the best use of resources need to achieve them' (Griffiths, 1988, para. 5.6). The analogy with a banker is surely false. The banker's clients not only initiate action, but bankers have their own resources and bear the risk, except when they make unsecured loans. A more useful analogy is the insurance company. The care manager holds the budget for a large number of cases and so is able to pool risks for more and less expensive cases. The effective maximum for annual case costs and the probability distributions of costs per case vary between client groups; and there are certainly client groups for which it is at first sight attractive to hold the budgets at higher levels in order to get greater risk pooling. However, it is unnecessary to separate case management from budget-holding. The budgets can be delegated to case managers subject to top-slicing for the creation of a fund for high-cost cases; and the same mechanism can be applied at several levels. There is some evidence of devices like that emerging in British authorities in which budgets are held by case managers. The use of the banker analogy in the Chapter 1 of the *Interim Report* was in the context of the SSD and service credit devices (Bebbington et al., 1985).

14 Some ways forward: (2) other implications

We shall discuss only three of the innumerable implications of setting out to achieve more effective targeting and to raise productivities, since it is these to which our evidence most relates. They are that authorities should: (i) raise the proportion receiving intensive support; (ii) work through the implications of achieving more predictable relationships between means and ends – a 'more determinate technology' – by developing outcome-focused performance indicators and standards for monitoring the implementation of clearer priorities and allocating resources; (iii) plan for the long term as well as the medium term, so helping to lay the foundations for long-run excellence not the continuation of short-run mediocrity; (iv) sponsor the development of national and local community care politics and polities, so that there is a more legitimate basis for choosing priorities and more sophisticated analysis and review of policy and performance; (v) create community care laboratories for experiment and teaching in each authority; and (vi) raise the ratio of investment to consumption spending before the demographic pressure on public spending intensifies.

1 Raise the proportion of cases with intensive support

The better matching of resources to needs is not synonymous with raising average intensity. Many of the authorities we studied were already (and are increasingly energetically) developing sharper targeting priorities and are taking steps to implement them. However, allocation norms are also needed. Indeed, the PSSRU community care experiments have been designed around budget-holding case managers with spending limits for individual cases. We have long believed that the way forward is prospectively to fix limits for first-line managers based on the marginal costs of the most likely institution-based mode of care and the probability that a case would shortly be admitted to it in the absence of more flexible and intensive community care. The PSSRU model sets both the total budget and a spending limit per case. The total budget is the more important. But the total budget has proved difficult to set equitably and realistically because area comparisons of the potential supply of inputs have been dated and unreliable, and because the provisions of other agencies have been difficult to predict into the future over even short planning periods. The importance of a spending limit per case is that by triggering management review, it clearly sets the limits to discretion and becomes a benchmark by which case managers compare the spending needs of cases. A leading American authority has independently reached the conclusion that managers of community services should work within budgets fixed in advance bearing in mind the costs of the most likely residential alternative and the probability of its utilisation. The conclusion was drawn from a review of the results of the American home care demonstration projects (Weissert, Cready and Pawelak, 1988).

1.1 International comparisons of intensity

It is clear that we have low levels of intensity of our basic community social services compared with some other countries. The average intensity is too low mainly because small proportions of recipients obtain more than standard levels of support. So Davies and Challis (1986, p.4) guesstimated that persons at high risk of admission to residential or hospital care living in their own homes each received resources costing the social services department less than one-seventh of their costs to the department once resident in homes.

Table 14.1 compares Cover and Intensity in France, four Scandinavian countries, the Netherlands, and England and Wales. Differences in service content as well as statistical convention make the comparisons imprecise. They are made more explicit in the studies coordinated by Age Care Research Europe (ACRE) (Jamieson, forthcoming) and the European Centre for Social Welfare Training and Research (Baldock, Davies, Evers, Johansson, Knapen, Thorslund and Tunissen, 1990). However, the crude data in the table strongly suggest that average intensity in the UK is lower than in the other countries. The exception is France, but the British figures may understate intensity compared with some of the other countries because it is based on the number of hours received by users not paid for by the agencies; the numbers paid for being 25 per cent greater than the numbers received in England and Wales in 1986. Not reported in the table because their bases are less well understood are the ACRE results for one area in Flanders. The study suggests relatively high and increasing intensity: from 3.1 hours per week in 1975, through 4.5 hours in 1980, to 5.0 hours in 1985 (Baro, De Bruyne, Moorthamer and Van den Bergh, 1989). In the new, ambitious and universalist Israeli personal care service, the average provision by 1988 was already 9.4 hours per week; between 1980 and 1988, both horizontal target efficiency and average intensity more than doubled; and, targeted on different recipients, average intensity for the homemaking service was 2.5 in 1988 (Factor, Habib and Be'er, 1988; Factor, Morginstin and Naon, 1989).

The history of average intensity in France is interesting, though apparently not well documented. It is likely that average intensity did indeed fall during the early 1980s. It seems that the central government sought the political benefits of a publicised increase in cover without increasing resource inputs. So the comparison between the national average intensity in 1984 and the departmental levels for the earlier years may correctly suggest the direction of the change which occurred nationally. We have been able to re-analyse our data to compare the earlier allocations in the three French areas with England and Wales. Applying the need definitions from the French study to our data shows English Intensity to be lower both for recipients 'in need' and 'not in need', so that the overall difference is unlikely to be due to differences in the populations served (Davies and Baines, 1989).

Table 14.1
Intensity and Cover in France, Scandinavia and
England and Wales

	Cover: Cases/Pop 65 and over	Intensity: Hours per week
France		
Haute Normandie, 1979-81	4.3[a]	5.0
Lille, 1979-81	8.3[a]	4.7
Ile de France, 1979-81, 1979-81	5.1	5.0
France, 1984		2.6
Scandinavia		
Denmark	20[b]	4.9
Finland	10[b]	3.4
Norway	14[b]	3.3
Sweden	14[b]	6.8
England and Wales		
1985	6.0	2.6[c]
1986	6.1	2.4[c]
1988	4.6	3.2

Sources: Ankri, J., Isnard, M.C. and Henrard, J.C. (1989); Brethouwer (1989); CIPFA (1987b, 1987b, 1990); Curtis and Bucquet (1987); Jansson and Wallberg (1988).
a In France home help is received only by those of low income.
b Proportion of elderly in households receiving home help.
c Hours received.

Averages conceal the range of provision, particularly the proportions of users receiving large inputs. Table 14.2 illustrates a system providing large inputs to a high proportion of its clientele. To the Commissioner for Social Services for the State of New York interviewed in 1988, it seemed to be a matter for shame that in three of the nine upstate counties, less than one half of the recipients received nine or more hours of service weekly. However, the New York system has too many sources of inefficiency for its allocations to be a model for us, despite the great interest to us of its experience as a technically progressive and interventionist policy committed to its complex mixed economy of welfare. Many British readers find European comparisons more interesting. For Denmark in 1983, Holstein et al. (1989) report that in 1984, 79 per cent of the clients of permanent home helps received no more than six hours per week, 13 per cent received between six and thirteen hours, and 7 per cent received thirteen hours or more. Among those aged 85 and over, 33 per cent received seven hours or more weekly.

Table 14.2
Hours per week of personal care service in the
State of New York, 1982: per cent of clients

Hours	Area		
	Up-state	Down-state	NY City
1-8	42.3	8.9	9.1
9-14	12.0	8.9	12.9
15-20	13.8	15.6	15.9
21-28	11.1	9.7	7.7
29-	20.7	56.9	54.5

Source: New York State Health Planning Commission, *Personal Care Survey*, 1982.

The evidence for other European countries also suggests that we have an unusually narrow range of allocations. Swedish policy analysts complain about the rigidity of their welfare state. However, the Swedes are successfully increasing the proportion of their resources allocated to those most at risk. In Stockholm in 1977, more than 50 per cent of home help hours were being consumed by 10 per cent of recipients (Sundstrom, 1987). In rural Tierp, 35 per cent were consumed by the 10 per cent of consumers receiving most, 53 per cent being received by 20 per cent of users (Thorslund, Norstrom and Wernberg, 1990). The Swedes widened the range of intensity by lowering the minimum as well as increasing the maximum allocation – surely a useful device during a period of transition to the concentration of state-provided service on the most vulnerable. In Stockholm, 18 per cent received less than one hour a week in May 1988, and another 15 per cent received one but less than two hours (Nyckeltal Och Matt, 1988); and in rural Tierp, the 20 per cent of users consuming least received only 2.3 per cent of the hours, 30 per cent receiving only 5 per cent and 60 per cent only 23 per cent.

The effect can be seen when we consider levels of consumption among those entering institutions immediately prior to admission. Sundstrom (1987) alludes to a local study which showed that, on average, they had received some three hours of home help daily. Virtually all had been recipients. In contrast, direct estimates made by Avon Social Services Department (1980) and Barnes (1980) and the indirect national estimate made in Davies and Challis (1986, p.4) illustrate that the number of hours received immediately prior to admission to British old people's homes is typically low. Neill, Sinclair, Gorbach and Williams (1988) like Avon SSD and Barnes, showed that only one-half of their study's entrants to old people's homes had previously received domestic help.

Swedish writers (Sundstrom, 1987; Thorslund and Johansson, 1987) describe how the municipalities have been attempting to concentrate more resources on the neediest, a development which has come later in the UK, as we showed in Chapter 1. Lowering minimum levels contributes to this (though the Swedes have also reduced cover), as does the policy of most municipalities to restructure user charges so as to make it more expensive to consume only a few hours, and less expensive to consume more than six hours per week (Sundstrom, 1987). Charging policy is similarly used in Denmark, where home help hours in excess of six per week have been free of charge. It is true that Chapter 2 demonstrated that there is only ambiguous evidence that consumers at high risk consume fewer home care hours when they face a higher price for the additional hours required to provide service of an intensity sufficient to make it an alternative to entering an institution for long-term care. However, it would surely be foolhardy to allow charging policies to be at odds with the need to increase the number of hours consumed by such cases when the additional consumption might be substantial. As we argued in the last chapter, there can be clear benefits additional to those received by the user, including the lower cost to society of maintaining persons in their home than in institutions.

1.2 By how much is it 'economic' to raise Intensity?

The White Paper and consultative documents demand that authorities show in their plans how they intend to 'improve the cost-effectiveness' (Department of Health, 1990a, para. 29) Some issues require further definition. Some are about the distribution of consumers between alternative 'modes' of care. What are the costs of 'equivalent' care outcomes in alternative modes by relevant cost criteria? to what extent should consumers choice of modes be constrained by the relative costs of alternatives? assuming that the relative costs of alternative modes should influence modal choice, how can we achieve an efficient distribution of consumers between modes? Earlier chapters illustrate that there are equivalent questions about distributions within modes of care.

We did not find sufficiently high marginal productivities for practicable increases in inputs to achieve reasonable target effects for the outcomes which most matter to substituting home for residential care. Had we done so, we should certainly seek to establish the upper limit of costs below which community services would be less expensive than residential-based modes for the production of broadly equivalent outcomes. However, we still lack the study of the relations between needs, resources and outcomes in residential care modes which would allow estimation of the costs of equivalent outcomes. And in this study we have shown that (i) what marginal productivities exist seem to be few and weak; (ii) they are undetectably small for some important outcomes for the achievement of modal substitution; and (iii) reasonable target outcomes for the few of the important effects which are attainable therefore require high and sometimes unrealistic levels of input when they are attainable at all.

Since the main effort should be to improve the marginal and average productivities of resources, the most interesting issue is not what resources are required to achieve targets given the present marginal productivities, but what improvements in productivities can be achieved by various levels and types of investment. This is a researchable question. It should be one of the key elements in a programme of research on the community services and their alternatives. But the big improvements possible are unlikely to be achieved quickly. The SSI letter about implementing the Act realistically states that case management arrangements need not be fully in place by April 1991, though authorities are to be required to include in their plans proposals for 'progressively introducing' case management with supporting budgetary frameworks' (Department of Health, 1990b, para. 46). Achieving the improved productivities will take time, and showing that they have generally been achieved will take longer. Until then, the more useful question is more modest: to what level could community service resources be allocated without causing costs to be higher than institution-based modes of care. That is the focus of this section.

Some of the literature, thankfully a diminishing stream, suggests territorially unvarying guideline estimates. Economic argument and much evidence implies that this is naive.

The reasons why it is naive to impose territorially unvarying guideline estimates follow from fundamental axioms about the nature of populations in need of long-term care and the nature of production processes in long-term care (Davies and Challis, 1986, Chap. 1). In particular, analyses which suggest unvarying estimates ignore three of these axioms:

- *The great potential substitutability of services and resources in the production of the desired care outcomes.* Because of the substitutability, the most efficient mixes of resources can and should reflect area variations in the relative supply and costs of resources, and the mixes of resources should accordingly differ between areas. Residential modes can be substituted for community services, community services can be substituted for one another irrespective of the agency which supplies them, informal care can substitute for agency inputs, and there can be countless forms of hybrid each partially substitutable for others.

- *The great variations between persons in the circumstances which would be taken into account in flexibly and entrepreneurially matching resources to needs to improve equity and efficiency.* So, for instance, one might be suspicious of the Swedish evaluation which concludes that it is uneconomic to substitute home care for care in service housing by means of an analysis which assumes that unless accommodated in the service housing, all the clients would require new purpose-built flatlets (Edebalk and Persson, 1988); or the many analyses which value informal care inputs at some level which assumes that all carers would otherwise use the time in paid employment.

- *The variations in costs with client characteristics in all modes and the differences between modes in the factors which influence care costs.* The former is at the core of the traditional economic argument about modal choice in care. The latter is not, but is quite fundamental to argument about how to develop community care. Community care is best for those for whom target levels of life and care quality are inexpensive in the community-based modes, but for whom residential-based care costs much the same as for others.

In this section, we shall establish that: (i) the levels of spending on home care beyond which is would be more efficient to choose residential care are likely to be higher than the cursory inspection of local authority financial statistics suggest, particularly for persons of most dependency; and (ii) the levels are likely to vary greatly between areas. Although we shall be unable to present simple orders of magnitude which could be applied by managers without heed to their local circumstances, we show that local investigation could establish useful if temporary local guidelines.

1.2.1 Towards guideline limits for community service costs

Diagram 14.1 summarises the traditional economic argument about what is the most efficient modal choice in the balance of care. On the diagram are drawn curves representing the relationships between costs and dependency correlates for each of several alternative care modes. The costs are implicitly assumed to be for outcomes of equal acceptability. The curves embody propositions about the relationships: in particular that residential care modes have higher average costs than community-based care but that differences in resident dependency affect costs less than in community-based care; and that average costs in long-stay hospitals are higher but less sensitive to dependency variations. It follows from the assumptions that the most cost-effective mode of care for a person with dependency levels between 0 and A will be community-based care; for a

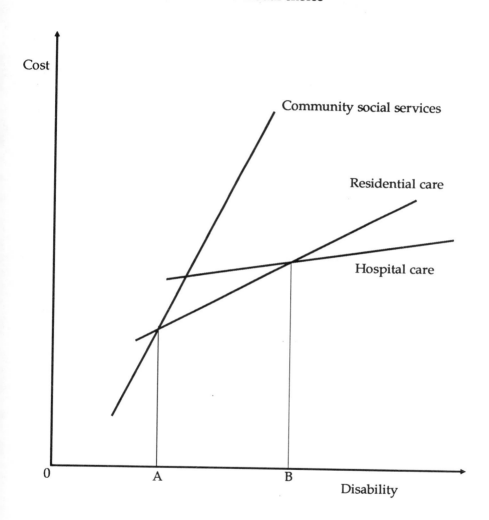

Diagram 14.1
Costs and modal choice

person with dependency levels between A and B will be a residential home mode; and for a person with a dependency level of more than B will be the long-stay nursing home or hospital.

However, the Audit Commission (1985) suggested that the local authorities would continue to be dependent to some degree on their existing stock of residential homes. Anne Parker, Director of Social Services of an authority with an admirable record of service to elderly people, made a similar assumption in 1983:

> I ... start from the base that residential care will continue to play a significant and continuing part in the continuum of services for the elderly, a service which will largely be provided in the 'public' and communal buildings which form the bulk of our present stock, ... I say 'in the sort of buildings we have today' because many local authorities will be left with their existing plant or a reduced and adapted stock. Few will be in the business of the wholesale development of new Part III accommodation ...

The situation has been changing rapidly. Many are responding quickly to incentives to divest themselves of their residential homes. What remains true is that most authorities still provide residential care in some of the capital stock they had created by the mid-1970s, and that this stock will continue to be the basis of the authority's own provision for some years.

Our first task is to look for the break-even point implied in Diagram 14.1 for persons who might realistically be considered by case managers to be on the margin where more intensive home support and residential care might seem to be alternatives. Then we add caveats to the argument about its level. We do so using the information in Diagram 14.2.

1.2.2 *Evidence about break-even costs*

Information in Diagram 14.2
Of the five pieces of information, the first three are among the costs criteria which could conceivably be applied to the production of guidelines: (i) the upper end of the distribution of our study estimates of the opportunity cost of community social services to the social services department; (ii) the upper end of the distribution of the opportunity costs to the health and social services of community health and social services taken together; (iii) predicted values of the opportunity costs to the community health and social services and informal carers predicted for clients with incapacities broadly equivalent to those for the more disabled of the residents postulated (shown in the last section of the diagram but perhaps more applicable to the penultimate section). (A wider range of criterion costs could be compiled from, for instance, the more thorough analysis of opportunity costs to and transfers from various interest groups contained in Davies and Challis (1986).

Diagram 14.2
Community services and residential care costs

The diagrams show (i) the average opportunity cost of care per week to the ssd for recipients living at home during the first six months (SSCOST), and (ii) average opportunity costs per week to the ssd and the community health services for people living at home during the first six months (SSHSCOST), (iii) the range of opportunity costs to the social service department of care for persons of that level of dependency in local authority old people's homes with the dependency needs found in 1981 (Homes, actual dependency mix), (iv) the range of opportunity costs for persons of that level of dependency in new local authority old people's homes, and (v) the sum of agency and opportunity costs to informal carers for persons of very high levels of dependency. Classification into group is by the circumstances of the most dependent client in the household. Frequencies are proportional to the area under the line.

The lines indicating the range of opportunity costs of places in local authority homes are from Davies and Goddard (1987). The opportunity costs to informal carers are estimated using the techniques described in *Community Services and the Social Production of Welfare* (PSSRU, 1991).

A. Long interval need, lesser informal support (Type 2)

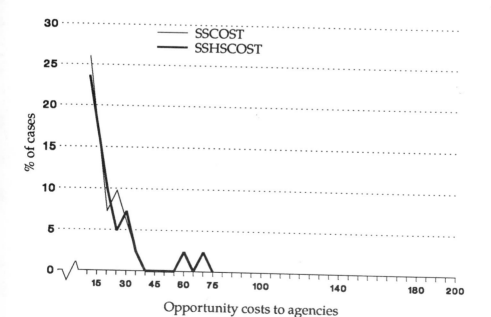

Opportunity costs to agencies
(£ 1985 prices)

B. Short interval need, greater informal support (Type 3)

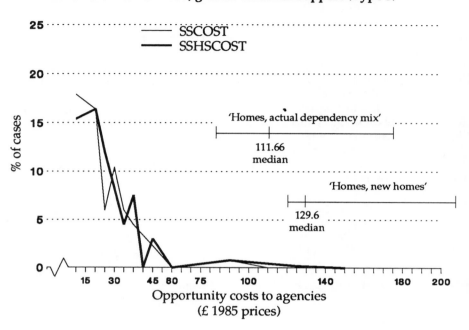

C. Short interval need, lesser informal support (Type 4)

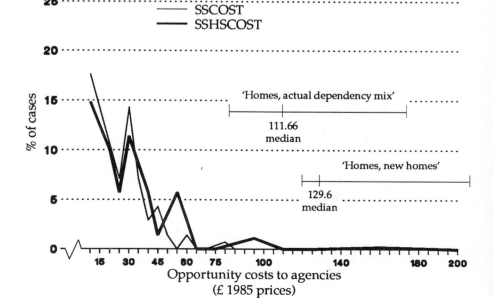

D. Critical interval need, greater informal support (Type 5)

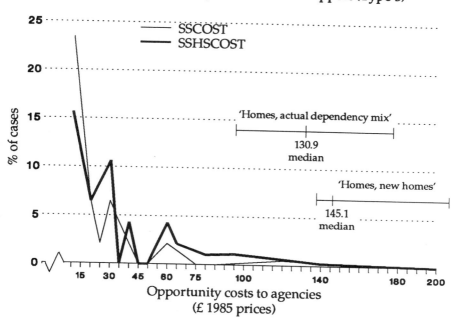

E. Critical interval need, lesser informal support (Type 6)

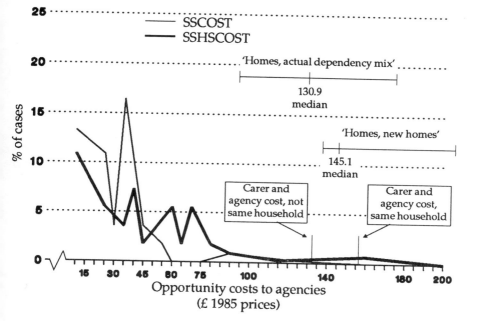

Policy-makers must choose the cost criterion. Since which criterion is chosen quite fundamentally defines the incentives for the system, the choice of criterion might well be made at the highest level in a system with unitary accountability, as was the case with pricing and investment criteria in public enterprises. Criterion (ii) would be better than criterion (i). Its degree of superiority would depend on the extent to which the resources were focused on those whose physical dependency was greatest and for whom, therefore, it was of the greatest importance to ensure that the costs of publicly-financed and agency-provided personal care, from whatever source, were taken fully into account. Chapter 3 of Davies and Challis (1986) described how a failure to do so made a nonsense of the budget-capped case management of community health and social services in Massachusetts. The State of New York created a similar cause of inefficiency.

The difference between criteria (ii) and (iii) describes limits to opportunity costs defined by extreme value judgements about what sharing of burdens between informal and formal carers would be equitable. Criterion (ii), like criterion (i), takes no account of opportunity costs to informal carers. Therefore it does not suggest to a hypothetical case manager applying the costs guideline that another mode would be preferable where the informal carer is bearing such a high cost that the combined cost to agencies and informal carers together exceeds the guideline. Of course, the case manager may be provided with separate guidelines for agency and carer costs; a sliding scale of opportunity cost with primary household income, for instance, as well as an agency cost criterion of type (ii). Again, the case manager need not be forced to take the costs guideline alone into account. If, for instance, the opportunity costs to carers are too difficult to estimate, other evidence might be taken into account. However, a type (iii) criterion does suggest the outside range for opportunity cost.

The importance of the distinction arises because of the covariation of the costs to informal and formal carers. As the last section of Diagram 14.2 implies, *Community Services and the Social Production of Welfare* will show that the proportion of the combined opportunity cost borne by carers of single clients was on average 52 per cent. However, it was 64 per cent for the neediest (critical interval) cases. This correlations between costs to agencies and costs to carers was also found in Cleveland, Ohio (see Davies and Challis, 1986, p.170). Such a pattern almost certainly reflects an inequitable degree of burden borne by many carers of the most dependent, given our results about the proportion of informal carers suffering severe malaise. *A priori*, too, one would expect that among the most dependent there would be higher proportions of caring time spent on tasks which most informal carers and their dependents would regard as repugnant, physically stressful, incompatible with healthy relationships between themselves and the dependents, and incompatible with the roles that they would wish for themselves and the formal services (Davies and Challis, 1986, p.187). (Evidence about Dutch intensive home care suggests that the formal services in the Netherlands contribute more to the personal care tasks and informal carers more to the tasks which they are most willing to undertake; see van den Heuvel, 1989.)

The diagram also contains information about the opportunity costs of residential care for the more dependent MYTYPOs, ranges of opportunity costs to the social services department of residential home places under differing targeting assumptions, and the average level of charges in private old people's homes in 1985.

The diagram reveals a big gap between the costs actually incurred in community-based modes of care and residential costs. At first sight, there seems to be a large safety margin for increased levels of resources for many recipients in community-based care, although, of course, residential care is more economic for some, particularly when the opportunity cost to the informal carer is taken into account.

Caveats to Diagram 14.2

The diagram oversimplifies the choice because it neglects (i) the proliferation of modes, (ii) the association of costs with incapacity in both modes of care when allowance is made for outcome variations, (iii) the higher costs of providing larger quantities of residential care, and (iv) various other flows which exaggerate the true costs of community-based care to public funds.

(i) The review of the evidence in Appendix 14 suggests that modes have indeed proliferated. It would be disappointing if the range of ways of securing social care were not to extend further in response both to imaginative development of independent and other suppliers seeking to capture a niche in the market in competition with others, and in response to the focus of case managers on matching resources to client needs and preferences. However, there is not yet great variety in most areas.

(ii) The review of the evidence about how costs of care in institutions vary with dependency suggests a substantial gradient. However it also illustrates how they also reflected (a) inheritances of capital stocks, (b) conventions about facility design, operation and resourcing which vary substantially between countries, and (c) the cost and price effects of financing mechanisms. Changes after 1991 will affect all of these. In particular, persons hitherto likely to be accommodated in long-stay hospital beds may be more likely to be supported in nursing homes, and the distinction between nursing and rest homes may be eroded by a payments system in which more costs are tied not to the status (as distinct from social services department provider agreements about the cost structure) of the home, but to the dependency of individual residents. Also new criteria and arrangements for quality assurance may lead providers to provide more resources to compensate for greater dependency. This could well make the total payment to the facility more sensitive to dependency, and make the most dependent paid for in residential facilities by the social services department more dependent than all but a small minority of current residents of old people's homes. Both these eventualities would make costs rise more steeply with dependency. To the social services department, it will seem relatively steeper still, since some of the common overhead hotel cost will be part of the 'housing benefit' allowance met by the Department of Social Security. So we could profitably look elsewhere to extend the range of evidence on which to base a judgement: for instance, American, Australian, and continental provision. Those which relate resource inputs to customer circumstances, regime and outcomes would be particularly valuable.

(iii) That the price that has to be paid tends to increase with the total number of places demanded is illustrated in Diagram 14.3. The diagram illustrates the shape of 'supply curves' of local authority residential homes for a selection of the authorities for which supply schedules under various circumstances were simulated by Davies, Darton and Goddard (1987). They vary in position, shapes and slopes. However, many authorities clearly would have to retain more expensive facilities if they imposed a higher demand. The appendix alludes to American argument about the shape of supply curves for independent providers. (The argument is summarised in Davies and Knapp (1988)). Again, it suggests a supply curve which increases with the quantity demanded.

However, one would suspect that in the long run, the gradient in prices and costs due to variations in demand would be relatively shallower than the gradients due to variation in the dependency-related characteristics of users over the range of quantities demanded and dependency mixes which the aggregation of case managers' decisions would yield among social services departments. The importance of that will become evident below.

(iv) After hidden costs to society are taken into account, too few customers still seem to have substantial expenditures made on them.

Conclusions
The arguments and evidence reviewed here and in Appendix 14 imply big local differences in optimal targeting criteria for modes of care. Persons whom it would be more costly to public funds to support at home in

Diagram 14.3
Costs[a] and the supply of local authority residential care:
area variations illustrated

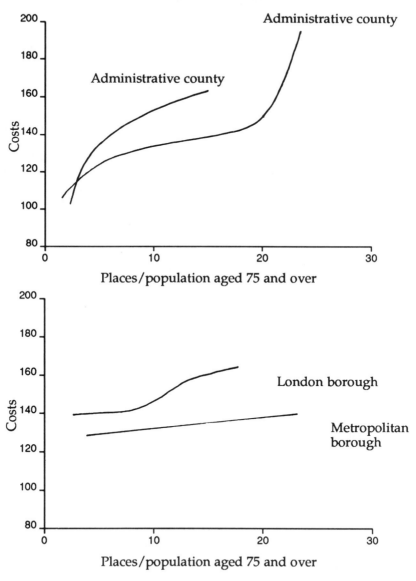

Notes:
a   Opportunity costs to the social services of accommodating heavily and
           appreciably dependent persons only assuming 'vacancy concentration'.
           Diagrams are illustrative only. See source for the precise schedules.
Source: Davies, Darton and Goddard (1987).

some areas would be less expensively supported thus in others. Evidence suggests that this is so also in other countries. For instance, the highest Medicaid nursing home cost – the permitted fee applicable to the whole area – among the five sites implementing the financial control model in the channelling demonstration was 37 per cent greater than the lowest (Carcagno et al., 1985, Table 8.3).

Moreover it is likely that the supply curves are highly responsive to financing arrangements. They will probably remain so after the changes in the stock of facilities we can expect during the next few years. Again, the costs of the most likely alternative residential mode of care differ greatly with the disabilities of users.

However, the evidence suggests that there remains a margin for increased community service spending when allowance is made for hidden costs to public funds. Of course it would be all too easy to provide guidelines which are too generous, and so to exacerbate the financing problems of the growing need for long-term care among persons who must be supported from public funds. The danger would be the greater because more intensive provision of community care may be thought to affect the actual probability of admission to institutions for long-term care without in fact doing so. But currently the gap between the upper limit of spending for most cases at greatest risk and the opportunity costs in residential care is so great that this danger is not great in practice in the UK, though it may well be in such countries as Sweden and the USA.

1.2.3. Choosing the parameters of a case-managed system

Discussion in Chapter 13, other chapters in this book and other PSSRU studies provide information about some elements required to set the parameters of a case-managed system with budgets and opportunities for flexible packaging of the kind advocated in the White Paper implementation documents.

Elements of the argument which together form the logic for parameter-setting are scattered through this book and Davies and Challis (1986). We here draw them together. To simplify the explanation, we postulate a simplified model. It focuses attention on the most important features of the management-designed structures and causal processes of PSSRU-style case-managed community care. In the following sections, we outline our simplifying assumptions, state the argument, and use the model to illustrate the implications of projects and arguments for the balance achieved between residential and community-based care modes.

1.2.4 Assumptions

First, we assume that *the alternative scenarios postulated are similar* in several respects:

Table 14.3
Definitions of case management model concepts

AVBUDG	Average weekly budget for home care excluding case management costs: ie TOTHCCOST less CMCOST.[a] AVBUDG = OTHHCCOST.
AVBUDG curve	The curve describing the relationship between AVBUDG, BUDGCAP, and TARGFLOOR.
BUDGCAP	The guideline weekly cost of home care which case managers should not exceed (or expect to exceed) over more than a short time without managerial review of the case. The text argues that BUDGCAP = CMCOST and an element which varies with AVBUDG in a way which reflects the distribution of the cost-determining characteristics of the persons between TARGFLOOR and BUDGCAP and the position of the HORIZTE curve.
CMCASELOAD	Number of cases per case manager.
CMCOST	Average weekly costs of case management.
DEPINDEX	Index of characteristics affecting costs of achieving equivalent outcomes in home care (given CMCASELOAD) associated with targeting criteria.
DEPINDEX curve	The curve describing the numbers of persons in the potential target population at every level of DEPINDEX.
DEPINDEX Integral	The area under the DEPINDEX curve between TARGFLOOR and BUDGCAP. The DEPINDEX Integral measures the total cost of home care (with equivalent outcomes) assuming 100 per cent target efficiency.
HOMEDUR	Average duration of stay cared for living at home.
HORIZTE curve	The curve describing the postulated or selected degree of horizontal target efficiency given the DEPINDEX score and which given DEPINDEX determines the AVBUDG required.
LIFEDUR	Average expectation of life: LIFEDUR = HOMEDUR + RESDUR.
OTHHCCOST	Average weekly cost of home care services other than case management.
OTHHCCOST curve	Curve describing the dependence of OTHHCCOST on AVBUDG given the level of CMCASELOAD.
RESCOST	Weekly care cost in residential facilities.[a]
RESCOST curve	Curve describing the dependence of RESCOST on RESDUR.
RESDUR	Average duration of stay in residential mode of care: RESDUR = LIFEDUR - HOMEDUR.
TARGFLOOR	The minimum level of DEPINDEX, the index of dependency-generating characteristics, for which care to be publicly funded.
TOTHCCOST	Total weekly cost of home care: TOTHCCOST = CMCOST + RESCOST

a Dependency or 'care' costs only; ie excluding 'housing benefit' costs for non-dependent persons.

- The alternative scenarios considered have identical distributions by characteristics which influence costs of home care given the mix of outputs desired. Also we specify a degree of horizontal target efficiency, so that a level of AVBUDG (the average cost of home care per week excluding case management) is associated with only one level of BUDGCAP (the level beyond which case managers must not spend without management review of the case). The variables are defined in Table 14.3.
- Alternative scenarios have identical average prices of residential care given the quantity demanded and the distribution by dependencies between modes.
- Case managers are similar in their priorities and competence.
- Home care services have the same degrees of technical efficiency, and face similar supply curves for inputs.
- Home care is preferred to residential care by all potential recipients, but efficiency in the production of care purchased from public funds takes precedence over consumer choice.

Secondly, we make *assumptions which reduce the number of stages in the argument* by simplifying the picture of reality in inessential respects.

- Case management is received only when customers are receiving home care.
- There are only two types of home care input: 'case management' (the matching of resources to individual needs and the procurement of service), and 'other home care inputs', which include respite, assessment, and other periods in social care institutions as part of the plan of care while the customer is based at home. Correspondingly, there are two components of costs, CMCOST and OTHHCCOST, expressed per week.
- Case management itself does not affect HOMEDUR.
- There are only two modes of care: care while living at home, and care while living in a residential facility. There are no episodes as hospital inpatients and no clients subsequently become independent of the social services department. So LIFEDUR = RESDUR + HOMEDUR; and the identity which explains the relationship between the two bottom quadrants of Diagram 14.4c, RESDUR = LIFEDUR − HOMEDUR.
- On average cases live for the same length of time irrespective of the values at which model parameters are set.
- All the consumers satisfy asset and income tests for financing by the social services department, which pays their entire care costs. Both OTHHCCOST and RESCOST cover care costs only. So all costs other than care costs will be met by sources other than the social services department; for instance, the social security system.
- What is being optimised is costs to the social services department, not, for instance, costs to public funds or social opportunity costs. All costs are of client and carer outcomes of equivalent value.

1.2.5 Core logic: maximising equity and efficiency

Management choices and POW relationships
The logic explores the relationship between parameters chosen by managers (TARGFLOOR, AVBUDG, BUDGCAP, CMCASELOAD) and the basic dependency-related characteristics of the population in need, and technological and economic relations of the production of welfare: the cost implications on the costs of producing home care of the distribution of the potential target population by DEPINDEX, the selection or acceptance of some rate of horizontal target efficiency, the effects of OTHHCCOST on HOMEDUR given CMCASELOAD, the effects of the quantity and nature of demand for residential care on RESCOST. They are described by the curves in Diagrams 14.4a, 14.4b and 14.4c.

The model is intended to clarify: the levels at which managers must fix those parameters within their control if equity and efficiency is to be maximised; the circumstances in which the selection of inconsistent parameters cause serious departures from equity and efficiency; the effects of differences in scenario for the characteristics of the most equitable and efficient solutions; and the assumptions implicit in arguments for different service arrangements.

Diagram 14.4a: AVBUDG, BUDGCAP, TARGFLOOR and DEPINDEX
We have seen how targeting has been seen as the most important key – by some, overwhelmingly the most important key – to improving equity and efficiency (Audit Commission, 1985; 1986c; Department of Health and Social Security 1987b; 1988a). Though we confirm the importance of low 'productivities' (and particularly low 'marginal productivities'), we do not deny the centrality of targeting. The discussion of the application of our management scanning logic in case management in Chapter 13 likewise suggests that our logic starts with target choices and their implications; for instance the strategic choice between aiming at achieving gains with the complex cases requiring large and skilful case management inputs, high cost cases not requiring such large case management inputs, and cases of lower cost and complexity.

There are two main targeting parameters which managers can set: TARGFLOOR and BUDGCAP.
- TARGFLOOR we conceive to be chosen on the basis of a broad statement of policy by local politicians and members. The broad commitment might be that publicly-funded home care should be used only for persons requiring more than help with the performance of domestic tasks, or that it should be available to persons requiring only help with domestic tasks of some kinds in certain general circumstances. Such definitions can be translated into practice guidelines in various ways. We elsewhere discuss how that can best be done.

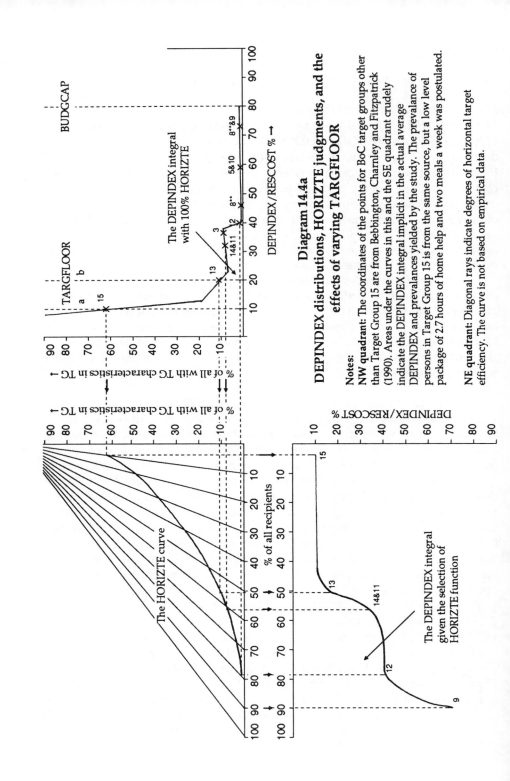

Diagram 14.4a

DEPINDEX distributions, HORIZTE judgments, and the effects of varying TARGFLOOR

Notes:

NW quadrant: The coordinates of the points for BoC target groups other than Target Group 15 are from Bebbington, Charnley and Fitzpatrick (1990). Areas under the curves in this and the SE quadrant crudely indicate the DEPINDEX integral implicit in the actual average DEPINDEX and prevalances yielded by the study. The prevalence of persons in Target Group 15 is from the same source, but a low level package of 2.7 hours of home help and two meals a week was postulated.

NE quadrant: Diagonal rays indicate degrees of horizontal target efficiency. The curve is not based on empirical data.

Diagram 14.4b

A DEPINDEX distribution for a case-managed community care caseload

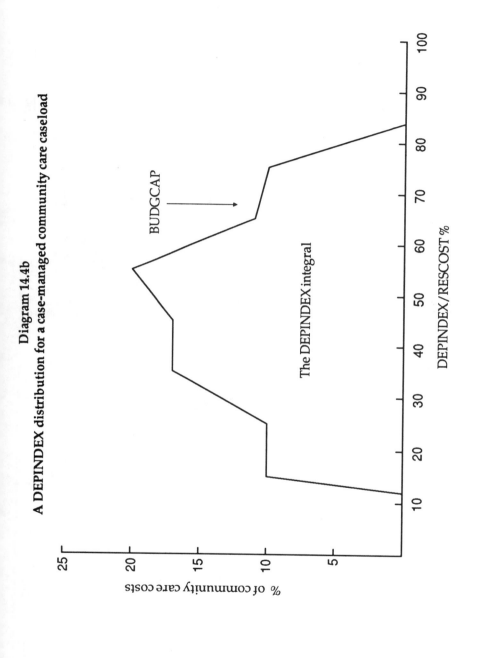

Diagram 14.4c
Cost relationships and case management parameters

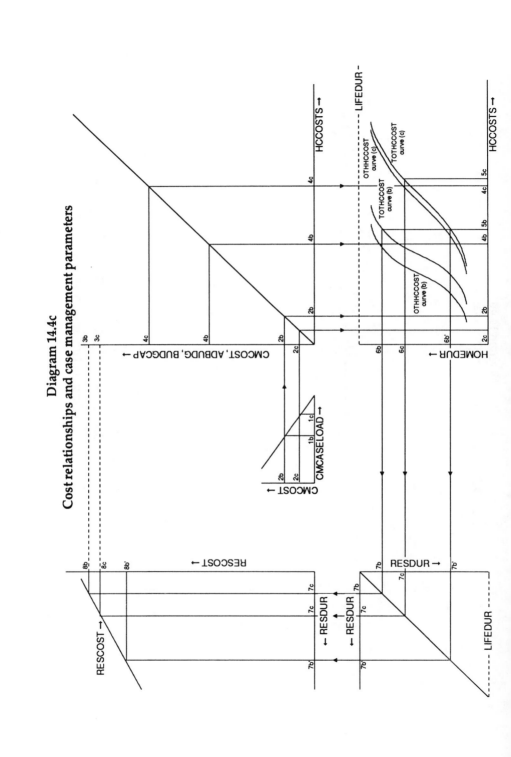

- BUDGCAP we see to be set as a budget guideline not as a set of client characteristics. Again, this is discussed elsewhere in this essay. So has the use of multiple budget caps for persons for whom the most realistic residential costs of care would differ.

Diagram 14.4a presents the implications of assumptions about matching resources to needs embodied in a recent application of the DH Balance of Care model (DHSS Operational Research Service, 1987).

The North-East (NE) quadrant of the diagram shows (i) the number of potential cases by DEPINDEX, (ii) hypothetical positions for TARGFLOOR, and (iii) the position chosen for BUDGCAP. In a system of needs-based planning, the evidence for the shape of the curve would take the form of estimates of numbers in target groups. The DH Balance of Care model distinguishes 16 target groups for the elderly, but care in the home is thought appropriate for persons in only 10 of them. The shape of the DEPINDEX curve shown in the NE quadrant of Diagram 14.4a reflects estimates of numbers in areas of one of the authorities in this study derived using a combination of balance of care and PSSRU needs indicator methodology (Bebbington, Charnley and Fitzpatrick, 1990).

It follows from the definition of DEPINDEX that the area under the curve between the selected levels of TARGFLOOR and BUDGCAP is the total cost of the home care required for that caseload (excluding case management costs and given CMCASELOAD). This is denoted by the integral of the DEPINDEX function between the TARGFLOOR and BUDG-CAP values. The value of the integral divided by the number of persons in the target group – the number at or above TARGFLOOR and at or below BUDGCAP – is the average cost of the home care implicit in the matching judgements contained in the model.

As we have shown in Chapter 1, social services departments generally achieve much less than 100 per cent horizontal target efficiency. Indeed, we have argued that we should choose a developmental strategy in which access to the new system would at first be limited (Davies, 1989). We argue this because there is now a chance to lay foundations for an excellent care system in the long run. But to achieve the excellence will require large investments of long gestation in structures and cultures. So, making ends meet by achieving less than 100 per cent Horizontal Target Efficiency can be an important device for reconciling inadequate short-term resources and investment in the foundations for a high quality but expensive system in the future. In short, we should choose to achieve less than 100 per cent horizontal target efficiency in the provision of the most complex forms of case-managed community care, leaving some for whom that would be beneficial to receive more standard services. That would not cause anyone to be worse off than they now are, though their interests are now badly served. For some other target groups, the system already achieves low levels of target efficiency.

So the North-West (NW) quadrant of Diagram 14.4a postulates the selection of degrees of horizontal target efficiency. The HORIZTE curve describes the relationship between the integral of the DEPINDEX function between TARGFLOOR and BUDGCAP and AVBUDG. (The diagonal rays from the horizontal axis show the postulated degree of horizontal target efficiency indicated by the numbers beneath the axis; the numbers beneath the axis also indicating the proportion of all recipients remaining after the targeting function is applied.) In practice, the degree of horizontal target efficiency selected is likely to vary between target subgroups, and so between levels of DEPINDEX. One would expect authorities and case managers themselves to choose a shape for the HORIZTE curve that was convex when viewed from the horizontal axis. The reason is that the political and humanitarian costs of failing to meet needs of the most vulnerable are much higher. However, authorities would probably judge that the most equitable and efficient allocations require a relationship between horizontal target efficiency and target group which is far more complex than the neat monotonic function between DEPINDEX and HORIZTE described in the NW quadrant. Indeed, there was a more complex relationship implicit in the professional judgements used in the study by Bebbington, Charnley and Fitzpatrick (1990).

Diagram 14.4a has important messages.

- If equity and efficiency is to be maximised, the manager can choose any two out of AVBUDG, BUDGCAP and TARGFLOOR, but not all three, unless s/he is willing to allow the degree of horizontal target efficiency to change. For instance, were TARGFLOOR to be precisely defined in terms of DEPINDEX, and if the managers were in addition to set both AVBUDG and BUDGCAP, it is unlikely that the case managers would have precisely the budget necessary to achieve the equitable and equivalent outcomes sought; they would respond by – deliberately or otherwise – achieving less than 100 per cent horizontal target efficiency and/or failing to achieve the equivalent outcomes to those in the residential mode for some or all home care clients and carers. A high BUDGCAP with an AVBUDG which is too low might cause the case managers to have to allow too few people to have costs near that limit and/or it might cause them to have to spend too little on those of lower DEPINDEX. Equivalent outcomes, and so equity could not be achieved. What the home help service has traditionally done is almost the reverse: it has accepted local conventions about TARGFLOOR and adopted a low AVBUDG thinly to serve 100 per cent of those referred, so resulting in a low implicit BUDGCAP.

- The AVBUDG which reconciles the targeting criteria, a selected level of HORIZTE and the shape of the DEPINDEX curve is unlikely to be the same multiple of TARGFLOOR or multiple of AVBUDG irrespective of the selected values of TARGFLOOR and BUDGCAP.

- We have assumed that the costs which are used as the criterion in weighting need-related circumstances to compute DEPINDEX are the costs of outcomes of equivalent values. Were we instead to assume that they are the costs of outcomes whose values varied directly with DEPINDEX, it is possible that the least damaging way of adjusting to selected values of BUDGCAP and AVBUDG between revisions of the parameters would be to allow case managers to vary TARGFLOOR. The community care projects partly resolved the dilemma in this way, and partly by adjusting the degree of HORIZTE.

- Knowing the shape of the DEPINDEX distribution, one can assess the implications of alternative levels of TARGFLOOR and variations in the HORIZTE judgements. The NE quadrant, which shows the distribution of DEPINDEX in the population as a whole, suggests that almost one half of the resources would be allocated to persons whose DEPINDEX scores would lie between the averages for the two BoC target groups judged to need the least social services department resources. To exclude Target Group 15 would allow much more ambitious goals to be set for persons of greater needs. One might argue that far more might be spent on the home care of those likely to join the 13 per cent of persons for whom residential care is judged appropriate.

- The SW quadrant shows the shape of the DEPINDEX curve after applying the HORIZTE function. The area under the DEPINDEX curve accounted for by persons with DEPINDEX scores between the averages for target groups 14 and 15 is smaller in relation to the total area under the curve than the equivalent area in the NE quadrant. Any set of targeting judgements in which horizontal target efficiency is greater for those with higher DEPINDEX scores will reduce the relative size of the DEPINDEX integral accounted for by target groups whose members are on average less needy.

- Combining the information in Diagram 14.5 with the information of Diagram 14.4a permits an analysis of the sensitivity of total cost commitment through time to varying judgements about packaging and degrees of horizontal target efficiency. This study has shown that the thorough reassessment of the needs of cases at regular intervals has been the exception rather than the rule. It is an objective of policy to avoid the indefinite commitment of resources, or indeed creating the expectation among consumers and others that there will be an indefinite commitment of resources, without reassessment. The diagram and the table suggest what post-review reductions in allocations would make cover the costs of reassessment, though again the questions and logic of the diagram and table are more generalisable than the actual calculations.

- We lack evidence about the likely scale of the reductions in allocations which would result from periodic reassessments. If these prove not to

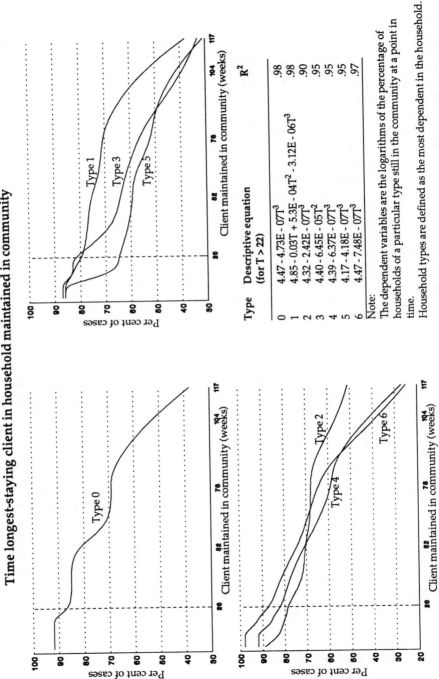

Diagram 14.5a

Time longest-staying client in household maintained in community

Type	Descriptive equation (for T > 22)	R^2
0	$4.47 - 4.73E - 07T^3$	.98
1	$4.85 - 0.03T + 5.3E - 04T^2 - 3.12E - 06T^3$	.98
2	$4.32 - 2.42E - 07T^3$	.90
3	$4.40 - 6.45E - 05T^2$	.95
4	$4.39 - 6.37E - 07T^3$	.95
5	$4.17 - 4.18E - 07T^3$	.95
6	$4.47 - 7.48E - 07T^3$	.97

Note:

The dependent variables are the logarithms of the percentage of households of a particular type still in the community at a point in time.

Household types are defined as the most dependent in the household.

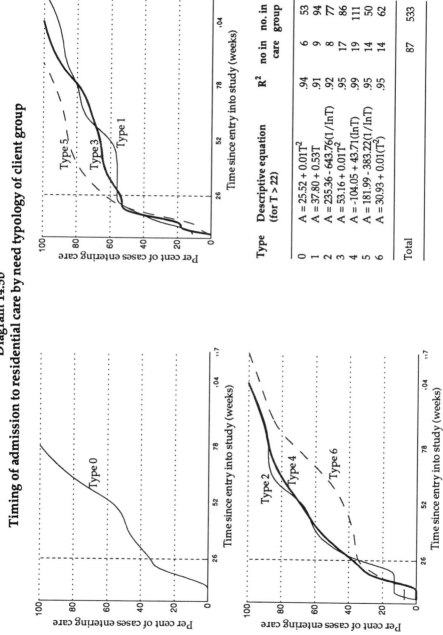

Diagram 14.5b

Timing of admission to residential care by need typology of client group

Type	Descriptive equation (for T > 22)	R^2	no in care	no. in group
0	$A = 25.52 + 0.01T^2$	.94	6	53
1	$A = 37.80 + 0.53T$	.91	9	94
2	$A = 235.36 - 643.76(1/\ln T)$	.92	8	77
3	$A = 53.16 + 0.01T^2$	.95	17	86
4	$A = -104.05 + 43.71(\ln T)$	.99	19	111
5	$A = 181.99 - 383.22(1/\ln T)$	.95	14	50
6	$A = 30.93 + 0.01(T^2)$	.95	14	62
Total			87	533

Table 14.4
Home care cost commitment and targeting decisions[a]

Col.1 MYTY-PO group	Col.2 Expected duration of consumption (weeks)	Col.3 Average weekly cost (£)	Col.4 Expected cost commitment (£)	Col.5 Equivalent BoC/-target groups	Col.6 COST/RES-COST1	Col.7 % of total target number (%)	Col.8 Relative cost commitment
2	100	7.62	762	15	10	3.6	6.483
				14	32	7.9	2.558
3	89	11.70	1041	11	32	0.6	.176
				12	40	1.4	.482
				13	19	11.5	1.898
4	67	12.60	844	8[b]	46	0.2	.055
				8[b]	73	0.9	.433
5	74	8.82	653	3	36	1.9	.504
				10	59	0.4	.159
6	65	18.84	1225	5	59	0.4	.148
				9	74	0.3	.138

a The computations are illustrative, not for application to other contexts, because of the absence of explicit judgments about HORIZTEs for target groups, the partial equivalence of Balance of Care (BoC) target groups and MYTYPOs, the assumed stability of service consumption, the reliance on integrating the equations over a range beyond the data from which they were fitted, and the neglect of the expected costs of residential care, the profile of whose consumption is described in Diagram 14.5b. Also the BoC model takes no account of capacities of clients to finance their consumption. (Baines and Davies, 1990, analyse the discounted present values of expected costs for changes in the utilisation of services through time.)

b The BoC model distributed persons in target group 8 between a package consisting only of community care and a more expensive package comprising community-based services and sheltered housing.

Col.1   The MYTYPO classification is for the most disabled client in the household at the time of the first interview.

Col.2   The estimated area under the curve describing the proportions continuing to receive community-based services. Estimated by integrating the equations in Diagram 14.5 over the period during which more than 5 per cent of recipients were expected to continue to receive services. The equations were fitted on data points from the six month, and six-monthly thereafter until the 27th month. The equations are for household consumption; ie they predict the percentage of households one or more of whose members continue to receive community social services at any subsequent point in time.

Col.3   Source: Bebbington et al., 1986, Table 6.10. The estimates are for what were there classified as 'typical' non-rural areas with median cost levels.

Col.4   The product of columns 2 and 3.

Col.5   BoC model target groups. The equivalence with MYTYPO groups is only approximate because the MYTYPO classifications were based on more detailed information about physical functional abilities, and judgments about informal support reflected the degree and nature of disability. The classification into BoC target groups takes explicit account of incontinence and mental health, rather than allowing for them through their effects on functioning. The ambiguities make it likely that some cases in each target group might have been assigned to other TYPOs than assumed above.

Col.6   COST/RESCOST%. Weekly costs. Both numerator and denominator are derived from Bebbington, Charnley and Fitzpatrick (1990).

Col.7   Per cent of the total number in all target groups receiving ssd resources.

Col.8   The product of columns 2, 6 and 8, divided by 10,000.

be large, the calculation of the cost commitment of current decisions, necessary for financial planning and control, should take into account the effects on the use of resources of the time duration over which services are likely to be received, the prevalence of persons with the target group characteristics in the community, and the relative costs of packages. In a system without the regular review of cases, so should decisions about horizontal target efficiency. Since on average the expected duration of consumption is longer in the more numerous target groups with low DEPINDEX scores, the effect of taking the expected duration of consumption into account is to increase the resources released for higher horizontal target efficiencies and richer packages for the needier target groups by setting higher TARGFLOORs. In a system with reviews, the parameters described in the diagram and its associated equations would change, but analogous information would be needed.

That the precise distribution described by the DEPINDEX curve is difficult to predict makes more important the proposition that we can set two but not all three targeting parameters. Many authorities are doing their planning sums on the basis of crude national guesstimates made by the Audit Commission (1985). However the distributions vary between areas. Taking the Audit Commission distribution may seriously misrepresent the local situation. Better methodologies are available – though they too will need improvement if needs-based planning is to be a reality – but even reasonable estimates would be expensive and time-consuming to make. Moreover, users tend to be unrepresentative of those in need because of arbitrariness in the selection of cases and of 'case management parameters' (see below), and because of differences in the degree of enforcement of the intended parameters. Also the distributions will change quickly. So the collection of evidence about the distributions should be one of the aims in the collection and analysis of community care data bases.

Diagram 14.4b: the DEPINDEX distribution in case-managed community care
The shape of the DEPINDEX curve in Diagram 14.4a reflects judgements for systems which have both neglected the performance of case management tasks and fixed the upper limit of spending on home care too low for efficiency. These result in excessive estimates of the proportions for whom residential care is appropriate.

The shape of the DEPINDEX curve can be different from that in Diagram 14.4a in a case-managed project which has clear substitution aims and so targets differentially across the range of persons in the broader target group. The distribution shown in Diagram 14.4b is for one of the PSSRU community care projects. This was a social care project with a relatively high ratio of AVBUDG to RESCOST. The case managers had clear targeting criteria. The shape therefore reflects the outcomes of an optimising process, though the Diagram 14.4b distribution also reflects both the attempts of case managers to postpone the admission to homes of residents who are in some cases irrationally reluctant to enter, and so may partly reflect departures from allocations yielding outcomes of equivalent value.

Distributions are not yet available which show the DEPINDEX curves for systems which have fully incorporated case-managed community care. So far, community care projects have always coexisted with a number in residential homes much in excess of the numbers receiving the case-managed community care, and the number of persons who could benefit from case-managed community care has always greatly exceeded the numbers for whom there were community care places given the constraints imposed on caseload numbers.

Diagram 14.4c: implications of parameter choices

Diagram 14.4c describes that part of the model which works through the interrelationships between the principal parameters of the production of welfare (marginal costs of LIFEDUR and of RESDUR) and the choice of AVBUDG and BUDGCAP given TARGFLOOR and the DEPINDEX distribution after the application of HORIZTE judgements.

Diagram 14.1 described the central postulate of standard economic theory of community care: the budget limit for spending on a case (BUDGCAP) receiving a mode of care should be set at the level at which cost equals that for the case in that mode of care which offers less independence and whose average cost is next highest. This is one, but only one, condition for making the best use of resources. The choice of budget limit must be logically related to the other parameters controlled by managers and to the basic relationships of the production of welfare.

So the logic of Diagram 14.4c is intended to analyse such matters as (i) what are the consequences of the choice of targeting and case management parameters and HORIZTE for RESCOST, (ii) what choices of parameters result in efficiency, (iii) under what circumstances can one envisage a straightforward mechanism which would automatically lead to equitable and efficient outcomes without deliberate and informed selection of case management parameters, (iv) what are the effects of differing local circumstances in production relations of welfare in home and residential care, and (v) what assumptions or characteristics alternative models argue (or imply) about the nature of the production of welfare, the setting of parameters, and the working of the process described in the diagram.

First we describe the general logic.

The argument of Diagram 14.4c

Diagram 14.4c shows the effects of the choice of case management parameters. It starts with the central segment and the north-east quadrant. Choices implied there are followed through the vertical and horizontal lines connecting quadrants. The causal direction is described by the arrows.

The outcome of each round is the level of RESCOST consistent with the choice of parameters given production of welfare relationships.

North-East (NE) Quadrant. We have argued that one starting point is targeting policy, since managers may expect politicians to have strong views about it, and will require their support for changed policies. Given the targeting parameters (TARGFLOOR, BUDGCAP, and HORIZTE) taken with the DEPINDEX distribution determine optimal AVBUDG and its relation to BUDGCAP and TARGFLOOR. The logic thus far takes us to the North-East (NE) quadrant of Diagram 14.4c in which AVBUDG is one of the variables measured on the vertical axis. AVBUDG and BUDGCAP can be varied regularly and quickly in response to learning about the parameters of the OTHHCCOST and RESCOST curves, to changes in them due to investment, and to other demands.

Centre Segment. Chapter 13 also argues that targeting should also affect the whole style of case management. The reason is that the initial choice of caseloads influences structures, procedures, case management policy, assumptions and expectations among those appointed, the styles of work they adopt, the skills they acquire, and other characteristics which (i) greatly affect ends, means and their interrelations, and (ii) once established, are difficult and expensive to change. The initial choice is not between a caseload of 24 and 26, 35 and 38, or 50 and 55. It is between caseloads of 25, 35 (40 per cent greater pressure than 25), and 50 (40 per cent more than 35).

As we have argued in Chapter 13, each level assumes different styles, complexity of the more difficult cases, and priority choices: all amounting to choices about who should benefit, by how much, and in what way. One example of the type of priority choices are the selection of types of benefit; for instance, higher Maslow goals like Morale improvement with lower order Maslow goals, or mainly the latter (Maslow, 1970). Another is the selection of benefits for some kinds of client more than others; for instance, dependants or informal carers, complex but low or medium cost cases requiring particularly skilful case management and counselling or straightforward high cost cases. Such choices will be reflected in generic targeting or specialist targeting, team skill level and composition, and the other parameters listed in Diagram 13.1. Once the parameters are broadly set, managers can readily only (i) make small adjustments or (ii) hive off a section of the target group to a specialist case management team. To make more drastic changes, they must be prepared to face major investments.

The relationship between CMCASELOAD and CMCOST is described in the segment in the centre of the diagram. The level chosen is carried over to the top right-hand quadrant and there deflected to the bottom right-hand quadrant.

South-East (SE) Quadrant. The SE quadrant describes the relationship between OTHHCCOST given CMCOST and HOMEDUR. This relationship reflects the same parameters of the production of welfare as are assumed in the DEPINDEX curve: the lower the marginal productivities, it follows, the lower the ratio of BUDGCAP to AVBUDG in the NE quadrant. It asserts that the choice of CMCASELOAD sets the average and marginal productivities of other home care inputs in terms of HOMEDUR. (The choice also affects other outputs, including those which do not affect HOMEDUR.) The low CMCASELOADs postulated when working through the model from CMCASELOAD = 1b cause the high average and marginal productivities illustrated in OTHHCCOST(a) and TOTHCCOST(a) curves. The lower productivities corresponding to CMCASELOAD = 1c are shown in OTHHCCOST(b) and TOTHCCOST(b).

Our estimates of marginal productivities of individual services reflect their technical efficiencies as well as the service 'technologies', the relations between resources and outcomes given complete technical efficiency. It is argued on page 22 of Davies and Challis (1986) and Diagram 6.1 above – that the performance of core case management tasks do not directly and immediately affect the development of the technology or the technical efficiency of any one service. But (i) their performance directly affects other forms of efficiency and so the efficiency of the package as a whole. The slope of the OTHHCCOST curve reflects the marginal productivity of the aggregate of all inputs, and so is influenced by better matching of resources to needs. Also, (ii), the effective performance of case management tasks can (and has) affected behaviour over time through the awareness of competition even where the alternatives are partial, and the system lacks formal structures and an ethos which deliberately fosters and uses competitive processes to secure more efficient and responsive performance. The existence and activities of the case managers could presumably affect the variety and prices of services, and could help to enrich the technology to a greater extent with a livelier competitive process as long as the focus of the competition were the real economics of production and real benefits to consumers.

High average productivity is denoted by high HOMEDUR given costs. High marginal productivity is denoted by curves with a steep slope. The shape of the curves reflect assumptions about the productivity of inputs. Diminishing returns to home care services are assumed beyond some level: that is, beyond that level additional home care inputs are assumed to have smaller effects on outcomes in general and HOMEDUR in particular. At very low levels, greater home care provision may increase average HOMEDUR less than at intermediate levels. If consumer choice is unrestricted by agency costs, one could in principle achieve a RESDUR of 0 at some home care cost. In that sense, the failure to provide care in the home for anyone who wants it can be seen as the result of a failure of the system as it is perceived in Wisconsin, not the result of the limit of the state's obligation to spend to extend consumer choice (McDowell, Barniskis, and Wright, 1989).

We have argued at the beginning of the last paragraph that the effects of OTHHCCOST on HOMEDUR depend on the level of CMCASELOAD chosen: the higher the chosen CMCASELOAD, the further to the left and the steeper is the OTHHCCOST curve. However, we would expect that successive increases in case management inputs would have ever smaller effects on the steepness and position of the OTHHCCOST curve; the effects on the average and marginal productivities of home care with respect to HOMEDUR and other outputs would diminish. Again, variations in CMCASELOAD when the caseloads are very high (as in the British home help services) would have little effect. So in this respect, too, there are variable returns.

BUDGCAP is a guideline which requires case managers to review with superiors cases whose spending over a period is anticipated to exceed it. The level of BUDGCAP should reflect managerial judgement about the point of intersection A in diagram 14.1. So BUDGCAP should be chosen to reflect the implications of the production of welfare relationships which are described by the OTHHCCOST and RESCOST curves and prior decisions about CMCASELOAD and AVBUDG. It should not be seen as an independent logical starting point of the process of designing case-managed community care. What the diagram describes is a system of simultaneous equations which must be solved for consistent values of BUDGCAP, RESCOST, CMCASELOAD, AVBUDG, LIFEDUR, and RESDUR, the solution being one which equalises BUDGCAP and RESCOST.

AVBUDG is the average budget overall *less* the chosen CMCOST. This is varied more easily than CMCASELOAD and the qualitative correlates reflected in investment costs in case managers and the case management system. So there is a sense in which decisions about CMCASELOAD should be seen by managers as logically prior to AVBUDG. We have seen that AVBUDG should depend on the distribution by dependency-generating characteristics of target clienteles.

South-East and South-West (SW) Quadrants. The choice of CMCASELOAD (in the centre of the diagram) and AVBUDG in the North-East quadrant determines OTHHCCOST and TOTHCCOSTS, the sum of CMCOST and OTHHCCOST; and OTHHCCOST determines HOMEDUR, as shown in the SE quadrant. By assumption, RESDUR = LIFEDUR – HOMEDUR. So the level of HOMEDUR sets the level of RESDUR. RESDUR in turn sets the level of RESCOST, as can be seen by following the connection between the SE quadrant through the SW quadrant to the NW quadrant.

North-West (NW) Quadrant. The quadrant shows the relationship between RESCOST and RESDUR; that is, it shows what any level of RESDUR implies for the level of RESCOST. The relationship reflects two features of the production of welfare. First, the higher is RESDUR, the greater will be the quantity of residential care demanded in the area, and so the lower the average supply price. This was illustrated earlier in the chapter. But secondly, the higher is RESDUR, the lower will be the average degree of dependency of residents; and therefore the lower will be RESDUR. We have only examples of marginal cost schedules for varying levels of supply for some local authority areas making varying assumptions about demand, and little hard evidence about the supply curves of independent provision. Likewise, the variations in costs and prices have been estimated for periods with very different market circumstances than those likely after April 1991. So we have little real evidence on which to base a judgement about whether RESCOSTS will rise or fall with RESDUR; whether the curve has on balance a positive or negative slope. The direction and certainly the slope of the curve will vary from place to place.

Finally we return to the NE quadrant to find the optimal level of BUDGCAP.

1.2.6 A logic to optimise efficiency

The managers will choose the initial parameters of the design of the case-managed community care (TARGFLOOR, CMCASELOAD, BUDGCAP with its associated AVBUDG) without precise knowledge of the production of welfare relationships (what OTHHCCOST curves are associated with varying levels of CMCASELOAD, and the RESCOST curve) and the implications for HORIZTE. Nevertheless it is essential for them to make an accurate guess about the level of RESCOST and to set AVBUDG and BUDGCAP accordingly.

Diagram 14.4c shows the implication of an inappropriate choice of BUDGCAP. Setting it incorrectly could cause a level of RESCOST greater than the level set. Should the managers then adjust BUDGCAP to that level of RESCOST, the level of RESCOST which would result once the effect of the new BUDGCAP level worked through, could again not be equal to the adjusted BUDGCAP, and again, there would be inequity and inefficiency: inconsistencies in budget guidelines and targeting criteria which would result in inappropriate placement, and so inequity between consumers, and inefficiency in the use of public resources. The result could either be a widening gap between BUDGCAP and RESCOST for a few rounds, or gaps which alternate in direction between rounds, depending on the starting point and the shapes of the OTHHCCOST and RESCOST curves. In circumstances in which RESCOST exceeded the BUDGCAP, there would be the gap which Diagram 14.2 suggests might exist; and with it too many persons either admitted to residential modes of care or queueing for them while supported with inadequate service. Should RES-COST prove less than BUDGCAP, there would likewise be inefficiency, and wasteful vacancies in facilities.

So the equation of BUDGCAP with the RESCOST which emerges during the previous period is insufficient to avoid inequity and inefficiency. Given TARGFLOOR, AVBUDG and HORIZTE, managers must set the BUDGCAP in the light of the RESCOST *expected in the light of the BUDGCAP and other parameters chosen.* So the manager must have some knowledge of the production relationships of care, at least over the expected range of variation of the parameters.

Diagram 14.4c suggests on what that range will depend. The variation in RESCOST associated with a change in BUDGCAP will be greater: (i) the steeper are the OTHHCCOST, and so the TOTHCCOST, curves: that is, the higher are marginal productivities of home care; and (ii) the steeper is the RESCOST curve, that is, the more sensitive is RESCOST to increases in the demand for care in residential facilities. That is in one sense bad news for social services managers. Social services departments are likely to strive hard to raise the marginal productivity of home care services during the next few years, in part by adopting case-managed community care. Success in doing so will make it more difficult as well as more important to develop tools to enable them to second-guess future RESCOST and to set BUDGCAP accordingly. However the tighter regulation of quality in residential facilities is likely to produce a clearer relationship between resources and the dependency of residents, so increasing the importance of the dependency effect compared with the supply curve effect. However the introduction of tighter assessments accompanied by more rigorous quality assurance after 1990 could drive out small low-cost homes in some areas. That might be followed by a period of expanding demand at a price which would attract new entrants. The elasticity of supply of places could then be much lower in such areas. That would increase the size of the supply curve effect by more than the increase in the dependency effect. That again would make it more difficult to choose the appropriate BUDGCAP.

There is a danger of quite the opposite kind. The Act demands the long-run development of case-managed community care, and official policy expressed in Implementation Documents and elsewhere has encouraged the adoption of forms of case-managed community care of the type which has yielded the improved productivity of home care. However, the documents realistically and rightly envisage the development of case management over a long period. They argue that the improvements will require large-scale cultural change – skill enhancement and some value change – as well as the creation of new field arrangements and systems to support them. The social services departments will be attempting to make these at the same time as they are required to make other large changes. So it is likely that many authorities will for some time be operating with OTHHCCOST curves more like (b) than (a). That would require them to set high BUDGCAPs and AVBUDGs. Moreover, the

OTHHCCOST curves flatten at high and low levels of HOMEDUR. Indeed, it would be reasonable to postulate from the results of this study that RESCOST would never be high enough to permit social services departments to operate with levels of BUDGCAP and AVBUDG putting them in the range of the OTHHCCOST curve at which variations in BUDGCAP would greatly affect HOMEDUR. In such circumstances, social services departments could not successfully use increases in AVBUDG to increase the proportion of persons in home care without lowering the quality of life of clients and carers, and they could not use changes in the balance of care to finance increased demand from a lesser increase in resources. However, current RESCOST would be a better predictor of future RESCOST, and on that account at least, the choice of BUDGCAP would technically be easier.

There could be two reasons for social services departments being trapped into levels of AVBUDG which are too low to impact on the balance of care. (i) The negotiations between the Department of Health and the Department of Social Security might result in the adoption of estimates of care costs in residential home which are small compared with the 'housing benefit level' for which the Department of Social Security would be responsible. A housing cost allowance of £80 would fix AVBUDG and BUDGCAP consistent with equity and efficiency so low that it could well force social services departments to operate over the flat bottom range of the OTHHCCOST curves. A settlement of £20 might allow them to operate in the steep region, even if the slope of OTHHCCOST curves were increased only moderately by the imperfect implementation of case-managed community care. So the policy goal of enabling more people to continue to live in private households would be seriously compromised were the settlement to be at the level which some pressure groups representing suppliers of housing would desire because it would give them independence of case management judgements. (ii) Authorities may find it impossible to raise their TARGFLOOR sufficiently to release enough resources for a high AVBUDG, either because local managers and politicians were uninformed or unconvinced by the evidence about the potential of case-managed community care, or because reasonable definitions of the target groups who should be benefited resulted in a TARGFLOOR incompatible with much reallocation of resources to those with high DEPINDEX scores. However the shape of the DEPINDEX curve shown in Diagram 14.4a suggests that higher AVBUDG could be achieved by raising TARGFLOOR (or, equivalent, lowering the degree of HORIZTE among groups with low DEPINDEX scores) by only a modest degree.

1.2.7 Sensitivity to POW parameters

Some parameters to which the efficiency effects of misjudgements are sensitive have been mentioned.

- Higher marginal productivities in home care make the system more sensitive.
- A RESCOST with a steep positive gradient makes the system more sensitive. The RESCOST curve will be positive when the positive supply curve effect more than offsets the negative dependency effect. (The supply curve effect is caused because increased supply demands more expensive upgrading of decreasingly suitable accommodation and increasing investment in decreasingly suitable staff and their quality control.The dependency effect occurs because high RESDUR is associated with lower average dependency in residential care and so lower RESCOST.)
- HORIZTE being held constant, the waste of resources due to misjudgement in the choice of BUDGCAP and AVBUDG would be greater, the higher is the proportion of those in the targeted range of the DEPINDEX distribution with higher DEPINDEX scores.
- The gap between RESCOST yielded by the cycle and the value of BUDGCAP set at the beginning of the cycle varies with the sum of the slopes of OTHHCCOST and RESCOST curves.
- The steeper and more convex to the origin is the HORIZTE curve shown in Diagram 14.4a, the greater the inefficiency would be caused by a misjudged BUDGCAP, because a higher proportion of total resources which will be allocated to consumers with DEPINDEX scores in regions within which the BUDGCAP is likely to be set. With a steep and concave HORIZTE curve, the effects of misjudgements about either AVBUDG or BUDGCAP will be felt primarily by clients of high need. The White Paper and Implementation Documents state the policy that these clients should have higher priority.

1.2.8 Various models interpreted

The PSSRU community care projects
We can paraphrase part of the argument of Davies and Challis (1986) thus: (i) Because of the low levels of case management input for those at risk of inappropriate admission to institutions for long-term care, spending more per case on home care services would not greatly reduce the utilisation of institutional care; that is, the slope of the OTHHCCOST curve with respect to duration of stay in home care would be slight. (ii) However with higher levels and more entrepreneurial and client-responsive case management, the OTHHCCOST curve could be steepened and its position shifted downwards.

The solution applied in the Thanet experiment and its descendants was (i) to set a high level of CMCASELOAD, and to undertake substantial investments in changing the assumptions and skills of case managers, and the structures, policies and procedures which comprise a case management system; (ii) to choose an AVBUDG and BUDGCAP which would allow the effective care of both complex and resource-intensive cases living in their own homes, the ratio of AVBUDG to RESCOST being 0.16 compared with proportions varying between 30 and 47 per cent in the financial control models of channelling (Carcagno et al., 1986, p.246); and (iii) to establish a BUDGCAP at what would have been the point of intersection A of Diagram 14.1 had the residential accounts distinguished care from living costs, and the latter were excluded – given our model's assumptions that all costs are care costs and all care costs are borne by the social services department, the level at which BUDGCAP would equal expected RESCOST. (Given who bore what costs at the time, BUDGCAP was set below expected RESCOST, partly because the social services department paid for hotel as well as care costs in what in the late 1970s was the dominant source of residential care, the PSSRU BUDGCAPs having been set with an eye on social opportunity costs, not just opportunity costs to the social services department.) The Thanet experiment and its descendants have clearly raised the average and marginal productivity of inputs with respect to the capacity to remain in the community with at least equivalent quality of life and care; that is, they have shifted the TOTHCCOST curve to the left and made it steeper.

The logic can be followed through the diagram. Starting with the component in the centre of the diagram, the value of CMCASELOAD was set at a level with consequences like level 1b of the diagram. With this went investment in the skills and attitudes of case managers and investment in the case management system. The CMCASELOAD of 1b was associated with a CMCOST of 2b. It was attempted to set AVBUDG and BUDGCAP at a level which would roughly equate BUDGCAP to the RESCOST emerging from the cycle once allowance was made between the divergence between the costs to the social services reflected in standard accounts and a broader concept of opportunity costs. (There was also a happy coincidence that at the same time the AVBUDG and BUDGCAP were compatible with a DEPINDEX distribution yielding improved quality of life and care, and that the clients who could thus be targeted were a substantial proportion of those at risk of admission to residential modes of care. But that is irrelevant to the pure efficiency argument explored here. So is the conventional criterion of success by which experiments are evaluated: that on average the costs of equivalent quality of life and care are lower.) The CMCOST of 3b was associated with an AVBUDG of 4b, OTHHCCOSTS of 4b and TOTHCCOSTS of 5b, with a HOMEDUR of 6b, a corresponding RESDUR of 7b, and a RESCOST of 8b. The value of RESCOST seemed to be approximately equal to BUDGCAP. That approximately satisfied the condition for optimisation established in Diagram 14.1.

Intensive home help provision

Some of the intensive home care schemes were based on an assumption that more of the same home care services would achieve the necessary diversion from institutions. An example is the Rhondda project. No explicit attention was paid to improving the performance of most of the core case management tasks.

Diagrammatically, let us assume an AVBUDG of 3b. There would be a high CMCASELOAD and a low level of CMCOST. Rhondda set a CMCASELOAD at, say, 1c. Taken with the associated investments in case managers and case management systems, this caused a CMCOST of 2c. The model predicts that the OTHHCCOST curve would be shallow and far to the right. Given the position of the OTHHCCOST and TOTHCCOST curves associated with that CMCOST, the HOMEDUR achieved from (a relatively high) AVBUDG of 4c would be only 6c at a TOTHCCOST of 5c, a RESDUR of 7c, and a RESCOST of 8c. Since a RESCOST of 8c is less than the BUDGCAP of 3c, too much would be spent on home care in relation to the costs of residential care. But the root of the problem is not the choice of AVBUDG, but the selection of CMCASELOAD and its associated investment costs. The results were compatible with this. The higher AVBUDG did not achieve the massively increased HOMEDUR. Chapter 13 mentioned the project. Its lack of success was ascribed by its evaluators to a failure to achieve the matching of resources to needs. The difference between 8b and 8c illustrates the difference made to the most efficient BUDGCAP by the lower productivity of TOTHCCOST(c) given the same AVBUDG as was assumed for the description of community care projects.

Intensive personal and rehabilitative care at home

Unlike the intensive home help model but like the PSSRU community care argument, this model might well postulate a high rate of return on investment. Investment can be in either or both the performance of case management tasks and case management systems, or raising the productivities of the services themselves. Assumptions about the relative returns on the two foci of investment distinguish the PSSRU argument from what is implicitly assumed by the designers of schemes with enhanced home care with a changed task mix and rehabilitative intent.

Implicitly, those aiming for more intensive home care with a shift to personal care and rehabilitation assume (i) that the rate of return on investment in case management systems would be low and/or (ii) that CMCASELOAD and so CMCOST would have little effect on the position and slope of the OTHHCCOST curve (the 'productivity' of home care services) and so on HOMEDUR. However, they believe that there can be a high rate of return on investment in individual home care services. For instance, it might be argued that a heavy emphasis on training home care workers in rehabilitative techniques and styles of work might have large effects. The PSSRU model assumes a high rate of return from investment in case management, and suggests that the rate of return is at least as high as the rate of return in the direct performance of other care tasks.

In terms of Diagram 14.4c, the argument is that it is investment in the home care services alone which will shift the OTHHCCOST curve, not a combination of investments in services and investment in case management and case management systems. These comments should not be interpreted as general approval. For example, versions of the model which put little weight on the performance of case management tasks, or do so without making case managers holders of budgets against which all care costs are charged, and without allowing case managers to procure care inputs from any of several sources, do not provide any obvious incentives to the case manager to help to improve efficiency while improving effectiveness. Concentrating the responsibility for performing case management tasks amounts to no more than a form of organisational consolidation. Concentration of the responsibility, authority and accountability, with fixed budgets which are flexibly used to channel most of the spending around the care supply system, adds powerful incentives to improve efficiency, and sets the case manager free to be responsive to user needs and values within the limit set by BUDGCAP. To the organisational consolidation is added powerful incentive effects. Chapter 13 has discussed the circumstances in which to forego these efficiency-improving mechanisms might be worthwhile.

The financial control model of the channelling demonstration
British readers will find descriptions of the basic and financial control models of channelling in Chapter 3 of Davies and Challis (1986). The former relied mainly on case management with gap-filling funds, did not have an AVBUDG or BUDGCAP, and so is more like child care workers with unusually generous access to section 2 money, or the St Pancras scheme (London Council of Social Service, 1963).

The financial control model was more like the PSSRU models: each site had a BUDGCAP and an AVBUDG; Federal and State funds were pooled and routed through the case managers who had the power to authorise the amount, duration and scope of services paid for from the pooled Federal and State funds; there were clear targeting criteria intended to capture a population at risk of admission to institutions for long-term care; (too late in the day) there were (excessively bureaucratic) information systems to secure financial and other forms of control; the projects were an attempt to achieve change in the local systems, albeit by means which gave them influence over a much smaller part of the local market than the PSSRU experiments.

The financial control and PSSRU models differ in the levels at which they set their AVBUDG, BUDGCAP, CMCASELOAD parameters, and their control of HORIZTE.

First, the financial control models set their BUDGCAP at 85 per cent of the site's approved Medicaid and Medicare nursing home rates. That almost certainly exceeded the value of RESCOST by our definitions. So the financial control models set BUDGCAP too high for efficiency either if our criterion is social opportunity cost, or if our criterion is the opportunity cost to a long-term care agency. (Like the PSSRU evaluations, the Mathematica evaluations of costs and benefits estimated costs by interest group; Thornton and Miller-Dunstan, 1986.)

Secondly, there were two differences in the handling of AVBUDG: (i) the logic applied to the choice of the initial AVBUDG and its subsequent adjustment; and (ii) the actual levels selected.

(i) The logics applied in the selection of AVBUDG were different in the two cases. The designers of the channelling experiment argued that clients in typical circumstances could be adequately cared for with a package costing about 60 per cent of nursing home costs. The Thanet project also had expectations about the costs of adequate home care for the target clientele. But the case management team was found to be achieving good outcomes with lower spending, and expected diminishing returns on higher spending. An apparent island of plenty in an ocean of scarcity both offended principles of equity and could arguably undermine the model's incentives to improve efficiency. Therefore AVBUDG was reduced. The Thanet AVBUDG provided a basis for fixing AVBUDG in subsequent projects. Also the Thanet parameters seemed more deliberately set so as to reduce the average costs of better care.

(ii) The financial control and Thanet models differed too in the actual AVBUDG set. One must distinguish between the AVBUDG intended and the AVBUDG which the costing research showed to have been actually achieved. We have seen that the AVBUDG for the financial control models was intended to be 60 per cent. Achieved AVBUDG for the channelling sites varied between 30 and 47 per cent and achieved AVBUDG for Thanet community care project turned out to be 19 per cent. The argument of Diagram 14.4c suggests that the consequences of a higher AVBUDG depends on the marginal productivities of home care services – the slope of the OTHHCCOST curve over the relevant range – and the slope of the RESCOST curve. Depending on these slopes, a higher AVBUDG may or may not pay off. In fact, the higher AVBUDG in the financial control models did not greatly affect HOMEDUR. Therefore there were few cost savings.

Thirdly, there were also the differences in the setting of the CMCASE-LOAD. As was described in Chapter 13, the financial control levels of CMCASELOAD were typically substantially higher than in the Thanet project and the PSSRU projects based on it – though not as much higher as AVBUDG: the proportion of total costs accounted for by case management costs was 23 per cent among the five financial control projects but only 17 per cent for Thanet. Probably as important, though only anecdotally illustrated rather than fully described and analysed in the channelling literature, there were policy and procedural differences which made the practice more bureaucratic and less client responsive. Channelling was attempting a systemic change with means which only marginally influenced the system as a whole, because its case managers did not allocate resources for a sufficiently large part of the market, and not entirely for those it served. Therefore the providers of home care were under less pressure to improve productivities. These differences may well have contributed to the smaller effects on HOMEDUR described in Chapter 13. Certainly interviews with providing agencies and time spent visiting cases with case managers from channelling as for other American sites suggest serious cost-affecting inflexibilities in supply.

Fourthly, there were differences in targeting between the PSSRU models and channelling. Without exception, PSSRU experiments have been placed on the procedural pathways to institutional long-term care. In this, the PSSRU experiments have been similar to the cost-saving American projects like the South Carolina CLTCP (Davies and Challis, 1986, chap. 3). So the extra funds did not result in an addition to the total number of persons provided with care more than could be financed by the difference between RESCOST and AVBUDG. That was not so in channelling. There, much of the benefit was enjoyed by persons not at high risk of admission to institutions, and much of the addition to AVBUDG seeped away into increased HORIZTE: seeped away in the sense that this was the very opposite of what was intended, though arguably worthwhile in its own right.

The literature stresses the failure of financial control channelling. The argument of Diagram 14.4c helps to explain this. The high BUDGCAP and failure to increase the slope of the OTHHCCOST curve have not had sufficient emphasis in the American literature. These were the roots for the real failure. But the failure has anyhow been exaggerated in that literature. Partly that is because of the concern of technical critics with issues of evaluation design. Partly also it is because of the understandable focus on whether the additional home care costs actually escalated the costs of home care. That focus on whether total costs were reduced distracted attention from the efficiency issues highlighted in Diagram 14.4c. In the absence of theory of the kind provided by Diagram 14.4c, it is easy to be distracted thus. The British discussion could similarly be distracted. The PSSRU evaluations too have paid great attention to the same criterion as the Americans: producing better than equivalent care for the same or less cost, and so helping to self-finance the modernisation of long-term care. We have insufficiently stressed that this was the results of a lucky selection of parameters as well as improvements in the real economy of care. (See Chapter 13. See also the comparison of results of the care in the community initiative projects for the former patients of mental illness and mental handicap hospitals; Knapp, Cambridge, Allen, Beecham and Darton, 1991).

2 Work through the implications of a more determinate technology

Nothing shows the technostructural achievement of the last two decades as clearly as the extensiveness, quality, depth and range of current discussion of community care. Compared with what is written during the Seebohm years, the state papers – the Griffiths Report, the White Paper, the community care Implementation Documents – focus much more on outcomes for consumers, on cost-effectiveness in the use of publicly-financed resources, and on relating resources to needs. Needs, resources and outcomes are being treated more consistently and in finer detail. 'Needs-based planning' was in vogue in the Seebohm years too, but Alan Williams' demon 'needologists' translated the situations of potential users directly into service requirements without considering alternative means of producing desired outcomes (Williams, 1974). Most of the guidelines used – and extensively applied at the local level well after they had been centrally renounced – were arbitrarily set (Webb and Falk, 1974), and reinforced the tendency to expand a narrow range of standard services. Now the emphasis is on structures and processes which will yield better outcomes and greater cost-effectiveness by means of flexibility, substitution and choice. In a sense, the focus on how to relate resources to needs and outcomes makes us all Production of Welfare planners now.

A main benefit of a production of welfare approach to the transformation of community care would be increased technological determinacy: greater predictability about the outcomes produced from resources. Production of welfare studies have shown some of the ways in which we can promote greater determinacy in subtle technologies. One is the development of community care data bases for each of the three most important conceptual categories of the production of welfare: needs, resources (particularly costs) and outcomes (including measures of the quality of life and care). Each successive generation of studies have improved measures. Most authorities have not kept abreast.

As important as the design of the collections is their analysis. Many performance issues are about the interrelationships between resources, needs and outcomes. The analyses must be fitted to the new definitions and divisions of responsibilities, and, because these will vary between areas, the focus must be on the development of general techniques and adaptable modules. A major focus should be the derivation of indicators. Had this study found a higher degree of technological determinacy, we would have based on it a new generation of 'Mark III' needs indicators and corresponding outcome indicators. These would have mirrored the theory of needs and output more closely than previous work (Davies, 1976). The objection to producing and using them is not technical. It is that they will only contribute powerfully when the world becomes sufficiently determinate. The development of outcome indicators for allocating resources and monitoring outcomes could strengthen the complementarity of devices for achieving improvements. The best systems will not rely on one model with its devices. Like the best American systems, each area will have a variety of models, each fitting a situation and further adapted to its local environment; and the models will be complemented by a variety of devices to provide checks and balances which will ensure that none of the competing objectives will acquire an unreasonable priority over the others.

A seemingly more esoteric way of promoting technological determinacy is to develop a lingua franca. We need a common language, common concepts, and an assumed common knowledge of arguments expressed in the common language. These must be usable by a wide range of workers in the development of community care. That is one reason why this chapter contains a formal model of the argument about the interrelations of efficiency-determining parameters in the general PSSRU model of case-managed community care. To recognise the need for a lingua franca is particularly important when we expect policy-makers, managers and field workers to adopt new ideas fast.

3 Plan for the long as well as the medium term

The new planning works from principles and priorities through implications for the new economy of care to structures and processes for implementing change. It is not about end-states seen as irrevocable, infallibly defined, and inviolable, though it is about time-scheduled programmes: mechanisms for 'ordering change' – the expression used in a critique of changing concepts of local planning in the 1970s – or 'managing change', its new managerialist form (Hart, 1973; Pettigrew, 1985). The new approach to planning recognises the importance of gaining the commitment of many to fundamental change. Long time horizons are essential.

The Social Services Inspectorate echo what others write about 'a process of evolutionary change', but adding that no less than a major cultural shift is required (Department of Health, 1990y, paras. 4.3 and 27.1) for the new case management ideas to be understood, accepted, and to have sufficient impact on actual practice, a change requiring long time horizons:

a sustained process of change, built upon a progressive shift of influence from those providing services to those seeking or securing them. That shift of emphasis will require a major change of culture in most local authorities or health authorities. Attitudes will have to change at every level ... Organisational structures, procedures and practices will also have to be amended.

Changes in structure and form are difficult enough to achieve. So is the new clarity of policy translating the broad principles into action-orientated plans, technical artifacts for implementing it, and devices for its monitoring. But they are as nothing compared with the changes in content required in handling matters of such complexity, because the changes which most count are those which require the understanding, reskilling and commitment of the vast number of persons who actually work with clients and carers.

So a three-year time horizon for some processes must be related to a much longer time horizon for critical forms of investment. Experience shows that it takes longer than three years to make a wholly constructive but large impact on a local system of community care. It was little short of a decade before Kent moved from the beginning of the implementation phase of the first community care project to a system of community care schemes in each area. The system is still developing fast in Wisconsin after a decade (McDowell, Barniskis, and Wright, 1989; Spann, 1987). It is not surprising that the Australian Commonwealth Department of Community Services and Health formally recognise that it will take 'perhaps 15 to 25 years' (Auditor General, 1989).

4 Sponsor the development of community care politics and polity

It would be a mistake to act as if we assumed that managers and care workers can between them secure the implementation of community care. In the era of the ideational hegemony of 'new managerialism', we may be biased towards overstating the influence on outcomes of 'good management'. The assumptions of care professions have clearly influenced the perceptions reflected in the policy framework and discussion. But community care is essentially 'redistributive'. So community care issues will be seen through political eyes. Therefore the success of a community care policy will depend on being able to work within the constraints and opportunities of broader political environments, and the sharpness of the distributive priorities defined and worked through in community care policies. One must ask whether good community care can be achieved without full and precise community care policy, and whether one can have full and precise community care policy without a rich and well-focused community care politics. If so, one must also ask whether there can be a rich and well-focused community care politics without a well developed community care polity: structures which represent interests and which define the issues, influence the bargaining, and channel the outcomes of the political process.

The style of planning advocated in the implementation documents could help to strengthen the local politics of community care. Quite how the principles are worked through in local authorities will influence the characteristics of the polities which emerge. Since who will benefit, and in what way, will be affected by most issues of structure and process in the development of community care, the existence of a politics of community care which provides checks and balances to executive action must depend on the degree to which the 'mobilisation of bias' is proportional to the effects of policy on interests. The consumers of community care do not find it easy to organise to present their views effectively. Few local consumer pressure groups have the resources for the sophisticated monitoring of the impacts of community care policy, or the development of local critiques which reflect national and international ideas.

There are examples of countries which have inserted into the polities organisations which can influence the mobilisation of bias. One example is the State and Area Administrations on Aging in the USA, and their broad state counterparts in Australia. Though their functions vary greatly in detail, the offices collect and report on data, and undertake policy analysis. They are often important in the politics of community care. In principle, they resemble the Low Pay Unit or the Equal Opportunities Commission. They are sufficiently separate from the agencies which perform care that they can work more closely with consumer interest groups.

The modernisation of long-term care is everywhere too recent for good histories to have been written. The Wisconsin history seems to be interesting (McDowell, Barniskis, and Wright, 1990; Spann, 1987). The interdependence of policy, politics, and the structure of the polity is clear. A new Secretary of the Department for Health and Social Services so organised arrangements for the development of community care that all client groups were subject to a similar policy framework. So the Wolfensberger normalisation arguments and the ideas of the independent living movement had an early impact. Arguments for all client groups were influenced. The Secretary recruited persons into the Department to play three roles: 'managerial enablers'; 'program translators' and 'missionaries'. 'Program translators' integrated and communicated management and advocacy concerns. Often single-minded and uncompromising, the missionaries aggressively defined and asserted the needs and interests of individual client groups at the program level. Translators and managers depended on the missionaries, because without which 'programs lack heart and concreteness and are vulnerable to failure in either the political arena or the operational context'. Among the recruits were 'vocal advocates'. The Secretary ensured that 'all relevant advocacy interests were represented in policy choices and program decisions', giving representatives of major advocacy organisations informal access to him, and ensuring that the shape of the program would be open to the influence of such of their ideas which bore rigorous examination. After the publication of planning guidelines, ten representative task forces (with state officials in the minority) tackled structured assignments, thus creating 'a coalition of categories' essential for widespread support. The process developed widespread enthusiasm for the programme.

Throughout Spann's account, the impression is created that the executive sought to develop the politics of community care and strengthen its polity. Key committee decisions were routinely presented to one of the translators 'to be transformed into ... descriptive language reflecting the agency's vision': 'compelling speeches and communiques humanised bureaucratic language, thereby influencing the attitudes and perceptions of both insiders and outsiders'. Translating the competing jargon of professional and other competing interest groups into clear and powerful vernacular helped to articulate the common and humanistic values. Debating issues in jargon restricts participation and so perceptions about what is important, and tends to imprison the participants in well-worn grooves reflecting their narrow professional concerns and sectional interests. This professional advocacy gave the program 'preeminence on the political agenda of the powerful network of advocates for the elderly'. The state official spent much time mobilising interest groups in the state: for instance talking in the evenings to consumer groups and agencies. The translators too worked to mobilise political strength in this way.

We see some British authorities doing something of the same (Jowell and Wistow, 1989). There must be ways in which national organisations could do more to help forward the development of local politics of community care.

5 Create community care laboratories for experiment, development and teaching

We have already argued the need for a lingua franca and a shared body of formal argument linking means and ends, both to promote and permit analysis of more technologically determinate community care. What might emerge are general but tightly-argued alternative models.

Each model would constitute a package consisting of structures and artifacts, expectations, skills and assumptions. Of course, they would not be off-the-peg precisely-specified blue-prints to which implementations must rigidly adhere in every detail. Diagram 13.4, it will be remembered, postulated a scanning process in which assumptions and local appreciations led to differences in the local variants created by applying the same universal principles. But they would be worked out and described in sufficient detail for them to be a useful basis for local adaptation.

It is undeniable that people moving into key positions find it easier to look for a fit between contexts and a model that already exists, and adapt the model. One could not simultaneously re-invent the modern car: the wheel, the mechanics, and the coachwork. Relying on invitations to invent anew is quite likely to encourage some areas smugly to produce the neolithic sledge. To avoid that, it is essential that we develop logically tough models, and expose them to evaluated demonstration of the kind which delivers the artifacts, assumptions, skills and expectations.

The original source of the models might be intensively evaluated research projects. However, some models have already been described in detail. For these models, a task which is quite as important is to establish expertise, confidence and commitment in each authority. Local demonstration projects could contribute greatly. They could be local laboratories for experiment and evaluated development, structured observation, learning and teaching: centres of excellence which mixed persons trained and experienced in the new methods with professionals for whom the experience would be an important part of their qualification for positions of influence in the outside world.

There are obvious dangers. In particular, to establish and maintain them successfully would require clear articulation of the model, close collaboration between the governmental sponsors and the host ssd in their development, and a contractual relationship between the two which ensured that the integrity of the demonstration was maintained over a long period. There is much less case for the casually commissioned demonstrations which are created when (small) pots of gold are offered with few strings to cash-starved providers as long as their protocols argue that the projects have some relevance to issues of current importance and make reference to fashionable concepts: the usual distracting model of central sponsorship in all the continents where we have had the chance to see centrally-funded innovation at work.

6 Raise the ratio of investment to consumption spending while the demographic pressure eases

The theme which unites many of these suggestions is the change to a new and more complex set of ends and means. This study illustrates the scale of the transformation needed. All agree that the development of community care will be difficult. We shall be able to add cubits to policy effectiveness only by large effort.

Industries which have and expect high rates of technical progress are characterised by high ratios of spending on their capacity to produce more efficiently to spending directly on production. We must raise the ratio of investment to other spending on the community social services.

Looked at more broadly even over a decade, it would be a great mistake to argue that this would be unaffordable. Whatever the macro-economic *nostre* of the day, vast increases in social expenditure are not necessary to cope with demographic change. Indeed, for a few years, demographic trends will actually lighten the burden on the public purse. This is illustrated in Table 14.5. Also illustrated is that later, we can again expect a steady increase in demands. What better time than this to make the investments which will allow the evolution of a system which will integrate the mixed economy with greater equity, efficiency, and above all, improved welfare? Successful investment in community care could be a political triumph bringing support from many voters. Failure to find the resources to make the investment could be electorally serious, and an opportunity to improve the quality of our national life permanently lost.

Table 14.5
Impact of demographic change on social expenditure and financing burdens, 1990-2030

Year	Social Expenditure	Financial burden/ population aged 15-64
1990	100	100
2000	99	98
2010	103	101
2020	107	106
2030	115	118

Source: OECD (1988), Table 22.
Assumes that real per capita benefits for quinquennial age groups remain the same over time. The benefits cover five major social programmes: education, health care, pensions, unemployment, compensation and family benefits. Tax expenditures are excluded. Some 90 per cent of total direct social outlays in the twelve OECD countries are covered. Index recalculated with 1990 = 100.

7 Conclusion

This study would have been easier to read (and to write) had there been clearer relations between needs, resources and outcomes in the services. However, it is worth remembering that one reason why the challenge seems to be so formidable is that policy-makers have implicitly set such difficult goals. The contributions used to justify additional spending on community care must be unambiguously demonstrable as well as real.

So the results of our analysis have been challenging indeed. Targeting has been neither as equitable nor as efficient as could be attained and marginal productivities seem to have been few and low. The 'goodies', authorities who by the criteria of the new managerialists have tried harder, seemed to be no more efficient than the 'baddies', though the difference in effort seemed great, and high spenders may have produced more equitable patterns of outcomes in some respects. Our analysis of structures and processes explains why the weaknesses exist, and show that the current arrangements do not have characteristics which will lead automatically to increased efficiency. Therefore, unless large investments are made and successfully yield high returns, the implicit policy of allowing most of the increase in demand for care to be met by raising levels of community services risks serious diswelfares and concomitant political opprobrium as the inevitable scandals break.

However, we cannot guarantee that the investments will yield the returns in better targeting and high productivities in the ways which are essential for the policy to be viable. No one close to the action and understanding the contrast between the new precepts and much current practice thinks that the required returns will quickly, certainly and automatically follow from the investments (Department of Health, 1990).

We return to the dilemma identified in the Preface. Changes of such magnitude, risk, and pervasiveness rarely work out with precisely the anticipated effects. There are no examples of authorities in this country or abroad which have worked them through entirely – in the one British authority which had in the decade since the first scheme started spread schemes for case-managed community care over the whole of its large area, the schemes still had a total caseload of only 31 per cent of the numbers in that authority's own residential homes and 14 per cent of the entire number in residential homes in its area. The scale in the authority with the second greatest cover was even smaller in relation to the numbers in the authority's own homes. Wisconsin, which had been developing the Community Options programme with great vigour, still supported many more residents in nursing homes. The history in the first British authority illustrates that even when starting from a stockaded scheme in each area, the quick removal of the stockade – the attempt to integrate the whole system around the new principles, the abandonment of the systems built to develop the stockaded oases – can drive out many of those who have learned to work in the new way, and swamp, isolate, and deprive others of influence on strategic development; and so force subsequent reinvention of assumptive, mechanical and structural wheels needed to make the model run. So we must not start on the process with illusions. The modernisation of long-term care will require resources and effort, and success cannot be guaranteed.

But Perestroika and Glasnost of some form or other has become essential: the existing system could not cope with the new worlds as adequately as with the old. Perestroika is already too far advanced for the clock to be turned back. And in the process, there is not a real alternative to tackling the basic parameters which determine equity and efficiency in community-based care. The alternative to shifting the balance of care by improving targeting and productivities in community-based care is a system which would rely unnecessarily and excessively on shelter-with-care. Shelter-with-care solutions are by definition a use of resources which reduces the degree of tailoring through time to changing individual circumstances: more of the resources are locked into services which produce benefits enjoyed collectively not individually. For many, the wastes which result more than cancel out the economies of scale and propinquity in the provision of services.

Also, we are now in a bad position from which to shift from the emphasis on improving community-based care to an emphasis on shelter-with-care. The public sector consists mainly of facilities which are obsolete by the criteria of best practice in the Netherlands or Denmark. Investment would almost certainly come substantially from the for-profit sector, whatever party were in power. It would be difficult for the nature of the provision to be other than supply-led, where the suppliers were continually favouring developments aimed primarily at privately financed demand made effective initially by tapping equity in owner-occupied housing. Privately-financed demand has proved to be price-inelastic in the US, and is probably so here when property prices are buoyant (Davies, 1986; and Davies and Knapp, 1988). The American experience suggests that with long-run excess demand for good quality accommodation, the State fights an up-hill battle to get an adequate supply of good quality service for those whom it finances, and attempts to do so have often escalated costs to public funds to an unnecessary degree. So this alternative policy of greater reliance on shelter-with-care raises still more complex problems. And it is not what most people really want.

So Griffiths and the government policy are right. However, we must not tie our fortunes to goals which cannot be achieved. We must not pretend to ourselves that we can achieve a massive short-run substitution for residential-based care by using community services without large long-run investments of resources and effort. And in the process we will have to recognise and engage issues which go beyond those already identified in current official thinking about implementing the White Paper, many and wide-ranging though they are by the criteria of only a few years ago. They must be the subject of another study.

Appendix to Chapter 2

Table A2.1
Predictor variables used in analysis of gross expenditure, cover, intensity, unit costs and the ratio of income from charges to gross expenditure for 1986/7

Need correlates

Estimated proportion of population aged 75 and over. Mean, 6.45; standard deviation, 1.27. CIPFA.

Total unemployment rate 1985.

Male unemployment rate 1985.

Female unemployment rate 1985.

Cost-raising factors

LABCOST 1985: DoE Local Government Labour Cost Index. Mean, 1.033; standard deviation, 0.052.

Sparsity: Hectares per thousand population. Mean, 273.1; standard deviation, 537.4.

Political characteristics of authority

Conservative control (CONCON) 1984. Conservatives hold more than 50 per cent of council seats after May elections. Mean, 0.328.

Labour control (LABCON) 1984. Analogous to CONCON. Mean, 0.422.

Solid Conservative control (SOLIDCON). Conservatives hold more than 50 per cent of council seats in 1974, 1979, and 1984. Mean, 0.215.

Solid Labour control (SOLIDLAB). Analogous to SOLIDCON. Mean, 0.259.

Swing to Conservatives (SWINGCON). Number of Conservative seats greater in 1984 than 1979, and greater in 1979 than 1974. Mean, 0.086; standard deviation, 0.413.

Swing to Labour (SWINGLAB). Analogous to SWINGCON. Mean, 0.026; standard deviation, 0.159.

Swing to other parties (SWINGOTH). Analogous to SWINGCON. Mean, 0.147; standard deviation, 0.355.

Volatility in party representation (INDXPOL). Absolute sum of differences in proportions held by each party between 1974 and 1979, and 1979 and 1984. Mean, 0.751; standard deviation, 0.406.

Fiscal circumstances and characteristics of authority 1985/6

Local rate and grant-borne expenditure estimates per head. Mean, 543.8; standard deviation, 1382.4.

Per cent rate and grant-borne expenditure met from rates. Mean, 60.5; standard deviation, 11.9.

Variation from Grant-Related Expenditure per head. Mean, -776.2; standard deviation, 8756.6

Per cent variation from Target expenditure. Mean, 1.32; standard deviation, 2.55.

Per capita Block Grant claim after Penalty. Mean, 162.8; standard deviation, 56.4.

Per cent increase in rate- and grant-borne expenditure met from the rates, 1979-1985. Mean, 133.4; standard deviation, 190.3.

Table A2.1 (continued)

Service policies and characteristics
Ratio of home help hours paid to hours received. Mean, 1.211; standard deviation, 0.174.
Ratio of home helps to organisers. Mean, 21.4; standard deviation, 7.8.
Ratio of home help organisers to cases. Mean, 0.004; standard deviation, 0.002.
Ratio of home help cases aged 75 and more to cases aged 65-74. Mean, 3.206; standard deviation, 0.981.
Per cent home helps part-time. Mean, 89.9; standard deviation, 18.6.
Minimum home help charge per week. Mean, 0.397; standard deviation, 0.642.
Flat rate home help charge. Mean, 0.824; standard deviation, 1.229.
Maximum home help charge per hour. Mean, 1.465; standard deviation, 1.437.
Minimum home help charge per hour. Mean, 0.070; standard deviation, 0.257.
Minimum home help charge per week. Mean, 0.397; standard deviation, 0.642.

Date of last review of home help charges.
Residents supported by the authority in all residential homes per thousand population aged 75 and over. Mean, 0.70; standard deviation, 0.096.
Net expenditure on meals-on-wheels per thousand population aged 65 and over. Mean, 6.508; standard deviation, 21.97.
Net expenditure on day centres per thousand population aged 75 and over. Mean, 24.62; standard deviation, 60.08.

Table A2.2
Intercorrelations of (log) cover, (log) intensity and (log) unit costs, and the proportions of the variance in (log) gross expenditure explained by each[a]

Variable correlations (log)	Variance in			Gross expenditure explained (per cent)
	Log intensity	Log unit costs	Log gross expenditure	
Log cover[b]	–	–	0.692	85.2
Log intensity[b]	1	–0.301	–	11.2
Log unit costs[b]		1	–	13.4
Log gross expenditure[b]			1	100.0

– not significantly different from zero
a Based on authorities making returns of data required for the computations of each variable published in CIPFA Social Services Statistics 1985/6
b per estimated population aged 75 and over

Table A2.3
Model results for log gross expenditure

	Parameter estimates	
	(a)	(b)
Regression coefficients		
Per cent population aged 75 and over	–0.128**	–0.116
Index of representational instability	–0.221	
Labour majority 1984	0.318**	
Labour cost index		3.186**
Residential homes provision		3.536**
Conservative majority 1984		–0.403**
Goodness of fit		
Adjusted coefficient of determination	0.244	0.546
Equation F-value	10.27***	23.86***

Column (a) reports the third step of an analysis. Had their coefficients been significant at the 10 per cent level, the analysis would also have allowed the admission of political and employment variables and sparsity. It is based on 87 authorities.
Column (b) reports the sixth step of an analysis. Had their coefficients been significantly different from 0 at the 10 per cent level, the analysis would also have allowed the admission of the provision of day centres and the provision of meals. It is based on 77 authorities.

All parameter estimates significantly different from zero at 10 per cent level of significance or below.
* Significantly different from 0 at 5 per cent level
** Significantly different from 0 at 1 per cent level
*** Significantly different from 0 at 0.1 per cent level

Table A2.4
Model results for log cover

	Parameter estimates	
	(a)	(b)
Regression coefficients		
Residents in all residential homes	20.581***	
Net expenditure on meals-on-wheels	–0.074***	
Conservative control at all three dates	–0.788***	
Ratio of older to younger elderly		–0.231**
Home help organisers per case		–109.678*
Population sparsity		0.000026
Goodness of fit		
Adjusted coefficient of determination	0.72***	0.117
F-value	53.56***	5.80**
Significance of partial correlations of omitted variables		
Labour control at all three dates	+***	
Labour majority	+***	
Swing to Conservatives	+***	
Population sparsity	–***	
Per cent of population aged 75 and over	–***	

Column (a) reports the third step of an analysis. Had their coefficients been significant at the 10 per cent level, the analysis would also have allowed the admission of political, fiscal and employment-related variables, the provision of day centres, sparsity, the labour cost index, and the proportion of the population aged 75 and over. It is based on 61 authorities.

Column (b) reports the third step of an analysis. Had their coefficients been significantly different from 0 at the 10 per cent level, the analysis would also have allowed the admission of the rate of home helps to organisers, the proportion of home helps part-time and the ratio of hours paid to hours secured by clients. It is based on 73 authorities.

*   Significantly different from 0 at 5 per cent level
**   Significantly different from 0 at 1 per cent level
***   Significantly different from 0 at 0.1 per cent level

Table A2.5
Correlations of log cover, log intensity and log unit costs with service operating characteristics

	Log cover	Log intensity	Log unit costs
Log cover	1		
Log intensity		1	
Log unit costs		–0.301	1
Ratio of home helps to organisers			–0.379
Per cent home helps part time			–0.286
Ratio of cases 75 and over to cases 65-74		–0.363	0.273
Ratio of hours paid to hours received		–0.218	0.295
Ratio of organisers to cases	–0.253		0.379
Population sparsity		0.295	

*   Significantly different from 0 at 5 per cent level
**   Significantly different from 0 at 1 per cent level
***   Significantly different from 0 at 0.1 per cent level

Table A2.6
Model results for log intensity

	Parameter estimates
Regression coefficients	
Population sparsity	0.0000148***
Ratio of hours paid to hours received	−0.326*
Ratio of organisers to cases	81.281***
Ratio of home helps to organisers	0.014***
Goodness of fit	
Adjusted coefficient of determination	0.30
F-value	8.81***

The results are reported for the fourth step. Had they reached the 10 per cent significance level, the analysis would also have allowed the admission of the proportion of home helps part-time and the ratio of the number of home help recipients aged between 65 and 74 to the number aged 75 and over. It is for 73 authorities.
* Significantly different from 0 at 5 per cent level
** Significantly different from 0 at 1 per cent level
*** Significantly different from 0 at 0.1 per cent level

Table A2.7
Model results for log unit costs

	Parameter estimates	
	(a)	(b)
Regression coefficients		
Labour cost index	2.020***	2.486***
Ratio of organisers to cases	43.083****	
Log intensity	0.282***	
Labour majority 1984	−0.048	
Ratio of hours paid to hours received	0.252**	
Variation of total spending from block grant target	0.018**	
Per cent increase expenditure financed from rates	0.0000190*	
Population sparsity	0.00000611*	
Index of representational instability		0.113*
Conservative majority in all three years		0.093*
Swing to Conservatives		0.122
Goodness of fit		
Adjusted coefficient of determination	0.70***	0.51***
F-value	21.31**	19.33***

Column (a) reports the eighth step of an analysis. Had the results reached the 10 per cent level of significance, the analysis would also have allowed the admission of political, fiscal, and employment-related indicators, the proportion of the population aged 75 and over, the ratio of home helps to organisers and the proportion of home helps working part-time. It is for 71 authorities.
Column (b) reports the fourth step of an analysis. Had the results reached the 10 per cent level of significance, the analysis would also have allowed the admission of political, fiscal, and employment-related indicators, sparsity, and the proportion of the population aged 75 and over.
All coefficients significantly different from zero at the 10 per cent level.
* Significantly different from 0 at 5 per cent level
** Significantly different from 0 at 1 per cent level
*** Significantly different from 0 at 0.1 per cent level

Table A2.8
Model results for the ratio of charges to gross expenditures

	Parameter estimates
Regression coefficients	
Minimum home help charge per week	0.047***
Flat rate home help charge	0.015**
Labour majority	–0.035*
Per cent increase in expenditure financed by rates	–0.0000064
Swing to Conservatives	–0.043
Goodness of fit	
Adjusted coefficient of determination	0.58***
F-value	12.84***

Estimates reported for the fifth step of an analysis. Had their coefficients been significantly different from zero at the 10 per cent level, the analysis would have admitted political, fiscal and employment-related indicators, sparsity, the proportion of the population aged 75 and over, the maximum charge per hour, the minimum charge per week and the date of the last review of charges.
All coefficients significantly different from zero at the 10 per cent level.
* Significantly different from 0 at 5 per cent level
** Significantly different from 0 at 1 per cent level
*** Significantly different from 0 at 0.1 per cent level

Table A2.9
Analysis of expenditure recovery ratios: dependent and independent variables

Dependent variables
Home help ratio 1977. Mean, 4.9; standard deviation, 4.1.; minimum, 0; maximum 18.4.
Home help ratio 1987. Mean, 5.9; standard deviation, 5.6; minimum, 0; maximum, 21.6. 1987/8.
Proportionate increase in home help ratio 1977-1987.
Meals-on-wheels ratio 1977. Mean, 28.7; standard deviation, 18.6; minimum, 0; maximum, 73.6.
Meals-on-wheels ratio 1987. Mean, 38.2; standard deviation, 21.4; minimum, 0; maximum, 100.
Proportionate increase in meals ratio 1977-87.
Day care ratio 1977. Mean, 15.6; standard deviation, 13.8; minimum, 0; maximum, 66.0.
Day care ratio 1987. Mean, 17.4; standard deviation, 14.5; minimum, 0; maximum, 89.2.
Proportionate increase in day care ratio 1977-87.
Authorities' own residential homes ratio 1977. Mean, 28.5; standard deviation, 3.5; minimum, 18.6; maximum, 46.3.
Authorities' own residential homes ratio 1987. Mean, 35.2; standard deviation, 6.4; minimum, 18.4; maximum, 46.9.
Proportionate increase in homes ratio 1977-87.

Table A2.9 (continued)

Party representational and representational volatility
Per cent seats held by Conservative party (CONPC). 1977. Mean, 51.0; standard deviation, 27.8; minimum, 0; maximum, 93.1. 1987. Mean, 31.8; standard deviation, 19.8; minimum, 0; maximum, 73.3.
Per cent seats held by Labour party (LABPC). 1977. Mean, 37.5; standard deviation, 27.5; minimum, 0; maximum, 100. 1987. Mean, 47.7; standard deviation, 25.4; minimum, 0; maximum 98.3.
Conservative control: Conservatives held more than 50 per cent of seats (CONCON). 1977: mean, 0.565. 1987: mean, 0.183.
Labour control (LABCON). 1977: mean, 0.322. 1987: Mean: 0.435.
Solid Conservative control: Conservatives hold more than 50 per cent of the seats in 1974, 1979, and 1987. (SOLIDCON). 1977: Mean 0.139.
Solid Labour control (SOLIDLAB). Mean: 0.204.
Index of representational volatility: Absolute sum of changes in the proportion of the seats held by each party. Mean, 1.05; standard deviation, 0.516; minimum, 0.11; maximum, 2.45.

Prevalence of low incomes in the target group
Low incomes in 1975 (LOIN). Source: DoE. Mean, 23273; standard deviation, 3762; minimum, 17190; maximum, 35720.
Supplementary benefit receipt in 1976 (SUPBEN). Source: DoE. Mean, 22831; standard deviation, 14852; minimum, 4561; maximum, 77415.
Supplementary pensioners per population aged 65 and over 1986 (UR1). Source: DoE. Mean: 21.6; standard deviation, 7.1; minimum, 7.26; maximum, 42.7.
Pensioner claimants per population aged 65 and over 1986 (UR2). Source: DoE. Mean, 21.1; standard deviation, 6.3; minimum, 11,1; maximum, 43.7.
Ratio of UR1 1986 to LOIN 1975. Predictor for ratios of ratios only.
Ratio of UR1 1986 to SUPBEN 1975. Predictor for ratios of ratios only.
Ratio of UR2 1986 to LOIN 1975. Predictor for ratios of ratios only.
Ratio of UR2 1986 to SUPBEN 1975. Predictor for ratios of ratios only.

Interactions between low income prevalence and political variables
The interaction terms were defined as (X - MEAN OF X)(Y - MEAN OF Y), thus retaining the the effects of the relative variation of the two variables on the interaction term but removing the effects of arbitrary scale effects in measuring them.
The effects of square and cube terms of variables were explored.

Table A2.10
Analysis of expenditure recovery ratios in 1977 and 1987: the effects of representational characteristics and high proportions of target populations – poverty

Ratio	Adjusted R^2	Predictor variable	Regression coefficient	Significance of coefficient	Number of authorities
Home help 1977	0.48	LABPC	-0.16052	0.0001	110
		(LABPC)^2	0.00113	0.0060	
		SUPBEN	-19.2487	0.0036	
		(SUPBEN)^2	9.71108	0.0196	
		CONSTANT	14.5216		
Home help 1987	0.36	CONÇON	3.555	0.0043	106
		(UR1)^2	-0.0049	0.0150	
		(UR1.LABPC)^2	-6.432	0.0011	
		CONSTANT	11.394		
Home help 1987/1977	0.15	CONCON77	-4346.8	0.0008	92
		LABCON87 BUT NOT 77	5629.3	0.0004	
		UR1	-231.8	0.0148	
		(UR1/LOINC77)	-33978.6	0.0685	
		CONSTANT	7956.7		
		UR1	24203.82	0.0000	
		(UR1)^2	-988.67	0.0000	
		(UR1)^3	12.96	0.0000	
		(UR1/LOIN79)	-91960.4	0.0655	
Meals-on-wheels 1977	0.11	LABCON	-15.1050	0.0002	
		(LOIN)^2	0.0920	0.0311	
		CONSTANT	30.2672		
Meals-on-wheels 1987	0.12	UR2	-1.2128	0.0002	99
		CONSTANT	64.98		

Table A2.10 (continued)

Ratio	Adjusted R^2	Predictor variable	Regression coefficient	Significance of coefficient	Number of authorities
Meals-on-wheels 1987/77 (UR186/LOINC75)	0.16	(INDXPOL.CONCH) 1584.6 CONSTANT	4774.6 0.0213 100.13	0.0008	84
Day care 1977		No relationships from which to construct model found.			
Day care 1987	0.25	(SOLIDLAB.UR1) (SOLIDLAB.UR1)^2 (SOLIDLAB.UR1)^3 CONSTANT	14.668 −3.588 0.2138 16.59	0.594 0.218 0.0057	92
Day care 1987/1977	0.02	LABPC87 LABCON77 (CONPC)^2 (CONPC)^3 LABCON 87 BUT NOT 77 UR1 CONSTANT	3.427 −195.62 0.251 −0.00309 −157.19 15.92 −387.81	0.237 0.231 0.171 0.243 0.310 0.044	81
Authorities' own residential homes 1977	0.24	SOLIDLAB (LOIN.SOLIDLAB) (LOIN.SOLIDLAB)^2 (LOIN.SOLIDLAB)^3 CONSTANT	−15.4864 7.879 −1.3050 0.0648 30.78	0.0508 0.0420 0.0193 0.0059	105
Authorities' own residential homes 1987	0.38	LABPC UR2 (SOLIDLAB.UR2)^3 CONSTANT	−0.0785 −0.5172 0.0172 49.18	0.0040 0.0000 0.0000	93
Authorities' own residential homes 1977/87	0.36	SOLIDLAB LABPC77 NOT CONCON87 BUT CONCON 77 CONSTANT	14.27 −0.620 −10.19 184.42	0.0067 0.0070 0.0067	91

Table A2.11
Raw variables from which were constructed the variables used in the exploration of the responsiveness of home help hours consumed to price

Need type of least handicapped client in household
Ability to undertake light housework at the first interview
Change in the ability to undertake light housework between the two interviews
Confusion at the time of the first interview
Change in confusion between the interviews
Death of spouse shortly preceding the first interview
Ability to care for self at first interview
Change in ability to care for self between the interviews
Meals-on-wheels inputs over period
Nursing inputs preceding first interview
Nursing inputs over period
Day hospital attendances
Days per week meals prepared by informal carers
Number of persons to do favour or run errands at time of first interview
Change in number of persons to do favours or run errands between the
    interviews
Number of persons to turn to in time of difficulty at time of first interview
Change in number of persons to turn to in time of difficulty at time of first
    interview
Neighbourhood: poor, good, rural
Bath or shower not shared
Central heating
Ownership of: washing machine; tumble drier; car; telephone; refrigerator; freezer
Special chair
Wheel chair
Walking aid
Handrail in bathroom
Special handrail on stairs
Hoist
Extension arm
Money difficulties at time of first interview
Money difficulties got worse
Urinary incontinence at time of first interview
Urinary incontinence worsened between two interviews
Faecal incontinence at time of first interview
Faecal incontinence worsened between two interviews
Satisfaction with housework at first interview
Satisfaction with housework at second interview
Satisfaction with social contact at first interview
Satisfaction with social contact at second interview
Ability to produce meals at time of first interview
Ability to produce meals at time of second interview
Need group of least dependent member of household
Single male
Single female
Whether multiple client household
PGC Morale score at time of second interview
Index of clients' felt vulnerability to risks
Ability to perform heavy instrumental activities of daily living
Attended a day hospital between first and second interview
Positive attitude to service receipt

Appendix to Chapter 3

Table A3.1
Definitions of need-related circumstances and characteristics of clients included in the statistical modelling

Variable label	Description	Mean	S.D.	Min. value	Max. value	No. of valid cases
Socio-economic variables at time of first interview						
CLEAN1	Whether adequate standard of cleanliness[a]	0.079	0.270	0	1	521
POOR	Whether neighbourhood poor[a]	0.108	0.310	0	1	575
OWNOCC	Whether house is owner occupied?	0.405	0.491	0	1	521
Dependency factors at time of first interview						
MYTYPO1	Whether typology category 1	0.158	0.365	0	1	575
MYTYPO2	Whether typology category 2	0.101	0.301	0	1	575
MYTYPO3	Whether typology category 3	0.163	0.370	0	1	575
MYTYPO4	Whether typology category 4	0.210	0.408	0	1	575
MYTYPO5	Whether typology category 5	0.106	0.308	0	1	575
MYTYPO6	Whether typology category 6	0.115	0.319	0	1	575
ADLSELF1	Ability to perform self-care domestic tasks[b]	8.205	3.904	0	14	518
ADLHOM1A	Ability to perform light care tasks[b]	4.260	2.143	0	6	516
ADLHOM1B	Ability to perform heavy domestic care tasks[b]	1.479	1.722	0	5	516
URIN1	Whether incontinent of urine	0.339	0.662	0	2	514
FAECAL1	Whether incontinent of faeces	0.132	0.413	0	2	507
CF1	Whether evidence of confusion	0.163	0.370	0	1	575
Dependency factors at time of second interview						
ADLSELF2	Ability to perform self-care tasks[b]	8.815	3.902	0	14	395
ADLHOM2A	Ability to perform light domestic care tasks[b]	4.354	2.124	0	6	291
ADLHOM2B	Ability to perform heavy domestic care tasks[b]	1.419	1.670	0	5	291
Change in dependency between first and second interviews						
ADLSELFX	Change in ability to perform self-care tasks[c]	0.327	3.574	-12	14	394
ADLHOMAX	Change in ability to perform light domestic care tasks[c]	-0.107	1.472	-6	6	289
ADLHOMBX	Change in ability to perform heavy domestic care tasks[c]	-0.014	1.364	-4	5	290
URINX	Change in urinary continence[d]	1.970	0.460	1	3	397
FAECALX	Change in faecal continence[d]	2.033	0.368	1	3	389
CFX	Change in state of confusion[d]	0.010	0.100	0	1	298
Life events in year before first interview						
ILLNESS1	Whether sudden serious illness	0.192	0.394	0	1	521
ACCID1	Whether serious accident/injury	0.127	0.333	0	1	521
HEALTH1	Whether health problem causing disability	0.345	0.476	0	1	521

Table A3.1 (continued)

Variable label	Description	Mean	S.D.	Min. value	Max. value	No. of valid cases
OTHPER1	Whether sudden serious illness/accident/injury of close person	0.058	0.233	0	1	521
DEATHSP1	Whether death of spouse	0.035	0.183	0	1	521
DEATHHH1	Whether death of other person in household	0.015	0.123	0	1	521
DEATHOT1	Whether death of close person outside household	0.102	0.303	0	1	521
MOVEHO1	Whether moved house	0.090	0.287	0	1	521
HOSP3M1	Whether been in hospital	0.370	0.483	0	1	521
AWAY1	Whether been away from home other than for holiday	0.044	0.206	0	1	521
MONEY1	Whether money difficulties	0.098	0.297	0	1	521
PRESSMO1	Whether pressure to move house	0.012	0.107	0	1	521
BURG1	Whether been burgled	0.012	0.107	0	1	521
NEIGH1	Whether problems with neighbours	0.035	0.183	0	1	521
HOUSE1	Whether house repair problems	0.048	0.214	0	1	521
Life events between first and second interviews						
ILLNESS2	Whether sudden serious illness	0.085	0.280	0	1	398
ACCID2	Whether serious accident/injury	0.053	0.224	0	1	398
HEALTH2	Whether health problem causing disability	0.204	0.403	0	1	398
OTHPER2	Whether sudden serious illness/accident/injury of close person	0.028	0.164	0	1	398
DEATHSP2	Whether death of spouse	0.038	0.191	0	1	398
DEATHHH2	Whether death of other person in household	0.008	0.087	0	1	398
DEATHOT2	Whether death of close person outside household	0.083	0.276	0	1	398
MOVEHO2	Whether moved house	0.025	0.157	0	1	398
HOSP2	Whether been in hospital	0.186	0.390	0	1	398
AWAY2	Whether been away from home other than for holiday	0.043	0.202	0	1	398
MONEY2	Whether money difficulties	0.083	0.276	0	1	398
BURG2	Whether been burgled	0	0	0	0	398
NEIGH2	Whether problems with neighbours	0.020	0.141	0	1	398
HOUSE2	Whether house repair problems	0.050	0.219	0	1	398
Social interaction variables at time of first interview						
COME1	Frequency of visits by friends/relatives	3.388	1.470	0	5	521
GOTO1	Frequency of visits to friends/relatives	2.349	0.809	2	5	521
FAVOURS1	Number of people willing to do small favours	0.944	0.775	0	3	519
DIFFTIM1	Number of people to turn to in times of difficulty	0.710	0.723	0	3	520

Table A3.1 (continued)

Variable label	Description	Mean	S.D.	Min. value	Max. value	No. of valid cases
Change in social interaction between first and second interviews						
COMEX	Change in frequency of visits by friends/relatives	-0.113	1.297	-5	5	398
GOTOX	Change in frequency of visits to friends/relatives	0.013	0.956	-3	3	398
FAVOURSX	Change in number of people willing to do small favours	-0.074	0.760	-2	3	394
DIFFTIMX	Change in number of people to turn to in times of difficulty	0.008	0.787	-2	2	393
LOSSCONF	Whether loss of confidante	1.796	0.403	1	2	393
Attitude to receipt of social services at time of first interview						
POSATT	Whether positive attitude to social services	0.530	0.500	0	1	575
NEGATT	Whether negative attitude to social services	0.157	0.364	0	1	575
Receipt of services						
AIDS	Number of physical aids/adaptations provided and used	0.762	1.128	0	8	395
DAYHOSP1	Whether attended day hospital during study period	0.068	0.253	0	1	-395
DAYHOSP2	Days at day hospital in fortnight before second interview	0.102	0.571	0	6	394
NURSE1	Whether community nursing input before first interview	0.426	0.495	0	1	521
NURSE2	Number of visits by nurse in fortnight before second interview	1.349	3.041	0	18	398
HHCINP	Average weekly hours of home help/care[e]	2.759	3.716	0	44.23	568
DCINP	Average weekly days of day care[e]	0.219	0.676	0	7.14	574
MOWINP	Average weekly meals on wheels[e]	0.883	1.698	0	7.10	565
STCINP	Average weekly days of short stay[e]	0.047	0.300	0	5	575
SWINP	Level of social work input during study period (none, low, medium, high)	0.817	1.193	0	3	574
Informal care support (at second interview)						
INFBED	Days per week informal care support with going to bed	0.089	0.726	0	7	575
INFMEAL	Days per week informal care support getting meals	0.635	1.821	0	7	575
INFHWK	Proportion of housework done by informal carer(s)	0.369	0.989	0	4	575

Table A3.1 (continued)

Variable label	Description	Mean	S.D.	Min. value	Max. value	No. of valid cases
Private sources of help						
PRIVNUR2	Whether private nurse attended during study period	0.015	0.122	0	1	398
PRIVNUR3	Whether private nurse visiting at time of second interview	0.015	0.122	0	1	398
PRIVHWK1	Whether private domestic help at time of first interview	0.050	0.219	0	1	397
PRIVHWK2	Whether private domestic help during study period	0.050	0.219	0	1	397
PRIVHWK3	Whether private domestic help at time of second interview	0.048	0.214	0	1	396
PRIVOTH1	Whether other private help at time of first interview	0.006	0.079	0	1	481
Voluntary sources of help during study period						
VOLHWK	Whether voluntary group helped with housework	0.008	0.087	0	1	398
VOLAD	Whether voluntary group gave any support or advice	0.050	0.219	0	1	398
VOLTR	Whether voluntary group provides transport	0.015	0.122	0	1	398
VOLOTH	Whether voluntary group gives other help	0.050	0.219	0	1	398

Notes:
a Assessed by interviewer
b 0 = lowest level of ability
c Positive scores indicate greater ability and vice versa
d Indicating onset or worsening of state
e Computed by dividing total receipt by number of weeks in study

Table A3.2
Simple correlations between significant need-related characteristics and service inputs

This table demonstrates the direct measures of association between need-related characteristics of elderly clients and the level of individual services (and service packages) received. Definitions of the variables appear in Table A3.1. Variables appearing in the models which have no significant direct association with the service concerned do NOT appear in this Table.

All households			Single person households		
I. Allocation of home help/home care services					
Socio-economic variables					
HHOLD1	0.11**		GENDER	0.09*	M
HHOLD2	–0.07*		OWNOCC	0.10*	
Dependency indicators					
MYTYPO1	–0.12***		MYTYPO1	–0.13**	
MYTYPO4	0.07*	M			
MYTYPO6	0.14***	M	MYTYPO6	0.11**	M
ADLHOM1A	–0.18***		ADLHOM1A	–0.29***	M
ADLHOM1B	–0.19***		ADLHOM1B	–0.22***	
ADLSELF1	–0.21***	M	ADLSELF1	–0.26***	
FAECAL1	0.08*		FAECAL1	0.10*	
ADLHOM2A	–0.33***		ADLHOM2A	–0.47***	
			ADLHOMAX	0.11*	
ADLHOM2B	–0.31***		ADLHOM2B	–0.35***	
ADLSELF2	–0.22***		ADLSELF2	–0.23***	
URINX	0.07*		URINX	0.08*	
Adverse life events					
DEATHSP1	0.07*	M			
MOVEHO1	–0.07*				
HOSP3M1	0.14***		HOSP3M1	0.18***	
AWAY1	0.06*				
MONEY1	–0.08*	M			
MONEY1	–0.09*				
HOUSE2	0.08*		HOUSE2	0.15**	M
			ILLNESS2	0.09*	
Social interaction factors					
GOTOX	–0.13***		GOTOX	–0.16***	
FAVOURSX	0.07*				
DIFFTIMX	0.07*	M	DIFFTIMX	0.18***	
Substitute services					
DAYHOSP1	0.12***		DAYHOSP1	0.08*	
NURSE1	0.15***		NURSE1	0.17***	
DAYHOSP2	0.14***	M	DAYHOSP2	0.11**	
NURSE2	0.17***	M	NURSE2	0.16***	M
SWINP	0.20***	M	SWINP	0.15***	M
DCINP	0.07*				
MOWINP	0.21***	M	MOWINP	0.14**	M
Informal support					
INFHWK	–0.09**				

Table A3.2 (continued)

All households			Single person households	
Support from the private sector				
PRIVHWK2	−0.11**		PRIVHWK2	−0.11**
PRIVHWK3	−0.10**		PRIVHWK3	−0.10*
II. Allocations of meals-on-wheels				
Attitude to service receipt				
POSATT	−0.11*			
NEGATT	0.14**			
Dependency indicators				
MYTYPO2	−0.10*			
MYTYPO4	0.13*			
MYTYPO6	0.12*			
ADLHOM1B	−0.16**			
ADLSELF1	−0.11*			
URIN1	0.11*			
ADLHOM2A	−0.31***			
ADLHOM2B	−0.24***			
ADLSELF2	−0.38***			
ADLHOMAX	−0.17**			
ADLSELFX	−0.17**	M		
FAECALX	0.15**	M		
Adverse life events				
ILLNESS2	−0.18**			
HEALTH2	0.13*			
DEATHSP2	−0.13*			
AWAY2	−0.13*			
Social interaction factors				
GOTO1	−0.18**			
LOSSCONF	0.15**			
Substitute services				
AIDS	0.23**			
DAYHOSP1	0.15**	M		
STCINP	−0.13**			
Support from the voluntary sector				
VOLTR	−0.16**			
VOLOTH	−0.15**			
III. Allocation of day care services				
Socio-economic variables				
POOR	−0.13*			
Dependency indicators				
MYTYPO4	0.21**	M		
ADLHOM1A	−0.14*			
ADLSELF1	0.15*			
URIN1	−0.20**	M		
CF1	0.18**			
ADLHOM2A	−0.23**			
ADLHOMAX	−0.26**			
CFX	0.32***			

Table A3.2 (continued)

All households			Single person households		
Adverse life events					
ACCID1	0.18**	M			
BURG1	–0.12*				
HOUSE1	0.17**				
HEALTH2	–0.19**				
HOSP2	–0.19**				
AWAY2	0.14*				
MONEY2	–0.15*				
Social interaction factors					
GOTOX	0.15*				
Substitute services					
AIDS	–0.20**	M			
Informal support					
INFBED	0.16**				
IV. Allocation of social work support					
Socio-economic variables					
HHOLD3	–0.12**				
POOR	0.16**		POOR	0.17**	
Dependency indicators					
MYTYPO1	0.13**		MYTYPO1	0.17**	
			MYTYPO3	0.13*	
			MYTYPO4	–0.09*	
URIN1	–0.11*				
FAECAL1	–0.11*		FAECAL1	–0.22**	
CF1	–0.14**		CF1	–0.16**	
ADLHOM2B	–0.17**		ADLHOM2B	–0.23**	
			URINX	–0.13*	M
Adverse life events					
ILLNESS1	0.13**	M	ILLNESS1	0.15*	
ACCID1	–0.15**				
OTHPER1	–0.18***				
DEATHHH1	–0.17***		DEATHHH1	–0.16**	
HOSP3M1	0.09*		DEATHOT1	0.12*	
DEATHHH2	–0.14**		DEATHOT2	0.17*	
Social interaction factors					
COME1	0.10*		COME1	0.19**	
FAVOURS1	0.14**		GOTOX	0.15*	
			DIFFTIMX	0.16*	M
LOSSCONF	–0.14**		LOSSCONF	–0.18**	
Substitute services					
			AIDS	0.19**	
DAYHOSP2	0.11*		DAYHOSP2	0.14*	
DCINP	–0.11*		HHCINP	0.13*	
Informal support					
INFBED	–0.09*		INFBED	–0.13*	

Table A3.2 (continued)

All households			Single person households		

V. Allocations of service packages

Socio-economic variables and attitude to service receipt

All households			Single person households		
HHOLD1	−0.31***	M			
HHOLD2	−0.13***				
POSATT	−0.07*				
NEGATT	0.14***		NEGATT	0.13**	

Dependency indicators

MYTYPO1	−0.17***	M	MYTYPO1	−0.21***	
MYTYPO2	−0.08**		MYTYPO2	−0.19***	
			MYTYPO3	0.09*	
MYTYPO4	0.12***		MYTYPO4	0.10*	
			MYTYPO5	0.11**	
MYTYPO6	0.15***		MYTYPO6	0.14***	
ADLHOM1A	−0.22***	M	ADLHOM1A	−0.43***	M
ADLHOM1B	−0.29***	M	ADLHOM1B	−0.34***	
ADLSELF1	−0.24***		ADLSELF1	−0.38***	M
URIN1	0.09**		URIN1	0.09+	
FAECAL1	0.11***		FAECAL1	0.14***	
CF1	0.18***		CF1	0.26***	
ADLHOM2A	−0.38***		ADLHOM2A	−0.49***	
ADLHOM2B	−0.38***		ADLHOM2B	−0.45***	
ADLSELF2	−0.31***		ADLSELF2	−0.45***	
ADLHOMAX	−0.09*	M			
ADLHOMBX	−0.11**	M	ADLHOMBX	−0.11*	
ADLSELFX	−0.13***		ADLSELFX	−0.15**	M
URINX	0.06*		URINX	0.09*	M
CFX	0.07*				

Adverse life events

ACCID1	−0.07*	M	ACCID1	−0.11	
BURG1	0.07*		BURG1	0.12**	
			MOVEHO1	0.11**	
			AWAY1	0.08*	
			MONEY1	−0.08*	
HOSP2	0.15***		HOSP2	0.16***	
AWAY2	0.10**		AWAY2	0.09*	
DEATHOT2	0.09**		MONEY2	−0.11*	

Social interaction factors

GOTO1	−0.12***		GOTO1	−0.19***	
FAVOURS1	−0.14***		FAVOURS1	−0.23***	M
			DIFFTIM1	−0.11**	
LOSSCONF	0.10**		LOSSCONF	0.08*	
DIFFTIMX	−0.07*		COMEX	−0.09*	

Substitute services

AIDS	0.07*		AIDS	0.13**	
DAYHOSP1	0.16***	M	DAYHOSP1	0.15***	M
DAYHOSP2	0.11***		DAYHOSP2	0.11**	
NURSE2	0.15***	M	NURSE2	0.14***	

Table A3.2 (continued)

All households		Single person households	
Informal support			
INFHWK	–0.11***		
Private and voluntary sector support			
PRIVHWK2	–0.11***	PRIVHWK2	–0.21***
PRIVHWK3	–0.10**	PRIVHWK3	–0.18***
PRIVOTH3	0.07*	PRIVOTH3	0.10*
SOCCLUB1	–0.08**	SOCCLUB1	–0.10**

Pearson correlations are used as the measure of association.
Significance levels are indicated as follows: * = 90 per cent; ** = 95 per cent; *** = 99 per cent.
'M' written after the measure of association denotes the presence of the variable in the model of service receipt.

Table A3.3
Definitions of levels of social work

Service	Level	Definition
Social work	Low	Low level of service. Cases where the situation was resolved after, at most, a couple of visits or one or two liaison phone calls.
	Medium	Medium level of service. Cases with heavier involvement, with up to eight or so face to face visits, more extensive liaison, or possibly a case conference.
	High	High level of service. Cases with much more considerable involvement, repeated face-to-face visiting, either very intensively or frequently over a longer period, usually amounting to at least eight visits over the study period, often associated with crises and entailing considerable liaison work.

Appendix to Chapter 5
Estimating the costs of the services provided to the elderly in the sample

This appendix outlines the methods of estimating the private opportunity cost for the social services provided to the elderly in our sample. Caveats in the estimation are also mentioned. It should be noted that the general principle of estimation is given, although where certain pieces of information were not available some alternative but similar approach was employed. All financial data used relate to that recorded for the 1984/85 financial year for the area being studied.

1 Domiciliary care services

This concerns home helps, home care assistants and community wardens. Here we shall describe the estimation for home helps. The method applied to the other two services was very similar.

We took the gross wage paid to a home help including any employer's National Insurance and superannuation contributions and multiplied it up by the ratio of paid hours to hours actually received by clients of social services. This allowed for the distribution of costs associated with guaranteed working hours, sick and holiday pay, training, etc. among clients. Clients receiving either service at weekends also had the cost marked up by the appropriate factor to reflect the higher wage costs of such working. Travel expenses for this analysis were distributed in proportion to the number of hours of service received by the client. Ideally this should be distributed in proportion to the number of visits received. However, this would require collection of data about the number of visits made to all clients over the year which is unavailable in local authorities and would deserve a separate study.

In addition to the costs of the home helps themselves, there is an overhead for the management and administration of the service. Here we include the costs of the home help (or home care) organisers and their supporting clerical staff as well as a portion of the area office costs for management, etc. that could not be directly attributed to a particular service. The latter apportionment was undertaken on the basis of the salaries of key workers who worked from the area office. A key worker was defined as someone with direct responsibility for a client group. Thus this included social workers and occupational therapists as well as the home help organisers and their assistants. This was felt to be a more robust method of distributing these costs than by, say, the number of full-time equivalent staff in each service over a year for which recording systems were in general more fallible. Implicitly, it also assumes that higher paid workers made more use of the resources for which costs could not be directly apportioned. In discussions in the areas this was felt to be not unreasonable.

For the overheads, we found little, if any, relationship between the activity of the home help organisers and the number of hours of service received by the client over a week. Instead, activity seemed to be related to the length of time over which the service was received, being mainly concerned with initial and follow-up assessments, routine monitoring and call-outs after particular incidents. For the opportunity costing, we therefore distributed the overheads not in proportion to the hours of service received but in proportion to the length of time over which a home help was going into the client's home. There is also, in theory, a capital element to be included in respect of housing the area office. However, the distribution of this among the clients in the manner used for other overheads represented a negligible quantity and was not pursued across all areas.

Table A5.1 shows the estimated costs by area and an example cost for a client receiving the median (in our sample) allocation of four hours home help per week.

Table A5.1
Estimated private opportunity cost of the home help service by area

	Area									
	1	2	3	4	5	6	7	8	9	10
Wages, travel and other employer costs per hour of service received	3.19	4.42	4.11	2.63	2.71	2.61	2.66	3.22	2.76	2.62
Overheads per week of service received	2.29	2.33	1.36	1.09	1.07	1.03	1.23	1.25	1.39	0.84
Cost per week for a client receiving four hours of home help per week	15.05	20.01	17.80	11.61	11.91	11.47	11.87	14.13	12.43	11.32

2 Meals-on-wheels

This is one of the most complex services to cost. In some authorities it is a straightforward matter as the responsibility is passed to an alternative agency. This may be the local district council or it may be a voluntary body, notably the WRVS. In these situations, both the revenue account cost and the private opportunity cost to the social services department coincide, being the cost per meal of the transfer payment to the agency. However, care does need to be exercised as there may have been historic capital inputs to these agencies which should be reflected in the opportunity cost.

In other authorities, the service is provided in part or in full by the social services. It is important to try and distinguish between the costs incurred for each of home deliveries and luncheon club deliveries. This particularly applies to the cost of transport. Also to be included is the cost of capital in providing kitchens for meal preparation. If meals are prepared on a small scale at residential homes, in schools or in the town hall, etc. this capital may be assumed to be negligible (the marginal cost attached to the capital input is then approximately zero). Where the kitchens were specially built with the aim of supplying meals for the service, the capital input should be recognised. However, crude estimates of this suggested that it was at most two or three pence per meal. Given the complexity of estimating this component, it was therefore not pursued.

The distribution of costs (Table A5.2) for this service is substantial. This reflects quite dramatically the level of input from other sources such as voluntary bodies or local district councils. High-cost areas were those with central kitchens and paid preparation and delivery labour. Low-cost areas were those where the service was the devolved responsibility of other agencies.

Table A5.2
Estimated cost of meals-on-wheels delivered to the home, by area

	Area									
	1	2	3	4	5	6	7	8	9	10
Cost per meal delivered	2.43	2.73	1.90	2.21	0.72	1.29	1.11	0.42	0.73	0.67

3 Day care

Here we distinguish between day care provided in residential homes and that provided in purpose-built day centres.

3.1 Day care in residential homes

Resource allocation and unit costing for day care in residential homes differs in style across the authorities. In some, it is very much a marginal resource used by only a handful of clients while in others it is the major form of day care provision. Similarly, authorities differ in the manner in which they recognise it as a cost centre. In Area 9, financial resources are input into a home when the take-up of day care places reaches six per day. Thus there is an implicit policy marginal costing of zero on homes not reaching this level. In Area 5, unit costs are calculated for a home on the assumption that two day care places consume financial resources at the same rate as one residential place; this gives a relatively high unit cost determined for a day care place compared with other methods. In contrast, Area 8 has separate cost centres in their accounts for the care assistants attached to day care and residential care as well as for transport. However, they do not separate the other operating and administrative costs.

With the exception of Area 8 we only considered the homes' operating costs. The capital input for day care was assumed to have a marginal value of zero. This is a reasonable assumption where day care is provided at a low level (i.e. only two or three places per day in a home with about 40 residential places) and where it involves little more than a sitting chair in the day lounge, a little time from care assistants, and a meal and drinks. This is the case in Areas 4, 7 and 10 as far as the study clients were concerned. In Areas 5, 6 and 9, slightly (but not substantially) higher use was made of homes for day care. In Area 8 homes, separate accommodation was made available for day care, effectively creating a day centre within a residential home. Indeed present policies in the authority plan group residential homes with extensive provision for day care. Here, therefore, a separate study was undertaken to cost day care and the costs presented include a capital element.

For the purposes of the costs of staff, provisions, supplies and services and other day-to-day running costs, three day care places were given the weight of one residential care place to reflect the higher staffing used during the day rather than at night and also the uptake of meals by day care recipients when compared with residents. All the costs of transport at a home were attributed to day care. In practice this overcosts the transport element, though in discussions it was found that little transport was used by permanent residents when compared with day care clients. In contrast, none of the premises' costs, such as maintenance and gardening, were included for day care. This was because day care recipients make little use of most of the facilities provided in a home compared to residents. We also only considered places taken up as far as day care was concerned though all available residential places in a home were recognised; this was felt to allow for the more marginal use of day care in the authorities presented here.

3.2 Day care in purpose-built day centres

The costing here is more straightforward than for day care in residential homes. In particular we derived a unit revenue account cost by dividing the total operating costs of the centre concerned by the number of places taken up. Care was exercised that the costs of transporting clients to the centre and any meals delivered to the centre were included.

Capital inputs here are critically important. These were discounted at a rate of 7 per cent.

Table A5.3 gives the cost of providing day care by area and by the type provided. Care must be taken in comparing costs directly between areas as there was a wide variety in the level and specialisation of activities provided.

Table A5.3
Private opportunity costs of day care, by area and type of provision

	Area									
	1	2	3	4	5	6	7	8	9	10
Cost in a residential home	–[a]	–	–	–	5.71[b]	6.94	–	11.29[c]	4.93	9.11
Cost in a purpose-built centre	8.18	7.82	15.14	11.70	–	9.99	8.15	–	3.10	18.00

a Missing costs imply no study client received the service in this form.
b In area 5, two different residential homes were used by clients in the study sample.
c In area 8, day care in residential homes is almost separate from residential care and on a large scale: a capital element is therefore included.

4 Short-term care in residential homes

The nature of problems in costing short-term care are much the same as in costing day care in that accounts rarely distinguish between permanent and short-term admissions. Indeed many homes do not identify certain beds as being solely for short-term admissions when they are available. In this latter situation it might be argued that the marginal cost of the bed is simply the sum of the costs of food and little else; this reflecting the use of an otherwise empty bed.

With respect to operating costs we have adopted the same approaches as with day care in residential homes. A cost of a place has been determined with short-term beds having equal weight as permanent beds and day places a weight as described earlier. Where there are formally identified short-term beds, the operating cost per occupied bed day has then been found by dividing the cost per place-day by the occupancy rate for the short-term beds. Where there is not this formal identification or where there is considerable use of long-term beds for short-term admissions as and when beds are available, we have used the cost of a place-day divided by the overall occupancy level for residential places in the home. For the opportunity cost we have added in a capital component in exactly the same manner as that used for day centres.

Table A5.4 shows the costs obtained for the three areas providing the service to study clients. The service is provided in most of the other areas though it is predominantly used as a form of carer relief or similar and so is not generally provided to the elderly living alone.

Table A5.4
Private opportunity cost for short-term care in the three areas providing it to study clients

	Area			
	8	9a[a]	9b[a]	10
Operating cost	15.31	14.94	15.36	10.90
Capital cost (discounted at 7 per cent)	3.22	3.22	3.89	3.30
Total cost per client day	18.53	18.16	19.25	14.20

a Two homes in area 9 provided short term care to study clients.

5 Social work

This is the other complex service to cost for the clients concerned. The role of many social workers was to act as a 'service broker' and the collection of time diary information in this context was flawed with problems: involvement was very short and was often not known about by other service coordinators. This generally involved initial assessments, placing the client in contact with other services and then maintaining a distant monitoring of the client's status. Thus much of the involvement was episodic in nature. There is very little evidence of constructive research for costing this field either in the academic literature or in the local authorities themselves.

Here we have adopted a simple approach based upon the time information that was collected. As with other labour inputs, we consider the revenue account costs and the operating component of the opportunity cost to be identical. Where possible we obtained the salary and travel expenses paid to the relevant social workers in the 1984/85 financial year. Where this was not possible average figures for groups of social workers identifying as closely as possible to the worker concerned were used (groups could be identified by looking at team structure and level of worker). We then calculated the cost per hour worked for each social worker assuming a 37-hour week and a 47-week year (for part-time workers and for those that only worked part of the year figures were adjusted accordingly).

Where time information was available from the social worker concerned the cost attributable to the case could then be obtained. For those cases with no time information we adopted a different approach. An 'expert team' was asked to classify each case (whether time information was available or not) according to whether they felt it involved a high, medium or low input of social work time. This was carried out on the basis of information collected from the case review conducted at the second stage of the project. For those cases with time information, we then found the median number of hours involved for each category of case identified. This gave figures of 23 hours for a high-rated case, thirteen hours for a medium-rated case and just five hours for low-rated cases over the six-month period. We then used these times for those cases with no direct time information. The vast majority of cases with no time inputs are those with a short episode of social work input as connected with, for example, making a day care application. For such cases the error will be small in magnitude and is dwarfed by the costs of the other service inputs.

In addition, an area office administration/management overhead was calculated using the same keyworker method as described for the home help organisers earlier, neglecting also the capital overhead of the office. Thus an overhead cost was apportioned to each social worker in the office based on their salary and this was then apportioned in proportion to the number of hours of time consumed by a particular case.

Commentary on the costs that were derived for Table A5.5 is difficult. The range of values shown is not a measure of the costs of fieldwork in

Table A5.5
Private opportunity costs for social worker involvement, by area

	Area									
	1	2	3	4	5	6	7	8	9	10
Cost[a] per	–[b]	7.57	7.80	12.09	10.73	7.54	11.28	10.67	13.18	7.53
social		6.80		10.44	7.56	7.27	10.83	8.53	10.33	
worker				7.85	4.61	7.27	7.97	9.57		
hour of time				6.13		8.82				

a Costs given are for each social worker involved with study clients.
b None of the sample in area 1 had extensive social work input. Input relating to day care was costed as part of the day care costs.

each of the local authorities but reflects the hourly costs of social workers that deal with elderly cases. In most of the authorities, the study clients nearly all received social work costs close to the lower end of the ranges shown. Those that had high social worker costs tended to be very involved cases. It is, however, an area that requires considerably more work particularly so as to include such costs as support received by lower grade workers from their seniors and in including the costs of roles undertaken by social workers, other than their casework, which have an impact on the elderly in the community.

Appendix to Chapter 6

Table A6.1
Performance of core tasks of case management in the study areas: case finding

Area		Arrangements
1	Inner London	Sessional outposting of individuals. Liaison arrangements with other professionals.
2	Inner London	Permanent outposting to sub-office. Liaison arrangements with community health personnel. Shared office – social workers and home help organisers.
3	Outer London	Sessional outposting of individuals. Regular meetings with district nursing staff (re. home care clients).
4	Metropolitan District	Permanent outposting to sub-office. Sessional outposting of individuals
5	Metropolitan District	Sessional outposting to sub-office. Liaison arrangements with GPs, community centre and volunteer bureau.
6	Metropolitan District	No special outposting arrangements. Volunteer group in area office.
7	English Shire: city	Permanent outposting to sub-office. Liaison arrangement with GPs.
7	English Shire: rural	No special arrangements.
8	English Shire	Permanent outposting of individuals. Liaison arrangements with police and housing.
9	English Shire	Sessional outposting of individuals. Close proximity to local community hospital.
9	English Shire	No special arrangements.
10	Welsh County	Sessional outposting of individuals. Special Resources Group for elderly people comprising social work and home care. Shared building with community nurse personnel. Close proximity to geriatric hospital.

Table A6.2
Performance of core tasks of case management in the study areas: screening

Area	Social workers	Home help organisers
1 Inner London	Duty officer uses 'Basic' referral form. Referral letters go to Admin: information supplemented with client permission.	Catholic acceptance of referrals by clerk or assistant organisers. No screening activity.
2 Inner London	Rotating duty officer completes referral sheets.	Some screening activity by home care organisers.
3 Outer London	Rotating duty officer within specialist team completes basic referral forms.	Referrals often taken by clerk. Basic card completed. Little screening activity.
4 Metropolitan District	Rotating duty officer completes basic referral forms.	Direct referrals using same forms as SWs. Not well completed. Little screening activity.
5 Metropolitan District	Rotating duty officer. Basic referral forms are thoroughly completed.	Separate duty system. Referral forms thoroughly completed. Some screening activity.
6 Metropolitan District	Rotating duty officer completes 3 forms for information, administration, and diary of outcomes.	Separate referrals directly to organisers. Little screening activity.
7 English Shire: city	2 Duty officers. Standard referral forms, thoroughly completed and used for statistical purposes by the authority.	Direct referrals using standard forms thoroughly completed. Screening to aid prioritisation.
7 English Shire: rural	Permanent duty officer (no supplementation) completes forms thoroughly for statistical use.	By organiser, clerk or duty officer. Forms thoroughly completed and screening occurs especially with GP referrals.
8 English Shire	Intake team deals with *all* referrals and redirect when appropriate. Standardised information, thoroughly collected and supplemented.	No separate referral system. Referrals passed on from the intake team.
9 English Shire	Rotating duty officer completes basic referral form.	Referrals taken by duty social worker. Information often inadequate for organisers.

Table 6.2 (continued)		
9 English Shire	Information is not supplemented.	Referrals usually through duty social worker, but some direct. Information often inadequate. No real screening activity.
10 Welsh County	Referrals channelled direct to specialist team. Referral forms completed and information supplemented.	90 per cent referrals taken directly. Detailed information collected and supplemented.

Table A6.3
Performance of core tasks of case management in the study areas: assessment

Area	Social workers	Home help organisers
1 Inner London	Performed by any worker. No standardised assessment except for Part 3 and day care. Liaison with other professionals/agencies and 'the community'	Within two days of referral. Free service therefore no financial assessment. Basic card used, describing difficulties in maintaining selves at home. Special arrangements for hospital discharge.
2 Inner London	Post allocation to worker. No standardised assessment. Liaison with other professionals and informal carers.	Varies from day of referral to 'months' later. Special arrangements for hospital discharge. No standardised form. Financial assessments made.
3 Outer London	Standardised assessment report form. Social workers and assistants allocated problems of different seriousness. Liaison with other agencies.	General assessment made within 1-2 days of referral. Case cards used to record supplementary information. Financial assessments made.
4 Metropolitan District	No standardised form but being developed. Liaison particularly with occupational therapists. Some joint assessment.	Varies from 1-2 days to weeks later. Hospital discharges take priority. Awareness of lack of assessment skills. This area being formally developed. Financial assessments made.

Table A6.4
Performance of core tasks of case management in the study areas: case co-ordination and care packaging

Area	Social workers	Home help organiser
1 Inner London	Social workers put packages together. Waiting list for many SSD services.	Tasks prescribed by home help organisers but not always followed in practice. Organisers responsible for allocation of meals.
2 Inner London	Key worker concept is recognised. Negotiations with other agencies are common.	Loose prescription of tasks. Efforts to match home help/client for long-term care. Organisers responsible for allocation of meals.
3 Outer London	Occasional service coordination if necessary for client.	Tasks prescribed but not adhered to. Matching of client and home help. Organisers responsible for allocation of meals.
4 Metropolitan District	Coordination of SSD and services from other agencies.	Tasks prescribed and are now wider, encompassing personal care tasks. Organisers can allocate meals.
5 Metropolitan District	No key worker as in child care. Service allocation, particularly Part 3, day care, and telephones, through panels.	Tasks prescribed and expected to be adhered to. Matching of home help and client where necessary. Organisers can arrange peripatetic wardens.
6 Metropolitan District	Keyworker notion exists and services are coordinated. Sometimes NHS provides keyworker.	No specification of tasks, but 'do and don't' guidelines. Organisers also allocate community warden sitting, tuck-in and meals service.
7 English Shire: city	Standard criteria for Part 3, telephone, day care. Little direct work. Multidisciplinary panel or specialist workers coordinate services but no responsibility as key worker.	Tasks prescribed but adaptable. Organisers also responsible for meals, incontinence laundry (city only), home care and good neighbours (rural only).
7 English Shire: rural	Formal guidelines for day care services. Service coordination within the SSD.	

		Table 6.4 (continued)	
8	English Shire	No standard criteria for Day Care or Part 3. 1 social worker coordinates day care placements. Limited counselling service offered.	Organisers give formal instructions but home helps do not always stick to them. Organisers not responsible for other services.
9	English Shire	Involved in service packaging and coordination. Flexible criteria for Part 3, short stay and day care.	Tasks prescribed but not always followed. Some tasks and nursing are 'banned'. Matching of home helps and clients where possible. Organisers allocate meals.
9	English Shire	Possible coordination of social services. Most elderly people already get health services. Strict criteria for Part 3. Less stringent for day care and short-stay.	
10	Welsh County	Social work staff act as coordinators and keyworkers.	Tasks unspecified except for confused clients. Matching of home help and client where possible. Organisers also arrange sitting services.

Table A6.5
Performance of core tasks of case management in the study areas: monitoring/reassessment

Area	Social workers	Home help organiser
1 Inner London	Supplemented 'review' system for elderly person discontinued. No formalised reassessment now.	Six-monthly in theory. But also occurs on hospital discharge, and weekly meeting with home helps for feedback.
2 Inner London	Structured through supervision.	Theory is of regular reassessment, but in practice weekly meetings with home helps are used for feedback.
3 Outer London	No formal system but structured through supervision.	In theory, six-monthly, but not achieved. Reassessment after hospital discharge and feedback from home helps, social workers, general practitioners and district nurses.

Table A6.5 (continued)

4	Metropolitan District	No formal arrangements.	Six-monthly in theory, but not achieved. Problem clients get reassessed, others do not. Reliance on feedback from home helps, recognised to be inadequate.
5	Metropolitan District	Day care and Part 3 placements reviewed regularly at area level.	Aim at six months review but not necessarily by visiting elderly person. Feedback from home help, other professionals etc.
6	Metropolitan District	Described as 'unrealistic concept', by social work practitioners.	No formal guidelines but aim at 12-monthly reviews. Problem cases get more attention.
7	English Shire: city	Reliance on primary health care team for feedback. Three- and six-monthly review system.	Two-weekly follow up after assessment possible then six-monthly reviews in principle. Feedback from home helps and social workers where involved.
7	English Shire: rural	No formal procedures but biannual reports to seniors.	Six-monthly reviews are achieved – shorter time scale if problems arise. Feedback from home helps.
8	English Shire	Formalised review system for long-term clients.	Standard check after two weeks. Formal reviews after six months (not always achieved). Feedback from clients, relatives, district nurses, home helps.
9	English Shire	Part 3 places reviewed after six months. Reliance on feedback from other service staff.	Usually reactive, e.g. after hospital discharge.
9	English Shire	Day care and Part 3 places get formal review.	Formally every six months but not achieved. Feedback from home helps and reassessment on hospital discharge.
10	Welsh County	Good deal of reliance on home helps and home care aides. More monitoring of cases where 'need for support'.	12-monthly reviews are achieved. Demanding clients get more attention.

Table A6.6
Performance of core tasks of case management in the study areas: case closure

Area	Social workers	Home help organiser
1 Inner London	No active policy. 'Usually on death'. Requires approval of team leader.	'Only occasionally because clients rarely improve'.
2 Inner London	'When things set up and running smoothly'. Requires approval by senior.	Requires case conference to remove service from client in need.
3 Outer London	When services set up. Quicker closure if monitoring possible through other service. Requires approval by senior.	Only on hospitalisation, if the client is away or specifically short term cases.
4 Metropolitan District	A case of 'self determination'. No active policy. Requires approval by Senior.	Where mental illness or personal care tasks are too demanding.
5 Metropolitan District	Where service set up and running. Active closure policy, needs approval by Senior.	Short term cases or where the elderly person displays severe behaviour problems.
6 Metropolitan District	Active case closure policy, needs approval by team leader.	'Not often'. Where the client moves or behaves badly or doesn't want the service.
7 English Shire: city	When intervention is thought unlikely to improve quality of life.	Where clients get better or exhibit difficult behaviour.
7 English Shire: rural	When services set up or where none are appropriate and therefore client referred elsewhere.	Recovery, death or institutionalisation.
8 English Shire	Active closure policy by intake team. Cases requiring long-term care placed on 'bank' system.	Where clients recover, behave badly, or require environmental health services. Also on refusal to pay for service.
9 English Shire	By 'mutual understanding'.	If clients get better or find substitute help.
9 English Shire	If no service is provided or where Part 3 becomes permanent.	Only if clients are better or not wanting the service.
10 Welsh County	Active policy to close where there is no clear decision to provide service.	Where environmental health services required, or consistently bad relations between client and home helps.

Appendix to Chapter 7

1 Introduction

The purpose of this Appendix is to outline the form of the dichotomous logit model which was used in the statistical analysis of 'risk', the main assumptions which underlie the model, and to explain the interpretation and predictive power of the results.

2 The dichotomous logit model

When constructing the model, we are estimating the probability of whether the elderly person is 'at risk' or not. This means that the dependent variable takes a dichotomous form:

$$Y_i = 1 \quad \text{if 'at risk'}$$
$$Y_i = 0 \quad \text{otherwise}$$

If we now transform this into probabilistic terms we get the following. The probability distribution of Y is given by:

$$P(Y) = p^y(1 - p)^{1-y}$$

where p is the 'odds' that Y = 1. The logit model assumes 'p' can be written as:

$$p = \frac{\exp{(\beta'X)}}{(1 + \exp{(\beta'X)})}$$

where X is a vector of independent variables and β is a vector of coefficients. The coefficients can be estimated from the data by standard maximum likelihood methods (see, for example, McCullagh and Nelder, 1983).

3 Interpretation of results

In the non-linear Logit model, the interpretation of the coefficients is not so simple as in Least Squares Regression models. We need to bear in mind that we have transformed the dependent variable into the probability that $Y_i = 1$. This means that we have to look at the estimates in probabilistic terms. Each coefficient represents the relative contribution of the corresponding independent variable compared with the others. Therefore, the greater the magnitude of an estimated coefficient, the greater the contribution of that independent variable to the estimated probability of being 'at risk'.

A logit analysis will generate an explanatory equation which is the weighted sum of the explanatory factors. Only statistically significant factors are retained in the 'final' equation, and so a series of logit analyses will be necessary in order to arrive at a satisfactory equation. This equation actually produces a prediction of the probability of a case with specified characteristics belonging to each of the group options. The prediction formula is:

$$P(Y_i = 1) = \frac{\exp (\hat{\beta}'X_i)}{(1 + \exp (\hat{\beta}'X_i))}$$

where X_i denotes the values for the ith person of the set of explanatory factors which appear in the 'final' equation and $\hat{\beta}$ denotes the estimated coefficients. Thus $\hat{\beta}'X_i$ is actually a weighted sum of characteristics, and the equation above is a conversion formula which generates a probability that an elderly person with a given set of characteristics and circumstances should be classified as being 'at risk'. However, it must be borne in mind that such an equation should not be applied mechanistically.

In building our 'final' equation the t-statistic is used to test the significance of each parameter, those which are insignificant being dropped. The overall goodness of fit of the model has been measured for the proportion of correct predictions (PCP). This is the number of individuals who would be assigned to the correct group on the basis of these probabilities, relative to the expected number of correct predictions given random assignment (see Amemiya, 1981).

Appendix to Chapter 12
The estimation of the costs of reducing stress among carers

1 The outcome variable

The inventory was intended 'to sample ... the different types of emotional disturbance seen in adults'; twelve of the 24 components being taken from the Cornell Medical Index Health Questionnaire, 'a useful indicator of emotional disturbance'. The inventory items relate to 'the emotions of carers and to aspects of the physical state which might have an important psychological component' (Rutter, Tizard and Whitmore, 1970, p.339).

Relevant to its use as an indicator of likely degree of disturbance and/or distress, Bebbington and Quine (1986) found a single dimension accounting for a 'moderate' proportion of the covariance in inventory scores, and 'pragmatic validity' in their analysis of scores for 200 carers of severely mentally handicapped children. They argued that their results gave 'support to the malaise construct and to the inventory' (pp.5,7), arguing that earlier work had been statistically flawed.

Predictor variables are shown in Table A12.1. *The cost function equation* is described in Table A12.2. *An overview of the results* is presented in Table A12.3.

2 Are the low marginal productivities a statistical artefact?

Section 1.2.2 alludes to the failure of other studies to find positive marginal productivities for service inputs on carer stress. It is possible (though not in all cases certain) that the statistical analyses have understated the impact of services. First, the score is an indicator of stress of only 'moderate' validity (Bebbington and Quine, 1986), and it is only imperfectly reliable (Rutter, Tizard and Whitmore, 1970, p.339). Errors in predictors attenuate estimates of slope terms. Secondly, though more is allocated to clients whose carers suffer high stress, insufficiently more may be allocated to reduce the stress to a level lower than the stress of others whose dependants are in a less stress-inducing state. The argument is analogous to one stated at the end of Chapter 4. It has been recognised by others also. Gilleard et al. elegantly express it almost in the same way as by an econometrician: resources and burden indicators 'may be unrelated because of the confounding interaction between demand and supply – the distressed supporter may receive more support, and the support may then ameliorate the distress to a level comparable with those initially experiencing little need for extra help and thus receiving little. The effect would be to cancel

Table A12.1
Costs of reducing stress on carers: predictor variables

MULTIPLE	Multiple client household dummy (16.7%)
TYPO	A variable representing a need typology, combining functional ability and the availability of informal support. See Table 3.1 for definitions and distribution.
MSTYP3	Malaise score x Type 3 interaction. Mean, 0.716; S.D., 2.081; Med., 0.000; First decile, 0.000; Ninth decile, 3.00.
URINBOTH	Incontinent of urine at both times (13.2%)
URINCH	Change in urinary incontinence (6.8%)
FAECALB	Incontinent of faeces at both times (5.4%).
FAECALCH	Change in faecal incontinence (8.4%)
CONFUSC	Highest confusion score in household. Mean, 1.543; S.D., 2.009; Med. 1.00; First decile, 0.00; Ninth decile, 5.00.
BEHAVC	Highest behavioural score in household. Mean, 1.885; S.D., 2.153; Med., 1.00; First decile, 0.00; Ninth decile, 5.00.
WANDERS	Elderly person ever wanders (4.1%).
DISTURB	Elderly person wakes carer (5.3%).
DANGER	Elderly person does dangerous things (19.5%).
CHAT	Elderly person has difficulty holding conversation (23.0%).
SAMEHH	Elderly person lives in same household as carer (13.5%).
TIMESH	Shared household: 1 = 2 years or more (12.0%). 2 = 10 years or more (7.2%). 3 = 50 years or more (5.3%).
ALONE	Can be left alone for: 1 = 1 day or more (75.6%) . 2 = 1 week or more (32.3%). 3 = 1 month or more (6.5%).
TRAVEL	Time carer spends travelling: 1 = 5+ minutes (60.5%). 2 = 20+ minutes (26.8%). 3 = 60+ minutes (8.3%).
DAUGHT	Carer is daughter (40.9%).
SON	Carer is son (21.2%).
DINLAW	Carer is daughter-in-law (5.3%).
OTHKIN	Carer is other kin (14.9%).
ONKIN	Carer is other non-kin (17.3%).
WORKFT	Carer works full time (34.0%).
WORKPT	Carer works part time (21.4%).
RETIRED	Carer is retired (17.5%).
FEELINGS	Carer feels s/he would act differently (5.8%).
PROBLEMS	Carer expects real problems (6.3%).
LOSTEMP	Carer has lost out in employment (45.7%).
RELSHIP	Carer feels caring has affected relationships (18.3%).
MORALE	Caring has an adverse affect on morale (72.2%).
PRESSURE	Carer feels under pressure (53.1%).
CONFIDE	Carer has someone to confide in, yes (89.0%).
CGOESOUT	Carer gets out at least once weekly (75.0%).
PASTREL	Carer had good past relations with elderly person (91.3%).
INTER1	Multiple x malaise. Mean, 0.742; S.D., 2.177; Med., 0.000; First decile, 0.000; Ninth decile, 3.00.

Variables used subsequent to the first round of exploratory modelling.

Table A12.2
Social care costs[a] of reducing Malaise score of principal informal carer: the selected equation[b]

Client characteristic	Regression coefficient	Significance
Malaise score	1.44	0.142
Malaise score squared	-0.14	0.090
Malaise if client Type 3[c]	1.36	0.009
Malaise if multi-person client household	-1.57	0.004
Client in multi-person household can be left one month or more	51.46	.000
Highest behavioural disturbance score[a]	1.85	0.000
Type 4[d]	9.08	0.002
Type 6[e]	8.08	0.027
Carer's sleep disturbed	-12.15	0.018
Type 6 in multi-person household	16.32	0.018
Constant	6.02	0.005

Adjusted R^2 = 23. F = 9.79. Significance of F = 0.0000
a Average weekly opportunity costs to the social services department for the 208 households with clients receiving home care for more than twelve weeks.
b Modelling strategy designed to find the effects of increased resources on Malaise reduction.
c Type 3 clients have short interval needs with greater informal support.
d Type 4 clients have short interval needs with lesser informal support.
e Type 6 clients have critical interval needs with lesser informal support.

Table A12.3
Costs of reducing the Malaise of non-spouse principal carers: an overview of results

Among the sample as a whole, higher levels of social service inputs seemed to have a sufficiently strong effect to reduce Malaise only among those with Malaise scale scores above the threshold suggested to find psychiatric cases. The Malaise score above which resources had a discernible effect varied between types of client. (The effect was present over the whole range of scores only for the 3 per cent of carers whose most disabled dependents suffered short interval need and lived with others but with little informal support). Unsurprisingly, for the 18 per cent of carers whose dependents were of short interval need dependents living alone with little informal support, the resource variation appeared not to have a strong enough effect on Malaise to have an impact on any but a small minority (Appendix 12.1 Tables 3 and 4).

For this sample, there was little sign that the sum of the spending on community health and social services reduced Malaise over any range.

The model suggested that the cost to the community social services of reducing carer Malaise to the threshold would add substantially to costs as they now are. For the carers whose malaise exceeded the threshold in the sample as a whole, the increase in costs would be 13 per cent. The increase in overall costs would be 5 per cent. Perhaps the most realistic estimate of the costs necessary to eliminate Malaise scores in excess of 5 is that predicted for those whose dependents have high scores on the Behavioural Disturbance index. This is shown in Table 12.9, which provides information for the groups whose costs of malaise reduction differs. The reader should make allowance for the downward bias in the cost estimates due to the scale of the error term in the Malaise indicator.

Variations in behavioural disturbance of carers have a large effect on the costs of malaise reduction and on the differences in the costs between client groups.

any ameliorative influence of support when viewed cross-sectionally' (1984, pp.174-5).

It is particularly important to be able to take into account carers' feelings of stress before the client acquired the stress-generating characteristics because there is evidence that the main influences on the Malaise score are carer circumstances and characteristics, not dependants' characteristics, as will be shown in the sequel to this volume. For some, circumstances other than dependency-related characteristics of the elderly person may be the main cause of stress; or the perception of stress may reflect the carer's personality as much as the reality of the position. Tarnopolski et al. (1979) illustrate the confounding of stress with burden. It is like the discussion of 'complainers' by those working with other indicators of psychiatric disturbance. Rutter, Tizard and Whitmore (1970) discussed the existence of 'grumble factors' as influences on scores, though they suggested that the grumble factors were no more important for high than low malaise scorers among their sample. We interviewed the carers only once. Our attempt to use simultaneous equation techniques did not yield good models which credibly separated out the impact of input differences on Malaise over the whole range of observations. So we can make an inference about the positive effects over the whole range only if one heroically assumes that the marginal cost of improvements is equal over the whole range of malaise scores and that it is the degree to the resources allocated are sufficient to compensate for the malaise differences which varies. Perhaps this might usefully be assumed to be the upper limit of the concealed positive impact.

That we are not basing our estimates on a full structural model is in one sense a red herring. The possible understatement of the stress-reducing effects of inputs does not in itself invalidate the use of the model to predict the consequences of resource variations.

Appendix to Chapter 14

Break-even costs

Caveats to the logic of Diagram 14.1: some evidence
Chapter 14 argued that Diagram 14.1 oversimplifies the argument about guidelines for modal choice because it ignores (i) the proliferation of modes; (ii) the association of costs with incapacity in both modes of care when allowance is made for outcome variations; (iii) the higher costs of providing larger quantities of residential care; (iv) various other flows which exaggerate or understate the true cost of community-based care to public funds; and (v) such other factors as the divergence between social

opportunity cost and the cost to public funds and Pandora effects. Evidence aoout each is discussed below.

1. Proliferation of modes

Modes have indeed proliferated; for example the rapid extension of boarding out schemes. However, these still provide care for few and their true costs remain unknown. More important are places in homes run by voluntary organisations. The charges for these were estimated by Darton, Jefferson, Sutcliffe and Wright (1987) to be some 15 per cent less than the charges for private homes, though the opportunity costs to the public funds of places in them are less different if allowance is made for hidden (and particularly quality assurance) costs.

2. Costs and incapacity

This is not the place to present detailed evidence. However, our argument requires that we sketch in broad orders of magnitude.

The variation of costs vary with disability and other dependency-generating characteristics both in community-based and residential care modes should make a substantial difference to the guidelines. Some American states and experimental schemes distinguish several 'levels of care', setting different budget limits for each. It is always difficult to allocate cases at the margin between the levels and so prevent cost escalation, because care professionals tend to err towards the over-generous assessment of patient needs. Often the assessors in those American schemes are physicians in independent practice. However, one should not therefore assume that multiple guidelines would on balance decrease efficiency. On the contrary, the variation in the cost variations due to dependency are so large that a guideline reasonable for some would be quite inappropriate for another; and one of the objectives of the community care experiments is to give incentives to those who make the allocations to try to achieve equity between clients of different care needs.

The point of having guidelines is to provide information in cases where substitution between modes is a possibility. So the guidelines should be defined for groups for whom the main substitution opportunity is the same.

One group is those for whom the choice is between residential modes of care and community services.

• Local authority residential homes.

The evidence for the effects of dependency on costs for local authorities' homes is now ageing. The PSSRU survey of 1981 was the most recent large collection (Darton and Knapp, 1984). A 20 per cent gradient between the 20 per cent most heavily dependent and the 40 per cent minimally dependent is assumed. The (varying) results of analyses of the relationships between costs and dependency are discussed in Davies and Challis (1986) and Davies and Knapp (1988).

- Private residential homes.
  For private old people's homes, a 10 per cent difference in the proportion who are heavily or appreciably dependent is associated with a 27.5 per cent variation in charges (Judge, Knapp and Smith, 1986).
- The averages around which the variations occur have clearly changed since 1981.
  Davies and Knapp (1988, p.320) suggested that the average costs of local authority homes were similar to average charges for private homes in 1985. The increase in board and lodging payments between April 1985 and April 1988 (18 per cent) has been similar to the increase in gross cost per week in local authority homes (21 per cent) between 1985/6 and 1988/9 (House of Commons, 1987, 23 November 1987, 123, Cols 79-81; CIPFA, 1986, 1989). A study by the Social Services Inspectorate (1985) found a cost of £501 for the initial registration of a home and an annual cost of quality assurance or £13.65. However, they stated the quality assurance costs to be underestimates because they did not cover inputs from other agencies. They also argued that the authorities had not yet mobilised sufficient resources for the quality assurance tasks. For these reasons, one might assume a mean for local authority and private homes of £140. This is little different from the cost of private homes assumed by the Audit Commission (1986c) study (£138.55).
  For some, the more realistic alternative mode is not residential care but the nursing home or the long-stay hospital. We have argued that this is a crucial target group. The development of community care cannot be considered a success unless its problems are well handled since the unit costs of its members is high.
- Opportunity costs in long-stay geriatric beds may have been almost twice those in residential homes. Costs in psychiatric hospitals might have been 50 per cent greater (Wright, Cairns and Snell, 1979; Davies and Challis, 1986).
- American literature suggests that the substitution for hospital beds by nursing home beds is more readily achieved than their substitution by community-based provision (Applebaum, Seidl and Austin, 1980; Eggert, 1983; Berkeley Planning Associates, 1987); but that more studies have focused on the reduction of nursing home utilisation than hospital costs because they are funded to reduce the Medicaid rather than the Medicare budget (Eggert, 1983; Davies and Challis, 1986; Eggert and Friedman, 1988; Kemper, 1988; Weissert, Cready and Pawelak, 1988). The limit for board and lodging allowances for private nursing home care was 42 per cent greater than its equivalent for residential care in April 1988, the differential having grown from 25 per cent in April 1985. The experimental NHS nursing homes were set up to have much the same unit costs as beds in long-stay hospitals, so we must look elsewhere for the costs of lower-level institutional alternatives to hospitals. Knapp, Cambridge, Darton, Thomason, Allen, Beecham and Leedham (1989,

Table 10.2) estimated the mean opportunity costs at 1986 prices of care in the community of persons discharged from hospitals. One group was discharged into two residential-based schemes for the elderly physically frail and two other groups to such schemes for the elderly mentally infirm. These costs were £299 and £207 respectively. However, they did not find good outcome reasons for the big variations in costs of schemes they discovered, so that there must have been great variation in efficiency in various senses. Wright and Haycox (1985) estimated marginal costs to be between 60 and 80 per cent of revenue costs for mental handicap hospitals. Martin Knapp and his colleagues (1989, Chapter 12), working against a background of bed closure, found that the marginal costs per inpatient day in psychiatric hospitals were only 80 per cent of average costs, an estimate nearer the lower range of those quoted from others in their discussion. They also used the experience of the care in the community projects to argue that the time taken to release the fixed cost element need not be long, since most of the costs are of manpower performing care and treatment tasks. We lack such sophisticated analysis for long-stay wards for the elderly. However, the same general argument must apply, though to a lesser extent, since in many areas the alternative is not hospital but ward closure.

We must also consider the costs of the inputs required for persons for which we seek to substitute for hospital care. There is evidence from schemes whose aim was to substitute for hospital care. Gibbins et al. (1982) designed their scheme for persons otherwise at risk of hospital admission. It was intended to provide a standard service of 21 hours of care per week; three episodes of care per day for seven days per week. The PSSRU's Darlington community care/care in the community project for persons at risk of needing long-stay nursing care in hospital required service three or four times each day, and so some 25 hours per week (Challis, Darton, Johnson, Stone, Traske and Wall, 1989). Townsend et al. (1988) found a reduction of hospital readmission among discharged patients with much smaller and shorter-term inputs of care attendance, but the patients were not particularly at risk of long-term care. Darlington's revenue costs to health and social care agencies over six months were clearly lower for the scheme beneficiaries than for the comparison group (Challis et al., 1989, Table 14).

Again community-based care for some could be more expensive than in the alternative provision. The implication is that case managers should have incentives to search for those cases who would be costly in residential and nursing home modes but whose disabilities and other need-related circumstances are such that they could be maintained in the community without great resources. The experiments show many who fit these criteria.

This brief review suggests that costs and prices reflect (i) inheritances of capital stocks, (ii) conventions about facility design, operation and resourcing which vary substantially between countries, and (iii) the cost and price effects of financing mechanisms. Persons of a wide range of dependency-generating characteristics are found in institutions facing quite different cost- and price-affecting influences of this kind. The result is a pattern of variation in inputs given needs. The variation cannot be satisfactorily explained, far less justified, by the matching of resources to needs and preferences. Changes after 1991 will affect all of these. So we could profitably look at a wider range of experience to extend the range of evidence on which to base a judgment. In particular, it might be useful to collate evidence from other countries.

3. Responsiveness of residential care supply to price
Diagram 14.3 illustrates supply curves for the local authority homes in the authorities for which opportunity costs were computed by Davies, Darton and Goddard (1987). Clearly the supply curves vary in slope and position between areas. We do not yet have estimates of supply curves for independent provision. However, we can speculate about their shape. Davies and Knapp (1988, Figure 4, pp.321-3) argued that the demand curve for private residential care was likely to have two discontinuities. If so there will be kinks in the supply curve to payers case-managed by the SSD from public funds using a prospectively determined and tightly constrained national benefit. In the short run one would expect the curve to commence with a shallow slope created by supply from providers whose charges are now highly sensitive to the levels of the social security entitlement. But beyond a certain point, one would expect the supply curve to have a steepness which reflected the elasticity of demand among private consumers. American estimates and *a priori* argument alike suggest that demand among private payers is highly elastic. There may be kinks in the supply curve for another reason. Much of the supply was originally provided in converted premises in areas which have a large number of former boarding houses purchaseable at lower prices per square foot than new buildings, the rise of the private residential home following the decline of the British seaside resort. Though more recent expansion has been greater elsewhere, in some areas the supply of such property seems to be scarce. Once exhausted, additional supply depends on more expensive building. Darton et al. (1987, Table 5.1) report mortgage interest and other capital costs to be 17 per cent of total costs of private residential homes for elderly persons. The higher the rate of expansion, the greater the percentage is likely to be on average.

4. Other cost adjustments
It is necessary to make allowance for other costs in setting the upper limit to community service allocations. Assuming the criterion to be costs to public funds, these are; (i) housing subsidies net of housing taxes (an addition to community-based costs), (ii) net differences in social security

benefits (an addition); (iii) taxes on consumption expenditures not made if the person were in residential care (a subtract); (iv) differences in length of stay in hospitals (probably an addition); and (v) taxes lost because community carers reduce their earnings in order to support their dependants (a subtract).

Detailed investigation is needed to establish these at the individual level, and the study collection of evidence lacks important items. Audit Commission (1986c) estimates for (i) and (ii) suggest that they amounted to £43 in 1985 and £59 if the dependent lived alone in local authority sheltered housing. Guesstimates for item (iii) based on 15 per cent of the average weekly consumption expenditures of persons aged 75 and over living alone and elderly couples living alone were £10.43 and £5.37. About (v), our evidence is that among carers as a whole, only 7 per cent actually lose earnings because they work fewer hours as a consequence of their caring responsibilities, but that among those who did work fewer hours the mean loss of earnings was estimated to be £24.60. For carers as non-spouse principal carers in general the mean was £1.80. An estimate of the loss of earnings due to giving up work to care for clients among the 5 per cent of carers to whom this was relevant was £12 per week, this figure being based on applying Joshi's estimates of the effect of career interruption on women's earnings to our carers' statements about giving up work. Over all non-spouse principal carers, the mean was £0.57. (The assumptions and evidence will be described in the sequel to this volume: *Community Services and the Social Production of Welfare*.) On average it is small.

We conclude that
- It is particularly important to take some account of the imputed social cost of housing in circumstances in which the housing would otherwise become vacant. However, the importance should not be overstated. (i) Those with surviving spouses or who had shared their home with other relatives would not generally be releasing accommodation for occupation by others. (ii) Accommodation is (and should often be) kept vacant until it is certain that the admission is irreversible. This period is often substantial compared with the survival time of the person admitted. So the cost saving might on average be small averaged over the whole period of survival in the facility. The taxes on expenditures vary less between consumers and apply over the whole period. They offset the housing costsse to a considerable degree for most persons. However the external costs vary greatly between persons and areas. Taking them into account would formidably complicate case management policy and create differences in the treatment of consumers which it would be difficult to explain and justify to politicians, far less consumers.
- For many, the distribution would still seem to have too few users with substantial home care costs.

5. *Other considerations*

The analysis has been based on some criteria only.

It can be argued that the criteria are incomplete; that social opportunity cost should be the criterion. Attempts to do so have been made in the evaluation of community care projects (Davies and Challis, 1986). This basis is not taken here partly because our argument fits mainly into contemporary policy argument being developed by the new managerialists, and their criteria are narrower; and partly because the conceptualisation and measurement of social opportunity cost yield figures which are still less precise.

Secondly we have chosen to ignore the Pandora effect: the consequences for the demand for services of the agencies providing care of higher quality, greater relevance to consumer needs, and in larger quantities for each consumer. We do so partly because it is most helpful to policy-makers to work out guidelines under the assumption that the supply of resources is sufficiently responsive to demands for us to ignore the reduction in intensity which would follow from spreading resources to meet greater need; and partly because we have not so far attempted to estimate the parameters of the Pandora process.

References

Abrams, M. (1978) *Beyond Three Score and Ten*, Age Concern Research Publications, London.

Abrams, P. (1977) 'Community care: some research problems and priorities', *Policy and Politics*, 6:2, 125-52.

Abrams, P. (1980) 'Social change, social networks and neighbourhood care', *Social Work Service*, 22, 12-23.

Abrams, P., Abrams, S., Humphrey, R. and Snaith, R. (1981) *Action for Care: A Review of Good Neighbour Schemes in England*, The Volunteer Centre, Berkhamsted.

Abrams, P. (1984) edited by M. Bulmer, 'Realities of neighbourhood care: the interactions between statutory, voluntary and informal social care', *Policy and Politics*, 12:4, 413-29.

Abrams P. (1985) edited by M. Bulmer, 'Policies to promote informal care: some reflections on voluntary action, neighbourhood involvement and neighbourhood care', *Ageing and Society*, 5:1, 1-18.

Adler, M. and Asquith, S. (1981) *Discretion and Welfare*, Heinemann, London.

Aiken, M. and Hage, J. (1966) 'Organisational alienation: a comparative analysis', *American Sociological Review*, 31, 497-507.

Aiken, M. and Hage, J. (1971) 'The organic organisation and innovation', *Sociology*, 5, 63-82.

Aldridge, H. (1979) *Organisation and Environments*, Prentice Hall, Englewood Cliffs, New Jersey.

Allan, G. (1983) 'Informal networks of care: issues raised by Barclay', *British Journal of Social Work*, 13:4, 417-33.

Allen, I. (1982) *Short Stay Residential Care for the Elderly*, Policy Studies Institute, London.

Amemiya, T. (1981) 'Qualitative response models: a survey', *Journal of Economic Literature* 19, 1483-1536.

Anderson, A., Banks, P. and Kerr, V. (1988) *Case Management: The Way Forward*, Choice, London.

Ankri, J., Isnard, M. and Henrard, J. (1989) *Home Help in France*, Laboratoire Santé et Vieillissement, Université René Descartes, Paris.

Applebaum, R.A. and Harrigan, M. (1986) *Channeling effects on the quality of clients' lives*, Mathematica Policy Research In., Plainsboro, New Jersey.

Applebaum, R., Seidl, F. and Austin, C. (1980) 'The Wisconsin community care organization', *The Gerontologist*, 20:3, 350-5.

Association of County Councils (1990) *Caring for People: meeting the challenge*, ACC Publications, London.

Association of Directors of Social Services (1988) *Community Care: Agenda for Action*, Response to Sir Roy Griffiths' Report, ADSS, London.

Audit Commission (1985) *Managing Social Services for the Elderly More Effectively*, HMSO, London.

Audit Commission (1986a) *Managing Social Work More Effectively*, HMSO, London.

Audit Commission (1986b) *Community Care and Joint Planning*, HMSO, London.

Audit Commission (1986c) *Making a Reality of Community Care*, HMSO, London.

Audit Commission (1987) *Developing Services for the Mentally Handicapped*, Occasional Paper 4, Audit Commission, London.

Audit Inspectorate (1983) *Social Services: Provision of Care for the Elderly*, HMSO, London.

Auditor General (1988a) *Efficiency Audit Report: May 1988*, Home and Community Care Program Working Group, Department of Community Services and Health, Australian Government Publishing Service, Canberra.

Auditor General (1988b) *First Triennial Review of the Home and Community Care Program: Final Report of the HACC Working Group*, Home and Community Care Program Working Group, Department of Community Services and Health, Australian Government Publishing Service, Canberra.

Austin, C. (1981) 'Client assessment in context', *Social Work Research and Abstracts*, 17:1, 4-12.

Austin, C. (1983) 'Case management in long-term care: options and opportunities', *Health and Social Work*, 8:1, 16-30.

Avon Social Services Department (1980) *Admissions to Homes for the Elderly: A Survey of Alternatives*, Avon County Council, Bristol.

Baines, B. and Davies, B. (1989a) *Institutional Admission, Heavy Service Use, and the Joint Consumption of Community Health and Social Services: Predictions Using Logit Analysis*, PSSRU Discussion Paper 636, University of Kent at Canterbury.

Baines, B. and Davies, B. (1989b) *Entry to Institutions for Long-term Care and the Joint Consumption of Community Health Services Among Users of Community Social Services: A Statistical Prediction Analysis*, PSSRU Discussion Paper 637, University of Kent at Canterbury.

Baldock, J., Davies, B. Evers, A. Johansson, L. Knapen, M., Thorslund M. and Tunissen, C., *Care for the Elderly: Significant Innovations in Three European Countries*, The European Centre for Social Welfare Training and Research, Praeger-Campus, Frankfurt and New York.

Baldwin, S. (1977) *Disabled Children: Counting the Costs*, Disability Alliance, London.

Baldwin, S. (1985) *The Costs of Caring: Families with Disabled Children*, Routledge and Kegan Paul, London.

Bamford, T. (1982) *Managing Social Work*, Tavistock, London.

Banks, P. (1988) 'Cutting the cloth to suit the client', *Social Work Today*, 19 May, 14-15.

Barclay Report (1982) *The Role and Tasks of Social Workers*, Bedford Square Press, London.

Barnes, C.D. (1980) *The Restless Tide: A Study of Admissions into Homes for the Elderly*, Surrey County Council SSD, Kingston-on-Thames.

Barrett, S. and Fudge, C. (1981) *Policy and Action*, Methuen, London.

Baro, F., De Bruyne, G., Moorthamer, L. and van den Bergh, H. (1989) *Home help service in Belgium: Paper for the ACRE consortium*, Catholic University of Leuven, Leuven, Belgium.

Barrowclough, C. and Fleming, I. (1986) *Goal Planning with Elderly People: Making Plans to Meet Individual Needs: A Manual of Instruction*, Manchester University Press, Manchester.

Baumol, W.J. (1982) 'Contestable markets: An uprising in the theory of industry structure', *American Economic Review*, 72, 1-16.

Baur, P. and Okun, M. (1983) 'Stability of life satisfaction in late life', *The Gerontologist*, 23:3, 261-5.

Bayley, M. (1973) *Mental Handicap and Community Care*, Routledge and Kegan Paul, London.

Bayley, M. (1978) *Community-Orientated Systems of Care*, Volunteer Centre, Berkhamsted.

Bayley, M. (1982) 'Helping care to happen in the city', in A. Walker (ed.) *Community Care: The Family, the State and Social Policy*, Blackwell, Oxford.

Bebbington, A. (1979) 'Changes in the provision of social services to the elderly in the community in fourteen years', *Social Policy and Administration*, 13, 111-23.

Bebbington, A. and Charnley, H. (1985) *Domiciliary Care Project: Entry into Care*, PSSRU Discussion Paper 441, University of Kent at Canterbury.

Bebbington, A. and Davies, B. (1980) 'Territorial need indicators: a new approach', *Journal of Social Policy*, 9:2 and 9:4, 145-68 and 433-62.

Bebbington, A. and Davies, B. (1982) 'Patterns of social service provision for the elderly', in A. Warnes (ed.) *Geographical Perspectives on the Elderly*, John Wiley, Chichester.

Bebbington, A. and Davies, B. (1983) 'Equity and efficiency in the allocation of the personal social services', *Journal of Social Policy*, 12:3, 309-30.

Bebbington, A. with Moennadin, R. (1989) *Target Efficiency in the Home Help Service in 1985*, PSSRU Discussion Paper 619, University of Kent at Canterbury.

Bebbington, A., Charnley, H., Davies, B., Ferlie, E. and Twigg, J. (1984) *Domiciliary Care for the Elderly Project: Protocol Paper (revised)*, PSSRU Discussion Paper 315, University of Kent at Canterbury.

Bebbington, A., Charnley, H., Davies, B., Ferlie, E., Hughes, M. and Twigg, J. (1986) *The Domiciliary Care Project: Meeting the Needs of the Elderly. Interim Report*, PSSRU Discussion Paper 456, University of Kent at Canterbury.

Bebbington, A. and Quine, L. (1986) 'A comment on Hirst's "Evaluating the Malaise Inventory"', *Social Psychiatry*, 22, 5-7.

Becker, B. (1982) 'The nursing home scoring system: a policy analysis', *The Gerontologist*, 22:1, 39-44.

Bedfordshire Social Services Department (1978) 'Meals services in Bedfordshire', *Clearing House for Local Authority Social Services Research*, 2, 15-58.

Begg, I., Moore, B. and Rhodes, J. (1983) *The Measurement of Inter-Authority Input Cost Differences*, Cambridge Economic Consultants, Cambridge.

Beland, F. (1985) 'Who are most likely to be institutionalised, the elderly who receive comprehensive home care services or those who do not?', *Social Science and Medicine*, 20, 347-54.

Benthall, J. and Polhemus, T. (eds)(1975) *The Body as Medium of Expression*, Allen Lane, London.

Beresford, P. and Croft, S. (1986) *Whose Welfare*, Lewis Cohen Urban Studies, Brighton Polytechnic.

Bergmann, K. (1973) 'Psychogeriatrics', *Medicine*, 9, 643-52.

Bergmann, K. (1982) 'Depression in the elderly', in B. Isaacs (ed.) *Recent Advances in Geriatric Medicine 2*, Churchill Livingstone, Edinburgh.

Bergmann, K. (1983) 'Psychogeriatrics', *Medicine*, 9, 643-52.

Bergmann, K. and Jacoby, R. (1983) 'The limitations and possibilities of community care for the elderly demented', in Department of Health and Social Security, *Elderly People in the Community: Their Service Needs*, HMSO, London.

Bergmann, K., Foster, E., Justice, A. and Matthews, V. (1976) 'Management of the demented elderly patient in the community', *British Journal of Psychiatry*, 132, 441-9.

Berkeley Planning Associates (1987) *Evaluation of the ACCESS Medicare Long-term Care Demonstration Programs: Final Report*, Berkeley, Cal.

Bligh, J. (1979) 'Clients' views of day centres for the elderly and physically handicapped in Hammersmith', *Clearing House for Local Authority Social Services Research*, 1, 1-49.

Bond, J. and Carstairs, V. (1982) *Services for the Elderly*, Scottish Home and Health Department: Health Services Studies no. 42.

Booth, T. (1978) 'Finding alternatives to residential care: the problem of Innovation in the PSS', *Local Government Studies*, July, 3-13.

Booth, T. (1981) 'Collaboration between the health and social services: Part 1. A case study of joint care planning', *Policy and Politics*, 9:1, 23-49.

Booth, T. (1985) *Home Truths: Old People's Homes and the Outcomes of Care*, Gower, Aldershot.

452 Resources, needs and outcomes

Bradburn, N. (1969) *The Structure of Psychological Wellbeing*, Aldine, Chicago.
Bradshaw, J. and Glendinning, C. (1981) *The resource worker project: final report*, Social Policy Research Unit, University of York.
Bradshaw, J., Clifton, M. and Kennedy, J. (1978) *Found Dead: A Study of Old People Found Dead*, Age Concern, Mitcham.
Bradshaw, J. and Lawton, D (1978) 'Tracing the causes of stress in families with handicapped children', *British Journal of Social Work*, 8:2, 181-92.
Brearley, C. (1982) *Risk and Social Work*, Routledge and Kegan Paul, London.
Brearley, C., Hall, M., Jefferys, P., Jennings, R. and Pritchard, S. (1982) *Risk and Ageing*, Routledge and Kegan Paul, London.
Brethouwer, D. (1989) *Ongelijkles in het Geltrush van Eezinsvergorgy*, Doctorial Dissertation, University of Groningen, The Netherlands.
Briggs, A. and Oliver, J. (1985) *Caring: Experiences of Looking After Disabled Relatives*, Routledge and Kegan Paul, London.
British Association of Social Workers, (1977) Guidelines, *Social Work Today* 12 April, 13.
British Crime Survey (1983) HMSO, London.
Brocklehurst, J.C., Carty, M.H., Leeming, J.T. and Robinson, J.M. (1978) 'Care of the elderly: medical screening of old people accepted for residential care', *The Lancet*, 8081, 141-2.
Brotherton, J. (1975) *The Need for Meals on Wheels and Luncheon Clubs in the Dover District of Kent: Final Report*, Kent County Secretary's Department, Research and Intelligence Department, Kent County Council, Maidstone.
Brown, R., Bate, S. and Ford, P. (1986) *Social Workers at Risk*, Macmillan, London.
Brown, G. and Harris, T. (1978) *Social Origins of Depression: A Study of Psychiatric Disorder in Women*, Tavistock, London.
Brown, T.E. and Learner, R.M. (1983) 'The South Carolina Community Long-term Care Project', *Home Health Services Quarterly*, 4, nos. 3/4.
Brown, R. and Phillips, B. (1986) *The effects of case management and community services on the impaired elderly*, Mathematica Policy Research, inc., Princeton, New Jersey.
Brunel Institute of Organisation and Social Studies (1974) *Organising Social Services Departments*, Heinemann, London.
Buckle, J. (1984) *Mental Handicap Costs More*, Disablement Income Group Charitable Trust, London.
Burden, R. (1980) 'Measuring the effects of stress on mothers of handicapped infants', *Child Care, Health and Development*, 6, 111-23.
Burley, L., Currie, C., Smith, R. and Williamson, J. (1979) 'Contribution from geriatric medicine within acute medical wards', *British Medical Journal*, 14 July, 90-94.
Cahn, E. (1986) *Service Credits: A New Currency for the Welfare State*, Welfare State Programme 8, STICERD, London School of Economics, London.

Callahan, J.J. (1989) 'Play it again Sam – There is no impact', *The Gerontologist*, 29, 5-6.

Camden Social Services Department (1983) 'Survey of current meals-on-wheels consumers', *Clearing House for Local Authority Social Services Research*, 9, 91-118.

Capitman, J. (1985) *Evaluation of Coordinated Community-oriented Long-term Care Demonstration Programs*, Berkeley Planning Associations, Berkeley, Cal.

Capitman, J., Haskins, B. and Bernstein, J. (1986) 'Case management approaches in coordinated community-orientated long-term care demonstrations', *The Gerontologist*, 26, 398-404.

Carboni, D. (1982) *Geriatric Medicine in the United States and Great Britain*, Greenwood, Westport, Conn.

Carcagno, G J, Applebaum, R., Christianson, J., Phillips, B., Thornton, C., and Will, J. (1986) *The evaluation of the national long-term care demonstration: The planning and operational experience of the channelling projects: Volume 1* Mathematica Policy Research, Inc., Princeton, New Jersey.

Carp, F. (1986) 'Neighborhood quality perception and measurement', in R. Newcomer, M. Lawton and T. Byers (eds) *Housing an Aging Society: Issues, Alternatives and Policies*, Van Nostrand Rheinhold, New York.

Carpenter, G.I. and Demopoulos, G.R. (1988) *Screening the Elderly in the Community: Final Report*, St Paul's Hospital, Winchester, Hants.

Coursey, D., Isaac, R.M. and Smith, V.L. (1984) 'Natural monopoly and contested markets: Some experimental results', *Journal of Law and Economics*, XXVII, 91-113.

Callahan, J.J. (1989) 'Play it again Sam – There is no impact', *The Gerontologist*, 29, 5-6.

Carpenter, M. (1983) *A Study of Community Care Services and their Relevance to the Elderly*, M.Sc. Thesis, School of Policy Sciences, Cranfield Institute of Technology, Cranfield.

Carstairs, V. and Morrison, N. (1971) *The Elderly in Residential Care*, Scottish Health Services Studies, 19, Scottish Home and Health Department, Edinburgh.

Carter, J. (1981) *Day Services for Adults: Somewhere to Go*, Allen and Unwin, London.

Cassel, J. (1976) 'The contribution of the social environment to host resistence', *American Journal of Epidemiology*, 104, 107-123.

Central Statistical Office (1987) *Economic Trends*, HMSO, London.

Challis, D. (1981) 'The measurement of outcome in social care of the elderly', *Journal of Social Policy*, 10, 179-208.

Challis, D. (1985) *Case Management and Consumer Choice: The Community Care Scheme*, PSSRU Discussion Paper 396, University of Kent at Canterbury.

Challis, D., Chessum, R., Chesterman, J., Luckett, R. and Woods, B. (1988) 'Community care for the frail elderly: an urban experiment', in B. Davies and M. Knapp (eds.) *British Journal of Social Work*, 18 (Supplement), 13-42.

Challis, D., Chessum, R., Chesterman, J., Luckett, R. and Traske, K. (1990) *Case Management in Social and Health Care: the Gateshead Community Care Scheme*, PSSRU, University of Kent at Canterbury.

Challis, D., Chesterman, J., Traske, K. and Von Abendorff, R. (1990) *Assessment and case management: some cost implications*, PSSRU Discussion Paper 682/2, University of Kent at Canterbury.

Challis, D., Darton, R., Johnson, L., Stone, M., Traske, K. and Wall, B. (1989) *The Darlington Community Care Project: Supporting Frail Elderly People at Home*, PSSRU, University of Kent at Canterbury.

Challis, D. and Davies, B. (1986) *Case Management in Community Care*, Gower, Aldershot.

Challis, D. and Ferlie, E. (1986) 'Changing patterns of fieldwork organisation: I. The headquarters view', *British Journal of Social Work*, 16, 181-202.

Challis, D. and Ferlie, E. (1987) 'Changing patterns of fieldwork organisation: II. The team leaders' view', *British Journal of Social Work*, 17, 147-67.

Challis, D. and Ferlie, E. (1988) 'The myth of general practice: specialisation in social work', *Journal of Social Policy*, 17, 1-22.

Challis, D. and Knapp, M. (1980) *An Examination of the PGC Morale Scale in an English Context*, PSSRU Discussion Paper 168, University of Kent at Canterbury.

Challis, D., Tong, M.S. and Traske, K. (1988) *Salisbury Health Authority: Survey of the Elderly 1988*, PSSRU Discussion Paper 614, University of Kent at Canterbury.

Chandler, A. (1962) *Strategy and Structure: Chapters in the History of the Industrial Enterprise*, MIT Press, Cambridge, Mass.

Charlesworth, A., Wilkin, D. and Durie, A. (1984) *Carers and Services: A Comparison of Men and Women Caring for Dependent Elderly People*, Equal Opportunities Commission, Manchester.

Charnley, H.M., Bebbington, A.C. and Fitzpatrick, A. (1990) *Balance of allocation of services to elderly people in Oxfordshire*, PSSRU Discussion Paper 700, University of Kent at Canterbury.

Charnley, H. and Ferlie, E. (1984) *Domiciliary Care Project: Process Protocol*, PSSRU Discussion Paper 366/2, University of Kent at Canterbury.

Chartered Institute of Public Finance and Accountancy (1986) *Personal Social Services Statistics, 1984-5, Actuals*, CIPFA, London.

Chartered Institute of Public Finance and Accountancy (1987) *Personal Social Services Statistics, 1985-6, Actuals*, CIPFA, London.

Chartered Institute of Public Finance and Accountancy (1988) *Personal Social Services Statistics, 1986-7, Actuals*, CIPFA, London.

Chartered Institute of Public Finance and Accountancy (1989) *Personal Social Services Statistics, 1987-8, Actuals*, CIPFA, London.

Chetwynd, S. (1981) *The Problem of Informal Health Care and its Costing*, Unpublished M.Sc. Dissertation, University of York.

Child, J. (1972) 'Organisational Structure, Environment and Performance: The Role of Strategic Choice', *Sociology*, 6:1, 1-22.

Clare, A. (1982) 'Social aspects of ill health in general practice', in A. Clare and R. Corney (eds) *Social Work and Primary Health Care*, Academic Press, London.

Clare, A. and Corney, R. (eds) *Social Work and Primary Health Care*, Academic Press, London.

Clarke, L. (1984) *Domiciliary Services for the Elderly*, Croom Helm, Beckenham.

Cloke, C. (ed.)(1983) *Caring for the Carers: A Directory of Initiatives*, 2nd edition, Mitcham.

Cmnd 3703 (1968) *Local Authority and Allied Social Services* (Report of the Seebohm Committee) HMSO, London.

Cohen, D., McCann, W., Murphy, J. and van Geer, T. (1973) 'Revenue sharing as an incentive device', in B. Stein and S. Miller (eds) *Incentives and Planning in Social Policy*, Aldine, Chicago.

Coid, J. and Crome, P. (1986) 'Bed blocking in Bromley', *British Medical Journal*, 10 May, 1253-6.

Collard, D. (1978) *Altruism and Economy*, Martin Robertson, Oxford.

Commonwealth of Massachusetts (1975) *Home Care: An Alternative to Institutionalization: Final Report*, Department of Elder Affairs, Commonwealth of Massachusetts, Boston.

Cooke, K., Bradshaw. J., Glendinning, C., Lawton, D. and Staden, F (1982) *1970 cohort 10-year follow up study. Interim report to the DHSS 108/682*, Social Policy Research Unit, University of York.

Corney, R. (1982) 'The extent of mental and physical ill health of clients referred to social workers in a local authority department and a general attachment scheme', *Psychological Medicine*, 9, 585-9.

Coursey, D., Isaac, R.M. and Smith, V.L. (1984) 'Natural monopoly and contested markets: some experimental results', *Journal of Law and Economics*, 91-113.

Creese, A. and Fielden, R. (1977) 'Hospital or home care for the severely disabled: a cost comparison', *British Journal of Preventative and Social Medicine*, 31:2, 116-21.

Crosbie, D. (1983) 'A role for anyone?: a description of social work with the elderly in two area offices', *British Journal of Social Work*, 13, 123-48.

Crowel, R. (1988) 'The integrated clinically managed housing network' in M.Harris and L.L. Bachrach, *New Directions in Mental Health Services*, 40, 63-7.

Culyer, A. (1973) *The Economics of Social Policy*, Martin Robertson, Oxford.

Culyer, A. (1974) 'Economics, social policy and disability', in D.S. Lees and S. Shaw (eds) *Impairment, Disability and Handicap: A Multidisciplinary View*, Heinemann, London.

Culyer, A. (1980) *The Political Economy of Social Policy*, Martin Robertson, Oxford.

Curtis, S. and Bucquet, D. (1987) 'Characteristics of elderly people receiving home-help in three regions of France', in *Rev. Epidém et Santé Publ.*, 35, 318-322.

Cyert, R. and March, J. (1963) *A Behavioural Theory of the Firm*, Prentice Hall, Englewood Cliffs.

Darton, R. and Knapp, M. (1984) 'Factors associated with variations in the cost of local authority old people's homes', *Ageing and Society*, 4:2, 157-83.

Dant, T., Carley, M., Gearing, B. and Johnson, M. (1989) *Co-ordinating Care: The Final Report of the Care for Elderly People at Home (CEPH) Project, Gloucester*, Open University/Policy Studies Institute, London.

Darton, R., Jefferson, S., Sutcliffe, E. and Wright, K. (1987) *The PSSRU/CHE Survey of Residential and Nursing Homes: The Costs and Charges of the Surveyed Homes*, PSSRU Discussion Paper 563/3, University of Kent at Canterbury.

Davies, B. (1968) *Social Needs and Resources in Local Services*, Michael Joseph, London.

Davies, B. (1971a) 'Causes of variations in the provision of local authority health and welfare services: a comparison between counties and county boroughs', *Social and Economic Administration*, April, 100-124.

Davies, B. (1971b) 'Welfare departments and territorial justice: some implications for the reform of local government', *Social and Economic Administration*, 235-52.

Davies, B. (1971c) *Planning Resources for Personal Social Services*, The James Seth Memorial Lecture, University of Edinburgh, Edinburgh.

Davies, B. (1976) 'Needs and outputs', in H. Heisler (ed.) *Foundations of Social Administration*, Macmillan, London.

Davies, B. (1978) *Universality, Selectivity and Effectiveness in Social Policy*, Heinemann, London.

Davies, B. (1981a) 'Strategic goals and piecemeal innovations: adjusting to the new balance of needs and resources', in E. Goldberg and S. Hatch (eds) *A New Look at the Personal Social Services*, Policy Studies Institute, London.

Davies, B. (1981b) *Community care projects: some proposals*, PSSRU Discussion Paper 182, University of Kent at Canterbury.

Davies, B. (1983) *Micro-predictability and the Macro Policy Process: Implications of the Results of a Field Experiment*, PSSRU Discussion Paper 286/1, University of Kent at Canterbury.

Davies, B. (1985) *The Production of Welfare Approach*, PSSRU Discussion Paper 400, University of Kent at Canterbury.

Davies, B. (1986a) 'American lessons for British policy and research on long-term care of the elderly', *The Quarterly Journal of Social Affairs*, 2 3, 321-55.

Davies, B. (1986b) 'American experiments to substitute community for institutional long-term care: lessons for evaluation and policy', in C. Phillipson (ed.) *Dependency and Interdependency in Old Age: Theoretical Perspectives and Policy Alternatives*, Croom Helm, Beckenham.

Davies, B. (1987) 'Equity and efficiency in community care: supply and financing in an age of fiscal austerity', *Ageing and Society*, 7:2, 161-74.

Davies, B. (1989) *Case Management in the UK: Current debate and future prospects. PSSRU Discussion Paper 672, University of Kent at Canterbury.*

Davies, B. (1990a) Comments on Australian Development: A British Perspective, in A. Howe, E. Ozanne, and C. Selby-Smith, eds. (1990) *Community Care Policy and Practice: New Directions in Australia*, Monash University, Melbourne, 260-4.

Davies, B. (1990b) 'New priorities in home care: Principles from the PSSRU experiments', in A. Howe, E. Ozanne and C. Selby-Smith (eds.) (1990) *Community Care Policy and Practice: New Directions in Australia*, Monash University, Melbourne, 47-72.

Davies, B. and Baines, B. (1989) *Cover, Intensity and Need: An Anglo-French Comparison*, PSSRU Discussion Paper 635, University of Kent at Canterbury.

Davies, B. and Baines, B. (1990) *Costs to the SSD and the CHS: A SPOW Analysis*, PSSRU Discussion Paper 671, University of Kent at Canterbury.

Davies, B. and Challis, D. (1980) 'A production relations evaluation of the meeting of needs in the community care projects', in E. Goldberg and N. Connelly (eds) *Evaluative Research in Social Care*, Heinemann, London.

Davies, B. and Challis, D. (1986) *Matching Resources to Needs in Community Care*, Gower, Aldershot.

Davies, B. and Coles, O. (1981) 'Towards a territorial cost function for the home help service', *Social Policy and Administration*, 15:1, 32-42.

Davies, B., Barton, A., McMillan, I. and Williamson, V. (1971) *Variations in Services for the Aged*, Bell, London.

Davies, B., Darton R. and Goddard, M. (1987) *The Effects of Alternative Targeting Criteria and Demand Levels for the Opportunity Costs to the SSD of Care in Local Authority Homes*, PSSRU Discussion Papers 484, University of Kent at Canterbury.

Davies, B. and Ferlie, E. (1982) 'Efficiency-promoting innovation in social care', *Policy and Politics*, 10:2, 181-203.

Davies, B. and Ferlie, E. (1984) 'Patterns of efficiency improving innovations: social care and the elderly', *Policy and Politics*, July, 281-95.

Davies, B. and Goddard, M. (1987) *The Development of the BRITSMO Concept*, PSSRU Discussion Paper 519, University of Kent at Canterbury.

Davies, B. and Grimley-Evans, J.(1982) *Gateshead IAP Community Care Project: Towards a health/social care model. Discussion Paper 258, Personal Social Services Research Unit, University of Kent, Canterbury.*

Davies, B. and Knapp, M. (1981) *Old People's Homes and the Production of Welfare*, Routledge and Kegan Paul, London.

Davies, B. and Knapp, M. (1988) 'Costs and residential social care', in I. Sinclair (ed.) *Residential Care: The Research Reviewed*, HMSO, London.

Davies, B. and Missiakoulis, S. (1988) 'Heineken and matching processes in the Thanet community care project: an empirical test of their relative importance', *British Journal of Social Work*, 18 (Supplement) 55-78.

Davies, L. (1981) *Three Score Years ... And Then?*, Heinemann, London.

Davies, R. and Duncan, I. (1975) *Allocation and Planning of Local Authority Residential Accommodation in Reading*, University of Reading: Operational Research Unit Report, Department of Applied Statistics.

Deitchman, W.S. (1980) 'How many case managers does it take to screw in a light bulb?', *Hospital and Community Psychiatry*, 31, 788-789.

Department of Community Services (1985), *Annual Report, 1984-5*, Australian Government Publishing Service, Canberra.

Department of Health (1990a) *Caring for People: Community Care in the Next Decade and Beyond: Implementation Documents, Draft Guidance on Planning*, Department of Health, London.

Department of Health (1990b) Caring for People: *Community Care in the Next Decade and Beyond: Implementation Documents, Draft Guidance on Assessment and Case Management* Department of Health, London.

Department of Health (1990c) *Care in the Community: letter from the Chief Inspector to Directors of Social Services*, Social Services Inspectorate, Department of Health, London.

Department of Health and Social Security (1974) *Report of the Committee of Enquiry into the Care and Supervision Provided in Relation to Maria Colwell*, HMSO, London.

Department of Health and Social Security (1976) *Priorities for the Health and Personal Social Services*, HMSO, London.

Department of Health and Social Security (1981a) *Growing Older*, Cmnd. 8173, HMSO, London.

Department of Health and Social Security (1981b) *Care in Action: A Handbook of Priorities for the Health and Personal Social Services in England*, HMSO, London.

Department of Health and Social Security (1981c) *Report of a Study on Community Care*, DHSS, London.

Department of Health and Social Security/Office of Population Censuses and Surveys (1985a) *1984 Hospital In-patient Enquiry*, HMSO, London.

Department of Health and Social Security (1985b) *HPSS Statistics for England*, HMSO, London.

Department of Health and Social Security (1985c) *Social Work Decisions in Child Care*, HMSO, London.

Department of Health and Social Security (1986) *Neighbourhood Nursing: A Focus for Care* (Chair Julia Cumberlege), HMSO, London.

Department of Health and Social Security (1987a) *Public Support for Residential Care: Report of a Joint Central and Local Government Working Party*, (Chairperson Mrs J. Firth) HMSO, London.

Department of Health and Social Security (1987b) *From Home Help to Home Care: An Analysis of Policy, Resourcing and Service Management*, Social Services Inspectorate, DHSS, London.

Department of Health and Social Security (1987c) *The Balance of Care Microcomputer System: Technical Guide*, Operational Research Service, DHSS, London.

Department of Health and Social Security (1988a) *Managing Policy Change in Home Help Services*, Social Services Inspectorate, DHSS, London.

Department of Health and Social Security (1988b) *Managing to Care: A Study of First Line Managers in Social Services Departments in Day and Domiciliary Care*, Social Services Inspectorate, DHSS, London.

Dexter, M and Harbert, W. (1983) *The Home Help Service*, Tavistock, London.

Domiciliary Care Project (1986) *Project Summary*, PSSRU, Kent.

Donabedian, A. (1982) *The Criteria and Standards of Quality*, Health Administration Press, Ann Arbor.

Dorner, S. (1975) 'The relationship of physical handicap to stress in families with an adolescent with spina bifida', *Developmental Medicine and Child Neurology*, 17, 765-76.

Douglas, M. (1973) *Natural Symbols: Explorations in Cosmology*, Penguin, Harmondsworth.

Douglas, M. (1975) *Implicit Meaning*, Routledge and Kegan Paul, London.

Doyle, D. (1981) 'Terminal care of the elderly', in J. Kinnaird, J. Brotherston and J. Williamson (eds) *The Provision of Care for the Elderly*, Churchill Livingstone, Edinburgh.

Dunnell, K. and Dobbs, J. (1982) *Nurses Working in the Community*, OPCS/HMSO, London.

Dunnell, K. and Ide, L. (1974) 'An attempt to assess the cost of home care', in D.S. Lees and S. Shaw (eds) *Impairment, Disability and Handicap: A Multidisciplinary View*, Heinemann, London.

Ebrahim, S., Hedley, R., Sheldon, M. (1984) 'Low levels of ill health among elderly non-consumers in general practice', *British Medical Journal*, 289, 1273-5.

Edebalk, P.E. and Persson, V. (1988) *Alderdomshem eller Hemmaboenole?*, Swedish Institute for Health Economics, Lund.

Eggert, G. (1983) *The ACCESS/Medicare Program: A Strategy to Redirect the Hospital and Nursing Home Utilization Pattern of the High User Group*, Monroe County Long-term Care Program Inc., Rochester, NY.

Eggert, G. and Friedman, B. (1988) 'The need for special interventions for multiple hospital admission patients', *Health Care Financing Review*, Annual Supplement.

Eggert, G.M., Zimmer, J.G. and Freidman, B. (1986) *Direct access versus brokerage: a comparison of case management models*, Monroe County Long-Term Care Program, Rochester, New York.

Elias, N. (1978) *The Civilizing Process: Vol I. The History of Manners*, Blackwell, London.

Enthoven, A. (1987) 'The health care economy in the USA', in G. Teeling-Smith (ed.) *Health Economic: Prospects for the Future*, Croom Helm, Beckenham, Kent.

Equal Opportunities Commission (1980) *The Experience of Caring for Elderly and Handicapped Dependents*, Manchester.

Equal Opportunities Commission (1982a) *Caring for the Elderly and Handicapped*, Manchester.

Equal Opportunities Commission (1982b) *Who Cares for the Carers: Opportunities for Those Caring for the Elderly and Handicapped*, Manchester.

Etzioni, A. (1961) *A Comparative Analysis of Complex Organisations*, Free Press, New York.

Etzioni, A. (ed.)(1969) *The Semi-Professions and their Organisation: Teachers, Nurses, Social Workers*, Free Press, New York.

Evandrou, M. and Winter, D. (1988) *The Distribution of Domiciliary and Primary Health Care in Britain*, Paper No. 26, Suntory Toyota International Centre for Economics and Related Disciplines, London School of Economics, London.

Evers, A. (ed.)(forthcoming) 'Report of the study of innovation in community-based servces for the elderly in England and Wales, the Netherlands and Sweden coordinated by the European Centre for Social Welfare Training and Research', Vienna.

Factor, H., Habib, J. and Be'er, S. (1988) *Evaluating the Need for Long-term Care Services and their Costs. Social Security: Special English edition.*

Factor, H., Morginstin, B., Naon, D. (1989) *Cross-national Analysis of Home Help Services: Development of Home Help Services in Israel*, Paper presented to the ACRE consortium, JDC-Brookdale Institute for Gerontology, Jerusalem, Israel.

Fare, R., Grosskopf, S. and Lovell, C. (1985) *The Measurement of Efficiency of Production*, Kluwer-Nijhoff, Boston.

Fare, R., Lovell, C. and Zieschang, K. (1983) 'Measuring the technical efficiency of multiple output technologies', in W. Eichorn, R. Henn, K. Neumann and R. Sheppard (eds) *Quantitative Studies on Production and Prices*, Physica-Verlag, Wurzburg.

Farrell, M. (1957) 'The measurement of productive efficiency', *Journal of the Royal Statistical Society*, A, 120.

Ferlie, E. (1982) *Sourcebook of Innovations*, PSSRU Discussion Paper 261, University of Kent at Canterbury.

Ferlie, E., Challis, D. and Davies, B. (1983) *A Guide to Efficiency Improving Innovations in the Home Care of the Frail Elderly*, PSSRU Discussion Paper 284, University of Kent at Canterbury.

Ferlie, E., Challis, D. and Davies, B. (1984) 'Models of innovation in the social care of the elderly', *Local Government Studies*, 10:6, 67-82.

Ferlie, E., Challis, D. and Davies, B. (1985) 'Innovation in the care of the elderly: the role of joint finance', in A. Butler (ed.) *Ageing: Recent Advances and Creative Responses*, Croom Helm, London.

Ferlie, E., Challis, D. and Davies, B. (1989) *Efficiency Improving Innovations in the Community Care of Frail Elderly People*, Gower, Aldershot.

Finch, J. (1984) 'Community care: developing non-sexist alternatives', *Critical Social Policy*, 3:3, 6-18.

Finch, J. (1986) 'Community care and the invisible welfare state', *Radical Commuity Medicine*, 28, 15-23

Finch, J. (1987a) 'Whose responsibility? Women and the future of family care', in I. Allen et al. (eds) *Informal Care Tomorrow*, Policy Studies Institute, London.

Finch, J. (1987b) 'Family ties', *New Society*, 20 March, 16-18.

Finch, J. and Groves, D. (1980) 'Community care and the family: a case for equal opportunities', *Journal of Social Policy*, 9:4, 487-511.

Finch, J. and Groves, D. (eds)(1983) *A Labour of Love: Women, Work and Caring*, Routledge and Kegan Paul, London.

Foster, P. (1983) *Access to Welfare*, Macmillan, London.

Fowler, N. (1984) Buxton speech to Joint Council of Social Services.

Friend, J., Power, J. and Yewlett, L. (1974) *Public Planning: The Intercorporate Dimension*, Tavistock, London.

Froland, C. (1980) 'Formal and informal care: discontinuities in a continuum', *Social Services Review*, 54.

Froland, C., Pancoast, D., Chapman, N. and Kimboko, P. (1981a) 'Linking formal and informal support systems', in B. Gottlieb (ed.) *Social Networks and Social Support*, Sage, Beverly Hills and London.

Froland, C., Pancoast, D., Chapman, N. and Kimboko, P. (1981b) *Helping Networks and Human Services*, Sage, Beverly Hills and London.

Fuss, M., McFadden, D. and Mundlak, Y. (1978) 'Functional forms in production theory' in M. Fuss and D. McFadden (eds) *Production Economics: A Dual Approach to Theory and Applications. Vol. 1*, North-Holland, Amsterdam.

Gath, A. (1978) *Down's Syndrome and the Family*, Academic Press, London.

Gavett, W., Drucker, W., McCrum, M. and Dickinson, J. (1985) *A Study of High-cost Inpatients in Strong Memorial Hospital: Final Report*, University of Rochester School of Medicine, Rochester, NY.

Gerard, D. (1987) *Charity and Change*, Unpublished Ph.D. Thesis, Faculty of Technology, Open University, Milton Keynes.

Gibbins, F.I., Lee, M., Davison, P.R., O'Sullivan, P., Hutchinson, M., and Murphy, D.K. (1982) 'Augmented home nursing as an alternative to hospital care for chronic elderly invalids', *British Medical Journal*, 284, 330-3.

Gilhooly, M. (1984) 'The impact of care-giving on carers: factors associated with the psychological well-being of people supporting a dementing relative in the community', *British Journal of Medical Psychology*, 57, 35-44.

Gilleard, C., Belford, E., Gilleard, J., Whittick, J. and Gledhill. K (1984) 'Emotional distress amongst the supporters of the elderly mentally infirm', *British Journal of Psychiatry*, 145, 172-7.

Gilligan, C. (1982) *In a Different Voice: Psychological Theory and Women's Development*, Harvard University Press, Cambridge, Massachusetts and London.

Glendinning, C. (1983) *Unshared Care*, Routledge and Kegan Paul, London.

Glendinning, C. (1986) *A single door: social work with the families of disabled children*, Allen and Unwin, London.

Glennerster, H. (1985) 'Decentralisation and inter-service planning', in S. Hatch (ed.) *Decentralisation and Care in the Community*, Policy Studies Institute, London.

Glennerster, H., Korman, N., Marslen-Wilson, F. and Meredith, B. (1982) *Social Planning*, London School of Economics, London.

Glennerster, H., Korman, N. and Marslen-Wilson, F. (1983) *Planning for Priority Groups*, Martin Robertson, Oxford.

Goldberg, E. and Connelly, N. (1982) *The Effectiveness of Social Care for the Elderly*, Heineman, London.

Goldberg, E. and Fruin, D. (1976) 'Towards accountability in social work: a case review system for social workers', *British Journal of Social Work*, 6:1, .

Goldberg, E. and Warburton, W. (1979) *Ends and Means in Social Work*, Allen and Unwin, London.

Goldberg, E., Mortimer, A. and Williams, B. (1970) *Helping the Aged: A Field Experiment in Social Work*, Allen and Unwin, London.

Goldberg, E., Warburton, W., McGuinness, B. and Rowlands, J. (1977) 'Towards accountability in social work: one year's intake to an area office, *British Journal of Social Work*, 7: 3, 257-83.

Goldberg, E., Warburton, W., Lyons, L. and Willmott, R. (1978) 'Towards accountability in social work: long term social work in an area office', *British Journal of Social Work*, 8:3, 253-87.

Goldberg, E., Gibbons, J. and Sinclair, I. (1983) *Problems, Tasks and Outcomes: The Evaluation of Task Centred Casework in Three Settings*, Allen and Unwin, London.

Gorbach, P. and Sinclair, I. (1981) *Pressure on Health and Social Services for the Elderly*, National Institute for Social Work, London.

Graham, H. (1983) 'Caring: a labour of love', in J. Finch and D. Groves (eds) *Women, Work and Caring*, Routledge and Kegan Paul, London.

Grant, G. (1986) 'Towards joint teams with joint budgets? The case of the all-Wales strategy', in J. Chant (et al.)(eds) *Health and Social Services: Collaboration or Conflict*, Policy Studies Institute, London.

Graycar, A. (1983) 'Informal, voluntary and statutory services: the complex relationship', *British Journal of Social Work*, 13, 379-94.

Greenwood, R. (1978) 'Politics and public bureaucracies: a reconsideration', *Policy and Politics*, 6:4, 403-20.

Greenwood, R. and Hinings, C. (1976) 'Contingency theory and public bureaucracies', *Policy and Politics*, 5:2, 159-80.

Griffiths, R. (1983) *NHS Management Enquiry*, DHSS, London.

Griffiths, R. (1988) *Community Care: Agenda for Action*, A Report to the Secretary of State for Social Services, HMSO, London.

Gunderson, E. and Rahe, R. (1974) *Life, Stress and Illness*, Charles C. Thomas, Springfield, Illinois.

Gurland, B., Kuriansky, J., Sharpe, L., Simon, R., Stiller, P. and Berkett, P. (1977) 'The comprehensive assessment and referral evaluation (CARE): rationale, development and reliability', *International Journal of Aging and Human Development*, 8, 9-41.

Gwynedd County Council (1977) *A Research Review of the Operation of the Home Help Services in Gwynedd*, Gwynedd County Council Social Services Department, Caernarfon.

Gwynne, D. and Fean, L. (1978) *The Home Help Service in Cumbria*, Cumbria Social Services Department, Carlisle.

Hadley, R. and McGrath, M. (1970) *Going Local*, Occasional Paper 1, National Council for Voluntary Organisations, London.

Hadley, R. and McGrath, M. (1984) *When Social Services are Local*, Allen and Unwin, London.

Hage, J. (1980) *Theories of Organization*, Wiley, New York.

Harris, A. (1968) *Social Welfare for the Elderly*, HMSO, London.

Harris, M. (1988) 'New directions for clinical case management', in M.Harris and L.L. Bachrach, *New Directions in Mental Health Services*, 40, 87-96.

Harris, M. and Bachrach, L.L. (1988) *New Directions in Mental Health Services: Clinical Case Management*, 40.

Harris, M. and Bergman, H.C. (1988) 'Clinical case management for the chronically mentally ill: a conceptual analysis' in M. Harris and L.L. Bachrach, *New Directions in Mental Health Services*, 40, 5-15.

Harrison, R. (1983) *A Survey of the Personal Characterisation and Consumer Satisfaction Among Home Help Clients*, London Borough of Bromley, Department of Social Studies.

Hart, D.A. (1973) 'Ordering change and changing orders', *Policy and Politics*, 2, 27-4.

Hasenfeld, Y. (1974) 'People-processing organisations: An exchange approach', in Y. Hasenfeld and R. English, eds., *Human Service Organisations*, University of Michigan Press, Ann Arbor, Michigan.

Hasenfeld, Y. (1983) *Human Service Organizations*, Prentice Hall, Englewood Cliffs, New Jersey.

Hochman, H.M. and Rodgers, J.D. (1969), 'Pareto optimal redistribution'', *American Economic Review*, 59, 542-57.

Haskins, B., Capitman, J., Collignon, F., Degraaf, B., and Yordi, C. (1985) *Final report: Evaluation of coordinated community orientated long-term care demonstration projects*, Berkeley Planning Associates, Berkeley, California.

Hedley, R. and Norman, A. (1982) *Home Help: Key Issues in Service Provision*, Centre for Policy on Ageing, London.

Henderson, S., Duncan-Jones, P., Byrne, D. and Scott, R. (1980) 'Measuring social relationships: the interview schedule for social interaction', *Psychological Medicine*, 10, 723-34.

Henderson, S., Byrne, D. and Duncan Jones, P. (1981) *Neurosis and the Social Environment*, Academic Press, Sydney.

Hendriksen, C., Lund, E. and Stromgard, J. (1984a) 'Consequences of assessment and intervention among elderly people: 3 year randomised controlled trial', *British Medical Journal*, 1984, 289, 1522-4.

Hendriksen, C., Lund, E. and Stromgard, J. (1984b) 'Home helpers and their job activities', *Ugeskr laeger*, 146, 138-41.

Hillingdon Social Services Department (1977) *Domiciliary Services Evaluation. Part III: The Home Help Service*, London Borough of Hillingdon.

Hirst, M. (1983) 'Evaluating the Malaise Inventory', *Social Psychiatry*, 18, 181-4.

Hodgson, J. and Quinn, J. (1980) 'The impact of the TRIAGE health care delivery system upon client morale, independent living and the cost of care', *The Gerontologist*, 20:3, 364-71.

Holstein, B., Due, P., Almind, G. and Holst, E. (1989) *Home Help for the Elderly in Denmark*, Paper presented to ACRE Consortium, Institute for Social Medicine, University of Copenhagen, Copenhagen.

Hooper, J. (1988) 'Case-finding in the elderly: does the primary care team already know enough?', *British Medical Journal*, 297, 1450-52.

Hounslow Social Service Department (1981) 'A survey of meals-on-wheels and luncheon club recipients in Hounslow', *Clearing House for Local Authority Social Services Research*, 2, 45-112.

House of Commons (1947) *Hansard*, Vol. 444, HMSO, London.

House of Commons (1987) *Hansard*, Vol. 123, No. 1429, HMSO, London.

House of Commons Public Accounts Committee (1983) Session 1982-1983, *HCP 160 and 160-i*.

House of Commons Social Services Committee (1985) *Community Care with Special Reference to Mentally Handicapped and Mentally Ill People*, Fourth Report of the Social Services Committee 1984/5, HMSO, London.

Howell, N., Boldy, D. and Smith, B. (1979) *Allocating the Home Help Service*, Bell, London.

Hughes, S.L. (1988) 'Apples and oranges: a review of evaluations of community-based long-term care', *Health Services Research*, 20, 249-259.

Hunt, A. (1970) *The Home Help Service in England and Wales*, HMSO, London.

Hunter, D. (ed.) (1988) *Bridging the Gap*, King Edward's Hospital Fund, London.

Hunter, D., McKeganey, N. and MacPherson, I. (1988) *Care of the Elderly: Policy and Practice*, Aberdeen University Press, Aberdeen.

Huntington, J. (1981) *Social Work and General Medical Practice: Collaboration or Conflict*, Allen and Unwin, London.

Hurley, B. and Wolstenholme, L. (1980) 'The home help study: a summary of the findings and implications of the (Bradford) social services research project', *Clearing House for Local Authority Social Services Research*, 1, 35-70.

Hyman, M. (1980) *The Home Help Service: A Case History Study in the London Borough of Redbridge*, Redbridge Social Services Department, Ilford.

Intagliata, J., Willer, B., and Egri, G. (1988) 'The role of the family in delivering case management services', in M. Harris and L.L. Bachrach, *New Directions in Mental Health Services*, 40, 39-51.

Isaacs, B. (1971) 'The concept of pre-death', *The Lancet*, 29 May, 1115-19.

Isaacs, B. and Evers, H. (1981) *Innovations in the Care of the Elderly*, Croom Helm, London.

Isaacs, B. and Neville, Y. (1975) *The Measurement of Need in Old People*, Scottish Health Services Studies no. 34, Scottish Home and Health Department, Edinburgh.

Isaacs, B. and Neville, Y. (1976) 'The needs of old people: the "interval" as a method of measurement', *British Journal of Preventive and Social Medicine*, 30, 79-85.

Jackson, R. and Himalsingami, C. (1973) 'Measurement and evaluation of health and personal social services of the elderly', in R. Canvin and N. Pearson (eds) *Needs of the Elderly for Health and Welfare Services*, Institute of Biometry and Community Medicine Publication No. 2, University of Exeter.

Jamieson, A.(Ed)(forthcoming) *Home Care for Older People in Europe*, Oxford University Press, Oxford.

Jansson, T. and Wallberg, E. (1988) *Care of the Elderly in the Nordic Countries: Costs, Quality, Management*, Statskontoret, SAFAD, Stockholm.

Johansson, L. (1987) *The Importance of Informal Care for the Elderly: Some Data from the Tierp Study in Sweden*, Department of Social Medicine, University of Uppsala, Uppsala.

Johnson, M. and Challis, D. (1983) 'The realities and potential of community care', in Department of Health and Social Security, *Elderly People in the Community: Their Service Needs*, HMSO, London.

Johnson, M., di Gregorio, S. and Harrison, B. (1981) *Ageing, Needs and Nutrition*, Policy Studies Institute Research Paper 81/8, Policy Studies Institute, London.

Jolliffe, I., Jones, B., Knapp, M. and Morgan, B. (1982) 'Classifications of the Elderly Population', *Ageing and Society*, 2:3, 331-56.

Jones, G. (1969) *Borough Politics*, Allen and Unwin, London.

Jones, T. and Prowle, M. (1984) *Health Service Finance*, 2nd edition, Certified Accountants Educational Trust, London.

Jones, D., Victor, C. and Vetter, N. (1983) 'Carers of the elderly in the community', *Journal of the Royal College of General Practitioners*, 33, 707-10.

Judge, K. and Matthews, J. (1980) *Charging for Social Care: A Study of Consumer Charges and the Personal Social Services*, Allen and Unwin, London.

Judge, K., Knapp, M. and Smith, J. (1986) 'The comparative costs of public and private residential homes for the elderly', in K. Judge and I. Sinclair (eds) *Residential Care for Elderly People*, HMSO, London.

Jowell, T. and Wistow G. (1989) *Give them a voice*, Birmingham Community Care Special Action Project, Birmingham City Council, Birmingham.

Kakabadse, A. (1982) *Culture of the Social Services*, Gower, Aldershot.

Kakabadse, A. and Worrall, R. (1978) 'Job satisfaction and organisational structure: a comparative study of nine SSDs', *British Journal of Social Work*, 8, 51-70.

Kane, R.A. and Kane, R.L. (1981) *Assessing the Elderly: A Practical Guide to Measurement*, Heath and Co., Lexington, Mass.

Kane, R.L. and Kane, R.A. (1982) *Values and Long-term Care*, Lexington Books.

Kane, R.L. and Kane, R.A. (1985) *A Will and a Way: What the United States can learn from Canada about caring for the elderly* Columbia University Press, New York.

Kane, R.A. (1988) 'The noblest experiment of them all: learning from the national chanelling evaluation', *Health Services Research*, 23, 189-198.

Kay, J. and Vickers, J., (1988) 'Regulatory Reform in Britain', *Economic Policy*, October, 285-351.

Kemper, P. (1988) 'The Evaluation of the National Long-Term Care Demonstration: Overview of the Findings', *Health Services Research* 23, 161-174.

Kemper, P., Applebaum, R. and Harrigan, M. (1987) 'Community care demonstrations: what have we learned?' *Health Care Financing Review*, 8, 87-100.

Kemper, P., Brown, R.S., Carcagno, G.J., Applebaum, R.A., Christianson, J.B.,Corson, W., Miller-Dunstan, S., Grannemann, T., Harrigan, M., Holden, N., Phillips, B., Schore, J., Thornton, C., Wooldridge, J. and Skidmore, F. (1986) *The evaluation of the national long-term care demonstration: Final report* Mathematica Policy Research, Inc., Princeton, New Jersey.

Kendall, J. (1989) *Efficient decision-making in the mixed economy: information and transaction cost considerations in the care of the mentally ill*, Personal Social Services Research Unit, University of Kent at Canterbury.

Klein, R. (1973) *Complaints Against Doctors: A Study in Professional Accountability*, Knight, London.

Knapp, M. (1984) *The Economics of Social Care*, Macmillan, London.

Knapp, M., Cambridge, P., Darton, R., Thomason, C., Allen, C., Beecham, J. and Leedham, I. (1989) *Care in the Community: Final Report*, PSSRU, University of Kent at Canterbury.

Knapp, M., Cambridge, P., Thomason, C., Allen, C., Beecham, J. and Darton, R. (1991) *Care in the Community: Evaluating a Demonstration Programme*, PSSRU Studies, Gower, Aldershot.

Laing, W. (1990) *Can Perestroika be pushed past its limits? Empowering elderly people in the care market*, Institute for Economic Affairs, London.

Land, H. and Rose, H. (1985) 'Compulsory Altruism for Some or an Altruistic Society for All', in P. Bean, J. Ferris and D. Whynes (eds) *In Defence of Welfare*, Tavistock, London.

Lapping, B. and Radice, G. (1968) *More power to the people: young Fabian essays in democracy in Britain*, Longman, London.

Larsen, R. (1978) 'Thirty years of research on subjective well-being of older Americans', *Journal of Gerontology*, 33, 109-25.

Larue, A., Bank, L., Jarvik, L. and Hetland, M. (1979) 'Health in old age: how do physician ratings and self-ratings compare?', *Journal of Gerontology*, 34, 678-961.

Latto, S. (1982) *The Coventry Home Help Project: Short Report*, Coventry Social Services Department, Coventry.

Lau, L. (1974) 'Comments on applications of duality theory', in M. Intagliata and D. Kandrick (eds) *Frontiers of Qualitative Economics II*, North-Holland, Amsterdam.

Lawrence, P. and Lorsch, J. (1967) *Organisation and Environment*, Harvard University Press, Boston, Mass.

Lawson, R. (1989a) *The Management of Change of Home Help Services in Four Local Authorities*, PSSRU Discussion Paper 621, University of Kent at Canterbury.

Lawson, R. (1989b) *Interorganisational Partnership in the Provision of Home Care for Elderly People*, PSSRU Discussion Paper 626, University of Kent at Canterbury.

Lawton, M.P. (1975) 'The Philadelphia Geriatric Centre Morale Scale: a revision', *Journal of Gerontology*, 30, 85-89.

Lawton, M.P., Brody, E.M. and Saperstein, A.P. (1989), 'A controlled study of respite service for caregivers of Alzheimers patients' *The Gerontologist*, 8-16.

Lee, G. (1985) 'Kinship and social support: the case of the United States', *Ageing and Society*, 5, 19-38.

Levin, E., Sinclair, I. and Gorbach, P. (1983) *The Supporters of Confused Elderly Persons at Home*, National Institute for Social Work, London.

Levin, E., Sinclair, I. and Gorbach, P. (1985) 'The effectiveness of the home-help service with confused old people and their families', *Research, Policy and Planning*, 3:2, 1-18.

Lipsey, R. and Lancaster, K. (1956) 'The general theory of second best', *Review of Economic Studies*, 24, 11-32.

Lipsky, M. (1980) *Street Level Bureaucracies*, Russell Sage, New York.

Litwak, E. and Kulis, S. (1983) 'Changes in helping networks with changes in the health of older people: social policy and social theory', in S.E. Spiro and E. Yuchtman-Yaar (eds) *Evaluating the Welfare State: Social and Political Perspectives*, Academic Press, London.

Local Government Training Board (1988) *Managing Tomorrow*, LGTB, London.

Lohmann, N. (1977) 'Correlations of life satisfaction, morale and adjustment measures', *Journal of Gerontology*, 32, 73-5.

London Council of Social Service (LCSS)(1963) *Day Care Service for the Aged in Their Own Homes*, National Council of Social Service, London.

Lowi, T. (1972) 'Four systems of policy, politics and choice', *Public Administration Review*, 32.

Lynch, J. (1977) *The Broken Heart*, Basic Books, New York.

McCullagh, P. and Nelder, J.A. (1983) *Generalised Line Models*, Chapman and Hall, London.

McDowell, D., Barniskis, L., and Wright, S. (1989) 'The Wisconsin Community Options Program: Planning and Packaging Long Term Support for Individuals', in A. Howe, E. Ozanne and C. Selby Smith, (eds.) *Community Care Policy and Practice: New Directions in Australia*, Monash University Press, Melbourne, 28-46.

McFadden, D. Puig, C. and Kirschner, D. (1977) *Determinants of the Long-Run Demand for Electricity*, Proceedings of the American Statistical Association (Business and Economics Section), 109-107.

McKegoney, N. and Hunter, D. (1986) '"Only connect ...": tightrope walking and joint working in the care of the elderly', *Policy and Politics*, 14:3, 335-60.

Marks, J. (1975) *The Home Help Service in West Sussex*, West Sussex County Council, Chichester.

Marshall, M. (1983) *Social Work with Old People*, Macmillan, London.

Maslow, A.H. (1970) *Motivation and Personality*, Harper and Row, New York.

Maurer, J., Ross, N., Bigos, Y., Papagiannis, M. and Springfield, T. (1984) *Final Report and Evaluation of the Florida Pentastar Project*, Florida Department of Rehabilitative and Preventive Services, Tallahassee, Florida.

Mauss, M. (1935) 'Les techniques du corps', *Journale de la Psychologie*, 32.

Means, R. (1981) *Community Care and Meals on Wheels: A Study in the Politics of Service Development at the National and Local Level*, Working Paper 21, University of Bristol School for Advanced Urban Studies, Bristol.

Means, R. and Smith, R. (1985) *The Development of Welfare Services for Elderly People*, Croom Helm, London.

Melia, K. and Macmillan, M. (1983) *Nurses and the Elderly in Hospital and the Community*.

Midwinter, E. (1986) *Caring for Cash: The Issue of Private Domiciliary Care*, Centre for Policy on Ageing, London.

Miller, J. (1976) *Towards a New Psychology of Women*, Allen Lane, London.

Miller, P. and Ingham, J. (1976) 'Friends, confidants and symptoms', *Social Psychiatry*, 11, 51-8.

Miller, L.S. and Pruger, R. (1977) 'The division of labour in a perfect people-changing agency', *Administration in Social Work*, 1, 171-185.

Moreland Commission on Nursing Homes and Residential Facilities (1976) *Moreland Report Vol. 3*.

Moore, B. (1984) *Privacy: Studies in Social and Cultural History*, M.E. Sharpe, New York.

Moroney, R. (1976) *The Family and the State: Considerations for Social Policy*, Longman, London and New York.

Mortimer, E. (1982) *Working with the Elderly*, Gower, Aldershot.

Moseley, L. (1968) 'Variations in socio-medical services for the aged', *Social and Economic Administration*, 2:3, 169-83.

Moxley, D. (1989) *The Practice of Case Management*, Sage, Newberry Park, California.

Mullen, E. and Dumpson, J. (1972) *Evaluation of Social Intervention*, Jossey Bass, San Francisco.

Municipality of Stockholm (1988) Some figures for the social services in Stockholm, Stockholms Socialforvaltung, Stockholm.

Murphy, E. (1988) *Home or Away: report of a working conference on home support schemes for elderly people with mental and physical disabilities*, National Union for Psyciatric Research and Development, United Medical Schools of Guys and St Thomas's Hospitals, London.

National Association of Probation Officers (1977) *Risk: An Analysis of the Problem of Risk in Social Work Practice*, NAPO, London.

Neill, J., Sinclair, I., Gorbach, P. and Williams, J. (1988) *A Need for Care? Elderly Applicants for Local Authority Homes*, National Institute for Social Work/Avebury, London.

Nerlove, M. (1965) *Estimation and Identification of Cobb-Douglas Production Functions*, North Holland, Amsterdam.

Netten, A. (1988) *Allocating Costs to Joint Households*, PSSRU Discussion Paper 566, University of Kent at Canterbury.

Newcastle-upon-Tyne Management Services Division (1979) *Home Help Service in Newcastle-upon-Tyne*, Report for Social Services Committee, Newcastle-upon-Tyne Metropolitan Borough.

Neugarten, B., Havighurst, R. and Tobin, S. (1961) 'Measurement of life satisfaction', *Journal of Gerontology*, 16, 134-43.

New York State Planning Commission (1982) *Personal Care Survey*, New York State Health Planning Commission, New York.

Nissel, M. and Bonnerjea, L. (1982) *Family Care of the Handicapped Elderly: Who Pays?*, Policy Studies Institute, London.

Norman, A. (1980) *Rights and Risk: A Discussion Document on Civil Liberty in Old Age*, National Corporation for the Care of Old People, London.

Nunnally, J. (1975) 'The study of change in evaluation research', in E. Spann, J. (1987) *The Community Options Program: A public choice for personal choice in long term support*, Robert M. LaFollette Institute of Public Affairs, University of Wisconsin, Madison, Wisconsin.

Nyckektal Och Matt (1988) *Aldreomsorgsstudie Stokholms Lan*, Municipality of Stockholm, Stockholm.

O'Brien, B. (1986) *What Are my Chances Doctor?: A Review of Clinical Risks*, Office of Health Economics, London.

Office of Economic Cooperation and Development (1988) *Ageing Populations: The Social Policy Implications*, OECD, Paris.

Office of Population Censuses and Surveys (1980) *Nurses Working in the Community*, HMSO, London.

Office of Population Censuses and Surveys (1982) *The General Household Survey 1980*, HMSO, London.

Office of Population Censuses and Surveys (1983) *General Household Survey 1981*, HMSO, London.

Office of Population Censuses and Surveys (1988a) *General Household Survey 1985: Informal Carers*, HMSO, London.

Office of Population Censuses and Surveys (1988b) *The Prevalence of Disability Among Adults*, HMSO, London.

On Lok (1987) *On Lok senior health services risk-based CCODA: Description of the Program*, On Lok Senior Health Services, San Francisco, California.

Ouchi, W. (1971) 'Relationship between organisational structure and organisational control', *Administrative Science Quarterly*, 22, 95-113.

Palmore, E. and Luikart, C. (1972) 'Health and social factors related to life satisfaction', *Journal of Health and Social Behaviour*, 13, 68-80.

Collins, A. and Pancoast, D. (1976) *Natural Helping Networks*, National Association of Social Workers, Washington DC.

Parker, G., Baldwin, S. and Glendinning, C. (1984) *Informal Care and Carers: A Research Review and Recommendations for Future Research*, Social Policy Research Unit, University of York.

Parker, J. (1965) *Local Health and Welfare Services*, Allen and Unwin, London.

Parker, R. (1976) 'Charging for the social services', *Journal of Social Policy*, 5:4, 359-74.

Parker, R. (1981) 'Tending and social policy', in E. Goldberg and S. Hatch (eds) *A New Look at the Personal Social Services*, Policy Studies Institute, London.

Parsloe, P. (1981) *Social Services Area Teams*, Allen and Unwin, London.

Parsloe, P. and Stevenson, O. (1978) *Social Services Teams: The Practitioners' View*, HMSO, London.

Parsons, T. (1951) *The Social System*, Routledge and Kegan Paul, London.

Pattie, A. and Gilleard, C. (1979) *The Manual of the Clifton Assessment Procedures for the Elderly (CAPE)*, Hodder and Stoughton, London.

Payne, M. (1977) 'Integrating domiciliary care into an area team', *Social Work Service*, 14, 54-8.

Perrow, C. (1970) *Organisational Analysis*, Tavistock, London.

Perrow, C. (1972) *Complex Organisations: A Critical Essay*, Scott Foresman, Chicago.

Peschek, D. and Brand, J. (1966) *Policy and Politics in Secondary Education*, London School of Economics, London.

Pettigrew, A. (1979) 'On studying organisational cultures', *Administrative Science Quarterly*, 24, 570-81.

Pettigrew, A. (1985) *The Awakening Giant*, Blackwell, Oxford.

Pilling, D. (1988a) *The Case Management Project: Summary of the Evaluation Report*, Department of Systems Science, City University, London.

Pilling, D. (1988b) *The Case Management Project: Report of the Evaluation*, Department of Systems Science, City University, London.

Plank, D. (1977) *Caring for the Elderly: Report of a Study of Various Means of Caring for Dependent Elderly People in Eight London Boroughs*, GLC Research Memorandum, London.

Polhemus, T. (ed.)(1978) *Social Aspects of the Human Body*, Penguin, Harmondsworth.

Pruger, R. (1987) *Making information work: The story of the Equity Project*, School of Social Welfare, University of California, Berkely, California.

PSSRU (1991) *Community Services and the Social Production of Welfare*, Gower, Aldershot.

Pugh, D. and Hickson, D. (1968) 'The comparative study of organisations', in D. Pym (ed.) *Industrial Society*, Penguin, Harmondsworth.

Pugh, D., Hickson, D., Hinings, C. and Turner, C. (1968) 'Dimensions of organisational structure', *Administrative Science Quarterly*, June, 65-105.

Quine, L. and Charnley, H. (1987) 'The Malaise Inventory as a measure of stress in Carers', in J. Twigg (ed.) *Evaluating Support to Informal Carers*, Papers presented to a conference held in York, Social Policy Research Unit, University of York.

Quine, L. and Pahl, J. (1985) 'Examining the causes of stress in families with severely mentally handicapped children', *British Journal of Social Work*, 15:5, 501-17.

Qureshi, H. (1984) *Decision Making about the Provision of Practical Help in Families*, Paper given to British Society for Gerontology Conference, Leeds.

Qureshi, H., Challis, D. and Davies, B. (1983) 'Motivations and rewards of helpers in the Kent Community Care Project', in S. Hatch (ed.) *Volunteers: Patterns, Meanings and Motives*, The Volunteer Centre, Berkhamstead.

Qureshi, H., Challis, D. and Davies, B. (1989) *Helpers in Case Managed Community Care*, Gower, Aldershot.

Ramsay, M. (1982) 'Mugging: fears and facts', *New Society*, 25 March.

Ratna, L. and Davis, J. (1984) 'Family therapy with the elderly mentally ill: some strategies and techniques', *British Journal of Psychiatry*, 145, 311-15.

Rawlings, C. (1981) *Social Work with the Elderly*, Allen and Unwin, London.

Raynes, N., Pratt, M. and Roses, S. (1979) *Organisational Structure and the Care of the Mentally Retarded*, Croom Helm, London.

Reid, W. and Hanrahan, P. (1981) 'The effectiveness of social work: recent evidence', in E. Goldberg and N. Connelly (eds) *Evaluative Research in Social Care*, Heinemann, London.

Reid, W. and Shyne, A. (1969) *Brief and Extended Casework*, Columbia University Press, New York.

Renshaw, J., Hampson, R., Thomason, C., Darton, R., Judge, K. and Knapp, M. (1988) *Care in the Community: The First Steps*, Gower, Aldershot.

Report, V, *Reimbursing operating cost: Dollars without sense*, The Commission, Albany, New York.

Richardson, A. (1990) *Case management in practice: reflections on the Wakefield case management project*, Nuffield Institute for Health Services Studies, University of Leeds, Leeds.

Rimmer, L. and Popay, J. (1982) *Employment Trends and the Family*, Study Commission on the Family, London.

Rimmer, L. and Wicks, M. (1983) 'The challenge of change: demographic trends, the family and social policy', in H. Glennester (ed.) *The Future of the Welfare State*, Heinemann, London.

Rossiter, C. and Wicks, M. (1982) *Crisis or Challenge: Family Care, Elderly People and Social Policy*, Study Commission on the Family, London.

Rowe, W. (1977) *Anatomy of Risk*, John Wiley, New York.

Rowlings, C. (1981) *Social Work with Elderly People*, Allen and Unwin, London.

Rutter, M., Graham, P. and Yule, W. (1970) *A Neuropsychiatric Study in Childhood*, Heinemann, London.

Rutter, M., Tizard, J. and Whitmore, K. (1970) *Education, Health and Behaviour*, Longman, London.

Sager, A. (1979) *Learning the Home Care Needs of the Elderly*, Levin Policy Institute, Brandeis University, Waltham, Mass.

Sager, A. (1982) *Living at Home: The Roles of Public and Informal Support in Disabled Older Americans*, Levinson Policy Institute, Brandeis University, Waltham, Mass.

Salvage, A.V. (1985) *Domiciliary Care Teams for the Elderly: Provision by Social Services Departments and Recommendations for their Introduction*, Vols I and II, Research Team for the Elderly, University of Wales College of Medicine, Cardiff.

Sanford, J. (1975) 'Tolerance of debility in elderly dependents by supporters at home: its significance for hospital practice', *British Medical Journal*, 3, 471-3.

Saunders, P. (1990) *Reflections on the Review of the HACC Program*, in A. Howe, E. Ozanne and C. Selby-Smith (eds.) (1990) *Community Care Policy and Practice: New Directions in Australia*, Monash University, Melbourne, 201-212.

Scheidt, R. and Windley, P. (1983) 'The mental health of small-town rural elderly residents: an expanded ecological model', *Journal of Gerontology*, 38, 472-529.

Schmale, A. (1958) 'Relation of separation and depression to disease: a report on a hospitalised medical population', *Psychosomatic Medicine*, 20, 259-77.

Scrivens, E. and Henheh, A. (1989) 'Working for patients: making the internal market effective', *Public Money and Management*, 9:4, 53-58.

Seelbach, W. and Hanson, C. (1979) *Morale among the Institutionalised and Non-institutionalised Elderly*, Paper presented at the annual meeting of the Gerontological Society, Washington DC.

Shanas, E., Townsend, P., Wedderburn, D., Friis, H., Milhoj, P. and Stehouwer, J. (1968) *Old People in Three Industrial Societies*, Routledge and Kegan Paul, London.

Sharpe, L. and Newton, K. (1984) *Does Politics Matter?*, Oxford University Press, Oxford.

Shen, J., Takeda, S. and Hennessy, C. (1985) *On Lok's risk-based CCODA: The impact of prospective capitation on comprehensive care to the elderly*, On Lok Senior Health Services, San Francisco.

Sinclair, I. Crosbie, D., O'Connor, P., Stanforth, L. and Vickery, A. (1984) *Networks Project: A Study of Informal Care, Services and Social Work for Clients Living Alone*, National Institute for Social Work, London.

Sinclair, I., Crosbie, D., O'Connor, P., Stanforth, L. and Vickery, A. (1988) *Bridging Two Worlds: Social Work and the Elderly Living Alone*, Avebury, Aldershot.

Staples, P. (1990), 'An Historical Perspective and Some Questions for the Future', in A. Howe, E. Ozanne and C. Selby-Smith (eds.) (1990) *Community Care Policy and Practice: New Directions in Australia*, Monash University, Melbourne, 2-7.

Steinberg, R.M. (1983) *Measuring Tendencies to Utilize Services: Accounting for the Value Preference, and Coping Styles of Difficult Clients*, Andrus Steinberg, R.M. and Carter, G.W. (1982) *Designing Care Management: A Handbook for Development Implementation and Evaluation of Case Coordination Programs for the Elderly*, Andrus Gerontology Center, Los Angeles, California. Gerontology Centre, University of Southern California, LA.

Stevenson, O. (1981a) *Specialisation in Social Service Teams*, Allen and Unwin, London.

Stevenson, O. (1981b) 'Caring and dependency', in D. Hobman (ed.) *The Impact of Ageing*, Croom Helm, London.

Stevenson, O. and Parsloe, P. (1978) *Social Services Teams: The Practitioners' View*, HMSO, London.

Stewart, J. (1986) *The New Management of Local Government*, Allen and Unwin, London.

Stocking, B. (1984) *Initiative and Inertia: Case Studies in the NHS*, Nuffield Provincial Hospitals Trust, London.

Strain, L. and Chappell, N. (1982) 'Confidantes: do they make a difference to the quality of life?', *Research on Aging*, 4, 479-502.

Struening and M. Guttentag (eds) *Handbook of Evaluation Research*, Sage, Beverley Hills.

Sumner, G. and Smith, R. (1969) *Planning Local Authority Services for the Elderly*, Allen and Unwin, London.

Sundstrom, G. (1987) *Old Age Care in Sweden: Yesterday, Today, Tomorrow*, The Swedish Institute, Stockholm.

Taylor, R. and Ford, G. (1983) 'The elderly as underconsulters: a critical reappraisal', *Journal of the Royal College of General Practitioners*, 33, 699-705.

Technical Working Group on Private Financing of Long Term Care for the Elderly (1986) *Report to the Secretary on Private Financing of Long Term Care for the elderly*, DHHS, Washington DC.

Tennant, A. and Bayley, M. (1985) *The Eighth Decade: Family Structure and Support Networks in the Community*, Department of Sociological Studies, University of Sheffield.

Test, M.A. and Stein, L. (1978) "Training in Community Living: Research Results and Design", in L.I. Stein and M. Test (eds.)(1978) *Alternatives to Mental Hospital Treatment, New York, Plenum.*

Thompson, E. and Eastwood, M. (1981) 'Survivorship and senile dementia', *Age and Ageing,* 10, 29-32.

Thornton, C. and Miller-Dunstan, S. (1986) *Analysis of the benefits and costs of channeling,* Mathematica Policy Research, Plainsboro, New Jersey.

Thornton, P. and Moore, J. (1980) *The Placement of Elderly People in Private Households: An Analysis of Current Provision,* University of Leeds.

Thornton, C., Will, J. and Davies, M. (1985) *The evaluation of the national long-term care demonstration: Analysis of channeling project costs,* Mathematica Policy Research, Inc., Princetown, New Jersey.

Thorslund, M. and Johansson, L. (1987) 'Elderly people in Sweden: current realities and future plans', *Ageing and Society,* 7, 345-55.

Thorslund, M., Norstrom, T. and Wernberg, K. (1990) *The Utilization of Home Help in Sweden: A Multivariate Analysis,* Department of Social Medicine, University of Uppsala, Uppsala.

Timms, E. (1983) 'On the relevance of informal social networks to social work intervention', *British Journal of Social Work,* 13, 405-16.

Tinker, A. (1982) *The Elderly in Modern Society,* Longman, London.

Tinker, A. (1984) *Staying at Home,* HMSO, London.

Titmuss, R. (1968) *Commitment to Welfare,* Allen and Unwin, London.

Tobin, S. and Lieberman, M. (1976) *Last Home for the Aged,* Jossey-Bass, San Francisco.

Townsend, J., Piper, M., Frank, A., Dyer, S., North, W. and Meade, T. (1988) 'Reduction in hospital readmission stay of elderly patients by a community based hospital discharge scheme: a randomised controlled trial', *British Medical Journal,* 297, 1043-1046.

Townsend, P. (1957) *The Family Life of Old People,* Routledge and Kegan Paul, London.

Townsend, P. (1962) *The Last Refuge,* Routledge and Kegan Paul, London.

Townsend, P. and Davidson, N. (1982) *Inequalities in Health: The Black Report,* Penguin, Harmondsworth.

Townsend, P. and Wedderburn, D. (1965) *The Aged in the Welfare State,* Bell, London.

Treas, J. (1977) 'Family support systems for the aged: some social and demographic considerations', *The Gerontologist,* 17:6, 486-91.

Trent Regional Health Authority (1984) *Better Health in Trent: A Plan for Action,* Trent Regional Health Authority, Sheffield.

Tunstall, J. (1966) *Old and Alone,* Routledge and Kegan Paul, London.

Turner, B. (1981) *Exploring the Industrial Subculture,* Macmillan, London.

Turner, B. (1984) *The Body and Society: Explorations in Social Theory,* Blackwell, London.

Twigg, J. (1983) *The Supporters of Elderly Mentally Infirm People in Hammersmith and Fulham*, Hammersmith and Fulham Social Services Department, London.

Ungerson, C. (1981) *Women, Work and the 'Caring Capacity of the Community': A Report of a Research Review*, Report to the SSRC, mimeo, University of Kent at Canterbury.

Ungerson, C. (1983) 'Women and caring: skills, tasks and taboos', in E. Garmarnikow, D. Morgan, J. Purvis and D. Taylorson (eds) *The Public and the Private*, Heinemann, London.

Ungerson, C. (1987) *Policy is Personal: Sex, Gender and Informal Care*, Tavistock, London.

van den Heuvel, W. (1989) *Home Help Service in the Netherlands*, Paper for the ACRE Consortium, Department of Health Sciences, University of Groningen, The Netherlands.

van Sonderen, F., Suurmeijer, P. and van den Heuvel, W. (1985) *Measuring the Home Help Service*, Vakgroep Medische Sociologie, Groningen, The Netherlands.

Vetter, N. (1987) 'Performance indicators in the care of the elderly', *Nursing Times*, April 1, 30-2.

Vetter, N., Jones, D. and Victor, C. (1984) 'The effects of health visitors working with elderly patients in general practice', *British Medical Journal*, 288, 369-71.

Vickery, A. (1981) *Consultation on 64 cases of elderly people living alone referred for social work help*, draft report, National Institute for Social Work, London.

Victor, V.R. and Vetter, N.J. (1988) 'Rearranging the deckchairs on the Titanic: failure of an augmented home help scheme after discharge to reduce the length of stay in hospital', *Archives of Gerontology and Geriatrics. 7*, 83-91.

Wagner, G. (1988) *Residential Care: The Research Reviewed*, HMSO, London.

Walker, A. (1982) 'The Meaning and Social Division of Community Care', in A. Walker (ed.) *Community Care: The Family, the State and Social Policy*, Blackwell, London.

Wallberg, E. (1988) *Dagens Nyheter*, Agency for Administrative Development, Stockholm.

Warburton, W. (1982) *What Social Workers Do*, Cambridgeshire Social Services Department, Cambridge.

Warner, N. (1990) *Implementing Community Care*, Department of Social Services, Kent County Council, Maidstone.

Wasser, E. (1971) 'Protective practice in serving the mentally impaired aged', *Social Casework*, 52:8, 511-22.

Webb, A. (1978) *Policy Innovation and the Balance of Social Care*, University of Kent, PSSRU/PSSC Conference on Developments in the Care of the Elderly, University of Kent at Canterbury.

Webb, A. and Falk, N. (1974) 'Planning the social services: the local authority ten year plans', *Policy and Politics*, 3, pp 33-54.

Webb, A. and Hobdell, M. (1980) 'Coordination and teamwork in the health and personal social services', in S. Lonsdale, A. Webb and T. Briggs (eds) *Teamwork in the Personal Social Services and Health Care*, Croom Helm, London.

Webb, A. and Wistow, G. (1980) 'Implementation, central-local relations and the personal social services', in G. Jones (ed.) *New Approaches to the Study of Central-Local Government Relationships*, Gower, Aldershot.

Webb, A. and Wistow, G. (1986) *Planning, Need and Scarcity: Essays on the Personal Social Services*, Allen and Unwin, London.

Weber, M. (1947) *The Theory of Social and Economic Organisation*, (trans.) A. Henderson and T. Parsons, Free Press, New York.

Weeks, D. (1973) 'Organisation theory: some themes and distinctions', in G. Salaman and K. Thompson (eds) *People and Organisations*, Longman, London.

Weick, K. (1976) 'Educational organizations as loosely-coupled systems', *Administrative Science Quarterly*, 21, 1-19.

Weisbrod, B. and Schlesinger, M. (1986) 'Public, Private, Non-profit Ownership and the Response to Asymmetric Information: The Case of Nursing Homes', in S. Rose-Ackerinan (ed.) *The Economics of Non-Profit Institutions*, Oxford University Press, Oxford.

Weiss, R. (1969) 'The fund of sociability', *Trans-Action*, 6, 36-43.

Weiss, R. (1974) 'The provision of social relationships', in Z. Rubin (ed.) *Doing Unto Others*, Prentice Hall, Englewood Cliffs, N.J.

Weissert, W., Cready, C. and Pawelak, J. (1988) 'The past and future of home- and community-based long-term care', *The Milbank Quarterly*, 66, 309-88.

Wellman, B. (1981) 'Applying network analysis to the study of support', in B. Gottlieb (ed.) *Social Networks and Social Support*, Sage, Beverly Hills and London.

Wenger, G. (1984) *The Supportive Network: Coping with Old Age*, Allen and Unwin, London.

West, P. (1981) 'Theoretical and practical equity in the National Health Service in England', *Social Science and Medicine*, 15C, 117-22.

West, P., Illsley, R. and Kelman, H. (1984) 'Public preferences for the care of dependency groups', *Social Science and Medicine*, 18:4, 287-95.

West Midlands Regional Health Authority (1984) *A Strategy for Health: 1. 1984-1994*, West Midlands Regional Health Authority, Birmingham.

Whittington, C. and Bellaby, P. (1979) 'The reasons for hierarchy in social services departments: a critique of Elliot Jacques and his associates', *Sociological Review*, 27:3, 513-39.

Wicks, M. (1978) *Old and Cold: Hypothermia and Social Policy*, Heinemann, London.

Wicks, M. (1982) 'Community care and elderly people' in A. Walker (ed.) *Community Care: The Family, the State and Social Policy*, Blackwell, Oxford.

Wilkin, D. (1979) *Caring for the Mentally Handicapped Child*, Croom Helm, London.

Williams, A. (1974) 'Need as a Demand Concept (with special reference to health)' in A.J. Culyer (ed.) *Economic Policies and Social Goals*, Martin Robertson, London.

Williams, A. (1977) 'Measuring the quality of life of the elderly', in L. Wing and A. Evans (eds) *Public Economics and the Quality of Life*, Johns Hopkins University Press, Baltimore, Maryland.

Willmott, P. (1986) *Social Networks, Informal Care and Public Policy*, Policy Studies Institute, London.

Wilson, E. (1982) 'Women, the "community" and the "family"', in Winnicott, D.W. (1971) *Playing and Reality*, Tavistock, London.

Wistow, G. (1982) 'Collaboration between health and local authorities: why is it necessary?', *Social Policy and Administration*, 16:1, 44-62.

Wooldridge, J. and Schore, J. (1986) *Channeling effects on hospital, nursing home and other medical services*, Mathematica Policy Research Inc., Plainsboro, New Jersey.

Wright, K. (1974) 'Alternative measures of output of social programmes: the elderly', in A. Culyer (ed.) *Economic Policies and Social Goals*, Martin Robertson, Oxford.

Wright, K. (1986) *The Economics of the Informal Care of the Elderly*, Centre for Health Economics, University of York.

Wright, K. and Haycox, A. (1985) *Costs of Alternative Forms of NHS Care for Mentally Handicapped Persons*, Discussion Paper 7, Centre for Health Economics, University of York.

Wright, K., Cairns, J. and Snell, M. (1979) *Research Project on Alternative Patterns of Care for the Elderly*, Draft Final Report, Institute for Social and Economic Research, University of York.

Wright, K., Cairns, J. and Snell, M. (1981) *Costing Care: The Costs of Alternative Patterns of Care*, Joint Unit for Social Services Research, University of Sheffield, Sheffield.

Young, K. (1981) 'Discretion as an implementation problem', in M. Adler and S. Asquith (eds) *Discretion and Welfare*, Heinemann, London.

Younghusband, E. (1959) *Report of the Working Party on Social Workers in the Local Authority Health and Welfare Services*, HMSO, London.

Zarit, S., Reever, K. and Bach-Peterson, J. (1980) 'Relatives of the impaired elderly: correlates of feelings of burden', *The Gerontologist*, 20:6, 649-55.

Zawadski, R.T. (ed.)(1984) *Community-based systems of long-term care*, Haworth Press, New York.

Zawadski, R.T. and Ansak, M.L. (1981) *On Lok's CCODA: The first two years*, On Lok Senior Health Services, San Francisco, California.

Zawadski, R.T. and Eng, C. (1988) 'Case management in capitated long-term care', *Health Care Financing Review*, Special Supplement.

Zawadski, R., Shen, C., Yordi, C. and Hansen, J. (1984) *On Lok's Community Care Organization for Dependent Adults: A Research and Development Project (1978-1983). Final Report*, On Lok Senior Health Services, San Francisco.

Glossary
Some PSSRU-speak decoded

All **variable names** used in statistical analysis are described in one of the following tables:

Table 3.1 (pp. 50-1) on the need types, MYTYPOs; Tables A2.1, A2.9 and A2.11 for variables used in Chapter 2; Table A3.1 for variables used in Chapters 3 and 7; Tables 4.1-3 (pp 79-82) for variables used in Chapter 4 and 12; Appendix to Chapter 5 for the cost variable used there; and Appendix 12 and particularly Table A12.1 for the variables used in the analysis of carer stress.

The following **conceptual 'parameters' of models of case management with delegated budgets** are defined in Table 14.3: AVBUDG and AVBUDG curve; BUDGCAP; CMCASELOAD; CMCOST; DEPINDEX, DEPINDEX curve, and DEPINDEX integral; HOMEDUR; HORIZTE and HORIZTE curve; LIFEDUR; OTHHCCOST and OTHHCCOST curve; RESCOST and RESCOST curve; RESDUR; TARGFLOOR; and TOTHCCOST. **Other case management model parameters** are described in Diagram 13.1, the associated text, and references quoted therein.

Case management 'arrangements' or 'parameters': Features or combinations of features of the kind outlined in Diagram 13.1 and Table 14.3 and the associated text.

Case management system: A managed system for the performance of case management tasks. Practice and experimental systems differ greatly. The elements of the PSSRU arrangements are outlined in Davies and Challis (1986).

Core tasks of case management: See Table 6.1.

Cover: The ratio of the number of recipients to the number in a target group.

Expenditure recovery ratio: The ratio of income from user charges to gross expenditure on a service.

Final outputs or 'outcomes': Effects of direct evaluative importance created by the application of resources. Contrasts with 'intermediate outputs', service quantities and effects of importance because they produce outcomes of evaluative importance in their own right.

Heineken process and effects: Causal processes or effects focusing on meeting such higher order Maslow needs as improving Morale by practice styles and techniques which focus on psychological well-being and relationships and which put emphasis on client perceptions of how the quality of their lives can be improved. See Davies and Challis (1986), Diagram 1.1. Compare the Matching and Exchange processes and effects there postulated.

Horizontal target efficiency: The proportion of those in the target group actually receiving service. (See, for example, Bebbington and Davies, 1983; and Knapp, 1984, which describes the concept diagrammatically.)

Input mix efficiency: The aspect of production efficiency which measures the degree to which inputs are mixed in the most efficient combination given their substitutability in the production of outputs and their relative prices. (See, for example, Knapp, 1984, pp 78-9, input mix there being called 'price' efficiency; and Bebbington et al. which describes the distinctions between the three types of productive efficiency diagrammatically.)

Intensity: Units of input per recipient.

Interest group evaluation: The classification and analysis of evaluation evidence by broad interest groups, e.g., the SSD, the NHS, carers and client, society as a whole. (See Davies and Challis, 1986.)

Lead agency: The agency with responsibility for developing and implementing local trade and industry policies (i.e. the prevention or correction of 'market failures') for a client group. (See Davies, 1986; Davies and Challis, 1986.)

Marginal cost of a final output: The increase in costs associated with an increase in output of one unit.

Marginal productivity (of services or inputs with respect to a final output): The increment of a final output associated with an increase in a resource or service input by one unit, given the level of output postulated and the need-related circumstances of the client. A distinction is made between 'general' and 'targeting effects' in the analysis of marginal productivities; the latter describing differential marginal productivities between clients varying in need-related circumstances. (See Chapters 4, 12 and 13.)

Marginal cost: The cost of an additional unit of 'final output'.

Opportunity costs: Resource costs; the costs measured in the next most desirable opportunity foregone. (See Knapp, 1984.)

Organisational locus: The locus of the case management team in relation to case-finding and the path to institutional long-term care. (See Chapter 13 and Davies and Challis, Chap. 13.)

Output mix efficiency: The aspect of allocative efficiency which measures the degree to which the mix of 'final outputs' approaches that specified as best given by a legitimate set of criteria given the circumstances. (See Bebbington et al., 1985, for a diagrammatic explanation.)

Pandora effect: The generation of increased demand due to the provision of more and better service.

Production function: The statistical description of the relationship between resources, quasi-inputs, and outputs. See Davies and Knapp, 1981, p.15-6 and Knapp, 1984, pp.112-4.

Production of welfare approach: The analysis of the relations between resources and outcomes of evaluative significance in their own right ('final outputs') for persons of different ('need-related') circumstances and different social care systems. The studies typically combine statistical analysis with the analysis of the characteristics which affect targeting, the production of welfare, equity and efficiency and why systems acquire the characteristics. (See, for example, Davies and Knapp, 1981; Knapp, 1984; Davies, 1985; Davies and Challis, 1986.)

Quasi-input: A factor whose level is assumed not to be affected by variations in resource inputs being analysed during the period studied either directly or indirectly, and which affects (or is postulated to affect) the relations between resources and outcomes. (See Davies, 1985.)

Scope: The range of case management tasks for which authority, responsibility and accountability are concentrated in persons or small teams; and a key manner in which case management arrangements can be varied to reflect goals and circumstances. (See Chapter 13 and Davies and Challis, 1986)

Social production of welfare approach: An intellectual framework for the analysis of the production of welfare from the perspective of dependents and their informal support networks.

Span: The range of substitute and complementary services and resources controlled or purchaseable from and charged to the case managers' budgets; a key way in which case management arrangements can be varied to reflect goals and circumstances. (See Chapter 13 and Davies and Challis, 1986.)

Substitutability and substitution: Substitutability describes the degree to which resources or services could potentially be used as alternatives to produce the same output mix; substitution describes the extent to which they are so used. (See Chapter 2.)

Technical efficiency: The aspect of productive efficiency which describes the degree to which the levels of 'final outputs' produced approach the maximum feasible given the output and input mixes. (See, for example, Knapp, 1984, pp.78-9; and Bebbington et al., 1985, for a diagrammatic explanation.)

Trade and industry policy: Policies to avoid or remove 'market failures'.

Vertical target efficiency: The proportion of beneficiaries who are in the target group (the recipients measure); or, the proportion of resources received by members of the target group (the resource measure). (See, for example, Bebbington and Davies, 1983; and Knapp, 1984, which describes the concept diagrammatically.)

Author index

Adler, M., 164
Age Care Research Europe (ACRE), 351
Aiken, M., 218
Allen, I., 240
Allen, C., 393, 443
Almind, G., 280
Amemiya, T., 437
Ankri, J., 352
Ansak, M.L., 295
Applebaum, R., 304, 307, 308, 309, 443
Asquith, S., 164
Association of Directors of Social Services, 318
Aston School, 210
Audit Commission, 5, 8, 9, 14, 15, 16, 17, 18, 29, 30, 75, 76, 143, 147, 210, 218, 228, 235, 237, 259, 282, 285, 314, 325, 358, 369, 379, 443, 446,
Auditor General, 322, 395,
Austin, C.317, 443,

Bachrach, L.L., 349
Baines, B., 271, 281, 352, 378
Bamford, T., 165
Bank, L., 97, 333
Banks, P., 337
Barclay, P., 76, 155, 237
Barnes, C.D., 354
Barniskis, L., 342, 343, 383, 395, 396
Barrowclough, C., 300
Barton, A., 23
Bate, S., 171
Baumol, W.J., 292
Baur, P., 97, 333
Bebbington, A., 8, 10, 16, 17, 23, 48, 94, 98, 162, 178, 220, 237, 259, 275, 288, 332, 349, 370, 373, 374, 378, 435
Becker, B., 296
Bedfordshire Social Services Department, 17
Beecham, J., 393, 443
Begg, I., 120
Belford, E., 275
Bellaby, P., 212
Benthall, J., 192

Bergmann, K., 86, 200
Berkeley Planning Associates, 443
Bernstein, J., 321
Bligh, J., 162
Boldy, D., 16
Booth, T., 17, 86, 118, 184, 234
Bradshaw, J., 174, 265, 337, 340
Bramley, G., 334
Brand, J., 25
Brearley, C., 163, 164, 170
Brethouwer, D., 352
British Crime Survey, 166
British Association of Social Workers, 162, 164
Brocklehurst, J.C., 270
Brody, E.M., 335
Brotherton, J., 17
Brown, G., 49, 86
Brown, T.E., 309
Brown, R., 171, 307
Brunel Institute of Organisation and Social Studies, 184
Bucquet, D., 352
Byrne, D., 49

Cairns, J., 119, 443
Callahan, J.J., 335
Cambridge, P., 393, 443
Camden Social Services Department, 17
Capitman, J., 308, 321, 332
Carcagno, G.J., 304, 307, 366, 388
Carley, M., 345
Carpenter, G.I., 17, 151, 272
Carter, J., 48, 52, 349
Carty, M.H., 270
Cassel, J., 86
Challis, D., 1, 3, 4, 5, 12, 15, 16, 21, 30, 31, 33, 34, 48, 52, 69, 78, 83, 83, 86, 93, 94, 96, 97, 122, 123, 129, 137, 142, 147, 163, 200, 211, 212, 214, 215, 224, 229, 233, 234, 236, 262, 265, 268, 272, 273, 274, 275, 280, 295, 296, 297, 298, 302, 301, 303, 304, 305, 306, 307, 308, 313, 216, 317, 318, 320, 321, 326, 327, 328, 337, 343, 347, 349, 351, 354,

Subject index